WHITE HOUSE STUDIES

WHITE HOUSE STUDIES COMPENDIUM

VOLUME 9

WHITE HOUSE STUDIES

Additional books in this series can be found on Nova's website under the Series tab.

Additional e-books in this series can be found on Nova's website under the e-book tab.

WHITE HOUSE STUDIES

WHITE HOUSE STUDIES COMPENDIUM

VOLUME 9

ANTHONY J. EKSTEROWICZ
AND
GLENN P. HASTEDT
EDITORS

Copyright © 2013 by Nova Science Publishers, Inc.

All rights reserved. No part of this book may be reproduced, stored in a retrieval system or transmitted in any form or by any means: electronic, electrostatic, magnetic, tape, mechanical photocopying, recording or otherwise without the written permission of the Publisher.

For permission to use material from this book please contact us:
Telephone 631-231-7269; Fax 631-231-8175
Web Site: http://www.novapublishers.com

NOTICE TO THE READER

The Publisher has taken reasonable care in the preparation of this book, but makes no expressed or implied warranty of any kind and assumes no responsibility for any errors or omissions. No liability is assumed for incidental or consequential damages in connection with or arising out of information contained in this book. The Publisher shall not be liable for any special, consequential, or exemplary damages resulting, in whole or in part, from the readers' use of, or reliance upon, this material. Any parts of this book based on government reports are so indicated and copyright is claimed for those parts to the extent applicable to compilations of such works.

Independent verification should be sought for any data, advice or recommendations contained in this book. In addition, no responsibility is assumed by the publisher for any injury and/or damage to persons or property arising from any methods, products, instructions, ideas or otherwise contained in this publication.

This publication is designed to provide accurate and authoritative information with regard to the subject matter covered herein. It is sold with the clear understanding that the Publisher is not engaged in rendering legal or any other professional services. If legal or any other expert assistance is required, the services of a competent person should be sought. FROM A DECLARATION OF PARTICIPANTS JOINTLY ADOPTED BY A COMMITTEE OF THE AMERICAN BAR ASSOCIATION AND A COMMITTEE OF PUBLISHERS.

Additional color graphics may be available in the e-book version of this book.

Library of Congress Cataloging-in-Publication Data

ISBN: 978-1-62618-681-1

ISSN: 2329-499X

Published by Nova Science Publishers, Inc. † New York

CONTENTS

Preface		ix
About the Contributors		xi
Chapter 1	Choosing a New Direction: The Presidential Election of 2008 *Glen Sussman*	1
Chapter 2	Congress on the Line: The 2008 Congressional Election and the Obama Presidency *Jesse Richman*	21
Chapter 3	Campaign Tactics and American Grand Strategy in the Election of 2008 *Joshua Rovner*	37
Chapter 4	Passing the Torch Through Political Time: Heir Apparent Presidents and the Governing Party *Donald A. Zinman*	53
Chapter 5	Bush's Adventures in the National Service Policy Arena and Five Lessons for President Obama *Richard Holtzman*	69
Chapter 6	Forging the Eagle's Sword: President Washington, the Congress and the Army *Ryan Staude*	87
Chapter 7	Wars of Choice: James Madison, George W. Bush and the Presidential Legacy Question *Anthony J. Eksterowicz and Glenn P. Hastedt*	103
Chapter 8	For Love or for Money?: William McKinley and the Spanish-American War *Jeffrey Bloodworth*	127
Chapter 9	War Counsel: Military Advice in the White House *Brent A. Strathman*	151
Chapter 10	Presidents and War: Notes on the End of Constitutionalism *James K. Oliver*	169

Chapter 11	Absorbing the First Blow: Truman and the Cold War *John M. Schuessler*	191
Chapter 12	*"It's Not Enough to Say We're in Viet-Nam Simply Because Ike Got Us There":* Lyndon Johnson and the Constraints of Continuity in Vietnam Policymaking *Nicole Anslover*	209
Chapter 13	Lonesome Dove: The Pope, the President, the Church, and Vietnam, 1963-1969 *Lawrence J. McAndrews*	225
Chapter 14	"No Winners, No Losers": Reagan, the Iran-Iraq War and the Gulf's Perpetual Security Dilemma *Bernd Kaussler*	247
Chapter 15	Speech on the Implementation of the GI Bill Extending Educational Benefits to Veterans *Barack Obama*	267
Chapter 16	The Presidency of James Wilson *Michael H. Taylor and Kevin Hardwick*	271
Chapter 17	Post-FDR Republican Presidents' Adherence to Core Conservative Values *Steven E. Standridge*	289
Chapter 18	Politicians Under the Microscope: Eye Blink Rates During the First Bush-Kerry Debate *Patrick A. Stewart and Jonathan "Chad" Mosely*	315
Chapter 19	Exploring Partisan Bias in the Electoral College, 1964-2008 *Phillip J. Ardoin*	331
Chapter 20	First Ladies and the Cultural Everywoman Ideal: Gender Performance and Representation *Jill Abraham Hummer*	345
Government Documents		367
Chapter 21	NSC 68: United States Objectives and Programs for National Security (April 14, 1950) (Excerpts)	369
Chapter 22	Report to the American People on Korea (April 11, 1951) *Harry S. Truman*	387
Chapter 23	Remarks on the Cessation of Bombing of North Vietnam (October 30, 1968) *Lyndon Baines Johnson*	393
Chapter 24	U.S. National Security Directive 114 "U.S. Policy towards the Iran-Iraq War" (November 26, 1983)	399

Chapter 25	U.S. National Security Directive 139, "Measures to Improve U.S. Posture and Readiness to Developments in the Iran-Iraq war (April, 5 1984)	**401**
Congressional Documents		**405**
Chapter 26	Gulf of Tonkin Resolution	**407**
Chapter 27	The War Powers Resolution	**409**
Chapter 28	The Iraq War Resolution	**415**
Index		**421**

PREFACE

The American presidency has become one of the most powerful offices in the world with the ascendency of American power in the 20th century. 'White House Studies Compendium' brings together piercing analyses of the American presidency - dealing with both current issues and historical events. The compendia are the bound issues of 'White House Studies' with the addition of a comprehensive subject index as well as rearranged.

ABOUT THE CONTRIBUTORS

Richard Holtzman has been an Assistant Professor of Political Science at Bryant University in Smithfield, RI, since completing his Ph.D. in Government at the University of Texas at Austin in 2006. He teaches courses on American government, the modern presidency, the politics of government and business, campaigns and elections, and political ideologies. His research interests include presidential rhetoric and power, national service, and the scholarship of teaching and learning.

Glen Sussman is Professor of Political Science at Old Dominion University. His research interests include the American presidency, environmental politics and policy and political behavior. He is the recipient of an Arthur Schlesinger, Jr. Research Fellowship that supported his study of conservation policy during the administration of President John F. Kennedy at the Kennedy Presidential Library in Boston.

Jesse Richman received his PhD from Carnegie Mellon University in 2005. He is an alumnus of the Summer Institute for Political Psychology and the Empirical Implications of Theoretical Models summer program. Dr. Richman spent a year as a visiting assistant professor at Vanderbilt University, and is now Assistant Professor of Political Science at Old Dominion University. His research has appeared in major Political Science journals including Legislative Studies Quarterly. He studies legislative and electoral politics at the state and national levels, with a focus on the interaction between political parties, ideology and the policy agenda.

Joshua Rovner is Assistant Professor of Strategy at the US Naval War College. His research focuses on intelligence, strategy, and American foreign policy. Prior to joining the faculty at the Naval War College, Dr. Rovner was the Stanley Kaplan Postdoctoral Fellow in Political Science and Leadership Studies at Williams College. He holds a Ph.D. in Political Science from the Massachusetts Institute of Technology.

Donald A. Zinman is an Assistant Professor of Political Science at Grand Valley State University in Allendale, Michigan. He obtained his Ph.D. in Government from the University of Texas at Austin in 2006. His research interests include the presidency, political parties and American political development.

Jeff Bloodworth is an assistant professor of history at Gannon University. In addition to articles in the Pacific Northwest Quarterly and Wisconsin Magazine of History, he is working on a history of American liberalism during the 1970s.

Anthony J. Eksterowicz is Professor of Political Science at James Madison University where he teaches courses on the Presidency, Congress, American Government, First Ladies,

Health Care and Political Reform. He has published over forty articles and five books on various subjects such as, Foreign Policy and the Presidency, First Ladies, Politics and Pain Care, Political Parties, Stem Cell Research, the Presidential Pardoning Power and Citizen Participation. His two latest books are; The President and Foreign Policy: Chief architect or General Contractor, NOVA Press 2005 and The Presidential Companion: Readings on First Ladies, Second Edition, University of South Carolina Press, 2006, forthcoming this summer.

Glenn Hastedt is Professor and chair of the Justice Studies Department at James Madison University. His areas of specialization are United States foreign policy and strategic intelligence with an emphasis on questions of intelligence failure and the politics of intelligence. His recent publications include American Foreign Policy: Past, Present, Future, 7the d (Pearson, 2008), American Foreign Policy 09/10 (McGraw Hill, 2008) and articles on intelligence in Intelligence and National Security.

James K. Oliver is Emma S. Morris Professor Emeritus at the University of Delaware where he completed 35 years of service in 2003. He is the recipient of the University's Excellence in teaching, Excellence in Graduate Advisement, and the College of Arts and science Distinguished Lifetime Service Award. He has published five books and more than twenty papers on American foreign policy and defense policy, international organization and governance, and international relations theory.

Ryan Staude is a Ph.D candidate at the University at Albany, SUNY. His dissertation explores George Washington's political philosophy and its effect on nationalism and national identity in the 1790s. Additionally, he is active in film studies and has presented several papers examining film's relationship to history, and how filmmakers treat the past cinematically. He is currently finishing his dissertation, and working on a study analyzing the depiction of colonial and Revolutionary America on film.

Brent A. Strathman is a Visiting Assistant Professor of Government at Dartmouth College, and the Editorial Assistant for Security Studies.

Nicole L. Anslover earned her PhD from the University of Kansas and is currently Assistant Professor of History at Indiana University Northwest, where she teaches classes on Cold War America. She is working on a book addressing the compulsion for continuity from Presidents Truman to Johnson.

Bernd Kaussler received his PhD from the School of International Relations at the University of St Andrews in Scotland and is currently Assistant Professor of Political science at James Madison University where he teaches U.S. Foreign Policy, Middle East Security and Political Islam. His research interests include Iranian and US foreign policies, political violence and human rights in Iran as well as Persian Gulf security.

Lawrence J. McAndrews is Professor of History at St. Norbert College in DePere, WI. He is the author of *Broken Ground: John F. Kennedy and the Politics of Education* and *The Era of Education: The President and the Schools, 1965-2001*.

John Schuessler is an Assistant Professor of Strategy and International Security at the Air War College. He received his PhD in 2007 from the Department of Political Science at the University of Chicago, specializing in international relations. Before coming to the Air War College, he was a Lecturer and Post-Doctoral Fellow with the Committee on International Relations, also at the University of Chicago, as well as a Research Fellow with the International Security Program at the Belfer Center for Science and International Affairs at Harvard University. He thanks the Belfer Center for their support, as well as the

Eisenhower Institute. He also thanks Robert McMahon and Sebastian Rosato for helpful comments on previous drafts. He can be contacted at john.schuessler@maxwell.af.mil.

Phillip Ardoin is an Associate Professor and serves as Program Director of the MA Program in Political Science at Appalachian State University. His research focuses on presidential elections and issues of partisan polarization.

Kevin Hardwick is an Associate Professor of History at James Madison University. His scholarship focuses on 17th and 18th century intellectual and constitutional history. His most recent article appears in the Journal of Southern History.

Jill Abraham Hummer (Ph.D., Virginia) is Assistant Professor of Political Science at Wilson College in Chambersburg, Pennsylvania. Her research focuses on the intersection Phillip Ardoin is an Associate Professor and serves as Program Director of the MA Program in Political Science at Appalachian State University. His research focuses on presidential elections and issues of partisan polarization.

Jonathan "Chad" Moseley is a Civics teacher at Westside High School in Jonesboro, Ar. He Received his B.S. from Northern Illinois University in 2001 and his M.A. in Political Science from Arkansas State University in 2005.

Steve Standridge holds an M.A. in Political Science from the University of Colorado – Denver; an M.S. in Management from Regis University and a B.S. in Business Administration from California Polytechnic (San Luis). He's currently a PhD student at Oklahoma State University's Fire and Emergency Management Program.

Patrick A. Stewart (Ph.D. Northern Illinois University, 1998) is an assistant professor in the Department of Political Science at the University of Arkansas. He previously served as Director of the Masters of Public Administration Program (MPA), and Co-Director of the Center for Social Research (CSR) at Arkansas State University from 2000-8. He has published over twenty five chapters and articles in such journals as American Review of Public Administration, Harvard International Journal of Press/Politics, Motivation and Emotion, Political Psychology, Politics and the Life Sciences, Review of Policy Research, and Technological Forecasting and Social Change. His current research concerns the influence of nonverbal communication on political impression formation and the analysis of Presidential primary candidates and their use of humor during debates.

Michael H. Taylor received an M.A. Education from Virginia Tech in 1995 and taught a U.S. Government course for seven years at Turner Ashby High School in Bridgewater, VA. He is currently completing an M.A. History at James Madison University and his thesis was entitled: *James Wilson: A Willing Target in the Battle for Ratification of the Constitution: The State House Yard Speech — October 6, 1787.*

Chapter 1

CHOOSING A NEW DIRECTION: THE PRESIDENTIAL ELECTION OF 2008

Glen Sussman
Washington State University, Pullman, WA., US

ABSTRACT

After a hotly contested primary campaign, especially on the Democratic side, Barack Obama and John McCain emerged as the nominees of their respective political parties. At the summer conventions, Obama presented Joe Biden as his running mate, a Senator who brought expertise in foreign policy while McCain introduced little known Alaska governor, Sarah Palin as his running mate. Together, the two campaigns offered American voters historical "firsts" - - the first African-American to head a major party ticket, the first woman to be nominated by Republicans as vice president, and McCain who would be the oldest president elected if he won on November 4.

The campaign was characterized by high points with the mobilization of young people joining in to participate in the presidential campaign as well as low points including profoundly disturbing economic conditions that will challenge the new president. Given the differences over policy positions held by the Obama and McCain campaigns, this election will have far reaching implications for U.S. domestic and foreign policy.

INTRODUCTION

In January 2001, George W. Bush, in a disputed election, moved into the White House after campaigning on a theme of "compassionate conservatism" and a commitment that he would be a "uniter not a divider." He inherited a balanced budget with a budget surplus and a country at peace. Eight years later, he left a legacy of record national debt and budget deficits, a huge trade deficit, an unpopular war in Iraq, charges of Constitutional violations related to his war on terrorism, home foreclosures, the collapse of financial institutions, infrastructure needs, and an automobile industry in trouble. Consequently, against a backdrop of an unpopular president, a country involved in two wars, and economic deterioration, the McCain-Obama presidential contest assumed increased salience and importance making the 2008 presidential campaign very consequential for the American electorate. It also provided American citizens with opportunities, surprises, and historic "firsts" in the two century traditional exercise of choosing a new president.

The study of presidential elections is important for several reasons. First, the American president represents the electorate at home and abroad. Candidates for the presidency must choose which domestic and foreign policy issues should receive prominence during their campaign. During the primary season, partisans acting through caucuses and primaries evaluate competing candidates who are seeking the nomination of their party.

Second, during the general election, candidates must propose to the American public their "plans" regarding how they will address the pressing problems relevant to the presidential campaign. This plays an important role as it shows a party's agenda, partisan differences, and insight into post-election presidential action.

Third, the public through the electoral process chooses who they want to lead them over the next four years. After a long primary season and Fall campaign, to what extent have the candidates mobilized their partisans and attracted Independents and the undecided? Obviously, this involves an assessment of the extent to which the electorate believes in a candidate and whether they can predict to their satisfaction, presidential performance as it relates to campaign promises.

Fourth, the candidates represent only one side of the presidential campaign. What is the character of the electorate? To what extent does it exhibit similarities to past elections or to what degree does it reflect changes in American society?

This study is guided by three research questions. First, what was the impact of several important factors usually associated with presidential elections? Second, what were the characteristics of the electorate in the 2008 presidential campaign? Third, how did the 2008 electoral map compare to the previous two presidential elections and why?

THE CAMPAIGN FOR THE PRESIDENCY

There are several factors that assume importance for an investigation into specific presidential elections - - namely, is the seat open or is there an incumbent, the state of the economy, war and peace, the choice of a running mate, the characteristics of the electorate, and how the electoral map compares to previous elections.

During the post-World War II period leading up to the 2008 presidential election, the United States has been represented by eleven presidents. Richard Watson and Norman Thomas pointed out two decades ago, "Incumbent presidents who are running for reelection start out with certain advantages in the electoral contest. They are typically better known to the voters than their opponents, who must strive to narrow the recognition gap between the two candidates." [1] It is interesting to note, however, that among the four presidents who served two full terms during this time - - Eisenhower, Reagan, Clinton, Bush (43) - - only one (Reagan) was succeeded by a partisan candidate for the presidency. Consequently, it is very difficult for the party in power to be successful in maintaining its claim to the White House. During this period, there have been ten contests with a sitting president and five open seats.

As Daniel Shea and Bryan Reece describe it, an "Open seat means the incumbent advantage . . . is not in play." [2] According to James Campbell, open seat contests are more likely to result in very close contests as almost "half of open seat elections have been near dead heats." [3] Campbell also informs us that open seat elections are "influenced to a much lesser degree by retrospective evaluations of the recent presidential administration than are elections in which the incumbent is running." [4]

The state of the nation's economy is a most important factor when examining presidential elections since the condition of the electorate's pocketbook plays a significant role in voters' evaluations of a candidate. In Brad Lockerbie's examination of voter's expectations and the role of the economy in presidential elections, he found that voters' "look to the future" as they evaluate how each candidate's economic plan will affect their personal pocketbook as they plan to make their vote choice. [5] When times are good, it is more likely that the party in power will gain benefits while the voters are more likely to penalize the party in power when economic conditions are deteriorating. [6] As Campbell explains, "The historical record indicates that voter expectations set a growth rate of about three percent as the politically neutral point between punishing and rewarding an in-party's economic record. [7]

War and international crises can be an ally of a president or can bring down a president. Research has shown that presidents tend to benefit from "rally around the flag" support from the American public at least in the short term. As Daynes, Tatalovich and Soden explain, "Sudden military confrontations rally Americans behind presidential leadership and if wars, declared or undeclared, and preemptive military strikes can be short, clean, and victorious, the president is always the winner in the polls. That seems to be the lesson from the history of warfare." [8] However, wars that are not short-lived can have a profound impact on the political fortunes of presidents and by extension, candidates for president who support an ongoing war. As Lyn Ragsdale clearly points out, "people worry when a war looks intractable or unwinnable." [9] Harry Truman suffered terribly in public opinion polls as the Korean War dragged on while Eisenhower benefited. John Kennedy took the blame for the Bay of Pigs fiasco yet benefited from the Cuban missile crisis. Lyndon Johnson who was a domestic policy president and Richard Nixon who had foreign policy expertise were both haunted by the Vietnam war. Jimmy Carter benefited from the Middle East accord he brokered with Israel and Egypt but suffered due to the American hostage crisis near the end of his term in office. Ronald Reagan's image was tarnished by the attack on a Marine barracks in Lebanon but benefited with his order of the invasion of Grenada. George Bush (41) benefited from the invasion of Panama and the first Persian Gulf War while Bill Clinton received mixed results as a result of problems in Haiti, Somalia, and southeastern Europe. Finally, George W. Bush benefited from the events of 9/11 but his invasion of Iraq in 2003 turned into an unpopular war despite his declaration of "Mission Accomplished" on the flight deck of an aircraft carrier.

The choice of a running mate is part and parcel of a presidential campaign. Although eight presidents have died in office, in addition to the resignation of Richard Nixon (one-fifth of all presidents) resulting in the vice president assuming the presidency, the role and impact of vice presidential candidates has been downplayed. Yet in recent years, presidents have been giving more responsibility to their vice presidents. The selection of vice presidential candidates has traditionally rested on the notion that the presidential candidate choose a running mate who offers additional resources to bolster the party or to "balance" the ticket in order to secure and enhance the collection of electoral votes. As Lee Siegelman and Paul

Wahbeck have shown, a variety of factors have been considered important in the selection of a running mate including region, demographics, religion, age, shoring up weaknesses in the presidential candidate, offering the position to a primary season rival or a state with electoral votes. [10] Over the last half century, for instance, we have seen tickets balanced by region and/or religion (Senator John F. Kennedy a northern Catholic and Lyndon Johnson a southern Protestant), office (Governor Bill Clinton choosing Senator Al Gore), gender (Vice President Walter Mondale selecting Congressperson Geraldine Ferraro) or youth (Vice President George H.W. Bush's selection of Senator Dan Quayle). [11]

The characteristics of the electorate play an important role in presidential elections. Seven decades ago, FDR established an important electoral coalition that provided the support he needed in four presidential campaigns and established a foundation for his Democratic successors through the 1960s. By the 1980s, however, the election of Ronald Reagan suggested the emergence of a Republican majority. Among the various demographic voting groups, age, race, and gender remain interesting factors to investigate in terms of the role they have played in American presidential electoral politics. As Joseph Pika and Richard Watson have pointed out, "African Americans and young people - - two groups who historically participate the least - - were formerly denied the franchise. . . . women, another group that traditionally had a comparatively low rate of participation, now vote more than men . . ." [12] Although turnout by women lagged behind that of men since the 19th Amendment was ratified, a "gender gap" emerged in 1980 as women voters turned out in larger numbers than men and gave more support to Democratic candidates. [13] African-Americans (and Latinos) have maintained support for Democrats as well. The year after the voting age was dropped to eighteen by Constitutional Amendment in 1971, approximately 55% of young voters turned out in the Nixon-McGovern presidential contest. However, their turnout has declined ever since leaving political observers waiting to find out when and to what extent the youthful cohort might participate in numbers that would compare to those in the 1972 election.

The electoral map that reflects the results of presidential elections provides a portrait of partisan success and failure every four years. In this regard, region of the country has played an important role for both parties. Where the Democrats were successful in holding Southern states since the Civil War, the character of the electorate began to change as white Southern voters began to shift to the Republican party beginning in 1948 and becoming more noticeable with the election of Richard Nixon in 1968 and Ronald Reagan in 1980. [14] Republicans also fared well in the American Southwest, Rocky Mountain West and Midwest Plains states. In contrast, Democrats' strength in presidential elections has been located in New England, the Northeast, Upper Midwest and the Coastal West. [15] During the last twelve elections (1960-2004), Democrats have won 5 times compared to Republicans who have been successful 7 times. In addition to the Midwest farm belt that has been very supportive of Republican presidential candidates, since the 1968 presidential campaign, Southern states have been more likely to vote Republican unless a Southern Democrat was in the race, thus helping Lyndon Johnson, Jimmy Carter and Bill Clinton. After twelve years of Republican dominance of the White House during the Reagan and Bush Administrations, the Clinton presidency maintained power throughout the 1990s only to see George W. Bush win back the White House for Republicans in 2000 and again in 2004. Against the backdrop of a two term administration, Republicans would have to wait until November to find out if Bush (43) could succeed as Reagan did before him in helping to retain the White House for his fellow Republican from the Southwest, John McCain, in 2008. Democrats would have to wait as well to see if Barack Obama, a Northern Democrat, could do what other Northern Democrats could not do.

Taking into consideration these factors, the two candidates who emerged as the nominees of their respective parties were, to a large degree, unexpected. As one observer of the primary process explained:

> As far as Democrats were concerned, Hillary Clinton was the front-runner and heir apparent for the Democratic nomination. On the Republican side, John McCain's faltering campaign in the early months of the primary season suggested that Republicans would end up selecting another nominee. [16]

Moreover, what heightened interest in the 2008 campaign for the presidency was the likelihood of a Democrat or Republican "first" - - the first woman (Hillary Clinton), the first African-American (Barack Obama), the first Morman (Mitt Romney), the first Latino (Bill Richardson), or the oldest nominee (John McCain).

THE PRIMARY SEASON

As the American people watched the primary season unfold, partisans among the American electorate had a variety of choices among Democratic and Republican contenders seeking the nomination of their respective parties. On the Democratic side, Hillary Clinton, Barack Obama and John Edwards were the leading contenders followed by a second tier of candidates including Bill Richardson, Joe Biden, Mike Gravel, and Dennis Kucinich who sought the nomination. However, it was Clinton and Obama who were locked in a very competitive race for the nomination of their party throughout the length of the primary season. Although Hillary Clinton entered the Democratic primary season as the "front runner," Barack Obama's victory in Iowa's first caucus of the season immediately changed the direction and character of the campaign. Obama captured 38% of the vote followed by John Edwards with 30% while Clinton finished in third place with 29%. [17] A week later, Obama was unable to ride his momentum to victory in New Hampshire as Hillary Clinton won in the country's first major primary of the season. Clinton picked up 39% of the vote to Obama's 36.4%. [18] The two candidates split the Super Tuesday states thus ensuring a contentious contest as the two campaigns moved into the later stages of the primary season. In the end, Senator Obama secured a sufficient number of delegates to win the Democratic nomination at the summer convention. As James Campbell explains, "Despite Clinton's winning many of the large states (including New York, California, Pennsylvania, and Ohio) and nine of the final fifteen primaries, Obama did well enough in the proportional representation primaries and in the caucus states, along with the party's super-delegates, to secure the nomination." [19]

On the Republican side, former Arkansas governor, Mike Huckabee defeated former Massachusetts governor, Mitt Romney in the Iowa caucuses but a week later came in third in New Hampshire. In the party competition for the Republican nomination that lacked a clear front runner, Senator John McCain rebounded in New Hampshire by winning 37 percent of the vote to Romney's 32% with Huckabee capturing a meager 11%. A resurgent McCain campaign began to push aside his partisan competitors including Mitt Romney, Mike Huckabee, Fred Thompson, Rudy Giuliani, and Ron Paul. McCain, seeking the Republican nomination for a second time, went on to perform very well in the winner-take-all system on Super Tuesday, thus setting the stage for the Arizona Senator to win the Republican nomination. Ironically, notwithstanding the enthusiasm for Obama among Democrats and Independents, another important problem confronting McCain was a backlash against him by the conservative base of his party who saw him as too liberal to represent Republicans in the November general election. [20]

The stage was set for the contest between two United States Senators - - namely, Democrat Barack Obama and Republican John McCain. In this case, the Democrats nominated the first African-American candidate of a major national party, a Senator with a liberal voting record. Republicans nominated a longtime Senator who, despite a reputation of being a "maverick," maintained a conservative voting record and would be, if elected, the oldest individual elected to the White House.

THE GENERAL ELECTION

The general election that takes place during the Fall brings the two nominees of the major party organizations into a heated contest for the White House. According to one political observer of the Obama-McCain contest:

> Eight years ago, the Bush Administration inherited a balanced budget, a budget surplus and a country at peace. However, life in the U.S. changed on 9/11 but more importantly in March 2003 with the invasion of Iraq by the U.S. Moreover, the economy has deteriorated with huge budget and trade deficits, home foreclosures, infrastructure needs and the collapse of financial institutions. Against a backdrop of a very unpopular Republican president, a country at war and economic deterioration, the McCain-Obama presidential contest has taken on added importance making the 2008 presidential election very consequential for the American electorate. [21]

The 2008 presidential contest reflected two distinct campaigns with tremendous "enthusiasm" for Obama among a sizable segment of the American electorate and, in contrast, a McCain campaign struggling to find its way. The discussion that follows examines the impact of several factors involved in the 2008 race for the presidency.

AN OPEN COMPETITIVE SEAT

Incumbency is an important advantage for presidents seeking a second term in office. The 2008 Fall campaign was, however, characterized by an open seat where the incumbent was not eligible to run again. The campaign was also distinct since the Vice President, Dick Cheney, decided not to seek the nomination of his party which resulted in several Republican partisans making the decision to seek the nomination of their party. As shown in Table 1, only one out of the five open contests during the period 1948-2004 resulted in the candidate of the party in power winning the presidential election. Despite George H.W. Bush's difficulties with the conservative base of the Republican party, riding on the coattails of

Ronald Reagan, he was able to retain the White House for Republicans in 1988. Having said this, could John McCain, riding on the coattails of George W. Bush replicate the success of George H.W. Bush two decades later?

An added dimension to the campaign was that the incumbent President George W. Bush was very unpopular with approval ratings dropping into the low 30s to mid-20s percentile. Although McCain indicated that he would retain his "maverick" approach to politics and that he disagreed with Bush on a number of issues, Bush's low approval ratings did not bode well for the Republican nominee. On the one hand, as Campbell has argued, "From an internal political science perspective, the 2008 election might be characterized as an open seat showdown between V.O. Key's retrospective voting perspective favoring Obama and Anthony Downs' prospective voting perspective that may favor McCain." [22] On the other hand, as Larry Sabato has argued, "It is undeniable that George W. Bush has been an unpopular president for longer than any of his predecessors, at least since the dawn of the age of polling in 1936" and he "ended up in the mid-20s right before Election Day - - an unprecedented level of unpopularity at just the wrong time" while only "27% of the actual voters on November 4 approved of President Bush's performance in office." [23] Consequently, McCain was confronted with a polling statistic that did not serve his campaign well as voters made their choice who to support for president. In short, the campaign could be characterized by both retrospective and prospective attitudes among voters as McCain was saddled with a very unpopular outgoing Republican incumbent while he, himself, was unable to articulate to voters how he would resolve a faltering economy and the war in Iraq.

Table 1. Open Seats in Presidential Elections, 1948-1952

Election Year	Candidates and Party	Which Party Won
1952	Eisenhower (R) Stevenson (D)	Out Party
1960	Kennedy (D) Nixon (R)	Out Party
1968	Nixon (R) Humphrey (D)	Out Party
1988	Bush (41) (R) Dukakis (D)	In Party
2000	Bush (43) (R) Gore (D)	Out Party

THE STATE OF THE ECONOMY

Although the war in Iraq had been a major factor in voter's calculations regarding the choice between Obama or McCain for the White House, the deteriorating economy was a major concern for voters by the summer of 2008. Lost jobs, collapse of financial institutions, a weakening automobile industry, individually and together, loomed over the presidential contest between McCain and Obama. Moreover, home foreclosures, delayed plans for retirement, and the increasing price of gasoline angered Americans who struggled during the first half of 2008 with continuing trouble on the horizon as the presidential campaign unfolded. During the Fall campaign, the "Wall Street meltdown crisis in financial institutions hit in mid-September, dominated the remainder of the campaign, and shifted a significant portion of the vote from McCain to Obama." [24] And as the Obama campaign reminded voters, as far as John McCain was concerned, the "fundamentals of our economy are strong."

The cumulative impact of a variety of economic problems presented the voters with serious concerns about which candidate could be trusted to successfully address the economic meltdown. A federal government stimulus plan amounting to $700 billion became a focal point for voters and the media. The prospect of additional taxpayer dollars added to voter anxiety. As reported in a Gallup poll in December 2007, one-third of the American electorate viewed the Iraq war as the most important issue facing the country, more than the economy and health care combined. [25] In February 2008 the Iraq war had been eclipsed by economic affairs as the number one issue and by October 2008 only ten percent of the American electorate cited the Iraq war as the primary issue facing voters. [26]

On election day, exit polls revealed that more than six out of ten voters (62%) cited the economy as the most important issue facing the country despite two wars (Iraq and Afghanistan) and concerns about health care among other issues. [27] While McCain performed well among voters who felt that their personal financial situation would get "better," those who believed that their financial situation would get "worse" supported Obama. [28]

WAR AND PEACE

It is a well-known axiom in presidential politics that when the country is confronted with an international crisis the American people will "rally around the president." Poll data shows that presidential approval ratings increase during the pre-to-post event. For instance, John F. Kennedy's approval increased during the Cuban Missile Crisis; Jimmy Carter saw increased support among the American people (in the short term) when Americans were taken hostage in the Persian Gulf; George Bush (41) gained benefits as a result of the first Persian Gulf War a year before re-election; and George Bush (43) saw his poll numbers skyrocket after 9/11 and again but not so high during the U.S. invasion of Iraq in March 2003.

Benefits are elusive, however, and some presidents might find themselves in trouble with the American electorate as good fortune turns into profound difficulties. Taking Jimmy Carter's example above, he initially gained the support of the American people and used this political capital to brush aside Senator Ted Kennedy's efforts to challenge him for the Democratic nomination in 1980. However, as the hostage crisis continued for over a year with nightly reminders for Americans put forth by network news anchors, it eventually assumed the role of a foreign policy nightmare for the president. The hostage crisis created a perception of Carter and the United States as weak, inept, and unable to resolve this lengthy tragedy. Bush (43) believed that the attack on the United States on 9/11 and the subsequent support he received from the American people provided the foundation upon which he could shift military strategy away from Afghanistan with a new focus on Iraq. Like his father before him during the first Persian Gulf War, Bush (43) saw his approval ratings increase substantially. However, as the Iraq war wore on, Americans tired of the conflict as casualties mounted and hundreds of billions of tax dollars were directed to the war rather than domestic needs. The considerable public support and goodwill that Bush had gained resulting from 9/11 and during the early stages of the Iraq war turned into strong opposition by the American citizenry as the country headed into the 2008 primary season.

Senator Obama reminded voters that he had opposed the Iraq War from the beginning while Senator McCain continued his support for the war reiterating his view that there was no substitute for victory. Notwithstanding research (albeit dated) that has shown that military heroes have been more successful at winning presidential votes than civilians, [29] civilian Obama defeated war hero McCain.

THE CHOICE OF A RUNNING MATE

During the 2008 presidential contest, to what extent did the two candidates choose running mates who brought strengths to the ticket? Joe Biden, a long time member of the U.S. Senate with substantial foreign policy experience including service as chair of the powerful Senate Foreign Relations Committee was chosen by Obama as his running mate. The selection of Biden helped to downplay Obama's lack of experience in international affairs and provided support from a longtime legislator with experience in the operation of the upper chamber of the U.S. Congress. In turn, John McCain surprised Democrats as well as his Republican supporters. The Arizona Senator could have selected Mitt Romney as his running mate, a candidate who would have shored up McCain's lack of experience in economic affairs. However, in an effort to bolster his campaign, demonstrate that he was what he claimed to be, a "maverick," and nail down his connection to the conservative base of the Republican party, McCain chose Alaska Governor, Sarah Palin, to serve on the Republican ticket. Here was a candidate who, according to the *New York Times* was a "conservative Christian who opposed abortion. She runs marathons. She fishes. She hunts" while she portrayed herself as a "needed outside agent of change . . . ." [30] Sarah Palin initially resonated well with the conservative base of the Republican party but over time, her weaknesses came to dominate her attempt to be a loyal and knowledgeable partner with McCain. For instance, with less than two months left in the Fall campaign, she was involved in a "troubling scandal involving allegations that she used her power as governor to fire the 'top cop' in Alaska because he refused to fire an Alaska state trooper who divorced Palin's sister." [31]

Although Biden brought baggage with him into the 2008 campaign (e.g., allegations of plagiarism in previous campaigns), he had been vetted and had the support of Obama and the Democratic Party. In contrast, Palin was a novelty, unknown, untested, and a likely target of the news media. In contrast to her Democratic counterpart, Joe Biden, Palin, whose political experience rested on her service as city council member and mayor of the small town of Wasilla and two years as governor of Alaska, was unable to demonstrate to American voters that she was prepared to be president. Moreover, her overall lack of experience made it difficult for Republicans to criticize Obama's lack of experience in foreign affairs. [32]]

THE CHARACTERISTICS OF THE ELECTORATE

Voting behavior among the American electorate has been a central aspect of research on American politics both by academic scholars and the news media. Concerns have been raised that since the Kennedy-Nixon presidential campaign in 1960 that attracted approximately 63% of Americans to the polls on election day, voter turnout has declined (see Table 2). Moreover, on a comparative scale, the low turnout of voters in Switzerland saves the U.S. from assuming the worst voting turnout among the advanced industrial democracies. Having said that, the Obama-McCain presidential contest reflected a level of enthusiasm not seen for decades as turnout among American voters almost reached that of the Kennedy-Nixon contest. This was a positive sign for American democracy in general and voter participation in particular.

Table 2. Voter Turnout in Presidential Elections, 1960-2008

Election Year	Turnout
1960	62.8%
1964	61.9
1968	60.8
1972	55.2
1976	53.6
1980	52.6
1984	53.1
1988	50.2
1992	55.2
1996	49.1
2000	51.3
2004	55.3
2008	61.7

Source: Data for 1960-2004 obtained from The American Presidency Project at www.presidency. ucsb. edu/data/turnout.php/. Accessed January 25, 2009. Data for 2008 obtained from the United States Elections Project at http://elections.gmu.edu/Turnout_2008G.html. Accessed January 25, 2008.

Notwithstanding the importance of the factors discussed above in presidential elections, what made the 2008 contest interesting and potentially consequential, was the change in the composition and character of the voting population, especially among two demographic categories - - namely, age and race. Among all age cohorts in election studies, the youthful cohort (18-29 years old) has been characterized by low turnout. Or as M. Margaret Conway reminds us, "voter turnout increases with age." [33] Moreover, Martin Wattenberg raised concerns in 2007 about the "relative lack among today's young people of a sense of civic obligation to vote. . . ." suggesting that since the "current generation of young people has a relatively weak sense of citizen duty, its current poor turnout rates may well be a constant state of affairs throughout their lifetimes." [34] As far as issues were concerned, young voters mirrored the sentiments of older voters as the economy and jobs, terrorism and the war in Iraq commanded their attention. On the other hand, young and older voters diverged when it came to technology- - its use by younger voters and its employment by the Obama campaign that targeted young voters. For instance, the Obama campaign used Facebook and YouTube among others in its communication efforts regarding young voters.

It has also been the case that African-American voters and Latino voters have voting rates that have remained less than of white voters. Having said this, the share of overall turnout among the young, African-Americans and Latinos increased for the 2008 presidential election. Young voters comprised approximately 21% of the 2008 electorate compared to 17% in 2004, African-Americans constituted 13% of all voters in 2008 up from 11% in 2004 while the Latino share of the electorate increased from 6% to 8%. [35]

As shown in Table 3, there is a strong relationship between age and candidate preference. Among voters aged 18-64, Obama was the preferred candidate. Moreover, young voters, in particular, supported the Democratic presidential nominee in large numbers. Only the age cohort 65 and older exhibited a pattern of voting at variance with the other age groups as these voters supported McCain by a ten point margin. There was also a strong relationship between race and voting preference. While Latinos and Asian-Americans voted strongly for Obama, African-American voters supported Obama overwhelmingly. In contrast, white voters split their votes with a sizable advantage going to McCain.

The increase among young voters, African-American voters, and Latino voters had an especially significant impact since their votes went primarily to Democrat Barack Obama. Although Asian-Americans constitute a smaller segment of the American electorate, these voters reflected a similar pattern to that suggested above - - namely, strong, partisan support for the Democratic presidential nominee. The high, partisan turnout among voters in these demographic groups suggests both high expectations among these voters and potential success for Democratic candidates at least in the near future.

Table 3. Voter Turnout by Sociodemographic Group, 2008

		Obama	McCain	PDI*
Age				
	65 & older	44	54	-10
	45-64	50	49	+1
	30-44	52	46	+6
	18-29	66	31	+35
Race				
	African-American	96	3	+93
	Asian-American	63	34	+29
	Latino	67	30	+37
	White	43	57	-14
Gender				
	Female	56	43	+13
	Male	49%	48%	+1
New Voters		68	31	+37

Source: Adapted from CNN at www.cnn.site.printthis.clickability.com/ and the BBC at http://newsvote.bbc.co.uk/mpapps/pagetools/print/news.bbc.uk/ Accessed January 17, 2009.

Women constitute another major demographic group of voters who have played an especially important role in presidential elections since the "gender gap" was identified in 1980 with women voting at a higher level than men in every presidential election since then.

Women have also been more likely to vote for Democrat presidential candidates over Republicans. [36] In the 2008 presidential election, the female voting cohort constituted approximately 53% of all voters compared to 47% for their male counterparts. As we noted above, where we have seen increases in voting turnout among young voters, African-Americans, and Latinos, the same can be said about women.

Moreover, the gender gap remained a conspicuous factor in the Obama-McCain presidential contest. On the one hand, male voters split their votes evenly for the Democrat and Republican candidate. On the other hand, a 13 point gap separated women and men as female voters leaned strongly in favor of Obama.

It is also important to note the role of new voters in the 2008 presidential election. Here was a cohort of voters who McCain and Obama could target in their appeal to gain votes. As reported by the British Broadcasting Corporation (BBC), in the 2004 presidential election, Democrat John Kerry secured 53% of new voters to 46% who supported Republican President George W. Bush while four years later, two-thirds of new voters supported the Democrat nominee, Barack Obama. [37]

Table 4. The Electoral College Map: 2000, 2004, 2008

State	2000 Dem	2000 Rep	2004 Dem	2004 Rep	2008 Dem	2008 Rep	Change
Alaska		x		x		x	NC
Alabama		x		x		x	NC
Arizona		x		x		x	NC
Arkansas		x		x		x	NC
California	x		x		x		NC
Colorado		x		x	x		+Dem
Connecticut	x		x		x		NC
Deleware	x		x		x		NC
Florida		x		x	x		+Dem
Georgia		x		x		x	NC
Hawaii	x		x		x		NC
Idaho		x		x		x	NC
Illinois	x		x		x		NC
Indiana		x		x	x		+Dem

State	2000 Dem	2000 Rep	2004 Dem	2004 Rep	2008 Dem	2008 Rep	Change
Iowa	x			x	x		+Dem*
Kansas		x		x		x	NC
Kentucky		x		x		x	NC
Louisiana		x		x		x	NC
Maine	x		x		x		NC
Maryland	x		x		x		NC
Massachusetts	x		x		x		NC
Michigan	x		x		x		NC
Minnesota	x		x		x		NC
Mississippi		x		x		x	NC
Missouri		x		x		x	NC
Montana		x		x		x	NC
Nebraska		x		x		x	NC
Nevada		x		x	x		+Dem
New Hampshire		x	x		x		+Dem*
New Jersey	x		x		x		NC
New Mexico	x			x	x		+Dem*
North Carolina		x		x	x		+Dem
North Dakota		x		x		x	NC
New York	x		x		x		NC
Ohio		x		x	x		+Dem
Oklahoma		x		x		x	NC
Oregon	x		x		x		NC

Table 4. (Continued)

State	2000 Dem	2000 Rep	2004 Dem	2004 Rep	2008 Dem	2008 Rep	Change
Pennsylvania	x		x		x		NC
Rhode Island	x		x		x		NC
South Carolina		x		x		x	NC
South Dakota		x		x		x	NC
Tennessee		x		x		x	NC
Texas		x		x		x	NC
Utah		x		x		x	NC
Vermont	x		x		x		NC
Virginia		x		x	x		+Dem
Washington	x		x		x		NC
West Virginia		x		x		x	NC
Wisconsin	x		x		x		NC
Wyoming		x		x		x	NC

Source: Adapted from results obtained from CNN at www.cnn.com/ELECTION/2004/pages/results/electoral.college/Accessed June 28, 2008 and November 20, 2008.
NC = No change
*States that alternated between the two parties in 2000 and 2004

THE ELECTORAL MAP

The Republican party won the White House in 2000 and retained it in 2004. Close observation of the electoral maps of the presidential elections of 2000 and 2004 show almost an identical outcome in states' support of the Democratic and Republican contenders. Democrats Al Gore (2000) and John Kerry (2004) won New England, the Northeast, Upper Midwest and the Coastal West while George W. Bush carried the Rocky Mountain West, Farm Belt plains states, Midwest, Ohio River valley, and the South.

Heading toward election day, a key question was the extent to which the Obama campaign could secure electoral support in states that were reliably Republican. As Table 4 shows, Obama was able to succeed on two fronts - - namely, holding on to Blue states and securing sufficient electoral support in several Red states. During the last two presidential elections, there were ten states that had voted Republican at least once and seven that voted Republican in both the 2000 and 2004 elections. In 2008, Obama won all ten of these states that demonstrated the range of his support geographically. From Colorado in the Rocky Mountains to Iowa in the Midwest, from Nevada in the West to Virginia in the South, Obama expanded the Democratic base of support. Moreover, he picked up Red states that had a large number of electoral votes including Ohio and Florida.

CONCLUSION AND SUMMARY PROPOSITIONS

The 2008 presidential election, as described by Alan Abramowitz, was indeed, a "campaign full of twists and turns" that eventually was "shaped by two dominant features of the political environment in 2008 - - a deteriorating economy and a deeply discontented but divided electorate." [38] Having said this, several other factors played a role, some larger, some smaller, in the final outcome of the election. In the end, Democrat Barack Obama defeated Republican John McCain 53% to 46% in the popular vote and 365 to 173 in electoral votes.

The presidential contest was characterized by high points including an increased level of enthusiasm among many voters, increased turnout in general and among several demographic groups in particular, and an election that gained the attention of citizens around the world. The election also exhibited several low points including a deteriorating economy and a country involved in two wars.

On the basis of this study, several propositions can be set forth regarding the 2008 presidential election. These summary generalizations also provide the basis for future research about presidential elections.

Proposition 1: Open seat competitive elections have, more often than not, benefited the out party.

As we have seen in this study, although fifteen presidential elections have occurred during the period 1948-2004, only five of them were open seat contests. More importantly, only 20% (1 out of 5) resulted in the party in power retaining the White House. The 2008 presidential election, once again, demonstrated the difficulty of the in party holding on to the presidency as Democrat Barack Obama defeated Republican John McCain. Moreover, despite research referred to earlier in this study, the Obama-McCain contest was not a close race as voters looked both retrospectively (low approval ratings for the leader of the in party) and prospectively (the extent to which the candidate of the party in power offered solutions to contemporary problems) as they made their voter preference known on election day. The candidate of the out party (Obama), won by seven percentage points in the popular vote and by more than 2 to 1 in the electoral vote far from a "dead heat" or "close contest."

Proposition 2: Economic problems remain a fundamental factor in making it difficult for the party in power to retain the White House.

Although the Iraq War was the major issue among the American electorate prior to the primary season, it was eventually overtaken by voters' increasing concerns about the state of the economy. In the midst of the economic meltdown, Obama reminded voters that McCain believed that the "fundamentals of the economy are strong." Obama benefited and McCain suffered as a deteriorating economy sent the stock market tumbling with Americans putting off their planned retirements. Home foreclosures, collapse of financial institutions, increasing unemployment among other bad news had a profound impact on the voters as they headed to the polls.

Proposition 3: International crises benefit the party in power in the short term but can become an albatross around the neck of the in party if the crisis continues for too long and the American people fail to see a resolution of the problem.

The tragedy of 9/11 benefited President George W. Bush as the country rallied around him in support of going after those responsible for the attack on the United States (Osama bin Laden and the Taliban government of Afghanistan that protected him). Moreover, the president's invasion of Iraq in March 2003 once again propelled Bush in the polls as the president announced that Saddam Hussein had weapons of mass destruction that threatened his neighbors as well as the U.S. However, the failure to capture bin Laden, the realization that Iraq did not have weapons of mass destruction, and a drawn out war in Iraq with increasing casualties turned the American people against the war. The contrast between the candidate of the out party, Obama, and the candidate of the in party, McCain, could not have been more clear as Obama reminded voters that he opposed the war from day one and that he intended to bring home the troops while McCain supported the war announcing that there was no substitute for victory.

Proposition 4: The role of the Vice Presidential running mate remains limited in presidential campaigns.

FDR's vice president John Nance Garner once stated that the vice presidency ain't worth a bucket of warm spit. This characterization of the office summed up the lack of importance of the office held by the person who, ironically, was only a heartbeat away from the presidency. However, in more recent years, we have seen presidents give more power and responsibility to their vice presidents including Walter Mondale serving with Jimmy Carter, Al Gore serving with Bill Clinton, and Dick Cheney serving with George W. Bush.

In the 2008 presidential campaign, Obama reached out to a long standing Senator and chair of the powerful Senate Foreign Relations Committee to join the Democratic ticket as McCain selected a little known governor of Alaska. Governor Sarah Palin's conservative ideology won the support of the Republican base but over time her weaknesses became more apparent as she became increasingly unable to demonstrate that she was able to take over the presidency in the event of a tragedy involving the president. Public opinion polls indicated that voters exhibited a concern about the candidates who might be called on to serve in the White House. According to CNN and the *Washington Post*, exit polls revealed that six out of ten voters felt that Governor Palin was not qualified to be president. [39] Having said this, voters remained focused on the two candidates at the top of the ticket.

Proposition 5: Voter mobilization, voter interest in the campaign, and voter enthusiasm for a presidential candidate remain important factors in presidential elections.

Since the Kennedy-Nixon presidential contest almost five decades ago, we have seen voting turnout decline in the U.S. and remain near the bottom of citizen participation compared to other advanced industrial democracies. The primary season and the Obama-McCain campaign for the presidency signaled a movement toward enhanced voter mobilization efforts, increased voter interest in the 2008 presidential election, and conspicuous enthusiasm among the voters, especially for Obama. Although Hilary Clinton was touted as the Democratic frontrunner, Barack Obama sent a clear signal beginning with the Iowa caucuses that he was a serious candidate and he intended to win the presidency. Obama's Republican counterpart, John McCain, overcame early problems with his campaign to surge ahead of his partisan competitors to win his party's nomination. Obama, in particular, used technological innovations to reach out to the voters while the enthusiasm level for Obama surged as the campaign for the presidency evolved.

Voter mobilization and increased enthusiasm reflected the changing character of the American electorate. In addition to increased voter turnout among all Americans, exit polls revealed that turnout also increased among African-Americans, Latinos and young voters. Moreover, these same demographic groups were associated with an increasing share of the total vote. Moreover, the gender gap favoring the Democratic candidate for president among female voters was evident on election day. It is still too early to make a broad generalization whether these changes bode well for the Democratic Party. Future elections will provide the answer whether and to what extent the character of the electorate that put Obama into the White House will remain or will, instead, be related to this specific election.

Proposition 6: The results of the 2008 presidential election indicate that Democrats can win on a national basis beyond New England, the Northeast, Upper Midwest, and Coastal West.

Since the election of New Englander John F. Kennedy, the only Democrats able to win the White House were identified with Southern states - - namely, Lyndon Johnson (Texas), Jimmy Carter (Georgia), and Bill Clinton (Arkansas). In contrast, Upper Midwesterners Hubert Humphrey (1968) and Walter Mondale (1984) and New Englanders Michael Dukakis (1988) and John Kerry (2004) were unable to win the presidency. In November 2008, Upper

Midwesterner Barack Obama became the first "Northerner" to win the presidency since JFK. In doing so, he was able to expand the base of support for a non-Southern Democrat candidate and win in all regions of the country including states that had voted Republican in the previous two presidential elections. External factors including the state of the economy and two wars along with a strong candidate and very effective voter mobilization enabled Democrats to make inroads in previously reliable Republican "Red" states.

In concluding this study, one final question concerns the issue of realignment. James Ceaser and Daniel DiSalvo define realignment as a "major electoral shift in the relative strength of the political parties (and therefore likely to endure for awhile), accompanied or sealed by a shift in the reigning political ideas that set government's agenda, plus a major change in the direction of public policy." [40] Very few elections have been identified as realigning elections with the last one occurring in 1932 with the election of FDR. While some observers thought that the 1980 election of Ronald Reagan would be a realigning election, it failed to exhibit the characteristics of this type of fundamental change. [41] Although the 2008 presidential election fulfilled one of the realignment criteria set forth by Watson and Thomas - - namely, an "unusually large number of new voters may also enter the electoral arena and cast their ballots disproportionately for one party's candidate," [42] the success of the Democrats in capturing the White House is only in its infancy. Sufficient time is required in order to look back and make an assessment of the extent to which the presidential election of 2008 signals a new direction in party politics.

REFERENCES

[1] Richard Watson and Norman Thomas, The Politics of the Presidency, 2nd ed. (Washington, DC: CQ Press, 1988), 78.

[2] Daniel M. Shea and Bryan Reece, 2008 Election Preview (Upper Saddle River, NJ: Prentice Hall, 2008), 7.

[3] James E. Campbell, "An Exceptional Election: Performance, Values, and Crisis in the 2008 Presidential Election," The Forum 6 (2008).

[4] James E. Campbell, "An Open-Seat Election in an Era of Polarized Partisan Parity: A Pre-Election Perspective on the 2008 Presidential Election," A paper prepared for delivery at the panel on "The 2008 Election in Long-Term Perspective" at the 2008 Annual Meeting of the American Political Science Association, August 28-31, 2008.

[5] Brad Lockerbie, "A Look to the Future: Forecasting the 2004 Presidential Election," PS: Political Science and Politics 37 (October 2004).

[6] See Ray C. Fair, "The Effect of Economic Events on Votes for President: 1984 Update," Political Behavior 10 (1988).

[7] Campbell, "An Exceptional Election." For those interested in the impact of fiscal policy as opposed to macroeconomic policy and its impact on presidential electoral fortunes see Alfred G. Cuzan and Charles M. Bundrick, "Fiscal Policy and Presidential Elections, 1880-1992," Polity 29 (Fall 1996).

[8] Byron W. Daynes, Raymond Tatalovich, Dennis L. Soden, To Govern A Nation: Presidential Power and Politics (New York: St. Martin's Press, 1998), 279.

[9] Lyn Ragsdale, Presidential Politics (Boston: Houghton Mifflin company, 1993), 150.

[10] Lee Siegelman and Paul J. Wahlbeck, "The 'Veepstakes': Strategic Choice in Presidential Running Mate Selection," American Political Science Review 91 (December 1997). See also Jay A. Hurwitz, "Vice Presidential Eligibility and Selection Patterns," Polity 12 (Spring 1980).
[11] Richard Pious, The Presidency (Boston: Allyn and Bacon, 1996), 128 and Lyn Ragsdale, Presidential Politics (Boston: Houghton Mifflin Company, 1993), 240.
[12] Joseph A. Pika and Richard A. Watson, The Presidential Contest (Washington, DC: CQ Press, 1996), 123.
[13] M. Margaret Conway, Gertrude Steuernagel, and David Ahert, Women and Political Participation (Washington, DC: CQ Press, 1997), 79 and Jeff Manza and Clem Brooks, "The Gender Gap in U.S. Presidential Elections: When? Why? Implications?" American Journal of Sociology 103 (March 1998).
[14] See Stephen J. Wayne, The Road to the White House 2008 (Boston: Thomason Wadsworth 2008), 99 and Paul Allen Beck and Frank J. Sorauf, Party Politics in America, 7th ed. (New York: Harper Collins Publishers, 1992), 249.
[15] Wayne, The Road to the White House 2008, 99.
[16] Glen Sussman, "The 2008 Presidential Campaign," Letras Internacionales 2 (September 2008).
[17] Larry Sabato, "Clinton as Truman, McCain as Lazarus, Obama-Mania, Hucka-Boom or Bust, and the Presidential Players," Sabato's Crystal Ball 6 (January 10, 2008).
[18] Sabato, "Clinton as Truman."
[19] Campbell, "An Esceptional Election," 7.
[20] CNN, "McCain Tangles with Conservatives," at *www.cnn.com/2008/POLITICS /02/05/conservative.backlash*. Accessed February 8, 2008.
[21] Sussman, "The 2008 Presidential Campaign."
[22] Campbell, "An Open-Seat Presidential Election," 9.
[23] Larry Sabato, "The 2008 Election in Perspective: Just What We Would Have Expected," Sabato's Crystal Ball 7 (January 2009), 1.
[24] Campbell, "An Exceptional Election," 13.
[25] Rick Maese, "Iraq War Pushed Aside As Campaign Issue," Baltimore Sun at *www.baltimoresun.com/news/world/iraq/bal-te.iraq31oct31002027,0,6808971*, print. Accessed January 26, 2009.
[26] Maese, "Iraq War Pushed Aside," and Frank Davies, "War in Iraq Looms As Campaign Issue" at *www.mercurynews.com/ci_8149197*. Accessed January 26, 2009.
[27] CNN, "Exit Polls: Obama Wins Big Among Young, Minority Voters" at *http://cnn.site.printthis.clickability.com/pt/cpt?action=cpt&title=Exit+polls%3A+Obama+*. Accessed January 17, 2009.
[28] Larry J. Sabato, "The 2008 Election in Perspective," 7.
[29] Albert Somit, "The Military Hero as Presidential Candidate," Public Opinion Quarterly 12 (Summer 1948).
[30] William Yardley, "Novice Stands Her Ground on Veterans' Turf in Alaska," New York Times at *www.nytimes.com/2006/10/29/us/politics/29alaska.html?_r=1&oref=slogin& pagew*. Accessed August 29, 2008.
[31] Sussman, "The 2008 Presidential Election."

[32] Robert Barnes and Michael D. Shear, "McCain Chooses Alaska Governor Palin as Running Mate," Washington Post at *www.washingtonpost.com/wp-dyn/content/article/2008/08/29/AR2008082901112_p*. Accessed August 29, 2008.
[33] M. Margaret Conway, Political Participation in the United States, 2nd ed. (Washington, DC: CQ Press, 17.
[34] Martin P. Wattenberg, Is Voting For Young People? (New York: Longman, 2007), 138.
[35] Michael McDonald, "The Return of the Voter: Voter Turnout in the 2008 Presidential Election," The Forum 6 (2008), 33 and United States Election Project, "America Goes to the Polls: 2008 Voter Turnout Brief" at *www.nonprofitvote.org*. Accessed November 6, 2008.
[36] Conway, Steuernagel, Ahern, Women and Political Participation, 79-80.
[37] .SteveSchifferes, "Who Voted for Obama?" at *http://newsvote.bbc.co.uk/mpapps/pagetools/print/news.bbc.co.uk/2/hi/americas/us_election*.Accessed
[38] Alan I. Abramowitz, The 2008 Election (New York: Longman, 2009), 2.
[39] CNN, "Exit Polls," and Alec MacGillis and Jon Cohen, "A Vote Decided by Big Turnout and Big Discontent with GOP," Washington Post at *www.washingtonpost.com/wp-dyn/content/article/2008/aa/04/AR2008110404088/p...* Accessed January 25, 2009.
[40] James W. Ceaser and Daniel DiSalvo, "The Magnitude of the 2008 Democratic Victory: By the Numbers," The Forum 6 (2008), 9.
[41] See Beck and Sorauf, Party Politics in America, 154, 174-176.
[42] Watson and Thomas, The Politics of the Presidency, 104.

Chapter 2

CONGRESS ON THE LINE: THE 2008 CONGRESSIONAL ELECTION AND THE OBAMA PRESIDENCY

Jesse Richman

ABSTRACT

This article explores the 2008 U.S. congressional election. The election outcome was shaped by the political context, by Democratic fundraising and candidate recruitment success, and by Democratic advantages on most salient public issues. What happened in the congressional races has substantial implications for the Obama presidency. The scope of the Democratic gains in Congress, along with the relationships and policy agendas developed in the campaign, will set the tone for the presidential/congressional relationship during the Obama administration, providing substantial opportunities for fundamental policy change.

INTRODUCTION

"Sometimes I wish I could be President and Congress too," Theodore Roosevelt once admitted (his fist clinched for emphasis). [1] Roosevelt is not likely to have been the only president to entertain this wish. Instead of being Congress too, presidents must strive to achieve policy success in a political system that gives Congress many opportunities to check and balance. While congressional support is never guaranteed, presidents who face an ideologically compatible Congress typically accomplish more of their goals. [2] Elections determine the partisanship and preferences of those on Capitol Hill and in the White House.

In 2008, elections for the House of Representatives and United States Senate were held on the same day as the presidential election. With its high profile, the presidential election dominated congressional races in the media. The presidential election mobilized millions of voters who otherwise would not have cast a congressional ballot. Both presidential candidates sought to influence congressional outcomes. Nevertheless, the presidential election was only one of multiple factors that shaped the outcome in individual congressional races.

Some aspects of the 2008 congressional elections reflect patterns well known to scholars of congressional politics. Most incumbents who ran for reelection won, reflecting both the institutional advantages enjoyed by incumbents and the dedication with which most pursue reelection. [3] Campaign finances influenced election outcomes, with a continuation of the trend towards a significant resource role played by political parties. [4] Although the results in particular races were shaped in part by local issues and the skills of individual candidates, national conditions, party identification, and presidential popularity continued to influence the overall partisan make-up of Congress. In some respects, however, the election was unusual. The 2008 election was only the second election since 1980 in which the winning presidential candidate's party gained seats in both the House and Senate. The election was the first since 1932 in which a party followed a gain of more than 30 House seats in the previous election with gain of more than 20 seats. [5] It was the first election since at least the 1970s in which the Democratic Congressional Campaign Committee raised more money than the National Republican Congressional Committee. The strength and scope of Democratic congressional gains was striking.

This article examines the 2008 congressional election, with a focus on what happened, why it happened, and what the consequences will be for American politics. The election created substantial yet bounded opportunity for policy movement by the Democrats.

THE CONTEXT

With the economy heading deeper into recession and two ongoing wars, the 2008 congressional election took place in the context of extraordinary public dissatisfaction with the direction of the country. In October 2008, polls suggested that 10.6 percent of Americans believed the country was going in the right direction, while 84.4 percent believed the country was on the "wrong track" or were dissatisfied with current conditions. [6] Reflecting this dissatisfaction, the House incumbent reelection rate (just under 93 percent) was the lowest since 1994.

The party that took the blame for the country being on the "wrong track" would lose the most seats in Congress. Because Republicans controlled the White House and Democrats controlled the Congress, both parties could potentially have shared blame for the country's problems.

Throughout 2008, job approval numbers for Republican President George W. Bush were low, averaging a mere 29 percent through the election. [7] Because unpopular presidents can drag down the approval numbers of their co-partisans, Republicans sought to distance themselves from President Bush. In several instances, Republicans running in Democratic-leaning areas sought to tie themselves to Democratic candidate Barack Obama as further insurance against the perception that they were like Bush. For example, an attack ad by Republican Phil English (PA, 3) featured Hillary Clinton and Barack Obama to bolster charges against his Democratic opponent. [8] Republican Senator Gordon Smith (OR) quoted praise of Smith by Obama in some television commercials. [9] The Bush shadow was not easily eluded, however. Smith and English still lost. Across the country, Democrats sought to make sure voters knew their opponents had backed the unpopular president. Jeanne Shaheen's "Where You Lead" ad in the New Hampshire Senate race echoed arguments made by Democratic candidates across the country, arguing that "Sununu followed Bush but failed New Hampshire." Shaheen won.

The presidency was not the only institution suffering low popular support during the 2008 campaign. Congress rarely achieves popularity equal to that of the president, but its popularity can also plumb depths no president has navigated. In January 2007, shortly after Democrats gained control of Congress, 34 percent of those polled approved of the job being done by Congress. As Figure 1 shows, through the next two years, public approval of Congress steadily eroded. [10] By October 2008, only 16 percent of poll respondents approved of Congress. Republicans sought to tie Democrats, particularly those running in conservative districts, to the positions and reputations of liberal members of the congressional leadership. [11]

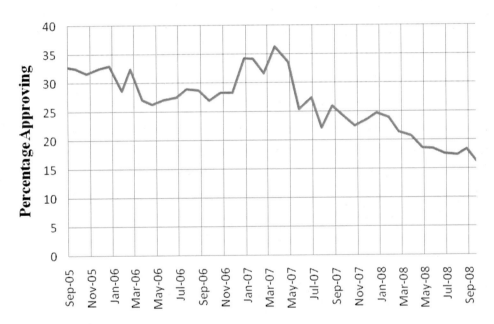

Figure 1. Approval of Congress: 2005-2008.

Fortunately for congressional Democrats, voters typically reward or punish incumbents in the president's party for economic conditions, instead of blaming the congressional majority party. [12] Republicans were particularly likely to take the blame for conditions in 2008 because they had controlled Congress from 1995 through 2006. A significantly smaller portion of Republican incumbents won reelection (88%) relative to their Democratic colleagues (94%). [13]

CANDIDATES AND DISTRICTS

Congressional elections are carried out district by district. Each campaign and each constituency is different. At the same time, the national parties have come to play an increasingly central role in recruiting, funding, and training promising candidates.

In the spring of 2008, the Republican congressional campaign operations in the House and Senate were in disarray. Stunned by a string of special election losses, including the loss of Speaker Hastert's former seat, Republicans sought to reorganize their campaign efforts. In the House, rank and file members added a supervisory board to oversee the operation of the Republican Congressional Campaign Committee. By contrast, Democratic House and Senate campaigns were coordinated by the leaders who had steered the party to victory in 2006.

A wave of retirements forced Republicans to play defense. Twenty six House Republicans voluntarily retired along with five Senate Republicans. A mere six House Democrats retired, and no Democratic Senators retired. In New Mexico multiple retirements combined with progressive ambition to create multiple losses. After Republican Pete Domenici retired from the Senate, Republicans Heather Wilson and Steve Pearce both decided not to run for reelection to the House and instead campaigned for the Senate. In the general election, Pearce lost to Democrat Tom Udall while the House seats vacated by Pearce and Wilson were both captured by Democratic candidates.

To win, parties must recruit effective candidates. [14] Events during the winter and spring of 2008 did not provide auspicious omens for Republicans weighing a House or Senate race. Three successive special election losses to Democrats in what had been safe Republican seats contributed to an unease that exacerbated Republican candidate recruitment challenges. Conversely, Democrats contemplated the possibility that 2008 would repeat the party's sweep of the 2006 elections. Because highly qualified candidates prefer to run when they have good prospects of success, Republicans faced recruitment challenges. John Ensign, the chair of the National Republican Senatorial Committee, argued that Republicans would have fared better if they had succeeded in recruiting several promising Senate prospects. [15]

Senate Democrats had the advantage of running in a year in which the minority party held most of the vulnerable seats. Senate Republicans faced the echo of their exceptional midterm victories in 2002. With 23 seats to defend relative to the Democrats' 12, Republican Senate campaign resources were stretched, and the party was particularly vulnerable to seat losses.

For some House Democrats, seats won in the 2006 midterm elections would prove difficult to hold. Gary C. Jacobson notes that "after 2006, forty-seven Democrats represented Republican-leaning districts, whereas only five Republicans represented Democratic-leaning districts." [16] The most vulnerable Democratic freshmen had won seats in solidly Republican districts after the incumbent was weakened by scandal. Several of these Democratic freshmen lost their reelection bids. In Florida's 16th district, this pattern had an ironic twist. Democratic freshman Tim Mahoney had won his Republican-leaning district in 2006 after Republican Mark Foley became embroiled in a sex scandal involving e-mails to former House pages. As part of a coordinated strategy to re-take seats lost due to scandal, Republican leaders helped Tom Rooney through the primaries and coordinated a post-primary endorsement of his candidacy by both of his primary election opponents. Then, in October 2008, sex scandals again rocked a FL-16th district incumbent. ABC News aired allegations that Mahoney employed and later paid $121,000 in hush money to a former mistress he was seeing during and after the 2006 campaign. [17] Consequently, Rooney won 60 percent of the vote.

Because they were often competing in traditionally Republican-leaning districts and the Democratic-controlled Congress was unpopular, Democrats facing competitive races had less incentive to nationalize the campaign in 2008 than in 2006, and Republicans had less incentive to seek a purely 'local' contest. A survey by the congressional newspaper *The Hill* found that "During the 2006 cycle, only 25 percent of Republicans in competitive congressional races declared their party affiliation on their campaign websites" compared with "70 percent of Democrats." In 2008, by contrast, "54 percent of Republicans and 44 percent of Democrats in tight races" indicated their party affiliation on their website. [18]

FUNDRAISING

2008 was a strong fundraising year for Democrats at the congressional level. Total spending numbers reveal the parties' dramatic reversal of fortunes. In 2008 the DCCC spent $169 million compared with only $116 million spent by the NRCC. This is all the more notable because in 2008 the Democratic committee out-spent its Republican counterpart for the first time since at least the 1970s. [19] With fewer resources, Republicans were able to offer less assistance to vulnerable incumbents and less aid to promising challengers. There were 38 races in which the DCCC spent more than one million dollars, but only four races in which the NRCC spent a similar amount. [20]

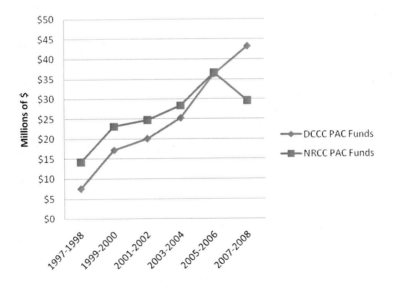

Figure 2. House Campaign Committee PAC Receipts 1997-2008. (2008 figures are through October 15th.)

The power conferred by majority status encourages interest groups to contribute. As shown in Figure 2, when House Republicans held the majority the Republican National Congressional Committee (NRCC) consistently collected more PAC (Political Action

Committee) money than the Democratic Congressional Campaign Committee (DCCC). In 2008, the tables were turned. The NRCC raised only $29 million PAC dollars for the 2008 campaign, while the DCCC raised $43 million. [21]

Faced with cash shortages, the Republican House leadership focused on recruiting independently wealthy challengers able to finance their own campaigns. Although such candidates might be able to run campaigns without national party help, the ability to self-finance does not ensure that a candidate has the skills and characteristics needed to build strong bonds with constituents and run an effective campaign. Self-financed candidates typically receive less electoral advantage per dollar spent than candidates who raised their money from other sources. [22]

Coordination with Obama's presidential campaign helped Democrats leverage fundraising advantages to compete in more states and districts, forcing Republicans to stretch thin resources to the break point. Democratic Senate Campaign Committee chair Chuck Schumer (D-NY) sought to exploit the Republicans' financial vulnerability by mounting effective challenges to so many Republican-held seats that the Republicans would lack the resources necessary to challenge potentially vulnerable Democratic incumbents. By late October, the Republican Senatorial Campaign Committee had been forced to drop funding for multiple formerly Republican-held open seats and the Republican effort to unseat Louisiana Democrat Mary Landrieu.

Forcing Republicans to play defense allowed Democrats to use their financial lead to best effect. Almost all studies of campaign spending effects suggest that challengers derive significant benefits from additional campaign dollars, and many studies find smaller effects for spending by incumbents. [23]

The sitting president is typically a valuable campaign asset for candidates in the president's party. [24] However, the unpopularity of President Bush made it more difficult for him to campaign for Republican candidates. Being seen as too close to the president was a major risk in many districts. Bush's 2008 fundraising numbers were down by 40 million from the equivalent figure for the 2006 congressional election cycle. Keeping a low profile, Bush held no rallies for GOP House or Senate candidates. [25]

CAMPAIGN ISSUES

Throughout the campaign, Republican candidates had to contend with the weakness of the Republican Party "brand." From 2006 through 2008, polls indicated that there were almost no issues on which the public trusted Republicans more than Democrats. According to a Pew survey conducted in February 2008, the only issue (out of 12) on which more respondents believed that Republicans would do a better job than Democrats was "Dealing with the terrorist threat at home," with 38 percent expressing more confidence in Democrats and 45 percent expressing more confidence in Republicans. On education, taxes, ethics, energy, the economy, Iraq, health care, and many more issues, Republicans began the campaign at a disadvantage relative to Democrats. [26]

Issues on which the Republican Party was at a disadvantage dominated the agenda in 2008. According to the exit poll, 63 percent of voters listed the economy as the most important issue in the election, followed by the Iraq war (10%) terrorism and health care (9%

each) and energy policy (7%). [27] Terrorism was the only Republican-advantaged issue seen as most important by a substantial number of voters. As discussed below, each of these issues played a role in many House and Senate races.

The economy came to dominate the 2008 election campaign. Although the financial meltdown had begun during the summer of 2007 with the emergence of severe problems in the subprime mortgage industry, by the fall of 2008 the problems had spread and deepened. The decision by Treasury Secretary Hank Paulson to allow Lehman Brothers to collapse precipitated a dramatic freeze in global credit markets that catapulted the economy to the very center of the campaign and placed a politically uncomfortable "Wall Street bailout package" on the legislative agenda.

The bailout package was the sort of legislation incumbent candidates would rather avoid in the months before an election. It was unpopular and extremely expensive. Initially the bailout package was rejected by the House of Representatives when Republican leaders were unable to provide the votes for the package that they had promised. Even though the package ultimately did pass Congress, vulnerable incumbents steered clear of voting for it. [28] Challengers from both parties sought to make opponents' votes in favor of the bailout a campaign issue. In the exit poll, Democrats edged ahead of Republicans on the economy, capturing 55 percent of the vote from those who ranked the economy as the most important issue.

The Iraq war was pushed from the center of the election campaign by a confluence of events. The successes won by General Petraeus reduced violence and US casualty rates. At the same time, negotiations between the Bush administration and the Iraqi government produced a status of forces agreement which called for a US troop withdrawal similar to that proposed by candidate Obama. The Iraq issue lacked the punch it carried in the 2006 midterm elections, but it continued to polarize the electorate. According to the exit poll, Republicans won 92 percent of the votes from those who "strongly approve" of the war, while Democrats won 86 percent of the votes from those who "strongly disapprove." Because more voters strongly disapproved than approved (41% versus 14%), the Iraq war issue helped Democrats. Democratic House candidates received 59 percent of the vote from those who ranked Iraq as the most important issue.

Terrorism and health care played predictable roles in voters' election calculations. Voters who believed terrorism to be the most important problem broke by more than three to one in favor of the Republicans. Democrats gained three fourths of the vote from voters who saw health care as most important.

High gas prices made energy policy a potent political issue by the summer of 2008. Republicans made a push to gain public trust on energy policy, forcing Democrats to parry. In the spring of 2008, former House Speaker Newt Gingrich promoted expanded domestic and offshore oil drilling. Gingrich argued that the United States should "drill here drill now" to alleviate high prices. House Republicans used procedural maneuvers by the Democratic leadership to justify their month long in-chamber protest during the August recess. At the time of the election, majorities in the public continued to support some form of expanded drilling. By early September the Gallup tracking poll briefly showed Republicans ahead of Democrats on the generic Congressional ballot, with some indications that this was because of the increased salience of the drilling issue.

After initial efforts to block policy change, Democratic leadership in the House of Representatives changed course. Using their control of the terms of House debate to ward off

Republican amendments, Democrats passed a limited expansion of offshore drilling. This move likely paid electoral dividends. In the exit poll 42 percent of those who favored offshore drilling voted for Democratic candidates, while a full 83 percent of those opposed to drilling supported the Democrats as well. The key positioning for the Democrats was among voters who "somewhat favor" offshore drilling. Although unpalatable for environmentalists, the Democrats' half-measures on drilling aligned with this group, and they won the support of 62 percent of these voters.

ELECTION OUTCOMES

Democratic successes in 2008 reflected a remarkable shift in voters' party loyalties. According to the exit poll, a full 19 percent of those who supported Bush in 2004 voted for a Democratic House candidate in 2008. Only 8 percent of those who supported Kerry in 2004 voted for a Republican House candidate in 2008. The Republican Party lost substantial support among political moderates, among voters unhappy with President Bush, and among voters who disapproved of the war with Iraq. [29] The 2008 Democratic coalition was predominantly urban and suburban. It included minority groups, lower-income voters, secular voters, and substantial numbers of well-educated professionals.

As a result of the 2008 election, representation in the 111th House of Representatives was more Democratic, more polarized, and more diverse than the 110th. Democrats held 257 House seats compared with Republicans' 178, a gain for Democrats of 22 seats. Democratic Senate gains were more substantial as a percentage of the chamber, with the Senate shifting from a 49-49 split (plus two independents caucusing with Democrats) to a sizable Democratic margin. [30]

The Democratic win expanded the party's share of congressional seats in all regions of the country. Table 1 presents the portion of House seats won by Democrats in the Northeast, Midwest, South, and West in the 2004, 2006, and 2008 elections. [31] Even in the South the Republican proportion (51.3 percent) was barely above 50 percent. Democrats continued to consolidate their lock on the Northeast with the defeat of Chris Shays (R-CT), the last House Republican from New England. Democrats also continued to gain House seats in the Midwest, capturing more than half of the seats.

Table 1. Election Outcomes by Region: Percentage of House Seats Won by Democrats

Census Region	109th (2004)	110th (2006)	111th (2008)	Net Change: 2004-2008	Number of Seats in Region
Northeast	60.2%	74.7%	79.5%	19.3%	83
Midwest	40.0%	49.0%	54.0%	14.0%	100
South	38.3%	42.2%	48.7%	10.4%	154
West	54.1%	58.2%	63.3%	9.2%	98
Total	46.4%	53.6%	59.1%	12.70%	435

For both parties, incumbent losses and retirements were concentrated among moderate members representing swing districts. As a result, surviving Democratic and Republican incumbents were somewhat more extreme in their political views than those who were defeated. [32]

The election also produced a more diverse Congress. The number of women elected to the US Congress in the 111th Congress was at an all time high for both the House and Senate. 75 women were elected to the House in 2008, up from 71 in 2006. In 2000 only 59 women were elected to the House. [33] Increased diversity was the result of Democratic gains. Reflecting the broader trend, 59 percent of Democratic female candidates won their races for Congress, whereas only 47 percent of Republican female candidates won. Republican Senator Elizabeth Dole lost her Senate seat in 2008, as did several Republican women in the House. Increasingly, the women in Congress are Democrats.

PRESIDENTIAL COATTAILS

Obama and House Democrats shared much of the same electorate. In the 2008 exit poll, a mere 8 percent of Obama's supporters reported voting for Republican House candidates, whereas 12 percent of McCain's supporters voted for Democratic House candidates. In 2004, 11 percent of Bush supporters voted for Democratic House candidates and 9 percent of Kerry supporters voted for Republican House candidates. In 2000, 17 percent of Bush supporters voted for Democratic House candidates. [34]

Democratic candidates benefited from Barack Obama's efforts to mobilize voters. In addition to coordinated campaign offices, Obama developed a parallel presidential campaign organization focused on mobilizing support among the crucial African American and youth constituencies. For example, in Virginia the campaign opened 49 Obama field offices in addition to twenty coordinated campaign offices. [35] Obama's efforts to motivate new voters would pay dividends for other Democratic candidates. According to the exit poll, 63 percent of new voters supported Democratic House candidates, compared with 52 percent of other voters. Members of Congress who believe that they won on the basis of presidential coattails may be more willing to take risks or make sacrifices to help the Administration achieve its goals.

Even as his campaign coattails arguably helped them win, Obama underperformed many Democratic congressional candidates. Nationwide, Obama won a smaller portion of the vote. According to the exit poll, House candidates ran ahead of Obama particularly among men and among voters for whom race was a factor in the 2008 presidential election. Among Democratic Senators running for reelection, only New Jersey Senator Frank Lautenberg received fewer votes in his state than Obama. [36] On the House side Obama ran ahead of only 17.5% of Democratic incumbents in their districts. [37] Candidates who win by larger margins in their district than the president sometimes use this to justify opposition to presidential initiatives. [38]

POLCY IMPLICATIONS

In his election-night victory speech, Obama promised to represent all Americans, not simply those who voted for him. But being president involves making policy tradeoffs and engaging in negotiations in which it can be difficult to satisfy all sides. The potential for policy gridlock will remain.

In order to pass legislation, Obama will typically need to achieve super-majorities in Congress. For instance, filibusters can block bills and appointments supported by more than half of the Senators. In U.S. politics it is difficult to pass legislation that is opposed by the floor median in either chamber, by more than 40 Senators, or by the president (unless veto-proof majorities can be constructed). Policies subject to such blocking are in what Keith Krehbiel terms the "gridlock interval." [39]

The Senate will be the crucial battleground for Obama administration legislative goals because the filibuster provides Republicans with their best hope of blocking Democratic policy initiatives. In the 110th Congress the filibuster provided Republicans with a virtually-assured means of blocking policies they opposed because Democrats needed the support of an often unattainable 9 GOP Senators to cut off debate. But 2008 Democratic gains in the Senate brought the party much closer to the 60 votes required to cut off debate and end filibusters. In the 111th Congress the support of only one or two moderate GOP Senators (e.g. Specter and Snowe) will suffice if the Democratic caucus is unified. This should allow the Senate to pass a broader agenda. As shown in Figure 3, the 2008 election produced the smallest gridlock interval since the 103rd Congress that greeted Bill Clinton's first term. [40]

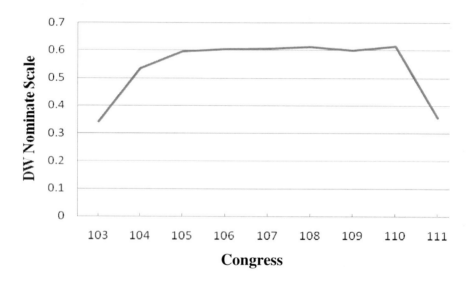

Figure 3. Size of the Pivotal Politics Gridlock Interval.

Although the changes in party power reflected in the smaller gridlock interval will make action easier on some issues, others are likely to prove difficult to change. Among the 45 taxing and spending issues examined by Project Vote Smart in its 2008 candidate survey, eight had status quo locations that were within the gridlock interval of the 111th Congress. Among the 37 issues potentially available for action were six that had been in the gridlock interval of the 110th Congress. [41] Most notable among issues no longer in the gridlock interval were income tax rates for families earning more than $180,001 per year. Still-gridlocked issues include several that were subject to debate in the 2008 presidential campaign, including defense spending, capital gains taxation, gasoline taxes, and corporate income taxes. [42] Substantial policy change is unlikely on these issues.

CONCLUSION

In 2008 Democrats won a noteworthy congressional victory to complement their presidential win. Gains in the House and Senate came from all regions of the country and reflected Democratic candidates' success in capitalizing on public dissatisfaction with the direction of the country and with President Bush. Financial resources, presidential coattails, and continued issue advantages helped Democrats consolidate their midterm election gains.

Victory held out for Democrats the tantalizing prospect of a long-term shift in the terms of political debate, but whether the election will inaugurate a significant realignment remains in doubt. Republicans can take comfort from the role played by short term presidential unpopularity in the election. With Bush gone, they may be able to escape the shadow of widely-perceived administration failures. Democratic gains in 2006 and 2008 were substantial, but the Democratic portion of all major party identifiers averaged only 57.6% in November and December 2008 Gallup polls. [43] Although near the high end, this is within the bounds of post-Reagan fluctuations in Democratic Party identification. [44]

Whether the electoral shift towards the Democrats proves enduring depends in the near term on whether Democrats in Congress and the Obama administration have substantial and popular policy successes. In 2008 Republicans were trusted less than Democrats to deal effectively with almost all major issues. If Democrats can maintain public trust, they are likely to continue winning elections.

Time to achieve policy success may well be short. In nearly every midterm election, the presidential party loses seats in the House of Representatives. Unless something very unusual happens, the 2010 midterm election will lead to losses for congressional Democrats. By 2010 the surge of new voters Obama brought to the polls will be a distant memory. Furthermore, opposition to administration actions may well galvanize Republican voters, even as Democrats find less reason to mobilize in the post-Bush politics of 2010. [45] Ideological balancing by moderate voters should also favor congressional Republicans. [46]

Although the American political system is not designed to facilitate rapid action, the configuration of preferences in the 111th Congress is the most favorable for Democratic policy goals since the 103rd. The congressional Democratic Party should be able to advance substantial parts of President Obama's legislative agenda.

REFERENCES

[1] Quoted in Arthur Meier Schlesinger Jr., The Cycles of American History (Mariner Books, 1999), 310.

[2] Jon R. Bond, Richard Fleisher, and B. Dan Wood, "The Marginal and Time-Varying Effect of Public Approval on Presidential Success in Congress" The Journal of Politics 65(1) 2003.

[3] For a discussion of the multiple sources of incumbency advantage see Paul S. Herrnson, Congressional Elections: Campaigning at Home and in Washington 5th Edition (Washington DC: CQ Press, 2008)

[4] For discussion of the relative efficiency of party campaign spending see Garrett Glasgow, "The Efficiency of Congressional Campaign Committee Contributions in House Elections," Party Politics 8 (1994) 657. For a general discussion of the effects of campaign spending on election outcomes see Gary Jacobson, The Politics of Congressional Elections Seventh Edition (New York: Longman, 2009), 45-51.

[5] The 30 followed by 20 statistic was brought to my attention by David Rhode, "Deciphering the 2008 Congressional Elections: Explaining and Assessing the Aggregate House and Senate Outcomes" (Southern Political Science Association Convention, January 9, 2009)

[6] This figure is the average of several polls taken in October 2008 that asked similar questions about the direction of the country. The specific poll questions differed slightly. Gallup: "In general, are you satisfied or dissatisfied with the way things are going in the United States at this time?" Pew Center for the People and the Press: "All in all, are you satisfied or dissatisfied with the way things are going in this country today?" Newsweek: "Are you satisfied or dissatisfied with the way things are going in the United States at this time?" CBS News / New York Times "Do you feel things in this country are generally going in the right direction or do you feel things have pretty seriously gotten off on the wrong track?" NBC News / Wall Street Journal "All in all, do you think things in the nation are generally headed in the right direction, or do you feel that things are off on the wrong track?" AP-GfK "Generally speaking, would you say things in this country are heading in the right direction or in the wrong direction?" LA Times / Bloomberg "Do you think things in this country are generally going in the right direction or are they seriously off on the wrong track?"

[7] Average of 155 national polls taken between January 1, 2008 and November 6, 2008 as reported in "President Bush: Overall Job Rating in National Polls" PollingReport.com (2009). *http://www.pollingreport.com/BushJob.htm*

[8] National Journal "Penn Pals" The House Race Hotline. (August 13, 2008). Downloaded on August 13th from *http://www.nationaljournal.com/hotline/hr_20080813_5345.php*

[9] Jonathan Weisman, "Candidates reach for Obama's coattails" The Washington Post (June 25, 2008).

[10] Figure is computed from the average of all national polls asking about Congressional approval, as reported in "Congress – Job Rating in National Polls" Pollingreport.com (2008). *http://www.pollingreport.com/CongJob.htm*

[11] Kimberly M Strassel, "Pelosi's Gang Feels the Pressure" The Wall Street Journal, September 12, 2008. *http://online.wsj.com/article/SB122117869912626029.html?mod=todays_columnists*

[12] Kevin B. Grier and Joseph P. McGarrity, "Presidential Party, incumbency, and the effects of economic fluctuations on House Elections, 1916-1996," Public Choice 110 (2002), 143. Some more knowledgeable voters do give the congressional majority credit or blame as well. See also: Brad T. Gomez and J. Matthew Wilson, "Causal

Attribution and Economic Voting in American Congressional Elections" Political Research Quarterly 56 (2003), 271-282.
[13] 94.3% of Democratic incumbents were reelected compared to only 88 percent of Republican incumbents. The difference is statistically significant t= 2.28, p<.05 two tailed.
[14] Gary C. Jacobson and Samuel Kernell, Strategy and Choice in Congressional Elections, 2nd ed. (New Haven, CT: Yale University Press, 1983).
[15] Aaron Blake, "Sen. Ensign paints a grim picture for GOP in November" The Hill, March 13, 2008. *http://thehill.com/leading-the-news/sen.-ensign-paints-a-grim-picture-for-gop-in-nov.-2008-03-13.html*.
[16] Gary Jacobson, The Politics of Congressional Elections Seventh Edition (New York: Longman, 2009).
[17] Emma Schwartz, Rhonda Schwartz and Vic Walter, "Congressman's $121,000 Payoff to Alleged Mistress,"ABC NEWS, October 13, 2008. *http://abcnews.go.com/Blotter/Politics/Story?id=5997043&page=1*.
[18] Martin, Anna. "More GOPers display party affiliation than in '06," The Hill, October 31, 2008.
[19] Total DCCC and RCCC disbursements data for 2008 calculated by the author from Federal Election Commission data. Data from 1988 to 2006 was calculated by Gary .C Jacobson, The Politics of Congressional Elections Seventh Edition (New York: Longman, 2009), 78.
[20] Michael Malbin, "A First Look at Money in the House and Senate Elections" George Washington University Campaign Finance Institute, November 6, 2008. *http://www.cfinst.org/pr/prRelease.aspx?ReleaseID=215*
[21] Calculation based on Federal Election Commission disclosure data *http://www.fec.gov/disclosure.shtml*.
[22] Brad Alexander, "Good Money and Bad Money: Do Funding Sources Affect Electoral Outcomes?" Political Research Quarterly 58 (2005), 353.
[23] Jacobson, Gary C., "Campaign spending effects in U.S. Senate elections: Evidence from the National Annenberg Election Survey," Electoral Studies 25 (2006), 195.
[24] Paul S. Herrnson and Irwin L. Morris, "Presidential Campaigning in the 2002 Congressional Elections," Legislative Studies Quarterly XXXII (2007), 628.
[25] Ryan Grim, "Bush fundraising down by $40 million," Politico.com, October 21, 2008. *http://www.politico.com/news/stories/1008/14799.html*.
[26] Pew Research Center for the People & the Press survey conducted by Princeton Survey Research Associates International. Feb. 20-24, 2008. N=approx. 750 adults nationwide. MoE ± 4.
[27] All exit poll results discussed here and later in the paper are from the National Election Pool, Edison Media Research, and Mitofsky International. "National Election Pool General Election Exit Poll" (Somerville, NJ: Edison Media Research/New York, NY: Mitofsky International [producers], 2006 and 2008).
[28] Aaron Blake, "Challengers say no to planned bailout – vulnerable incumbents follow suit." The Hill, September 29, 2008. *http://thehill.com/campaign-2008/*
[29] David W. Brady, Douglas Rivers and Laurel Harbridge, "The 2008 Democratic Shift" Policy Review No. 152. (December 2008 and January 2009).

[30] In Minnesota a contested recount and subsequent election challenge left the seating of Democrat Al Franken in doubt through March 2009. If Franken is seated, Democrats will control 59 Senate seats.

[31] Regional categories are derived from U.S. Census Bureau regional codes. Election data is from the New York Times.

[32] Based on author's calculation using DW Nominate 1st dimension common space scores reported by Keith Poole on his website (*www.voteview.org*).

[33] "Record Numbers of Women to Serve in Senate and House" Center for American Women in Politics. *http://www.cawp.rutgers.edu/press_room/news/documents/Press Release_11-05-08.pdf.*

[34] 2000 figure is derived from Paul R. Abramson, John H. Aldrich and David W. Rhode, Change and Continuity in the 2000 Elections (Washington DC: CQ Press, 2002) p. 249. 2004, 2006 and 2008 figures are based on the Voter News Service Exit Poll cited in footnote 16.

[35] Dr. Quentin Kidd. "The Virginia Election" (Panel presentation at Old Dominion University October 27, 2008).

[36] The relatively moderate McCain ran ahead of half of the Republican incumbent Senators in their own states.

[37] Data on presidential candidate performance in congressional districts is from Swing State Project. Downloaded on March 24, 2009 from *http://www.swingstateproject.com/showDiary.do?diaryId=4161*

[38] Richard F. Fenno, Learning to Legislate: the Senate education of Arlen Specter (Washington DC: CQ Press, 1991).

[39] Keith Krehbiel, Pivotal Politics: A Theory of U.S. Law Making (Chicago: University of Chicago Press, 1998).

[40] In the calculations underlying the figure, ideological locations are estimated using the first dimension from Keith Poole's DW-Nominate common-space scores as reported on Poole's website (*www.voteview.org*). I assume that Obama's replacement in the Senate is more liberal than Senator Specter (R-PA) and that Al Franken will win the Minnesota Senate race.

[41] To estimate policy status quo locations I used results from the National Political Courage Test administered by Project Vote Smart (*www.votesmart.com*) to estimate the ideological location most likely correspond with a preference for maintaining the current policy status quo. For more details on the measurement strategy see Jesse Richman "Parties Versus Pivots," Paper presented at the Southern Political Science Association Annual Convention New Orleans, January 10, 2009.

[42] Additional issues with status quo estimated to be in the gridlock interval of the 111th Congress: United Nations funding, research and development of new weapons, alcohol taxes, and international aid.

[43] Average of polls conducted from November 7 through December 16, 2008 as reported in "Selected Trend on Party Affiliation: 2004-2008" Gallup (2008) *http://www.gallup.com/poll/15370/Party-Affiliation.aspx*

[44] Michael F. Meffert, Helmut Norpoth and Anirudh V.S. Ruhil, "Realignment and Macropartisanship," American Political Science Review 95 (2001), 953.

[45] For a rigorous behavioral explanation of midterm loss see John Wiggs Patty "Loss Aversion, Presidential Responsibility, and Midterm Congressional Elections." Electoral Studies 25(2) (2006): 227-247. Surge and decline theory would anticipate a particularly large decline in Democratic support in the midterm election to the extent that the election was characterized by strong presidential coattails. For a discussion of surge and decline theory see James Campbell, "The Revised Theory of Surge and Decline," American Journal of Political Science 3(4) (1987): 965–979.

[46] Walter R. Mebane and Jasjeet S. Sekhon, "Coordination and Policy Moderation at Midterm," American Political Science Review 96 (2002), 141.

Chapter 3

CAMPAIGN TACTICS AND AMERICAN GRAND STRATEGY IN THE ELECTION OF 2008

Joshua Rovner [1]
Williams College, Williamstown, MA, US

ABSTRACT

Conventional wisdom holds that last year's election was a contest between candidates with utterly different visions for American grand strategy and foreign policy. John McCain was supposed to represent hawks who recognized the present dangers to US interests and who were ready to use American military power to confront them. Barack Obama was supposed to represent doves who believed in restoring fractured diplomatic relations and using soft power to repair America's image abroad. On the other hand, some critics believe that a bipartisan consensus had already emerged on grand strategy. These critics argue that Democrats and Republicans agreed on the nature of world politics, the character of contemporary threats, and the importance of preserving a large forward military presence in order to spread and protect American values abroad. If the critics are correct, then the campaign debates were superficial and had the effect of masking the deeper agreement on the trajectory of US grand strategy and foreign policy. This article evaluates both arguments in the immediate aftermath of the election. It concludes that while the campaign revealed important near-term policy disputes, both candidates hewed to the same underlying grand strategy.

INTRODUCTION

Foreign policy and national security affairs largely decided the party primaries in 2008, and they also played an important role in the general election. The war in Iraq was a springboard for John McCain and Barack Obama to win their respective party nominations, though for very different reasons. Senator Obama distinguished himself in the Democratic primary race for his early opposition to the war. His main rivals, especially Hillary Clinton, could not escape their Senate votes to authorize military action in 2002. Clinton and Obama agreed on most other issues, and Obama's antiwar stance energized party progressives who saw congressional Democrats as craven and needlessly deferential on foreign policy and national security. There were other reasons why Obama was able to overcome Clinton's early lead, to be sure, but it is hard to imagine that he could have done so without the war. Meanwhile, Senator McCain doggedly supported the troop surge in Iraq during 2007, long after public opinion had turned against the war. Declining violence in Iraq appeared to validate his position late in the year, and he was able to claim that he alone had the foresight and political courage to be commander in chief. McCain used the surge debate to emphasize his self-described status as a "maverick" in the Republican Party who could effectively distance himself from an unpopular lame duck administration.

A host of strategic issues served as a backdrop for the general election. The Beijing Olympics rekindled discussions about the rise of China and the appropriate U.S. response. Russia's invasion of Georgia led to a flurry of debates about whether another Cold War was on the horizon. Iran tried to exploit U.S. difficulties in Iraq in order to expand its influence in the Middle East, and it continued to move towards an indigenous nuclear weapons capability, despite American efforts to coordinate diplomatic nonproliferation efforts. Efforts to reverse North Korea's nuclear progress also stalled. The Taliban insurgency grew more ferocious on both sides of the Afghanistan-Pakistan border, forcing the United States to reconsider its strategic goals in the region. Finally, al Qaeda was still threatening, and Osama bin Laden was still alive. The McCain campaign tried to steer the debate towards these issues in order to highlight Obama's inexperience and capitalize on McCain's reputation on national security affairs. It also wanted to shift the debate away from the sputtering economy, especially after polls found that voters blamed Republicans for the expanding financial crisis by a two-to-one margin. [2] Failure to change the debate would force McCain into the unenviable position of running against a charismatic opponent as well as the recent legacy of his own party.

Maneuvering the election towards national security required that McCain draw stark contrasts between the candidates' experience and ideas. To this end, the McCain camp criticized Obama's pledge to negotiate with autocratic regimes without preconditions. His running mate, Gov. Sarah Palin of Alaska, described this as "beyond naiveté," and "downright dangerous." [3] McCain also hammered Obama for his opposition to the surge in Iraq, and for his unwillingness to accept the conclusion that the surge was successful. McCain went as far to suggest that Obama's political goals determined his foreign policy proclamations. "Behind all of these claims and positions by Senator Obama lies the ambition to be president," he declared in a speech to the Veterans of Foreign Wars. "What's less apparent is the judgment to be commander in chief." [4] In sum, McCain used national security and foreign policy to emphasize his experience against his younger opponent, and to contrast his political independence from his opponent's political opportunism.

Senator Obama had two basic responses to these attacks. First, he attempted to tie McCain's foreign policy to the Bush administration. Far from a maverick, Obama argued that McCain hewed to neoconservative principles on key issues. Moreover, he stressed that the neoconservatives' belligerent approach to diplomacy had been counterproductive because it caused states like North Korea and Iran to harden their positions and accelerate their nuclear weapons programs. Second, he repeatedly criticized McCain's outspoken support for the war in Iraq. As he had done in the primary campaign, Obama used the 2002-2003 arguments over regime change to criticize McCain's strategic judgment:

The war started in 2003, and at the time when the war started, you said it was going to be quick and easy. You said we knew where the weapons of mass destruction were. You were wrong. You said that we were going to be greeted as liberators. You were wrong. You said that there was no history of violence between Shiite and Sunni. And you were wrong. [5]

For Obama, the wisdom of a strategic adjustment five years into the war was less important than the wisdom of going to war in the first place. He counted on the fact that a strong majority had become permanently opposed to it, and that broad disillusionment cut against McCain's support for the surge.

These differences seemed to present a clear contrast in the candidates' approach to strategy, national security, and foreign policy. McCain stressed his experience in military matters and declared that he would support prudent policies even if they were politically unpopular. On the campaign trail, McCain and Palin also implied a more muscular philosophy: McCain was committed to victory and his opponent was committed to retreat; McCain would defeat America's enemies while his opponent would appease them; McCain would use American power but his opponent would squander it. Obama responded by arguing that McCain represented a continuation of President Bush's disastrous foreign policy. He also sought to distinguish himself by tying his positions on national security to his overarching theme of hope and optimism. In op-eds and stump speeches, he stressed the need to restore America's image abroad and revitalize frayed alliances.

Despite the candidates' attempts to distinguish themselves by highlighting different strategic priorities, a number of commentators argued that these differences were superficial, and that a fundamental consensus had emerged between the parties. According to this view, leaders on both sides of the aisle had agreed on a set of basic principles that govern U.S. diplomacy and military strategy. These principles include the idea that national security is at risk from "rogue states" and non-state actors, and that national interests are best served by promoting democracy and free-markets abroad. To this end, the United States should maintain a substantial military presence abroad, and be prepared to use it even when immediate national security interests are not at stake. The result, according to critics, is that bipartisanship starts at the water's edge: both parties believe that American ideas are good for the world, and both agree that spreading liberal values will result in peace and prosperity at home. As one observer put it, "Republicans and Democrats perceive the same threats, advance the same forward strategy for dealing with them, and place significant emphasis on the same coercive might and liberal assumptions." [6]

The election offers an excellent opportunity to assess this argument. Both parties had large incentives to stress their differences and explain why their respective strategies were superior. Republicans emphasized national security issues in order to highlight McCain's military service and his long experience. Indeed, the GOP had long benefited from the presumption that it was more serious about foreign affairs and more reliable in protecting national security. Democrats believed that public discontent over the war in Iraq would tie McCain to an unpopular administration and highlight Obama's vision of change. Because each side had strong incentives to highlight their different philosophies, the election is a hard test for the hypothesis that the consensus on grand strategy has emerged. Given the electoral stakes, we should expect to see vast differences in the strategies offered by the candidates and their supporters. On the other hand, indications of underlying agreement would represent powerful evidence that the strategic debate has narrowed.

I proceed as follows. The first section outlines the argument that the two candidates represented wholly different strategic philosophies. The second section discusses the opposite claim: that the differences were superficial and that a deep bipartisan agreement on American grand strategy had emerged by 2008. The third section evaluates the campaign through the prism of these two competing arguments. The conclusion summarizes the results and briefly discusses some of the implications. In brief, the candidates did express important differences on key issues, meaning that the election had important consequences for the near-term policy decisions. However, their public statements revealed basic agreement on their underlying strategic principles. The implication is that the long-term trajectory of American grand strategy would have remained the same, regardless of the election's outcome.

"Profoundly Divergent Attitudes": How the Candidates Tried to Set Themselves Apart

During the campaign season, partisans from both sides agreed that the election was in part a referendum on grand strategy and American foreign policy. Supporters of John McCain and Barack Obama declared that each side represented a profoundly different view about the appropriate direction of American strategy. McCain supporters lauded their candidate as a sober leader with a clear understanding of national security threats and the personal courage to confront them. They pointed out that McCain supported the surge in Iraq long after the war had become unpopular. McCain stood alone while congressional Democrats were demanding an end to U.S. military involvement in Iraq. In addition, they applauded McCain's strong stand against the Russian incursion into Georgia in August 2008, while simultaneously accusing Obama of claiming moral equivalence in that crisis. [7]

From these episodes, McCain's supporters drew two lessons. First, McCain could be expected to take a stand against looming dangers, whether they came in the form of resurgent great powers or from rogue states like Iran or North Korea. His willingness to buck domestic political expedients was something that earned him maverick status among Republicans. His willingness to accept personal and political risks also stood in contrast to his rival. Second, Obama had a naïve view of the world, putting too much stock in cooperation from allies and foolishly believing that America's adversaries could be satiated through negotiation and compromise. His rhetoric also suggested that he would increase U.S. vulnerability by cutting defense spending and otherwise encouraging less vigilance against clear and present dangers. In sum, Obama trusted that negotiations and multilateralism could solve American security problems; McCain believed that security required the unilateral threat of force. The two candidates could not be more different.

Obama's supporters agreed: their candidate represented a wholly different strategic philosophy. They portrayed McCain as a fire-breathing hawk, a thinly veiled neoconservative who had not learned anything from the Bush administration's failures. On the other hand, Obama understood that the United States had squandered its moral authority and had lost friends and influence as a result. While McCain could be expected to keep burning bridges, Obama would mend damaged relations with erstwhile allies and set the United States on a sustainable diplomatic course. Richard Holbrooke wrote during that campaign that the election showcased two men with "profoundly divergent attitudes toward the role of diplomacy… (And) contrasting visions for the United States." Obama would backstop creative diplomacy with the use of force, seeking opportunities to explore new kinds of interaction with long-time U.S. adversaries. McCain, on the other hand, revealed a "deep, visceral aversion" to negotiations and instead recommended an extremely hawkish view towards states like North Korea and Iran. As if the United States hadn't suffered enough in two simultaneous ongoing wars, McCain seemed almost eager to risk another one. [8]

The fact that rival candidates sought to highlight differences is hardly surprising. But the apparent differences between John McCain and Barack Obama seemed to be more than normal election year window dressing. The two men seemed to have fundamentally different perceptions of national security threats and opportunities, as well as unique approaches to solving foreign policy problems. Other observers, however, believed that these differences were largely superficial.

ALL TOGETHER NOW: THE EMERGING LIBERAL CONSENSUS

A grand strategy is "a political-military, means-ends chain, a state's theory about how it can best 'cause' security for itself." [9] It is *not* synonymous with military strategy, though military questions are critical components of any grand strategy. Operating in peacetime and in war, grand strategies define the logic that translates state power into security and prosperity. An effective grand strategy identifies threats to national security and opportunities to achieve national interests. It declares the capabilities and limits of available military, economic, and diplomatic tools. Most importantly, it explicitly connects those tools to a state's political objectives. This connective logic is what separates a grand strategy from a laundry list of national goals; strategies that ignore or elide over this "means-ends chain" are fatuous. Although the complexity of international politics and the *sturm und drang* of the foreign policy process make it difficult to adhere to a single coherent grand strategy, recent U.S. leaders have been more self-conscious about defining their military and defense policies in these terms. [10]

Analysts of grand strategy have identified numerous options for the United States. [11] On one end of the spectrum is a grand strategy of *neo-isolationism*, which would sharply reduce the U.S. military presence abroad and only recommend military action when core national security interests are at risk. Neo-isolationists argue that the United States remains safe behind two oceans and can rely on its large nuclear arsenal to deter aggression. Except in very rare cases military actions abroad constitute needless provocations and are counterproductive. Moreover, international markets are strong and resilient and do not rely on U.S. power to operate efficiently. For these reasons, the United States can afford to spend relatively little on defense while still profiting from international trade and finance. At the other end of the spectrum is *primacy*, a grand strategy premised on the idea that U.S. national interests demand a committed effort to maintain a preponderance of force. Primacists believe that political order depends on the existence of a hegemonic state who is willing to act as international custodian, ensuring stability in strategically important regions, protecting trade routes, and preventing the rise of would-be "peer competitors" who would challenge the dominant power and potentially upset the international status quo. [12]

Between these two poles are the grand strategies of *restraint, selective engagement* and *liberal internationalism*. [13] Like neo-isolationists, advocates of restraint argue for a limited military presence abroad, partly because of the intrinsic defensive advantages of American geography but also because scaling back U.S. activities will encourage other states to take on more of the burden of maintaining international stability. [14] Selective engagers also define the national interest in terms of security and worry about the unintended consequences of military action. However, they recommend the use of force abroad to maintain a balance between the great powers. According to this view, the primary purpose of military force should be to preserve the status quo and prevent the kind of great power competition that can lead to international catastrophe. Recent versions of selective engagement have considered other issues that warrant U.S. involvement, but the chief concerns remain the prevention of attacks against the United States and the preservation of the balance of power abroad. [15]

Liberal internationalists begin with different assumptions about the nature of international politics. They have faith in the power of international institutions and law to mitigate the perils of anarchy. While neo-isolationists and selective engagers view international relations through realist theory, which assumes that self-interested nation states are the primary actors on the world stage, liberals believe that institutions and norms can moderate state egoism. Great power politics are less dangerous and cooperation is possible when great powers participate in international regimes, which set the boundaries of acceptable behavior and reveal the significant opportunity costs for noncompliance. [16] Liberals also emphasize the consequences of economic and political interdependence, arguing that globalization has made it impossible for the United States to insulate itself from regional crises. The ripple effects from distant wars and economic breakdowns ultimately affect great power interests, even if no great powers are directly involved. As Mikhail Gorbachev famously put it, "peace is indivisible." [17]

Liberal internationalists recommend a set of basic principles that should guide U.S. foreign policy. First, enduring threats to security will come from *illiberal* actors like dictatorships, failed states, and terrorist groups. Even though these actors have limited capabilities, their rejection of liberal values means that they will eventually challenge American interests. Second, long-term security requires spreading free-markets and democracy while simultaneously eroding the legitimacy of illiberal ideas. It also requires a deeper U.S. commitment to international institutions as an alternative to the rough-and-tumble of politics under conditions of anarchy. Finally, any serious effort to expand the liberal sphere will demand a large, permanent, forward military presence. No other great power has the capabilities needed to respond quickly to regional breakdowns and preserve the peace. Moreover, the United States needs to invest in the military and non-military tools to counter threats from illiberal actors. This means investing in organizations dedicated to non-traditional missions like counter-terrorism, counterinsurgency, and state-building. Past military buildups have emphasized the kinds of forces that are necessary to defeat conventional threats from other nation-states. For liberal internationalists, the military must be prepared to confront a variety of non-state armed groups that reject liberal values.

A number of commentators have concluded that a bipartisan consensus had coalesced around the grand strategy of liberal internationalism by 2008. According to this argument, policy elites agree that the main threats to the United States come from illiberal actors, and that the way to achieve security is by using force abroad to spread liberal values. For this reason, the Bush administration was criticized not for its ideas but for its poor implementation of an otherwise sound strategy. Andrew Bacevich, a trenchant critic himself, nonetheless concludes that the president represented the culmination of a long-term trend in the American foreign policy tradition. While Bush was more active in his espousal of aggressive unilateralism in the name of spreading American values abroad, he shared with his critics some fundamental beliefs:

> President Bush's critics and his dwindling band of loyalists share this conviction: that the forty-third president has broken decisively with the past, setting the United States on a revolutionary new course. Yet this is poppycock. The truth is this: Bush and those around him have reaffirmed the pre-existing fundamentals of U.S. policy, above all affirming the ideology of national security to which past administrations have long subscribed. Bush's main achievement has been to articulate that ideology with such fervor and clarity as to unmask as never before its defects and utter perversity.

For Bacevich, the main defect of this grand strategy is that it substitutes ideological conviction about the moral rectitude of the United States for a clear-eyed appreciation of the limits of American power. American elites believe that they are charged with carrying the standard of democracy and freedom to all corners of the globe and that "for the American way of life to endure, freedom must prevail everywhere." Moreover, Americans have sustained this belief by deluding themselves that endless expansion can fuel their economic appetites. Bacevich concludes that the American strategic consensus has consolidated around the ideas that peace is indivisible and the United States is indispensable. The two parties may stake out different positions on some issues, but these are "superficial distinctions." [18]

In an effort to distill a more conservative and feasible alternative, Barry Posen confronts what he sees as the same converging view of strategy. "Republican and Democratic foreign policy experts," Posen writes, "now disagree little about the threats the United States faces and the remedies it should pursue." In a face of threats from rogue states, failed states, and terrorists with potential access to WMD, the consensus holds that the United States must pursue a policy of "international activism" and work to preserve its dominant military position. "Beyond uses of force," he continues, "the United States should endeavor to change other societies so that they look more like ours. A world of democracies would be the safest for us, and we should be willing to pay considerable costs to produce such a world." [19] The end of the Cold War signaled the end of any nation-state peer competitor to U.S. interests, creating a permissive environment for U.S. leaders to pursue more grandiose ambitions. Thus while Posen had previously advocated for a grand strategy of selective engagement, the growing consensus finally persuaded him that the United States could not resist its liberal impulses during a period of overwhelming economic and military strength. As he put it recently, "Years of Clinton and Bush administration foreign policy activism have convinced me that there is something about our situation that takes the selectivity out of selective engagement." [20]

Critics also note that more restrained grand strategies have been marginalized and do not play an important part in the current strategic discourse. Strategies of restraint are derided as isolationist, which is considered a dirty word in polite company. [21] Strategies of selective engagement are based on realist theory, which conceives of world politics in terms of self-interested nation-states competing for power and security under conditions of anarchy. A realist foreign policy counsels humility and self-control and warns against letting moral impulses overwhelm reason. The problem, as two observers from opposite sides of the political spectrum recently noted, is that liberal internationalists tap into a deep reservoir of American exceptionalism and crusading spirit, while Americans harbor a "deep aversion to strategies based on a 'classical' realism free of all moral constraints and aims." [22] Indeed, American realists have always struggled against the liberal aspirations of their compatriots. However intellectually compelling, realists like Hans Morgenthau, George Kennan, and Reinhold Niebuhr were not able to stem the liberal tide during the Cold War. And in the aftermath of that conflict, when liberal internationalists became infatuated with the opportunities presented by economic globalization, Robert Gilpin ruefully concluded, "No One Loves a Political Realist." [23]

Gilpin's lament rings true for contemporary critics of American foreign policy, who believe that liberal internationalism has become *the* mainstream position and that debates over grand strategy usually boil down to different sides of the liberal coin. If they are correct, no serious contender for high office can afford to stray too far from the liberal mainstream. [24]

COMPARING THE CANDIDATES

What did the election represent? Did John McCain and Barack Obama represent two opposite approaches, or did they adhere to the same basic grand strategy? Did the election provide evidence of a new strategic consensus?

The candidates' foreign policy positions differed in several respects. They espoused different views toward diplomacy and the role of international institutions. They also appeared to take different positions on the war in Iraq and the confrontation with Iran. However, close inspection of the campaign reveals basic agreement on the assumptions underpinning their grand strategies, despite the fact that each side had large incentives to emphasize the differences in such a closely contested election. In other words, the results tend to support the claim that a liberal internationalist strategic consensus has emerged. A caveat is in order, however. The fact that the two candidates shared basic liberal assumptions did not stop them from arguing on near term strategic dilemmas, nor will it prevent future political rivals from clashing. Rather, the emergence of a consensus will pare down the menu of acceptable options about the long-term direction of American foreign policy. [25]

PLUS CA CHANGE ...

The candidates' speeches and interviews reveal a few important differences in their diplomatic preferences. One of the most obvious is their different view towards the role of international institutions. Obama consistently argued that the United States should invest in existing intuitions and standing multilateral treaties like the Nuclear Nonproliferation Treaty. This was part of his broader goal of "renewing American diplomacy," which was based on the idea that the transnational character of conteporary problems could only be addressed by strengthening existing institutions. "On challenges ranging from terrorism to disease, nuclear weapons to climate change," he wrote, "we cannot make progress unless we can draw on strong international support." [26]

McCain was more skeptical. While he supported NATO publicly and paid lip service to other multilateral forums, he also implied that institutions could constrain U.S. foreign policy because they lacked the "political and moral advantages offered by united democratic action." [27] To share the international burden without becoming hamstrung by inflexible institutions populated by U.S. adversaries, McCain supported the creation of a "League of Democracies" that would cooperate to achieve common ends. He was particularly taken with Phillip Bobbitt's argument that such a league was best-suited to deal with illiberal actors who threaten what Bobbitt calls the "market state of consent." [28] (McCain called Bobbitt's *Terror and Consent* "the best book I've ever read on terrorism" and shared it with his campaign staffers and journalists on the trail. [29]) The logic was straightforward: the international order is based on the success of market-oriented liberal states; illiberal actors threaten that order; therefore, a coalition of motivated democracies will be most effective in combating them. Critics of such a league feared that it would undermine the UN, however, and this may have explained Obama's reluctance to sign on despite the fact that some of his advisors were attracted to the idea. [30]

Obama and McCain also differed on their willingness to negotiate with potentially hostile states. Obama argued that the United States, operating from a position of strength, could afford to sit down with its rivals. He lauded the "tough, thoughtful, realistic diplomacy" that characterized traditional U.S. foreign policy, and he believed that revitalizing cooperation with great powers like Russia was necessary to manage a number of shared problems. [31] Obama also argued that negotiations would have important secondary effects in the battle of ideas in the war on terrorism. As he put it, shrinking "the pool of potential recruits" to terrorist organizations "involves engaging the Islamic world rather than vilifying it." [32] McCain, on the other hand, warned against negotiating with rogue states like Iran, Syria, and North Korea, and proposed excluding Russia from the G-8 group of economic powers as punishment for its invasion of Georgia. He chided Obama rewarding undemocratic states with legitimacy and diplomatic respect when they had done nothing to earn it. McCain's supporters also warned that Obama's desire to negotiate was akin to the allies' willingness to appease the Fascist powers in the 1930s. As John Bolton ominously concluded, "negotiations – especially those 'without precondition' as Mr. Obama has specifically advocated – consume time, another precious asset that terrorists and rogue leaders prize…While the diplomats of European democracies played with their umbrellas, the Nazis were rearming and expanding their industrial power." [33]

The candidates' different positions on negotiations implied a deeper difference in their world views. Obama recognized that there were dangerous actors but believed their behavior could be managed, and that hard-line positions would be needlessly provocative. McCain countered that some actors are incorrigible, and they must be treated as threats of indefinite duration. No surprise, then, that McCain favored expanding ballistic missile defense while Obama expressed concerns about its technological feasibility as well as the diplomatic fallout of deploying BMD. [34]

One of the more controversial foreign policy distinctions had to do with the candidates' views towards Iran. Obama argued that diplomatic overtures could bear fruit and suggested that the United States might provide security guarantees and economic incentives for Iranian cooperation on nuclear issues. [35] His hedging position on missile defense – that it was attractive in theory but technologically immature – was probably also informed by the idea that deploying BMD to Europe would undermine rapprochement with Tehran. McCain was not interested in negotiations; he had other solutions in mind. At a campaign stop during the primary season he jokingly replaced the lyrics to the classic pop song "Barbara Ann" with "Bomb Iran." This event was overblown, as it certainly was not a statement of policy, but to his critics it suggested that he was unserious about the problem and too cavalier about the use of force. (At another campaign stop McCain joked that rising cigarette exports to Iran might be "a way of killing 'em." [36]) Jokes aside, McCain consistently used confrontational rhetoric when discussing Iran. He described Iran as "the world's chief sponsor of terrorism." Warning that it was determined to acquire nuclear weapons, he spelled out the implications for U.S. national security. "Protected by a nuclear arsenal," McCain reasoned, "Iran would be even more willing and able to sponsor terrorist attacks against any perceived enemy, including the United States and Israel, or even to pass nuclear materials to one of its allied terrorist networks." The appropriate response was a combination of sanctions, military threats, and accelerated deployment of missile defense around Iran's perimeter. [37]

Of course, the biggest controversy concerned U.S. strategy in Iraq. McCain strongly supported the war as well as the surge of new forces into Iraq in 2007, and pledged to keep U.S. troops in Iraq for as long as the mission required. The war in Iraq had become the central front in the battle against Islamic extremists, and the United States should not pass up the opportunity to destroy them in detail. McCain also believed that the surge and the adoption of a new approach to counterinsurgency were producing measurable progress. These gains would be lost in the event of a precipitous withdrawal, meaning that Iraq would be at risk of becoming a failed state and new base of operations for al Qaeda. McCain tried to align his position with Gen. David Petraeus, the popular military commander in Iraq who was largely responsible for implementing major changes to the U.S. approach.

Obama argued that the war was misguided from the start, opposed the surge, and called for a withdrawal of combat forces within sixteen months if he was elected. While McCain tied the war in Iraq to the war on terrorism, Obama viewed it as a disastrous distraction from the real battle with al Qaeda in Afghanistan. "We did not finish the job," he told an audience in 2007. Worse, the war in Iraq was the result of "a deliberate strategy to misrepresent 9/11 to sell a war against a country that had nothing to do with 9/11." Obama criticized not just the decision for the war but the conduct of the occupation, and he demonstrated more willingness to "push back" against Gen. Petraeus. [38]

Obama's position on Iraq suggested a realist critique of American strategic assumptions about what it could accomplish with the use of force. McCain, on the other hand, appeared to steer in the direction of neoconservatism, especially in his unapologetic embrace of unilateralism and his concerns about international institutions. Closer inspection, however, reveals that both Obama and McCain drew deeply on the liberal internationalist tradition in American grand strategy.

…Plus c'est la même chose

At first glance the differences between the two candidates were profound, suggesting philosophical differences about how to think about strategy and America's role in the world.

The fact that they butted heads on everything from institutions to Iraq suggests that the notion of a liberal consensus is misleading – or simply wrong. But the campaign revealed important similarities. Both McCain and Obama identified the same basic set of threats to the national interest. They agreed that the principal threat came from transnational terrorists, and the biggest danger was that terrorists would strike the United States or its allies with nuclear, biological, or chemical weapons. They also identified illiberal regimes such as Syria, Iran, and North Korea as security problems. Finally, both expressed concern about failing or failed states, which they believed could become the wellspring of new terrorist movements. In sum, the illiberal world was the source of pervasive threats to national interests, while the community of liberal democratic states was benign.

Because of this shared worldview, both agreed with the basic logic of using American power to spread liberal values. Obama stressed the moral obligation to respond to humanitarian disasters, and McCain emphasized the need to preserve national honor, but they both recommended the same active approach abroad. [39] Each candidate accepted the basic notion that security is indivisible. There was no other way to create a durable peace.

McCain and Obama wanted to increase the number of available U.S. ground forces, and they both supported President Bush's plan to add 27,000 marines and 65,000 soldiers. (McCain ultimately called for an increase of up to 150,000. [40]) Both believed that U.S. troops, badly overstretched by the wars in Afghanistan and Iraq, were nonetheless needed to prevent states from failing and to repair those that already had. Neither candidate seriously considered reducing the U.S. presence abroad as another way to deal with the problem of overstretch. [41] They also recommended maintaining the large defense budgets that had accumulated in the Bush years, while seeking to cut spending on high-technology weapons platforms that had no obvious bearing on counterinsurgency and counterterrorism. McCain was a well-known critic of wasteful Pentagon spending and large investments in dubious future technologies. Obama pledged to review every major weapons system, and his running mate declared that "we cannot afford…a trillion dollar-commitment to 'Star Wars', a thousand-ship navy, (or) the F-22 Raptor." [42] In other words, both wanted to beef up the military's ability to attack illiberal non-state actors and conduct nation-building, while seeking to offset those costs by scaling back on weapons more suited to conventional inter-state conflict.

Both agreed that the primary role of the military was to expand the liberal sphere and prevent the spread of illiberal ideas or lawless territory where such ideas could fester. To that end, Obama and McCain each recommended maintaining a large forward military presence. While they argued about where the bulk of those forces should reside (e.g. Iraq or Afghanistan), there was no question that the United States should keep large numbers of military forces around the Middle East and other regional hot spots. While Obama was outspoken about using "soft power" in order to repair the United States' image abroad, he was not shy about finding new missions for the instruments of hard power. For instance, he suggested that U.S. forces could support stronger efforts to stop the ongoing crisis in Darfur, possibly including the creation of a no-fly zone to protect civilians from the Sudanese air force. He also proposed expanding the area of operations in the ongoing war in Afghanistan by supporting hot pursuit missions into Pakistan in order to kill or capture top al Qaeda leaders. Obama clearly desired a greater military investment in counterterrorism operations, even though that carried substantial diplomatic risks in the region. [43]

The candidates' differences on key issues, though non-trivial, were not as large as it first appeared. On Iran, Obama was explicit about stating that he would keep the military option available even as he sought to improve diplomatic relations. A military strike would be a "terrible" choice, according to an Obama spokesman, but "it may be that in some terrible world we will have to come to grips with such a terrible choice." [44] McCain's position on Iran, though clearly harder edged, was also somewhat ambiguous. In short, McCain leaned towards force but held out the hopes that economic sanctions could lead to some future compromise, while Obama leaned towards negotiation but held in reserve the threat of military action.

Surprisingly, the candidates also moved towards a common position on Iraq. Despite starting from very different positions, both ended up expressing a similar vision for U.S. forces: a substantial reduction in ground forces by the end of the first term with a residual force in place to continue military training, advising, and counterterrorism operations. Their goals were also the same: a stable and sovereign Iraqi government capable of protecting its borders, denying sanctuary to terrorists, and helping to preserve regional stability. [45] Obama promised to withdraw U.S. troops, but also indicated that he would consult with military officials before making any final decisions. This suggested some flexibility for retaining land forces in Iraq. Indeed, while rejecting "an open-ended commitment of the sort that John McCain and George Bush have advocated," he promised that there would be a residual force and assiduously avoided putting a number on its size. [46] Meanwhile, McCain stressed that he did not support an indefinite commitment to Iraq and suggesting that the gains made after the surge might provide the opportunity for a substantial drawdown by January 2013.

This convergence of views was no accident. Rather, it demonstrated that the candidates operated according to the same strategic playbook. They arrived at the same conclusions because they began with the same assumptions about the nature of world politics and the role of force in American foreign policy. Their divergent positions on international institutions represented the only genuine difference in their approach to grand strategy. Obama expressed more faith in the positive effects of existing institutions, while McCain sought to create new alliances out of whole cloth. But on all other basic questions about national security and the use of force, the candidates were squarely in the liberal internationalist mainstream.

CONCLUSION

Foreign policy and grand strategy played important roles in the 2008 presidential campaign. Both candidates expected a close outcome, and both sought to criticize the other for what they considered misguided and potentially dangerous strategic ideas. Moreover, they seemed to represent caricatures of opposite foreign policy traditions: McCain the rock-ribbed conservative hawk and Obama the soft-power wielding liberal diplomat. But despite a few genuine policy disagreements, McCain and Obama revealed a set of shared strategic assumptions. Given the incentives to emphasize their differences, the surprising amount of common ground suggests that there is indeed an evolving elite consensus on American grand strategy. Politicians with every reason to distinguish themselves from their rivals nonetheless agreed on a set of basic underlying assumptions about the nature of world politics. The main threats to national security come from illiberal actors; the spread of liberal ideals is necessary for American security and prosperity; and the United States should maintain a substantial forward military presence in order to achieve its goals.

The emergence of a strategic consensus does not mean the end of the debate over near-term strategic options. On the contrary, controversies over diplomacy and the use of force are inevitable. But if the election is any indication, debates over military and foreign policy will increasingly focus on *how* to spread liberal ideas to illiberal parts of the world, regardless of whether this makes sense in the first place. Rather than revisiting the foundations of American grand strategy, analysts may end up occupying themselves with the mechanics of liberal expansion.

REFERENCES

[1] The views expressed here are solely those of the author. They do not necessarily represent the views of the Naval War College, the U.S. Navy, or the Department of Defense.

[2] CNN/Opinion Research Corporation survey, September 22, 2008.

[3] Transcript of the Vice Presidential debate, October 3, 2008; *http://edition.cnn.com/2008/POLITICS/10/02/debate.transcript/*.

[4] Elisabeth Bumiller and John M. Broder, "In V.F.W. Speech, McCain Attacks Obama on War," *New York Times*, August 18, 2008.

[5] Transcript of the first Presidential debate, September 26, 2008; *http://edition.cnn.com/2008/POLITICS/09/26/debate.mississippi.transcript/*

[6] Brendan Rittenhouse Green, "Less Strategic than Grand: America's Foreign Policy Consensus," *Précis*, the Newsletter of the MIT Center for International Studies (Fall 2007), p. 6.

[7] For a summary of these arguments, see Rudolph Giuliani, speech at the Republican National Convention, September 3, 2008; *http://www.americanrhetoric.com/speeches/convention2008/rudygiuliani2008rnc.htm*.

[8] Richard Holbrooke, "The Next President: Mastering a Daunting Agenda," *Foreign Affairs*, Vol. 87, No. 5 (September-October 2008). For a similar overview of their differences, see *New York Times*, "Barack Obama for President," October 24, 2008.

[9] Barry R. Posen, *The Sources of Military Doctrine: France, Britain, and Germany Between the World Wars* (Ithaca, NY: Cornell University Press, 1984), p. 13.

[10] One reason is that Congress now requires periodical National Security Strategy statements from the White House.

[11] The following section is based on Barry R. Posen and Andrew L. Ross, "Competing Visions for U.S. Grand Strategy," *International Security*, Vol. 21, No. 3 (Winter 1996-1997), pp. 5-53.

[12] Other benefits of primacy are outlined in Bradley A. Thayer, "In Defense of Primacy," *The National Interest*, No. 86 (November-December 2006), pp. 32-37.

[13] Posen and Ross refer to liberal internationalism as "cooperative engagement." I prefer the term liberal internationalism because it emphasizes the liberal assumptions upon which the strategy is based.

[14] Eugene Gholz, Daryl G. Press, and Harvey M. Sapolsky, "Come Home America: The Strategy of Restraint in the Face of Temptation," *International Security*, Vol. 21, No. 4 (Spring 1997), pp. 5-48; Gholz, Press, and Sapolsky, "Come Home, America," *The American Conservative* (June 2004); and Barry R. Posen, "The Case for Restraint," *The American Interest* (November-December 2007).

[15] Robert J. Art, *A Grand Strategy for America* (Ithaca, NY: Cornell University Press, 2004).

[16] Robert O. Keohane, *After Hegemony: Cooperation and Discord in the World Political Economy* (Princeton, NJ: Princeton University Press, 1984).

[17] Mikhail Gorbachev, "Nobel Lecture," June 5, 1991; http://nobelprize.org/nobel_prizes/peace/laureates/1990/gorbachev-lecture.html.

[18] Andrew J. Bacevich, *The Limits of Power: the End of American Exceptionalism* (New York: Henry Holt & Co., 2008), pp. 73-74.

[19] Posen, "The Case for Restraint."

[20] Barry Posen, Director's Statement, MIT Security Studies Program Annual Report, 2007-2008, p. 3; *http://web.mit.edu/ssp/program/MIT_SSP_AnnualReport2007-08.pdf*

[21] Sapolsky, Gholz and Press work hard to avoid the isolationist tag, noting that a grand strategy of restraint requires neither total military withdrawal nor economic protectionism. See Sapolsky, Gholz, and Press, "Come Home, America," (1997), pp. 5-6. On the use of the word to stifle critics of ambitious strategies, see Andrew J. Bacevich, "What Isolationism?" *Los Angeles Times*, February 11, 2006, p. B11.

[22] Anatol Lieven and John Hulsman, *Ethical Realism: A Vision for America's Role in the World* (New York: Pantheon Books, 2006), p. xiv. For an intellectual history of the liberal tradition in American foreign affairs, see Michael C. Desch, "America's Liberal Illiberalism: The Ideological Origins of Overreaction in U.S. Foreign Policy," *International Security*, Vol. 32, No. 3 (Winter 2007/08), pp. 7–43.

[23] Robert Gilpin, "No One Loves a Political Realist," *Security Studies*, Vol. 5, No. 3 (Spring 1996), pp. 3-26.

[24] Cindy Williams found evidence of this trend in her review of the major party candidates' foreign policy views as expressed in their respective essays for the journal Foreign Affairs. Barack Obama, John McCain, and Hilary Rodham Clinton all identified terrorism, non-state actors, and weak or failed states as serious threats to the national interest, and all argued that U.S. leadership and the use of force abroad was necessary to combat them. While they all supported efforts to expand NATO, they also argued for unilateral military action as circumstances required. Obama and Clinton both noted their approval. McCain did not mention this in his article, but elsewhere he was a strong supporter of unilateralism. The distinctions between the candidates were differences of degree, not of kind. Barry Posen, "A Grand Strategy of Restraint," in Michèle A. Flournoy and Shawn Brimley, eds., *Finding Our Way: Debating American Grand Strategy* (Washington, DC: Center for a New American Security 2008), p. 90.

[25] For extended discussions on the complex relationship between strategy and policy, see Richard K. Betts, "Is Strategy an Illusion?" *International Security*, Vol. 25, No. 2 (Fall 2000), pp. 5-50; and Hew Strachan, "The Lost Meaning of Strategy," *Survival*, Vol. 47, No. 3 (Autumn 2005), pp. 33-54.

[26] Barack Obama, "The Change We Need: Foreign Policy," *www.barackobama.com issues/foreignpolicy/*

[27] John McCain, "An Enduring Peace Built on Freedom," *Foreign Affairs* (November-December 2007).

[28] Philip Bobbitt, *Terror and Consent: The Wars for the Twenty-First Century* (New York: Alfred A. Knopf, 2008).

[29] Jeffrey Goldberg, "The Wars of John McCain," *The Atlantic Monthly* (October 2008), p. 52.

[30] Anatol Lieven and Charles Kupchan note that the idea of a league of democracies was also popular in some liberal circles. For Lieven's blistering review of the idea, see "League of Demagoguery," The *National Interest* online, September 2, 2008; http://www.nationalinterest.org/Article.aspx?id=19696. See also Charles Kupchan, "Minor League, Major Problems," *Foreign Affairs*, Vol. 87, No. 6 (November-December 2008); and Thomas Carothers, "A League of Their Own," *Foreign Policy*, No. 167 (July-August 2008).

[31] CNN, interview with Barack Obama, July 2008; http://www.cnn.com/2008/POLITICS/07/13/zakaria.obama/

[32] CNN, interview with Barack Obama, July 2008. See also Obama, "The Change We Need: Foreign Policy."

[33] John R. Bolton, "Bring on the Foreign Policy Debate," *Wall Street Journal*, May 18, 2008.

[34] Bob Deans, "Defense Spending: Where They Stand," *Raleigh News & Observer*, October 13, 2008, p. 3.

[35] Gordon and Zeleny, "Obama Envisions New Iran Approach."

[36] Reuters, "McCain Jokes About Killing Iranians with Cigarettes," July 8, 2008.

[37] McCain, "An Enduring Peace Built on Freedom." On missile defense and Iran, see "McCain, Obama Slam Iran's Missile Test," CNN.com, July 9, 2008.

[38] Michael R. Gordon, "Rivals Present Sharp Divide on Iraq Goals," *New York Times*, October 6, 2008.

[39] Robert G. Kaiser, "Nominees Have Similar Views on Use of U.S. Force," *Washington Post*, October 27, 2008, p. 4.

[40] Kaiser, "Nominees Have Similar Views."

[41] Benjamin H. Friedman, "More Troops for What?" *Foreign Policy* (online), July 2007; http://www.foreignpolicy.com/story/cms.php?story_id=3907

[42] Bret Stephens, "Will Obama Gut Defense?" *Wall Street Journal*, October 28, 2008, p. 15.

[43] McCain criticized Obama's stance by arguing that it was wrong to telegraph military decisions in advance. However, McCain previously agreed that hot pursuit missions would be appropriate if U.S. forces located bin Laden across the border. See Transcript of Interview with Sen. John McCain, *Military Times*, October 16, 2007; http://www.militarytimes.com/news/2007/10/military_mccain_transcript_071016w/

[44] Carol Giacomo, "New Beltway Debate: What to do About Iran," *New York Times*, November 3, 2008, p. 3.

[45] While both sought the same goals, Obama was more concerned about the financial and human costs of continuing the war, as well as the opportunity cost of failing to focus on the war in Afghanistan. Compare McCain's "Strategy for Victory in Iraq," www.johnmccain.com; and the *CBS Evening News* interview with Barack Obama, July

22, 2008; *http://www.cbsnews.com/stories/2008/07/22/eveningnews/main 4283623.shtml*

[46] CNN Interview with Barack Obama, July 2008. See also Michael R. Gordon and Jeff Zeleny, "Obama Envisions New Iran Approach," *New York Times*, November 2, 2007.

Chapter 4

PASSING THE TORCH THROUGH POLITICAL TIME: HEIR APPARENT PRESIDENTS AND THE GOVERNING PARTY

Donald A. Zinman
Grand Valley State University, Allendale, MI, US

ABSTRACT

Presidents who succeed a particularly dominant and transformative president of their own party find themselves in the predicament of the heir apparent. These presidents not only inherit their predecessor's policy agenda, but also the dominance of their party. We assess the performance of heir apparent presidents and their parties in presidential and congressional elections, in comparison to the performance of their predecessors' party performance in presidential and congressional elections. During the heir apparent's presidency, the governing party's dominance weakens in both presidential and congressional elections. Problems associated with a weakening dominant political order, or "regime", accelerate during the tenure of the heir apparent president, as the opposition party gains strength.

INTRODUCTION: THE POLITICS OF THE HEIR APPARENT PRESIDENCY

Writing in Federalist #72, Alexander Hamilton suggested that a president would be inherently predisposed to act in the shadow of his predecessor. [1] Presidents must weigh competing demands to continue the policy legacy of their predecessor on the one hand, while at the same time charting a separate and distinct course of action that will uniquely define their presidency. Under a party system, presidents inherit a coalition of supporters, and conversely, an organized team of adversaries. Supporters expect certain policy commitments to be fulfilled. Adversaries, now locked out of power, must find effective ways to challenge the incumbent president by depicting his agenda as timeworn and his administration as incompetent. Presidents who ascend to the office following a particularly transformative and significant president of their own party are likely to find themselves in the predicament of the heir apparent.

These presidents govern in an environment of a weakened governing party, while facing an increasingly mobilized opposition party. Their electoral records are generally less impressive than their predecessors, and their party tends to weaken at the congressional level during their tenure. Potentially, their ability to actively set their own course of action in office is limited by the agenda established by their predecessors, as well as a stronger opposition party.

The political position of the heir apparent president is a unique one that warrants more attention than it has been given in the presidential literature. In his assessment of the 1992 presidential election, Walter Dean Burnham noted that so-called "third - term understudies" (presidents who followed a two-term reign of their own party) face considerable difficulties with re - election. [2] These presidents often have trouble continuing the reformist impulses of their predecessors. When they succeed historically significant presidents who achieved transformative policy changes, heir apparent presidents are prone to significant difficulties amid a generally less supportive political environment than their predecessors experienced. It is important for us to appreciate the political environment of heir apparent presidents because it establishes the context of their leadership dilemma in office.

SECOND IN LINE IN POLITICAL TIME

The most historically significant presidents warrant scholars' attention because they left a lasting legacy upon the structure and function of American government. Presidents Thomas Jefferson, Andrew Jackson, Abraham Lincoln, Franklin Roosevelt, and Ronald Reagan arguably changed the American political landscape for decades to come, in ways that shaped the boundaries of political action for subsequent presidents. These presidents constructed an entirely new political order, or "regime" as Stephen Skowronek suggests. These presidents came into power as part of a major reaction against a crumbling and discredited political order. They have political authority to tear down most of the old order and begin building a new one. Subsequent regime - affiliated presidents (of the same party as the regime's founding president) face the tensions of serving their regime's constituencies and adhering to the reigning governing philosophy, while at the same time seeking to make a contribution of their own to the dominant political order. [3]

Other presidents have governed in opposition to the prevailing political order of their time. These "opposition presidents" came in to office at a time when their party was not the nation's long - term governing party. Presidents such as Grover Cleveland, Woodrow Wilson, and Dwight Eisenhower entered office leading a party that did not dominate the terms and conditions of American politics and governmental action. As David Crockett argued, these presidents faced the difficult choice of either fully confronting the dominant governing order, or accommodating themselves to the political realities of the environment in which they had to operate. In the accomodationist stance, the opposition president "places more effort on steady administration of the law, seeking to trim the edges of the reigning governing philosophy by moderating the received agenda, perhaps along lines more compatible with the principles of his own party." [4] They are most likely to be successful, he argues, if they pursue a course of moderation and accommodation within the framework of the dominant governing order. [5]

Opportunities and limitations for presidential action are shaped in large part by what Skowronek calls "political time", which refers to the president's place within the timeline of a dominant political order. Presidents are either affiliated with the dominant regime or opposed to it, governing at a given point in the life - cycle of that regime. [6] Skowronek chose several affiliated presidents who governed at the approximate mid-life of their regimes to illustrate the dilemma of the so - called "articulator" president, who faces the demands for innovation on the one hand, and loyalty to the tenets of the governing regime on the other hand. The governing party's unity becomes increasingly fragile under the tenure of these presidents and the opposition party grows progressively more formidable. The mid - life regime presidents under Skowronek's scrutiny are those "who rearticulated the old formulas in the greatest leap forward on received commitments." [7] The presidents he chose (James Monroe, James Polk, Theodore Roosevelt, and Lyndon Johnson) for his principal case studies in this category did not succeed a president who built the foundations of a new political regime. It is important for us to examine the political context of the presidents who do follow in the immediate footsteps of these regime builders, so as to better understand how political time moves. An heir apparent president should be considered an important sub - category of these numerous articulator presidents, for many of the problems articulator presidents face in office first manifest themselves when the regime builder has left the presidency.

A president who plays the greatest role as an heir apparent is one who enters office following the establishment of a new political equilibrium by a particularly transformative president of his own party. We define an heir apparent president as the first president to succeed the regime builders, as identified by Skowronek, of their own party. The heir apparents include James Madison, Martin Van Buren, Ulysses S. Grant, Harry Truman, and George H.W. Bush. Under this classification, Grant is the heir apparent to Lincoln because Andrew Johnson was not formally a Republican, having been a Democrat in his political career and running with Lincoln in 1864 on the ticket of the National Unity Party. Grant was the first Republican elected after Lincoln's death, making him the first subsequent president who was formally affiliated with the new dominant regime of American politics.

The heir apparent president is second in line in political time, because he assumes office as the first subsequent president of the regime builder's party. More than any other president who succeeds a president of his own party, heir apparent presidents have the largest shoes to fill, assuming office in the greatest shadow of a predecessor who transformed fundamental assumptions of American government and politics. For example, Democrat James Buchanan's succession of Democrat Franklin Pierce does not compare to Van Buren's succession of Jackson because Buchanan did not succeed a president who built the foundations of a new political order. Similarly, Grant's presidency was followed by three consecutive Republican presidents, none of whom succeeded a president who transformed the political order. Gerald Ford's succession of Richard Nixon should also not be considered an heir apparent presidency because he succeeded a president who resigned in disgrace, and because the Republican Party of the 1970's stood in opposition to the governing regime of the time. [8]

In office, the heir apparent faces a stronger opposition party, which establishes the political context for subsequent presidents under a given governing regime. Compared to their predecessors, heir apparent presidents are likely to have fewer opportunities for innovation and independent action that will uniquely define their presidencies in a significant and positive way. They act as the custodians of their predecessors' paradigm - shifting policies, though not entirely without their own policy innovations. They must deal with the consequences of their predecessors' significant departures in public policy. For example, Grant was the custodian of Lincoln's plan for a moderate course of Reconstruction after the Civil War. Truman was the custodian of the new world order envisioned by Franklin Roosevelt, though his administration was also the architect of Cold War American foreign policy. George H.W. Bush presided over the end of the Cold War envisioned by Reagan, though his administration also faced even more complicated international problems in a new multi - polar world order.

These heir apparent presidents have fewer opportunities to dramatically depart from the orthodoxies of their predecessors. The political order remains defined by their larger than life predecessors' policy achievements and consequences. Opportunities for more significant departures in public policy can come years later, after the passage of time and the growing saliency of new issues create a political environment more hospitable to reform. The Grant Administration, for example, was preoccupied by Reconstruction, but decades later Theodore Roosevelt could be an economic reformer. Truman had to chart a more moderate course of action on civil rights than Lyndon Johnson would years later. George H.W. Bush was the first custodian of post-Cold War American foreign policy, but it was George W. Bush who more dramatically reshaped the nation's foreign policy assumptions.

ELECTING AN HEIR APPARENT PRESIDENT

Jefferson, Jackson, Lincoln, Franklin Roosevelt, and Reagan each wedded their reformist programs to the virtue of popular will, believing themselves to be defenders of the American people against powerful interests. They stretched the boundaries of accepted presidential behavior, and used the office to enhance the president's leadership role and relationship with the American people. They were popular, even revered, figures who redefined the limits of government action and redrew the power equilibrium in American politics.

An heir apparent is elected by reassembling the political coalition that placed his predecessor in the presidency. The challenge for the heir apparent seeking election to the office is to maintain his predecessor's coalition of political supporters. Those who succeeded did so by promising continuity, committing themselves to sustaining their predecessors' programs and approaching new reforms with caution. After many years of reform under a transformative and significant presidency, voters might understandably wish to slow down the pace of social and economic change, preferring to maintain and absorb the recently implemented policy changes. As a candidate, the heir apparent is likely to hitch himself to the popular reforms enacted under his predecessor, pledging to competently administer the policies, programs and government agencies created by the outgoing president's reform agenda. The heir apparent may promise to correct administrative deficiencies that exist in his predecessor's reform programs, but he will also pledge to defend his predecessor's reforms from opposition forces seeking to undo them. For example, Truman promised to protect and defend the New Deal, calling it "the pattern for what we want to do." [9] George H.W. Bush was elected on the basis of a famous promise to protect the Reagan tax cuts from congressional Democrats. [10]

As Table 1 demonstrates, predecessors do have a better record of winning second terms, compared to their heir apparents, who tend to win elections by smaller margins than their predecessors enjoyed. In their second term elections, each predecessor expanded upon his electoral vote margin from four years earlier. This pattern also manifests itself in the popular vote totals of predecessor presidents, with the minor exception of Jackson's re - election in 1832, when his popular vote total dropped by 1.74 percent from his 1828 tally. Three of the four heir apparents who stood for election twice achieved smaller electoral vote totals in their second election, in comparison to their electoral vote totals four years earlier. In addition, three out of the five heir apparent presidents identified here were succeeded by a president of the opposition party. Madison left office with the Federalist opposition disorganized and weakened at the national level and was succeeded by Monroe, a Democratic - Republican. Ever since then, however, heir apparents have left office with their party in a weakened condition at the presidential level. Grant was succeeded by Republican Rutherford B. Hayes, but only after a disputed election in 1876, in which Democrat Samuel Tilden won the popular vote.

Table 1. Electoral Records of Heir Apparents and Predecessors [12]

President	Won Second Term?	First Term Election	Second Term Election
Jefferson	Yes	Electoral Votes: 52.90%	Electoral Votes: 92.05%
Madison	Yes	Electoral Votes: 69.32%	Electoral Votes: 58.72%
Jackson	Yes	Electoral Votes: 68.20% Popular Vote: 55.97%	Electoral Votes: 76.04% Popular Vote: 54.23%
Van Buren	No	Electoral Votes: 57.82% Popular Vote: 50.83%	Electoral Votes: 20.41% Popular Vote: 46.81%
Lincoln	Yes	Electoral Votes: 59.41% Popular Vote: 39.65%	Electoral Votes: 90.99% Popular Vote: 55.03%
Grant	Yes	Electoral Votes: 72.79% Popular Vote: 52.66%	Electoral Votes: 81.25% Popular Vote: 55.58%
FDR*	Yes	Electoral Votes: 88.89% Popular Vote: 57.41%	Electoral Votes: 98.49% Popular Vote: 60.80%
Truman	Yes	NA	Electoral Votes: 57.06% Popular Vote: 49.55%
Reagan	Yes	Electoral Votes: 90.89% Popular Vote: 50.75%	Electoral Votes: 97.58% Popular Vote: 58.77%
Bush	No	Electoral Votes: 79.18% Popular Vote: 53.37%	Electoral Votes: 31.23% Popular Vote: 37.45%

Heir Apparent presidents are identified in italics.
* FDR's third term re-election resulted in the incumbent winning 84.56% of the Electoral Vote and 54.74% of the Popular Vote. In his fourth term re-election, he polled 81.36% of the Electoral Vote and 53.39% of the Popular Vote.

Table 2. Means of Electoral Records of Heir Apparents and Predecessors

President	Electoral Votes	Popular Vote
Predecessor	81.78%	54.08%
Heir Apparent	58.64% (Winners Only: 68.02%)	49.46% (Winners Only: 52.40%)

Heir apparent presidents average weaker electoral and popular vote totals than predecessors (Table 2). This trend persists even when we exclude the losing re - election campaigns of Van Buren in 1840 and George H.W. Bush in 1992. Madison, governing at a time when a fully mature two - party system had not yet materialized, was elected and re - elected by smaller margins than Jefferson's reelection in 1804. Van Buren reassembled a smaller Jacksonian Democratic majority in 1836, and then went down to defeat four years later. Truman fell just short of winning the popular vote in 1948, and he amassed far fewer electoral votes than his predecessor had earned in four elections to the presidency. George H.W. Bush never equaled his predecessor's electoral vote totals, though in 1988 he surpassed Reagan's first popular vote accumulation. In 1988, Bush carried 40 of the 49 states Reagan won in his 1984 re - election landslide, but Bush only won 18 of these states in his unsuccessful re - election contest in 1992.

The Civil War and Reconstruction elections present a more nuanced picture. Grant stood for election in 1868 with the Democratic South under federal Reconstruction supervision. At the time of his election, three former Confederate states had yet to be re - admitted to the union. Grant was elected with a larger electoral and popular vote margin than Lincoln achieved in the multi - candidate, regionally polarized election of 1860. [11] Lincoln did not have to worry about Southern Democratic electoral opposition in the wartime election of 1864, but Grant had to stand for re - election in 1872 at a time when all former Confederate states had re - entered the union and the Democratic Party was rebuilding itself as a force of opposition. Grant was reelected by a very slightly larger popular vote margin than Lincoln's 1864 reelection, but his margin in the Electoral College was less impressive than Lincoln in 1864.

Gathering Opposition

The tendency for heir apparent presidents to either lose their reelection contests or win elections by margins smaller than their predecessors enjoyed suggests that opposition to the governing party gains momentum during the tenure of an heir apparent president. Many problems build up over the course of eight or more years with one party controlling the executive branch, causing the presidential party's mandate to govern to recede. After a long record of controlling the executive branch, policy consequences, intended and unintended, land in the lap of the heir apparent president. The heir apparent's party increasingly assumes ownership of the problems his party came to the White House to solve, as well as the policy consequences of his party's policies, and any new problems that may arise. His party assumes the identity as the governing party, making it possible for opposition forces to build a credible alternative. For example, Van Buren acted as the faithful custodian of Jacksonian economic and monetary policies, but he also faced the consequences of an economic collapse that was brought about by those policies. During Van Buren's tenure, the Whig Party regrouped at the national level, united around a single presidential candidate, and adopted highly effective campaign tactics to defeat the president's bid for reelection in 1840. [13]

All presidents come in to office with a mandate to govern, but the predecessors identified here enjoyed the widest mandate to tear down an established political order. Jefferson, Jackson, Lincoln, Franklin Roosevelt, and Reagan came into office with a mandate to solve vexing problems and crises, and to reject established governing formulas. To varying degrees, these presidents also had the strengths of their personalities and popular appeal with the American people. They also faced determined opposition forces, but within a much more supportive political environment than their successors.

The fate of the president's party in midterm congressional elections is one way for us to assess the currents of the political environment. House elections are particularly indicative of the public opinion environment concerning the presidential party. Senate elections can also reveal a national political trend, though the partisan shift of the Senate will be diluted by the fact that only one third of the seats are up for election every two years. Even though universal direct election of senators was not written into the Constitution until 1913, the selection of senators by elected state legislatures reflects the political currents in those particular states. To account for the changing size of the House and Senate across time, we will measure congressional party gains and losses in terms of percentages, rather than raw seat gains and losses.

Like all presidents, heir apparents are inclined to see their party suffer losses in midterm congressional elections. Some heir apparents suffered worse party losses than their predecessors, while others actually performed better in one or both houses. However, heir apparents generally presided over a weakening congressional party to a greater degree than their predecessors. As Table 3 reveals, in midterm elections, predecessors averaged a party loss of 3.9 percent in the House of Representatives and a gain of 0.8 percent in the Senate. Heir apparents averaged a party loss of 7.1 percent in House midterm elections, and 5.6 percent in Senate elections.

Table 3. Midterm Congressional Party Seat Gains and Losses of Heir Apparents and Predecessors by Percentage [14]

Election Year	President	House	Senate
1802	Jefferson	9.0	23.5
1806	Jefferson	1.4	2.9
1810	*Madison*	10.0	3.9
1814	*Madison*	2.4	-9.4
1830	Jackson	-4.7	-2.1
1834	Jackson	-0.5	-4.2
1838	*Van Buren*	-1.2	-9.6
1862	Lincoln	-12.3	1.5
1870	*Grant*	-14.4	-8.1
1874	*Grant*	-33.0	-3.0
1934	FDR	2.1	10.4
1938	FDR	-16.6	-7.3
1942	FDR	-10.3	-9.4
1946	*Truman*	-12.4	-12.5
1950	*Truman*	-6.4	-5.2
1982	Reagan	-6.0	1.0
1986	Reagan	-1.1	-8.0
1990	*Bush*	-1.8	-1.0
Predecessor Mean		-3.9	0.8
Heir Apparent Mean		-7.1	-5.6

Heir Apparents are in Italics

Table 4. Congressional Party Seat Gains and Losses in Successful Presidential Elections for Heir Apparents and Predecessors by Percentage

Election Year	President	House	Senate
1800	Jefferson	20.2	18.8
1804	Jefferson	7.7	5.9
1808	*Madison*	-16.9	-2.9
1812	*Madison*	-12.2	-5.6
1828	Jackson	10.8	-4.2
1832	Jackson	0.4	-8.3
1836	*Van Buren*	-6.2	17.3
1860	Lincoln	10.3	22.6
1864	Lincoln	23.7	8.8
1868	*Grant*	-6.2	0.0
1872	*Grant*	12.2	-12.2
1932	FDR	22.3	12.5
1936	FDR	2.8	7.3
1940	FDR	1.1	-3.1
1944	FDR	4.6	0.0
1948	*Truman*	17.2	9.4
1980	Reagan	7.8	12.0
1984	Reagan	3.7	-1.0
1988	*Bush*	-0.5	0.0
Predecessor Mean		9.6	5.9
Heir Apparent Mean		-1.8	0.9

Heir Apparents are in Italics.

This trend continues in presidential election years. Compared to predecessors, heir apparent presidents also bring weaker party coattails with them upon their election to the White House. Table 4 reveals that predecessors average a party gain of 9.6 percent in the House and 5.9 percent in the Senate in their presidential election years. When heir apparents were elected, however, they averaged a party loss of 1.8 percent in the House and a gain of only 0.9 percent in the Senate.

Heir apparents tend to leave office with their party in a weaker position, sometimes even weaker than when their predecessor began in office. Figures 1 through 5 reveal the congressional party breakdown by percentages in both houses from the first election of the predecessor through the final election when the heir apparent was in office. Van Buren, Grant, Truman, and the elder Bush all left office with their party in the minority in at least one house of Congress. Bush entered office with Republican minorities already established in both houses (only 40.2% in the House), which may have complicated the ability of the Democrats to make further substantial gains. Republicans lost only one Senate seat and eight House seats in the 1990 midterm elections. [15] In contrast, Reagan enjoyed a Republican Senate for his first six years in office. Madison's Democratic - Republicans maintained commanding congressional majorities during his tenure. Still, opposition Federalists did make a minor comeback in middle of Madison's presidency, but it was largely confined to New England and Delaware. Federalist disintegration resumed after the War of 1812 concluded. A competitive, popularly-based two party system had not yet crystallized, and the Federalists were reluctant, if not resistant, to build a party organization that would offer the American electorate an alternative. [16]

Party Control by Percentage: House [17]

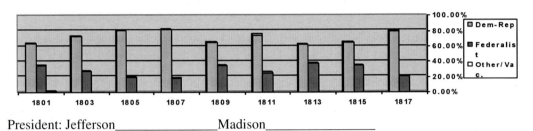

President: Jefferson_____Madison_____

Party Control by Percentage: Senate [18]

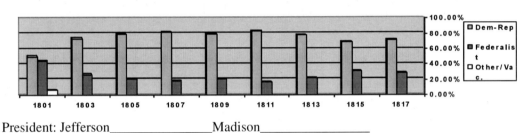

President: Jefferson_____Madison_____

Figure 1. Jefferson and Madison

Party Control by Percentage: House

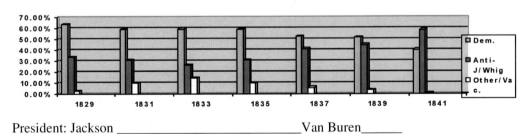

President: Jackson_____Van Buren_____

Party Control by Percentage: Senate

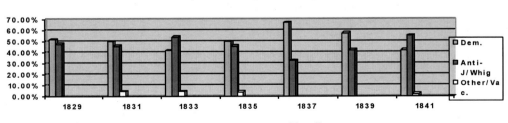

President: Jackson_____Van Buren_____

Figure 2. Jackson and Van Buren [19].

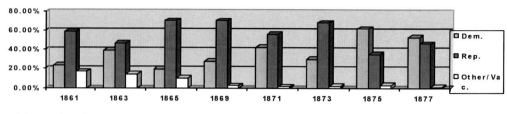

President: Lincoln _____ Grant_____

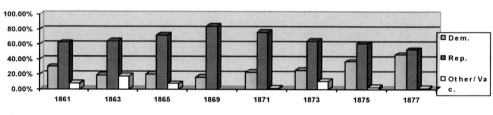

President: Lincoln _____ Grant_____

Figure 3. Lincoln and Grant.

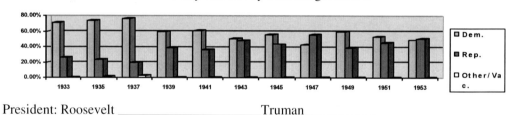

President: Roosevelt _____Truman_____

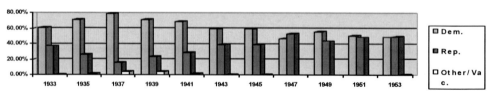

President: Roosevelt _____Truman_____

Figure 4. F.D. Roosevelt and Truman.

As a body more reflective of popular will, and subject to election every two years, the partisan composition of the House of Representatives reflects the reduced political support enjoyed by heir apparent presidents. Tabulations in Table 5 reveal that predecessor presidents averaged a party composition of 60.5 percent in the House. Heir apparents averaged a congressional party composition of 55.9 percent in the House.

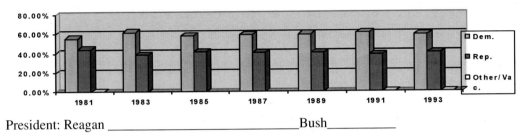

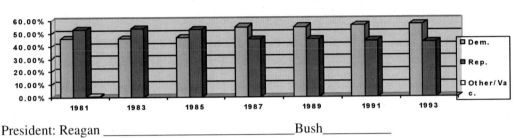

Figure 5. Reagan and Bush.

Table 5. Presidential party composition in Congress by Mean [20]

President	House	Senate
Predecessors	60.5%	61.5%
Heir Apparents	55.9%	64.0%

In the Senate, predecessors and heir apparents enjoyed comfortable party majorities more often than not. Heir apparents actually averaged a 64.0 percent party majority, while predecessors averaged a 61.5 percent party majority. As one third of Senate seats stand for re-election every six years, heir apparent presidents are likely to be the beneficiaries of Senate majorities that were installed during their predecessors' tenure. As Tables 3 and 4 reveal, predecessors usually outperformed their heir apparents in midterm and presidential year Senate elections. As a result, heir apparents often came into office enjoying the residual benefits of their predecessors' party coattails, or their predecessors' ability to limit the party's losses in Senate elections. Staggered six year terms also made some heir apparents the beneficiaries of their predecessors' electoral coattails. For example, Madison benefited from the large Senate majorities Democratic – Republicans accumulated under Jefferson's tenure, including an 82.4 percent majority at the start of the Tenth Congress in 1807. Every heir apparent president identified here presided over a diminishing party in the Senate during his tenure. Madison, Van Buren, Grant, and Truman all began their terms with Senate majorities left over from their predecessor, but progressively experienced party deterioration between their inauguration and the conclusion of their final midterm election before leaving office.

CONCLUSION: THE HEIR APPARENT PRESIDENCY IN POLITICAL TIME

We draw two central conclusions. First, heir apparent presidents—defined as presidents who succeed a regime - building president of their own party—generally achieve a reduced level of electoral success compared to predecessors. Heir apparents are more likely to lose their bids for second term, and their average electoral vote and popular vote performances are below the averages of predecessor presidents. Second, heir apparent presidents, to a greater degree than predecessors, face an opposition party of growing strength, as measured by the presidential party's performance in congressional elections for both midterm and presidential election years. Predecessors typically enjoy larger party majorities in the House than heir apparents do. Heir apparents average slightly larger party majorities in the Senate, but the heir apparents' party typically performs worse than the predecessors' party in Senate elections.

These findings suggest that heir apparent presidents are more likely to govern within a less supportive political environment compared to predecessors. Not only did heir apparent presidents confront a growing opposition party in elections, but they also faced more severe party divisions than their predecessors experienced. At the electoral level, the heir apparent presidents have experienced far more serious internal party disruptions when they stood for a second term. Madison's opponent in 1812 was New York Democratic - Republican, DeWitt Clinton, as part of a fusion ticket of Federalists and anti-war Democratic - Republicans. In 1872, Grant contended with a similar problem, facing a fusion ticket of the Democratic Party and the Liberal Republican Party, which denounced Grant's Reconstruction policies. The Democratic National Convention in 1840 refused to re - nominate the controversial incumbent Vice President Richard Johnson for a second term under President Van Buren. The party had no national nominee for the vice presidency, but allowed state parties to choose their own nominee. [21] Truman faced seemingly disastrous defections from four Southern state Democratic Party organizations lining up behind South Carolina governor Strom Thurmond, who ran in response to Truman's overtures in support of civil rights for blacks. Offended by Truman's new Cold War foreign policy, a faction of liberal Democrats also splintered from the national party and backed the candidacy of Henry Wallace. Before the 1948 campaign, some Democrats even openly mused about replacing Truman as the party nominee. [22] In the 1992 Republican primaries, George H.W. Bush faced the defection of former Reagan Communications Director Patrick Buchanan, who attacked Bush's economic record, his trade policies and his recalcitrance to push for a socially conservative policy agenda. [23] Even in the general election, some 13 percent of Republicans cast their ballots for Independent candidate Ross Perot. [24]

By contrast, predecessors have enjoyed a more unified party when they stood for re-election. Reagan, for example, won 96 percent of support from Republican voters in 1984. [25] Jefferson was unanimously re - nominated by the Democratic - Republican congressional party caucus in February, 1804, though Vice President Aaron Burr was dropped from the ticket without a controversy inside the caucus. [26] In comparison to heir apparents, predecessors did not face the same degree of high - level party defections in their reelection contests. Policy differences within the party did not result in disastrous defections of a high - level political figure that brought along a large number of voters. Jackson faced the election year resignation of Vice President John C. Calhoun as a consequence of the South Carolina nullification crisis in 1832. This defection, however, did not damage Jackson's Southern electoral support. Jackson carried every Southern state outside of South Carolina. Radical Republicans mounted a challenge to Lincoln's reelection in 1864, but their candidate, John C. Frémont, dropped out later in the summer. [27] Franklin Roosevelt began to face opposition from Southern Democrats as early as his second term. He even tried, and mostly failed, to "purge" several Southern Democrats in the 1938 primary elections. [28] Roosevelt, however, continued to enjoy overwhelming support from voters in Southern states in 1940 and 1944. Nor did Roosevelt's failed confrontation with Southern Democrats result in a defection of its leading politicians to a third party, much less the Republican Party.

The heir apparent presidency occupies an important place in the cycle of political time. Under the tenure of the heir apparent, problems associated with a weakening governing party began to crystallize. While many presidents successfully pass on their office to a successor of their own party, the heir apparents identified here faced the challenge of governing in the shadow of a president who built the foundations of a new political order. Entering office, they inherited not only a policy agenda to fulfill, but also the political supremacy of their party. Upon leaving office, all of these presidents, save for Madison, left their party in a less dominant and more vulnerable position. Even under Madison, the Federalist opposition experienced a modest comeback in the middle of the president's tenure. Under each heir apparent president examined here, the opposition party did not become the dominant party, but the opposition party did find more opportunities to be more competitive in elections and increase party representation in Congress.

REFERENCES

[1] Alexander Hamilton, "Federalist #72", in Clinton Rossiter, ed., *The Federalist Papers* (New York: Penguin Books, 1961), pp. 435-40.
[2] Walter Dean Burnham, "The Legacy of George Bush: Travails of an Understudy", in Gerald M. Pomper, ed., *The Election of 1992* (Chatham, NJ: Chatham House Publishers, 1993), pp. 1-38.
[3] Stephen Skowronek, *The Politics Presidents Make: Leadership from John Adams to Bill Clinton* (Cambridge: Belknap Press, 1997), pp. 34-39.
[4] David Crockett, *The Opposition Presidency: Leadership and the Constraints of History* (College Station, TX: Texas A&M University Press, 2002), p. 49.
[5] Ibid., p. 8.
[6] Skowronek, pp. 30, 49-52.
[7] Ibid. p. 58.
[8] Crockett, pp. 151-74.
[9] "Truman Declares Democrats Design Better Life in U.S.", *New York Times*, October 22, 1948.
[10] "Transcript of Bush Speech Accepting Presidential Nomination", *New York Times*, August 19, 1988.
[11] The Republican Party had no substantive organization in the Southern states on the eve of the Civil War. Lincoln won 48.48 percent of the non-Southern popular vote in 1860

(author's calculation from "Dave Liep's Atlas of US Presidential Elections", *www.uselectionatlas.org*.).

[12] Electoral data comes from Dave Liep's presidential election website, "Atlas of US Presidential Elections*", http://www.uselectionatlas.org/*. We begin counting the popular vote in 1828, as popular selection of presidential electors did not become widespread until 1824.

[13] Michael F. Holt, *Rise and Fall of the American Whig Party* (Oxford: Oxford University Press, 1999), pp. 87-111.

[14] Numbers come from the total seat gains and losses based on the author's calculation from the official House and Senate lists of party membership at the start of each new Congress, *http://clerk.house.gov/art_history/house_history/partyDiv.html* and *http://www.senate.gov/pagelayout/history/one_item_and_teasers/partydiv.htm*. These totals are based on Election Day results. Jackson's Democratic Party is listed as "Jacksonian" until 1837 in the official lists.

[15] A second Republican Senate loss should be noted in a 1991 special Pennsylvania election. "A Stunning Upset", *New York Times*, November 6, 1991. This election was depicted as a harbinger of danger for Bush's re-election prospects in 1992.

[16] Richard Hofstadter, *The Idea of a Party System: The Rise of Legitimate Opposition in the United States, 1780-1840* (Berkeley: University of California Press, 1969), pp. 178-79. On Federalist efforts to build an opposition party, see David Hackett Fischer, *The Revolution of American Conservatism: The Federalist Party in the Era of Jeffersonian Democracy* (New York: Harper & Row, 1965).

[17] Numbers come from the official House list of party membership at the start of each new Congress. Numbers are based on Election Day results, *http://clerk.house.gov/art_history/ house_history/partyDiv.html*.

[18] Numbers come from the official Senate list of party membership at the start of each new Congress. Numbers are based on Election Day results. Party designations are the same as the official House list, *http://www.senate.gov/pagelayout/history/one_item_and_teasers/partydiv.htm*.

[19] In the official House and Senate lists, Democrats during the Jackson presidency are referred to as "Jacksonians", while opponents are referred to as "Anti-Jacksonians". The label "Whig" was used beginning in 1837.

[20] Figures are compiled from the official House and Senate lists of party membership at the start of each new Congress. Tabulations cover the tenure of each predecessor and heir apparent president identified in this study, beginning with the congressional party composition established in the president's first election through the final midterm election under the president's tenure. In the case of Harry Truman, the first congressional party composition credited to him comes as a result of the elections of 1946, as Truman inherited the presidency in April 1945 upon the death of Roosevelt. The congressional party composition established by the election of 1944 is credited to Roosevelt.

[21] Joel H. Silbey, *Martin Van Buren and the Emergence of American Popular Politics* (Lanham, MD: Rowman & Littlefield, 2002), p. 148.

[22] One possibility was Dwight Eisenhower. Gary A. Donaldson, *Truman Defeats Dewey* (Lexington: University of Kentucky Press, 1998), pp. 136-44.

[23] On the Buchanan candidacy, see Peter Goldman, et al., *Quest for the Presidency 1992* (College Station, Texas A&M University Press, 1994), pp. 318-40.
[24] Gallup Poll Monthly, November, 1992, 9, reproduced in Nelson W. Polsby and Aaron Wildavsky, *Presidential Elections: Strategies and Structures of American Politics*, 10th Edition (New York: Chatham House, 2000), p. 322.
[25] Gallup Poll, November, 1984, in Polsby and Wildavsky, p. 321.
[26] Jules Witcover, *Party of the People: A History of the Democrats* (New York: Random House, 2003), pp. 93-94.
[27] Paul F. Boller, Jr., *Presidential Campaigns*, Revised Edition (Oxford: Oxford University Press, 2004), pp. 116-18.
[28] On the 1938 "Purge Campaign", see Sidney M. Milkis, *The President and the Parties: The Transformation of the American Party System Since the New Deal* (New York: Oxford University Press, 1993), pp. 83-87.

In: White House Studies Compendium. Volume 9   ISBN: 978-1-62618-681-1
Editors: Anthony J. Eksterowicz and Glenn P. Hastedt   © 2013 Nova Science Publishers, Inc.

Chapter 5

BUSH'S ADVENTURES IN THE NATIONAL SERVICE POLICY ARENA AND FIVE LESSONS FOR PRESIDENT OBAMA

Richard Holtzman
Bryant University, Smithfield, R.I., US

ABSTRACT

As candidates, both Barack Obama and John McCain criticized George W. Bush's failure to call for sacrifice and service from the American people in the wake of 9/11. However, criticizing the mistakes of a past president is not the same as learning from them. Obama has referred to service as the "cause of my presidency." If Obama is indeed committed to following through on this campaign rhetoric, what lessons can he learn from Bush's experiences? This essay offers an analysis of Bush's adventures in national service policy and, in particular, his failures of presidential leadership in this arena. Its purpose is to identify and elucidate five lessons derived from these experiences that will help President Obama better navigate this policy issue.

INTRODUCTION

On September 11, 2008, Senators John McCain and Barack Obama suspended their presidential campaigns for the evening to speak in support of national service at the Service Nation Presidential Candidates Forum at Columbia University. During back-to-back interviews with PBS anchor Judy Woodruff and *TIME Magazine* editor Richard Stengal, each candidate suggested that had he been president, he would have called for sacrifice from the American people in the wake of September 11, 2001. McCain referred to President George W. Bush's failure to emphasize the need for volunteerism and service during that period as "one of the biggest mistakes that we ever made after 9/11." Obama added: "I think that had the president very clearly said, this is not just going to be a war of a few of us, this is going to be an effort that mobilizes all of us, I think we would have had a different result." [1]

As this essay illustrates, these criticisms of Bush's tardy response to the civic awakening that emerged following the events of 9/11 are justified. However, recognizing and criticizing the mistakes of a past president is not the same as learning from them. President Obama has indicated that his call for Americans to serve will not be "issued in one speech or program; this will be a cause of my presidency." [2] If Obama is indeed committed to following through on this campaign rhetoric, what lessons can he learn from the experiences of his predecessor?

The following is an analysis of Bush's adventures in the realm of national service policy and, in particular, his failures of presidential leadership in this arena. Its purpose is to identify and elucidate five lessons derived from these experiences that will help President Obama better navigate this policy issue. [3]

LESSON #1: CRISES CREATE OPPORTUNITIES FOR BOLD PRESIDENTIAL POLICY-MAKING; YET, THEY ARE FLEETING AND DEMAND A TIMELY RESPONSE

Unforeseen events can serve as triggering devices that transform these events into pressing policy issues. John W. Kingdon conceptualizes the opportunities created by such triggering devices as policy windows, which open infrequently and only remain open for short periods of time. [4] In Kingdon's terms, the events of 9/11 established a favorable political environment for bold policy-making steps by President Bush. In his assessment of American civic engagement in the immediate aftermath of 9/11, Robert D. Putnam agreed that a "window of opportunity has opened for a sort of civic renewal that occurs only once or twice a century." [5]

"An Outbreak of Civic-Mindedness"

The weeks after 9/11 were marked by a significant shift in civic attitudes among Americans. [6] As one commentator remarked: "In the days that followed, we all witnessed an outbreak of civic-mindedness so extreme that it seemed American character had changed overnight." [7] Data suggest that a measurable change did take place during this period. According to one November 2001 poll, 81 percent of those surveyed "are looking for a way to contribute to the nation and support efforts by the federal government to facilitate such efforts" and 70 percent supported "dramatically enlarging America's national service program." [8] Another found significant increases in levels of political consciousness and engagement compared to findings from the previous year. In particular, it identified a renewed trust in national government (+44 percent) and one's neighbors (+10 percent), an increased interest in politics (+14 percent), and a heightened expectation of local cooperation during times of crisis (+6 percent). [9]

According to Democratic pollster Stanley B. Greenberg, the American people responded "with a strong emphasis on unity, coming together, community, seriousness of purpose, freedom of choice, and tolerance." [10] Charles C. Moskos interpreted the transformation as an "apparent awakening of a long-dormant patriotism." [11] Noting this widespread change in attitudes, an opinion piece in the *Los Angeles Times* proclaimed: "Something's Happening Here." However, its author did not overlook the fundamental question raised by this observation, subsequently asking: "Is America Going to Change Now?" [12]

Significantly, while polls identified a notable increase in civic trust and political interest among Americans in the weeks immediately following 9/11, there was no measurable movement in civic behavior. For example, comparing findings from 2000 with those documented in late 2001, there were no statistically significant differences in the willingness of Americans to join community groups (+0 percent) or attend public meetings (+1 percent). [13] As Paul C. Light remarked: "At least on the surface, Americans appear ready to [undertake] acts of goodness and kindness. Unfortunately, little of this civic enthusiasm has spilled over into volunteering." [14]

As explained by civic engagement scholars Putnam and Theda Skocpol, a change in public attitudes, while necessary, is not a sufficient condition for genuine civic revitalization. [15] They agree that it must be accompanied by a change in behavior to have any sort of long-term social effect. Yet, they argue that a large-scale transformation of civic attitudes into civic behavior will not occur spontaneously among American society; government commitment and action — in the form of popular leadership, resources, and the provision of meaningful service opportunities — is a necessity. Moreover, to be effective, the government reaction needs to be timely. In late 2001, Putnam and Skocpol warned that without the widespread and timely translation of attitudes into behavior, any civic goods generated in response to the events of 9/11 would be fleeting.

Bush Fails to React

In the immediate weeks following 9/11, however, President Bush and his aides were silent on the issues of civic engagement and national service. Concerning this silence from the White House, David Gergen, former advisor to Presidents Ronald Reagan, George H.W. Bush, and Bill Clinton, remarked that "President Bush clearly supports the idea. What is lacking, though, is a clarion call, a 'certain trumpet' that breaks through, along with a sweeping plan for action." [16] Incredulous and frustrated by what they perceived as Bush's lack of leadership, many civic engagement advocates implored the president to tap into the palpable, collective outpouring of civic emotion by calling for shared sacrifice and channeling this popular energy toward the achievement of common goals. The growing calls for the White House to take action were summed up in an October 16 headline in the *Christian Science Monitor*: "Public Feels the Urge to Act — But How?" [17]

The frustration of civic engagement advocates generated by Bush's silence was exacerbated when he passed on opportunities to take up the issue in response to questions from the White House press corps. For instance, during a press conference four days after the attacks in New York and Washington, D.C., Bush was asked about the sacrifices that ordinary Americans would now be expected to make in their daily lives. He responded: "Our hope, of course, is that they make no sacrifice whatsoever. We would like to see life return to normal in America." [18] Yet, for civic engagement advocates, the return to pre-9/11 normalcy meant a return to a society in civic decline and, more tragically, an historic opportunity for civic renewal squandered. As 2001 came to an end without a clear, civically-oriented policy response by the Bush Administration, there was a growing concern that the historic "window of opportunity" was quickly closing.

According to Obama, "President Bush squandered an opportunity to mobilize the American people following 9/11 by not asking them to serve." [19] In his principle policy speech on the national service issue, delivered as a Democratic primary candidate in Mt. Vernon, IA, on December 5, 2007, Obama argued: "We had a chance to step into the currents of history. We were ready to answer a new call for our country. But the call never came." [20] In fact, Bush did ultimately issue a "call to service" in his State of the Union address on January 29, 2002; four and a half months after the terrorist attacks. The problem was not a lack of interest or commitment on Bush's part, but one of timely presidential leadership.

LESSON #2: DESPITE A VAST WHITE HOUSE STAFF, A SINGLE POLICY ENTREPRENEUR WITH THE RIGHT IDEAS, CHARACTER, AND COMMITMENT IS INDISPENSABLE

The "call to service" issued by President Bush in his 2002 State of the Union address asked Americans to pledge two years of their lives to the service of others and introduced the USA Freedom Corps, which sought to reorganize and refocus the federal government's service apparatus. However, he had made the key decision that led to the development of this proposal much earlier. It was not an answer to the question of what the national service policy response should look like or how it would seek to translate the widespread shift in civic attitudes into a significant change in civic behavior. Instead, it addressed the question of "Who?" Bush's answer was John M. Bridgeland.

The Policy Entrepreneur Extraordinaire

According to interviews with White House staff members, political appointees, and leaders in the nonprofit sector [21], Bridgeland ("Bridge" to those who know him) was almost singularly responsible for developing the president's national service policy response to the events of 9/11. According to the former Director of the White House Office of Faith-Based and Community Initiatives, John J. DiIulio, Jr.:

> [The administration said,] "OK, what can we do constructively? Bridge, figure it out. Bridge, give us a plan. Bridge, be the guy." And it's really Bridgeland's ideas that, as far as I can tell, set the framework. This one guy, Bridgeland, *is* the story. They had a problem in search of a solution and he was the solution. [22]

Bridgeland was the rare breed of Beltway insider whose sincere civic-mindedness contributed to the image that he was somehow above politics. Although not a publicly-recognized figure, Bridgeland was widely recognized in halls of government as "a very respected person who had the president's ear and who was a very forceful advocate who could talk to both sides" of the aisle. [23]

A graduate of Harvard University and the University of Virginia Law School, Bridgeland entered into government service in 1993 as chief-of-staff for then-Representative Rob Portman, later Bush's Director of the White House Office of Management and Budget. Bridgeland joined the Bush presidential campaign in 2000 as Deputy Domestic Policy Director, provided legal advice during the ballot counting fiasco in Florida, and co-directed the policy transition team with Joshua Bolton, who later served as White House chief-of-staff. When Bush took office, Bridgeland was named Deputy Assistant to the President and head of the Domestic Policy Council, quickly establishing himself as a "go-to" guy in the administration.

And when it came to designing a national service policy response to 9/11, Bush once again called upon Bridgeland. In an interview, Bridgeland recalled: "I was in the Oval Office with the president. He looked at me and said 'Bridge, I want you to develop an initiative,' and these were the words he used, 'to create a culture of service, citizenship, and responsibility.'" [24] Along with his assignments to design, develop, and later direct Bush's citizen service initiative as the new "Service Czar," Bridgeland was promoted to the rank of Assistant to the President, which granted him direct access to the Oval Office.

"...And Then He Came Up with A Plan"

After presidential approval, it was left to Bridgeland to fill in the details. As a consequence of this model of policy-making, the particulars of this initiative were determined by a surprisingly limited array of factors. The most influential factor, according to interviews with those involved in the process, was Bridgeland himself. Again, DiIulio:

> The [answer to the] question: "Why not other options or models?" is that nobody asked [for anything specific]. I mean they gave it to one guy and didn't give him much staff and didn't give him any other real support and said "Do what you can" and then he came up with a plan. I know it's an overly simple, overly parsimonious explanation; but what you're looking at when you're looking at the components of Freedom Corps are things that he believed in, was able to get some support for, and was able to do. There wasn't anybody else and there hasn't been anybody else focused on Freedom Corps. [25]

Bridgeland relied upon his own resources by personally calling upon an eclectic group of "consultants" who broke the conservative mold. These consultants included Sargent Shriver, former head of John F. Kennedy's Peace Corps and Lyndon B. Johnson's Office of Economic Opportunity, which oversaw the VISTA program; Harris Wofford, a former Democratic Senator from Pennsylvania who assisted in the formation of the Peace Corps and AmeriCorps, and was the original CEO of Clinton's Corporation for National Service; and Robert Putnam, the prominent scholar of American civic engagement at Harvard University. Bridgeland also took advantage of his close relationship with DiIulio, a self-defined born-again Catholic Democrat, who had resigned as Director of the White House Faith-Based Office in August 2001 and returned to his professorship at the University of Pennsylvania.

As a candidate, Obama employed a similar approach. According to Steven Waldman, a self-described "service junkie" who serves as the editor-in chief of Beliefnet.com and has authored a book on the creation of Clinton's AmeriCorps program, Obama surrounded himself with the "best service advisors in the country." [26] These included Wofford, Alan Khazei, the founder of City Year and Be the Change, Vanessa Kirsch, the founder of Public Allies and New Profit, Inc., and DiIulio. However, beyond a team of advisors, the experiences of the Bush Administration indicate the benefit of having, in Kingdon's terms, a policy entrepreneur like Bridgeland who invests his time, energy, and reputation in managing every facet of the service issue and keeping it on the president's agenda. [27] Whether Obama will be able to find such an individual is an open question.

LESSON #3: UNDERLYING THE NATIONAL SERVICE ISSUE ARE IDEOLOGICAL BATTLE LINES CONCERNING THE ROLE OF GOVERNMENT THAT CANNOT BE IGNORED

While Bush's "call to service" and introduction of the USA Freedom Corps was prominently featured as one of the four main pillars of his 2002 State of the Union address alongside the global struggle against terror, homeland security, and the need for tax cuts and job creation, the speech offered no clear explanation of what exactly this citizen service initiative would look like. Policy specifics that were left publicly unaccounted for included the structure and organization of the USA Freedom Corps, the nature of its relationship with the nonprofit volunteer and community service sector, the means by which it would pursue its mission to "promote a culture of responsibility, service, and citizenship" [28] and just what this mission meant in practical terms.

A New Citizen Service Initiative

Prior to its introduction, public discussions had focused almost exclusively on the possibility of responding to 9/11 with a massive expansion of Clinton's AmeriCorps program.[1] However, what was presented to the American people in the president's address was not a proposal to "take AmeriCorps to scale" through a substantial increase in federal appropriations that would increase its number of corps members from less than 50,000 to 250,000 or more. Nor did it involve the development of a new program based on the traditional national service model that underlies the Peace Corps, VISTA, and AmeriCorps. It was instead something qualitatively new, referred to in Bush Administration policy papers as an "integrated citizen service initiative." [30]

---

[1] See David Broder, "A Service To the Country," *The Washington Post*, October 7, 2001; Edward Epstein, "New Push for National Service: Sept. 11 Revives Interest in Citizenship Duty for Youth," *San Francisco Chronicle*, January 6, 2002; Gergen, December 12, 2001; Richard Just, "Suddenly Serviceable: Is This the Moment for National Service?" *American Prospect* 13, no.1 (January 2002); Nancy Korman, "A Call for Heroes," *Boston Globe*, October 19, 2001; Putnam, October 19, 2001.

The USA Freedom Corps represents an organizational umbrella under which the aforementioned national service programs, as well as pre-existing, service-oriented offices housed in a range of federal departments and agencies, were incorporated. Its primary mission is administrative; namely, to coordinate these programs and integrate them with the efforts of the nonprofit volunteer and community service sector. According to Bridgeland, the phenomenon of citizen service should be considered an enterprise of wide-ranging scope, which not only moves beyond the more limited concepts of national service, volunteerism, and community service, but incorporates them. Bridgeland's model is focused on establishing and sustaining lasting partnerships between governmental and social institutions by supporting and, ultimately, culturally embedding an ethic of service among all levels of the state and civil society.

The initiative's innovative nature comes into sharp relief when placed in the context of long-standing ideological debates, situated at the heart of the service issue, concerning the desired relationship between the government and civil society. Past efforts by presidents to promote and facilitate service can be divided into two distinct paradigms, around which two deeply entrenched camps have formed. The first is a government-funded national service model, which provides the structural framework for Kennedy's Peace Corps, Johnson's VISTA program, and Clinton's AmeriCorps. According to the principles of this model, it is the responsibility of government to provide meaningful opportunities for citizens to become civically engaged; a responsibility that is satisfied by the creation of an organized service corps. In exchange for a one- or two-year, full-time commitment, corps members receive federally-funded stipends and are guaranteed incentives, such as grants for higher education. These programs are wholly dependent on appropriations by Congress and, as a result, have historically provided a relatively small number of funded slots for potential corps members. They also have frequently become fodder in partisan battles over federal spending. As a result, expanding service opportunities by increasing the number of available slots has proven to be a difficult task.

The other paradigm is orientated toward what might be called the traditional volunteerism model. This model is grounded in the Tocquevillian image of America as a nation of joiners who, through organized associations and self-sacrifice, can address community problems without the assistance or imposition of government. [31] These classic notions of limited government and responsible citizenship were at the heart of George H. W. Bush's Thousand Points of Light initiative, as well as the rhetoric of Ronald Reagan, who began the 1980s by invoking the American spirit of service "that flows like a deep and mighty river through the history of our nation." [32] This approach advocates community service, but eschews the creation of federal programs and appropriation of federal funds to support these efforts. The support offered is instead wholly rhetorical — calling on Americans to become engaged in their communities and praising those who do through public recognition. Underlying this model is the notion that expanding the reach of the federal government to coordinate and fund service activities is not only wasteful but counterproductive. Advocates of this paradigm consider the concept of paid volunteers as simply "an oxymoron." [33]

A "Third Way" for National Service Policy

According to Bridgeland: "USA Freedom Corps was an improvement from previous national service initiatives in that it bridged the divide between these two very, quite frankly, hostile and divisive camps." [34] It did so by providing support in the form of federal appropriations for structured service opportunities as well as through the rhetorical promotion and recognition of traditional volunteerism. Bill Bentley, former Executive Vice President of the Points of Light Foundation, agreed in an interview that this balance is essential:

> [W]e've got to integrate this because at the end of the day, traditional volunteers will always be here, always; and the government will never ever, ever put enough money into stipended service to meet the needs of local communities. So it's got to be a marriage. [35]

Through the incorporation of Citizen Corps, the Peace Corps, and the Corporation for National and Community Service under the umbrella of the USA Freedom Corps, Bridgeland was able to satisfy the dictates of compassionate conservatism by consolidating control over the government's faith-based, community-, and service-oriented agencies and offices, systematize and institutionalize a supportive relationship between these governmental entities and the mediating structures of civil society, and do so with a minimal expenditure of federal funds. While conceptually innovative, however, Bridgeland's model could not make up for the president's failure to take advantage of the temporary spike in civic interest after 9/11.

Obama's proposals do not seek to strike the same balance between the service paradigms that was sought by Bridgeland. Instead, his plans fall squarely in the tradition of the government-financed programs established by past Democratic presidents. These include expanding AmeriCorps to 250,000 slots from its current level at 75,000, more than doubling the size of Peace Corps to 16,000 volunteers from its current 7,800, and establishing new programs such as America's Voice Initiative to recruit and train foreign language speakers to strengthen public diplomacy abroad and the Green Job Corps to assist youth in gaining experience in energy-focused career fields. According to the Obama campaign, these and other service programs are projected to have a total cost of $3.5 billion per year.[36]

LESSON #4: BUSH'S CITIZEN CORPS HAS THE POTENTIAL TO SIGNIFICANTLY IMPACT THE PUBLIC CAPACITY FOR DISASTER RESPONSIVENESS IN THE U.S.

President Bush established the White House Office of the USA Freedom Corps, housed within the Executive Offices of the President (EOP), by Executive Order on January 30, 2002. This order's most concrete contribution was the creation of Citizen Corps, which Bush introduced in his 2002 State of the Union address as a means to "harness the power of every individual through education, training, and volunteer service to make communities safer, stronger, and better prepared to respond to the threats of terrorism, crime, public health issues, and disasters of all kinds."[37]

Citizen Participation, Beyond the War on Terror

The idea for Citizen Corps emerged from the Presidential Task Force on Citizen Preparedness in the War Against Terrorism in November 2001. While Bridgeland, who served as the Task Force co-chair, understood that most positions in the developing homeland security apparatus would be filled by trained professionals, he recognized the need to identify meaningful opportunities for citizen participation as well. He argued that these service opportunities should not be primarily focused on protecting the nation's security, but rather on strengthening local communities. The reason, he explained when interviewed, is that "if people get bored and if there's no threat, which in most communities there won't be, it's not going to be sustained." Therefore, the goal was to encourage service opportunities that address "on-going community needs...but also will give a surge capacity in the case of an attack."[38]

With the help of Elizabeth DiGregorio, then chief-of-staff at the Federal Emergency Management Agency (FEMA) and later Director of Citizen Corps, Bridgeland again developed a model that drew upon the support of local neighborhoods, churches, and voluntary associations rather than turning to direct intervention by the federal government. The mission of Citizen Corps is not to provide citizens with service opportunities, but to coordinate these opportunities through a loose framework offering organizational assistance to a national network of autonomous, locally-established Citizen Corps Councils, each responsible for developing strategies to meet the particular needs of their communities. According to "Citizen Corps: A Guide for Local Officials," these strategies include designing community action plans, assessing potential threats, and identifying available resources to prepare for and respond to terrorist attacks and natural disasters. [39]

These local Citizen Corps Councils have grown in strength and effectiveness by partnering with existing programs and professional first responders within their communities. Among these partners are Volunteers in Police Service (VIPS), enhancing the capacity of law enforcement by performing administrative duties to free up first responders during crisis situations; Community Emergency Response Teams (CERT), providing disaster preparedness education and training in basic disaster response skills; the Fire Corps, augmenting the capabilities of resource-constrained fire departments; Medical Reserve Corps (MRC) units, aiding local medical personnel in emergency response programs, public health initiatives, immunization programs, and blood drives; and Neighborhood Watch, administered by the National Sheriffs' Association, bringing residents together and providing public education to address its crime prevention mission, as well as emergency preparedness and response needs.

The day-to-day operations of Citizen Corps were first managed by FEMA, but were transferred to the Office of Disaster Preparedness within the Department of Homeland Security (DHS) when the latter was established by Congress in November 2002. Soon after, Citizen Corps published "An In-Depth Guide for Citizen Preparedness" in partnership with FEMA and the DHS "Are You Ready?" public awareness campaign. This comprehensive guide aids families, workplaces, and community organizations in developing local emergency plans and supply kits, provides in-depth information on specific hazards, and outlines other necessary information and skills for disaster preparedness. Additionally, the CitizenCorps.gov website serves as an on-line clearinghouse providing descriptions and contact information for dozens of volunteer opportunities in communities across the country.

Up to Speed After a Slow Start

During its first year of existence, President Bush regularly promoted Citizen Corps in public appearances and speeches. However, the program's efforts to engage citizens locally were hindered by two early difficulties. First, Congress only approved $74 million of the president's $230 million budget request for the 2003 fiscal year. As a result, the new program was unable to effectively coordinate the swelling number of interested volunteers. Additionally, public perceptions of Citizen Corps were stained by controversy surrounding one of its proposed components, Operation TIPS (Terrorism Information and Prevention System). This ten-city pilot program was an $8 million national reporting system that involved certain sectors of the American workforce in the homeland security effort. Truckers, postal workers, train conductors, ship captains, utility employees, flight attendants, and others were asked to act as the eyes and ears of law enforcement by reporting suspicious activities through a direct telephone hotline to the Justice Department. In 2002, House Majority Leader Dick Armey, with support from the American Civil Liberties Union (ACLU), went on the offensive against TIPS, arguing that it encouraged "Americans to spy on one another." [40] This public criticism was followed by a wave of negative attention on editorial pages across the nation, prompting the Bush Administration to abandon the program.

The reach of Citizen Corps, however, continues to expand. As of 2008, more than 2,300 local Citizen Corps Councils have been created through the initiative of citizens in every state. [41] While this success falls far short of establishing the "culture of service" that Bush rhetorically promoted, it does suggest that this piece of Bridgeland's model may offer a foundation upon which the Obama Administration could build. According to his campaign website, Obama's proposal to expand AmeriCorps to 250,000 slots involves a plan to develop five new corps under its purview: "a Classroom Corps to help teachers and students, with a priority placed on underserved schools; a Health Corps to improve public health outreach; a Clean Energy Corps to conduct weatherization and renewable energy projects; a Veterans Corps to assist veterans at hospitals, nursing homes and homeless shelters; and a Homeland Security Corps to help communities plan, prepare for and respond to emergencies." [42] Akin to Citizen Corps, Obama's Homeland Security Corps would work in concert with FEMA, yet it would involve the funding of full-time members to assist local community volunteers. Obama has not indicated his intentions regarding the Bush program that he has inherited.

LESSON #5: PRESIDENTIAL LEADERSHIP INVOLVES MORE THAN RHETORICAL SUPPORT FOR NATIONAL SERVICE; IT DEMANDS ENGAGEMENT WITH CONGRESS

In his 2002 State of the Union address, President George W. Bush pledged that the "USA Freedom Corps will expand and improve the good efforts of AmeriCorps and Senior Corps to recruit more than 200,000 new volunteers." [43] Less than a year later the AmeriCorps program was nearly dead. In December 2002, Congress drastically slashed its budget for the 2003 fiscal year and, as a result, its recruitment of future corps members was halted. Advocates for civic engagement, outraged by the prospect that opportunities to serve in governmental national service programs would plummet well below pre-9/11 numbers, implored the president to save the embattled program. Yet, the president remained silent on the matter, even while he continued "going public" to promote his "call to service" and use the reminder of 9/11 to actively encourage Americans to get involved. Bush offered no words in support of AmeriCorps, nor did he personally undertake any behind-the-scenes efforts to persuade members of his own party on Capitol Hill to come to its defense.

The reason was that while Bush was spending a substantial amount of his time in 2002 talking to the American people about his "call to service" and USA Freedom Corps, [44] little communication took place between the White House and Congress. In particular, it was the unwillingness of the White House to spend the political capital necessary to engage Republican leaders in the House of Representatives, specifically then-Majority Leader Armey and then-Majority Whip Tom DeLay, which ultimately caused the most damage to Bush's service initiative. On two occasions — during the quiet demise of the *Citizen Service Act*, the legislative centerpiece of the USA Freedom Corps, in 2002, and the AmeriCorps funding crisis in 2003 — the president opted to remain silently on the sidelines while long-time congressional opponents of government-run service initiatives challenged the president to back up his rhetoric with action.

Failure of the Citizen Service Act

On April 9, 2002, President Bush introduced his principles for the reauthorization of the Corporation for National and Community Service (CNCS), which served as the blueprint for the *Citizen Service Act* [H.R. 4854]. In an effort to meet the increased public demand that had arisen in response to 9/11, the primary intent of the bill was to overhaul and expand opportunities for service through accountability reforms and a dramatic increase in funding for CNCS. On May 24, 2002, the *Citizen Service Act* was taken up by the House Education and the Workforce Subcommittee on Select Education, chaired by Representative Peter Hoekstra, who was also one of the bill's authors and primary sponsors. While formerly a staunch opponent of AmeriCorps during the Clinton Administration, Hoekstra cited his support for the new accountability provisions included in the bill and predicted that it would pass through the House "relatively quickly and on a bipartisan basis." [45]

Despite Hoekstra's optimism, Bridgeland recognized that the strongest opposition to the *Citizen Service Act* would come from members of his own party in the House. Representing the views of many House Republicans who were unwilling to publicly criticize the Bush Administration on an issue that the president had rhetorically linked to 9/11, one unidentified member said: "The federal government getting more involved in Bill Clinton's program of national service is the silliest idea I have ever heard of." [46] Not only was the House Republican leadership adamantly opposed to the notion of "paid volunteers," but Clinton's AmeriCorps was, according to DiIulio, "the thing they love most to hate. They can't stand the very word — they call it AmeriCorpse." [47]

Bridgeland knew that persuading the House Republican leadership to not only embrace but agree to fund the significant expansion of the Clinton program that they had long targeted would be a difficult if not impossible task. His concerns were justified. On June 12, 2002, the *Citizen Service Act* successfully made it out of committee. But with no comment or explanation by the agenda-setters in the House, it disappeared into legislative limbo, never to be brought to the floor for debate or vote. In response, the White House made a strategic decision to abandon negotiations with Congress and accomplish as much as possible through presidential executive order.

Once committed to the rhetorical policy initiated by Bush's "call to service" and sealed with the decision to abandon the *Citizen Service Act* on Capitol Hill, Bridgeland understood that nothing less than a full-time, well-mounted publicity campaign for the USA Freedom Corps would be needed to grow the number of Americans who chose to commit themselves to service. Yet, despite a $23 million publicity campaign by the Ad Council and a constant stream of opinion pieces, speaking engagements, and radio show appearances by Bridgeland, most Americans did not appear to understand the structure and purpose of the USA Freedom Corps, or even be aware of its existence. This was most evident by the negligible changes in civic behavior that marked the years following its introduction.

Between September 2001 and September 2002, 59.8 million Americans over the age of sixteen volunteered. During the following twelve months, this number increased to 63.8 million. Accounting for the increase in population during this period, these figures indicate that the volunteer rate among those over sixteen years of age rose from 27.4 to 28.8 percent. [48] Between September 2003 and September 2004, the number of volunteers increased slightly to 64.5 million, which held the volunteer rate steady at 28.8 percent. [49] A White House press release on the three-year anniversary of the USA Freedom Corps in January 2005 boldly proclaimed: "Americans are answering the President's Call to Service." [50] However, the number of Americans answering the call had reached a plateau long before and already had begun to fall. [51]

The AmeriCorps Funding Crisis

Efforts to engage the public in national service after 9/11 were further hindered when the House of Representatives drastically slashed the budget of AmeriCorps in December 2002, which left Bridgeland's office consumed with securing its future financial viability. As DiIulio remarked: "Unfortunately, the defining event of what [the USA Freedom Corps] could be becomes the battle over AmeriCorps." [52] And it was a battle in which Bridgeland could do no other than take the leading role. According to interviews, the effort to destroy AmeriCorps had been in the making for years, as conservative critics had long riddled it with charges of wastefulness, liberal advocacy, and over-blown claims of success without accompanying evidence.

As a result, Bridgeland was forced to turn his time and attention to saving AmeriCorps, rather than expanding the scope and impact of the USA Freedom Corps. He explained:

> Everyone will tell you that I was wildly aggressive very early…pushing this thing because it was the right thing to do. And Congress wasn't willing to fix it; they wanted there to be pain. They wanted there to be a lot of pain. They've been waiting for there to be a lot of pain in the AmeriCorps program since it was passed. And this was a golden opportunity. [53]

Editorials and columns in major dailies across the country called on Bush to match his rhetoric on service with action by putting pressure on the Republican leadership in the House; particularly, then-Majority Leader DeLay. Open letters signed by a bipartisan majority of state governors and a bipartisan majority of Senators asked the president to publicly come to the defense of the very same program that he had, only a year prior, promised to expand. However, despite the president's continuing rhetorical promotion of service to the American people, he neither turned up the heat on DeLay nor offered a public statement in support of the embattled AmeriCorps program.

As a result of the budget cut, the program was forced to cap its enrollment at 50,000 and was left without the financial resources it needed to recruit new corps members. Consequently, it turned away thousands of interested applicants during a four month "enrollment pause" between November 15, 2002 and March 11, 2003. In the midst of this pause, in January 2003, Bush declared that the year which had passed since the introduction of the USA Freedom Corps had seen a great expansion in national service opportunities as a result of his administration's program. However, rather than the 75,000 corps members projected to serve in 2003, the cap at 50,000 equaled the number of volunteers who were enrolled during the previous year. More revealingly, this number came up short of pre-9/11 enrollment numbers, which totaled 53,000 in 2000 and 59,200 in 2001.

On the legislative front, the primary roadblock to Bush's national service initiatives was the leadership of his own political party and their antipathy toward AmeriCorps. Today, these individuals are no longer on Capitol Hill and Obama has the benefit of sizeable Democratic majorities in both the Senate and House of Representatives. Yet, as all presidents discover, Congress will throw its weight around in the domestic policy arena. Bush's experiences suggest that "going public" is not always a viable alternative to engaging in difficult negotiations with the Congress. Effective presidential leadership demands the skillful employment of both strategies.

CONCLUSION

George W. Bush's adventures in the national service policy arena demonstrate that a president's effectiveness is not determined simply by the powers of the office, but also by the incumbent's leadership abilities. As Michael A. Genovese clarifies:

> Leadership is a complex phenomenon revolving around influence — the ability to move others in desired directions. Successful leaders are those who can take full advantage of their opportunities, resources, and skills. [54]

To borrow an analogy from Genovese, Bush was dealt an extremely promising hand of cards in the wake of 9/11, but he played these cards poorly. By declaring four days after the attacks that Americans would have to "make no sacrifice whatsoever," Bush rendered his future efforts in this arena effectively obsolete. He had all of the resources that he needed at his disposal — historically-high approval ratings, a compliant Congress, a skillful aide in Bridgeland and, most importantly, an already-mobilized American public. As a result, John DiIulio argues, success with the national service issue should have been the equivalent of the most reliable shot in basketball — it's one of those things "that would look and appear to be so easy…it's just a lay-up. Freedom Corps ought to [have been] a lay-up." [55]

The opportunity was squandered because Bush waited too long to take his shot at the basket. As Obama's White House chief-of-staff, Rahm Emanuel, explained in reference to the current financial crisis: "You never want a serious crisis to go to waste…it's an opportunity to do things you could not do before." [56] In the aftermath of 9/11, the Bush Administration aggressively embraced this mantra in pursuit of its foreign policy and national security agenda; and yet, this wisdom was ignored in the arena of national service policy-making.

As Bush's "window of opportunity" closed in the months following 9/11, his resources quickly dissipated and he did not possess the skills to succeed with so little, so late. According to Genovese:

> A president who can play to optimum the cards of opportunity, resources, and skill has a chance of succeeding. Such a leader can resemble a superman or leviathan rather than Gulliver, who was tied down by thousands of lesser figures. But unusual is the president who maximizes power. More often, the president resembles the helpless giant enchained by scores of Lilliputians. [57]

In other words, the story of failed leadership is a common one among American presidents. In the national service policy arena, Bush failed to lead and ended up a "helpless giant." Akin to Bush after 9/11, Obama has been dealt some tremendous cards at the outset of his term. But how will he play his hand?

In his speech on December 5, 2007, in Mt. Vernon, IA, Obama framed the issue of national service as the heart of what it means to be an active American citizen facing the challenges of the 21st century:

> Your own story and the American story are not separate — they are shared. And they will both be enriched if we stand up together, and answer a new call to service to meet the challenges of our new century...
> We need your service, right now, in this moment — our moment — in history. …I am going to ask you to play your part; ask you to stand up; ask you to put your foot firmly into the current of history. I am asking you to change history's course. [58]

It was an echo of Bush's "call to service" delivered almost six years earlier in his first State of the Union address after the events of 9/11:

> [A]fter America was attacked, it was as if our entire country looked into a mirror and saw our better selves. We were reminded that we are citizens, with obligations to each other, to our country, and to history.
>
> This time of adversity offers a unique moment of opportunity — a moment we must seize to change our culture. [59]

As president, George W. Bush failed to seize the moment of opportunity and change American culture. If Barack Obama truly seeks to change history's course through national service, he must heed the lessons of his predecessor.

REFERENCES

[1] For a transcript of the McCain and Obama interviews at the Service Nation Presidential Candidates Forum, see *http://www.bethechangeinc.org/servicenation/summit/transcription*

[2] Barack Obama, "Speech in Mt. Vernon, IA," December 5, 2007. *http://www.barackobama.com/2007/12/05/obama_issues_call_to_serve_vow.php*

[3] While the term "national service" is a familiar part of the American political lexicon, there is little consensus as to its meaning. This lack of a shared understanding, according to Williamson M. Evers, has left the usage of this term "in a muddle." See Williamson M. Evers, "Introduction: Social Problems and Political Ideals in the Debate Over National Service." In *National Service: Pro & Con*, edited by W.M. Evers (Stanford: Hoover Institution Press, 1990).

For the purposes of this paper, national service is defined broadly as community service and volunteerism that is supported by government, whether financially, institutionally, or rhetorically.

[4] John W. Kingdon, *Agendas, Alternatives, and Public Policies* (Boston: Little, Brown and Company, 1984).

[5] Robert D. Putnam, "Bowling Together: The United State of America," *The American Prospect* 13, no.3 (February 2002): 22.

[6] The notable increase in levels of civic activity that swept across the nation in reaction to the events of 9/11 was not unique. In fact, according to Theda Skocpol and her coauthors, "new bursts of civic engagement" have regularly accompanied periods of national crisis. See Theda Skocpol, Ziad Munson, Andrew Karch, and Bayliss Camp. "Patriotic Partnerships: Why Great Wars Nourished American Civic Voluntarism." In *Shaped by War and Trade: International Influences on American Political Development*, edited by M. Shefter (Princeton: Princeton University Press, 2002).

[7] George Packer, "Recapturing the Flag," *New York Times Magazine*, September 30, 2001.

[8] Mark J. Penn, "Poll: How Americans Feel About Politics After 9/11," Democratic Leadership Council, December 13, 2001. *http://www.ndol.org/ndol_ci.cfm?contentid=250017&subid=269&kaid=127*

[9] Thomas H. Sander and Robert D. Putnam, "Walking the Civic Talk After Sept. 11," *Christian Science Monitor*, February 19, 2002.

[10] Stanley B. Greenberg, "'We'—Not 'Me': Public Opinion and the Return of Government," *The American Prospect* 12, no.22 (2001): 25.

[11] Charles C. Moskos, "Patriotism-Lite Meets the Citizen-Soldier." In *United We Serve: National Service and the Future of Citizenship*, edited by E.J. Dionne, K.M. Drogosz and R.E. Litan (Washington, D.C.: Brookings Institution Press, 2003), p.33.

[12] John Balzar, "Something's Happening Here: Is America Going to Change Now?" *Los Angeles Times*, October 3, 2001.

[13] Sander and Putnam, 2002.

[14] Paul C. Light, "Volunteers," National Public Radio, February 7, 2002. *http://www.npr.org/templates/story/story.php?storyId=1137657*

[15] See Robert D. Putnam, "A Better Society in a Time of War," *New York Times*, October 19, 2001; "Bowling Together: The United State of America," *The American Prospect* 13, no.3 (February 2002): 22; Theda Skocpol, "Will 9/11 and the War on Terror Revitalize American Civic Democracy?" *PS: Political Science and Politics* XXXV, no.3 (2002): 537-540; "Will September 11 Revitalize Civic Democracy?" In *United We Serve: National Service and the Future of Citizenship*, edited by E.J. Dionne, K.M. Drogosz and R.E. Litan (Washington, D.C.: Brookings Institution Press, 2003).

At its most basic level, the concept of civic engagement implies the active participation of citizens in civic life. According to Michael Walzer, this notion is based on the normative claim that the preferred setting and most supportive environment for the "good life" is within an organized political community in which we are "politically active, working with our fellow citizens, collectively determining our common destiny." See Michael Walzer, "The Idea of Civil Society: A Path to Social Reconstruction." In *Community Works: The Revival of Civil Society in America*, edited by E.J. Dionne (Washington, D.C.: Brookings Institution Press, 1998), p.125.

[16] David Gergen, "A Time to Heed the Call," *U.S. News & World Report*, December 12, 2001.

[17] Abraham McLaughlin, "Public Feels Urge to Act—But How?" *Christian Science Monitor*, October 16, 2001.

[18] George W. Bush, "Remarks by the President," Camp David, September 15, 2001. *http://www.whitehouse.gov/news/releases/2001/09/20010915-4.html*

[19] See "Barack Obama and Joe Biden's Plan for Universal Voluntary Public Service," Obama-Biden For President campaign website. *http://www.barackobama.com/pdf/NationalServicePlanFactSheet.pdf*

[20] Obama, December 5, 2007.

[21] Among those interviewed for this research project were Bill Bentley, former Executive Vice President and Chief Operations Officer of the Points of Light Foundation; John Bridgeland, former Director of the White House Office of the USA Freedom Corps and Assistant to the President; Elizabeth DiGregorio, Director of Citizen Corps in the Office of Disaster Preparedness at the Department of Homeland Security; Dr. John J. DiIulio, Jr., Professor at the University of Pennsylvania, former Director of the White House Office for Faith-Based and Community Initiatives and Assistant to the President; Jane Eisner, columnist for *The Philadelphia Inquirer*; Henry Lozano, former Director of the White House Office of the USA Freedom Corps and Deputy Assistant to the President; Marc Magee, Director of the Center for Civic Enterprise at the Democratic Leadership Council-Progressive Policy Institute; Dr. Robert Putnam, Professor at Harvard University and former "consultant" for the USA Freedom Corps; Patricia Read, Senior Vice President for Public Policy and Government Affairs at Independent Sector; and Jim Towey; former Director of the White House Office for Faith Based and Community Initiatives and Deputy Assistant to the President.

[22] John J. DiIulio, Jr., Interview by Richard Holtzman, Philadelphia, PA, May 20, 2004.

[23] Jane Eisner. Interview by Richard Holtzman, Philadelphia, PA, May 20, 2004.

[24] John M. Bridgeland, Interview by Richard Holtzman, Washington, D.C., May 19, 2004.

[25] DiIulio, May 20, 2004.

[26] Steven Waldman, "A Junkie's Take on Obama's National Service Plan," *Beliefnet.com*, July 7, 2008. *http://blog.beliefnet.com/stevenwaldman/2008/07/a-junkies-take-on-obamas-natio.html*
[27] Kingdon, 1984.
[28] "USA Freedom Corps Policy Book," The White House, January 30, 2002, p.3. *http://www.whitehouse.gov/news/releases/2002/01/freedom-corps-policy-book.pdf*
[29] See David Broder, "A Service To the Country," *The Washington Post*, October 7, 2001; Edward Epstein, "New Push for National Service: Sept. 11 Revives Interest in Citizenship Duty for Youth," *San Francisco Chronicle*, January 6, 2002; Gergen, December 12, 2001; Richard Just, "Suddenly Serviceable: Is This the Moment for National Service?" *American Prospect* 13, no.1 (January 2002); Nancy Korman, "A Call for Heroes," *Boston Globe*, October 19, 2001; Putnam, October 19, 2001.
[30] "USA Freedom Corps Policy Book," p.3.
[31] See Richard Holtzman, "Voluntarism and Volunteering." In *Social Issues in America: An Encyclopedia, Vol.7*, edited by J. Ciment (Armonk, NY: M.E. Sharpe, Inc., 2006).
[32] Quoted in Harris Wofford, "The Politics of Service." In *United We Serve: National Service and the Future of Citizenship*, edited by R.E. Litan (Washington, D.C.: Brookings Institution Press, 2003), p.43.
[33] Bill Bentley, Interview by Richard Holtzman, Washington, D.C., February 17, 2004.
[34] Bridgeland, May 19, 2004.
[35] Bentley, February 17, 2004.
[36] For details on Obama's proposed programs and yearly cost estimate, see the Obama-Biden National Service Plan Fact Sheet at *http://www.barackobama.com/pdf/NationalServicePlanFactSheet.pdf*
[37] George W. Bush, "State of the Union Address," Washington, D.C., January 29, 2002. *http://www.whitehouse.gov/news/releases/2002/01/20020129-11.html*
[38] Bridgeland, May 19, 2004.
[39] "Citizen Corps: A Guide for Local Officials," Citizen Corps, Department of Homeland Security. *http://www.citizencorps.gov/pdf/council.pdf*
[40] Quoted in Nat Hentoff, "The Death of Operation TIPS," The Village Voice, December 17, 2002. *http://www.villagevoice.com/2002-12-17/news/the-death-of-operation-tips/*
[41] "Citizen Corps Councils Around the Country," Citizen Corps, Department of Homeland Security. *http://www.citizencorps.gov/cc/CouncilMapIndex.do*
[42] "Barack Obama and Joe Biden's Plan for Universal Voluntary Public Service."
[43] Bush, January 29, 2002.
[44] In his interview, Bridgeland noted that Bush made 26 public appearances in support of his "call to service" and USA Freedom Corps between their introduction on January 29, 2002, and the end of the year.
[45] Quoted in Sara Hebel, "Onetime Critics of AmeriCorps Praise President's Plan to Expand It," *Chronicle of Higher Education*, April 12, 2002.
[46] Quoted in Kate O'Beirne, "Corps-Crazy: The Administration and its New, Needless Initiatives," *National Review*, February 25, 2002.
[47] DiIulio, May 20, 2004.
[48] "Increase in Volunteering," Bureau of Labor Statistics, U.S. Department of Labor, December 19, 2003. *http://www.bls.gov/opub/ted/2003/dec/wk3/art05.htm*

[49] "Volunteer Rates in 2004," Bureau of Labor Statistics, U.S. Department of Labor, December 17, 2004. *http://www.bls.gov/opub/ted/2004/dec/wk2/art05.htm*

[50] "Fact Sheet – USA Freedom Corps Marks Three-Year Anniversary," The White House Office of the USA Freedom Corps, January 29, 2005. *http://www.usafreedom corps.gov/about_usafc/newsroom/announcements_dynamic.asp?ID=856*

[51] "Volunteering in the United States, 2006," Bureau of Labor Statistics, U.S. Department of Labor, January 10, 2007. *http://www.impactgiveback.org/PDF/VolunteeringUnited States2006.pdf*

[52] DiIulio, May 20, 2004.

[53] Bridgeland, May 19, 2004.

[54] Michael A. Genovese, *Memo to a New President: The Art and Science of Presidential Leadership* (New York: Oxford University Press, 2008), pp.40-41.

[55] DiIulio, May 20, 2004

[56] Rahm Emanuel, "Comments at the Wall Street Journal CEO Council," Washington, D.C., November 19, 2008. *http://online.wsj.com/video/rahm-emanuel-on-the-opportunities-of-crisis/3F6B9880-D1FD-492B-9A3D-70DBE8EB9E97.html*

[57] Genovese, 2008, p.41.

[58] Obama, December 5, 2007.

[59] Bush, January 29, 2002.

Chapter 6

FORGING THE EAGLE'S SWORD: PRESIDENT WASHINGTON, THE CONGRESS AND THE ARMY

Ryan Staude
SUNY Albany, New York, US

ABSTRACT

President George Washington and Congress battled over military policy in the early republic due to the administration's early military failures. Having seen the Continental Congress's inefficiency in prosecuting the Revolutionary war, and well aware of the nation's bias against standing armies, Washington sought to build an army that could simultaneously quell the Northwest Indians and not stir objections among the legislature or the populace. When his efforts in 1790 and 1791 failed, the Congress tried to wrest control of the army from the executive branch. The debate focused on what type of soldier (professional or militia) should compose the American army. Washington and Secretary of War Henry Knox argued for professionals, while a vocal group of congressmen encouraged the legislature to establish a citizen soldier army. This essay examines the establishment of a nascent military force in America, and Washington's struggle with the Congress to maintain control over the army in the early 1790s.

INTRODUCTION

From 1784 to 1798 the American army never numbered more than 3,000 men. In theory it was a professional army, but in practice it was nothing more than a frontier constabulary. However, in the first half of the 1790s the army was at the center of a debate between President George Washington and Congress. The contest centered on which branch of government would exercise greater control over the nation's military policy. The resolution to the debate set the precedent for future civilian control over the military, and more importantly, it decided how the army would be used to pacify the natives in the Northwest Territory.

This essay examines the struggle between the executive and legislative branches over control of military policy in the early republic. American victory in the Revolutionary war confirmed the nation's independence, but whereas Americans once looked to London for guidance on issues of defense, the questions of protection and national self-defense now had to be answered within the country. Old prejudices against a professional army insinuated themselves into the national dialogue about a military establishment. Equally vociferous were the proponents of a standing, albeit very small, army. During the Confederation period (1783-1787), the Congress put together a patchwork solution to keep peace on the frontier. Satisfactory to very few people, the issue of national defense was one of the many items which propelled politicians and elites to call for a new constitutional convention in 1787 [1].

The Constitution provided that the president was the commander-in-chief of the military, but Congress controlled the purse. This idea needed to be translated into reality during George Washington's first presidential administration. The crucible for the debate was the Northwest Indian Wars of the early 1790s. As Americans streamed into the Ohio territory, they encountered hostile Shawnee, Miami, and Wabash Indians. Washington favored using a professional force to subdue the natives, while Congress argued that a militia was more suitable to the task. This was an important debate from which Washington did not shrink. The president held his ground because he witnessed the Continental Congress's inefficacy during the Revolutionary war, and while he agreed with the principle of civilian rule, he thought it better if that rule were exercised within a clear chain-of-command with the president at the top. In addition to the implications over executive/legislative control of the military, the resolution had practical ramifications for the settlement of the frontier. Washington's firm decision that military policy and strategy fell into the provenance of the executive branch established the model which all subsequent wartime presidents (and Congresses) have followed.

THE CONFEDERATION YEARS

As there was no executive branch in the Articles of Confederation, the question was not who controlled the army, but whether there would be a professional army at all. Upon George Washington's resignation as commander-in-chief, and the subsequent discharging of most of the Continental army, the new nation was left with a paucity of soldiers. For most of the summer of 1784, the American army consisted of 80 soldiers under ranking officer Captain John Doughty at West Point, New York [2].

It was by no means clear what type of force would protect the nation after the Revolution. Congressman Alexander Hamilton of New York chaired a committee charged with gathering information. Writing to General Washington in April 1783, Hamilton asked the general's opinion on what type of post-war military structure "...may best be adapted...with the principles of our governments."[3] Washington asked several of his officers for their opinions, and after compiling their ideas, composed his "Sentiments on a Peace Establishment."[4] In the letter, Washington made four recommendations for the nation's military establishment: (1) a regular army of 2,631 officers and men to "awe the Indians, protect our Trade, prevent the encroachment of our Neighbours of Canada and the Florida's, and guard us at least from surprises; Also for security of our Magazines."[5] (2) a "well-organized militia" to augment the army in times of war; (3) the establishment of three general deposits to hold munitions and supplies; and, (4) the Congress should establish military academies to "keep alive and diffuse the knowledge of the Military Art..."[6] However, even the "sunshine of the General's [Washington's] name" could not overwhelm the traditional American fear of standing armies as a danger to liberty [7].

The Congress debated Hamilton's plan, to no resolution, for much of the summer and autumn of 1783. After Virginia's cession of its western lands in early 1784, the need for a military establishment became even more imperative. The Congress recognized the need for "some [frontier] garrisons...to be maintained...at the expense of the United States."[8] With Hamilton and his allies still clamoring for a professional army, Massachusetts Congressman Elbridge Gerry rose to deliver an impassioned speech against standing armies on May 26. The spokesperson for the anti-army side, Gerry personified the republican fear of classical standing armies as dangers to liberty. Charging Hamilton and the Nationalists, those who favored a stronger central government, with trying to empower the national government at the expense of the states Gerry waxed melodramatically, "...standing armies in time of peace are inconsistent with the principles of republican governments, dangerous to the liberties of a free people, and generally converted into destructive engines for establishing despotism." The fiery rhetoric fulfilled its mission as, a week after the speech, Congress, behind a solid bloc of the New England states, voted to disband the last remaining regiment of the Continental army stationed at West Point. The following day, June 3, Congress "recommended" that four states recruit 700 soldiers from their militia for one year's service on the frontier. The legislature adjourned not having resolved the basic issues surrounding the place of the peace establishment in the new republic; nevertheless, a peacetime army had been created [9].

Designated the First American Regiment, these 700 soldiers were tasked with the mission of patrolling the Northwest Territory: an area that encompassed 248,000 square miles, and was four times the size of England and Wales combined.[10] Pennsylvania was given the selection of the lieutenant-colonel commandant of the Regiment by dint of its furnishing the largest number of men for service. On the recommendation of its president, Thomas Mifflin, Congress appointed Josiah Harmar to the position on August 13, 1784. The Revolutionary war veteran relished the opportunity and wrote to his friend, John Dickinson, that he would give "steady attention to the duties of this appointment [and] ...render every possible service to my country..."[11] The commandant, though, was hamstrung by a number of difficulties, including poor soldiering by his troops, lack of financial support and material support from the government, and the need to report both to Congress and the to the Supreme Executive Council of Pennsylvania.[12] Harmar had barely 30 percent of his authorized force when he was ordered to move west in September 1784 [13].

The army's life on the frontier was arduous. Its main tasks were to evict white squatters from federal lands, keep peace between Indians and the whites, and provide protection for the government officials tasked with surveying the land and negotiating with the Indians. Harmar fought to keep his command intact even though the force was rife with desertion and his soldiers spent a considerable amount of time inebriated. Two years after the act of 1784, the army was still 182 soldiers short of its authorized strength.[14] Whites kept moving west, but the Congress hesitated to augment the army. As the Americans further encroached on Indian lands, the natives began to retaliate against the whites, and the army. In 1787 a Wyandot

Indian hunting party kidnapped and killed a federal soldier, then proceeded to parade his scalp through various Indian villages. It was the first time the Indians had attacked the army; the significance was understood by everyone involved: by assaulting the symbol of the U.S. on the frontier, the Indians were declaring war against the United States [15]. At the close of 1787, the frontier was a powder keg ready to explode, and the officers and soldiers of the United States army were ill-equipped to deal with the impending firestorm.

THE ARMY AND THE CONSTITUTION

Historian Walter Millis wrote that the Constitution was "as much a military as a political and economic charter."[16] The confluence of events in the mid-1780s including a slight economic depression, Shays' Rebellion in western Massachusetts, and the unrest on the frontier, forced the men gathered at Philadelphia to seriously examine the Confederation's military policies. A majority of the 55 delegates gathered in Philadelphia had been involved intimately with the Revolution either as soldiers or politicians. After watching the debacle of Massachusetts militia refusing to fire at Daniel Shays in 1786, and through their own experiences in the war, most favored the employment of regulars over militia. Even the small state advocate, William Patterson of New Jersey, in presenting his plan of government said, "there must be a small standing force to give every government weight."[17] Only anti-standing army diehard, Elbridge Gerry, spoke against giving the government the power to raise a permanent, perhaps limitless, federal army.

The final military provisions mirrored the spirit of checks and balances that pervaded the document: the president would be commander-in-chief of the army, thereby maintaining civilian control, but Congress would be the financier. Any appropriation of money could last no longer than two years. The vital difference between the Constitution and the Articles of Confederation was the centralization of the military power in the hands of the federal government. The national government was charged with recruiting and supporting federal soldiers; also, the federal government alone held the responsibility of providing the nation with external security and internal tranquility.

The states had to ratify the document before it became the law of the land. Opponents of ratification, called anti-Federalists, were determined to defeat the Constitution, and were prepared to play the venerable standing army card to do it.[18] The anti-Federalists tied the issue of raising armies to the larger issue of the states conceding sovereignty to the newly created federal government. Writing in the New York Journal, fiery anti-Federalist Robert Yates proclaimed,

> It might be here shown, that the power in the federal legislature, to raise and support armies at pleasure, as well in peace as in war, and their controul over the militia, tend, not only to a consolidation of the government, but the destruction of liberty.[19]

Elbridge Gerry was joined by prominent statesmen like Patrick Henry of Virginia in his denunciation of the Constitution's military clauses. The new government, according to the latter, was a "government of force," and the standing armies clause was the "genius of despotism expressly."[20] The Federalists, though, won the debate over ratification; partly because they tied the central government's authority to control the military with the continued survival of the republic. Indeed, the Federalists opined that "the establishment of a militarily independent national government was essential for the survival of republican institutions in America."[21] In the Ohio wilderness, Lt. Colonel Harmar followed with rapt attention the events unfolding back east. Upon hearing of the Constitution's acceptance, Harmar wrote to a subordinate with the hopes that the "wheels of government will now be soon in motion," and that a "proper force" would be raised to chastise the Indians [22]

THE HARMAR CAMPAIGN OF 1790

Even before he was officially elected as president, Americans were already turning to George Washington for his advice concerning frontier unrest. Harry Innes wrote to Washington in December 1788 informing him of a possible British conspiracy involving the Indians in the Ohio territory. Not knowing to whom he should turn, Innes sent his letter to Washington because "whatever tends to disturb the peace" of the United States would surely "distress and injure" Washington's "tranquility and repose."[23] Less than two weeks after he was inaugurated on April 30, 1789, Washington received a letter from Arthur Campbell on the best method of dealing with the Indians, stating that regular troops (and not militia) were needed to "foment divisions and play off the interests, and view of one Tribe against that of another…"[24]

Frontier warfare escalated significantly in 1789. "Murders, scalpings, the stealing of horses and even of livestock, and the most dreaded fate of all, Indian captivity, were prevalent throughout the entire frontier."[25] Westerners pleaded with the president for assistance.[26] For pragmatic reasons, the country's lack of funds, and the paucity of soldiers, Washington initially favored a peaceful approach to dealing with the Indians. However, even though peace was to be preferred, the new president warned the territorial governor, Arthur St. Clair, that the "national dignity" may demand war.[27] As 1789 drew to a close, the situation began to deteriorate faster than ever before. St. Clair wrote Washington, "The constant hostilities between the Indians who live upon the river Wabash and the people of Kentucky must necessarily be attended," but should force be required, the "handful of troops, sir, that are scattered in the country, though they may afford protection to some settlements, can not possibly act offensively by themselves." Appearing to be at the end of his tether, St. Clair asked the president for instructions. In his response Washington still hoped to avoid war because it would jeopardize "the security of the frontier inhabitants, the security of the troops, and the national dignity." "But," he added,

> If, after manifesting clearly to the Indians the dispositions of the General Government for the preservation of peace, and the extension of a just protection to the said Indians, they should continue their incursions, the United States will be constrained to punish them with severity.[28]

Washington concluded his letter by instructing St. Clair to send an emissary to the Wabash Indians to inform them of the government's intentions, and to gauge the tribes' attitudes [29].

The president delivered his first annual address to Congress on January 8, 1790. He had been in office for approximately nine months, and the Indian hostilities continued to be one of the most pressing problems confronting the nation. In consultation with his Secretary of War, Henry Knox, and St. Clair, Washington had decided on negotiations to try and stem the violence. While some Indians would negotiate with the government, many of the hostiles (with British support) refused to yield. Mindful of America's small military, Washington began his first State of the Union address with a frank discussion of the nation's need for a stronger military. Arguing that the common defense merited the Congress's "particular regard," President Washington asserted that "To be prepared for war [was] one of the most effectual means of preserving peace." Immediately after calling for a stronger army, the president advanced the idea that the time may soon approach where the nation would be required to "punish aggressors" on the frontier if the peace initiatives failed.

Initially, the House of Representatives gave the president wide latitude to conduct diplomacy, and military operations against the Indians. In its response to the president's address, the House lamented that the "pacific arrangements pursued with regard to certain hostile tribes of Indians, have not been attended with that success which we had reason to expect from them." Essentially giving the president carte blanche to deal with the problem, the House went on to say that they would not "hesitate to concur in such further measures as may best obviate any ill effects which might be apprehended from the failure of those negotiations."[30] The House's willingness to approve of Washington's conduct stems from two sources. First, the House was engaged in two particularly thorny issues: the question of the location of the permanent national capital, and the assumption of the state debts advocated by Secretary of the Treasury Alexander Hamilton. Indeed, since the beginning of the national government, the Congress had dealt with other issues leaving Indian affairs totally to the president's purview. The Congress did not hesitate to take up the question of the frontiers, but "Hitherto it has been necessarily excluded by subjects of prior necessity."[31] Second, the legislature intimately trusted the president's judgment because he had more "than common knowledge of western and Indian affairs…"[32] These two factors allowed Washington to formulate military policy with almost no recourse to the legislative branch.

What the Congress did not know was that they had already given Washington the authority to start an Indian war. In September 1789, Washington transmitted a letter from St. Clair to the Congress detailing the escalating troubles on the frontier. In his covering letter he asked the Congress for permission to call forth the militia to "embrace the cases apprehended by the Governor of the Western Territory." The Congress, in complying with the request, laid the groundwork for the administration's first attempt to defeat the Indians [33].

The expedition, however, was a failure. Knox, St. Clair, and Harmar planned a two-pronged attack against the Indians. Lt. Colonel Harmar would march from Ft. Washington (present-day Cincinnati) with 300 regulars and 1,200 militia to the Miami Indian villages at Kekionga. Meanwhile, Major John F. Hamtramck would move up the Wabash River from Fort Knox with 100 regulars and 300 militia to attack the Indians at Vermillion, thereby diverting attention from Harmar's column.[34] The plan was put into action in late September 1790. Hamtramck's column never reached Vermillion as the Kentucky militia threatened to desert and the major returned to Ft. Knox rather than risk mutiny. Harmar fared no better. He did raze some Indian villages, but on two separate occasions, Indians routed detachments from his main force. Claiming victory, Harmar trekked back to Ft. Washington. Though, St. Clair and Harmar sent official reports back to the administration at Philadelphia claiming that the Indians' "headquarters of inequity" had been destroyed, the rumors and letters from westerners convinced Washington otherwise.[35] Washington hesitated to make any official report to Congress, in mid-November he wrote Knox that his "...forebodings with respect to the expedition against the Wabash Indians are of disappointment; and a disgraceful termination under the conduct of B. Genl. Harmar." His worst fears had been realized – the campaign had produced nothing but "expence without honor or profit."[36]

DEFEAT AND DESPAIR: THE ST. CLAIR CAMPAIGN OF 1791

The New Year did not alleviate the problems on the frontier. In January, Washington's old comrade from the Revolutionary war, Rufus Putnam, wrote him from the Marietta settlement in the Ohio territory. The recent victories over Harmar had emboldened the Indians, and Putnam feared a general uprising once spring reached the wilderness. "...the war, which was partial before the campaign of last year, is, in all probability become general...We are in the utmost danger of being swallowed up."[37] Secretary Knox admitted that Harmar's expedition had been a failure, and the nation faced an increasingly hostile enemy. Knox presented the president with an even greater fear that, "their [the Indians] own opinion of success, and the number of trophies they possess, will probably not only encourage them to a continuance of hostilities, but may be a means of their obtaining considerable assistance from the neighbouring tribes."[38] The specter of a united Indian resistance, the discontent of the western settlers, and the need to redeem the national honor pushed Washington to call for another campaign.

Together Knox and Washington decided to ask Congress for an increased professional military establishment. The two men believed that the poor performance of the militia was to blame for Harmar's defeat; therefore they determined to use more regular soldiers in the 1791 campaign. Both realized that Congress would scrutinize more closely their handling of military policy, and that cries from western constituents for a greater reliance on militia would reach the ears of pliant representatives. Virginians and Kentuckians advocated using militia and not regulars for fighting because "militia officers and privates having their all at stake, and well accustomed to rifles, and the Indian mode of warfare are preferable to the best regular troops, armed with muskets."[39] Some Congressmen also began to question the administration's motives in conducting the war. The most vociferous of these opponents was Senator William Maclay. He made known to all who would listen that the war was "undertaken without the shadow of authority from Congress," and that Congress, instead of "begging our own servants to spare the effusion of human blood," should initiate a line of inquiry into the executive's conduct of the war.[40]

Maclay's calls, however, were in vain, as the president and Secretary of War were able to devise a solution which they thought would placate the Congress and meet their needs for a stronger, federal army. Washington furthered the ideas of using levies, short-term volunteers that would fall under federal control. This was a compromise between having to use militia and enlarging the regular army. Levies would fall under federal supervision and discipline, but would be dismissed at the expiration of their enlistment terms. Washington was confident that a corps of levies combined with a strengthened regular army could quell any Indian resistance.

Accordingly, Knox officially submitted the administration's plan to the Congress. Since the current army was "utterly inadequate" for disciplining the Indians, Knox proposed a three-step plan,

> First – That the situation of the frontiers requires an additional defensive protection, at least until offensive measures shall be put into operation – The plan of a regiment of rangers is therefore submitted.
>
> Secondly – That the peculiar situation of the frontiers requires the augmentation of one regiment of regular troops to consist of nine hundred and twelve non commissioned Officers and privates.
>
> Third – That another expedition which shall effectually dispose the Wabash and other hostile Indians to peace, seems indispensable.[41]

Knox's letter contained the troop numbers he and Washington thought would be enough to overwhelm the Indians: 1,200 regular soldiers, 500 rangers, and 1,300 levies. The government, Knox concluded, must "regulate events instead of being regulated by them."[42]

As in the previous year, Congress complied with the administration's request, but they did not pass the authorization until March 3, 1791 – the last day of the First Congress. An additional regiment of 912 non-commissioned officers and privates was to be raised, and the Congress also gave the president authority to "engage a body of militia to serve as Cavalry," and "a Corps, not exceeding two thousand non-commissioned officers, privates and musicians...under the denomination of Levies..."[43]

Satisfied with their new establishment, Washington and Knox put their plans in motion. While the new and enlarged federal army was being recruited, the two men authorized Brigadier General Charles Scott of the Kentucky militia to fulfill the "ranger" component of the mission. As Knox told Scott, quick, penetrating raids would carry "the war into the enemy's country, [and] prevent in a great degree their invading the frontiers."[44] After directing Scott to begin his raids, Knox consulted with the newly commissioned Major General Arthur St. Clair, and his second-in-command Brigadier General Richard Butler. The army, under St. Clair, would march north to the Maumee Valley (the same destination of Harmar's campaign) building a chain of forts along the way. When the army reached the Miami villages it was to draw the enemy into battle, and, afterwards, establish a permanent post on the site of the towns [45]. President Washington wrote that the post "was the primary object of the campaign," after building it, "every thing else would be easy." One of Harmar's most trusted subordinates shared the President's ideas, "The Indians can never be subdued by just going into their towns and burning their houses and corn, and returning the next day, for it is no hardship to an Indian to live without..." In order for the government to be able to dictate terms, "respectable garrisons in the most important parts of their country," must be established.[46] As St. Clair was preparing his army he was to send out peace offerings to the hostile Indians, and as such President Washington composed a message to the Indians stating that a war with the United States would mean "absolute destruction to you, your women and your children."[47]

A variety of delays kept St. Clair and his force in the vicinity of Ft. Washington until mid-September. He began his campaign with 2,000 regular soldiers (including levies) and 400 militia. Stopping at various points to build forts, the first snow of the season had already fallen when the force (now numbering just under 1,400 due to desertions, illness, and garrison duty), reached the banks of the Wabash river on November 4, 1791. That morning, 1,000 natives attacked the force shortly after reveille. The resulting battle was one of the worst losses in the army's history. The Indians stormed through the camp while the regulars sought to maintain discipline amidst the fleeing militia. After trying to salvage the situation, St. Clair ordered a retreat. Lieutenant Ebenezer Denny accurately captured the mood of the fleeing soldiers when he wrote that to "Delay was death." The Indians' lack of discipline had compelled them to stop fighting and begin plundering the American camp. This hesitation allowed the survivors to make their way back to the relative safety of Ft. Jefferson, thirty miles distant from the battlefield. When battle casualties were finally tallied it was discovered that of the 1,400 American combatants, 900 were either killed or wounded. The Indians had virtually annihilated the American army [48]

THE EAGLE'S SWORD

As with Harmar's defeat, rumors trickled into Philadelphia before St. Clair's official report made its way to the capital. On December 4, Henry Lee wrote to Washington of the "late disaster in the west," and included a testimony from Kentuckian John Rogers of St. Clair's defeat. Newspapers began reporting rumors of the terrible loss on Monday, December 5.[49] As with Harmar's campaign, Washington waited for official word which he received on December 9. On the following Monday he submitted the following message to both houses of the U.S. Congress,

> It is with great concern that I communicate to you the information received from Major General St. Clair, of the misfortune which as befallen the troops under his command.
> Although the national loss is considerable, according to the scale of the event, yet it may be repaired without great difficulty, excepting as to the brave men who have fallen on the occasion, and who are a subject of public as well as private regret.
> A future communication will shortly be made of all such matters as shall be necessary to enable the Legislature to judge of the future measures which it may be proper to pursue.[50]

With this message, Washington launched into a protracted battle with Congress over the fate of who exerted more control over military policy. The contest lasted for most of 1792 and took the form of two issues: did the Congress have the right to investigate an executive action without looking to impeachment, and what would the next step in the campaign against the Northwest Indians look like?

THE INVESTIGATION OF MAJOR GENERAL ST. CLAIR

On March 27, 1792, William Giles of Virginia put forward a motion in the House of Representatives which called on the president to "institute an inquiry into the causes of the late defeat of the army under the command of Major General St. Clair..." Most particularly the Congress was interested in whether the "the detentions or delays which are suggested to have attended the money, clothing, provisions, and military stores, for the use of the said army..." caused the defeat.[51] Debate quickly began over whether the House had the authority to direct the president to begin an investigation. Congressman Giles answered his critics by stating that the "House was the proper source as the immediate guardians of the public interest."[52] In addition to the question of whether the House could ask the president to investigate a matter of the executive branch, a second issue arose: was the executive the correct person to even investigate the situation? Abraham Baldwin of Georgia was,

> Convinced the House could not proceed but by a committee of their own. Such a committee would be able to throw more light on the subject, and then the House would be able to determine how to proceed; and, if any failure had taken place on the part of the Executive officers, he should then be prepared to address the President, and to request him to take the proper steps in the case.[53]

The debate continued until both motions (Giles's and Baldwin's) were put to a vote. The motion to direct the president to investigate the defeat lost by a vote of 35 to 21, but Baldwin's motion (to have the House investigate the defeat) won by a margin of 34 votes.[54] For the first time in American history, the legislative branch of the government investigated actions taken by the executive branch.

The House referred the matter to a select committee and on March 30 it subsequently asked Secretary of War Knox to submit papers relevant to the expedition for the committee's consideration. The president convened his cabinet on the following day to discuss the appropriate response to the Congress's request. In his memorandum on the meeting, Secretary of State Thomas Jefferson asserted that Washington "neither acknowledged nor denied, nor even doubted the propriety of what the house was doing."[55] The president did feel, however, and the cabinet agreed that Congress should make their requests of the department heads *through* the president and not directly to the secretaries. Washington wanted it clear that the secretaries were members of the executive branch and answered to him *before* they answered to Congress. The fact that Washington did not have issue with the House's inquest belied the fact that he felt the executive branch had acquitted itself in the preparations for the campaign, and secondly, it revealed that he had his own problems with St. Clair's expedition. According to Jefferson, the president had always disapproved of "two lines of St. Clair's conduct." First, he had never gathered enough intelligence about the Indians, and he did not keep "his army in such a position always to be able to display them in a line behind trees in the Indian manner at any moment." A House investigation would bring the expedition's errors to light and vindicate the executive's line of conduct.

Washington's wishes, however, were not fulfilled. Indeed, though the final report does not directly blame the executive for St. Clair's defeat, there was enough veiled criticism to raise Washington's and Knox's ire. In its report of May 8, 1792, the committee gave three causes for the defeat. They first blamed the "delay in furnishing the materials and estimates" for the campaign. Second, the delays in the quartermaster's department caused a "want of provisions" on the frontier. Lastly, the "want of discipline and experience in the troops" caused the defeat. General St. Clair was exonerated for his "coolness and intrepidity." Secretary Knox objected to the report because he thought it sullied his reputation. After further consideration the committee confirmed its initial findings in February 1793.[56] The president's personal reputation remained unscathed, but the legislature had won a victory over the executive. For the next campaign, the Congress would take a more active role in the type of force that would compose the military establishment.

THE PRESIDENT'S WAR

While it investigated St. Clair's defeat, the Congress made ready to receive the president's next plan for the war against the Indians. Knox presented the administration's plan to Congress with the warning that the Indians' victories would make them deaf to any peace pleas; therefore, a "strong coercive force" was needed.[57] The plan called for raising the two existing regiments to their full strength, and adding three more regiments for a total troop complement of 5,168 men.

The subsequent Congressional debate mirrored the public's divided opinion over the administration's approach to the protection of the frontiers, and also the growing sentiment among congressmen that the legislature needed to exercise a greater voice in making military policy. The debate began with an excoriation of the war and the statement that it was "unjustly undertaken as it has since been unwisely and unsuccessfully conducted..."[58] The main arguments against the bill took two lines: the first was financial, the second was tactical. The cost of this new army was a large halter around the government's neck, according to some of the legislators. The plan called for expenditures up to $1.1 million – a sum that was twice the amount budgeted for the other branches of government [59].

The real contest, though, centered on the policy aspect of the question; namely, what type of soldier was best suited to protect the frontiers? Washington firmly believed that only the discipline and numerical strength of a professionally trained army could offer hopes of victory.

Many congressmen, finally responding to their constituents' cries, urged the use of militia to solve the problem. The arguments offered in favor of citizen-soldiers centered on their experience fighting the Indians, and their trustworthiness as opposed to regular soldiers. Most agreed that regulars were fine for garrison duty, but "as to active service, the frontier militia and rangers were pronounced to be by far preferable to regular troops..."[60] Aspersions were cast on the men who joined the regular establishment as the dregs of society. Mostly from cities, the Indians frightened these urban poor, whereas frontier militia was accustomed to the "war whoop," it did "not strike them with that degree of terror with which it inspires those men who enlist in the regular establishment"[61].

Some Congressmen questioned the administration's needs for such a large force. The "strange policy" to "raise five or six thousand men to oppose a handful of Indian banditti, whose utmost amount does not...appear to exceed twelve hundred" troubled the legislators. There was a conspiratorial mention of the "secrets of the [president's] Cabinet" as the only place where the truth was known. Just when it appeared that the naysayers would triumph, reason was restored with the plain fact that between 1783 and 1790, 1500 settlers had been killed or captured on the frontier. The militia had not been able to stem this violence, and may have, with their punitive raids, further incited it.

One need only look at the militia's performance in the Harmar and St. Clair campaigns to see that a "very trifling disaster, or a slight cause of discontent, is sufficient to make them disband and forget all subordination, so far as even to neglect the means of self-defence..."[62] When the final vote was called, the president's plan triumphed, notwithstanding the opposition's efforts. Ten months after the bill was passed, in January 1793, the Congress again took up the question of the military establishment, this time over a motion to eliminate the three additional regiments called for in the March 1792 act. Once again, the president emerged victorious, but not before the motion was given considerable vocal support on the House floor [63].

CONCLUSION

Washington and Knox were vindicated when their army won a smashing victory against the Indians in August 1794 at Fallen Timbers in the Maumee valley. The president selected Revolutionary war veteran Anthony Wayne to command the new army, and "Mad Anthony" spent two years training and disciplining his army before launching a campaign in the summer of 1794. After defeating the Indians, Wayne marched to the nearby British-held Ft. Miamis and dared the commander to stop him. Not wanting to precipitate an international incident, Wayne backed down, but his primary goal had been accomplished: in 1795 at the Treaty of Greeneville the Indians signed over most of the present-day state of Ohio to the American government [64].

The Northwest Indian War from 1790-1794 was the first armed conflict the new American government, under the Constitution, faced. Armies were raised and employed in an aggressive manner and all understood that precedents would be set for future conflicts. The Constitution made the president commander-in-chief of the military, but gave Congress the power to declare war. Did this mean that the president could use the military at his pleasure? As commander-in-chief, was he solely responsible for the composition of the army? The Constitution was silent on these questions and it was left to the first administration to answer them. After the defeats in 1790 and 1791, the Congress felt obliged to insert itself in military matters which Washington interpreted as his purview. The administration held fast even when the cry to use militia instead of regulars arose in Congress and among the public. In addition to the practical consequences for the northwest frontier, the clash marked an important victory for the executive branch in fashioning military policy. Washington knew that public opinion demanded he use militia in some capacity, but he wanted regular soldiers to provide the backbone of the United States army. Through Congressional questioning and investigations he held his ground on the matter, and Wayne's victory at Fallen Timbers justified his tenacity. In future conflicts the Congress and president would spar over the latter's wartime powers, but never again did the legislature seriously battle the executive branch over the composition of the military, if only because Washington's firmness had made the question moot. The Constitution gave the president the power on paper to be commander-in-chief, but it was George Washington who made that authority real and tangible.

REFERENCES

[1] The most succinct study on military policy during the Confederation is Lawrence Delbert Cress, *Citizens in Arms: The Army and the Militia in American Society to the War of 1812* (Chapel Hill: University of North Carolina Press, 1982). See also Richard H. Kohn's seminal study *Eagle and Sword: The Federalists and the Creation of the Military Establishment in America, 1783-1802* (New York: Free Press, 1975).

[2] Don Higginbotham, *The War of American Independence: Military Attitudes, Policies, and Practicies, 1763-1789* (New York: Macmillan, 1971; reprint, Boston: Northeastern University Press, 1983), 445; Russell F. Weigley, *History of the United States Army* (New York: Macmillan, 1967), 80-81; James Ripley Jacobs, The Beginning of the United States Army, 1783-1812. (Princeton: Princeton University Press, 1947)14-15.

[3] The committee also included James Madison, Samuel Osgood, James Wilson, and Oliver Ellsworth. Alexander Hamilton, *The Papers of Alexander Hamilton*, ed. Harold C. Syrett, in 27 volumes (New York: Columbia University Press, 1961-1987), III, 322.

[4] George Washington, *The Writings of George Washington*, ed. John C. Fitzpatrick, in 39 volumes (Washington, DC: Government Printing Office, 1931-1944), XXVI, 374-398. (Hereafter referred to as *Writings GW*)

[5] Ibid., 375.

[6] Ibid., 396-397.

[7] Edmund C. Burnett, ed., *Letters of Members of Continental Congress*, in 8 volumes (Washington, DC: Carnegie Printing Institute, 1921-1936), VIII, 842. (Hereafter referred to as *LMCC*).

[8] Worthington C. Ford, ed., *Journals of the Continental Congrss, 1774-1789* in 34 volumes (Washington, DC: Manuscript Division of the Library of Congress, 1904-1937), XXIV, 806-807. (Hereafter referred to as *JCC*)

[9] For Gerry's speech see *JCC*, XXVII, 433-434; for the decision to reduce the army see Ibid., 524. For the politics behind the vote see Kohn, *Eagle and Sword*, 54-60. For the resolution of June 3 see *JCC*, XXVII, 530-531.

[10] William Guthman, *March to Massacre: A History of the First Seven Years of the United States Army, 1784-1791* (New York: McGraw-Hill, 1975), vii.

[11] Alan S. Brown, "The Role of the Army in Western Settlement: Josiah Harmar's Command, 1785-1790," *Pennsylvania Magazine of History and Biography* 93 (1969), 163-164; Jonathan Heart, *The Journal of Captain Jonathan Heart*, ed. Consul Willshire Butterfield (Albany: John Munsell's Sons, 1885), 30-31.

[12] Kohn, 63.

[13] Ibid.; Brown, 164-165.

[14] For army life on the frontier see Jonathan Heart, *The Orderly Book of Captain Jonathan Heart, September 7, 1785 to May 2, 1788*, Record Group 94, National Archives; and Josiah Harmar to Jonathan Heart, April 17, June 1 1787, *Letter Book of Captain Jonathan Heart, April 17, 1787 to January 26, 1788*, Record Group 94, National Archives.

[15] Kohn, 68.

[16] Walter Millis, *Arms and Men: A Study in American Military History* (New York: G.P. Putnam's Sons, 1956), 47.

[17] Dave R. Palmer, *1794: America, Its Army, and the Birth of a Nation* (San Rafael: Presidio Press, 1994), 104-108; Max Farrand, ed., *The Records of the Federal Convention of 1787*, in 4 volumes (New Haven: Yale University Press, 1937), III, 145. (Hereafter referred to as *Records*).

[18] For Anti-Federalist ideology see Cecelia M. Kenyon, "Men of Little Faith: The Anti-Federalists on the Nature of Representative Government," *William and Mary Quarterly* 12 (1955): 8-43; Jackson Turner Main, *The Anti-Federalists: Critics of the Constitution, 1781-1788* (Chapel Hill: University of North Carolina Press, 1961), 119-186; Gordon

S. Wood, *The Creation of the American Republic, 1776-1787* (Chapel Hill: University of North Carolina Press, 1969), 485-523.
[19] *New York Journal*, October 10, 1787
[20] Jonathan Elliot, ed., *The Debates in the Several State Conventions on the Adoption of the Federal Constitution*, in 5 volumes (Buffalo, NY: William S. Hein, 1891), III, 378-396. (Hereafter referred to as *Debates*).
[21] Cress, 105.
[22] *Outpost*, 100, 137
[23] George Washinton, *The Papers of George Washington: Presidential Series*, ed. W.W. Abbot, et al., 14 volumes to date (Charlottesville: University Press of Virginia, 1987-), I, 187-189. (Hereafter referred to as *Papers: GW*)
[24] Ibid., II, 253-255.
[25] Wiley Sword, *President Washington's Indian War: The Struggle for the Old Northwest, 1790-1795* (Norman: University of Oklahoma Press, 1985), 75.
[26] *Papers: GW*, II, 314-315.
[27] Ibid., III, 140-142.
[28] Arthur St. Clair, *The St. Clair Papers: The Life and Public Services of Arthur St. Clair*, ed. William Henry Smith, in 2 volumes (Cincinnati: Robert Clarke and Company, 1882), II, 123-126.
[29] Ibid.
[30] "Proceedings January 12, 1790," *Annals of Congress*, House of Representatives, 1st Congress, 1st Session, ed. Joseph Gales, Sr. (Washington, DC: Gales and Seaton, 1849), 1089 (Hereafter referred to as *Annals*)
[31] James Madison, *The Papers of James Madison*, ed. Robert Rutland, et al., 17 volumes to date (Charlottesville: University Press of Virginia, 1962-), XII, 318.
[32] Ibid.
[33] Kohn, 97-98; *Annals*, 927-928.
[34] Jacobs, 50-52
[35] *American State Papers: Indian Affairs*. 2 volumes (Washington, DC: Gales and Seaton, 1832-1834), I, 104. (Hereafter referred to as *ASP: IA*).
[36] *Papers: GW*, VI, 668.
[37] Ibid., VII, 208-209.
[38] Ibid., 262-268.
[39] Ibid., 187.
[40] William Maclay, February 17, 1791, March 1, 1791, *Papers of William Maclay*, Library of Congress
[41] Linda Grant DePauw, ed., *A Documentary History of the First Federal Congress, 1789-1791*, 14 volumes (Baltimore: Johns Hopkins University Press, 1971-1986), V, 1367-1370. (Hereafter referred to as *Documentary History*).
[42] Ibid, 1369-1371
[43] Ibid., 1302-1303
[44] *ASP: IA*, I, 130-131
[45] Ibid., 131-137.
[46] *Writings: GW*, XXXI, 449; St. Clair, II, 197.
[47] *Papers: GW*, VII, 549-551.

[48] Winthrop Sargent, "Winthrop Sargent's Diary while with General Arthur St. Clair's Expedition Against the Indians," *Ohio State Archaeological and Historical Quarterly* 33 (1924), 263.
[49] *Papers: GW*, IX, 249-250; Douglas Southall Freeman, *George Washington: A Biography*, 7 volumes (New York: Charles Scribner & Sons, 1948-1957), VI, 336.
[50] *Annals*, 2nd Congress, 1st Session, 48.
[51] Ibid., 490.
[52] Ibid.
[53] Ibid., 492
[54] Ibid., 493-494
[55] *Papers: GW*, X, 169.
[56] *American State Papers: Military Affairs*. 7 volumes (Washington, DC: Gales and Seaton, 1832-1861), I, 36-39, 41-44 (Hereafter referred to as *ASP: MA*).
[57] *ASP: IA*, I, 197-198
[58] *Annals*, 2nd Congress, 1st Session, 337.
[59] Ibid., 763.
[60] Ibid., 339.
[61] Ibid., 341.
[62] Ibid., 343, 347.
[63] See Ibid., 773-802 for the debate.
[64] For the Battle of Fallen Timbers see Paul David Nelson, *Anthony Wayne: Soldier of the Early Republic* (Bloomington: Indiana University Press, 1985), 264-266; for the Treaty of Greeneville see *ASP: IA*, I, 577-583.

Chapter 7

WARS OF CHOICE: JAMES MADISON, GEORGE W. BUSH AND THE PRESIDENTIAL LEGACY QUESTION

Anthony J. Eksterowicz and Glenn P. Hastedt
Department of Political Science
James Madison University, Virginia, US

ABSTRACT

This article examines the presidential legacy question for presidents who conduct wars of choice. We first discuss the variables associated with wars of choice placing them on a continuum. We then assess these variables as applied to two presidents that have conducted wars of choice, James Madison and the War of 1812 and George W. Bush and the Iraq War. We then draw some conclusions concerning the presidential legacies of not only these two presidents but also other presidents who have conducted wars of choice.

What can be noted about the legacy of a president who conducts a war of choice? To exemplify such a situation let us assume that a president has, at one time or another, stated various reasons for the conduct of such a war. So much so that average citizens find it difficult to ascertain the fundamental and real reasons for such an action. Furthermore, the president has cloaked the language justifying the war in the language of necessity (national defense) not choice. The president plays fast and loose with the facts to convince the public by using worst case analysis to bolster the need for war. The president has not prepared the nation for the waging of this war in that no direct individual taxes have been raised nor has the population been asked to sacrifice any material goods for the war effort. The president and his allies reassure the public that the war will be won with a minimal amount of violence and that the opposing forces will be defeated in short order. In addition, the economic costs of war will be low. The president appeals to the patriotism of the nation to unify citizens behind the cause. He simultaneously characterizes opposition figures and arguments as dangerous to the cause of victory at best and traitorous at worst. The president asserts executive powers that serve to provoke the opposition forces. He notes that all diplomatic efforts have been exhausted and the enemy still resists the nation's demands. There appears to be no alternative to war from the president's and his party's perspective. While the president portrays unity of purpose there seems to be concern in military circles about the effectiveness of our fighting forces. In addition, there is concern within the president's party and among the opposition for the nature of the president's leadership abilities. This is displayed by arguments among cabinet members about the necessity, justification, preparedness and leadership required of a successful war effort. The president is aware of such criticisms but asserts his justifications for war in no uncertain terms and acts as though making tough decisions reflects bold leadership.

Many of the above characteristics can be applied to President George W. Bush in his conduct of the Iraq war. However, we present them as not only applicable to President Bush but also applicable to James Madison in his conduct of the War of 1812. Wars of choice present presidents with similar circumstances and how they manage such circumstances contribute to their legacy.

In the last year of his presidency, President Bush was thinking of his legacy and particularly about the impact of the Iraq War upon such a legacy. In fact, a group of scholars and pundits have suggested that Bush will be treated better in history's long run than he is today. Some go as far as suggesting he might turn out to be another Truman. Harry Truman was a president who left office with extremely low popular approval ratings and yet somehow today is revered for his tough and decisive decisions. These decisions have withstood the test of time. All of this occurs before the Bush economic collapse but their analysis was limited to the foreign policy area.

Forgetting the fact that presidents do not get to choose which other presidents they will be compared to and that when these comparisons are made they usually encompass the entire policy realms of an administration, wars of choice have remarkably contributed to negative assessments for many presidents. We posit that understanding the problems associated with such efforts can go a long way in determining just how presidents are treated legacy wise. Thus, there is great utility in examining Madison's efforts in the War of 1812 and Bush's efforts in the Iraq War for similarities and contrasts.

In this article we discuss the problems associated with determining wars of choice and wars of necessity. Then we examine President Madison's War of 1812. We first discuss the international and domestic political environment within which the war takes place. We note the causes expressed for the war both real and contrived. We also attempt to ascertain the true causes as best we can. We cite the nature of expectations and leadership associated with the war. We cite logistical and military strategies and problems with the war. We also examine the nature of the opposition to the war. We then examine President Bush's Iraq war and scrutinize it among the lines above. Finally we draw some conclusions concerning wars of choice and their legacy upon presidents.

WARS OF CHOICE OR NECESSITY

Early in the 2004 presidential election year President Bush was asked on *Meet the Press* if he considered the Iraq War a war of choice or necessity. Mr. Bush was not prepared for the question. He replied, "That's an interesting question," as if to give him time to think through the implications. He even asked the questioner to elaborate on that a bit. Finally he answered with certainty that it was a war of necessity[1] One can forgive the president for hesitating because it is not an easy answer.

How can we distinguish wars of choice from wars of necessity? Any given war is to some extent in the eye of the beholder. So it is possible for two different people to see the same war but one may see it as a war of necessity and the other as a war of choice. Thus someone like a Charles Krauthammer sees the Vietnam War as a war of necessity [2] while another like Richard Hass views it as a war of choice.[3] The criteria for distinguishing the two are often cloaked by policymakers who wish to turn a perceived war of choice into a perceived war of necessity in order to rally the nation behind a noble cause which only they may see clearly. That is why the reasons for initiating such a war are often cloaked in the language of necessity. Furthermore, there may be many reasons for the initiation of the war articulated by various policymakers at various times. These reasons may swing from national defense to the promotion of democracy to the protection of resources vital to the functioning of a democracy. But which is the real and paramount reason? It is difficult to tell among the various reasons given by policymakers. It is also difficult to define what the national interest is at any given moment for great powers have many interests. Finally, can wars of choice turn into wars of necessity and vice versa?[4] For example did the War of 1812, which we argue was a war of choice, turn into a war of necessity once the British invaded the United States and burnt the capital building and the White House?

On this last question we may have an answer. We would argue that it is the initial decision to go to war that is of paramount importance. One cannot blame a big bully for retaliating against a smaller foe if that foe deliberately poked him in the eye with a stick. It is the initial act of poking that is important. The other questions are much more difficult to handle. We would suggest that there are a number of criteria that distinguish a war of choice from a war of necessity. With regards to some wars it may be self evident that they are either one or the other. For example, World War II is generally believed to be a war of necessity despite Patrick J. Buchanan's arguments to the contrary.[5] There is a certain amount of "I know it when I see it" mentality here. Other wars are much more difficult to distinguish. For example, how would one characterize the Civil War? It would depend upon which perspective was stressed the North's or South's. In any event, there are a number of characteristics associated with a war of choice.

A war of choice is offensive in character. There is am emphasis upon the danger to national interests in waiting for an attack or invasion. There is much more of an emphasis upon prevention and even preemption. In addition all diplomatic means toward neutralizing the crisis may not have been exhausted even though top national policymakers may claim otherwise. In other words there are always a few more diplomatic steps left on the table. Wars of choice are often portrayed as low cost, low risk endeavors. A quick and easy end to them seems to be the watchword. Policymakers usually do not take draconian measures to prepare the nation for such wars. National taxes may not be raised. There may be little to no attempts at rationing goods necessary to the war effort. Standards of living will not take an immediate hit therefore the nation is not prepared for the longevity of the struggle by being asked to make sacrifices. It can be termed war on the cheap if not for the inevitable, long run, losses of life and investments. The protection of the state from physical attack or invasion is usually not of immediate concern although policymakers may threaten dire outcomes if nothing is done. Another characteristic of such wars is initial high public support because of the expectation of a quick victory and low costs. This, in turn, leads to an increase in opposition to such wars as they drag on and these initial expectations fail to be realized.[6]

Another characteristic of these wars is their call for patriotism and characterization of the opposition as unpatriotic or even traitorous. This is especially the case if these wars are initiated during election years.

The great problem here is that wars of choice may not be perceived that way until they progress and begin to bog down. Their danger lay in their initial framing. We suggest that it may be useful to place wars along a continuum. At one end there are clearly the wars of choice like Vietnam, the War of 1812 and Iraq. At the other end, wars of necessity may be represented by World War II and the Revolutionary War. The more a war exhibits the characteristics of a war of choice it would fall closer to the choice side of the continuum. Thus any war may possess more or less of these characteristics but we may still be able to determine its nature.

Using this method both the War of 1812 and the Iraq War under the leadership of James Madison and George W. Bush appear to be wars of choice. We now turn to the analysis of these wars and what they portend for presidential legacies.

MADISON AND THE WAR OF 1812

The International and Domestic Environment

The international and domestic environment that led to the War of 1812 was one of war between France and England. For many years preceding Mr. Madison's war France and England were fighting for economic domination in trade and commerce in the European theater. Their colonies were producing goods and products that had to be protected from one another. The threat to Britain was Napoleon and his dreams of conquest. Empires literally collided from approximately the 1790s to Napoleon's defeat by the British at Leipzig in 1813 and again at Waterloo in 1815. The war was fought on land and sea. Two great naval armadas met for battle on the high seas. As such the burgeoning country of America, formally neutral, found itself caught between these two great powers. No matter what agreement was made with one country the other would take offense as did France after the United States signed the Jay Treaty with England in 1794. This treaty regulated commerce and defined neutral rights during the war between France and England. The French resented the treaty so much that there was a sort of mini naval war between America and France from 1798 to 1801 [7]

From the American perspective there was a changing of the guard politically with the election of Thomas Jefferson in 1800. Before this election the Federalist Party under Alexander Hamilton's influence wanted to prepare the nation financially for war and build up its defense establishment. There were various threats that existed on American boarders from the potential Spanish and French threats in the south and southwest to the British threat in Canada and their increasing alliance with Native American tribes in the north and northwest. However Jefferson's election changed the American response. Jeffersonian Republicans were against big government programs and worked to cut taxes and reduce national debt. This meant that defense spending declined under Jefferson. He preferred defensive measures such as gunboats to protect American ports. He believed them to be cheap and effective [8].

During this time American neutrality was severely tested by both the British and the French. They were competing economically by restricting each others' most important trading goods via quarantines and blockades. Napoleon's Continental System served to restrict British manufacturing and trade. The British Orders in Council sought to do the same to France.[9] These two decisions confounded Jefferson and America around 1806-07 but there was another important issue that would lead to Jefferson's embargo of British goods and that was the British practice of impressments.

Naval war consumed ships and as the War of 1812 approached the British fleet experienced shortages of lumber which England increasingly had to obtain from Canada due to French and Russian actions regarding the closing of Baltic ports exporting such goods.[10] During this time the British experienced shortages of material and other goods that hindered their ability to build and maintain a large fleet. As 1812 neared British shipbuilding declined.[11] As early as the issuance of Orders in Council the British experienced a shortage of sailors to man their ships. Many British sailors deserted the spartan quarters and harsh treatment aboard British vessels for the more accommodating American vessels. British ships began the practice of boarding American ships in search of such sailors but inevitably American sailors were *impressed* by the British to serve on their ships. This practice caused much distress between Britain and America and led to Jefferson's embargo of British goods in retaliation. Near the beginning of the War of 1812 nearly 6000 American sailors had been impressed by the British and nearly one quarter of the men aboard American ships were British.[12]

Domestically, America was divided. The Federalist Party was strong in the northeast and in New England. They were opposed to the war and believed that President Madison was too close to France. They preferred the British Crown to the Emperor Napoleon. However, Madison's own party was split between his supporters and the supporters of the New York Republican Clintons; DeWitt and George. In fact George Clinton ran against Madison in 1808 as an Independent Republican and DeWitt Clinton ran against him in 1812 as a Federalist. The Clintons and their followers believed that the Republican Party should have adhered to greater Federalists principles. Thus they disliked Madison for not preparing properly for war. The so called "invisible Republicans" also wanted an increase in military preparedness and they despised Secretary of the Treasury Albert Gallatin. John Randolph of Roanoke Virginia, a Republican, disliked Mr. Madison for towing too much of a Federalist line.[13] The election of increasing numbers of Republican War Hawks to Congress after 1810 and Republican majority control of both houses of Congress in 1812 did much too politically spur on war [14]

Thus on the eve of the War of 1812, America had been dealing with her neutrality rights between two great powers fighting for economic superiority and world empire. Any move in this environment would be tricky at best and quite hazardous at worst. Tensions mounted between all three nations as the war approached. Domestically things were not much better. The nation was split three or four ways. There were splits in Mr. Madison's Republican party and he was not a well liked person within his party. In addition, the nation was not yet the

United States of America. That would come only after a bitter Civil War. It was Mr. Madison's task to unify the nation and it would not be easy.

The Causes for War

The War of 1812 has become known as Mr. Madison's war precisely because he made the choice. It was not strictly speaking a defensive war although President Madison attempted to cloak it in that language. The nation was not prepared for war. There existed no professional military in place.[15] The nation did not raise taxes to fund the effort preferring to borrow loans to finance the war.[16] In addition, there were expectations of a quick victory encouraged by government policymakers and Mr. Madison. Most of the criteria we developed for a war of choice apply to the War of 1812.

The causes for the war can largely be found in the objectives for war. We should note that scholars are still debating the primary cause for the war and at this time it may never be known with certainty. One reason for war was the British issuance of Orders in Council which affected American trade with other nations allied with either France or Britain. Closely related to this was the practice of British impressments of American sailors. As Hickey noted the war was fought for"free trade and sailors rights."[17]

There was an economic component to the need for war. America fought to free up trade with the European continent.

A second reason concerns the Northwest Territory. British officials in Canada were arming Indian tribes there. America feared the possibility of war from Canada and coercion of the increasing number of Americans settling in Canada.[18] While there were tensions along the boarder there also seems to be a bit of pre-emptive mentality in this reason.

A third reason flows from the second and can be attributed to the Federalists critics of the Madison administration. They believed that Mr. Madison wanted to annex Canada. This reason appears sound since the initial war plans called for an invasion of Canada. The protection of American settlers there was also one of the professed aims of the Republican War Hawks. Irving Brant claims that Madison disavowed this goal to the British shortly after the war began. According to Brant, the invasion was only strategic to defeat enemy troops within reach of America.[19] There is disagreement concerning this goal.

Stagg has argued that as the war approached the British believed that Canada could supply timber, fish and livestock that their West Indies colonies needed. Therefore the British could continue to obtain sugar and coffee from the West Indies. Canada's importance only increases after Russia denies the British access to her Baltic ports. At the same time American settlers rush to Canada where they find cheap land. With the American embargo failing Canada becomes even more crucial to American interests [20]

A fourth reason concerns the domestic political reality at the beginning of the war. President Madison was the leader of a deeply divided party doing battle with a Federalist Party. The war was one way of unifying all of these factions within the Republican Party and forging a governing base after the war. It would also have the effect of weakening the Federalist Party and silencing their opposition.[21] This view places much responsibility upon the "War Hawks" in Congress for the drumbeat to war.

Finally, there was the reason of national honor. We went to war to preserve our republican institutions. We went to war to demonstrate that we believed in our patriotic principles. We would not allow any empire to continue to disgrace us. Our prestige as a nation was at stake.

What can be noted of these reasons for war? Well they all appear to contain a grain of truth because all were expressed formally or informally encouraged by President Madison, his Republican Party leaders, members of his party in Congress, and the Federalist opposition among others. How do we determine the primary cause of the war after all of these years? It may be impossible for the scholarly community is still divided over this as a few of our cited sources demonstrate. One thing is clear, these objectives went largely unmet. The British government decided to stop the practice of impressments and revoked their Orders in Council before a shot was fired. Due to travel times in those days and a lag in communication Madison was unaware of this. War could have been avoided with further diplomatic overtures and more decision time for the Congress. It was an unnecessary war if we believe these reasons were the main ones. Ironically, Madison attempted to get the slow moving Congress to declare war a bit faster by revealing the letters of a man named John Henry who he portrayed as being in league with the British in Canada, Henry's purpose was to stir up trouble among the war resisters in New England. Madison actually paid for these dubious letters.[22] There was an impatience displayed by the Madison administration and a few diplomatic steps or maneuvers were left on the table.

Perhaps the closest we will get to the true cause of the war lies in the combination of political and economic reasons. Canada became crucial for American trade and the divisions within Madison's own party and the nature of the Federalist opposition all seemed to make war more likely. However, when assessing the success of the war, President Madison achieved very little beyond the unification of his own party and an increase in patriotism and national pride.[23] These are hardly reasons that justify the loss of life and national economic treasure that the war brought about. In fact, the cost of war was estimated at about 105 million dollars and it took, two decades to pay off this debt.[24] The war also failed to achieve its purpose of spreading republican institutions and democracy into Canada via conquest.[25]

National Expectations and Leadership

National military leaders, Republican Party leaders, the War Hawks in Congress and President Madison thought this would be a quick and decisive war. They believed that the British were too far away to protect Canada adequately and that the French and American settlements would help welcome Americans as they invaded Canada. In the eyes of some, Canada was there for the taking.[26] Others thought that the British were too occupied with Napoleon and would immediately give in when war was declared. Many American newspapers did not believe that Britain would invade America[27]. This would lead to a bloodless victory.[28] All of these beliefs were founded in wishful thinking and reflected the unwillingness to prepare seriously for war or at least a moderately long term struggle. This, in turn, reflected a lack of leadership in various circles.

The nature of the preparations for war or the lack thereof was stunning. We have already noted that the Republican Party was fiscally stringent eschewing keeping large numbers of men under arms during peacetime. There was also an unwillingness to increase taxes for the war preferring instead to borrow through loans for the effort. A naval build up was also needed but largely ignored for the preference of increasing the Army.[29] As a result, at the outset of the war the nation needed men, equipment, money, leadership, a realistic strategy for success and an appreciation that this endeavor might last a while. All of this reflected the type of leadership available to the nation.

Leadership suffered due to a number of problems. There were divisions within President Madison's own Republican Party which we have noted previously. It was a very difficult party to lead on the eve of war. It suffered from excessive argumentation and factions within its cabinet. These are problems that strong presidents must overcome but what type of a leader was James Madison?

Gary Wills notes that Madison was primarily a legislator whose best accomplishments came by working in secret. He was small in stature and prone to social isolation. While brilliant in drafting legislative and constitutional documents and in argumentation he was very provincial in his outlook. He was the only Secretary of State who never traveled abroad. This resulted in a naiveté about world politics and his fellow men. To Madison isolationism was a good thing.[30]

These are not characteristics that foster leadership in presidential circles. Add to this that 1812 was an election year and Madison was pressing the Congress for action that would help to unify the Republican Party. But it is proper to ask if war for the sake of political unity is leadership? Therefore the unrealistic expectations surrounding the war effort, the necessity to act in an election year, the problems associated with leadership all lead to America's lack of preparation for war and inevitability for conducting it.

Strategic and Military Problems

The first struggle the nation faced was the raising of an army for the war effort. There was a debate concerning troop levels. Madison wanted to rely upon short term volunteers and militia largely because he believed it would be a short war. However Congress raised the level of regular troops but they also engaged in a debate concerning the use of state militias. This threatened to decentralize the war to the leadership of governors in the states. There was also concern that militias could not legally engage in foreign wars on Canadian soil. In addition, Congress would not support a proposed expansion of the navy. Many believed that we simply could not compete with Great Britain on the high seas. The final compromise on troops was a combination of volunteers, regulars and militia in numbers hardly adequate for a long struggle.[31] The leadership of this army was also problematical.

In 1808 General Winfield Scott provided a scathing assessment of the military officer corps. He noted that the appointments to the officer corps were bad and influenced by party politics. Very few Federalists were appointed to the corps. The remainder of Republicans were not very educated leading to ignorant men as officers. This was the case particularly among New England Republicans. Other appointees were generally unfit for any duty.[32] Political patronage infected the appointment process so much that many believed the army was politicized. During the beginning of the war Madison's administration selected new generals from the pool of aging Revolutionary Republican veterans. Many of them were ex politicians.[33] There were no preparations for these officers to recruit for or organize their regiments. There were shortages of pay, supplies and equipment all of which directly led to early defeats in land battles in the north and northwest.[34] We should note that the army did get better as the war progressed. By the end of the war it was a professional, highly educated and socialized tool for defense.[35] This did not help the nation in the early going.

The military strategy was also a problem. Madison's administration thought a great deal about land war but the administration and the Congress neglected the Navy. Ironically some of the most accomplished military commanders like Perry and McDonough were in the Navy. Their exploits and defeats of the British along the Great Lakes were legendary. However, the British remained far superior along the east coast where they burned towns, plundered property and pillaged villages including Washington D.C.. Mr. Madison was lucky to escape their wrath.

The land war strategy was lacking. The best plan was a frontal assault on Montreal with all available troops. However that would require the cooperation of the New England states through which invading forces would travel. This section of the country was heavily Federalist and opposed to the war effort. Therefore, a three pronged attack was launched through the New York/Niagra, Montreal, Dearborn/Detroit areas. All of which met with humiliating defeat and surrender of American troops. It did not help that the War Department was in disarray, payment of soldiers was lacking and there was a shortage of food and doctors.[36] A war of choice should offer opportunities for far superior organization and preparation but ironically history would seem to demonstrate the opposite.

Federalist Opposition

As Hickey notes the War of 1812 provoked the most opposition of any American war effort. The grisly riot by Republicans against a Federalist newspaper and its staff and editor was but an example of this.[37] Federalist's arguments against the war were framed by the highly politicized environment of the times. Republicans, though divided, controlled the presidency and both houses of Congress. Mr. Madison did not obtain a single Federalist vote in the House of Representatives or the Senate for war. In fact only 61% of all votes in both houses were for war. The closest of any war vote in the nation's history.[38] Mr. Madison would lose support and Republican representatives in Congress all through the war until after the signing of the Treaty of Ghent.

Federalists had many reasons to oppose the war. They noted the obvious problems associated with preparation for the war. They did not buy the spreading of democracy to Canada argument. Federalists did not consider a conquered people fertile soil for republicanism. They argued that the federal government would become too big and unconcerned with civil liberties. In order to curtail smuggling of British goods through Canada and New England the Madison administration and Congress granted the Customs Department increased powers to search and seize illegal goods. Federalists, especially those on the boarder of Canada, deemed this an invasion of their rights. They considered it spying on Americans and became particularly agitated that it was done through an expansion of Madison's executive order power. Federalists also condemned the war as being political and exploitative of the divisions in the country. They warned of national control of state militias.

Federalists complained bitterly that they were being portrayed as traitors who were unpatriotic to the American cause. They stressed their rights to free and open debate. Federalists also feared the effect of the war upon domestic politics [39]

The New York Federalists were particularly incensed. They railed against the projected costs of the war in money and lives. Because of the war Republicans lost control of the New York State legislature after 1812. The New Yorkers warned of confrontations between soldiers and civilians. In this way the war would be brought home against American citizens. They questioned their rights to free speech during this war. In 1814 the Republicans campaigned against New York Federalists and the Federalists lost control of the New York state assembly. Despite these circumstances the New York Federalists campaigned against the war electorally citing its unconstitutional nature. Peace societies sprung up throughout New York and New England after the war [40].

John Lowell produced a passionate but cogent critique of the war in his Dispassionate Inquiry entitled, Mr. Madison's War. He noted that this was a war against Great Britain due to Mr. Madison's preferences for France. He provided extensive reasons as to why the war was wrong least of which was its offensive nature. He noted that we could have settled with Great Britain over the issue of impressments and that the section of the nation hardest hit with impressments was the section most opposed to war. He questioned Mr. Madison's motives, strategies and moral judgment in conducting what he considered to be an immoral and unjust war.[41] The opposition to the war was concentrated in the New York/ New England area but as intense as any opposition ever seen since. With all of these problems how did Mr. Madison fare historically?

Mr. Madison's Legacy

Immediately after the war the Republicans claimed that they had won the war. They fostered the political unity that the war brought about. The Republican Party was finally a unified force and the Federalist Party was in decline. There was a reveling in the new found patriotism which would be manifest in the Monroe Doctrine under yet another Virginia president. However the deep divisions between sections of the nation that the war revealed would come into play again in the decade before the Civil War. Did Madison win this war? He did not achieve most of his objectives and he was lucky to win the peace if not the war. The costs of the war were enormous; the divisions in the nation were not healed by the effort but rather muted for a time. Mr. Madison's judgment has been severely challenged by modern day historians. His saving grace was the Treaty of Ghent. Madison sent the best possible negotiating team to this conference. The British sent their second or third string team. They were concerned with the peace talks at the Congress in Vienna. To the British Ghent was a side show. The British were tired of the costs of the Napoleonic wars. While some of the British wanted to extract revenge others simply wanted it over. Besides the British had prevented the American conquest of Canada. When all was said and done both sides agreed to a peace treaty which reverted to the status quo before the war.[42] This made the concept of winning irrelevant. Mr. Madison may have won the peace but it was one he could have had at much less cost to the nation.

The scholarly assessment of Mr. Madison's effort has fluctuated a bit over the years. In the immediate aftermath of the war historians like Henry Adams castigated Madison for being a weak and unprepared leader. This affected his legacy in the negative direction. After World War II Irving Brant (cited here in this work) adopted a kinder explanation for Madison's usurpation of power and his abilities as commander in chief. However, more recently, scholars like Donald Hickey (also cited here) have taken the position that Madison lost the War of 1812 due to his inadequacies as commander in chief. What are we to make of this and Madison's legacy? As Wills notes, historians have not considered him a failure but have not seen fit to move him from the average category.[43] One must wonder if that rating has anything to do with Madison's accomplishments before and after his presidency. In any event the War of 1812, a war of choice probably has a lot to do with this average assessment. Is this a celing for war choice presidents? We now turn to another president at another time engaged in a war of choice.

BUSH AND THE IRAQ WAR

Domestic and International Environment

George W. Bush assumed the presidency under highly polarized circumstances, a condition that did not change for his entire tenure in office except for a period of national unity following the terrorist attacks of September 11, 2001. He was the first candidate since 1888 elected president with less than a majority of the popular vote and his election was affirmed by the Electoral College only after Florida began a controversial recount of the votes cast for president and the Supreme Court ordered the recount suspended.

George W. Bush was the first Republican president since Dwight Eisenhower to have a majority in both Houses of Congress on taking office, even though it was by the slimmest of margins, 10 seats in the House of Representatives and the tie breaking vote by Vice President Dick Cheney in the Senate. This working majority did not last long as in 2001 Senator Jeffords switched sides and joined the Democratic caucus. Bush regained a majority with the 2002 midterm elections which saw him campaign more vigorously for his party's candidates than was the norm for a sitting president. It was also a campaign marked by highly partisan language in which Democratic incumbents were widely and loosely condemned as soft on terrorism and had their patriotism questioned.

Bush was reelected in 2006 by the slimmest margin of any president since the Civil War and the Republican Party continued to hold a majority in Congress. As in 2000 his election owed far more to the outpouring of support from the Republican Party base than it did to support from swing voters.[44] In 2000, 52% of his vote came from party stalwarts while in 2004 it rose to 59%. Democrats regained control of Congress in the 2006 mid term election in what was generally held to be a nationwide vote repudiating his policy on Iraq.

Once again polarization was evident in the voting patterns of the American public. In May 2006 only 4% of Democratic voters approved of Bush's performance as president. No previous president had ever recorded an approval rating in the single digits from members of the opposition. In stark contrast, in January 2007 89.5% of Republicans approved of the job he had done as president. The average difference between Democratic and Republican respondents in the last quarter of 2004 was 79 points, 13 points higher than it had been during the Clinton administration [45]

The international environment that greeted the Bush administration when it took office looked anything but daunting. It was in most respects quite calm although the storm that would become 9/11 was already brewing beneath the surface. With the end of the Cold War now a decade removed the agenda of American foreign policy seemed increasingly preoccupied by "B" list threats rather than core national security problems. The most troubling military engagements of the Clinton era had either been brought to a conclusion such as Haiti and Somalia or were reaching that point as was the case in the former Yugoslavia. It was the calm and not the coming storm that the Bush administration's national security team (along with virtually all others) focused on as the 2000 presidential election neared.

National Security advisor Condoleezza Rice wrote in *Foreign Affairs* in January 2000 that the United States was "in a remarkable position.[46] Powerful secular trends are moving the world toward economic openness and —more unevenly—democracy and individual liberty…In such an environment, American policies must help further these favorable trends by maintaining a disciplined an consistent foreign policy that separates the important from the trivial." The failure to do so was the Republican Party's primary critique of Clinton's foreign policy. His administration Rice went on had replaced the national interest with humanitarian interests which she defined as there being "nothing wrong with" but as also being of a "second order effect." Perhaps most tellingly, in criticizing Clinton's "epidemic" penchant for seeking out "largely symbolic agreements and its pursuit of, at best, illusory 'norms' of international behavior" Rice pointed to the need to focus on the behavior of the few big powers that can radically affect international peace, stability and prosperity. Nowhere to be found in her discussion of the U.S. national interest was a reference to terrorist groups.

Rice promised that a new Republican administration would 1) ensure that America's military could deter war, project power and fight in defense of its interests if deterrence fails 2) promote economic grown and political openness by fostering free trade and a stable international monetary system 3) renew strong and intimate relations with allies who share American values 4) focus U.S. energies on comprehensive relations with big powers and 5) deal decisively with the threat of rogue regimes an hostile powers. She cautioned that the military is a special instrument and one not designed to be used as a civilian police force, political referee and "certainly not designed to build a civilian society."

This complacent view of the international system was shaken to its core by the terrorist attacks on the World Trade Center and Pentagon so much so that not long after 9/11 Deputy Secretary of State Richard Armitage asserted "history starts today."[47] In focusing on the terrorist threat the Bush administration cast the attack on the U.S. in global terms embracing a world view in which there was no middle ground. They were not just directed at the U.S. but against freedom, democracy and human rights. "Either you are with us or you are with the terrorists" stated President Bush.

The new more muscular U.S. foreign policy initially encountered little opposition. Traditional allies came to the U.S.'s side as did current adversaries such as Russia. Even those the Bush administration had labeled as rogue states such as Iran and Syria provided the U.S. with quiet support as it prepared for the invasion of Afghanistan and overthrow of the Taliban regime. The first U.S. Special Forces entered Afghanistan on October 19. Conventional forces arrived on November 25, and the last Taliban stronghold fell on December 16. Osama bin

Laden, whose group al Qaeda was held responsible for the 9/11 attacks, remained at large. By year's end a multiethnic interim government led by Hamid Karzai was in place.

The climate of widespread international support for the U.S. began to change as the administration turned its attention to Iraq and sought to build the case for war against it at the United Nations in 2002 and 2003. In making its case the U.S. relied upon both behind the scenes arm twisting and the public presentation of intelligence. Central to the administration's argument was Iraq's possession of weapons of mass destruction. When these diplomatic efforts failed the U.S. to sway key Security Council members China, Russia, Germany and France the U.S. along with Great Britain proclaimed they would create a "coalition of the willing" to remove Saddam Hussein from power.

On March 16, 2003 President Bush met with British Prime Minister Tony Blair and leaders from Spain and Portugal in the Azores to announce that the "moment of truth" had arrived for Saddam Hussein. The following day Bush issued an ultimatum requiring Saddam to leave Iraq in 48 hours, and on March 19 Brush ordered the invasion of Iraq. A "shock and awe" military campaign was begun that was designed to overwhelm and demoralize Iraqi forces, allowing the coalition forces to move swiftly to Baghdad. On April 9 Baghdad came under the control of U.S. forces, and on May 1 President Bush declared an end to major combat operations on the USS Abraham Lincoln against the backdrop of a huge banner declaring "mission accomplished."

Expecting to be greeted as liberators, U.S. forces soon came to be viewed as occupiers and became the target of terrorist attacks. Looting and vandalism were common. In September 2004 U.S. casualties had reached the 1,000 mark. As American casualties mounted, the nature of the conflict changed as well. Terrorist attacks directed at the United States and its Iraqi allies now took place alongside a heightened sectarian conflict between the Shia and Sunnis that increasingly took on the character of a civil war.

The conflict also brought forward vivid images of mistreatment of prisoners by American military personnel at Abu Ghraib prison, which served to enflame anti-American sentiment in Iraq and antiwar feelings in the United States. American casualties reached the 3,000 mark by the end of 2006; the United Nations estimated that 34,452 Iraqi civilians died in 2006 and that 30,842 people were detained in Iraq, including 14, 534 in U.S. military–run prisons.

Two years later the political-strategic landscape of Iraq looked very different. The Bush administration's decision after the November 2006 midterm elections to sending additional forces to Iraq, popularly known as the "surge," along with a change in strategy put into place by General David Petraeus that emphasized counterinsurgency tactics against U.S. enemies and working with Iraqis rather than trying to secure victory through battlefield successes against them led to a reduction in the violence and increased political stability. By the time President Barak Obama took office there was widespread agreement that U.S. troop withdrawals from Iraq could take place.

What did not look different in 2008 were continued problems with Iran and North Korea, the two other members of the axis of evil identified by President Bush. Neither had been dissuaded from their pursuit of nuclear power by attempts at diplomatic isolation, economic sanctions, or veiled threats of preemptive military action. Problems also began to resurface in Afghanistan where the Taliban had regrouped and were now once again viewed as a significant national security threat that demanded a U.S. military presence there. More generally a sense had developed that the administration's goal of spreading democracy through the region had been replaced by a support for stability.

Finally because the Bush Doctrine had been so heavily focused on terrorism it seemed to provide little guidance for other national security threats. A case in point was Russian intervention into Georgia during the 2008 Summer Olympics on the side of pro-Russian separatists. The U.S. response was little more than a series of declaratory policy statements of disapproval and support for Georgia. Nothing was done to change the situation on the ground.

Causes of War

The shifting rationales provided by the Bush administration about its urgency is a major contributing factor to the assessment that the Iraq War was one of choice and not of necessity. The two overarching arguments provided by the administration centered on a link between Iraq and al Qaeda along with its possession of weapons of mass destruction. Although invoked repeatedly neither claim was substantiated, a failure that gave rise to the assertion that administration had either politicized intelligence or simply ignored.

A third frequently expressed rationale for war was the need to bring democracy to the region. Global democratization formed a key tenet in the neo-conservative foreign policy agenda. A world of democratic states was held to be critical to furthering U.S. security in the region. Just as critical to the neo-conservative perspective was the belief that the U.S. had the ability to do so. While the democratic peace argument had already become a central fixture of the debate on U.S. foreign policy before Bush took office it remains a contested position with some arguing there are important differences between liberal and illiberal democracies and between new and established democracies in their peacefulness. Terrorism experts are similarly divided over the relationship between democracy and the origins of terrorist movements.

The subjective nature of the Bush administration's most frequently argued reasons for why the Iraq war was necessary gave rise to speculation that other reasons were really at work. One such argument focused on access to (cheap) oil. A second argument was that George W. Bush was driven to complete the removal of Saddam Hussein from power that his father began but did not finish in the Persian Gulf War. A variant of this argument held that his obsession with Saddam Hussein from power stemmed from a failed assassination attempt on his father. Still another conspiracy theory harkened back to arguments about the influence of the military-industrial complex. In this view the war was designed to provide large profits to companies doing business with the military. Fueling this view were the huge profits earned by Halliburton. Vice President Dick Cheney had served as its Chief Executive Officer from 1995-2000.

National Expectations and Leadership

The tragic events of 9/11 led to a dramatic reversal of the public's evaluation of George W. Bush. Where prior to that day his approval rating was at or near 50% after 9/11 it hovered near the 90% mark. Neither Bush personally nor his administration as a whole was able to translate this leap in public standing into a long term working foundation on which to govern. It did, however, provide support for a series of national security measures such as the USA

Patriot Act in the short term. Long term, his administration's domestic agenda stalled and his personal approval rating decreased steadily as the Iraq War progressed spiking occasionally after such positive events as the capture of Saddam Hussein in 2003 and the Iraqi election in 2005.

Perhaps most significantly Bush was never able to overcome the polarized context within which his actions were evaluated. Far more than was the case with the Korean War, the Vietnam War, the Persian Gulf War, fighting in Kosovo or the invasion of Afghanistan a gap existed between Democratic and Republican support for this war. The average difference in support level from July 2004 through the end of 2005 was about 62 percentage points.[48]

Echoes of the polarized pubic attitudes toward the Bush administration were found in the Bush administration's view of the public and its opponents. Governing from his Republican Party base Bush employed "binary rhetoric" in dealing with its opponents. Criticism and debate were characterized as undercutting the war effort, unpatriotic and bordering on treasonous.[49] Perhaps not surprisingly Republicans tended to stand by Bush and the Iraq War effort even as evidence mounted that the principal arguments for going to war, Saddam Hussein's possession of weapons of mass destruction and his links to al-Qaeda, were flawed while Democrats abandoned him. Just after the war began over 80% of Republicans agreed that Iraq was a national security threat to the U.S. and at least 60% would continue to hold this belief. In contrast, only 46% of Democrats saw Iraq as a threat at the start of the war and by October 2004 this number had fallen to 12%.[50]

This leadership strategy for engaging his opponents was at variance with that promised by Bush in his campaign for the presidency in 2000 and after taking office in 2001. Then he spoke of being a unifier and not a divider. By 2004 his public rhetoric had taken on a very different quality. After winning re-election he announced in his first press conference "I earned capital in the campaign, political capital, and now I intend to spend it. It is my style." It was not one, however, that Bush invented. As Richard Skinner notes the presidency was becoming increasingly partisan since the Reagan administration.[51]

The partisan and binary nature of Bush's approach to dealing with opposition was also evident in how he structured his White House decision making system [52]. White House appointees overwhelmingly tended to have personal ties with the Bush 2000 presidential campaign or his term as governor of Texas. Some 30% of Executive Office of the President staffers hailed from Texas and more than 80% had worked on the campaign. Collectively they ran interference for him in dealing with the bureaucracy or ran offices from the White House that made policy in their stead. For example, Chief of Staff Andrew Card was a key driving force in an early administration initiative on immigration reform that was widely seen as an effort to attract Hispanic voters to the Republican Party. As war with Iraq approached Card organized the White House Iraq Group to coordinate policy and ensure that the administration spoke with one public voice.

Partisan staffing was reinforced by a centralized decision making process that ensured as one staffer put it, the president would get the information he wanted but not necessarily the information he needed. A poignant example comes from a meeting between national security advisor Stephen Hadley and a strategy review group appointed to review Iraq policy at the same time that the Iraq Study Group was conducting its inquiry. As the meeting progressed Hadley spoke up: "you have got to give the president the option of a surge in forces…he will want to see it and he'll want to know what it means. You can take your positions for or against or in between, but you have to present him that as an option.

Moreover that information would not necessarily come through formally established channels but often through direct one-on-one conversations with key decision makers such as vice President Cheney and Secretary of Defense Donald Rumsfeld. Bob Woodward recounts one White House foreign policy meeting in the following terms:

> Rice began going through a long paper on issues that everyone was supposed to have read and understood. Rumsfeld leaned back and made it pretty clear he was not paying much attention. The president also seemed bored. "Don, what do you think about this?" Bush asked, interrupting Rice. . . . the discussion drifted off and the decision was left hanging. . . . It was as if Rice and the NSC had one serious, formal process going on while the president and Rumsfeld had another one—informal, chatty and dominant.[53]

Firm in his convictions, Bush did not seek out debates or an exchange of views on policy matters. His preference was to make a quick decision based on his personal assessment of the problem and then move forward. Meetings were designed to inform not elicit information. Two incidents highlight the resulting dynamics of Bush's leadership style for his administration's decision making processes. First, before the Iraq War Richard Haass who headed the State Department's policy planning unit met with national security advisor Condoleezza Rice and raised the need to discuss the pros and cons of war. Rice responded to the effect that Haas shouldn't bother because the president has made a decision.[54] Second, is another description of a White House foreign policy meeting by Woodward:

> Rumsfeld made his presentation while looking at the president, while Powell looked straight ahead. Then Powell would make his presentation to the president with Rumsfeld looking straight ahead. They didn't even comment on each other's statements or views. So Bush never had the benefit of a serious, substantive discussion between his principal advisors. And . . . the president did not force a discussion.[55]

Strategic and Military Problems

Pre 9/11 the Bush administration's foreign policy could be defined one of two ways. From the perspective of foreign leaders it was the equivalent of the saying "no" strategy employed with great effect during the early Cold War years by Charles DeGaulle and more recently by Alexander Putin. Whatever was asked of the United States the answer was "no." Where DeGaulle and Putin sought to reestablish the image of France and Russia respectively as major world powers, Bush said "no" in order to drive home the hegemonic power of the U.S. From the perspective of American domestic politics the essence of his foreign policy was captured by the phrase "ABC," anything but Clinton. Consistent with Condoleezza Rice's view of the American national interest the U.S. would no longer engage in the type of multilateral undertakings of its predecessor.

After 9/11 the Bush Doctrine would become the signature statement of the administration's strategy to deal with terrorism and the challenges of world politics more generally. It does not emerge in full form from any one document but rather is found throughout a series of statements made by George W. Bush beginning with his 2001 State of the Union address which predated the 9/11 terrorist attacks in which he identifies terrorists and rogue states as "emerging threats" but does not put forward a strategy for responding to them nor did he identify a linkage between the two. In his nationwide address following the 9/11 attacks Bush proclaims that the U.S. is now involved in a war against terrorism and those who support it.

The first statement of a strategy for dealing with terrorists and other hostile threats to the U.S. came in his June 2002 speech to the graduating class at West Point where Bush stated, "Our security will require all Americans to be forward-looking and resolute, to be ready for preemptive action when necessary to defend our liberty and to defend our lives." He also asserted that "the gravest danger to freedom lies in the crossroads of radicalism and technology." To these observations the September 2002 *National Security Strategy* added, "We cannot let our enemies strike first," that the United States will use its power to encourage free and open societies, and that it will never allow its military supremacy to be challenged.[56] Bush's January 2002 State of the Union Address further developed the linkage between terrorist and their supporters when he identified Iran, North Korea and Iraq as members of an axis of evil.

Observers disagree as to characterize the actual content of the Bush Doctrine although its essential features are generally agreed upon. Steven Hook identifies two core pillars on which it is based.[57] The first is American primacy in world politics. The world is unipolar and the U.S. is the dominant power. The second is preemptive war, the right to attack first in self defense. Together, American primacy and preemptive war laid the foundation for what Hook describes as an American protectorate over the interstate system. Ilan Peleg constructs a more expansive definition of the Bush Doctrine and divides its key elements into three parts.[58] Substantively the Bush Doctrine calls for opposition to terrorism, preemptive military action to defend U.S. security and promoting the spread of democracy. In terms of methods it relies upon unilateral action and where necessary the construction of coalitions of the willing instead of acting through international institutions. Finally, in terms of tone, the Bush Doctrine adopts a moralistic stance in which the American definition of values and goals is taken as a given to be the correct definitions.

Several aspects of the Bush Doctrine brought forward questions about the strength of its intellectual foundations with some asserting that it was not a strategic road map that guided policy but an opportunistic response to the events of 9/11 that allowed the administration to address real and longstanding foreign policy problems in the Middle East.

At its most general level the debate over the Bush Doctrine has pitted conservative realists against neoconservatives. Five key themes form the foundation for neoconservative thinking about world politics.[59] First, the internal character of regimes matters. Second, American power should be used for moral purposes. Third, neoconservatives are skeptical about the legitimacy and effectiveness of international law and institutions to achieve security and justice. Fourth, the United States should act unilaterally whenever possible. And fifth, military power ought to be considered as a primary instrument of American foreign policy. Conservative realists are in partial agreement with neoconservatives on such matters as the importance of military power in world politics and a de-emphasis on the role of international organizations and international law in world politics. But they take exception elsewhere. For realists there is a fundamental difference between national interest and global interest. Any foreign policy that does not recognize the difference will result in overreaching and in the long run result in dilution of a country's power, which will, in turn, threaten its ability to protect its national security. Moreover, what matters in world affairs is the nature of a country's foreign policy and not its domestic policies in areas such as human rights and democracy. They argue that the link between democracy and peace is not as iron-clad as many world make. New democracies, for example, tend to be prone to war. Finally, realists assert that although international law and institutions cannot protect countries from national security threats, they do provide a means for legitimizing the use of power, thus reducing both resistance to it and the costs of using it.

Specific aspects of the Bush Doctrine have also brought forward challenges. The most prominent point of controversy is the concept of preemption. At issue here was the blurring of a long-standing distinction in international politics between preemption and prevention. Both are based on the principle of striking first in self-defense. In the case of preemption, the feared attack is imminent. In the case of prevention, it is more general and future-oriented. International law recognizes the legitimacy of preemptive strikes but not necessarily of preventive strikes on an enemy. Critics argued that in casting the Iraq War as a preemptive one, the Bush administration used the imagery of preemption in a situation that was more legitimately characterized as prevention, especially when it was later found that Iraq did not possess weapons of mass destruction.

Another line of criticism questioned the assertion that containment deterrence could not work against rogue regimes and supporters of international terrorism.[61] Defenders of these strategies argued that they continued to be useful, and they attributed Libya's decision to abandon its quest for weapons of mass destruction to them. Critics also questioned the assertion that deterrence could not work because of the irrational nature of these regimes; making the argument that rationality is a matter of degree and not an all-or-nothing quality. Rogue regimes concerned with their survival could be expected to act rationally enough in the face of U.S. deterrence threats.

Democratic Opposition

Formulating a single policy stance on the Iraq War proved to be a challenge that the Democratic Party was never fully able to master during the Bush administration. In part, the problem involved tactics and timing. The terrorist attack of 9/11 along with the immediate success of the invasion of Afghanistan led to a rally-around-the-flag effect put opponents of the war on the defensive. By casting opposition in unpatriotic terms President Bush was able to secure passage of the USA Patriot Act and regain Republican control of the Senate in the 2002 midterm election. Bush did encounter opposition in his plans for creating an Office of Homeland Security in the White House but it was largely institutionally based and not partisan in nature. Placed in the White House this office would be beyond the reach of congressional overseers.

Later Democratic opposition to war related policies such as warrantless wiretaps and the selection of interrogation tactics was hindered by the rules put in place for briefing key congressional leaders. The "Gang of Eight" (the leaders of the two parties from the House and Senate and the ranking majority and minority members of the two intelligence committees) were sworn to secrecy and briefed in the absence of their aides.

Political memories also undercut Democratic attempts at crafting an opposition position on Iraq. Not only were the Democrats the party of Vietnam, they were also associated with the highly politicized anti-war movement of that era. Polls leading up to the 2004 presidential election showed that while Kerry was rated higher by the public on such domestic issues as health care, social security and the economy, Bush received higher ratings on his ability to handle Iraq and terrorism. At the same time as the Iraq War progressed pressure from grass roots Democrats for ending it mounted placing pressure on the Democratic Party leadership to address the issue if they wished to hold on to their electoral political base.

Senator Russ Feingold was first to openly challenge the Bush administration in August 2005 calling for the withdrawal of U.S. troops from Iraq by December 31, 2006. John Kerry would later join Feingold and other Democrats in the Senate in calling for a July 1, 2007 withdrawal date. Representative John Murtha along with Senate Minority leader Harry Reid proposed a redeployment of U.S. forces from Iraq to other cites in the region. In contrast Senator Joe Lieberman, while still a Democrat, called for supporting the president stating "it is time for Democrats who distrust President Bush to acknowledge that he will be the commander-in-chief for three more critical years and in matters of war we undermine presidential credibility at our nation's peril."

Absent the ability to formulate a unified position on Iraq the Democrats pursued a second-based opposition strategy of calling for Secretary of Defense Donald Rumsfeld's removal and the creation of a bipartisan committee to examine U.S. policy toward Iraq and the options open to it. Such a committee, the Iraq Study Group was created by Congress on March 15, 2006 and issued its report on December 6, 2006. Just over one week later Rumsfeld resigned. The Iraq Study Group's report painted a bleak picture of the situation in both Iraq and Afghanistan. It strongly urged a large pull back of U.S. forces from Iraq and a stepped-up transfer of power to Iraqi officials so that a more rapid withdrawal of U.S. forces might be arranged.

It should also be noted that opposition to going to war with Iraq also existed within the Republican Party. This opposition was expressed most openly by Brent Scowcroft who served as President George H.W. Bush's national security advisor. In a *Wall Street Journal* essay he cautioned that attacking Iraq at this time would threaten to undermine if not destroy the global anti-terrorist campaign the U.S. had begun.[62] More generally President George W. Bush's Iraq policy created a split within the Republican Party between traditional realists (who lost) and neo-conservatives (who won).

MADISON AND BUSH COMPARED

As we noted in the beginning of this article the similarities between the Madison and Bush are remarkable. With respect to the causes for war both presidents justified their action for numerous different reasons or causes. For Madison it was the British impressment of American sailors or an invasion of Canada or the protection of the Northwest territories. For Bush it was weapons of mass destruction, the inhumane Iraqi regime, peace in the Middle East. There were also the rumored reasons like the protection of the Iraqi oil fields and other economic considerations or perhaps a personal vendetta against the inhumane leader of Iraq who attempted to assassinate his father. With so many reasons it was difficult to isolate one that served as the true cause in either Madison or Bush's case. The reasons for war in both cases are muddled and are likely to remain so.

In terms of national expectations and leadership both Bush and Madison suffered from perceived leadership problems. Madison was a legislator with no battlefield experience. Bush was someone who supposedly flew fighter jets over American airfields and not Vietnam targets. Both naively believed that American forces would be welcomed with open Canadian and Iraqi arms. Both wrongly believed that their war efforts would be short. Both suffered from a lack of preparation for the war effort; Madison in the very beginning of his war and Bush after the initial "shock and awe" campaign. Both were surprised by these sets of circumstances. Neither president asked the nation to suffer either economically nor individually for the war effort. Both left national debts as a result of their war efforts.

As far as the international setting goes both Madison and Bush failed to understand that neither international system demanded the kind of U.S. involvement that it received. In Bush's case the link between international terrorism and Iraq was manufactured. In Madison's case the British would have and did resolve the impressment situation over time. Domestically both faced political opposition. Madison faced severe opposition from the Federalist Party and there were rifts within his own party which he successfully navigated. Bush faced Democratic opposition especially as time passed after the initial campaign. Both presidents dealt with the opposition by characterizing opponents as being unpatriotic or treasonous.

In terms of strategy and military problems these abounded in both cases. Madison's original strategy was faulty. Bush's plans for a long occupation of Iraq were virtually non existent. In addition, the war effort of both presidents faced significant politicization rather than national unity.

Conclusion

We have isolated a number of variables or factors that can be used to assess whether a president engages in a war of choice. We have also suggested that this takes place on a continuum. In other words, the more of these factors that are present the more likely the war in question is one of choice. We have also suggested that Madison and Bush both engaged in wars of choice. What does this imply for their historical legacies?

The more a president engages in this type of activity the higher the chance he or she will damage their historical legacy absent other redeeming actions. Madison fares much better than Bush here. He probably gets some credit for luck with respect to the War of 1812. After all the British were mainly concerned with Napoleon and European politics thus Madison escapes the potential harsh British retributions for the war. In addition, Madison probably gets a bit of a pass for being the "Father" of the Constitution and other significant legislative accomplishments. Despite all of this Madison has never risen above an average rating as president.

President Bush is in worse shape as far as his legacy goes. Not only do we have the criticisms surrounding the effort in Iraq ,which we have cited, there are other developments that subtract from his legacy. For example two of the greatest accomplishments touted by the Bush Administration are the No Child Left Behind Act and the Bush tax cuts. By 2009 both accomplishments are viewed as problematical. The act was not fully funded and the tax cuts were leading to heavy budget deficits. When one adds the near fiscal collapse, the nationalization of the American financing system and the disastrous emergency response to the Katrina hurricane there seems to be no where to go but down in legacy for the Bush administration. Unlike Madison there appears to be a paucity of redeeming circumstances that could aid the Bush legacy.

We close by noting that presidents cannot pick the previous presidents they wish to be compared to. That is up to historians. Thus George W. Bush has less in common with President Truman (the president he wishes to be compared to) and more in common with James Madison. Unfortunately, this comparison holds the promise of diminutive historical returns.

ACKNOWLEDGMENT

Dr. Eksterowicz would like to thank his Graduate Assistant, Andrew Sullivan for his research efforts on Madison and the War of 1812.

REFERENCES

[1] Joe Klein, "Why the 'War President' Is Under Fire," *Time* (February 15, 2004).
[2] Charles Krauthammer, "Wars of Choice, Wars of Necessity'" *Time* (November 5, 2001).
[3] Richard N. Hass, *Wars of Choice; Wars of Necessity*, New York: Simon and Schuster, 2009.
[4] See the discussion of this point in John Schuessler, "When Wars of Necessity Become Contested as Wars of Choice," Paper delivered at the 2004 Annual Meeting of the American Political Science association, September 2-5.
[5] Patrick J. Buchanan, *Churchill, Hitler and "The Unnecessary War": How Britain Lost Its Empire and the West Lost the World*, New York: Crown Publishers, 2008.
[6] For a discussion of these and other reasons see, Schuessler, "When Wars of Necessity…" 1-19.
[7] Donald R. Hickey, *The War of 1812: The Forgotten Conflict*, Chicago: Illinois University Press, 1990, pp. 1-9.
[8] Gary Wills, *James Madison*, New York: Times Books, 2002, pp. 109-110.
[9] John K. Mahon, *The War of 1812*, Gainesville: University of Florida Press, 1972, p.7.
[10] J.C.A. Stagg, "James Madison and the Coercion of Great Britain: Canada, the West Indies and the War of 1812," *The William and Mary Quarterly*, Third Series, Vol. 38, No. 1, p.26, 32-34.
[11] Richard Glover, "The French Fleet, 1807-1814; Britain's Problem; and Madison's Opportunity," *The Journal of Modern History*, Vol. 39, No. 3, pp.235-236.
[12] Hickey, The War of 1812: A Forgotten Conflict, p. 11.
[13] Ibid. pp.29-33.
[14] J.C.A. Stagg, "James Madison and the 'Malcontents': The Political Origins of the War of 1812," *William and Mary Quarterly*, Third Series. Vol. 33, No.4, pp.557-585.

[15] For a discussion of the plight of the officer corps before and after the war see, William B. Skelton, "High Army Leadership in the Era of the War of 1812: The Making and Remaking of the Officer Corps," *The William and Mary Quarterly,* Third Series, Vol.51, No.2, pp.253-274.

[16] Irving Brant, *James Madison: The President 1809-1812,* (New York, The Bobbs Merrill Company, Inc., 1956), p.402.

[17] Hickey, *The War of 1812...,* p.1.

[18] Irving Brant, "Madison and the War of 1812," *The Virginia Magazine of History and Biography,* Vol. 74, No. 1, Part One, p.56.

[19] Ibid. p.56.

[20] Stagg, "James Madison and the Coercion of Great Britain…" pp. 5-6, 7, 26-27, 32-34.

[21] Hickey, *The War of 1812...,* p.1.

[22] Reginald Horsman, *The War of 1812,* (New York: Alfred A. Knopf, 1969), p.21.

[23] For a discussion of national pride and patriotism as a reason for the war see, Norman K. Risjord, "1812: Conservatives, War Hawks and the Nation's Honor," *The William and Mary Quarterly,* Third Series, Vol. 18, No.2, pp. 196-210.

[24] Mahon, *War of 1812,* p. 385.

[25] Hickey, *The War of 1812,* p. 27.

[26] Robert Allen Rutland, *The Presidency of James Madison,* (Lawrence: The University Press of Kansas, 1990), p. 88.

[27] Lawrence S. Kaplan, "France and Madison's Decision for War 1812," *The Mississippi Valley Historical Review,* Vol. 50, No. 4, p. 662.

[28] Hickey, *The War of 1812, p.47.*

[29] Rutland, *The Presidency of James Madison,* p. 89.

[30] Wills, *James Madison,* pp.3-7.

[31] Hickey, *War of 1812,* pp. 30-35.

[32] Skelton, "High Army Leadership…," p. 253.

[33] Ibid. 255.

[34] Ibid. pp. 264-65.

[35] Ibid. p. 273.

[36] Hickey, *The War of 1812,* pp. 75-90.

[37] Ibid., pp.52-71

[38] Ibid. p. 46.

[39] For a discussion of these and other Federalist criticisms see, Lawrence Delbert Cress, "Cool and Serious Reflection': Federalist Attitudes toward War in 1812," *Journal of the Early Republic,* Vol. 7, No.2, pp. 123-145.

[40] Harvey Strum, "New York Federalists and the Opposition to the War of 1812,"

[41] John Lowell, *Mr. Madison's War. A Dispassionate Inquiry,* (Boston: Russell and Cutler, 1812), passim.

[42] For a discussion of the Treaty of Ghent see, Francis F. Beirne, *The War of 1812*(Hamden, Connecticut: Archon Books, 1965), pp. 374-387.

[43] Wills, *James Madison,* p.153.

[44] James E. Campbell, "Presidential Politics in a Polarized Nation: The Reelection of George W. Bush in Colin Campbell, Bert Rockman and Andrew Rudalevige (eds.), *The George W. Bush Legacy* (Wasnington, D.C. Congressional Quarterly Press, 2008), 21-44.

[45] Gary C, Jacobson, "George W. Bush, Polarization and the War in Iraq," in Campbell, et. al., *The George W. Bush Legacy*, pp. 62-91.
[46] Condoleezza Rice, "Promoting the National Interest," *Foreign Affairs* 79 (2000), 45-62.
[47] Quoted in Andrew Bacevich, "The Real World War IV," *Wilson Quarterly* (Winter 2005), 60.
[48] Jacobson, "George W. Bush, Polarization and the War in Iraq."
[49] Colin Campbell, Bert Rockman and Andrew Rudalevige, "Introduction," in Campbell, et. al., *The George W. Bush Legacy*, p.11.
[50] Jacobson, "George W. Bush, Polarization and the War in Iraq."
[51] Richard Skinner, "George W. Bush and the Partisan Presidency," *Political Science Quarterly* 123 (2008-9), 605-622.
[52] Andrew Rutalevige, "The Decider: Issue Management and the Bush White House," in Campbell, et. al., *The George W. Bush Legacy*, 135-163.
[53] Bob Woodward, *State of Denial, Bush at War, Part III* (New York: Simon and Schuster, 2006), p. 276.
[54] Glenn Kessler, "U.S> Decision on Iraq has Puzzling Past," *Washington Post*, January 12, 2003.
[55] Woodward, *State of Denial*, p. 241.
[56] White House, *"The National Security Strategy of the United States of America,"* September 2002, *www.whitehouse.gov/nsc/nss*.
[57] Steven Hook and John Spanier, *American Foreign Policy Since World War II*, seventeenth edition (Washington, D.C.: Congressional quarterly Press, 2009), pp. 324-28.
[58] Ilan Peleg, *The Legacy of George W. Bush' Foreign Policy: Moving beyond Neoconservatism* (Boulder: Westview Press, 2009).
[59] G. John Ikenberry, "The End of the Neo-Conservative Moment," *Survival,* 46 (2004), 7–22; Francis Fukuyama, *America at the Crossroads* (New Haven: Yale University Press, 2006).
[60] On the distinction between preemption and prevention, see Lawrence Freedman, "Prevention, Not Preemption," *Washington Quarterly,* 26 (2003), 105–114.
[61] Robert F. Trager and Dessislava P. Zagorcheva, "Deterring Terrorism: It Can Be Done," *International Security,* 30 (2005/6), 87–123; and Jeffrey Record, "The Bush Doctrine and War with Iraq," *Parameters* (Spring 2003), 4–21.
[62] Brent Scowcroft, "Don't Attack Saddam," *Wall Street Journal*. August 15, 2002, p. 22.

Chapter 8

FOR LOVE OR FOR MONEY?: WILLIAM MCKINLEY AND THE SPANISH-AMERICAN WAR

Jeffrey Bloodworth
Gannon University
Erie, Pennsylvania, US

ABSTRACT

The Spanish-American War occupies complicated historiographical territory. Because foreign policy specialists realize the war's imperialist results and assume an isolationist influence upon the Midwestern-born William McKinley, their histories bear this imprint.

Despite the allure of categorizing eras into "isolationism" versus "internationalism," an examination of the 1890s milieu and McKinley's foreign policy reveals the bankruptcy of simple foreign policy dichotomies, regional stereotypes, and tidy morality plays. Indeed, during the long nineteenth century, individual Americans were thoroughly involved with and committed to transforming the wider world: the very definition of internationalism. Moreover, though "Humanitarianism" does not usually play a significant role in most historical treatments of nineteenth century international history, humanitarian sensibilities did influence American foreign policy.

In this way, Spanish atrocities in Cuba and humanitarian concerns significantly shaped McKinley's path to war. From grassroots church leaders who wrote thousands of letters urging intervention to political elites close to the president, calls for a "humanitarian intervention" were major factors in McKinley's decision-making. Thus, even though the conflict had an imperial consequence, the president's rationale should be considered separate from the war's results. McKinley took America to war under the banner of righteous humanitarianism, only to succumb to the lures of empire once the conflict ended. McKinley's humanitarian motives and hubris led him to war while also blinding him to the dangers of its aftermath.

In the spring of 1892, news of a calamitous famine in Russia reached American shores. While Congress groused about the Tsar's lackluster famine relief and even threatened to sever diplomatic relations over his government's poor efforts, the lives of an estimated 20 million peasants hung in the balance. With Congress dithering, Iowans sprang to action. Spurred by the *Davenport* (Iowa) *Democrat's* editor, Benjamin Franklin Tillinghast, and Governor Horace Boies's "Iowa Russian Famine Relief Commission," the Hawkeye State's farmers donated 3,000 tons of grain. Though Congress eventually refused to ship the foodstuffs the grain reached the starving before summer's end. [1]

The bounty's arrival elicited much hue and cry. To one hungry Russian the unsolicited aid from faraway strangers meant "Christ is risen," while Leo Tolstoy claimed Iowa's beneficence signaled the "dawn of universal brotherhood."[2] Hyperbole aside, the connection between Tillinghast, Iowa's farmers, Tolstoy, and Russia's peasants complicates a typical dichotomy in the history of American foreign policy: 19th century isolationism followed by 20th century internationalism. [3] Indeed, the episode reveals that even during the supposed "isolationist" nineteenth century, humanitarian concerns fueled a nascent internationalism and American interventionism.

"Isolationism" originally entered the political lexicon as a partisan cudgel wielded against opponents of the Spanish-American War. Thus, the term was and remains problematic.[4] Though any number of foreign policy specialists regularly debunk "isolationism" as a myth which has never accurately described US foreign relations, many historians regularly employ the term, nevertheless. From Arthur Schlesinger, Jr. who describes US foreign policy during the 1920s, as a return to the "womb[of] familiar and soothing isolationism," to Frank Ninkovich who terms late nineteenth century America "hopelessly isolationist," if nothing else, the concept's sheer ubiquity forces historians to grapple with it.[5]

Since many specialists still take the term's existence for granted and relatively few actually study it, "isolationism" generally remains what *Washington Post* editor Felix Morley once called, "something highly reprehensible that nobody attempts to define." [6] Moreover, when historians have sought to identify its sources, they have drawn a specious and poorly buttressed connection between it and the agrarian Midwest. The paucity of work on the Midwest and isolationism should hardly surprise. Decades ago, Richard Leopold presciently warned his fellow diplomatic historians, "[by] ignor[ing] the international aspects" of the Midwest, "glib generalizations" would eventually replace well-resourced understandings of the region. [7]. Thus, textbooks and monographs not only routinely depict the nineteenth century as an isolationist era; they identify the Midwest as its haven.

With the still-entrenched assumption that isolationism reigned throughout the "long nineteenth century," the 1898 Spanish-American War has become a natural point of departure separating America's non-interventionist tradition from the twentieth century's swash-buckling internationalism. Mirroring this belief, Walter McDougall cleaves US foreign policy into an Old and New Testament, in which the long nineteenth century was marked by neutrality and non-intervention while the twentieth century featured a "Crusader State" mentality and action. [8] To McDougall, the Spanish-American War was the watershed moment where "a newly prideful United States began to measure its holiness by what it did, not just by what it was." [9] Likewise, Alan Dawley pinpoints the Spanish-American War as the spot in time where the "new internationalism" replaced the "isolationist moorings" of George Washington's Farewell Address and the Monroe Doctrine. [10]

As both a watershed moment separating isolationism from internationalism and the proverbial ugly imperialist stepchild of American diplomatic history, the Spanish-American War occupies complicated historiographical territory. Because foreign policy specialists realize the war's imperialist results and assume an isolationist influence upon the Midwestern-born William McKinley, their histories bear this imprint. [11].Despite the allure of categorizing eras into "isolationism" versus "internationalism," an examination of the 1890s milieu and McKinley's foreign policy reveals the bankruptcy of simple foreign policy dichotomies, regional stereotypes, and tidy morality plays.

It is clear that nineteenth century American foreign policymakers avoided Jefferson's "entangling alliances," however, it does not necessarily follow that nineteenth century Americans were then isolationist. [12] Rather than interpreting the federal government's reluctance to enter into alliances as proof of "isolationism," a number of scholars: George Herring, James Field, and David Hendrickson, have looked beyond state officials in their assessment of US foreign policy. According to them, during the long nineteenth century, individual Americans were thoroughly involved with and committed to transforming the wider world: the very definition of internationalism. [13]

In light of this more nuanced interpretation of US foreign policy, Tillinghast's humanitarian efforts and Congress's refusal to ship the foodstuffs are explicable, as both hew to the dominant themes of early diplomatic history: individual internationalism and governmental detachment. Tillinghast's labors reveal more than this. His activism reflects the emergence of an "international humanitarian" zeitgeist which appeared in—of all places—the American Midwest. This nascent humanitarian sensibility became so powerful, on both sides of the Atlantic, that humanitarian considerations influenced the foreign policies of democratic nations. Thus, even though Congress refused to ship famine relief to Russia, Iowa's governor responded to popular pressure by creating the "Iowa Russia Famine Relief Commission." In a similar fashion, McKinley heeded public outrage at Spain's gross human rights violations by launching a humanitarian intervention.

"Humanitarianism" does not usually play a significant role in most historical treatments of nineteenth century international history. Indeed, the nineteenth century has a well-deserved reputation as the heyday of European imperialism and *realpolitik*. In spite of this reality, humanitarian sensibilities did influence Western foreign policies. Whether it was British agitation against Ottoman atrocities and the Indian suttee (the self-immolation of widows), the multilateral 1885 Berlin Treaty eradicating the slave trade, or American aid to Russian peasants, a distinctly modern version of "humanitarianism" informed many Western citizens' views of the world in the mid-to-late nineteenth century. Consequently, and in democratic societies, humanitarians influenced policy [14].While William McKinley's decision for war was not solely prompted by humanitarian concerns, the president's policymaking occurred in a complicated international milieu in which humanitarianism increasingly influenced public opinion and American foreign policy.

Spanish atrocities in Cuba and humanitarian concerns significantly shaped McKinley's path to war. From grassroots church leaders who wrote thousands of letters urging intervention to political elites close to the president, calls for a "humanitarian intervention" were major factors in McKinley's decision-making. Thus, even though the conflict had an imperial consequence, the president's rationale should be considered separate from the war's results. Rather than judge the forces for war distinct from the conflict's consequences, the dominant historiographical interpretations fail to make this division. Instead, historians assume the conflict's architects always sought an imperial outcome. Instead, they pinpoint global capitalism's inherent imperial structure and/or McKinley's expansionist designs as the war's prime causes [15].These views are not only reductionist; they betray an *inverted* Whig interpretation of history. In contrast to the classic Whig interpretation of inevitable societal progress, the inverted Whigs emphasize the opposite. In their histories, the children of darkness continually, almost inevitably, triumph over the progeny of goodness and light; a pattern of which McKinley's war was yet another example.

In addition to a general inverted Whigishness coloring the dominant interpretations, most historians of the 1898 Spanish-American War stress four basic causal categories: international, national, regional, and individual. Scholars bandying the international analytical perspective look at the "macro-analytic" global viewpoint to reveal how shifts in geopolitical structures shaped events. From the macro-analytic position, the late nineteenth century was an era of living and dying powers during which ascendant nations; the United States, challenged descending empires: Spain. For macro-analytics, the Spanish-American War was predictable. [16]

Emphasizing the intersection of the national *and* international context, William Appleman Williams and Walter LaFeber of the Wisconsin School, argue that war with Spain was part and parcel of a conscious program of imperial expansion designed to expand markets and reduce domestic tensions [17].In league with the Wisconsin School's national and international context are regionalists, like Louis Perez, who emphasize the capitalist and imperialist structure of the world system which shaped McKinley's drive for regional hegemony. For Perez, McKinley's decision for war was a "[s]hrewd, purposeful, and calculated" move to secure a "dependent socio-economic system" before Cuban freedom fighters could gain independence from Spain. [18]

The macro-analytic, Wisconsin School, and regional perspectives all share a presentist bias. Since the scholars realize the imperial war's imperial outcome, they naturally assume McKinley harbored expansionist tendencies from the start. The Spanish-American War had imperial consequences and led to a gruesome American counter-insurgency in the Philippines. This historical reality does not necessarily mean the conflict's architect, McKinley, was guided by nefarious motives. Instead, the war is a prime example of the role "irony" plays in the course of human events.

McKinley took America to war under the banner of righteous humanitarianism, only to succumb to the lures of empire once the conflict ended. In this way, the Spanish-American War neatly jives with Reinhold Niebuhr's definition of irony and history: "[t]he powerful person…is involved in an ironic contrast only if his weakness is due to some pretension of strength…it is clear that the great evils of history are caused by human pretensions" [19].

In this way, McKinley's humanitarian motives and hubris led him to war while also blinding him to the dangers of its aftermath. McKinley's declaration that his war would be fought "[i]n the cause of humanity and put an end to barbarities, bloodshed, starvation, and horrible miseries now existing there," should not be cynically viewed as a smokescreen for ulterior motives. [20] Rather the Spanish American War is part and parcel of a rich and ironic tradition in American foreign policy that George Kennan identifies. Echoing Niebuhr, Kennan claims that American moralism "rooted as it unquestionably is in a desire to do away with war and violence, makes violence more enduring, more terrible, and more destructive…than did the older motives of national interest." [21]

Unlike a Niebuhrian reading of McKinley's motives, which understands how quickly high moralism quickly devolves into selfishness and self-interest, the inverted Whigs ignore irony and moral complexity. To them, McKinley was always guided by "populism, jingoism, and imperialism," and little else. [22] Thus, the accrued weight of Social Darwinism, cultural chauvinism, missionary zeal, and American big business rendered McKinley's decision predestined and inevitable. [23] Taken together, the accumulated mass of the isolationist-internationalist dichotomy, unsupported regional stereotypes, and the inverted Whigs have so skewed the historical treatments of McKinley's Spanish-American War that James Field has rightly termed the writings on conflict and the 1890s, "The Worst Chapter in Almost Any Book." [24]

INDIVIDUAL PERSPECTIVE

In terms of the Spanish-American War and William McKinley, the individual perspective has undergone the most profound interpretive transformation. For decades, historians regarded William McKinley as little more than a tool of northeastern business interests and his political handler, Mark Hanna. Since the 1980s, revisionists, led by Lewis Gould, have successfully resuscitated McKinley's reputation. In their view, he was the first "modern" president who used the bully pulpit to shape public opinion and bend Congress to his will. For them, it was McKinley—rather than GOP philosophy, an imperialist world system, or business interests who spelled the difference between war and peace. The president historical context also substantially shaped his policy. As the leader of an emergent power which sought to expunge European imperialism from the Western Hemisphere, McKinley operated within the framework of the Monroe Doctrine and the nation's long-held, yet ambiguous, desire to "control" Cuba.

INTERNATIONAL LEVEL

Though regional and national factors were substantial, this article argues that the international context and individual level were the most significant factors shaping McKinley's decision for war. In the mid-nineteenth century, international organizations and agreements dedicated to humanitarian ideals were founded and signed across the North Atlantic world. Starting with the "World Anti-Slavery Convention" in 1840, and extending to the "International Red Cross" and the "Geneva Conventions" in 1864, Western European and American activists lobbied and convinced their governments to sign onto a series of humanitarian-inspired treaties and agreements.

Initially catalyzed by the "teeming mass of ideas" linked to the American and French Revolutions, the humanitarian "association mania," as the *London Times* dubbed it, reflected the materialization of humanitarian ideals and movement. [25] Humanitarianism was a decidedly liberal project premised on the Enlightenment's fundamental hypothesis that all human life is equal. [26] The American and French Revolutions' emphases on "natural rights" along with the emergence of the mass press, public opinion, and democratic (responsive) governments helped transform humanitarianism into a mass movement. More importantly, these ideological and institutional developments made humanitarian interventionism, governments acting to protect human life beyond its borders, both politically possible and popular. [27]

Contemporary observers have dubbed public outcry at images of human suffering and attendant calls for governmental action the "CNN effect." However, media's ability to depict individual anguish, shape public opinion, and create calls for intervention existed prior to cable news. Indeed, rising literacy rates across Western Europe and America caused the proliferation of mass media in the form of newspapers and magazines which enabled nineteenth century print media to perform the same function as television does today. In this way, Benedict Anderson's pioneering work, *Imagined Communities*, which details the ways in which media built "imagined" national communities, helps account for the creation of transnational identities and the emergence of humanitarianism. [28]

It was in this technological, cultural and intellectual milieu that a Swiss businessman, Henri Dunant, successfully founded the International Red Cross. In the summer of 1859, Dunant stumbled into the gory aftermath of a battle between French and Austrian forces. Without proper medical care available, Dunant witnessed the slow and torturous death of wounded soldiers who after days of suffering finally expired where they fell. Deeply affected by what he saw, Dunant penned a memoir of the battle's aftermath, *Memory of Solferino*, which became an unexpected bestselling sensation across Europe. Dunant sensed he had touched a nerve. Thus, in 1863, Dunant, Gustav Moynier, and other European humanitarians convened the Geneva Convention. There, they founded the International Red Cross and unveiled the Geneva Treaty. [29] As the first codified humanitarian principles of international law governing war, the sixteen signatory nations to the "Geneva Treaty and Convention" gave the International Red Cross unfettered access to treat and aid the wounded on the battlefield. [30]

At the very time Dunant was organizing the Geneva Convention, Clara Barton was also leaping into the humanitarian fray across the Atlantic. Similar to Dunant's reaction to Solferino, Barton was horrified at the primitive level of care available for Union soldiers. She took it upon herself to provide medical aid for the wounded and care for prisoners-of-war, thus, becoming a folk hero in the North. [31] After the war, Barton spent the better part of the 1870s unsuccessfully lobbying presidents to sign the Geneva Convention. [32]. In the 1880 election, Barton used her considerable cache with Union veterans to campaign for James Garfield, whom she believed might support the treaty and an American branch of the Red Cross. [33]

Reflecting America's status as an emergent power and increasing dependence on foreign trade, Garfield and his Secretary of State, James Blaine, devised a foreign policy that looked beyond the Western Hemisphere. Though Garfield signaled his intent to ratify the Geneva Convention, he was felled by an assassin's bullet. [34] Garfield's successor, Chester Arthur, however, was even more committed to cultivating ties with Europe. [35] From standardizing postal regulations and time zones to finally ratifying the Geneva Convention, Arthur made US foreign policy more closely mirror Americans' individual internationalism.

The administration backed the Geneva Convention as little more than an afterthought. Nevertheless, Barton used Arthur's treaty endorsement to found and champion an American chapter of the Red Cross.[36] By 1892, the Red Cross had become America's *defacto* provider of domestic humanitarian relief, an activity the federal government had foresworn. Indeed, in 1890, Congress had rebuffed calls for federal relief to drought-stricken Great

Plains farmers. A mere two years after Congress claimed it had "no [constitutional] authority" to aid its own citizens, the Senate voted to transport relief to Europe. The House defeated the Senate measure, leaving the Red Cross to transport Iowa's foodstuffs. Nonetheless, the vote revealed how popular humanitarian sentiment was slowly changing Congressional conceptions of federal power, relief, and foreign policy. [37]

Though Congress refused to ship famine relief, it did eventually commission the "Russian Famine Relief Committee of the United States." Headed by a former President, Rutherford B. Hayes, and Vice President, Levi Morton, as well as senators, congressmen, and Supreme Court Justices, The commission's very existence exemplified the famine relief movement's effectiveness in pushing the federal government into the international humanitarian fray. [38] Moreover, the entire Russian famine relief effort raised Barton's and the American Red Cross's visibility further convincing humanitarian activists of their ability to mobilize voters and move government to ameliorate the world's ills.

Though Tillinghast, who was involved with the Red Cross and close to its leaders, and Barton slowly brought government toward international relief work, events slowly made "humanitarian intervention" palatable to the public and policymakers. Because Russia was a signatory to the Geneva Conventions and Leo Tolstoy was literally begging for international aid, the Tsar had little choice but to accept Barton's help. Two years later, when Americans called for the Red Cross to relieve Armenians in the Ottoman Empire, Barton dealt with a government that was not only the perpetrator, Turkish officials believed American missionaries were to blame for the "troubles" in Armenia.[39]

In large part, humanitarians pushed for global action, due to the influx of news enabled them to read about and view images of human suffering as never before. During the 1890s, the international telegraph, along with the maturation of *Reuters* and *Associated Press* news services, enabled newspapers and magazines to more easily report international news.[40] For example, the *Christian Herald* and *Harper's* regularly publicized Turkish atrocities committed against Armenians. In tandem with new communication systems were advances in photographic technologies, which rendered human suffering all the more real to readers. For example, *Harper's* 1895-96 series "The Troubles in Armenia," editors used photographic reproductions and image-making to bring Armenian anguish to life.

With eleven-by-sixteen photolithographs and drawings graphically depicting the Armenians' "utter extinction," American opinion leaders, like Julia Ward Howe and Charlotte Gilman Perkins, called for American intervention. [41] Gilman believed American intervention in Armenia would "usher in the new age of global social consciousness… [by] using her great strength to protect it [liberty] everywhere." [42] In conjunction with newspapers and magazines were books, like Frederick Greene's bestseller, *The Armenian Crisis in Turkey*, which further highlighted the slaughter. Similar to Gilman and Howe, Greene called also for American involvement: "I care not what parties are in power, or how the games stands on the diplomatic chessboard, the Eastern Questions will be settled…and one more blot will be wiped out from the annals of the world."[43]

Despite the activism, Grover Cleveland refused to act. Mirroring Congress's refusal to aid Great Plains farmers in 1892, the president claimed he lacked the constitutional power to act. [44] After years of Cleveland ignoring pleas for American involvement, the 1896 Republican Platform explicitly called for action to "bring these atrocities to an end."[45] With scores of local Armenian relief organizations raising money and calling for intervention, including Tillinghast's Davenport Iowa Relief Committee, a reluctant Clara Barton finally negotiated access to the Armenians and directed the Red Cross's first "intervention."[46]

Barton's move into Ottoman territory was a significant first step toward establishing the precedent of humanitarian interventions with the American public. For example, the *New York Tribune's* editors believed the "Armenian venture" had "established the precedent that it is not necessary that two countries should be at war in order to admit of the intervention of the Red Cross on behalf of the suffering." [47] Moreover, the "right of humanitarian interventionism" was not invented in American. In the 1880s, Britain's Prime Minister William Gladstone received Parliamentary approval for armed intervention to stop Turkish atrocities against Bulgarian Christians.[48] In this way, the concept of "humanitarian interventionism" was well entrenched during the 1890s.[49]

Despite the Red Cross's intervention, an estimated 186,655 Armenians died in the autumn of 1896 alone. [50] Thus, the memory of "Armenia" loomed large in Americans' collective consciousness when their attention turned to Cuba. Indeed, in the days leading to McKinley's declaration of war, the *New York Times* equated Armenia with Cuba: "The barbarities of the Spaniard, like the barbarities of the Turk, are...essential to his rule...[a]s Europe recognizes that to put a stop to Turkish misrule it is necessary to put a stop Turkish rule...so we must recognize that to pacify Cuba Spain must go."[51] In this way, Cuban rebel leaders used the specter of "Armenia" as a propaganda tool to maintain the American public's interest in the conflict. Maximo Gomez, the leader of the Cuban insurgency, told the *New York Journal's* readers "[t]he horrors of Armenia are not as deserving of the attention of the American Congress as the barbarous and atrocious conduct of the butcher, Captain-General Weyler." [52]

In McKinley's "declaration of war" message to Congress, he referred to the "many historical precedents where neighboring States have interfered...to check the hopeless sacrifices of life by internecine conflicts beyond their borders."[53] He directly addressed the issue of violating sovereign borders in the name of humanitarian ideals, "[i]t is no answer to say this is all in another country, belonging to another nation, and is therefore none of our business. It is specially our duty, for it is right at our door."[54] In this way, the Red Cross's intercession into the Armenian crisis was yet another model and precedent for intervention into another state's internal affairs. Concurrently, it revealed the impotency of doing so solely through a humanitarian agency.

THE INDIVIDUAL LEVEL: MCKINLEY'S PATH TO WAR

Taken together, the emergence of the Red Cross, international news services, and a coherent humanitarian movement set the stage for McKinley's humanitarian intervention into Cuba. Americans' long held designs on the island coupled with domestic politics undoubtedly played a role in the president's decision-making. Still, the precedent and public support for humanitarian action existed and proved decisive in McKinley's decision for war. McKinley, though, entered office both publicly and privately forswearing any intent to intervene in Cuba or wage war against Spain: A seeming carbon copy of his predecessor's policy. While Cleveland is given credit for revitalizing the Monroe Doctrine, restraint largely defined his foreign policy and sense of executive authority. Whether he was resisting pressure to annex

Hawaii, refusing to ship famine relief to Russia, or refusing to intervene in Cuba, Cleveland retained a limited vision of presidential powers. Nonetheless, during discussions with Spanish authorities and in public statements it was he who originally made humanitarianism America's primary pretext for war.[55]

The evening prior to his inauguration, McKinley dined with Cleveland and praised the outgoing president for his restraint, telling his soon-to-be predecessor, "if I can only go out of office…with the knowledge that I have done what lay in my power to avert [war]…I shall be the happiest man in the world." [56] Though inverted Whigs dismiss this oft-cited statement as little more than cornpone, at best, and a smokescreen, at worst, historians should look no further than to McKinley's military service for proof of his sincerity.

McKinley's intimate familiarity with war made him quite hesitant to launch one of his own. Though he looked back on his service in the Union army with pride, his experience at Antietam and other minor, yet bloody, skirmishes led the president to recount "as I have grown older, I have come to understand…[that] it [war] means empty houses, empty hearts, and empty futures." [57] Despite his efforts to avert conflict, 13 months into his presidency, he signed a congressional resolution that amounted to a declaration of war. Though revisionists have restored the 25th president's reputation through a handful of balanced and sober works, insofar as the Spanish-American War is concerned, the inverted Whigs remain dominant. In their accounts, McKinley remains either a secret imperialist, feckless, or a combination of the two.

McKinley revisionists and the inverted Whigs share one thing in common, however: Little direct documentation of the president's private deliberations [58]

In life, McKinley was famous for "the masks he wore," shielding even his closest associates from his intimate thoughts. [59]. The tribune of Middle America, the *Emporia Gazette's* William Allen White, once complained even he could not penetrate "that plaster cast which was his public mask" and find the "real" McKinley.[60] The president's biographers believe a series of personal tragedies rendered the president more reserved and aloof than what was "normal" for his era. Thus, aside from his early stance against intervention, McKinley left little in the way of a personal written record through which to understand his evolving policy on Cuba.[61] Consequently, historians are left to piece together the evolution of his policy via an array of eye-witness accounts, speeches, memoranda, and educated conjecture.

With a foot in both the nineteenth and twentieth centuries, the source of William McKinley's popular appeal and basic personality has eluded many of his biographers. The modern half of McKinley might have successfully restructured the presidency; but the nineteenth century portion remained decidedly Victorian. Thus, when the president used media to build support for his agenda, he appears familiar. However, the personal side of the final Civil-War-vet-cum-president appears antiquated, especially when measured against his high-flying successor: Theodore Roosevelt.

McKinley assumed office at a key juncture in the history of American foreign policy. The nation's messianic vision to transform the world had always animated Americans' individual view of their role in the world. But by the late nineteenth century, the emergence of the United States as a significant global power alongside the materialization of mass media and non-governmental organizations made increased diplomatic activism inevitable. In this way, intervention into the Spanish-Cuba conflict was likely, if not inevitable.

While McKinley forged a modern foreign policy, his entrée into international policy, tariffs and reciprocity were the political fault lines of a different era. Similar to the way in which McKinley occupies the intersection of two political eras, in hailing from Canton, Ohio, the president's hometown straddled the junction of a modern industrial era and an agrarian America. As a Congressman, McKinley's voters were mostly farmers. However, his constituents and district also included B.F. Goodrich and Harvey Firestone, who transformed Akron into the world's rubber capitol, Joshua Gibbs, who made Canton America's foremost producer of farm machinery, and William Hoover, who based his vacuum cleaner company out of McKinley's adopted hometown. [62]

As a Congressman and Governor, McKinley focused almost exclusively upon domestic issues, such as tariffs. As a staunch protectionist advocating stiff duties on imports, McKinley was hardly distinct from his Republican brethren, who elevated such a stance to party orthodoxy.[63] As chair of the powerful Ways and Means Committee, he mastered the issue by authoring the landmark 1890 tariff bill, was commonly called the "McKinley Tariff." [64] Some critics might dismiss the Congressman's policy bailiwick as little more than carrying water for Ohio's business interests. Still, McKinley believed high tariffs protected American farmers and workers against low foreign wages. [65]

McKinley's single-minded focus upon high tariffs was only altered by James Blaine's concept of "reciprocity." Reciprocity was the brainchild of the contentious two-time Secretary of State who popularized the idea as a legislative crow-bar to pry foreign markets open to American goods. Contemporary reciprocal trade agreements are commonly associated with liberalized trade policies. For McKinley, though, reciprocity was a means to stop "free trade" which he believed resulted in "sending too much money out the country, or getting too little in, or both."[66]

While McKinley's embrace of reciprocity merely reemphasizes his long-held protectionism, it would be a mistake to narrowly associate the president's trade policy with isolationism. As America's world trade boomed, McKinley and other Republican protectionists realized they would have to allow more foreign goods into America as a carrot for reciprocity agreements and access to international markets. In a strange twist of fate, McKinley's protectionism actually led him and his administration toward greater internationalism and bi-lateral cooperation.[67]

As president, McKinley remained an internationalist and emphasized reciprocity agreements as a key to economic growth, claiming the nation could "no long[er] indulge in the sentiment that we can sell everything and buy nothing."[68] While McKinley came into office focused on relieving "the glut" through foreign trade, the issue of Cuba demanded his immediate attention. Though his formative governing experience was overwhelmingly comprised of domestic affairs, he was no small town rube controlled by business interests. As McKinley's experience with reciprocity reveals, he was a quick study who could learn and embrace new theories with relative aplomb. Moreover, McKinley ran and "dominated" his government's foreign policy, yet another attribute of the first "modern" president. [69]

The president's Cabinet revealed both his Midwestern roots and his desire to pursue Cleveland's Cuba policy: home rule (autonomy) and an end to the civil war. Indeed, with tariff policy and an international conference on bimetallism as his most pressing and immediate foreign policy issues, McKinley's choices for Secretary of War, Russell Alger, and State, John Sherman, reflects a president preparing for the hum-drum work of bi-lateral trade agreements rather than imperial expansion. [70] As a general in the Civil War and former governor of Michigan, Alger might have appeared fit for his position on paper. However, he lacked the bureaucratic and organizational capacity for the job. John Sherman's choice for State was similarly uninspired. Sherman revealed his shortcomings when he suggested threatening American intervention into Cuba for the president's inaugural address, leaving McKinley to rely upon his personal friend William Day, who served as the assistant secretary of state, to handle Cuba. [71]

McKinley sincerely wished to avoid war with Spain. The president, unlike his predecessor, had realistic hopes of maintaining party unity in the highly partisan and closely fought electoral thicket of the day even as he advanced America's strategic and moral interests. Nevertheless, his sense of presidential powers combined with the political calculus of the situation and the ongoing conflict made war likely, if not inevitable.

Historians posit that Spain's newly installed liberal government could only remain politically viable if it maintained its most prized colonial possession, a position increasing the likelihood of American intervention. Since the Cuban rebels lacked the firepower to expel the estimated 60,000 Spanish troops, who occupied well-entrenched positions in the island's urban centers, and Spain lacked the power to defeat the rebels or the political will to admit defeat and end 400 years of colonial control, McKinley's program of "escalating pressure" could only lead in one direction. [72] Further complicating the situation was the Cuban Junta, which operated in New York City. As the leaders of the Cuban rebels-in-exile, the Junta raised money and sent arms to its forces on the island, a situation that the Spanish government called for McKinley to stop. [73]

If the president had merely cared only about acquiring Cuba, he had ever geo-strategic and political reason to immediately launch a war. In addition to Cleveland's prescient warning to McKinley that "[n]othing [could] stop" war from coming, it was in the president's political interest to launch the conflict. [74] Armed with the economic and military firepower to enforce the Monroe Doctrine, if the policy were to retain any meaning, McKinley had to end the bloody anti-colonial conflict located at America's doorstep.

With Americans consistently supporting anti-colonial independence movements throughout the nineteenth century from the Greeks to the Armenians, war was a political winner. In the bubble-and-boil of Gilded Age partisan politics, control of Congress was at stake in every election. In the twenty years following Reconstruction's end and McKinley's election, Republican presidential candidates had never earned a majority of the vote and only held the Congress and the White House simultaneously for one congressional session, 1889-1891. [75] Thus, from McKinley's perspective, if the recent past was indicative of the future, the 1898 midterms could spell the end of a united GOP government. It was not only Democrats McKinley had to worry about, but the six so-called "silver" Republicans who were McKinley's implacable foes over bimetal currency *and* Cuba, and up to thirteen Senate otherwise loyal Republicans who were ready to buck their president in support of the Cuban rebels. [76]

Though historians' claims that Republican congressional leaders pushed for war to control Washington, rather than Cuba, has merit, domestic political considerations played a minor role in shaping McKinley's policy. [77] A Democratic Congress was not the equivalent of a political earthquake. The president surely wanted a Republican Congress, but he had come of age in a time where divided government was the norm rather than the exception. More importantly, McKinley had already fought in a bloody civil war and had no taste for sending American troops into war unnecessarily. [78] Indeed, McKinley told General

Leonard Wood "I shall never get into a war until I am sure that God and man approve. I have been through one war; I have seen the dead piled up; and I do not want to see another."[79]

While political and geo-strategic considerations pushed McKinley toward war, moral concerns over the human costs of continued Spanish rule, more than any other single factor, account for the timing of McKinley's decision for war. By 1897, the full humanitarian consequences of Weyler's latest offensive were coming to light and the August assassination of Spanish Prime Minister Antonio Canovas left an already anarchic political scene in even greater chaos.[80]

Similar to any other incoming president, McKinley used his initial months in office to reassess his predecessor's policy and configure his own positions. He stalled while Congress pressed the president to recognize the "belligerent rights" of the rebels. Under the paper-thin guise of investigating the death of Dr. Ricardo Ruiz, a Cuban-born naturalized American citizen who died while in custody of Spanish authorities, McKinley sent a personal envoy, William Calhoun, to investigate and report. But if McKinley were so primed for conflict, as many inverted Whigs claim, why send Calhoun? After all, America's consul-general in Havana, Fitzhugh Lee, who favored intervention, would have supplied the White House with pro-invasion arguments. [81]

Though McKinley claimed Calhoun's report would have to "differ very materially from the overwhelmingly facts already in my possession," to alter his Cuba policy, his decision to send a personal envoy is revealing. Far from an executive pushed by yellow journalism, jingoism, and big business, McKinley cautiously collected facts and calibrated policy. [82] Rather than hit the administration like a bombshell, Calhoun's May, 1897 report merely re-emphasized what McKinley already understood: with Cuba "wrapped in the stillness of death and the silence of desolation," Spain had lost sovereignty and the ongoing humanitarian nightmare had no end in sight. [83] Significantly, Calhoun believed the rebels would reject the compromise of "autonomy" meaning the bloodletting and violence would continue until Spain capitulated.

Calhoun's report, however, helped prepare the way for McKinley's turn toward war. Though the president refused to recognize the Cuban insurgency, he maintained the option to intervene on behalf of suffering Cubans. Regardless, McKinley used the report as a pretext to call for Spain's actions in Cuba to "at least be conducted according to the military codes of civilization." [84] In authorizing funds to feed and clothe destitute Americans in Cuba, McKinley might have meddled in Spain's internal colonial affairs but he stopped well short of what his pro-war foes wanted [85].

McKinley showed similar flexibility when his Ambassador to Spain, Stewart Woodford, first reported the new president's policy to the Spanish government. The president's blunt call for a resolution "in conformity…with the feelings of our people, the inherent rights of civilized man, and…of advantage both to Cuba and Spain" seemingly set the two nations on a collision course toward war; at the time, an eventuality Woodford believed would occur before December, 1897.[86] Ironically, Spanish leaders were relieved to hear McKinley's "demands." The newly installed liberal government, headed by Prime Minister Práxedes Sagasta, believed its autonomy program could meet McKinley's hopes for "Cuban peace…and protection of American interests."[87] Moreover, once Sagasta recalled Weyler from Cuba, McKinley believed Spain was committed to Cuban autonomy.[88] After hearing these encouraging signs, the president did call "intervention upon humanitarian grounds" the rationale receiving his "most anxious and earnest consideration," but he refused to recognize the Cuban insurgents as "belligerents" or endorse Cuba's outright independence [89].

While McKinley was committed to avoiding war via Sagasta's autonomy program, he was constrained by domestic politics from fully aiding the program's success. In December, 1897 Spain's Queen Regent, Maria Cristina, begged Ambassador Woodford to stop the New York-based Junta from sending arms to Cuba, a reasonable request in light of her government's rapid shift toward autonomy.[90] Though Madrid could not stop the rebellion and implement autonomy without Washington's help, McKinley, could not impede the Junta without creating a political firestorm at home. Rather than a cynical ploy to prompt war while appearing innocent, McKinley's refusal to buttress Spain's autonomy program reveals the extent to which any president is constrained by domestic politics. Unfortunately for both sides, without an American crackdown on the Junta, autonomy was destined to fail; a reality the Spanish government understood.

In the interim between Sagasta's October, 1897 negotiations with Woodford and the April, 1898 outbreak of war, McKinley's major policy moves regarding Cuba were exclusively devoted to humanitarian measures. From sending aid to American citizens living in Cuba to a wholesale aid program overseen by Clara Barton, the president might have been privately mute about his motives, but his actions reflect a leader who was unsure about the resolution of the crisis but resolutely sought to ameliorate Cubans' suffering.

MCKINLEY'S RELIGIOSITY

Inverted Whigs may see the president's humanitarianism as little more than a smokescreen for his "real" aims, but McKinley's religiosity matters. Separated from their subject by time and cultural distance, many historians have failed to fully value McKinley's decidedly middle class sensibilities. Central to understanding McKinley moral worldview is Methodism: The most popular nineteenth century American denomination. In McKinley's youth, nearly 12,000 Methodist preachers evangelized the American Midwest and frontier bringing over a million Americans to the Christian faith and the Methodist Church. Among these converts was a young Will McKinley.

In comparison to his ebullient successor, Theodore Roosevelt, McKinley is a boring fuddy-duddy. The president's Methodism, while a significant source of his deep religious faith, merely reemphasizes McKinley's Middle American roots, a cultural context which, as Christopher Lasch has noted, most scholars either implicitly distrust or refuse to understand.[91] Methodism was the religious equivalent of kudzu, growing from four ministers and 300 lay people in 1771 to 8,000 preachers and 1.5 million members 1850, making it most numerous of all American denominations.[92]

Spread by the energy and zeal of itinerant frontier preachers, Methodism found most of its converts among the newly settled frontier's petty bourgeoisie. The defining feature of American Methodism, lay preachers, leveled the differences between "gentlemen and commoner" by offering leadership positions and other trappings of social mobility to otherwise humbly-born congregants.[93] Like thousands of other upwardly mobile Americans, the McKinleys switched from Presbyterianism to become founding members of their Niles, Ohio congregation and were so active it was said "they ran the church."[94] No longer the "boiling hot religion" of the eighteenth century, McKinley's Methodism was a mass social movement fit for those "hungry for advancement" and spiritual nourishment.[95].

While the McKinley's denominational switch had a worldly dimension, the family and young Will were deeply devout. Teetotalers, fervently anti-slavery, yet religiously tolerant, the McKinley clan were the quintessential mid-century Yankee Protestants. Indeed, the minister who oversaw young McKinley's conversion and baptism, Reverend Aaron Morton, was quietly active in the Underground Railroad. Moreover, McKinley's hometown, Poland, Ohio, was not only a veritable hotbed of abolitionist sentiment his brother-in-law was a former bodyguard for John Brown.[96]

Though McKinley's Methodism might seem milquetoast to contemporary observers, his religious faith was both deep and sincere. Though he did not become a minister, as his mother had hoped, he remained a committed Christian throughout his life. As a self-described "soldier of Jesus" who served in "the psalms-singers of the Western Reserve" Civil War regiment, McKinley claimed "I felt more of the love my God in my heart at these [church] meetings than I have felt for some time."[97] In his postwar career, McKinley remained active as president of his local YMCA.[98] Indeed, the YMCA embodied McKinley's straight-arrow Protestant reformism. Ostensibly a vehicle for evangelizing unattached young men, in the decades following the Civil War the YMCA lost its proselytizing zeal in favor of a more generic "social betterment." [99]

It was McKinley's spiritual life and Christian moorings, which proved decisive in his decision to launch a humanitarian intervention into Cuba. Both McKinley's brother and his political adviser, Mark Hanna, noted that the outpouring of petitions, letters, and pressure for intervention put forth by "religious people" played a significant role in pushing the president to war. [100] Thus, it was not merely McKinley's personal spirituality that drove his Cuba policy, but that of his constituents as well. McKinley was operating in an environment in which middle class sentiment had made charity and humanitarianism the "highest achievements of civilization."[101] In this way, McKinley's hopes of stopping Spain's brutality in Cuba made intervention both viable and politically popular.

The president was a committed churchgoer whose religiosity was influenced by what Henry May called "Progressive Social Christianity." A middle class movement dedicated to enacting the New Testament's social principles via reform, the Social Gospel (as it is commonly called) had become a powerful force in late nineteenth century American Protestantism.[102] Thus, whether McKinley literally embraced the Social Gospel is irrelevant because the movement shaped the entire climate of intellectual and religious opinion. Insofar as the Spanish-American War is concerned, Protestant church leaders, influenced by this perspective, offered stirring moral endorsements for war.

One leading Social Gospel adherent, Josiah Strong, reveals the way in which church leaders brought their religious worldview to the foreign policy. Seeking to contrast America's role in the world with that of Europe, Strong called for an "imperialism of righteousness" rather than an imperialism of conquest.[103] Strong's "imperialism of righteousness" and his influential book, *Our Country* reeks of chauvinism and racist language to contemporary eyes. While Strong was undoubtedly naïve and filled with hubris, *Our Country* was a clarion call for an American foreign policy to serve as a source of good in the world. With the Social Gospel and Strong's "imperialism of righteousness" gaining sway with America's middle class and educated Protestants, a climate of opinion supportive of humanitarian activism paved McKinley's path to war.

MCKINLEY'S WAR

In conjunction with Calhoun's visit and the increasing public scrutiny of the situation in Cuba, in May, 1897, McKinley asked Congress to appropriate funds to aid 800 "destitute" Americans living in Spain's notorious *reconcentrados* compounds.[104] The policy, wholly consistent with international law, was also a first step toward intervention.[105] Soon after and with Armenia still fresh in the memories of humanitarian activists and American politicians, McKinley urged Clara Barton to visit Cuba to assess the situation and report to him. Upon her return, Barton called the island's situation tantamount to a war zone and asked for the president's endorsement to organize relief. McKinley gave his explicit and implicit approval to Barton's request. Pushing Spanish sovereignty aside, McKinley claimed "he would ignore any objection that might come from…the sending of food…and let Spain take the initiative by any overt act she might choose." [106] In late December, 1897, the president formed the Central Cuban Relief Committee (CCRC), and anonymously donated $5,000 to it. Under the direction of Barton, the CCRC was a coalition of philanthropic organizations designed to solicit and funnel charitable aid to Cuba.[107]

When historians consider non-governmental organizations (NGOs) in diplomatic history, they usually study contemporary bodies. The Red Cross and the CCRC were, however, early prototypes of what has now become ubiquitous. Lacking any legal clout, the CCRC and Barton possessed the very same "moral authority" to act and intervene that contemporary NGOs have. Thus, once both organizations entered Cuba in early 1898, the processes that Samuel Huntington terms the "transnational organizational revolution," were set into motion. Transnational organizations are founded upon values emphasizing the international bonds binding all humans together, and therefore represent ideas and values antithetical to national sovereignty. Thus, NGOs, by their very existence and nature, "act as a solvent against the strictures of sovereignty."[108] Consequently, with McKinley demanding that Spain conduct its warfare under "military codes of civilization," and then forming and sending the CCRC to ameliorate and monitor the existing crisis, the US had already compromised Spanish sovereignty over Cuba months before the war began.[109]

The CCRC's fundraising efforts lagged until Barton made vivid accounts of *reconcentrados*' suffering central to her appeals. Barton wrote of the *reconcentrados* children "[a]lmost every living child among them represents the sacrifice of a heroic mother. When there was little food the mother went without and died. The children ate and lived."[110] Though money soon poured in, officials estimated the CCRC required $20,000 per day to feed Cuba's 200,000 *reconcentrados*, a sum most considered beyond the reach of a private charity.[111] Thus, as Americans grew more involved in Cuba, the government realized private charity alone could not ameliorate the situation.

The De Lome letter and the *Maine*'s explosion are rightly credited with rousing mass sentiment for war. However, elite opinion regarding the humanitarian situation in Cuba was much more significant in shaping McKinley's policy than headlines in the penny press. Since the president had always sought the peaceful separation of Cuba from Spain and pursued policies designed to realize these ends, he had shown a disregard for popular pro-war sentiment from the time he had taken office. Deliberate and focused on ending Spain's domination over Cuba, the president slowly pursued what he believed to be an achievable goal. Hardly rushing headlong into war, it was the first-hand reports from Clara Barton and

Senator Redfield Proctor which decisively proved that Spain's autonomy program had failed. [112]

The war's proponents could have scarcely chosen a better spokesman for intervention than Proctor. The reserved and conservative Vermont senator was highly-regarded among his Senate colleagues, the White House, and the northeast business community. Consequently, those most opposed to intervention, conservatives and businessmen, were those most likely to be swayed by Proctor. The founder of what became the world's largest marble producing operation, Vermont Marble Company, and a political giant in his state, Proctor was a quintessential conservative.[113] While his conservatism was unquestioned, Proctor was privately and adamantly supporting the Cuban rebels.[114] Thus, when he announced his impending fact-finding trip to Cuba, many assumed the quiet and unassuming senator was disposed to counter American intervention.

Proctor's significant role was an accident of coincidences, false assumptions, media hype, and the senator's own sensibilities. Far from journeying to Cuba at the president's behest, Proctor extended his Florida vacation to include a tour of the island at the very last possible moment. By chance, Proctor's vacation coincided with the February 15, 1898 explosion of the *Maine*, which only increased media scrutiny of the senator's trip. Despite intense public interest in the *Maine*, the senator was in no hurry to capitalize on the combustible situation. After a week of fishing, Proctor finally set sail for Cuba from Key West. [115]

The much ballyhooed "Yellow Press" did hype Proctor's Cuba visit. Hearst's newspapers made all sorts of extravagant and unfounded claims, speculating that the former Secretary of War went to the island to plan invasion routes. [116] Rather than diagramming invasion scenarios, Proctor's two weeks were spent meeting with officials, attending a bullfight, visiting the wreck of the *Maine* and most significantly, observing *reconcentrados* conditions. In Matanzas, a city 50 miles north of Havana, Proctor saw what Barton called "all the diseases, incident to exposure, physical want and mental woe, from gaunt, lingering hunger down to actual starvation and death typical of the *reconcentrados*."[117] While visiting *reconcentrados* hospitals, the senator came upon several dead who still lay in their beds. Proctor described what he saw: "[a]ll my conception of wrong that could be inflicted on people falls short of this reality."[118]

After visiting four of Cuba's six provinces, meeting with Barton, and touring some of the worst of the *reconcentrados* camps, Proctor returned to the Capitol more convinced than ever of the necessity for intervention. Significantly, he kept his own counsel and remained mute on the subject—a stance that only added to media speculation. The senator's visit and belief in intervention hardly made him distinct. Nonetheless, his conservative bona fides, perceived relationship with the president, and the sense of drama rendered his pronouncement favoring intervention into a political bombshell. After refusing interview requests, Proctor penned a simple "statement" which he planned to release to the press. By happenstance on a Friday morning, March 18, Proctor bumped into Senator William Frye. According to Proctor, Frye literally "pushed me into the Senator chamber" to deliver his report. [119]

After a roll call which ensured Proctor of a full senate and plenty of gallery watchers, the understated New Englander let loose. Describing the "desolation and distress, misery and starvation" that was Cuba, Proctor painted the picture of a full-fledged humanitarian nightmare. He was known for his quiet, conservative, and understated manner. Thus, the senator's claim, "[t]orn from their homes, with foul earth, foul air, foul water and foul food or none, what wonder that one half have died and that one quarter of the living are so diseased that they can not be saved," rebutted those who believed the conditions were the creation of the yellow press. It was not only the religious and the moralists who were swayed; but also the business community, which finally backed intervention.

Proctor's speech rallied the business community and wary business journalists to the cause. Convinced that "an American Armenia" was festering 100 miles away, the *Wall Street Journal* and the *New York Commercial Advertiser* threw its weight behind intervention. As one New York banker, R.J. Kimball, said of Proctor's speech, "I do not remember of a speech, or document receiving in my observation and association among business men, such universal commendation."[120] Proctor's speech further solidified the moral and religious justifications for war and firmly brought the business community into the interventionist camp. With conservatives and the business community firmly backing what one Protestant journal called "the will of Almighty God that by war the last trace of this inhumanity of man to man shall be swept from this Western Hemisphere," McKinley had the moral backing of the religious and business elites [121].

Conclusion

After 13 months in office, McKinley finally opted for war. Though it is impossible to completely separate humanitarian considerations from domestic political and foreign policy concerns, the former were fundamental to the president's policy. If McKinley was solely concerned with domestic politics or simply in acquiring territory, he had ample opportunity to launch a war upon his inauguration. Why wait and further alienate silver Republicans and give Democrat's an issue? What if Spain's autonomy program would have worked and the US would have lost its chance to grab Cuba? The president chose war to end a bloody and seemingly irresolvable conflict that lay 90 miles from American shores. Indeed, with the humanitarian impetus at high tide and the Cuban revolution threatening to continue into the foreseeable future, how could McKinley have acted otherwise?

McKinley, like any human being, was pushed and pulled by self-interest, moral concerns, and above all an overweening faith in his own goodness and benevolent intentions. In the weeks between the end of the fighting and the 1898 Treaty of Paris, which officially ended the war, Americans organized "Peace Jubilees" to celebrate the conflict' close. First organized in 1869 by composer Patrick Gilmore to commemorate the American Civil War, "Peace Jubilees" were celebrations of what Gilmore called the coming "permanent tranquility." Though Boston and Atlanta hosted their own celebrations, President McKinley chose Philadelphia's "Peace Jubilee" for a major address.[122]

In his keynote, the president claimed America waged Spanish-American War so "that oppression at our door should be stopped" while warning his countrymen to "face the obligations that came with victory."[123] Echoing McKinley's self-righteous apology were the editors' of the Christian magazine *The Advance* who wrote "most Christian men believe that there are worse things than war, and that it [war] may be resort[ed] to as a last resort…for the overthrow of great wrongs, and for the defense of justice and humanity."[124].

The editors, like McKinley, remained convinced of their moral clarity and humanity's ability to pursue just ideals without contamination by base motives.

Within weeks of the "Peace Jubilee," however, McKinley struck a treaty which definitively set the nation on an imperialist path. In addition to adding Cuba, Puerto Rico, and Guam, by1899, the US, like the Spanish before them, was fighting its own an anti-colonial rebellion in the Philippines.

REFERENCES

[1] Merle Curti, *American Philanthropy Abroad: A History*, New Brunswick: Rutgers University Press, 1963 p. 114; "Another Cargo for Russia," *New York Times* April 21, 1892 , p. 8; Clara Barton, *The Red Cross, A History of this Remarkable International Movement in the Interest of Humanity; a Vivid and Authoritative Account of Relief from Suffering by War, Pestilence, Famine, Flood, Fires and other National Calamities*, Washington, D.C.: American National Red Cross, 1898, p. 178; Francis Reeves, *Russia Then and Now, 1892-1917; My Mission to Russia During the Famine of 1891-1892, With Data Bearing Upon Russia of Today*, New York: Putnam's Sons, 1917; *Final Report of the Russian Famine Relief Commission to the Governor of the State of Iowa*, June 1, 1892, Davenport: The Democrat Company, Printers, 1892.

[2] Curti, *American Philanthropy Abroad*, p. 113.

[3] Curti, *American Philanthropy Abroad*, p. 117; Barton, *The Red Cross*, p. 178.

[4] Walter McDougall, *Promised Land, Crusader State: The American Encounter with the World Since 1776*, Boston: Houghton Mifflin, 1997 p. 40-41.

[5] George Herring, *From Colony to Superpower: U.S. foreign Relations Since 1776*, New York: Oxford University Press, 2008, p. 1, 482; Frank Ninkovich, *The Wilsonian Century: U.S. Foreign Policy Since 1900*, Chicago: University of Chicago Press, 1999, p. 20; See Wayne Cole's *Senator Gerald P. Nye and American Foreign Relations*. Cole makes Europe the linchpin of American isolationism by defining "isolationists" as, people "opposed to [American] intervention in European wars." Broadening the term's applicability beyond US-European relations, Justus Doenecke claims "isolationists" are perfectly willing to act abroad but prefer do so without the constraints of multilateral agreements.

[6] David Hendrickson, *Union, Nation, or Empire*, Lawrence: Kansas University Press, 2009, p. 360-361; Ronald Powaski, *Toward An Entangling Alliance*, Santa Barbara: Greenwood Press, 1991 p. xi-xii; Justus Doenecke, "The Strange Career of American Isolationism," *Peace and Change* 3 (Summer-Fall 1975): 79. With mid-century historians such as Charles Chatfield declaring "no prominent [nineteenth century] American c[ould] be meaningfully described as [an] internationalist" and Hans Morgenthau calling the whole era an "intellectual, barren…political desert," nineteenth century isolationism has become a truism. Taken from, "Internationalism as a Current in the Peace Movement: A Symposium," in *Peace Movements in America*, ed. Charles Chatfield, New York, Schocken Books, 1973, p. 174-175; Hans Morgenthau, *In Defense of the National Interest*, New York: Knopf, 1951, p.4.

[7] Richard Leopold, "The Mississippi Valley and American Foreign Policy," *The Mississippi Valley Historical Review*, Vol. 37, No. 4 (Mar., 1951), p.626; Wayne Cole, *Senator Gerald P. Nye and American Foreign Relations*, Minneapolis, University of

Minnesota Press, 1962, p. 7; Glen Smith, *Langer of North Dakota: A Study in Isolationism, 1940-1959,* New York: Garland Pub., 1979, p. 212-213.

[8] McDougall, *Crusader State*, p. 120-121.

[9] McDougall, *Crusader State*, p. 120-121.

[10] Alan Dawley, *Changing the World: American Progressives in War and Revolution*, Princeton: Princeton University Press, 2003 p. 14-16 and 107-108.

[11] James Field, "American Imperialism: The Worst Chapter in Almost Any Book" *American Historical Review* 83 (June 1978): 644-83.

[12] Bradford Perkins, "Interests, Values, and the Prism: The Sources of American Foreign Policy," *Journal of the Early Republic,* Vol. 14, No. 4 (Winter 1994), p. 466; George Herring, *From Colony to Superpower: U.S. foreign relations since 1776*, New York: Oxford University Press, 2008, p. 2-3.

[13] Hendrickson, *Union, Nation, or Empire*, p. xiv-xv; James Field, *America and the Mediterranean World, 1776-1882*, Princeton: Princeton University Press, 1969, p. 25-26; Herring, *From Colony to Superpower*, p. 4-5.

[14] Nancy Cassels, "Bentinck: Humanitarian and Imperialist—The Abolition of the Suttee," *The Journal of British Studies*, Vol. 5, No. 1, November 1965, p. 77-87; Peter Marsh, "Lord Salisbury and the Ottoman Massacres," *The Journal of British Studies*, Vol. 11, No. 2, May, 1972, p. 63-83; Gary Bass, *Freedom's Battle: The Origins of Humanitarian Intervention*, New York: Alfred A. Knopf, 2008, p. 7; Geoffrey Robertson, *Crimes Against Humanity: The Struggle for Global Justice*, New York: New Press, 2000, p.12-13.

[15] Field, "The Worst Chapter in any Book," p. 645.

[16] Michael Mandelbaum, *The Fate of Nations: the Search for National Security in the Nineteenth and Twentieth Centuries*, Cambridge; Cambridge University Press, 1988.

[17] Joseph Fry, "From Open Door to World Systems, Economic Interpretations of Late-Nineteenth-Century American Foreign Relations," *Pacific Historical Review* 65 (May 1996): 277-303 p. 279.

[18] Louis Perez, *Cuba between Empires, 1878-1902,* Pittsburgh: University of Pittsburgh Press, 1983, p. 378-379; Louis Perez, *Cuba and the United States: Ties of Singular Intimacy,* Athens: University of Georgia Press, 1990.

[19] Reinhold Niebuhr, *The Irony of American History*, New York: Scribner, 1952, p. 154-155, 158-159.

[20] Message of POTUS Communicated to Congress 'Relations of the United States to Spain by Reason of Warfare in the Island of Cuba, April 11, 1898, p. 11.

[21] Alan Geyer, *Piety and Politics: American Protestantism in the World Arena*, Richmond, Virginia: John Knox Press, p. 60.

[22] James Field, "American Imperialism: The Worst Chapter in Almost Any Book," *American Historical Review,* Volume 83, No. 3, June 1978, p. 644.

[23] Louis Perez, *Cuba Between Empires*, p .178.

[24] James Field, "American Imperialism: The Worst Chapter in Almost Any Book," *American Historical Review,* Volume 83, No. 3, June 1978, p. 644.

[25] Douglas Maynard, "Reform and the Origin of the International Organization Movement," *Proceedings of the American Philosophical Society*, Vol. 107, No. 3, June, 1963, p. 220.

[26] Karen Halttunen, "Humanitarianism and the Pornography of Pain," *American Historical Review,* Vol. 100 No. 2, April, 1995, p. 303; Kevin Rozario, "'Delicious Horrors': Mass Culture, the Red Cross and the Appeal of Modern American Humanitarianism," American Quarterly, Vol. 55 No. 3, September, 2003.

[27] Gary Bass, *Freedom's Battle*, p.8 and 22-23.

[28] Benedict Anderson, *Imagined Communities: Reflections on the Origin and Spread of Nationalism,* London: Verso Editions, 1983.

[29] Caroline Moorehead, *Dunant's Dream: War, Switzerland and the History of the Red Cross,* New York: Carroll and Graf, 1999, p. 8.

[30] Moorhead, *Dunant's Dream* p. 23.

[31] Moorhead, *Dunant's Dream* p. 88-89.

[32] Moorhead, *Dunant's Dream* p. 92; Elizabeth Pryor, *Clara Barton: Professional Angel,* Philadelphia: University of Pennsylvania, 1988, p. 190; Moorhead, *Dunant's Dream* p. 93.

[33] Pryor, p. 202.

[34] Ira Rutkow, *James A. Garfield,* New York: Times Books, 2006 p. 73-74.

[35] Hendrickson, *Union, Nation, or Empire*, p. 261; John Rollins, *Frederick Theodore Frelinghuysen, 1817-1885: The Politics and Diplomacy of Stewardship,* Ph.D. dissertation, University of Wisconsin, Madison, 1974, p. 358-361; Pryor, *Clara Barton: Professional Angel,* p. 207-209; Clara Barton: What is the Red Cross?, Reel 68, File: International Red Cross Conferences, Sixth International Red Cross Conference, Vienna, Austria, Sept., 1897-97, Clara Barton Papers, Library of Congress.

[36] Pryor, *Professional Angel*, p. 263-65, 266; Bass, *Freedom's Battle*, p 28; George McMichael, *Journey to obscurity; the life of Octave Thanet*, Lincoln: University of Nebraska Press, 1965, p. 127; Moorhead, *Dunant's Dream*, p. 96-98; B.F. Tillinghast, "A Far-Reaching Charity," *The Midland Monthly*, p. 325-339; William Barton, *The Life of Clara Barton: Founder of the American Red Cross*, New York: Houghton Mifflin, 1922, p. 271.

[37] Extract from House Proceedings, William Jennings Bryan, Speech, January 6, 1892, Reel 81, Series IV, William McKinley Papers, Library of Congress.

[38] *Report of the Russian Famine Relief Committee of the United States*, Washington, D. C., John Hoyt, Washington, D.C., 1893, p. 1; Pryor, *Professional Angel*, p. 270.

[39] James Eldin Reed, "American Foreign Policy: The Politics of Missions and Josiah Strong, 1890-1900," *Church History*, Vol. 41, No. 2, June 1972, p. 234.

[40] Gary Bass, *Freedom's Battle*, p. 316; Pryor, *Professional Angel*, p.315-1317.

[41] Peter Balakian, *The Burning Tigris: The Armenian Genocide and America's Response*, New York: Harper Collins, 2003, p. 126; Bass, Freedom's Battle, p. 316.

[42] Balakian, *Burning Tigris*, p. 132.

[43] James Eldin Reed, "American Foreign Policy: The Politics of Missions and Josiah Strong, 1890-1900," *Church History*, Vol. 41, No. 2, June 1972, p. 235.

[44] *The Armenian Massacres, 1894-1896: U.S. Media Testimony*, ed. Arman Kirakossian, Detroit: Wayne State University Press, 2004, p. 41.

[45] Balakian, *Burning Tigris*, p. 64.

[46] Moorhead, *Dunant's Dream*, p. 99-101; Pryor, *Professional Angel*, p. 298-300; Balakian, *Burning Tigris*, p.70.

[47] Moorhead, *Dunant's Dream,* p. 103.

[48] Robertson, *Crimes Against Humanity*, p. 14-15.
[49] Ibid.
[50] *The Armenian Massacres, 1894-1896: U.S. Media Testimony*, ed. Arman Kirakossian, Detroit: Wayne State University Press, 2004, p, p. 51.
[51] "Armenia and Cuba," *New York Times*, April 15, 1898, p.6.
[52] New York Journal: The Purpose to Exterminate Rural Population, p.1" Reel 97, Series 12, Volume 20-26 William McKinley Paper, LOC.
[53] Message of POTUS Communicated to Congress 'Relations of the United States to Spain by Reason of Warfare in the Island of Cuba, April 11, 1898, p 11.
[54] Message of POTUS Communicated to Congress 'Relations of the United States to Spain by Reason of Warfare in the Island of Cuba, April 11, 1898, p. 11.
[55] Henry Graff, *Grover Cleveland*, New York: Times Books, 2002, p. 124-126.
[56] Lewis Gould, *The Spanish-American War and President McKinley*, Lawrence: University Press of Kansas, 1982, p.1.
[57] William Armstrong, *Major McKinley: William McKinley and the Civil War*, Kent, Ohio: Kent State Press, p. 127.
[58] See John Offner *An Unwanted War, The Diplomacy of the United States and Spain Over Cuba, 1895-1898*, Chapel Hill: University of North Carolina Press, 1992.
[59] Lewis Gould, *The Presidency of William McKinley*, Lawrence: University Press of Kansas, 1982, p.6.
[60] William Armstrong, *Major McKinley: William McKinley and the Civil War*, Kent, Ohio: Kent State University Press, 2000, p. 2.
[61] Thomas Paterson, "United States Intervention in Cuba, Interpretations of the Spanish-American-Cuban-Filipino War," *History Teacher* 29, May, 1996, p. 348.
[62] Kevin Phillips, *William McKinley* (The American Presidents), New York: Times Books, October, 2003 p. 14.
[63] Gould, *The Presidency of William McKinley*, p.6.
[64] Ibid.
[65] *Ideas and Foreign Policy: Beliefs, Institutions, and Political Change*, edited by Judith Goldstein and Robert O. Keohane, Ithaca: Cornell University Press, 1993, p. 91-93; McKinley Speech, The North West and Middle West in Foreign Trade, Series 4, Reel 81, William McKinley Papers, Library of Congress.
[66] "Letter Accepting Republican Nomination for President, 1896, p 12, Series 4, Speeches Reel 85, William McKinley Papers, Library of Congress; William McKinley, *The Tariff in the Days of Henry Clay and Since: An Exhaustive Review of Our Tariff Legislation, From 1812-1860*, New York: Kraus Reprint Co., 1970.
[67] Phillips, *William McKinley*, p. 113-115.
[68] Speech, The Mississippi Valley and Latin American Trade, p. 17, Series 4, Speeches, Reel 81, William McKinley Papers, Library of Congress.
[69] Offner, p. 38. Richard Hamilton, *President McKinley, War and Empire, Volume I*, New Brunswick: Transaction Publishers, 2006, p. 95-98.
[70] Gould, *The Presidency of William McKinley*, p. 16-19.
[71] Gould, *The Presidency of William McKinley*, p. 18-19; Offner, p. 227-228.
[72] Gould, *The Presidency of William McKinley*, p. 66.
[73] Offner, p.226.
[74] Offner, p. 41.

[75] Paul Kleppner, *The Cross of Culture: A Social Analysis of Midwestern Politics, 1850-1900*, New York: Free Press, 1970, p. 5-6.
[76] Offner, p. 43.
[77] Offner, p. 233-234.
[78] Armstrong, p. 18-20.
[79] Armstrong, p. 127-128.
[80] Offner, p. 51-53.
[81] Gould, *The Presidency of William McKinley,* p. 66; Newspaper Article, Starvation in Cuba, in *The Baltimore American*, Reel 97, Series 12, Volume 20-26, William McKinley Papers, Library of Congress.
[82] Newspaper Article, Preemptory Demand Will be Made that Independence of the Island Be Acknowledged, by Herbert Jervin Browne, *New York Journal,* Reel; 97, Series 12 Volume 20-26, William McKinley Papers, Library of Congress
[83] Newspaper Article, The Light Breaking in Cuba, *New York Journal And Advertiser*, June 1 ,1897, Reel 97, Series 12, Volume 20-26, William McKinley Papers, Library of Congress.
[84] Gould, *The Presidency of William McKinley*, p. 67.
[85] Relief of Destitute American Citizens in Cuba, 55TH Congress 1st Session, Senate, Document No. 86 Message from the President of the United States "Appropriations for the Relief of Desstitute American Citizens in the Island of Cuba, May 17, 1897.
[86] Offner, p. 57-58.
[87] Offner, p. 62-63.
[88] Offner, p. 77.
[89] Message of the POTUS Communicated to Houses of Congress at the Beginning of the 2nd Session of the 55th Congress, 55th Congress, 2nd Session, Document No. 1, Washington Government Printing Office , 1897. Series 14, Box 6, F Message of POTUS to Congress, December 6, 1897. Message of the POTUS Communicated to Houses of Congress at the Beginning of the 2nd Session of the 55th Congress, 55th Congress, 2nd Session, Document No. 1, Washington Government Printing Office , 1897, p. 12.
[90] Offner, p. 92.
[91] Christopher Lasch, *The True and Only Heaven: Progress and Its Critics*, 1991.
[92] Nathan Hatch, "The Puzzle of American Methodism," Church History,Vol. 63, No. 2 (June, 1994): p 178.
[93] Hatch, p. 180.
[94] William Armstrong, *Major McKinley: William McKinley and the Civil War*, Kent, Ohio: Kent State University Press, 2000, p. 7; Quentin Skrabjec, *William McKinley, Apostle of Protectionism*, p. 44.
[95] Hatch, p. 181; Skrabjec, p. 44.
[96] Armstrong, p. 7.
[97] Armstrong, p. 11.
[98] Phillips, *William McKinley*, p. 15-17.
[99] Zald, *The Political Economy of the YMCA*, p. 54-57.
[100] Hamilton, *President McKinley, War, and Empire*, p. 113.

[101] Kevin Rozario, "'Delicious Horrors': Mass Culture, The Red Cross, and the Appeal of Modern American Humanitarianism," *American Quarterly*, Vol. 55, No. 3, (September 2003): p. 418.

[102] *The Social Gospel in America, 1870-1920*, edited by Robert T. Handy, New York: Oxford University Press, 1966, p. 10-11.

[103] *The Social Gospel: Religion and Reform in a Changing America*, by Ronald C. White, Jr. and C. Howard Hopkins, Temple University Press, p. 115-116.

[104] "A Policy from the Senate," May 15, 1897, *New York Times*, p. 6A; Teemu Ruskola, "Canton Is Not Boston: The Invention of American Imperial Sovereignty," *American Quarterly*, Volume 57, Number 3, September 2005, p. 859-884.

[105] Gould, *The Spanish-American War and President McKinley*, p. 30-31.

[106] "President Plans to Stop Suffering" Reel 112, File 1898- Spanish American War a charitable act that remained secret until his death.

[107] "Minister De Lome on Charity," *New York Times*, December 29, 1897, p. 2.

[108] Steve Charnovitz, "Nongovernmental Organizations and International Law," *The American Journal of International Law*, Vol. 100, No. 2, April, 2006, p. 348; Samuel Huntington, "Transnational Organizations in World Politics," *World Politics*, Vol. 25, No. 3, (April, 1973) p. 365-368.

[109] Clara Barton, *The Red Cross*, p. 365.

[110] Clara Barton, "Relieving the Cuban Reconcentrados," The Indpendent, Clara Barton Ppaer, Seriew IV Civil War and Relief, LOC.

[111] "Cubans Dying of Hunger," *New York Times*, January 12, 1898, p.4; Offner, p. 92.

[112] Moorhead, *Dunant's Dream*, p. 104.

[113] Chester Winn Bowie, *Redfield Proctor: A Biography*, Ph.D. dissertation, University of Wisconsin, Madison, 1980. p. 1.

[114] Ibid, p. 356.

[115] Ibid, p. 356-360.

[116] Ibid, 360-362.

[117] "Cuba as Proctor Saw It," *New York Times*, March 18, 1898,p .1. Ibid, 363-364.

[118] Ibid, 363-364.

[119] Ibid, p.368.

[120] Ibid. 373-375.

[121] McDougall, *Crusader State*, p. 112.

[122] "The Jubilee at Boston," *New York Times*, Jun 16, 1869; pg. 1.

[123] Ibid, p. 5.

[124] The Advance, p. 1, Box 1, Series 13, F "Peace Jubilee" Clara Barton Papers.

Chapter 9

WAR COUNSEL:
MILITARY ADVICE IN THE WHITE HOUSE

Brent A. Strathman
Dartmouth College

ABSTRACT

Many accounts of American foreign policy prominently feature advisors in presidential decision making. Yet the question of advisory influence has not been fully examined. What is the role of advisors in decisions of war and peace?

This paper argues the extent of advisory influence is tied to how presidents ease credibility problems in the White House. Presidents and advisors have an uneasy relationship, and presidents learn to structure the foreign policy system to limit bias. The ways in which presidents inculcate trust and avoid bias determines the extent and type of advisory influence. Decisions of war and peace are connected to not only how presidents see the world, but also how presidents manage trust in the inner circle.

The logic of the argument is explored in a case study of the Spanish-American War. Unfortunately for the President, his inner circle was unable to ease the endemic uncertainty surrounding the crisis on the island. The inability of McKinley to manage the process allowed imperialists to execute their design for empire. The competition between advisors in the McKinley Administration manifested a war plan that ignored the imbalance of power between the United States and Spain.

INTRODUCTION

The night of February 15, 1898 was quiet and calm, as sailors of the USS Maine returned from a bullfight in Havana. At 9:40 in the evening, an explosion in the aft of the ship lifted the hull out of the water and tossed scores of sailors into the air. Out of 354 officers and men assigned to the ship, over 2/3 (266 in total) died in the explosion. Within six months, the United States joined the pantheon of world sea powers by defeating Spain in Cuba and the

Philippines. As the American ambassador to London would go on to say at the time, "It has been a splendid little war, begun with the highest motives, carried on with magnificent intelligence and spirit, favored by that fortune which loves the brave."[1]

President William McKinley viewed the war in a different light. When looking back at the events of April 1898, McKinley saw himself as the victim of war fever. The president did not want a war, even after an independent inquiry into the explosion of the Maine implicated Spain. Though the public wanted to fight (urged on by a sensationalist press and eager Congress), the president stalled for time, hoping diplomacy would force Spain to relent. As the crisis in Cuba deepened, the president became more uncertain in the solution to the crisis. Imperialists in Congress and the administration used this strategic uncertainty to place the United States on a war footing. In the end, McKinley approved a decision that he believed was wrong. The president confided in a former secretary that the "declaration of war against Spain was an act which has been and will always be the greatest grief of my life. I never wanted to go to war with Spain. Had I been let [alone] I could have prevented [it]."[2] For McKinley, this was a "dirty little war"[3] that he wanted to avoid.

The decision to go to war in Cuba highlights an important question of foreign policy making in the White House: who advises the president? Presidents perceive advisors differently, and these personal beliefs limit or constrain the inner circle. President George W. Bush, for example, relied heavily on those around him to make foreign policy decisions; in effect, he 'out-sourced' decision making to his inner circle. Like-minded advisors – the self-named 'Vulcans' – in the Bush Administration used their placement in the foreign policy hierarchy to support a war in Iraq.[4] But other presidents are not as dependent on their inner circle. President Kennedy famously questioned the utility of military advisors after the Bay of Pigs fiasco, warning future presidents to "watch the generals and to avoid feeling that just because they were military men their opinions on military matters were worth a damn."[5] The perception of bias limited the role of the inner circle in decisions for war.[6]

What is the role of advisors in the decision for war? How does competition between members of the inner circle impact presidential decisions? And most importantly, how does trust in advisors change executive level deliberations? This article continues in several parts. First, the paper examines the politics of advice in the White House. Political advising is an interaction between what a president wants to hear, and what an advisor can provide. But leaders are naturally wary of their advisors, concerned with personal and professional bias. As a result, presidents learn to structure the foreign policy hierarchy to limit bias by either quieting or encouraging competition between advisors. Decisions of war and peace are connected to how presidents manage trust in the inner circle.

The logic of the argument is explored in a case study of the Spanish-American War. McKinley was unsure of the proper solution to the Cuban problem. Unfortunately for the president, his inner circle was unable to ease the endemic uncertainty surrounding the crisis on the island. Though Congress, members of the media, and the American public wanted war, McKinley was unconvinced that force could solve the 'Cuba problem.' The attack on the USS Maine changed the decision. Political elites used the sinking of the Maine to push a new doctrine of American power, putting "their shoulders to the wheel of the wagon of jingoistic ballyhoo"[7]. The inability of McKinley to manage the process allowed imperialists to execute their vision of American grand strategy. This drive for empire, hidden behind a moralist veneer, led McKinley to approve a war that he dreaded.

An examination of the Spanish-American War is important for two reasons. First, conventional explanations of the "splendid little war" argue that public opinion – aroused by Congress and the media – was responsible for the decision. But a focus on advisors provides a different interpretation. Internal debate between competing conceptions of American interest split the McKinley Administration. Importantly, McKinley's mismanagement of the advisory system magnified the disagreement. The president was unable to find a solution to the 'Cuba problem', mostly due to the selection of the inner circle and his management style. The Spanish-American War is a prime example of how unchecked competition within the White House can lead to a military adventure.

And second, an exploration of the McKinley White House provides leverage on the question of who is responsible for quagmires: leaders or advisors? While the Spanish-American War was successful, the aftermath was not, as the United States becomes trapped in a lengthy engagement in the Philippines. In American foreign policy, it is common to blame advisors for quagmires. For example, McMaster argues that advisors did not do their duty, unable or unwilling to persuade President Johnson to change his Vietnam strategy.[8] Failed advising was responsible for the adventure in Southeast Asia. Likewise, conventional explanations of the Iraq War focus on the competition and machinations of neo-conservative advisors. According to these accounts, advisors played a large role in both planning the war, and persuading the president to approve their plan. A case study of decision making in the Spanish-American War examines the validity of the claim, while answering why these engagements persist.

THE CREDIBILITY PROBLEM IN THE WHITE HOUSE

French President Georges Pompidou once remarked there were three ways for a politician to ruin his career: chasing women, gambling, and trusting experts. He continued, saying "The first . . . was the most pleasant and the second the quickest, but trusting experts was the surest."[9] Pompidou realized experts and advisors have their own biases, and leaders who fail to question their inner circle risk mistakes. The question of who to trust – what I call the credibility problem of advising – is a constant feature of presidential decision making.

The dilemma facing presidents is not different from other, more mundane choices that feature information asymmetries and biased advisors. One example is investment planning. For most individuals, investment planning is complex and uncertain. Individuals not only lack basic knowledge of the available options, but the variety of choice is prohibitively large. More importantly, most of us do not have the time or resources to fill this information gap. The decision is too difficult without outside counsel. The solution is to hire an expert, such as an investment manager, to recommend a set of options that maximize returns. In other words, most individuals out-source their decisions to an expert. The decision making process closely resembles 'Judge-Advisor' models from organizational psychology [10] Instead of comparing and contrasting specific options, the decision maker evaluates the validity of the expert. Experts, in effect, act as cognitive shortcuts, collecting relevant information and generating a recommendation. In terms of investment planning, the decision to invest in a stock is tied to perceptions of the investment manager.

Decision making in the White House follows a similar process. Whenever a decision arises, bureaucracies mobilize to collect information and forward policy recommendations. These alternative policies are then relayed to the president through key members of the foreign policy team. In making the decision, presidents solicit two types of information: incoming intelligence on the strategic problem, and advice on which policy option would be most successful. But the credibility problem changes the decision, and leaders attribute sinister motives to members of the inner circle.[11] As a result, decision makers discount or under-weigh contributions from counselors because they are unable to trace the reasoning behind the recommendation; a psychological effect known as egocentric discounting.[12] More importantly, dysphoric cognition increases mistrust and paranoia.[13] Instead of collecting all relevant information and constructing a decision that best serves the nation, presidents are forced to evaluate their inner circle. In effect, decision making is a task of selecting which advisor (or advisors) to follow, and leaders who do not have faith in their advisors suffer from decision making errors [14] Foreign policy is a product of nested and competitive social relationships between advisors and leaders where trust is the coin of the realm [15].

One of the main tasks of presidential decision making is to inculcate trust by eliminating the bias created by the advisory process. Presidents traditionally reduce bias by either minimizing or encouraging conflict. In the first approach, leaders limit the competition between advisors by emphasizing consensus. Debate and disagreement are kept at a minimum, and leaders pressure advisors to create consensus. Advisors do not persuade or compete with other members of the White House; instead, counselors bolster a decision or policy that a president has previously made. By keeping debate at a minimum and dominating their subordinates, presidents minimize bias.

In this view, advisors censor discordant views, hoping to make the decision making process easier and more efficient. In effect, presidents that dominate their advisors limit their role in decisions for war. For example, President Lyndon Johnson silenced dissenters in his administration through his dominating personality and 'Tuesday lunches' [16] By quieting dissent, the president could concentrate on his plans for the 'Great Society' and maintain a positive view of Vietnam. Daalder and Lindsay argue that the Bush Administration followed a similar pattern [17] The Bush inner circle was responsible for verifying central pillars of neo-conservatism. Advisors simply mimicked the beliefs already held by the president.

But consensus is difficult to enforce or guarantee. Some presidents instead prefer multiple advocacy, encouraging an array of viewpoints supported by motivated proponents [18]. Instead of eliminating disagreement, presidents structure the process to guarantee active competition among bureaucracies. In these structures, advisors fill 'institutional roles,' representing their bureaucracies as faithful agents [19]. The pulling and hauling among advisors creates a marketplace for opinion that dilutes or balances individual bias. Successful and effective presidents learn to use the competition within the inner circle as a sounding board, matching the structure of the advisory process to their personality [20].

The key to effective decision making in this perspective is the experience of the president in managing competition. For example, President Kennedy changed his advisory process after the Bay of Pigs fiasco to compensate for group decision making errors [21] Kennedy recognized the danger of consensus, implementing new rules for ExComm to produce better decisions. The president took an active role in guaranteeing the free flow of ideas, and minimizing the conditions that quieted debate. But the mere presence of competition does not guarantee effective advocacy. Instead, leaders must judiciously and carefully arrange advocates to limit any bias introduced by an unequal distribution of advisor capacity and viewpoints [22]. By opening up the decision making process to many actors, leaders cancel out advisory bias.

Presidents ease the credibility problem – the question of who to trust – either by limiting advisory opinion, or diluting it. But solutions for the credibility problem present their own difficulties. For example, presidents with too much control of the process will unduly quiet or limit valid viewpoints; they receive bad advice from counselors who refrain from speaking truth to power. Policy stagnates, unable to evolve and change. Moreover, a competitive inner circle is difficult to control. Effective advising requires a hierarchy that complements the strengths of the president [23] Though competition among advisors minimizes the effect of bias, it places a strain on presidents who must balance the egos of the inner circle. A competitive advisory structure can backfire on presidents without prior experience, leading to problems such as groupthink or deadlock [24] Presidents can create a marketplace of ideas that rewards well-considered foreign policy, but only when they force advisors into specific roles. Otherwise, competition increases backbiting and discontent in the inner circle.

The Spanish-American War illustrates the problems associated with an inexperienced president that incorrectly manages the advisory system. McKinley was unsure of what to do regarding the Cuba problem. The president realized the United States was at a military disadvantage, as Spanish forces outgunned the American military. But McKinley's advisors did not ease his uncertainty. The president was confident in his leadership, appointing advisors that were unprepared for the rigors of foreign policy. In effect, the president eliminated bias by appointing weak advisors that he did not intend to follow. As a result, the president ignored the advice of his inner circle, and as the crisis on the island deepened, McKinley stalled the decision to go to war.

More importantly, the decision to rely on his own judgment provided a space for rivals who supported an expansionist foreign policy doctrine. As diplomacy continued, media reports of Spanish atrocities inflamed American public opinion. Imperialist allies in Congress and the Department of Navy used this opportunity to push a new offensive grand strategy.

MILITARY ADVICE AND THE SPANISH-AMERICAN WAR

What convinced the president to go against his better judgment and commit the United States to war? A decision that not only went against his own pacifism, but also created an empire that many in the United States did not want? The case study is divided into two parts. The first section reviews the events leading up to the explosion of the USS Maine. The debate over the 'Cuba problem' reflected a growing division within the government over the future of foreign policy. McKinley and his allies believed the United States did not have enough military power for an offensive grand strategy; he was wary of Spanish power in the Caribbean, and believed diplomacy provided the best solution to the conflict. But his imperialist opponents (best personified by Theodore Roosevelt, Henry Cabot Lodge, and Alfred T. Mahan) disagreed.

The United States needed a new, offensive grand strategy to not only protect the Caribbean from European influence, but also gain access to Asian markets. War provided the best means to accomplish both. The second part of the case study argues McKinley wilted in the face of his opponents, largely due to his own failures in selecting and using his advisors. In general, McKinley never solved the credibility problem, and the muddled decision to commit to war was soon followed by a quagmire in the Philippines.

A Disagreement of Doctrine

American interest in Cuba began well before 1898. In 1820, Thomas Jefferson echoed popular sentiment when he told Calhoun that "[we] ought, at the first possible opportunity, to take Cuba."[25] In the years leading up to the Civil War, many political elites considered an expansion into Cuba – with its large slavery population and natural resources – as economically and militarily wise. The United States gained territory and supported the Monroe Doctrine by forcing the Spanish out of the Caribbean. Several presidents even approached Spain to purchase Cuba, with the most serious proposal coming from Polk who offered $100,000,000 for the island [26].

American foreign and domestic policy struggled with the 'Cuba problem' in the years directly prior to the Maine explosion. As the insurgency in Cuba gained strength, conflict between Americans and the Spanish fleet increased. American gun-runners were frequently fired on by the Spanish navy as they fled their docking ports. On several occasions, these confrontations nearly ended in war. For example, Spanish authorities captured the Virginius off the coast of Jamaica in 1873. Spain charged the crew with piracy, eventually executing over 50 crewmembers. The capture and trial of the ship enraged the American public, but President Ulysses Grant resisted using force. The crisis ended after officials discovered the ship's registry was fraudulent [27].

A bigger problem for American diplomacy was the humanitarian crisis on the island. Continued domestic instability encouraged Spanish leaders to strong-arm insurgent groups. In February 1896, 'Butcher' Weyler was given control of the island. To end guerrilla activities, Weyler began a program that herded rural Cubans into camps, where starvation and torture were common. Soon, a majority of Americans received daily reports of Spanish atrocities from the cadre of bored reporters sent by Hearst's Journal and Pulitzer's World. Weyler instituted harsh censorship policies as a response – which only forced reporters to fabricate stories for an eager public [28] Personalized accounts of Spanish policies convinced the masses that a response was morally necessary. Leagues and groups arose across the American West pleading for action and collecting money to help the cause. Relief agencies even persuaded McKinley to donate money [29].

The president was not immune to the current of opinion. On the contrary, McKinley carefully studied mass opinion for direction, reading newspaper editorials and making public appearances [30] Some historians argue this fascination with the electorate and the public mood was the secret to his success as a politician. By understanding what the public wanted, McKinley could deftly change his policies to match trends in public attitudes. Yet the president did not relent to the war fever gripping the country. Personal experiences during the Civil War traumatized McKinley, convincing him that war was not to be celebrated. When speaking with confidantes, this pacifist streak stood out. As the president remarked to a friend, "I shall never get into a war until I am sure God and Man approve. I have been through one war; I have seen the dead piled up; and I do not want to see another."[32]

But there were other reasons for his lack of enthusiasm. First, the American military was weak and poorly funded. In 1898, the army stood at 28,000 troops with roughly 100,000 members in the National Guard. In comparison, Spain had 80,000 to 150,000 troops in Cuba [33]. Some newspapers even compared American uniforms to "cavemen" skins and their weapons to clubs [34]. Though the American Navy fared better (enjoying newer technology, a better trained corps, and more 'modern' battleships), Spain had more ships (in tonnage and number), and they were more maneuverable in battle. On the eve of the war, one American admiral wrote his wife "It is impossible for me to give you an idea of the surprise and consternation experienced by all on the receipt of the order to sail ... for nothing can be expected of this expedition except the total destruction of the fleet or its hasty and demoralized return ... With a clear conscience I go to the sacrifice."[35] Moreover the American economy continued to struggle in the aftermath of the 1893 economic depression. War would be bad for business, and powerful business groups urged the president to withstand the public clamor. Henry Cabot Lodge noted this reluctance in his account of the war, arguing the only brake on the march to war were business interests who "exerted their great force to stop every forward step along the inevitable path."[36]

Yet there was a deeper issue within the Administration. Officials struggled with defining the role of the United States in world affairs, and the instability in Cuba brought this disagreement into relief. For McKinley, the United States was unprepared for the demands of an empire. Militarily and economically, the United States could not compete with other great powers. Supporting an insurgency in Cuba did not advance American interests, nor did it improve commercial and military power. The best balance between the demands of the public and the wishes of business groups was diplomacy. As a result, McKinley hoped to pressure Spain to change their Cuba policy without resorting to the use of force.

Influential imperialists in Congress and government disagreed. War would be good for the country and satisfy the demands of Manifest Destiny. McKinley was too timid, and many agreed with Theodore Roosevelt's characterization that the president had "no more backbone than a chocolate éclair"[37]. More importantly, war justified greater military spending and a stronger role in international affairs. Cuba was an opportunity to extend American power and implement a new, global policy that balanced European gains [38] The greatest threat to American power was not Spain, but rather a rising German presence in the Caribbean. Roosevelt told Captain Alfred Mahan "Until we definitely turn Spain out of those islands (and if I had my way that would be done tomorrow), we will always be menaced by trouble there . . . by turning Spain out [we] should serve notice that no strong European power, and especially not Germany, should be allowed to gain a foothold by supplanting some weak European power" [39] The United States would best be served through military action and an offensive military doctrine; the greatest threat to American power was the failure to not do enough.

Cuba presented a dilemma for the president. The growing discontent in the public and government could best be satisfied through war. An offensive strategy in the Caribbean not only ended the humanitarian crisis on the island, but also served notice to European powers. But war with Spain was risky. A failed effort to release Cuba from the Spanish — a likely outcome considering the weak American military — would encourage other European states to extend their influence into the region, sap American military and economic strength, and weaken McKinley's chances for re-election.

The dilemma was particularly acute for the president. McKinley was inexperienced in foreign relations, and his political rivals used this inexperience to their advantage. His real forte was domestic politics and outflanking his opponents through public opinion. More importantly, McKinley preferred to micromanage decision making, trusting his own ability to read the political environment [40]. In choosing his cabinet, McKinley opted for well-known public figures, hoping to weaken domestic political opponents and minimize disagreement within the White House. For his Secretary of State, McKinley appointed John Sherman, a noted Senator and member of the Senate Foreign Relations Committee who was widely seen as the most able statesmen for the post. Though critics noted his advanced age (74), many believed Sherman increased the international and domestic stature of the president.[41] Secretary of War Russell A. Alger (a war hero, successful businessman, and a candidate for the Presidency) and Secretary of the Navy John Long (a popular governor of Massachusetts and Congressman with no previous experience with matters of the Navy) were chosen for similar reasons. By placing Sherman, Alger and Long in the cabinet, McKinley maintained control of the decision making process and ended the critiques of his inexperience.

McKinley's cabinet was a carefully constructed political ploy to quiet his critics. Yet his own foreign policy inexperience, combined with the inexperience of his main advisors, only complicated the Cuba decision. These factors would come to a head after McKinley ordered the USS Maine to Havana in late January 1898 as a response to rumors of a German-Spanish treaty [42] Within 45 days of the explosion, Congress increased defense spending; within 70 days, Congress declared war.

FROM PEACE TO WAR

On December 6, 1897, McKinley delivered his annual address to Congress. A significant portion of the speech reviewed Administration policy concerning Cuba. Though popular opinion and certain elements of Congress pushed war, the incremental approach favored by McKinley was effective. Diplomatic pressure and military threat forced Spain to recall Weyler, end the policy of concentration camps in the cities, and granted the release of American prisoners [43] More importantly, a change in policy risked war. The most dangerous option – and the one favored by many in Congress – was recognition of the insurgents as legitimate representatives of Cuba. In the speech, McKinley connects recognition to war; a step that he was unwilling to take [44]. War was too risky, the benefits were too few, and in his speech, the president reminded Congress that few options just short of armed conflict remained on the table.

But the argument of the president changes. By March 26, 1898, McKinley offered ultimatums, urging the Spanish to give up its fight against guerrillas and institute reforms. "The concentration of men, women, and children in the fortified towns and permitting them to starve is unbearable to a Christian nation," he wrote. "All this has shocked and inflamed the American mind, as it has the civilized world."[45] On April 11, 1898, McKinley asked Congress for the authority to commit war. The speech outlined Spain's broken diplomatic promises. For McKinley, it was now necessary to end the humanitarian crisis on the island, extend rights of self-determination to the Cuban people, protect American commercial activities, and end the threat to the homeland caused by the conflict on the island. The explosion of the Maine was "impressive proof of a state of things in Cuba that is intolerable ... thus shown to be such that the Spanish government cannot assure safety and security" of their own seaports.[46] Diplomacy failed to solve the Cuban problem, and war was justified by the continued failures of Spanish authorities.

What caused the dramatic change in American policy? How did McKinley – the noted pacifist – become a proponent of an offensive strategy? Previous explanations of the war generally focus on the political pressure brought to bear by domestic actors. Congress realized the explosion of the Maine presented an opportunity, and imperialists in both legislative bodies pressured the president. Congress simply needed to reflect the mood of the day to push the president into war, since the public "had made up their minds that the only real and possible solution was the end of Spanish rule in Cuba."[47] Soon, Congressmen began to frame the intervention as a moral crusade. The most notable political ploy was a speech delivered by Redfield Proctor on March 17. Proctor, who visited the Cuban reconcentrado camps in December 1897, spoke of his travels, combining appeals to national security with moral truth – war would open "opportunities among a capable people whose racial and temperamental characteristics were compatible with those of Americans."[48] The speech continued by denouncing McKinley and his connection to American big business. McKinley clearly felt the impact of the speech, lamenting to a friend "Congress is trying to drive us into war with Spain ... and we haven't enough ammunition on the Atlantic seacoast to fire a salute"[49].

More importantly, members of the media used the Maine tragedy to stoke anti-Spanish public opinion. The 'Cuba problem', hyped by newspaper headlines, was a microcosm of the frustration at social and economic conditions at home. Sensational reports provided by the media only confirmed popular perceptions of Spain. As a result, many histories of the Spanish-American war argue that McKinley was forced to declare war. President McKinley had no other choice but relent to popular demand arising everywhere in the United States [50].

But for others, this was McKinley's war. The image of McKinley as an inexperienced president pushed around by an agitated public does not fit with historical accounts. McKinley did have control of the process, and he continued to resist the call to arms by pushing back at political rivals. For example, on April 13, the Senate Foreign Relations Committee (moved by powerful imperialists such as Lodge) recommended the president intervene in Cuba and support the independence movement, introducing legislation that would essentially force the president to take action. Though Congressional imperialists advised the president that war was the surest and best way to solve the Cuban crisis, McKinley recognized the weakness of the American military. The president believed the United States would get involved "when it could fight in a manner that would allow it to shape foreign affairs in crucial and long lasting ways"[51]. Diplomacy was a stalling tactic that protected business interests, while providing time for a military buildup. A much weaker Joint Resolution eventually passed both legislative bodies on April 19th, but only after Congress relented by dropping the call for recognition [52].

War became "unavoidable" only after McKinley made the decision that Spain needed to relinquish Cuba [53] The question, then, turns to what changed in McKinley's mind; what made war unavoidable. Indeed, very little had changed on the ground. The arguments used by

McKinley to resist war did not waver in the months following the explosion in Havana harbor: the military balance continued to favor Spain, business interests were still threatened by an independent Cuba, and war with Spain favored the expansionists. A better explanation for McKinley's change is found in the relationship between the president and his inner circle.

McKinley's choice of advisors haunted him on the eve of war. To limit biased opinion, the president appointed weak and inexperienced advisors; advisors that he could easily dominate. But as diplomacy stalled and conditions on the island worsened, McKinley became confused over the direction of foreign policy. Unfortunately, the inexperience of the inner circle could not help the president in his decision making, and McKinley began making strategic missteps. For example, Alfred Mahan argued the fascination with Havana was a mistake. An attack on Puerto Rico should have been the first move, due to its geo-strategic position as a base for supplies and reinforcements. The US would have been better off by dropping the cause of Cuban independence and competing with the declining Spanish empire. If the US used a strategic rationale for war, "our leading object in such case would not have been to help Cuba, but to constrain Spain."[54] By not appointing experienced advisors, McKinley was unable to formulate an efficient policy.

More importantly, problems in war planning were exacerbated by the mismanagement of the military. The navy, while professional and top-heavy with an experienced officer corps, suffered from a lack of ships and ammunition. The destruction of the Maine reduced the American fleet to seven armored battleships, giving the Spanish navy a large advantage in the Caribbean. The United States not only had fewer ships, but also no reserve forces on the east coast. According to Mahan, the Spanish did not realize "the fact that we had not a battleship in the home ports that could in six months be made ready to replace one lost or seriously disabled."[55] He continued, "If we lost ten thousand men, the country could replace them; if we lost a battleship, it could not be replaced."[56] The War Department and Department of the Navy rushed to purchase more ships, only to find a bidding war with Spain [57] A bigger problem for the navy was a lack of ordnance. Even with an imminent war, the navy could not adequately arm their ships. Indeed, Dewey began the Battle of Manila with his ammunition holds half full [58].

The army was likewise poorly funded, ill-prepared, and disorganized. Army supplies could not meet demands, and soldiers confronted too little food, too few cots, and too few supplies for war. As Gould remarks, "Had all the soldiers who had been mobilized seen combat, there would not have been enough bullets for them."[59] And more importantly, officers were unable to deal with the mass of men that they now commanded. Officers could not even efficiently load troops onto boats, stalling the invasion several times. As conditions worsened at army camps in Tampa (the staging area for the invasion), McKinley grew frustrated, finally ordering the flotilla to leave with whatever force they could in early June. Though McKinley was the first modern war president (directing the war from the White House), he was continually thwarted by a pre-modern requisition system that weakened troop strength and mobility.

The choice of military advisors not only created uncertainty and military mismanagement, but also exacerbated competition within the administration. The critics were correct in their judgment of both Sherman and Alger. Secretary Sherman began to experience memory less and decaying mental acuity, largely due to the added stress of the foreign policy crisis [60] More and more duties fell to the Assistant Secretary of State, William R. Day. While Day was a longtime friend and confidante of McKinley, [61] he was inexperienced in foreign policy; his only previous experience in government was his post as a federal district judge. Secretary of War Russell A. Alger suffered a similar fate, wilting under the demands of his position. A declaration of war required a reorganization of the Department of War to equip a military that would become ten times the size of current force structures [62] Alger was not up for the job, and instead, Elihu Root took on many of the duties of the Secretary.

John Long likewise struggled with the pressures of his office, often looking to medical doctors to ease his pains. As a result, Long was often absent from the decision making. The real power belonged to his Assistant Secretary, Theodore Roosevelt. While McKinley disagreed with Roosevelt's approach to politics, he was experienced in naval affairs and many supported the young Roosevelt's position. Roosevelt's first public address as the Assistant Secretary brought this difference into relief. Where McKinley dreaded war, Roosevelt celebrated it as an activity to strengthen the nation. "War is the most effective means to promote peace," according to Roosevelt, and "It is through strife ... that a nation must win greatness" [63] Importantly, Roosevelt had allies in government and Congress. His friendship with Mahan gave him an ally on the Board of Directors of the Navy, while Henry Cabot Lodge supported his imperial vision of American power in Congress. And when war seemed likely, Roosevelt took advantage of his position.

In January, the Assistant Secretary wrote a letter to Long outlining a deployment plan for the navy to destroy the Spanish fleet and invade Cuba, hoping to push an activist role for the navy in any upcoming conflict. And when Long failed to show up to his office (due to a doctor's visit) on Feb. 25th, 1898, Roosevelt used his position to implement a policy of expansion [64] Without Long's knowledge, Roosevelt contacted Dewey, ordering him to assemble his fleet and prepare for offensive operations. Long was shocked by the actions of his undersecretary when he returned to his office the following morning, remarking that Roosevelt "has come very near causing more of an explosion than happened to the Maine ... the very devil seemed to possess him."[65] Only the charisma and ambition of the Assistant Secretary was necessary to place the Navy on a course for war [66].

Roosevelt continued his push for an offensive doctrine, regardless of the president's intentions. For example, Roosevelt publicly attacked Senator Mark Hanna at a public appearance in March, imploring the White House and opponents in Congress to step away from business interests [67] The advisory system, built from McKinley's belief in his own ability to read and respond to public pressure, provided a space for Roosevelt to compete successfully against the more staid, conservative diplomatic solution to the Cuban problem. McKinley eventually relented to the beat of war drums.

The decision to go to war with Spain did not emerge solely from national tragedy, nor from a sense of moral outrage. And it did not arise from a favorable balance of power; the United States did not have a material advantage in the sea or on the ground. Instead the decision for war resulted from an internal battle between competing conceptions of American empire. The president assumed he could dominate his cabinet and rely on his own policy judgments. Yet his choice of advisors, combined with his own inexperience in foreign policy, provided a space for imperialists to satisfy their own vision for American foreign policy. A war that began with freeing Cuba from Spain ended in a global war of expansion, fueled by imperialists in Congress and the foreign policy bureaucracy [68]

CONCLUSION

This paper began by asking the question of how the competition between advisors impacts presidential decisions for war. Put simply, who do presidents trust in their decision making? In general, three broad conclusions can be drawn from the example of McKinley and his management of the advisory system.

1. Solutions to the Credibility Problem Present Their Own Difficulties

Conventional accounts argue that domestic actors were responsible for the Spanish-American War. Congress and the media used the humanitarian tragedy on the island and the explosion of the Maine to their advantage. Redfield Proctor's speech in March, combined with media accounts of Cuban atrocities, influenced public attitudes concerning war [69] McKinley recognized his chances for re-election would increase with a declaration of war. It made political sense to pursue a military solution.

But the historiography provides a more complicated account of the decision. For example, public opinion was generally calm in the weeks following the destruction of the Maine. Instead, the precipitating event was the release of the report on the explosion in March 1898. Only after the board of inquiry released their findings did the public blame the Spanish [70] In other words, Congress and the media did not create the public support of war; they followed a trend that was already present. More importantly, McKinley resisted public opinion. The president recognized the United States military was unprepared for war. A devastating military loss to the Spanish (a likely consequence) would hurt his chances for re-election. An offensive grand strategy only satisfied a vocal minority, while limiting his political future. Though public opinion was a contributing factor to McKinley's decision, it was far from decisive.

A focus on advisors provides a different interpretation of war-making in the White House. In general, the inner circle is a cognitive shortcut, collecting information and forwarding policy recommendations. Unfortunately, the information gap creates doubt and suspicion; what I termed the credibility problem. And in the McKinley White House, solutions to this credibility problem only created confusion. McKinley was a micro-manager, relying on his own political skill to read the political environment. But his top-down control of the foreign policy process manifested uncertainty. First, his major foreign policy advisors were inadequate, chosen for their political symbolism rather than their insight. His Secretary of War and Secretary of State were incapable of aiding the president. As a result, McKinley struggled with the decision, stalling the decision to commit war, even going so far as to ignore his advisors for days before committing to minor strategic decisions, such as the decision to send Dewey to the Philippines in April 1898 [71].

This lack of direction encouraged competition between members of the foreign policy bureaucracy. It was not uncommon to find lower levels of the administration flouting bureaucratic rules and going beyond their job descriptions [72] And more importantly, an imperialist coalition rose to take advantage of the vacuum and push McKinley towards war. The offensive grand strategy that produced both the drive to Havana and occupation of the Philippines was a product of individuals with strategic positions in the government. First,

Henry Cabot Lodge used his position on the Senate Foreign Relations Committee to rally Congressional support for war. Mahan, a well-known figure who published articles in popular magazines, was the intellectual energy behind the strategy. The ex-Navy flag officer supplied the strategic rationale behind an offensive grand strategy, and publicly supported Senator Lodge. But more importantly, Mahan gave political cover for Theodore Roosevelt. Roosevelt used his position to move the navy into a war-footing, while arguing within the Administration for an offensive grand strategy. In effect, this 'trinity' – Lodge provided the moral reasoning for war, Mahan the military doctrine and strategic rationale, and Roosevelt the 'push' within the administration – built a coalition that McKinley could not out-compete. By failing to properly manage his advisors, the president provided the incentive and the political space for his opponents to win. And the combined energy of the three men successfully bargained for a stronger navy and supported a colony in the Philippines.

2. Advice Is 'Sticky'

Before the explosion of the Maine, the president resisted an offensive grand strategy. But this changes after the war. McKinley instead defers to his advisors, supporting plans for overseas territories. And after the decision was made, McKinley never revisited the logic of empire pushed by the imperialists.

For some, this change is to be expected. For example, work in organizational psychology finds that advice is 'sticky.' Placing faith in the inner circle promotes certainty and increases confidence, and decision makers are hesitant to change course after a decision is made [73] By connection, a president that follows their inner circle is hesitant to question their decision to accept advice, and as a result will ignore discordant evidence in order to maintain that trust. In the case of the Spanish American War, McKinley simply followed this heuristic. But while the war was short and successful, the aftermath was not, as the initial success in the Philippines is replaced by a quagmire.

First, an influential anti-war campaign (funded by Carnegie) challenged the plans for expansion. To Carnegie, European imperialism should not be replaced by American imperialism. The United States did not have a history of overseas expansion, and they were ill prepared to run a colony. Mistakes would naturally follow empire. More importantly, anti-war activists argued jingoists were leading the United States down a path that promoted greater conflict with the Europeans. Empire naturally entailed a greater chance for war.

Carnegie's warning would prove prophetic. After the successes of Dewey in Manila Harbor (May 1), the Battles of El Caney and San Juan Hill (both on July 1), and the destruction of a Spanish flotilla in Santiago, Chile (on July 3), the imperialists were proven correct. The success in the Caribbean allowed the coalition of imperialists to turn their attention to South Asia. But the planning for the Philippines was slapdash and confused [74] The president never intended to occupy the island, only changing his plans after the rousing success of Dewey. Many in the Administration were unfamiliar with the politics of the island, the strength of the insurgency, and even the geography. McKinley hurriedly created a Pacific command, ordering 5000 troops to deploy to the Philippines (which would quickly grow) to help defeat the Spanish in a meeting on May 6th. The first 2500 arrived on June 4, followed by another 3500 on July 17th.

The initial optimism of a colony in Southeast Asia soon faded. Dewey believed the insurgents could help the United States take the Philippines at a lower cost; and as a result, Dewey supported Aguinaldo and his leadership of the insurgency. But the guerrilla leader turned against the Americans. Filipinos wanted self-rule, and as the Spanish left the island (from the summer through the fall), Aguinaldo's rebels became better armed and gained support from the population. The American agreement to take control of the island infuriated the insurgents, and they began targeting American soldiers. On Feb. 4, 1899, an American sentry fired upon insurgents, starting a revolt that would last for several years. When the war ended on July 4, 1902, the US had suffered 4200 casualties, while killing roughly 20000 insurgents [75]. And more importantly, the United States lost the moral upper hand. In fact, planners borrowed a tactic used by Weyler on Cuba: separating civilians from guerrillas by forcing populations into camps. Though the US gained a vital seaport, the cost was high.

In general, the case demonstrates the problem of too much trust. By following advice, leaders can become trapped, unwilling to question their advisors in future deliberations. On its face, this makes sense. Advisors are vital cognitive shortcuts that ease decision making. A good advisor can simplify foreign policy. But there is a cost to following the inner circle. Too much trust in an advisor creates the conditions for policy stagnation and foreign policy quagmires.

3. Advisors Matter to the Extent Leaders Let Them Matter

Presidents form an advisory system to control the flow of information in the White House, and advisors are constrained by the structure they populate. But there are tradeoffs. For example, presidents can limit competition by stressing consensus and appointing advisors that can be easily controlled. Advisors realize they serve at the president's leisure. Because advisors want to participate in decision making, they hold their tongues, unwilling to speak truth to power. But limiting advisory opinion leads to stagnant foreign policy. While consensus limits backbiting and competition in the inner circle, it promotes tunnel vision. As a result, presidents who limit debate are often given bad advice.

A president that encourages competition faces a similar tradeoff. Competition and multiple advocacy guarantee motivated proponents with differing policy positions. Advisors are not shy from giving their advice, and leaders are given more and better information. But this complexity taxes the president. While competition dilutes individual bias through a marketplace of ideas, it also encourages advisors to subvert the policy making process. Advisors begin to compete with each other for influence, rather than provide unbiased advice. And more importantly, a competitive system is difficult to control. Inexperienced presidents are unable to manage the bruised egos of the inner circle, and the quality of advice quickly declines. The competition eventually overwhelms the decision making system and creates a space for advisors to hijack the decision.

The problems of both approaches arise during the Spanish-American War. McKinley wanted an advisory council that he could dominate. He believed in his own capabilities, convinced that he would be able to make foreign policy decisions without the help of his advisors. Unfortunately, when he needed help – in choosing a policy path and in planning the war – these same advisors were unable to aid his decision making. More problematic for

McKinley was the emergence of policy entrepreneurs. The failure of McKinley to control the process granted a space for imperialists to enact their own plans for war. By not taking control of the process, the president created a power vacuum that was filled by motivated political opponents.

Advisors matter to the extent that leaders allow; the important question for presidents is the manner and type of that participation. In general, the structures presidents use to constrain or control the advisory process present opportunities for participation. Advisory influence in decisions of war is connected to how presidents ease the credibility problem. Trust, in effect, is a two-way street. Leaders want to have faith in the inner circle to ease the demands of decision making and receive unbiased advice. But this can only occur if presidents give their advisors freedom to speak truth to power. Likewise, advisors want to have faith in the president to take control of the decision, and do what they think is best for the country. Unfortunately for presidents, the best policy is to limit competition and stress consensus. The solutions to credibility problems in the inner circle manifest their own problems. Each president chooses which costs to pay.

REFERENCES

[1] George J. A. O'Toole, *The Spanish War: An American Epic*, 1898 (New York: WW Norton and Co., 1984), 18.

[2] Quoted in Gerald F. Linderman, *The Mirror of War: American Society and the Spanish-American War* (Ann Arbor: The University of Michigan Press,1974), 35.

[3] Harvey Rosenfeld, Diary of a Dirty Little War: The Spanish-American War of 1898 (Westport, CT: Praeger, 2000), 2.

[4] James Mann, *Rise of the Vulcans* (New York: Viking, 2004).

[5] Benjamin Bradlee, *Conversations with Kennedy* (New York: Norton, 1975).

[6] Richard K. Betts, *Soldiers, Statesmen, and Cold War Crises* (Cambridge, MA: Harvard University Press, 1977).

[7] Gregory Mason, *Remember the Maine* (New York: Henry Holt and Co., 1939), 32.

[8] H. R. McMaster, Dereliction of Dury: Lyndon Johnson, Robert McNamara, the Joint Chiefs of Staff, and the Lies that Led to Vietnam (New York: HarperCollins Publishers, 1997).

[9] Guy Benveniste, *The Politics of Expertise*, 2nd edition (San Francisco: Boyd and Fraser Publishing Company, 1977), 4.

[10] Janet A. Sniezek and Timothy Buckley, "*Cueing and Cognitive Conflict in Judge-Advisor Decision Making*," Organizational Behavior and Human Decision Processes 62 (2): 159-174 (1995).

[11] Roderick M. Kramer, "Paranoid Cognition in social systems: Thinking and Acting in the Shadow of Doubt," Personality and Social Psychology Review 2:251-275 (1998), 262-263.

[12] See Michael Ross and Fiore Sicoly, "*Egocentric bias in availability and attribution*," JPSP 37:322-326 (1979); and Susan T. Fiske and Shelley E. Taylor, Social Cognition (Reading, MA: Addison-Wesley, 1984).

[13] See Roderick M. Kramer, "Paranoid Cognition in social systems: Thinking and Acting in the Shadow of Doubt," Personality and Social Psychology Review 2:251-275 (1998); and Roderick M. Kramer, "In dubious battle: Heightened accountability, dysphoric cognition, and self-defeating bargaining behavior." In Roderick M. Kramer and David M. Messick, eds., *Negotiation in its Social Context* (Thousand Oaks, CA: Sage, 1995).

[14] See Brian Uzzi, "Social structure and compeition in interfirm networks: the paradox of embeddedness," Administrative Science Quarterly 42:35-67 (1997); and Roderick M. Kramer, "Trust and Distrust in Organizations: Emerging Perspectives, Enduring Questions," *Annual Review of Psychology* 50:569-598 (1999).

[15] Ivo H. Daalder and I.M. Destler, *In the Shadow of the Oval Office* (New York: Simon and Schuster, 2009).

[16] See Robert Dallek, Flawed Giant: Lyndon Johnson and his Times, 1961-1973 (New York: Oxford University Press, 1998); and Henry F. Graff, The Tuesday Cabinet: Deliberation and Decision on Peace and War under Lyndon B. Johnson (Englewood Cliffs, NJ: Prentice-Hall, 1970).

[17] Ivo H. Daalder and James M. Lindsay, America Unbound: The Bush Revolution in Foreign Policy (Hoboken, NJ: Wiley and Sons, Inc., 2005).

[18] Alexander L. George, "The Case for Multiple Advocacy in Making Foreign Policy", American Political Science Review 66(3): 751-785 (1972).

[19] See I.M. Destler, Presidents, Bureaucrats, and Foreign Policy (Princeton, NJ: Princeton University Press, 1972) ; Colin Campbell, Managing the Presidency: Carter, Reagan and the Search for Executive Harmony (Pittsburgh, PA: University of Pittsburgh Press, 1986); and Charles E. Walcott and Karen Hult, "Organizing the White House: Structure, Environment and Organizational Governance," *American Journal of Political Science* 31(1): 109-125 (1987).

[20] See Margaret G. Hermann and Thomas Preston, "Presidents, Advisors and Foreign Policy: The Effect of Leadership Style on Executive Arrangements," Political Psychology 15(1): 75-96 (1994); and Thomas Preston, The President and His Inner Circle (New York: Columbia University Press, 2001).

[21] Irving L. Janis, *Victims of Groupthink* (Houghton-Mifflin, Boston, 1972).

[22] Alexander L. George, Presidential Decision-Making in Foreign Policy: The Effective Use of Information and Advice (Boulder, CO: Westview Press, 1980), 191-208.

[23] Ibid.

[24] Paul A. Kowert, Groupthink or Deadlock: When Do Leaders Learn from Their Advisors? (Albany, NY: State University of New York Press, 2002).

[25] Quoted in Richard Barnet, The Rocket's Red Glare: When America Goes to War (New York: Simonand Schuster, 1990), 107.

[26] Charles S. Olcott, William McKinley, Part of the American Statesmen, Second Series (Houghton Mifflin Company, New York, 1916), 383-384.

[27] Ibid., 386.

[28] Marcus M. Wilkerson, Public Opinion and the Spanish-American War: A Study in War Propaganda (Baton Rouge, LA: Louisiana State Press, 1932) 13.

[29] Olcott, William McKinley (1916), 396-397.

[30] Kevin Phillips, William McKinley, part of the series, The American Presidents, Arthur M. Schlesinger, Jr., editor. (New York: Times Books, Henry Holt and Company, 2003), 34-35.

[31] Paul T. McCartney, Power and Progress: American National Identity, the War of 1898, and the Rise of American Imperialism (Baton Rouge, LA: Louisiana State University Press, 2006), 117.
[32] Quoted in Phillips, William McKinley (2006), 92.
[33] See Mason, Remember the Maine (1939); and Jack Cameron Dierks, A Leap to Arms: The Cuban Campaign of 1898 (New York: J. B. Lippincott Company, 1970).
[34] Linderman, *The Mirror of War* (1974).
[35] Dierks, *A Leap to Arms* (1970), 46.
[36] Henry Cabot Lodge, *The War with Spain* (New York: Harper and Brothers, Publishers, 1899), 32.
[37] Mason, Remember the Maine (1939), 46.
[38] Lewis L. Gould, The Presidency of William McKinley (Lawrence, KS: The Regents Press of Kansas, 1980), 63.
[39] O'Toole, *The Spanish War* (1984), 99.
[40] Phillips, William McKinley (2003), 87.
[41] Olcott, William McKinley (1916), 329, 333-334.
[42] O'Toole, The Spanish War (1984).
[43] Phillips, William McKinley (2003), 91.
[44] Harry J. Sievers, ed., William McKinley, 1843-1901, Series Editor Howard F. Bremer (Dobbs Ferry, NY: Oceana Publications, Inc., 1970), 38.
[45] Ibid., 42.
[46] Ibid., 52.
[47] Lodge, The War with Spain (1899), 33.
[48] Linderman, The Mirror of War (1974), 42.
[49] David Traxel, 1898 (New York: Alfred A. Knopf, 1998), 120-121.
[50] David F. Trask, The War with Spain in 1898 (New York: Macmillan Publishing Co., Inc., 1981), 58.
[51] McCartney, Power and Progress (2006), 113.
[52] John A. Corry, 1898: Prelude to a Century (New York: Fordham University Press, 1998), 115-116.
[53] Gould, *The Presidency of William McKinley* (1980), 62.
[54] Alfred T. Mahan, Lessons of the War with Spain (and Other Articles) (Boston, MA: Little, Brown, and Company, 1899), 27.
[55] Ibid., 185.
[56] Ibid., 186.
[57] Traxel, 1898 (1998), 109-110.
[58] Ronald Spector, Admiral of the New Empire (Columbia, SC: University of South Carolina Press, 1988), 42.
[59] Gould, The Presidency of William McKinley (1980), 105.
[60] Olcott, William McKinley (1916), 335.
[61] Corry, 1898: Prelude to a Century (1998), 19.
[62] Olcott, William McKinley (1916), 337.
[63] Corry, 1898: Prelude to a Century (1998), 20.
[64] Gould, The Presidency of William McKinley (1980), 94-95.
[65] Traxel, 1898 (1998), 111.
[66] Corry, 1898: Prelude to a Century (1998), 188.

[67] Ibid., 97-98.
[68] Ibid., 121.
[69] See Wilkerson, Public Opinion and the Spanish-American War: A Study in War Propaganda (1932) 13; and John William Tebbel America's Great Patriotic War with Spain: Mixed Motives, Lies, and Racism in Cuba and the Philippines, 1898-1915 (Manchester Center, VT: Marshall Jones Co., 1996).
[70] Louis A. Pérez Jr., The War of 1898 (Chapel Hill, NC: The University of North Carolina Press, 1998), 66-68.
[71] Traxel, 1898 (1998), 123.
[72] Corry, 1898: *Prelude to a Century* (1998), 188.
[73] Janet A. Sniezek and Lyn M. Van Swol, "Trust, Confidence, and Expertise in a Judge-Advisor System," *Organizational Behavior and Human Decision Processes* 84(2): 288-307 (2001).
[74] Gould, *The Presidency of William McKinley* (1980), 97-103.
[75] Corry, 1898: *Prelude to a Century* (1998), 331-332.

Chapter 10

PRESIDENTS AND WAR:
NOTES ON THE END OF CONSTITUTIONALISM

James K. Oliver
University of Delaware, Emeritus
Newark, Delaware, US

ABSTRACT

The preponderance of contemporary institutional analysis concerning the president and war is that the exigencies imposed by world politics and the modalities of conflict in the late 20th and early 21st centuries ineluctably push the American political system away from Madison's constitutionalism towards an expansion of presidential power at the expense of the Congress. This paper will review the contemporary war powers relationship between President and Congress including the recent recommendations of the National Warpowers Commission. The focus of this analysis is on the period since the end of the Cold War for it is during the last two decades that the theory and practice of presidential primacy or "presidentialism" has reached its zenith, surpassing even the "imperial presidency" of the middle Cold War period, i.e. the 1960s and early 1970s. This presidentialism confronts the constitutionalism that Madison and his associates sought to codify at the turn of the 18th into the 19th century and invites analysis of the challenge to and whether the Madisonian vision retains relevance for the institutions and processes of US foreign and national security policy making.

James Madison's stature as a founding father is based on his seminal role as drafter of the Constitution and expositor of the institutional balance critical to constitutionalism; his presidency, notes one of his biographers, "is semi-forgotten."[1] In foreign affairs he consistently over-estimated US economic power vis-à-vis England and persisted in his conviction that an embargo against Britain would ultimately force the British to recognize US commercial and maritime rights and stop the impressments of American sailors. The embargo failed and Madison sought and fought a war with England with insufficient land and naval forces, launched a disastrously failed invasion of Canada, and suffered the humiliation of British forces sacking Washington. A late run of western and naval victories and Andrew Jackson's spectacular rout of British forces attacking New Orleans saved Madison's and his Administration's popularity. Britain, preoccupied with reconstituting a conservative order in Europe, negotiated a peace that returned North America to the *status quo ante* – an outcome seemingly beyond the reach of the American negotiators at Ghent [2].

Madison wanted war with Britain so that he might advance his problematic "commercial strategy to its logical conclusion."[3] Madison's strategic vision was seriously flawed. More important for the present study, however, was his conviction that war must be fought within the new constitutional framework. Madison, of course, was as sensitive as any of the founders to the dangers posed by war to the Constitutional framework.[4] In correspondence with Jefferson, he had emphasized that the Constitution presupposes "that the Executive is the branch of power most interested in war, and most prone to it. It [the Constitution] has accordingly with studied care, vested the question of war in the Legislature."[5] Thus, as Madison approached war, there were, "constitutional doubts" for

> [T]his would be the first war undertaken after the ratification of the Constitution. The Constitution gives to the Congress alone the power of declaring war. There is no specific mention of a presidential role at this stage. The president's power is to conduct the war once it has been declared. Should the president just wait for congressional action, or should he try to guide it? [6]

Madison, working with James Monroe and Henry Clay, "coordinated ways to choreograph congressional developments."[7] He did so, however, within the strictures of the Constitution, that he, as much as any man, had conceived and embedded in the Constitution, especially the prerogatives of Congress. In the end, therefore, he got his declaration and congressional authorization without resort to any "inherent" or "plenary" powers or fabricated emergencies designed to create a fait accompli for the Congress. Moreover, and in bold contrast to his 20th and 21st successors,

> [H]e did not himself violate the civil rights of a citizenry at war. . . . He did stretch the Constitution at times; but the most notable examples of this occurred before the war, not because of the war. He seized West Florida by presidential fiat . . . [and reimposed] nonintercourse without congressional authorization. But during the war itself, as if to prove that the Constitution did not have to be jettisoned in a crisis, he was truer to its strictures than any subsequent war president.[8]

The preponderance of contemporary analysis concerning the relationship of the president and war is that the exigencies imposed by world politics and the modalities of conflict in the late 20th and early 21st centuries ineluctably push the American political system away from Madison's example towards an expansion of presidential power at the expense of the Congress. That is, the exercise of world power and leadership require – or so a succession of President's asserted and, generally, Congress has acceded to – an enhancement of executive foreign and national security policy power at the expense of the balances of the late 18th century constitutional framework. By the end of George W. Bush's Administration an even more radical reading of the Constitution was advanced – one which elevated the President to a position of primacy and thereby displaced Madison's constrained definition and restrained exercise of the president's war powers.

In anticipation of a new presidency a conclave of notables – a National Warpowers Commission chaired by former Secretaries of State James Baker III and Warren Christopher – was convened by the Miller Center at the University of Virginia to consider the status and future of the war powers. The commission published a report in July of 2008 advancing a draft "National Powers Consultation Act" based on the principles of "pragmatism," and the hope that "our proposal maximize the likelihood that the President and Congress productively consult with each other on the exercise of war powers."[9]

This paper will review the contemporary war powers relationship between president and Congress including the recommendations of the National War Powers Commission. This review is not, however, primarily an historical reconstruction of the institutional relationship. Such histories are numerous and comprehensive.[10] Rather, the focus of this analysis is on the period since the end of the Cold War for it is during the last two decades that the theory and practice of presidential primacy or "presidentialism" has reached its zenith, surpassing even the "imperial presidency"[11] of the middle Cold War period, i.e. the 1960s and early 1970s. This presidentialism confronts the constitutionalism that Madison and his associates sought to codify at the turn of the 18th into the 19th century and invites analysis of the challenge to and whether the Madisonian vision retains relevance for the institutions and processes of US foreign and national security policy making.

CONSTITUTIONAL TWILIGHT AND THE DAWN OF "PRESIDENTIALISM"

The course of post-World War II presidential primacy begins with President Harry Truman's assertion that his military response to the North Korean invasion across the 38th parallel in June 1950 did not require *any* Congressional authorization. The president's inherent power as commander in chief and chief executive as well as authority derived from US treaty obligations and permanent membership on the Security Council of the United Nations were deemed sufficient to initiate and prosecute war.[12] Truman's assertions of authority for the presidential commitment of military forces without Congressional authorization constitute the most common ground from which presidential authority has been justified for the succeeding fifty-eight years.

Truman's claimed ambit of presidential power was grounded in the 1936 Supreme Court decision in the case of *United States v. Curtiss-Wright*, [13] a case that stands as the foundation of all subsequent claims of inherent and unencumbered presidential powers in foreign and national security affairs. Chief Justice George Sutherland asserted the arguable notion that the national government was the recipient of sovereignty from Great Britain and as such, the "investment of the Federal government with the powers of external sovereignty did not depend upon the affirmative grants of the Constitution." More important for the war powers and foreign affairs,

> In this vast external realm, with its important, complicated, delicate and manifold problems, the President alone has the power to speak or listen as a representative of the nation.

... As Marshall said in his great argument of March 7, 1800 in the House of Representatives, "The President is the sole organ of the nation in its external relations and its sole representative with foreign nations." [14]

Notwithstanding more than fifty years of scholarly attack, the "precedent" of *Curtiss-Wright* persists and is employed regularly by presidents and their advocates, to justify seemingly infinitely expandable presidential claims of foreign policy and war powers.[15] In Truman's case these extended to "emergency powers" which, the president argued, authorized seizing and managing vital domestic industries – in this instance, steel mills threatened by strikes. The case ultimately ended up before the Supreme Court and gave rise to a second construction of the executive-legislative war powers relationship; one in which the president must operate in a much more constrained constitutional environment.

The Court's 1952 ruling in *Youngstown Sheet and Tube v. Sawyer* [16], did not deny the existence of unenumerated powers but it rejected the *Curtiss-Wright* notion of broad inherent powers derived from some extra-constitutional reservoir of presidential power or an "emergency."[17] Justice Robert Jackson in his oft referenced landmark concurring opinion, sought to illuminate the fundamental reality of the constitutional design: diffused institutional power which "enjoins upon its branches separateness but interdependence, autonomy but reciprocity. Presidential powers are not fixed but fluctuate, depending upon their disfunction or conjunction with those of Congress." Inevitably, he concluded, "there is a zone of twilight in which he and Congress have concurrent authority"[18].

During the Cold War, only Dwight Eisenhower occupied a position closer to Jackson's understanding of the Constitution. In the three instances in which Eisenhower deployed military forces – the Formosa Crisis of 1954-1955, in the Middle East in 1957, and the Lebanon Crisis of 1958 – he refused to resort to sweeping and pre-emptive claims of inherent presidential power. Even so, he successfully resisted attempts to limit what he understood to be his power as commander-in-chief to move US troops wherever and whenever he deemed it appropriate.[19] In each instance Eisenhower sought Congressional support in the form of permissively worded "Area Resolutions" authorizing and legitimizing his preferred course of action. Furthermore, when Eisenhower did not want to intervene or escalate a situation, such as in Vietnam, he set for Dulles – a proponent of intervention – a precondition of gaining Congressional support for the action calculating that Congress would be unlikely to provide such support in the immediate aftermath of the Korean Conflict. The critical element for Eisenhower was coordinated and mutually supportive inter-branch decision-making and stronger foreign policy he thought likely when such cooperation was operative.[20]

John F. Kennedy's assertion of presidential initiative and denial that Congress was a constitutionally necessary partner in the management of the Cuban Missile Crisis was a decisive return to Truman's presidentialism. On September 13, 1962, Kennedy announced that he was prepared to engage Cuba and the Soviet Union on his own constitutional authority as Commander in Chief.[21] And when asked if there was any "virtue" in a Congressional authorizing resolution, Kennedy replied "No, I think it would be useful, if they desired to do so, for them to express their view. I'd be very glad to have those resolutions passed if that should be the desire of the Congress."[22] But, when Kennedy proclaimed a quarantine of Cuba in order to interdict the shipment of missiles and military supplies, he did so under "the authority entrusted to me by the Constitution as *endorsed* by the resolution of the Congress." He continued in his proclamation that he was "acting under and by virtue of the authority conferred upon me by the Constitution and statutes of the United States, in accordance with the aforementioned resolution of the United States Congress and of the Organ of Consultation of the American Republics."[23]

That is, nothing was authorized by Congress which the president did not already possess though there was no specification of what authority found in the Constitution and/or statutes Kennedy was referring to in this claim. Finally, reference to the Organ of Consultation of the American Republics (Organization of American States) as an "organ" of international engagement and commitment was no more legally compelling than Truman's specious claim that US membership in the UN and the existence of UNSC resolutions satisfied compliance with U.S. constitutional procedures authorizing the use of U.S. military forces.

Lyndon Johnson's response to purported attacks on US warships in the Tonkin Gulf, August 3, 1964, bore some superficial resemblance to Eisenhower's approach to the war powers. The immediate retaliation against North Vietnam was followed by consultation with the congressional leadership and a request by Johnson for a joint resolution from Congress, the model for which would be Eisenhower's Formosa and Middle East area resolutions and Kennedy's Cuba Resolution. However, the language of the Tonkin Gulf Resolution had been prepared by the Administration three months earlier and in the interim the United States Navy undertook operations along the North Vietnamese coast designed to provoke a North Vietnamese response.[24] The resolution itself was rushed through the Congress with limited hearings and debate and provided "That the Congress approves and supports the determination of the President, as Commander in Chief, to take all necessary measures to repel any armed attack against the forces of the United States and to prevent further aggression."[25]

Putting a constitutional gloss on the executive-legislative interaction in his signing statement, Johnson said the military response stemmed from his authority as Commander in Chief and "was mine – and mine alone." He conceded that he also had a responsibility "of submitting our course to the representatives of the people, for them to verify it or veto it."[26] The language of the Resolution is clear, however, and notwithstanding subsequent efforts by members of Congress to deny it, [27] they approved and supported – by 88-2 and 416-0 votes in the Senate and House respectively – what the President had already initiated under his authority as Commander in Chief.

AFTER VIETNAM: CONGRESSIONAL GOVERNMENT TRUNCATED AND PRESIDENTIALISM REDUX

Richard Nixon's constitutionally dubious expansion of the Vietnam conflict to include Cambodia led to Congress reasserting itself as a co-participant in the exercise of the war powers. This ultimately took the form of the War Power Resolution passed over Nixon's veto in 1973, the operational core of which centers on two mechanisms. The first involves a set of 60-90 day deadlines on presidentially initiated military action without Congressional approval. Congressional inaction would be sufficient to end the use of force. However, the countdown to closure is not triggered unless the president reports under Section 4(a) (1) of the Resolution that US forces have been introduced into circumstances in which "hostilities" are imminent. As Fisher notes: "For fairly obvious reasons, Presidents do not submit reports under that section. Instead they report more generally."[28] Thus in more than 120 instances since the passage of the Resolution, presidents have filed general informational reports that are deemed *by them* "consistent" with the War Powers Resolution. In only two instances – the *Mayaguez* incident during the Ford Administration and Reagan's Lebanese intervention in 1983– did the reports fall under Section 4(a)(1) . In the former case the report did not reach Congress until hostilities had ended, and in the latter, Congress passed a resolution authorizing Reagan to maintain the US presence for up to eighteen months [29]

The mechanism whereby Congress could terminate the use of US military forces at any time would be the passage of a concurrent resolution directing the president to remove US forces from hostilities. However, such "legislative vetoes" were declared unconstitutional by the Supreme Court in the case of *I.N.S. v. Chadha* because concurrent resolutions do not meet the "presentment" requirements of the Constitution. Because the powers ostensibly constrained by Congress are constitutionally granted in part to the president, the president must be presented with a bill or joint resolution for signature or veto [30]

With, therefore, its operational mechanisms presumptively unconstitutional and/or circumvented by every president who has operated under the War Powers Resolution, the Resolution has remained essentially inoperative. Ford, Carter, Reagan, and George H.W. Bush all employed force unilaterally either asserting that they were undertaking limited force to effect rescues, repel attacks on US forces, protect US nationals or property, or under cover of international treaty obligations. In other instances where major military involvements seemed more likely, presidents followed the pattern set by Kennedy and Johnson and undertook consultation with the leadership of Congress and solicited Congressional resolutions of support. Nonetheless, no president unambiguously acknowledged that they did not possess the authority as Commander in Chief and Chief Executive to act without Congressional affirmation however politically useful the latter might be.

Immediately following the Vietnam War and Watergate, the resort to force declined with Ford and Carter using military force in only three cases, all of which involved to some degree a rescue operation. Ford and Carter may have felt restricted by the events of the immediate past and their likely effect on domestic and Congressional support. Perhaps, also, the presence and lack of experience with the newly passed War Powers Resolution introduced greater caution.[31] However, under Reagan and the first Bush, a decidedly more robust inclination towards the use of force ensued. Along with eight major commitments of US forces, Reagan and Bush filed fourteen and seven reports respectively under the War Powers Resolution though none of them were submitted under the strictures of Section 4(a)(1). At every turn, the prerogatives of the Commander in Chief were asserted and deemed sufficient to initiate the use of force.

The major military action taken during the period was Bush's response to Saddam Hussein's invasion of Kuwait in August of 1990. Bush immediately sent American troops to the region, proclaimed the action defensive and fully within his powers as commander in chief, and explicitly denied that any Congressional authorization was necessary.[32] Simultaneously, the Administration worked assiduously to establish global support and legitimacy for its actions via construction of a coalition of financial and/or military support in the Arab world and among US allies and in the United Nations Security Council securing a Resolution on November 29, 1990 authorizing "all means necessary" to force the Iraqi's from Kuwait.[33]

With the hours before launching war counting down, Bush sought a resolution of support for his actions, and both houses passed authorization for the president to take offensive actions against Iraq. Nonetheless, in a signing statement Bush again rejected the notion that such authorization was necessary:

> As I made clear to congressional leaders at the outset, my request for congressional support did not, and my signing this resolution does not, constitute any change in the long-standing positions of the executive branch on either the President's **constitutional authority** to use the Armed Forces to defend vital U.S. interests or the constitutionality of the War Powers Resolution.[34]

Or, as Bush stated more pungently during the 1992 presidential campaign, "I didn't have to get permission from some old goat in the United States Congress to kick Saddam Hussein out of Kuwait."[35]

THE APOTHEOSIS OF PRESIDENTIALISM

Even as the tensions and foreboding atmosphere of the Cold War evaporated, the claims for presidential supremacy grew more bold and preemptory, peaking during the administrations of Bill Clinton and George W. Bush. Clinton used military force more frequently than any president since the Second World War and like his predecessors claimed in every instance the power to do so as commander in chief and chief executive without Congressional authorization. But it was Clinton's successor, George W. Bush through the initiative of his Vice President Richard Cheney, who formulated an expansive "New Paradigm" of war powers proceeding from an institutional foundation of presidentialism and a neutered Congress.

BILL CLINTON AND THE PRACTISE OF PREEMPTORY PRESIDENTIALISM

During his eight years in office, Bill Clinton forwarded 60 reports to Congress under the War Powers Resolution, none of them under Section 4(a) (1).[36] Ten of Clinton's uses of military force entailed "imminent" or actual hostilities. Four involved missile or air strikes and in a fifth case, deployment of American combat forces in anticipation of an invasion of Haiti to remove the military leader General Raoul Cedras (1994). Clinton abjured Congressional authorization, arguing that he possessed authority as commander in chief to respond to threats against American citizens abroad (Iraq, 1993), attacks against American embassies (Sudan/Afghanistan, 1998) or in response to UN Security Council Resolutions authorizing member state use of force (Haiti and air strikes against Iraq in 1998).

With the 1996 strikes against Iraq following Saddam's attacks on Irbil, however, Clinton advanced a justification different from those employed by his predecessors: the missiles "sent the following message to Saddam Hussein: When you abuse your own people or threaten your neighbors, you must pay a price."[37] The argument was and remains disconcerting for it justified preemptory attacks solely on the authority of the president whenever the commander in chief determined that *any* state posed an imminent threat, not just to the United States, but to the targeted state's own population or its neighbors. This justification for war is "both novel and startling"[38] but also an harbinger of the pre-emptive war powers concept advanced by George W. Bush in response to the 9/11 attacks and as the centerpiece of his global war on terrorism.

Finally, combat operations in Somalia in 1993 were justified in terms of protection of US nationals and their property and as a continuation of the humanitarian and peacekeeping intervention begun under Security Council authority during the Bush Administration. Congress sought to constrain the Administration, but failed to pass binding resolutions.

The most sustained and potentially dangerous engagement of US military forces during the Clinton years occurred in the Balkans. The first round of actions in Bosnia entailed the 1993 deployment of US combat aircraft in support of humanitarian flights and the enforcement of a no-fly zone. Subsequently, US forces were ordered by Clinton to undertake airstrikes against Serbian militias in Bosnia (1994), and, finally, the introduction of US ground troops in support of the Dayton Accords ending the fighting in Bosnia in 1995.

Throughout this escalation, Clinton never conceded that Congressional authorization was necessary. He reported his actions to Congress, sought support for them, but never explicitly requested authorization though he averred that he would "welcome and encourage congressional authorization of any military involvement in Bosnia."[39] When, however, Congress approached restrictions on his actions, he invariably asserted that these constituted encroachments on his powers as commander in chief and chief executive. [40] When in 1994 and 1995 US engagement escalated to airstrikes and then the introduction of ground troops, Clinton asserted that he had sufficient authorization from the United Nations Security Council and NATO.

Congressional reaction was fragmented, inconsistent, and incoherent.[41] Clinton's initiatives provoked debate and much rhetoric concerning the prerogatives of Congress to limit the President via a priori limitations on the introduction of US troops into Bosnia, appropriations restrictions, but also "respect" for the President's authority as ". . . Commander in Chief to conduct foreign policy . . . [T]here is no greater threat to American lives than a Congress that attempts to micro-manage foreign policy."[42] In the end, the Congress failed to pass anything stronger than non-binding measures supporting US forces deployed in the Balkans while dissociating the Congress from the President and his policies.

Three years later in Kosovo, Clinton again asserted a unilateral prerogative to place American forces in harm's way – in this instance an attack on a sovereign state – without congressional authorization. The scope and implications of Clinton's decision are as expansive as his earlier justification for the punishment of Saddam for the attack on Irbil: "Yesterday I decided that the United States would vote to give NATO the authority to carry out military strikes against Serbia if President Milosevic continues to defy the international community."[43] Louis Fisher summarizes the scope and gravity of Clinton's action:

> Note the language: "*I* decided that the United States . . . ." Clinton alone would decide America's policy. The decision to go to war against another country rested in the hands of one person, exactly what the framers thought they had avoided. Moreover, Clinton would be giving *NATO* authority, instead of the Congress giving the *President* authority.[44]

Congress subsequently passed confused and inconsistent concurrent resolutions authorizing, in the House version, peacekeeping, and in the Senate, support for military operations. Even if the substance of the resolutions had been synchronized, however, neither constituted legal authorization for Clinton's actions because concurrent resolutions are not legally binding. [45].

THE NEW PARADIGM OF PRESIDENTIALISM

If Bill Clinton succeeded in asserting, elaborating, and using unilateral presidential war power more extensively than any of his predecessors, he never really grounded his activism in an explicitly articulated constitutional argument or doctrine. George W. Bush's Administration on the other hand, synthesized the historical strands of a presidentially centered construct of foreign affairs. The driving force behind this effort was Vice President Richard Cheney. Before examining this doctrinal framework and justification for presidentialism, it is important to address a seeming paradox of the administration's use of the war powers.

The Administration is defined by two applications of force: [46] the "war on terrorism" commenced in Afghanistan after the 9/11 attacks and the invasion of Iraq in March 2003 followed by a war stretching beyond the Bush Administration into that of his successor. Both the Afghanistan and Iraq wars were formally covered by broadly permissive Congressional resolutions authorizing the use of force.[47] Bush and Congress seemed, therefore, to act in concert and within the framework established in the Constitution and the War Powers Resolution. While not declaring war, the Congress nonetheless authorized the use of force.

However, Bush and his Administration understood the two "authorizing" resolutions as supplementary and not antecedent to the inherent powers of the President acting as commander in chief and chief executive. In neither case did the President accede to or act pursuant to Congress's authorization powers. Indeed, in signing statements, Bush informed Congress, first, regarding Afghanistan: he acted "pursuant to my constitutional authority to conduct U.S. foreign relations as Commander in Chief and Chief Executive." Further,

> I am providing this report as part of my efforts to keep the Congress informed, consistent with the War Powers Resolution and Public Law 107-40 . . . . I appreciate the continuing support of the Congress, including its enactment of Public Law 107-40, in these actions to protect the security of the United States of America and its citizens, civilian and military, here and abroad.[48]

Then, with respect to the Iraq resolution, Bush characterized the "authorization" as a "resolution of support" and that, he did not regard it as "constitut[ing] any change in the long-standing positions of the executive branch on either the president's constitutional authority to use force to deter, prevent, or respond to aggression or other threats to U.S. interests or on the constitutionality of the War Powers Resolution."[49]

Some have wondered why, given the sweeping authority extended to the president in Public Law 107-40, Bush did not utilize the statute as his source of authority rather than the claim of inherent constitutional powers [50]. The answer would seem to lie in the argument advanced by the Administration, primarily through Vice President Cheney, that the president's authority as the sole and essential agent of US relations with the international system is not dependent upon statutory definitions of authority.

From the beginning of his government career Cheney maintained, as he stated in the Minority Report on the Iran-Contra Affair in 1987, that a proper reading of the Constitution and constitutional history must acknowledge that

> . . . Presidents exercised a broad range of foreign policy powers for which they neither sought nor received Congressional sanction through statute.
>
> This history . . . leaves little, if any, doubt that the President was expected to have the primary role of conducting the foreign policy of the United States. Congressional action to limit the President in this area therefore should be reviewed with a considerable degree of skepticism. If they interfere with the core presidential foreign policy function, they should be struck down. Moreover, the lesson of our constitutional history is that doubtful cases should be decided in favor of the President. [51]

Obviously, Cheney is paraphrasing the "plenary powers/sole organ" argument advanced in the *Curtiss-Wright* decision and reiterated by every president since World War II. What is distinctive here is that George W. Bush's declaration exploited the 9/11 terrorist attacks to not only initiate an open-ended "Global War on Terrorism" and an invasion of Iraq, but also expanded the argument justifying presidential primacy beyond that articulated by Sutherland into a far more comprehensive doctrine of presidential plenary foreign policy and war powers extending beyond conventional distinctions between foreign and domestic affairs.[52]

The central element in the effort to solidify a coherent doctrine of presidentialism was the summary codification of the several dimensions of the presumptive exclusive plenary foreign affairs and war powers of the president after 9/11. Two weeks after the 9/11 attacks, Deputy Assistant Attorney General John C. Yoo from his position in the Justice Department's Office of Legal Counsel submitted the first of many memoranda to the White House, the Department of Defense, Central Intelligence Agency, senior officials in the Office of Legal Counsel and Justice Department. "The President's Constitutional Authority to Conduct Military Operations against Terrorists and Nations Supporting Them," provided the basic reading of the Constitution from which subsequent specific interpretations would be derived.

Quoting liberally from Hamilton's numbers in the *Federalist Papers*, Yoo sought to elevate to legal readings and interpretations, repeated post-World War II Presidential assertions and practice including: (1) "The *centralization of authority* in the President *alone* is particularly crucial in matters of national defense, war, and foreign policy, where a *unitary executive* can evaluate threats, consider policy choices, and mobilize national resources with a *speed and energy that is far superior to any other branch*." [53] (2) "[T]he *process* used for conducting military hostilities is different from other government decisionmaking" in that it requires the speed and centralization that distinguishes the presidency. (3) The *powers* allocated to the Congress and the President are qualitatively and substantively different because Congress's powers are restricted to those enumerated in the Constitution whereas the President possesses unenumerated foreign affairs powers unique and *exclusively* available to the president. Yoo insists, therefore, that the *Curtiss-Wright* Court's reading of presidential power is correct: "This foreign affairs power is *exclusive*: it is "the very delicate, plenary and exclusive power of the President as sole organ of the federal government in the field of international relations - a power which does not require as a basis for its exercise an act of Congress."

Finally, Yoo undertakes a crucial conceptual move by conflating foreign affairs and war powers uniquely available to the president and not the Congress. Specifically, the conduct of military hostilities is characterized as "a central tool for the exercise of the President's plenary control over the conduct of foreign policy." Thus, "the President's broad constitutional power to use military force to defend the Nation, recognized by the Joint Resolution itself, would allow the President to take whatever actions he deems appropriate to pre-empt or respond to terrorist threats from new quarters." Moreover, and crucial for the entire presidentialist paradigm:

> In both the War Powers Resolution and the Joint Resolution, Congress has recognized the President's authority to use force in circumstances such as those created by the September 11 incidents. *Neither statute, however, can place any limits on the President's determinations as to any terrorist threat, the amount of military force to be used in response, or the method, timing, and nature of the response. These decisions, under our Constitution, are for the President alone to make.*

Subsequently, the OLC issued numerous memoranda [54] affirming the legality of Administration initiatives regarding: seizure, incarceration, and rights (Guantanamo and military tribunals) of belligerents including moving prisoners to other countries for interrogation ("rendition"); the detention of U.S. citizens; and several rulings on methods of interrogation understood to violate international agreements on torture, [55] but opining that such agreements might be suspended and did not bind the president. In addition, the OLC extended opinions authorizing warrantless surveillance under the Foreign Intelligence Surveillance Act (FISA). Perhaps the most expansive and broadly implicative of these opinions was an October 23, 2001 memorandum concluding: ". . . the President has the independent, non-statutory power to take military actions, domestic as well as foreign, if he determines such actions to be necessary to respond to the terrorist attacks upon the United States on September 11, 2001 and before." Yoo, having asserted that the use of military force domestically falls within the president's plenary powers as commander in chief, went on to suggest that, "First Amendment speech and press rights may also be subordinated to the overriding need to wage war successfully," and "the current campaign against terrorism may require even broader exercises of federal power domestically."[56]

With this last opinion, Yoo and his associates crossed a bright redline drawn by Justice Jackson in his *Youngstown* opinion.

> . . . [N]o doctrine that the Court could promulgate would seem to me more sinister and alarming than that a President whose conduct of foreign affairs is so largely uncontrolled, and often is unknown, can vastly enlarge his mastery over the internal affairs of the country by his own commitment of the Nation's armed forces to some foreign venture.
> . . . [T]the Constitution did not contemplate that the title Commander in Chief *of the Army and Navy* will constitute him also Commander in Chief of the country, its industries and its inhabitants. He has no monopoly of "war powers," whatever they are. . . No penance would ever expiate the sin against free government of holding that a President can escape control of executive powers by law through assuming his military role. . . .

> Loose and irresponsible use of adjectives colors all non-legal and much legal discussion of presidential powers. "Inherant" powers, "implied" powers, "incidental" powers, "plenary" powers, "war" powers and "emergency" powers are used, often interchangeably and without fixed or ascertainable meanings.
>
> ... The claim of inherent and unrestricted presidential powers has long been a persuasive dialectical weapon in political controversy. ... But prudence has counseled that reliance on such nebulous claims stop short of provoking a judicial test".[57]

Unfortunately for the Bush Adminsitration and advocates of the extraordinary presidentialist claims outlined by the OCL, these claims provoked a judicial test – *Hamdan v. Rumsfeld* [58] – and failed. Most important, the Court "refused to accept the government's core premise that a new 'crisis paradigm' required that ordinary legal rules be jettisoned"[59] and that in these extraordinary circumstances, the president's prerogatives as commander in chief constituted a sufficient and constitutional warrant not only for foreign affairs, but domestic affairs – including judicial process – as well. The Court rejected Bush's claim that the president's inherant or plenary powers authorized acting without Congressional authorization in establishing military tribunals for dealing with alien detainees including diminution of their rights established in the Uniform Code of Military Justice and the Geneva Conventions.

More broadly, *Hamdan*, in reasserting presidential deference to legislative authorization, judicial prerogatives, and treaty obligations

> ... not only gives broad direction on how a war on terror may be constitutionally conducted but also disproves exorbitant claims already made during that war regarding the President's supposed freedom to authorize torture and cruel treatment ant to carry out widesprread warrantless domestic wiretapping in the face of contrary statutes.[60]

The Administration immediately secured from Congress the Military Commissions Act of 2006 which authorized the President to establish and convene military commissions quite similar to those previously declared unconstitutional "because they did not comport with the UCMJ and the Geneva Conventions."[61] Nonetheless, the Bush Administration acceeded to the Court's ruling.

Moreover, even as the implications of Hamdan reverberated through Administration, Congress and the judicial system, the political ground was cut from under the administration as popular and Congressional skepticism coalesced. The decisive moment came with the 2006 election and Republican loss of control of the Congress. Details of the OLC materials emerged and investigative reporters belatedly began working in earnest. Cheney's closest aid, Lewis Libby, was indicted and convicted of illegally leaking the name of a CIA analyst, Valerie Plame whose husband, Joseph C. Wilson, a former ambassador, had publically challenged and discredited the veracity of Bush's claims of Iraq's acquisition of nuclear raw materials from Niger. Finally, in October of 2008 and again on January 15, 2009, the OLC itself repudiated Yoo's previous analysis.[62]

Though Yoo et al's memos have been withdrawn in most cases, the central claim of presidential primacy has not. Bush's successor has not rejected the notion of inherant constitutional powers possessed by the President. In addition, the War Powers Resolution has not been redeemed and remains in a state of limbo. Indeed, the only recent attempt to assess the Resolution, The Warpowers Commission, rendered a negative verdict concerning its utility. More important, the Commission advanced a set of procedural recommenadations which if adopted, would leave presidentialism still very much in control of the institutional initiative.

"Something That Would Work"[63]

The War Powers Commission deals with the conflicted history of the war powers by simply summarizing the post Cold War positions taken by Presidents and Congress. However, the positions taken and claims made by Presidents and/or proponents of Congressional prerogatives are not subjected to any analysis or critique. Thus, for example the Commission simply observes: "Advocates of congressional power cite Truman's decision as a turning point in the war powers debate, when Presidents began asserting more and more power. Advocates of presidential power dispute that the Korean War represented a sea change"[64]

The Commission concludes from this cataloging of "President says"/"Congress says" tit-for-tat that because for every claim there is an opposite and no less intensely held counter-claim, the war powers are ambiguous and there can be no resolution of the constitutional questions until the courts decide. And "Because the courts have not ruled on the merits in these cases, the questions of which branch may exercise which war powers remain open."[65] Thus, "We take no position on the underlying constitutional questions. Nor do we judge the actions of any President or Congress. We merely note the persistence and intensity of the debate, as it informs any recommendations we can reasonably and practically make"[66].

It is clear, however, that they do in fact judge negatively the actions taken by the Congress, i.e. the constitutionality of the War Powers Resolution of 1973.[67] And when they turn to "recommendations we can reasonably and practically make", there is little doubt where the Commission's sentiments lie.

On each point of their summary of criticisms of the 1973 Resolution, the President's complaints are privileged. Moreover, in their exegesis of the *Chadha* case the Commission reveals that it *does* believe that the Supreme Court has ruled negatively on the most fundamental operational principle of the Resolution: the practice of using one-house "legislative vetoes" of administrative actions. Furthermore, "The general view is that if the War Powers Resolution were put to the same test in *Chadha*, Section 5(c) of the Resolution, and perhaps other provisions, would fail."[68] Finally, Mr. Baker asserted in July of 2008, "[The 1973 Resolution] is not effective, at best. It's unconstitutional at worst. It's a bad law that ought to be replaced with a good law, something that would work."[69]

The "War Powers Consultation Act"

The proposed War Powers Consultation Act encompasses: (1) a mandatory executive-legislative consultation process in the event of "significant military actions" and (2) a process whereby Congress would be required to vote approval or disapproval of military actions taken by the president. In the event both houses of Congress pass a joint resolution of disapproval, the resolution would be presented to the president who could exercise a veto which could, in turn, be overridden by a two-thirds vote in both houses. Failure to override would mean the president's war would proceed.

Required Consultation

The proposed consultation process requires that the president meet with a newly constituted Joint Congressional Committee consisting of: the Speaker of the House and the Senate Majority Leader and the Minority Leaders of the House and the Senate as well as the bipartisanship leadership of the House and Senate Committees on Foreign Relations/Affairs, Armed Services, Intelligence, and Appropriations.[70] The president is required to consult with, not merely notify, the Joint Committee before armed forces are deployed in any "significant armed conflict." The only exception to this requirement is in the event of covert operations in which case, the president must consult with the Joint Committee within three calendar days of the deployment of forces.

The notion of "significant armed conflict" is obviously pivotal in this process and is understood as meaning: "(i) any conflict expressly authorized by Congress, or (ii) any combat operation by U.S. armed forces lasting more than a week or expected by the President to last more than a week."[71] Significant armed conflict does not extend to: (i) repelling attacks, or preventing imminent attacks; (ii) limited reprisals against terrorists or states that sponsor terrorism; (iii) humanitarian missions in response to natural disasters; (iv) investigations or acts to prevent criminal activity abroad;(v) covert operations; (vi) training exercises; or (vii) missions to protect or rescue American citizens or personnel abroad.[72] Should any of these actions escalate into a significant military action, the President is required to undertake consultation with the Joint Committee.

Several of these exceptions constitute exclusions from Congressional authorization of the use of force heretofore within the province of Congress. With the possible exception (i), (vii) and perhaps (iii)[73], the effect is, therefore, to replace the presumption that *all* uses of force must be *authorized* by Congress with the constitutionally problematic notion of "consultation." As Fisher notes,

> The Constitution is not designed to ensure that Congress will be "consulted" before the president initiates war. It is written to place singularly in the hands of Congress the decision to take the country from a state of peace to a state of war. The president needs authorization or a declaration from Congress, in *advance*, and not simply "consult" with a few senior lawmakers before committing U.S. forces to an offensive war.[74]

Moreover, "consultation" entails no obligation to act on the advice rendered, nor does the requirement of consultation and the admonition that it be serious necessitate anything more substantive than "consultation" with the leadership of the Congress than in the past.

In addition, presidentially initiated covert operations and "limited" reprisals against terrorists and/or states supporting terrorists provide the president substantial and statutorily covered range of opportunities for initiating wars. For example, presumably any state placed on the State Department's list of sponsors of international terrorism would be "pre-approved" for a presidentially initiated use of force. And if the operations were covert, the President would be free to delay "consultation."[75]

CONGRESSIONAL APPROVAL OR DISAPPROVAL OF PRESIDENTIAL ACTIONS

The process whereby Congress approves or disapproves a president's actions is designed to force the Congress to act and present the president with a joint resolution requiring presidential signature before it can become law. If no authorization of declaration of war has been passed by Congress within 30 days of the president initiating significant military action, the Chair and Co-chairs of the Joint Committee must introduce identical joint resolutions approving the action in their respective houses of Congress which must be voted on within twelve calendar days. If the resolution is disapproved, any member of the House and Senate may introduce a joint resolution of disapproval of the military action which must be voted on within five calendar days. However, "The effect of the passage of this joint resolution shall not have the force of law unless presented to the President and either signed by the President or subsequently approved by Congress over the President's veto."[76]

This procedure retains one of the most heavily criticized elements of the War Powers Resolution, i.e. providing at least two months time during which a Congressionally unauthorized war might be initiated and fought. In addition, the process whereby Congress registers its support or disapproval, is decidedly tilted against Congress. Thus, either a Congressional resolution of disapproval or one introduced by any member is likely to elicit a presidential veto leading to the necessary two-thirds override vote in both houses. "In other words, the president could initiate a war and continue it as long as he has one-third plus one in a single chamber. The procedure is flatly unconstitutional."[77]

In sum, the Commission, under the self-imposed requirement that it produce, "something that would work," is constitutional, and perceived as fair and balanced by all parties, fails its own test. It fails because their paradigm of what "works" is the constitutionally dubious presidentialism asserted by Truman, practiced by all his successors with the possible exception of Eisenhower, and tendentiously codified during George W. Bush's presidency. "The Baker-Christopher Commission fails to offer a solution for war powers disputes," Fisher concludes

> Because it never addressed the central tenets of the Constitution, including the principle of popular government and the explicit text that places the war power with Congress. The commission's draft bill weakens Congress, plays to executive strengths, and undercuts the rule of law. It does great damage to the core structural safeguard of separation of powers and checks and balances. . . .[78]

MOVING BEYOND PRESIDENTIALISM?

The post-Cold War expansion and elaboration of presidentialism has been, slowed as it was in the 1950s and again in the 1970s by the erosion of military, political, and popular support for a divisive, presidentially initiated war as well as in the case of the Korean War, a crucial judicial decision. Harold Hongju Koh has suggested that "In *Hamdan*, the Supreme Court has given us a *Youngstown* for the twenty-first century,"[79] for ". . . *Hamdan* goes a long way toward restoring the constitutional vision that the [Bush Administration] had turned upside down. It marks a major step toward reestablishing what Justice Jackson termed in his *Youngstown* concurrence the "equilibrium established by our constitutional system."[80]

The analysis undertaken in this paper suggests that however major and necessary a step has been taken, it is far from sufficient. However, elegant and compelling Jackson's concurrence in *Youngstown*, it was overwhelmed in less than a decade by the terrifying exigencies of the nuclear duel at the brink of Armageddon off Cuba. It was deemed necessary to set aside Madison's equilibrated constitutionalism for the presidentialism required to prosecute first, global containment and then a global war on terrorism. Moreover, what the Court gave, it could take away as *Chadha* cast a pall over the War Powers Resolution and the flawed reassertion of "Congressional government" in the decade after Vietnam.

Madison's constitutional equilibrium assumes that presidential aggrandizement is a near inevitable concomitant of war, his restraint in the War of 1812 notwithstanding to the contrary. However, Madison and the framers also theorized that the Congress would jealously guard its war power prerogatives and "push back" a too assertive president. The Tonkin Gulf Resolution experience led Senator J. William Fulbright to conclude the contrary:

> In adopting a resolution with such sweeping language, however, Congress committed the error of making a *personal* judgment as to how President Johnson would implement the resolution when it had a responsibility to make an institutional judgment, first as what *any* President would do with so great an acknowledgment of power, and, second, as to whether, under the Constitution, Congress had the right to grant or concede the authority in question.[81]

The subsequent behavior of Congress suggests, however, that the problem is deeper than a situational "error" of judgment; that it reflects a fundamental structural weakness; a conceptual flaw in the Madisonian design. Is the contemporary Congress – a collective body comprised of self-interested politicians preoccupied with their short-term electoral needs – any longer capable of the far-seeing "institutional judgments" necessary to the constitutionlist paradigm of 1787? By the time Clinton undertook his sustained campaign of unilateral uses of force, and presidentialism approached its apogee under George W. Bush, Congress's "institutional judgment" continued to be rendered through resolutions of "support," eleventh hour "authorizations," and often incoherent but politically expedient legislation encompassing "support for the troops" but not the president's policy. None of this conforms to the institutional role envisioned by Madison and his associates, an institution whose constitutional prerogatives and authority a President Madison respected and engaged with care.

Jackson observed that in a Constitution of concurrent authority, ". . . congressional inertia, indifference or quiescence may sometimes, at least as a practical matter, enable, if not invite, measures on independent presidential responsibility."[82] Within eight years of his landmark opinion, congressional quiescence; indeed, deference – the operational corollary of presidentialism – had become thoroughly instantiated in the executive-legislative relationship culminating in the second Bush Administration's extraordinary "New Paradigm" of presidential primacy. The more extreme formulations of presidentialism advanced by the George W. Bush's Administration have been set aside. Nonetheless, the Warpowers Commission has rendered a report recommending a presidentialism in which Congress is to play a ritualistic and, arguably unconstitutional "consultative" role.

President-Elect Barrack Obama entered office at least rhetorically committed to a presidency consultatively engaged with Congress on foreign and national security policy and during the transitional period, met with the National Warpowers Commission.[83] Though Obama has not explicitly endorsed the Commission's recommendations, during his campaign, he outlined a more open and cooperative relationship with the Congress including the strengthening of traditional and the fashioning of new institutional and consultative linkages between executive and legislative branches.[84]

It remains to be seen if the "traditional and . . . new institutional and consultative linkages between executive and legislative branches" will challenge presidentialism's status as the default executive-legislative relationship.

REFERENCES

[1] Garry Wills, James Madison (New York: Times Books/Henry Holt and Company, 2002): 1.
[2] Wills' history of Madison's presidency along with Robert Allen Rutland's The Presidency of James Madison (Lawrence, Kansas: University Press of Kansas, 1990) and J.C.A. Stagg's Mr. Madison's War: Politics, Diplomacy, and Warfare in the Early American Republic, 1783-1830 (Princeton: Princeton University Press, 1983) are essential sources.
[3] Wills: 94 and Rutland: 188.
[4] See Louis Fisher, "Studies on Presidential Power in Foreign Relations, Study No. 1: "The 'Sole Organ' Doctrine," (The Law Library of Congress, August 2006): 6 and the shorter, "*The Law*: Presidential Inherent Power: The 'Sole Organ' Doctrine," Presidential Studies Quarterly 37 (March 2007): 139-152.
[5] Quoted by Fisher, "The 'Sole Organ' Doctrine": 6.
[6] Wills: 94.
[7] Ibid.
[8] Wills: 154. See also, Rutland: 189.
[9] National Warpowers Commission Report: 9 *ttp://millercenter.org/dev/ci/system/ application/views/_newwebsite/policy/commissions/warpowers/report.pdf* ; (Hereafter, WCR).
[10] Among the best of these are: John Hart Ely, War and Responsibility: Constitutional Lessons of Vietnam and Its Aftermath, (Princeton, NJ: Princeton University Press, 1993); Louis Fisher, Presidential War Power, second edition revised (Lawrence, Kansas: University Press of Kansas, 2004); Michael J. Glennon, Constitutional Diplomacy, (Princeton, NJ: Princeton University Press, 1990); Louis Henkin, Foreign Affairs and the US Constitution, 2d edition, (New York: Oxford University Press, 1996) and Henkin, Consitutionalism, Democracy, and Foreign Affairs, (New York: Columbia University Press, 1990), and Harold Hongju Koh, The National Security Constitution: Sharing Power after the Iran-Contra Affair, (New Haven: Yale University Press, 1990). A comprehensive casebook of foreign affairs and national security law is Thomas M. Franck, Michael J. Glennon, and Sean D. Murphy eds., Foreign Relations

and National Security Law: Cases, Materials, and Simulations, 3d edition, (St. Paul, Minnesota: West Publishing, 2007).

[11] The term is that of Arthur Schlesinger, Jr., The Imperial Presidency, (Boston: Houghton Mifflin Company, 2004).

[12] Subsequently, Truman restated the argument for the Administration's decision to send US troops to Europe, again claiming that the President possessed the inherent power to do so as commander in chief as well as authority under the then new North Atlantic Treaty.

[13] United States v. Curtiss-Wright (1936).

[14] U.S. v. Curtiss Wright.

[15] Perhaps the most thorough critique of Sutherland's opinion has been that provided by Louis Fisher. See in addition to Presidential War Powers, "The 'Sole Organ' Doctrine," and "*The Law*: Presidential Inherent Power: The 'Sole Organ' Doctrine": 139-152.

[16] Youngstown Sheet and Tube Co. v. Sawyer, 343 U.S. 579 (1952).

[17] Thus Associate Justice Hugo Black stated unequivocally in his majority opinion: "The President's power, if any, to issue the order [to seize the steel mills] must stem either from an act of Congress or from the Constitution itself." Ibid.

[18] Ibid.

[19] Fisher notes, for example, Eisenhower's successful opposition to Senator Wayne Morse's attempt to amend the Middle East Resolution to restrict the President's armed forces deployment prerogatives. Presidential War Power: 122-123.

[20] Presidential War Power: 124-125.

[21] Public Papers of the Presidents, 1962: 674.

[22] Ibid: 679.

[23] Ibid: 807 and 810; emphasis added.

[24] See Stanley Karnow, Vietnam: A History, (1991): 373ff, William Conrad Gibbons, The U.S. Government and the Vietnam War: Executive and Legislative Roles and Relationships, Part II: 1961-1964, (1986): 228-235 and 291-292, and Joseph C. Goulden, Truth Is the First Casualty: The Gulf of Tonkin Affairs – Illusion and Reality, 1969.

[25] The Southeast Asia (Tonkin Gulf) Resolution, August 7, 1964. 78 Stat. 384 (1964).

[26] Public Papers of the Presidents, 1963-1964, II: 946.

[27] Ely systematically obliterates Fulbright's claims of Johnsonian duplicity; see War and Responsibility: 19-30.

[28] Fisher, Presidential War Powers: 150.

[29] See Fisher's discussion at ibid as well as Richard F. Grimmett, "Congressional Research Service, War Powers Resolution: Presidential Compliance", CRS Report RL33532, 12-14 (June 12, 2007) and Michael J. Glennon, "The War Powers Resolution: Sad Record, Dismal Promise," (excerpts from 17 Loy. L.A. L. Rev. 657, 658-70 (1984), in Foreign Relations and National Security Law: Cases, Materials, and Simulations: 717-720 and 721-723.

[30] I.N.S. v. Chadha, 462 U.S. 919 (1983).

[31] Apparently, it also produced great resentment among the foreign policy staffers in the Ford Administration and no one felt it more intensely than Ford's Chief of Staff, Richard Cheney. See Charlie Savage's "Takeover: The Return of the Imperial Presidency," at The Rule of Law and the Global War on Terrorism: Detainees,

Interrogations, and Military Commissions Symposium at the Washburn University School of Law, November 13, 2008: 310.
[32] "Crisis in the Persian Gulf Region: U.S. Policy Options and Implications," hearings before the Senate Committee on Armed Services, 101st Cong., 2d Sess, 1990: 701-702.
[33] United Nations Security Council Resolution 678, November 29, 1990. Reprinted in part in Foreign Relations and National Security Law: 657-658.
[34] Public Papers of the Presidents, 1991, I: 20.
[35] Cited by Fisher, Presidential War Power: 172.
[36] In contrast, the five other Presidents who have served under the War Powers Resolution of 1973 filed 61 reports.
[37] Public Papers of the Presidents, 1996, II: 1469.
[38] Fisher, Presidential War Powers: 192.
[39] Public Papers of the President, 1993, I: 1455.
[40] Ibid: 1768.
[41] The latter term is Fisher's characterization of a compromise bill passed by the Senate in response to Clinton's dispatch of 20,000 troops to Bosnia in a peacekeeping mission. Fisher, Presidential War Power: 190 and 183-192 for Bosnia.
[42] Statement of Representative James B. Longley Jr. (R-Maine) among the twelve Republicans who ultimately voted against a measure designed to restrict Clinton's capacity to introduce American troops into Bosnia. Quoted by Fisher, Presidential War Power: 188.
[43] Public Papers of the Presidents, 1998, II: 1765.
[44] Fisher, Presidential War Power: 198.
[45] See Fisher's discussion of this critical point at ibid: 199.
[46] Though Bush filed more than 35 reports to Congress under the War Powers Resolution. This total was exceeded only by Bill Clinton who filed 60 or almost half of all the reports filed under the War Powers Resolution. See Grimmett, in Foreign Relations and National Security Law: 717-719.
[47] "Authorization for Use of Military Force Against Perpetrators of 9/11," S.J. Res. 23, Pub. L. No. 107-40, 115 Stat. 224 (Sept. 18, 2001) and "Authorization for Use of Military Force against Iraq Resolution of 2002," H.J. Res. 114, Pub. L. No. 107-243, 116 Stat. 1498 (Oct. 16, 2002). Both excerpted in Foreign Relations and National Security Law: 671-672 and 680-684 respectively.
[48] 37 Weekly Compilation of Presidential Documents: 1447 and 1448.
[49] 38 Weekly Compilation of Presidential Documents: 1778 .
[50] Fisher: 210.
[51] Report of the Congressional Committees Investigating the Iran-Contra Affair with Supplemental, Minority, and Additional Views. S. Rpt. No. 100-216 and H. Rpt. No. 100-433, 100th Cong., 1st Sess., November 17, 1987. Michael Malbin drafted the Minority Report, but Cheney, as the ranking minority member of the Committee, was the intellectual source of the arguments therein. See Paul Starobin, "Imperial Presidency Has Long History," National Journal (February 22, 2006) at http://www.govexec.com/story_page_pf.cfm?articleid=33442.
[52] Crucial elements of the Cheney operation included Louis "Scooter" Libby a long time Cheney associate and David Addington, who had served as a staffer for the Minority at the time of the Iran-Contra congressional hearings. Addington served as Cheney's

Legal Counsel and Chief of Staff during the second term and was the pivotal operative in a network of "presidentialists" including John C. Yoo, Deputy Assistant Attorney General in the Office of Legal Council in the Justice Department, between 2001 and 2003, Jay S. Bybee, director of the OLC during the first Bush Administration (and now a federal appellate court judge), and Steven G. Bradbury, the director during the second Bush Administration. The legal opinions crafted in the OLC by this group, apparently under Addington's oversight, Cheney and Bush's "New Paradigm" of Presidential power. See Jane Mayer, "The Hidden Power: The legal mind behind the White House's war on terror, The New Yorker (July 3, 2006), *www.newyorker.com/archive/2006/07/03/060703fa_fact1*.

[53] All quotes in the next two paragraphs are from John C. Yoo, ""The President's Constitutional Authority to Conduct Military Operations Against Terrorists and Nations Supporting Them," Memorandum of Opinion for the Deputy Counsel to the President, September 15, 2001; emphasis added.

[54] The following OCL memoranda are relevant: John C. Yoo, "Constitutionality of Amending Foreign Intelligence Surveillance Act to Change the "Purpose" Standard for Searches," OCL, September 25, 2001; John C. Yoo and Robert J. Delahunty, "Authority for Use of Miliatary Force to Combat Terrorist Activities Within the United States, OCL, October 23, 2001; John C. Yoo and Delahunty, "Authority of the President to Suspend Certain Provisions of the ABM Treaty," OLC, November 15, 2001; Yoo, "The President's power as Commander in Chief to Transfer Captured Terrorists to the Control and Custody of Foreign Nations," OLC, March 13, 2002; Patirck Philbin, "Swift Justice Act," OLC, April 8, 2002; Jay S. Bybee, "Determination of Enemy Belligerency and Military Detention," OLC, June 8, 2002; Memorandum to Daniel J. Bryant, Assistant Attorney General, Office of Legal Affairs, Applicability of 18 U.S.C. 4001(a) to Military Detention of United States Citizens," OLC, June 27, 2002.

[55] OLC Memorandum for John Rizzo, Acting General Counsel of the Central Intelligence Agency, "Interrogation of al Qaeda Operative [Abu Zubaydah], OLC, August 1, 2002; Memorandum for John A. Rizzo, Senior Deputy General Counsel, Central Intelligence Agency, Application of 18 U.S.C. 2340-2340A to the Combined Use of Certain Techniques in the Interrogation of High Value al Qaeda Detainees," OLC, May 10, 2005; Memorandum for John A. Rizzo, Senior Deputy General Counsel, Central Intelligence Agency, "Application of 18 U.S.C. 2340-2340A to the Combined Use of Certain Techniques in the Interrogation of a High Value al Qaeda Detainee," OLC, May 10, 2005; and Memorandum for John A. Rizzo, Senior Deputy General Counsel, Central Intelligence Agency, "Application of United States Obligations Against Torture to Certain Techniques that May Be Used in the Interrogation of High Value al Qaeda Detainees," OLC, May 30, 2005.

[56] See Yoo and Delahunty, Re: Authority for the Use of Military Force to Combat Terrorist Activities Within the United States," Department of Justice, Office of Legal Counsel, October 23, 2001: 14, 24-25 and Neil A. Lewis, "Memos Reveal the Scope of Power Bush Sought in Fighting Terror," The New York Times, March 3, 2009 at *www.nytimes.com/2009/0303legal.html*.

[57] Jackson's concurring opinion in Youngstown Sheet and Tube Co. v. Sawyer in Foreign Relations and National Security Law,

[58] 126 S.Ct. 2749-2825, 165 L.Ed.2d 723 (2006).
[59] Harold Hongju Koh, "Setting the World Right," 115 Yale L.J., 2350-2367 (2006) excerpted in Foreign Relations and National Security Law: 93-97; quotation is at 94.
[60] Ibid: 96. Legal challenges to the constitutionality of the MCA are now working their way through the judicial system.
[61] Thomas Frank, "U.S. Presidential Power in 'Wartime'," 5 International Journal of Constitutional Law, 7 (2007) quoted in Koh, "Setting the World Right," Foreign Relations and National Security Law: 98.
[62] Steven A. Bradbury, Principal Deputy Assistant Attorney General, "Memorandum for the Files, Re: October 23, 2001 OLC Opinion Addressing the Domestic Use of Military Force to Combat Terrorist Activities," October 6, 2008 and Bradbury, "Memorandum for the Files Re: Status of Certain OLC Opinions Issued in the Aftermath of the Terrorist Attacks of September 11, 2001, "January 15, 2009.
[63] James Baker quoted in Peter Baker, "Obama to Hear Panel on Changes to War Powers Act." For another of Louis Fisher's critiques – to which this summary is indebted – see his, *"The Law:* The Baker-Christopher War Powers Commission," Presidential Studies Quarterly, 39 (March 2009): 128-140.
[64] WCR: 19.
[65] Ibid.
[66] Ibid: 17.
[67] Ibid: 25.
[68] Ibid: 23.
[69] Peter Baker, "Obama to Hear Panel on Changes to War Powers Act," The New York Times, December 12, 2008. *http://www.nytimes.com/2008/12/12us/politics/11web-baker.html?*
[70] WCR: 45-46. The Chairmanship and Vice Chairmanship of the committee would alternate between the Speaker of the House and the Majority Leader of the Senate.
[71] Ibid: 45, Section 3(A). Definitions.
[72] Ibid: Section 3(B).
[73] Repelling imminent attacks and rescues have, been understood as the only exceptions to a priori Congressional authorization of the use of force since the drafting of the Constitution.
[74] Fisher, "The Baker-Christopher War Powers Commission": 137.
[75] Ibid: 137-138.
[76] Ibid: Section 5(C): 48.
[77] Fisher, "The Baker-Christopher War Powers Commission": 139.
[78] Ibid.
[79] Koh, "Setting the World Right," in Foreign Relations and National Security Law": 95.
[80] Ibid: 97.
[81] "U.S. Commitments to Foreign Powers," Hearings before the Senate Foreign Relations Committee, 90th Congress, 1st Sess. 3 (1967). Language from S. Rept. No. 129, 91st Cong., 1st Sess. 8 (1969): 23. Emphasis in the original.
[82] Jackson in *Youngstown*, excerpted in Foreign Relations and National Security Law: 28.
[83] "Obama to Hear Panel on Changes to War Powers Act."

[84] *http://www.barackobama.com/issues/foreign_policy/index.php.* See also Charlie Savage, "Barack Obama's Q and A," The Boston Globe, December 20, 2007, *http://www.boston.com/news /politics/2008/specials/Candidate QA/Obama QA. Transcript.*

Chapter 11

ABSORBING THE FIRST BLOW: TRUMAN AND THE COLD WAR

John M. Schuessler
Department of Leadership and Strategy
Air War College, Montgomery, Alabama, US

ABSTRACT

In the historiography on the Cold War, a common assertion is that the Truman administration had to use overheated rhetoric to shock the public into supporting its containment policy. Ideological excess aside, however, what stands out about the Cold War is the relatively forthright way in which the Truman administration escalated the conflict. One finds few of the evasions and distortions that characterize American entry into World War II or Vietnam. The argument of this article is that the administration was able to be transparent about its intentions because, in contrast with the latter cases, it was not looking to provoke a fight with its adversary. However aggressive its containment strategy, it was the Soviet side that made the first overt move by giving the green light to the Korean War. Responding to what was widely seen as blatant aggression, Truman was able to deploy forces to Korea with little pushback from Congress or the public, even though he had failed to consult with them. Indeed, popular fears of a "garrison state" gave way to a massive military buildup and stronger commitments to NATO. If Truman had to contend with any opinion problem at the time, it was not isolationist sentiment but its opposite, as 1950 marked the high tide of preventive war agitation. In all these ways, the case attests to the political advantages of absorbing the first blow, advantages that Roosevelt and Johnson had to do largely without as they were mobilizing support for war.

The views expressed in this academic research paper are those of the author and do not reflect the official policy or position of the US government or the Department of Defense.

In the historiography on the Cold War, a common assertion is that the Truman administration had to use overheated rhetoric to shock the public into supporting its containment policy.[1] Ideological excess aside, however, what stands out about the Cold War is the relatively forthright way in which the Truman administration escalated the conflict. One finds few of the evasions and distortions that characterize American entry into World War II or Vietnam. The argument of this article is that the administration was able to be transparent about its intentions because, in contrast with the latter cases, it was not looking to provoke a fight with its adversary. However aggressive its containment strategy, it was the Soviet side that made the first overt move by giving the green light to the Korean War. Responding to what was widely seen as blatant aggression, Truman was able to deploy forces to Korea with little pushback from Congress or the public, even though he had failed to consult with them. Indeed, popular fears of a "garrison state" gave way to a massive military buildup and stronger commitments to NATO. If Truman had to contend with any opinion problem at the time, it was not isolationist sentiment but its opposite, as 1950 marked the high tide of preventive war agitation. In all these ways, the case attests to the political advantages of absorbing the first blow, advantages that Roosevelt and Johnson had to do largely without as they were mobilizing support for war.

The article unfolds in six sections. First, it briefly discusses the conditions under which one might expect leaders to deceive, using World War II and Vietnam as illustrations. It then takes up the Cold War case. It provides an overview of its origins; outlines the evolution of the containment policy; focuses on the events surrounding the outbreak of the Korean War; and discusses the escalation of the Cold War that Korea made possible. The final section concludes.

Explaining Deception

Why do leaders resort to deception to sell wars to their publics? Elsewhere the author has argued that the need to generate public consent is itself to blame.[2] Specifically, leaders resort to deception when they anticipate domestic opposition to an open declaration of hostilities, and deception promises to blunt that opposition. Such dissent is especially likely in cases where the benefits of using force do not clearly outweigh the costs. As a general rule, the less substantial and imminent the threat and the less assured a quick and decisive victory, the more contentious a use of force is likely to be. Preventive war, for example, is usually contested on these grounds.[3] In such cases, leaders have incentives to preempt debate by escalating the use of force incrementally, taking pains to shift responsibility for hostilities onto the adversary. The process culminates in a manufactured crisis that justifies open warfare. Deception is entailed insofar as leaders conceal their designs, exploit pretexts to justify escalation, and oversell the use of force.

The American experiences in World War II and in Vietnam provide illustrations [4] Starting with the former, Roosevelt feared that if Hitler were able to dominate Europe he would pose an intolerable threat to the Western Hemisphere. To stall the Nazi advance, the U.S. extended assistance to those powers resisting Hitler, first Great Britain and then the Soviet Union. Such assistance was limited to lend-lease aid and convoy protection, but by the fall of 1941 leading officials had concluded that the defeat of Germany would require

American belligerency. The problem was that there was widespread opposition to expanded involvement in the war. A diverse anti-interventionist movement, with significant representation in Congress, had mobilized to challenge administration initiatives, and this movement fed off a deeply ambivalent public opinion, which supported aid to the allies but was strongly opposed to formal belligerency.

Roosevelt was sensitive to the domestic mood and believed that an effective policy abroad required a consensus at home. Given the persistence of anti-interventionism, such a consensus was bound to be elusive in the case of a declaration of war. The president thus maneuvered the country in the direction of open hostilities while assuring a wary public that the country would remain at peace. This strategy entailed three types of deception. First, Roosevelt went to some lengths to conceal his belligerent intentions, for example by pledging to keep the U.S. out of the fighting even when the thrust of official thinking suggested that full-scale intervention would be required. Second, when the Nazis threatened to overrun the Allies in 1941, he sought out pretexts that would justify escalation. He was less successful in the Atlantic, where naval "incidents" such as the *Greer* episode failed to excite popular opinion, than in the Pacific, where the Pearl Harbor attack finally united the country behind war with the Axis. FDR may not have deliberately allowed the Pearl Harbor attack to happen, but it does appear that he brought matters to a head with Japan in order to have some "back door" into the European war. Finally, he indulged in rhetorical overkill at critical junctures, amplifying the Nazi threat to the Western hemisphere and exaggerating the liberal credentials of allies to justify expanded American involvement on their behalf.

Turning to the Vietnam case, Johnson confronted the same dilemma as Roosevelt- how to take the country into a war that was sure to meet with considerable skepticism - and ended up resorting to the same tactics. The situation in South Vietnam had deteriorated rapidly since he had assumed office, and trusted advisers agreed that only American military power could turn the situation around. Like his predecessors, Johnson feared that if he did not contain communism in Indochina, then dominoes would fall both abroad and at home. The problem was that while there was certainly a vocal minority calling for stronger action, this did not amount to a groundswell of support for intervening in another land war in Asia. LBJ could not ignore the fact that powerful segments of elite opinion were opposed to intervention and that the public was ambivalent at best.

To avoid a divisive debate on the subject, Johnson chose to escalate incrementally, exploiting a series of pretexts to justify the bombing of North Vietnam and the deployment of ground forces. All the while, he denied that a major change in policy was in the offing. This strategy entailed three types of deception. First, it required that the administration conceal its ultimate intent. To this end, Johnson and his advisers made early promises that the U.S. would not take over the fighting, did their planning in secret, pressured Congress to limit debate once escalation got underway, and advanced half-hearted peace initiatives to appease liberal critics. Second, it required that they exploit a series of pretexts to justify progressively stronger military measures. Among these, the most notable were the Gulf of Tonkin "incident," which yielded a supportive Congressional resolution, and the Pleiku attack, which resulted in the Rolling Thunder bombing campaign. Rolling Thunder, in turn, provided the rationale for the introduction of ground forces, which were ostensibly needed to protect airbases but were soon taking the fight to the Viet Cong. Finally, it entailed engaging in rhetorical "oversell." Leading officials relied on crude versions of the domino theory to make the case that a communist takeover would be catastrophic and fostered the impression that victory was in sight, despite internal predictions of a long war with an indeterminate outcome. As in the World War II case, these deceptions were crucial for overcoming domestic aversion to a wider war.

As the behavior of Roosevelt and Johnson attests, leaders are most prone to deceive when they anticipate opposition to a declaration of war. The puzzle that remains is how Truman was able to overcome domestic resistance to a stronger containment policy without the evasions and distortions that characterize the latter two cases. I begin to unravel this puzzle by reviewing the origins of the Cold War.

THE ORIGINS OF THE COLD WAR

As the end of World War II approached, the United States became increasingly wary of its Soviet ally. With the impending defeat of Germany and Japan, vacuums of power were opening up in Europe and Asia that American leaders feared Russia would fill. After all, Soviet armies had played the leading role in defeating the Nazis, now occupied much of Eastern Europe, and were poised to enter the war against Japan. Moreover, other key allies, such as Great Britain, had been gravely weakened, leaving the Soviet Union as the only great power in the region. As the Office of Strategic Services (OSS) warned in April 1945, "Russia will emerge from the present conflict as by far the strongest nation in Europe and Asia – strong enough, if the United States should stand aside, to dominate Europe and at the same time to establish her hegemony over Asia. Russia's natural resources and manpower are so great that within relatively few years she can be much more powerful than either Germany or Japan has ever been. In the easily foreseeable future Russia may well outrank even the United States in military potential."[5]

Having just fought to prevent the Axis powers from dominating Eurasia, American leaders were hardly keen to allow the Soviets to do so. Their primary concern was not military aggression. Top officials knew that the Soviet Union had suffered immensely at the hands of the Nazis and would focus on reconstruction for the time being. It would be the height of folly for them to provoke a war with the United States in their current state of weakness. As the OSS concluded in January 1945, "Russia will have neither the resources nor, so far as economic factors are governing, the inclination, to embark on adventurist foreign policies which, in the opinion of Soviet leaders, might involve the USSR in a conflict or a critical armament race with the great Western powers."[6] Rather, the primary concern was that Communist parties would capitalize on political and economic instability in Europe and Asia to seize power, indirectly enlarging the Soviet sphere of influence. Through such a process of psychological conquest, the Kremlin could capture or co-opt the industrial infrastructure, natural resources, and skilled labor of Eurasia.[7]

This development was anathema to the national security of the United States because if a totalitarian state like the Soviet Union became too powerful, it, like Nazi Germany, could stir up trouble in the Western Hemisphere and threaten the homeland with strangulation or attack. Recent advances in airpower, in combination with the atomic bomb, made the latter prospect especially frightening [8] In the event that the United States found itself isolated in a totalitarian world, it was feared that a "garrison state" would be the result, as Americans would be forced to sacrifice political and economic liberties for the regimentation required for national defense [9] The National Security Council summed up the dangers in March 1948, "Between the United States and the USSR there are in Europe and Asia areas of great potential power which if added to the existing strength of the Soviet world would enable the latter to become so superior in manpower, resources, and territory that the prospect for the survival of the United States as a free nation would be slight"[10].

As the end of World War II approached, these were still long-term concerns. At the time, leading officials held out hope that they could cooperate with the Soviet Union in the postwar world. Roosevelt, for example, had envisioned the United States and the Soviet Union working together to keep the peace as two of the Four Policemen [11]. Over the course of the war, a range of disagreements had come to sour relations between the two sides, however. First was the issue of a second front. From the time of Pearl Harbor, Stalin had pressed Roosevelt and Churchill to open a second front in Europe in order to relieve Nazi pressure on the Soviet Union. After leading Stalin to expect such a front in 1942, Roosevelt opted instead to endorse a British proposal to invade North Africa, delaying the Normandy invasion until 1944. It does not appear that it was Roosevelt's intent to exhaust the Russians by making them carry the main burden of the fighting [12]. He wanted to take the offensive against Hitler as quickly as possible, but also wanted to maximize the chances of success while minimizing casualties. All of these considerations pointed toward a landing in North Africa. Stalin, however, suspected that the allies had deliberately let the Soviet Union bear the brunt of the fighting, exacerbating his distrust of them.

Second was the problem of Germany. Until the end of the war, the Roosevelt administration remained divided over how to deal with a defeated Germany. The Treasury Department, with Roosevelt's support, was inclined toward dismemberment, in order to prevent the resurgence of German power. The State Department, however, wanted to integrate a disarmed but united Germany into the world economy, in order to foster democracy there and promote the economic recovery of Europe. The Soviets, for their part, had suffered immensely at the hands of the Nazis and did not look kindly upon the prospect of a rehabilitated Germany. In particular, they were determined to exact reparations in order to facilitate reconstruction and circumscribe Germany's military potential. With the end of the war, the economic situation in Europe grew desperate, triggering fears that Communist parties would exploit the resulting instability to seize power. From that point on, the United States' top priority was to revive German coal production in order to spur European economic recovery. This meant that reparations shipments to the Soviet Union would have to take second place to German rehabilitation. Still reeling from the war, the Soviets could not help but look on these developments with bitterness [13].

The strong stand on reparations was part of a larger strategy on the part of the United States to withhold reconstruction assistance from the Soviet Union in the hopes of extracting political concessions [14]. Of particular concern to leading officials was the Soviets' heavy-handed behavior in Eastern Europe, especially in Poland. Because of its sensitive location, the Soviets wanted a Poland they could depend on after the war, which meant one ruled by Communists. Roosevelt had been prepared to concede to Stalin a sphere of influence in Eastern Europe, but wanted it to be a relatively open one. He accepted that the countries of the region would be closely aligned with Russia on matters of foreign policy, but hoped that they would enjoy a measure of domestic autonomy. By way of the Four Freedoms and the Atlantic Charter, he had certainly led the American people to expect as much. When the Soviet Union recognized the Communist-dominated Lublin Committee as the provisional government of Poland in early 1945, some measure of conflict was unavoidable. At Yalta, Roosevelt attempted to secure Stalin's agreement to reorganize the Polish government on a broader democratic basis, but the Soviet leader had no intention of following through on promises of free elections. Upon succeeding to the presidency, Truman fared little better. He wanted to remove the "Soviet blackout" in Eastern Europe, but understood that he had limited leverage while Russian armies occupied the region. He more or less gave up on trying to save democracy in Eastern Europe by the end of 1945. By that point, the damage had been done: Leading officials had prodded the Soviet Union to accept an open sphere in Eastern Europe as a litmus test of their intentions. By imposing police states in Poland, Rumania, and Bulgaria, the Kremlin had failed that test, triggering fears that they were intent on wider expansion [15].

Those fears were seemingly confirmed at the beginning of 1946 when the Russians tried to make inroads into the eastern Mediterranean and the Middle East, an area that was particularly sensitive to Great Britain. They were slow to withdraw their forces from northern Iran, abetting separatist movements there, and pressed Turkey for the right to build military bases in the Dardanelles area. The Soviets eventually backed down in both crises, but not before elements of the Truman administration had become convinced that they sought world domination. This assessment was articulated most forcefully by George Kennan, deputy head of the U.S. mission in Moscow, in the "Long Telegram" of February 22, 1946. The central thrust of Kennan's analysis was that the Soviet Union was a totalitarian regime which depended on the exploitation of external threats to justify its repressive rule at home. In the Kremlin, the United States confronted "a political force committed fanatically to the belief that with [the] US there can be no permanent *modus vivendi*, that it is desirable and necessary that the internal harmony of our society be disrupted, our traditional way of life destroyed, the international authority of our state broken, if Soviet power is to be secure" [16]. The "Long Telegram," together with the Kremlin's provocative behavior in the Near East, convinced leading officials that accommodation with them was futile and that it was time to "get tough with Russia."

Around this time, a new policy began to take shape which aimed to induce Russian restraint by impressing them with American "patience and firmness." Its first public expression came on February 28, 1946 in a speech delivered to the Overseas Press Club by Secretary of State James Byrnes. In the speech, Byrnes put the Soviets on notice, informing them that "we will not and we cannot stand aloof if force or the threat of force is used contrary to the purposes and principles of the [United Nations] Charter."[17] From that point on, no major concessions were made, on issues ranging from the postwar treatment of Germany to the international control of atomic energy. This reorientation of American policy culminated in the Truman Doctrine of March 12, 1947. In that speech, Truman portrayed the Soviet-American conflict as a clash between two mutually irreconcilable ideologies and famously declared that "it must be the policy of the United States to support free peoples who are resisting attempted subjugation by armed minorities or by outside pressures" [18] If there had been any ambiguity before, the Cold War was now officially underway [19].

CONTAINMENT

From the Truman Doctrine onward, the United States moved aggressively to contain Soviet influence in Europe and Asia. The essence of the strategy, as articulated by Kennan, was threefold: (1) to restore the balance of power by building up "strongpoints" in Western Europe and Japan; (2) to bring about fragmentation within the international communist movement by encouraging nationalism; and (3) to gradually moderate Soviet behavior by the steady exertion of "counterpressure" [20]. The aim, in the end, was "strength at the center; strength at the periphery; the retraction of Soviet power and a change in the Soviet system." [21]. In this way, leading officials hoped to perpetuate American preponderance.

However ambitious their goals, it is important to emphasize that the Truman administration did not expect a military confrontation with the Soviet Union when they moved to implement containment, nor was it their intent to provoke one. Intelligence assessments at the time repeatedly concluded that the Russians were too weak to risk war with the United States, their conventional superiority in Europe outweighed by American advantages in atomic weapons and industrial capacity [22]. Privy to this intelligence, leading officials saw the threat from the Kremlin as primarily political, rather than military, in character [23]. The fear was that demoralized populations in Europe and Asia would succumb to Communist rule in the face of economic dislocation and social unrest, enlarging the Soviet sphere of influence. As Kennan told a National War College audience in October 1947, "Remember that…as things stand today, it is not Russian military power which is threatening us, it is Russian political power…If it is not entirely a military threat, I doubt that it can be effectively met entirely by military means"[24].

Accordingly, the first initiatives pursued by the Truman administration were in the political, economic, and diplomatic spheres. The Truman Doctrine, for example, was designed to mobilize domestic opinion behind aid to Greece and Turkey at a time when Great Britain was suspending assistance to those governments because of financial constraints. The situation was especially dire in Greece, where a communist-led insurgency threatened to topple the government and align Greece with the Soviet Union. Leading officials worried that if Greece fell to communism, then Turkey, Iran, and possibly even Italy and France would follow by way of a domino effect. The only alternative seemed to be a massive infusion of aid to prop up the Greek regime. The Truman Doctrine constituted a form of ideological "shock therapy" meant to bring a reluctant Congress and public on board [25].

Beyond immediate aid to Greece and Turkey, the Truman administration's top priority in spring 1947 was to promote Western Europe's economic reconstruction. At the time the situation looked dire. For example, on May 27, Undersecretary of State for Economic Affairs William L. Clayton reported, "It is now obvious that we grossly underestimated the destruction to the European economy by the war…Without further prompt and substantial aid from the United States, economic, social, and political disintegration will overwhelm Europe"[26]. Assessments such as these stirred the administration into action. On June 15, Secretary of State George C. Marshall launched the European Recovery Program. The Marshall Plan, as it was called, was motivated primarily by geopolitical and ideological factors [27]. Administration officials feared that local Communists would capitalize on the economic disarray to seize power, enlarging the Soviet sphere of influence. As Truman explained to Congress in his special message on the Marshall Plan:

> Our deepest concern with European recovery is that it is essential to the maintenance of the civilization in which the American way of life is rooted. It is the only assurance of the continued independence and integrity of a group of nations who constitute a bulwark for the principles of freedom, justice and the dignity of the individual. The economic plight in which Europe now finds itself has intensified a political struggle between those who wish to remain free men living under the rule of law and those who would use economic distress as a pretext for the establishment of a totalitarian state. The next few years can determine whether the free countries of Europe will be able to preserve their heritage of freedom. If Europe fails to recover, the peoples of these countries might be driven to the philosophy of despair – the philosophy which contends that their basic wants can be met only by the surrender of their basic rights to totalitarian control [28].

The Marshall Plan was intended to avert just such a deterioration in the balance of power by building up Western Europe as a bulwark against Soviet expansion.

It was widely understood among leading officials that the economy of Western Europe could not recover fully without a substantial German contribution. Ruhr coal was considered especially crucial [29]. By the spring of 1947, the Truman administration wanted to do more than revive German industry, however. Around this time, the "western strategy" began to take shape [30]. According to this strategy, the United States, Britain, and France would "organize" their zones of occupation into a West German state, which would be tied to the western powers in a variety of ways. The United States and Britain had already taken the first important steps in this direction when they had merged their zones of occupation the previous summer. The thinking behind the "western strategy" was that an occupied Germany could not contribute fully to European recovery, but that a divided Germany was to be preferred to a unified one that succumbed to Soviet control or grew powerful enough to play off East against West. As Secretary of State Dean Acheson later framed the issue, "We are concerned with the integration of Germany into a free and democratic Europe. We have made and are making progress to this end with the part of Germany which we control and we shall not jeopardize this progress by seeking a unified Germany as in itself good." In time, leading officials hoped, this west German state could be integrated into a European political community, a "Third Force" capable of balancing Soviet power and containing Germany without a permanent American military presence[32] The United States and its allies had reached sufficient agreement on these points to move forward with the creation of a west German state in early 1948 [33]

Like the other major initiatives of the early Cold War period, the creation of a west German state was primarily a political, economic, and diplomatic exercise. It reflected the thinking among leading officials that the reconstruction of Western Europe had to come before rearmament [34]. This assessment was shared even at the Pentagon. Frustrated as he was by the widening gap between commitments and capabilities, Secretary of Defense James Forrestal agreed that the objectives of U.S. policy were "economic stability, political stability and military stability...in about that order."[35]. This is not to say that there was no military component to containment. By 1948, the Truman administration had secured an extensive system of overseas bases from which to project power in the event of war, enjoyed a monopoly over atomic weapons, and was considering extending alliance guarantees to Western Europe in the form of a North Atlantic Treaty [36]. Nor is it to suggest that leading officials were unaware that their initiatives were provocative, especially the creation of a west German state [37] The important point, however, is that the Truman administration did not expect Soviet *military* aggression. It was for this reason that policymakers felt able to rebuild Western Europe while postponing rearmament.

In the meantime, the Truman administration was counting on its atomic monopoly to deter any residual threat of Soviet adventurism. The United States had demobilized rapidly after World War II, and by 1947 very little was left of the military machine that had been built up during the war [38] This meant that the United States had to settle for a tripwire strategy in Western Europe [39]. According to this strategy, Russian armies would overrun the continent at the outset of any war, but the United States would ultimately prevail by way of a sustained campaign of atomic bombardment. The upside of the tripwire strategy was that the United States did not have to maintain a large military establishment or deploy ground forces in order to deter Soviet aggression in Europe. Limited resources could be devoted instead to the Marshall Plan. The downside, however, was that the United States would have to bomb her own allies in the event of a war, yielding at best a Pyrrhic victory. Administration officials were more than aware of the tripwire strategy's liabilities. Omar Bradley, then U.S. Army chief of staff, remarked in April 1949 that "It must be perfectly apparent to the people of the United States that we cannot count on friends in Western Europe if our strategy in the event of war dictates that we shall first abandon them to the enemy with a promise of later liberation." [40]. Around the same time, Truman reminded the NATO foreign ministers that "a Soviet attack today, while we could eventually defeat it, would involve an operation of incalculable magnitude in which, even if eventual victory is sure, the consequences to the U.S., and particularly to Western Europe itself, might well be disastrous" [41]. The prospect of such a war was sufficiently sobering that American leaders felt they could not pursue a firm policy of containment in the 1948-49 period. The Truman Doctrine notwithstanding, the administration decided against interventions in Italy and Greece to ward off Communist takeovers [42].

NSC-68 AND THE KOREAN WAR

The tripwire strategy was by no means ideal, but it did promise to deter war at moderate cost as long as the United States retained its monopoly over atomic weapons. This explains why the test explosion conducted by the Soviet Union in September 1949 set off such alarm bells in Washington [43]. A Soviet atomic capability meant that victory in a third world war could no longer be taken for granted, compromising the American deterrent. Leading officials feared the diplomatic consequences. One concern was that if the Europeans concluded the United States would not risk atomic retaliation on their behalf, they would back away from provocative initiatives like the rehabilitation of Germany. Another was that atomic weapons would enhance the Kremlin's penchant for risk-taking. Surveying Soviet moves in February 1950, Paul Nitze, director of the State Department's Policy Planning Staff, reported:

> In the aggregate, recent Soviet moves reflect not only a mounting militancy but suggest a boldness that is essentially new – and borders on recklessness, particularly since in the present international situation great stakes are involved in any USSR move, and any move directly or indirectly affects the US and risks US counter action. Nothing about the moves indicates that Moscow is preparing to launch in the near future an all-out military attack on the West. They do, however, suggest a greater willingness than in the past to undertake a course of action,

including a possible use of force in local areas, which might lead to an accidental outbreak of general military conflict. Thus the chance of war through miscalculation is increased [44]

Together with the "loss" of China, the breaking of the atomic monopoly contributed to a perception among leading officials that the Communist side was seizing the initiative in the Cold War.

In light of Soviet atomic capabilities, the Truman administration conducted a comprehensive review of its strategic posture in the spring of 1950. The culmination of this exercise was NSC-68, formally titled "United States Objectives and Programs for National Security"[45]. Authored by a State-Defense Policy Review Group under the direction of Nitze, NSC-68 reaffirmed the goals of the containment policy while calling for a "rapid build-up of political, economic, and military strength in the free world" to offset Soviet gains [46]. The fear was that U.S. credibility would erode with its military advantage, undermining deterrence. Sensing American weakness, key allies would be intimidated while the Soviets would be emboldened. In NSC-68's terms, "Without superior aggregate military strength, in being and readily mobilizeable, a policy of 'containment' – which is in effect a policy of calculated and gradual coercion – is no more than a policy of bluff"[47]. The point of maximum danger would come in the mid-1950's when it was estimated that the Soviets would have enough atomic bombs to launch a surprise attack. The arms buildup was intended to avert general war by restoring deterrence. This would require large nuclear and conventional forces, the first to launch a decisive attack on the Soviet homeland in the event of war and the second to allow the "forward defense" of Europe [48]. The problem was that while this buildup was underway, the country was going to have to cross a kind of danger zone in which the Soviets might be tempted to risk war while conditions were favorable. "The assumption," in Trachtenberg's words, "was that a 'window' favoring the Soviets had opened, and that the American attempt to close it might well lead to a war"[49].

Evidence of Soviet risk-taking was not long in coming. On June 25, 1950, North Korean armies poured across the 38th parallel into South Korea. It was taken for granted that the Soviets had authorized the invasion and could be planning for aggression in more vital areas, such as the Middle East and Europe [50] When it became clear that Soviet action elsewhere was unlikely and that only U.S. troops could save South Korea, Truman approved the deployment of two divisions from Japan, reversing the prior policy of military disengagement from the peninsula.

The president, like his advisers, feared the consequences of inaction. He believed that "If we let Korea down, the Soviets will keep right on going and swallow up one piece of Asia after another...If we were to let Asia go, the Near East would collapse and no telling what would happen in Europe"[51] Determined to draw the line, Truman was ready to assume the defense of South Korea [52]

The public, rallying around the flag, saw matters in much the same way [53] They were shocked by the blatant nature of the North Korean attack and, convinced that the war would be a short one, strongly supported intervention. Assured of public backing, Truman was able to commit the country to a limited war in Korea with little pushback from Congress, even though he had failed to consult with them.

On July 19, 1950, the president explained his decision to the people: "The free nations have now made it clear that lawless aggression will be met with force. The free nations have learned the fateful lesson of the 1930's. That lesson is that aggression must be met firmly. Appeasement leads only to further aggression and ultimately to war"[54]

ESCALATING THE COLD WAR, TO A POINT

The consensus surrounding Truman's decision to intervene in Korea is surprising given the domestic constraints that had been placed on his prosecution of the Cold War thus far [55] Deep-rooted strands of anti-statism and isolationism in American political culture meant that there were limits on how quickly the administration could build up a peacetime military establishment and take on new commitments worldwide. The common fear was that a "garrison state" would result, not from hemispheric isolation as Truman warned, but from the demands of the containment policy. A strategy that required military preparedness and "entangling alliances," after all, was bound to concentrate unprecedented power in the executive branch. As journalist Hanson Baldwin posed the dilemma, "How can we prepare for total war without becoming a 'garrison state' and destroying the very qualities and virtues and principles we originally set about to save?"[56].

Fears of a "garrison state" were articulated most forcefully by Republicans such as Senator Robert A. Taft. Like Baldwin, Taft feared that "an all-out war program in time of peace might mean the final and complete destruction of those liberties which it is the very purpose of the preparation to protect."[57]. It was for this reason that he and his conservative allies in Congress opposed the tax increases and budget deficits that would have been necessary to fund an expansion of the national security state. Partisan politics aside, Truman was every bit as determined to reconcile military and economic considerations as the Republican opposition. From 1945 on, the president had resisted demands from the Pentagon that he sanction larger defense budgets, mainly because he did not want to run deficits. Rather, he settled on a "tripwire strategy" that promised to deter war at a moderate cost by relying on air-atomic power. As Hogan argues, this strategy was closer to the "Fortress America" concept championed by conservatives than many realized at the time [58]. Even after the Soviet nuclear breakthrough, Truman wanted to hold the line on defense spending. His initial reaction to NSC-68 was to shelve it until its cost implications became clear, and he told a press conference in May 1950 that "the defense budget next year will be smaller than it is this year" [59].

With the onset of the Korean War, Truman's attitude quickly changed. The Soviets had demonstrated their penchant for risk-taking, and would only become more aggressive as their capabilities increased. The heightened risk of global war convinced him, along with many in the opposition, that rearmament could not be postponed any longer. The result was the massive military buildup that had been ruled out up to that point. Over the coming years, the armed forces would double in size, fueled by a staggering 262 percent increase in defense appropriations. Only a fraction of this increase was earmarked for the fighting in Korea. The rest was meant to restore deterrence by enabling victory in a general war. "The North Korean invasion," as Wells argues, "made the case for a rapid U.S. military buildup that Paul Nitze and his associates had not been able to do" with NSC-68 [60] One of the primary objectives of the buildup was the "forward defense" of Europe. To shore up weaknesses in this area, the administration launched a series of initiatives to strengthen the NATO alliance [61]. These included a push for European rearmament, the appointment of Dwight Eisenhower as Supreme Commander to lead NATO forces, and the deployment of four divisions to serve under him. Truman made the latter move over strong Republican objections. They questioned the wisdom of stationing American troops in Europe at a time of continued fighting in Korea and challenged the president's right to deploy them without congressional approval [62]. The fact that Truman prevailed in this debate is another indicator that domestic opinion was ready to assume commitments that had been politically untenable prior to the Korean War. As Acheson confided to the British and French foreign ministers in September 1950, "The Government of the United States has searched its intentions deeply…and has come to decisions which I think can only be described as a complete revolution in American foreign policy and in the attitude of the American people."[63].

The problem that Truman had to contend with during the Korean War was not isolationist sentiment but its opposite, as 1950 marked the high tide of preventive war agitation [64]. In mid-August, a Congressional delegation warned Acheson, "There is a growing disposition on the part of the American people to support the concept of preventive war. This growing attitude is sired in fear and will continue to grow in volume unless some bold alternative course of action is presented by the Government"[65]. Fuel was added to the fire on August 25 when Francis P. Matthews, the secretary of the navy, gave a controversial speech calling on Americans to become the world's first "aggressors for peace"[66]. The administration immediately disowned the speech, with Truman reminding the public on September 1 that "We do not believe in aggressive or preventive war. Such war is the weapon of dictators, not of free democratic countries like the United States"[67].

Official sanction of the preventive war option was so unwelcome because Truman was generally determined to say and do nothing that might provoke the Soviet Union at a time of relative weakness[68]. This was a sentiment shared throughout the administration. For example, General J. Lawton Collins, the Army Chief of Staff, recommended on January 12, 1951 that "Since the United States is not now prepared to engage in global war, and will not be ready before 1 July 1952, we should take all honorable means to avoid any action that is likely to bring Russia into open conflict with the United States prior to that date"[69]. It was agreed that this ruled out a major escalation of the Korean War, which had become a live issue when China intervened in late November 1950 and threatened to drive U.S. forces off the peninsula [70].General Douglas MacArthur, the local commander, wanted to retaliate against the Chinese mainland with air power and use Chiang Kai-shek's troops to offset the enemy's superior numbers. The Joint Chiefs, however, overruled him, with Omar Bradley famously testifying before Congress that such a strategy "would involve us in the wrong war, at the wrong place, at the wrong time, and with the wrong enemy."[71] Having finally secured domestic support for a stronger containment policy in Europe, administration officials did not want to undermine it by way of a wider war in Asia.

CONCLUSION

Truman's refusal to escalate the Korean War in the face of stalemate contributed to its growing unpopularity and provided a political opening for Republicans, who charged the administration with underestimating the Communist threat in Asia. Public support for the larger policy of containment, however, remained robust. In June 1951, an opinion survey of popular attitudes toward NSC-68 found that the public "appears by all reliable objective criteria to be favorably disposed," with 83 percent wanting to continue current levels of spending on rearmament, 52 percent supporting economic assistance to allies, and 57 percent favoring sending U.S. troops to Europe [72]. These numbers reflect the fact that, however unhappy they were with the situation in Korea, the public had largely come around to the administration position on the Cold War.

In this respect, the case attests to the political advantages of absorbing the first blow. Truman was able to escalate the Cold War because he waited for the Soviet Union to make the first overt move, which turned out to be in Korea. It was the Korean War, in turn, which overcame domestic resistance to a stronger containment policy [73].It is a testament to Truman's political instincts that he did not press the issue earlier and jeopardize the Cold War consensus in the process. In contrast, Roosevelt and Johnson were intent on picking a fight before they had secured a domestic consensus for war. The result was that they had to resort to deception to preempt opposition to their designs. The enduring lesson is that, whatever disadvantages might accrue to a policy of restraint, the damage to the democratic process can be severe when a policy of preemption is pursued.

REFERENCES

[1] This is a point made in Steven Casey, "Selling NSC-68: The Truman Administration, Public Opinion, and the Politics of Mobilization, 1950-51," *Diplomatic History*, Vol. 29, No. 4 (September 2005), pp. 655-656. He cites John Lewis Gaddis, *The United States and the Origins of the Cold War, 1941-1947* (New York, NY: Columbia University Press, 2000), pp. 351-352; Gaddis, *Strategies of Containment: A Critical Appraisal of Postwar American National Security Policy* (Oxford, UK: Oxford University Press, 1982), pp. 107-109; and Thomas J. Christensen, *Useful Adversaries: Grand Strategy, Domestic Mobilization, and Sino-American Conflict, 1947-1958* (Princeton, NJ: Princeton University Press, 1996), pp. 49-58, 122-127, among others.

[2] John Schuessler, "Doing Good by Stealth? Democracy, Deception, and the Use of Force" (PH.D. dissertation, University of Chicago, 2007).

[3] Randall L. Schweller, "Domestic Structure and Preventive War: Are Democracies More Pacific?" *World Politics*, Vol. 44, No. 2 (January 1992), pp. 235-269.

[4] Chapter 2 of the dissertation deals with World War II while chapter 3 deals with Vietnam.

[5] Cited in Dale C. Copeland, *The Origins of Major War* (Ithaca, NY: Cornell University Press, 2000), p. 151.

[6] Cited in James McAllister, *No Exit: America and the German Problem, 1943-1954* (Ithaca, NY: Cornell University Press, 2002), p. 41.

[7] Melvyn P. Leffler, *A Preponderance of Power: National Security, the Truman Administration, and the Cold War* (Stanford, CA: Stanford University Press, 1992), Introduction.

[8] Aaron L. Friedberg, *In the Shadow of the Garrison State: America's Anti-Statism and its Cold War Grand Strategy* (Princeton, NJ: Princeton University Press, 2000), pp. 36-38.

[9] On postwar fears of a "garrison state," see Michael J. Hogan, *A Cross of Iron: Harry S. Truman and the Origins of the National Security State, 1945-1954* (Cambridge, UK: Cambridge University Press, 1998) and Friedberg, *In the Shadow of the Garrison State*.

[10] *Foreign Relations of the United States*, 1948, Vol. I, p. 546. Cited in Gaddis, *Strategies of Containment*, p. 57.

[11] The other two Policemen would be Great Britain and China. See Gaddis, *The United States and the Origins of the Cold War*, pp. 9-13.

[12] Gaddis argues that "Roosevelt generally resisted efforts to deploy forces for the dual purposes of defeating the Germans and containing the Russians." See Gaddis, *Strategies of Containment*, p. 6 and Gaddis, *The United States and the Origins of the Cold War*, chapter 3.

[13] On the German question, see Gaddis, *The United States and the Origins of the Cold War*, chapter 4; Leffler, *A Preponderance of Power*, pp. 63-71; Copeland, *The Origins of Major War*, pp. 153-155; and McAllister, *No Exit*, pp. 49-55. Trachtenberg argues that, by the summer of 1945, the United States and the Soviet Union had tacitly agreed to partition Germany, to let each side do what it wanted in its own occupation zone. See Marc Trachtenberg, *A Constructed Peace: The Making of the European Settlement, 1945-1963* (Princeton, NJ: Princeton University Press, 1999), pp. 15-33.

[14] Gaddis, *The United States and the Origins of the Cold War*, chapter 6 and Copeland, *The Origins of Major War*, pp. 155-156.

[15] On Eastern Europe, see Gaddis, *The United States and the Origins of the Cold War*, chapter 5; Leffler, *A Preponderance of Power*, chapter 1, esp. pp. 34-36 and 49-54; and McAllister, *No Exit*, pp. 56-66. Trachtenberg argues that by the end of 1945 the United States had come to accept Soviet predominance in Eastern Europe as the basis for a larger spheres of influence settlement. See Trachtenberg, *A Constructed Peace*, pp. 4-15.

[16] *Foreign Relations of the United States*, 1946, Vol. VI, p. 706. Cited in Gaddis, *The United States and the Origins of the Cold War*, p. 303.

[17] Cited in Gaddis, *The United States and the Origins of the Cold War*, p. 305.

[18] *Public Papers of the Presidents of the United States*: Harry S. Truman, 1947 (Washington, DC: United States Government Printing Office, 1963), pp. 178-179.

[19] On the reorientation of American policy in 1946, see Gaddis, *The United States and the Origins of the Cold War*, chapters 9-10; Gaddis, *Strategies of Containment*, pp. 19-24; Leffler, *A Preponderance of Power*, chapter 2, esp. pp. 77-81, chapter 3, esp. pp. 106-110, chapter 4, esp. pp. 142-146; and Trachtenberg, *A Constructed Peace*, chapter 2.

[20] Kennan, *Strategies of Containment*, chapters 2-3.

[21] Leffler, *A Preponderance of Power*, p. 18.

[22] Gaddis, *Strategies of Containment*, p. 62 and Leffler, *Preponderance of Power*, pp. 5-6, 149, 218-219, 261-262, and 306-308.

[23] Leffler, *A Preponderance of Power*, chapter 4, esp. p. 180.

[24] Cited in Gaddis, *Strategies of Containment*, p. 40.

[25] Christensen, *Useful Adversaries*, pp. 49-54; Gaddis, *The United States and the Origins of the Cold War*, pp. 346-352; and Leffler, *A Preponderance of Power*, pp. 142-146.

[26] *Foreign Relations of the United States*, 1947, Vol. III, pp. 230-232. Cited in Leffler, *A Preponderance of Power*, p. 159.
[27] Leffler, *A Preponderance of Power*, pp. 157-164. See also McAllister, *No Exit*, pp. 124-135.
[28] *PPPUS*: Truman, 1947, pp. 516-517. Cited in Leffler, *A Preponderance of Power*, p. 200.
[29] Leffler, *A Preponderance of Power*, pp. 151-157.
[30] Trachtenberg, *A Constructed Peace*, p. 55.
[31] *Foreign Relations of the United States*, 1949, Vol. III, pp. 872-873. Cited in Gaddis, *Strategies of Containment*, p. 76.
[32] On "third force" planning, see McAllister, *No Exit*, chapter 4 and Sebastian Rosato, "The Strategic Logic of European Integration," (Ph.D., The University of Chicago, 2006), chapter 3.
[33] Trachtenberg, *A Constructed Peace*, p. 78.
[34] Leffler, *A Preponderance of Power*, pp. 148-151.
[35] Cited in Gaddis, *Strategies of Containment*, p. 61. Forrestal elaborated elsewhere, "As long as we can outproduce the world, can control the sea and can strike inland with the atomic bomb, we can assume certain risks otherwise unacceptable in an effort to restore world trade, to restore the balance of power – military power – and to eliminate some of the conditions which breed war." Cited in McAllister, *No Exit*, p. 122.
[36] On overseas bases, see Leffler, *A Strategy of Preponderance*, pp. 56-59, 226-228 and Copeland, *The Origins of Major War*, pp. 152-153. On the atomic monopoly, see Leffler, *A Preponderance of Power*, pp. 94-96, 114-116 and Copeland, *The Origins of Major War*, pp. 162-164. On the origins of NATO, see Trachtenberg, *A Constructed Peace*, pp. 83-86 and McAllister, *No Exit*, pp. 141-156. Trachtenberg points out that the United States was pulled into the NATO system reluctantly.
[37] The Berlin blockade was a direct response to the policy of establishing a west German state. See Trachtenberg, *A Constructed Peace*, pp. 78-86.
[38] On the rapid pace of demobilization, see Gaddis, *The United States and the Origins of the Cold War*, pp. 161-163.
[39] Trachtenberg, *A Constructed Peace*, pp. 89-91, 96-97. On U.S. war planning, see also Marc Trachtenberg, *History and Strategy* (Princeton, NJ: Princeton University Press, 1991), pp. 119-121, 153-158 and Leffler, *A Preponderance of Power*, pp. 110-114, 221-226.
[40] Cited in Trachtenberg, *A Constructed Peace*, pp. 100-101.
[41] Cited in Trachtenberg, *A Constructed Peace*, p. 90.
[42] Trachtenberg, *A Constructed Peace*, pp. 86-89.
[43] On the implications of the end of the atomic monopoly, see Leffler, *A Preponderance of Power*, pp. 323-333 and Trachtenberg, *A Constructed Peace*, pp. 96-103.
[44] *Foreign Relations of the United States*, 1950, Vol. I, pp. 145-146. Cited in Leffler, *A Preponderance of Power*, p. 330.
[45] The full report can be found in *Foreign Relations of the United States*, 1950, Vol. I, pp. 235-292. On the context surrounding NSC-68, see Samuel F. Wells, Jr., "Sounding the Tocsin: NSC 68 and the Soviet Threat," *International Security*, Vol. 4, No. 2 (Autumn 1979), pp. 116-158; Trachtenberg, *History and Strategy*, pp. 107-115; Leffler, *A*

[46] *Preponderance of Power*, pp. 355-360; and Christensen, *Useful Adversaries*, pp. 122-127. For a strong critique, see Gaddis, *Strategies of Containment*, chapter 4.
[46] *Foreign Relations of the United States*, 1950, Vol. I, p. 282.
[47] *Foreign Relations of the United States*, 1950, Vol. I, p. 253. Cited in Leffler, *A Preponderance of Power*, p. 357.
[48] Trachtenberg, *A Constructed Peace*, p. 100.
[49] Trachtenberg, *History and Strategy*, p. 112.
[50] Kim Il-sung did, in fact, secure Soviet and Chinese approval before attacking. See William Stueck, *Rethinking the Korean War: A New Diplomatic and Strategic History* (Princeton, NJ: Princeton University Press, 2002), pp. 69-77.
[51] Cited in Leffler, *A Preponderance of Power*, p. 366.
[52] On the American decision to intervene, see Leffler, *A Preponderance of Power*, pp. 364-369 and Stueck, *Rethinking the Korean War*, pp. 78-82.
[53] On public opinion during the Korean War, see John E. Mueller, *War, Presidents, and Public Opinion* (New York, NY: Wiley, 1973), esp. chapter 3 and Benjamin I. Page and Robert Y. Shapiro, *The Rational Public: Fifty Years of Trends in Americans' Policy Preferences* (Chicago, IL: The University of Chicago Press, 1992), pp. 209-214.
[54] *Public Papers of the Presidents of the United States*: Harry S. Truman, 1950 (Washington, DC: United States Government Printing Office, 1965), p. 538.
[55] On these domestic constraints, see Christensen, *Useful Adversaries*, pp. 39-49; Hogan, *A Cross of Iron*; Friedberg, *In the Shadow of the Garrison State*, chapters 1-2.
[56] Cited in Aaron L. Friedberg, "Why Didn't the United States Become a Garrison State?" *International Security*, Vol. 16, No. 4 (Spring 1992), p. 112.
[57] Cited in Gaddis, *Strategies of Containment*, p. 120.
[58] Hogan, *A Cross of Iron*, pp. 335, 467.
[59] Cited in Gaddis, *Strategies of Containment*, p. 113. On Truman's reaction to NSC-68, see Wells, "Sounding the Tocsin," pp. 137-138 and Hogan, *A Cross if Iron*, pp. 302-304.
[60] Wells, "Sounding the Tocsin," p. 140. On the military buildup, see Gaddis, *Strategies of Containment*, p. 113; Leffler, *A Preponderance of Power*, pp. 369-374; and Hogan, *A Cross of Iron*, pp. 304-312.
[61] On the NATO initiatives, see Gaddis, *Strategies of Containment*, pp. 114-115; Leffler, *A Preponderance of Power*, pp. 383-390, 406-418; Trachtenberg, *A Constructed Peace*, pp. 96-103; and McAllister, *No Exit*, pp. 183-192. The latter two are primarily concerned with the question of German rearmament.
[62] On the so-called "Great Debate," see Hogan, *A Cross of Iron*, pp. 322-335.
[63] *Foreign Relations of the United States*, 1950, Vol. III, p. 316. Cited in Gaddis, *Strategies of Containment*, p. 114.
[64] Trachtenberg, *History and Strategy*, p. 122. See also Casey, "Selling NSC-68" and Casey, "White House Publicity Operations During the Korean War, June 1950-June 1951," *Presidential Studies Quarterly*, Vol. 35, No. 4 (December 2005), pp. 691-717.
[65] *Foreign Relations of the United States*, 1950, Vol. III, p. 199. Cited in Casey, "Selling NSC-68," p. 675.
[66] Trachtenberg, *History and Strategy*, p. 117 and Casey, "Selling NSC-68," p. 676.
[67] *PPPUS*: Truman, 1950, p. 613. Cited in Casey, "Selling NSC-68," p. 677.
[68] Casey, "White House Publicity Operations," p. 701.

[69] Cited in Trachtenberg, *History and Strategy*, p. 124.
[70] Trachtenberg, *History and Strategy*, pp. 118-126; Leffler, *A Preponderance of Power*, pp. 399-406; and Stueck, *Rethinking the Korean War*, chapter 5. American leaders became increasingly willing to escalate the Korean conflict as the military buildup bore fruit. See Trachtenberg, *History and Strategy*, pp. 126-130.
[71] Cited in Trachtenberg, *History and Strategy*, p. 125.
[72] Cited in Casey, "Selling NSC-68," p. 688 and Casey, "White House Publicity Operations," p. 708.
[73] Robert Jervis, "The Impact of the Korean War on the Cold War," *The Journal of Conflict Resolution*, Vol. 24, No. 4 (December 1980), pp. 563-592.

Chapter 12

"IT'S NOT ENOUGH TO SAY WE'RE IN VIET-NAM SIMPLY BECAUSE IKE GOT US THERE": LYNDON JOHNSON AND THE CONSTRAINTS OF CONTINUITY IN VIETNAM POLICYMAKING

Nicole Anslover

ABSTRACT

Lyndon Johnson felt compelled to follow the Vietnam policies put in place by his predecessors, particularly John F. Kennedy. LBJ suffered this "compulsion for continuity" several reasons. He was so far removed from Kennedy's inner circle, however, that he had difficulty determining exactly what those policies were. He relied on his own anti-communist feelings, and what Truman and Eisenhower had done, and continued the eventually disastrous policy of "one more step." It was his obsessive need to ensure continuity with the Kennedy memory that led to many of his decisions; Johnson did not fully let his own foreign policy ideology develop. Johnson also made a concerted effort to obtain Eisenhower's approval on all Vietnam policies. The desire to be consistent with policies already in place is an important motivating factor in foreign policy decision-making, and Johnson's Vietnam policies clearly demonstrate that fact.

When Lyndon Johnson unpredictably became president in November 1963, he had an exceptionally perilous set of problems to face. He needed to calm a fearful nation, honor the memory of a slain leader, and cope with multiple foreign entanglements. When asked months later what his first priority was during the transition, Johnson stated, "I recognized that our first great problem was to assure the world that there would be continuity in transition…". [1] This need for continuity would become a factor in many of Johnson's decisions, particularly in terms of the Vietnam War.

In the recent historiography of the Vietnam War, "blame" is one of the most common words historians use. In research and writing, trying to discern who is to blame for the escalation and mismanagement is often the primary goal. Lyndon Johnson is frequently the scapegoat. But we need a new perspective on how and why Vietnam-related decisions were made. Presidents feel the need to follow the examples of their predecessors in terms of foreign policy—in other words, a "compulsion for continuity". Regardless of whether or not continuity with previous administrations is the right choice, it is an important factor in presidential decision-making. LBJ was committed to continuity with JFK's policies; however, he was never part of Kennedy's inner circle and therefore had difficulty determining exactly what those policies were. To assure himself, and the nation, that he was following a plan already in motion, Johnson sought approval from Dwight Eisenhower and attempted to prove cohesion with his policies, too.

Johnson did not intend to make Vietnam his priority – he had grandiose plans for domestic reform. He wanted to be able to devote his time in office to building his Great Society, but feared (correctly) that he would have to focus on foreign policy. His days in the Senate and as vice president gave LBJ plenty of his own foreign policy experience to draw on. But his major concern was that the public expected him to carry forward Kennedy's policies. Johnson sought to appear outwardly confident that he could do this, and early on, repeatedly assured the public that he would not allow the conflict in Vietnam to spiral out of control. He promised his constituents: "The United States still seeks no wider war. We threaten no regime and covet no territory. We have worked and will continue to work for a reduction of tensions, on the great stage of the world. But the aggression from the North must be stopped." [2]

Despite assurances to the contrary, Lyndon Johnson dramatically escalated American involvement in Vietnam. That is an undeniable fact. After being presented with a "blank check" from Congress in the form of the Gulf of Tonkin Resolution, Johnson escalated involvement through initiatives such as Operation Rolling Thunder and the introduction of combat ground troops. However, what is still open to interpretation is *why* Johnson took the steps he did to advance American military intervention. Was it due to his ideology, some rigid anti-communist stance? Was it faulty advice from his military advisors? Or was he simply a power-hungry president afflicted with the curse of hubris? Certainly, when one studies the literature of the Johnson era, all of these possible explanations alone and in tandem are addressed at some point. [3] Johnson's strong, almost manic, personality marred by self-doubt must be taken into consideration, as well.

JOHNSON ATTEMPTS TO ENSURE CONTINUITY WITH KENNEDY

However, scholars must heavily weigh another explanation. Because of his own insecurities, Lyndon Johnson had an almost obsessive need to ensure continuity with his predecessors. [4] One might assume that as vice president, Johnson had been privy to Kennedy's foreign policy plans—this assumption is incorrect. Indeed, Johnson considered the vice presidency to be the most "insignificant office" of any in government; this judgment was compounded when he was rarely asked for his opinion on foreign affairs.

However, Kennedy did want to keep Johnson relatively happy and realized that perhaps he could be of some assistance in foreign affairs. Shortly after the inauguration, Kennedy wrote to Johnson acknowledging the need to have a Vice President "who is fully informed and adequately prepared" in matters of national security, particularly foreign and military policies. Kennedy also assured his second in command that he wanted to form a "closer working relationship" than some previous executives enjoyed. In order to accomplish these goals, Kennedy authorized Johnson to preside over National Security Council meetings in his absence and granted him access to pertinent information from all agencies concerned with foreign policy. [5]

Some historians and former Kennedy supporters argue that Kennedy was actively searching for a way out of Vietnam; his public and private statements well into 1963 demonstrate otherwise. Kennedy's own rigid anti-communism led him to consider plans to use a "significant number of United States forces to signify United States determination to defend South Vietnam". [6] Because of Kennedy's offer to provide his VP with all pertinent information, Johnson would have been aware that Kennedy considered engaging U.S. troops.

Despite being aware of most policy decisions, Johnson was not an active participant in them. When he abruptly assumed command, he needed to reassess America's Vietnam policy due to Kennedy's sudden death; the murder of South Vietnam's President Diem further complicated the state of affairs . Paul Kattenburg, a senior member of the State Department, went to South Vietnam to assess the situation. Upon observing the political unrest in the country, he noted that "the time has come again for very careful stock-taking and analysis," and he stressed, "a great sense of urgency is unquestionably required." Kattenberg concluded that while there did not appear to be any new leadership firmly taking charge, the political climate was somewhat positive: "Generally, the country is breathing a deep sigh of relief after the elimination of the dictatorship and is feeling its way in the new freedom." [7] The changing of the guard, as it was, in South Vietnam, required American officials to come up with new ideas on how to shape policy.

Kattenburg intended to offer concrete suggestions in his report, but this was difficult because he, and others, were confused as to what U.S. objectives actually were. He could not offer a clear definition of policy but stated optimistically: "I am assuming that our objective in the broadest sense continues to be to assist the Vietnamese in 'winning the war'." Unfortunately, according to Kattenburg, some of the South Vietnamese generals either did not understand that objective or simply interpreted it differently. If one did assume that the main objective was victory (however defined), Kattenburg cautioned that there would definitely be problems achieving this goal. He warned "nothing repeat nothing at all will really be achieved toward that objective until we manage to overcome the overwhelming feeling among the mass of Vietnamese population that the other side is winning and not ours." Therefore, Kattenburg suggested that the primary policy objective should be to "maximize our bargaining posture in the international arena vis-à-vis Viet-Nam," because that might be the arena where success could actually be measured. [8] From the beginning of his time in office, LBJ received vague reports such as Kattenburg's; unfortunately, many others within the administration seemed as confused about policy as he himself was, making it even more difficult to follow Kennedy's path.

JOHNSON'S RELIANCE ON KENNEDY'S AIDES

To help him gain his footing, it was logical for Johnson to retain the majority of Kennedy's advisors during his early days in office; he learned to rely on some of them and many stayed on to advise LBJ even after the 1964 election. Key voices on Vietnam that continued from the Kennedy years were Robert McNamara, Dean Rusk, and McGeorge Bundy. Many of these advisors emphasized the theme of continuity, thereby increasing it's importance to LBJ. Johnson's attention to continuity was probably heightened because it was a matter to which his senior advisors paid close attention. Dean Rusk, of whom Johnson had been very fond since his days as Vice President, emphasized past policies in several of his speeches. Shortly after the 1966 State of the Union, Rusk gave an address discussing the reasons for continued commitment in Southeast Asia. Not only was the security of Vietnam essential to the security of the U.S., according to Secretary Rusk, but it had deep reaching roots. In fact, "That determination was made first, before the Korean War, by President Truman, on the basis of protracted analysis in the highest councils of the government." [9] Rusk and Johnson often respected one another's opinions; this issue is simply one more area where they found common ground.

Walt Rostow was another holdover from the Kennedy administration that Johnson worked well with. Johnson often relied on Rostow's optimism and dogged attitude regarding the military in Vietnam (until March 1968, that is). Rostow was emphatic that not only was escalation the right decision for Johnson, but that it was also what Kennedy would have done. Rostow took it upon himself to point out how closely Johnson was adhering to what Kennedy would have done. Frequently, Rostow and others made compilations of Kennedy quotes on the topic, marking the most significant passages for Johnson's attention. The quotes were worthwhile – Rostow remarked that he was surprised at how adamantly the Kennedy statements supported continued involvement in Vietnam. Rostow told Johnson that after re-reading these quotes, he realized the "basic elements in President Kennedy's position" were quite striking. For Rostow, the elements Kennedy highlighted were "his explicit linkage of the commitment in Viet Nam to the SEATO Treaty; his flat acceptance of the domino theory in Southeast Asia," and "his recurrent linkage of Viet Nam to Berlin, and the general theme that the fate of our own liberty was involved in Viet Nam." For Rostow, these themes were particularly important because this record of statements could possibly help Johnson refute detractors of his escalation policies. After all, Rostow remarked, "I don't believe any objective person can read this record without knowing that President Kennedy would have seen this through whatever the cost." [10] With encouragement like this, it becomes more understandable that Johnson would feel so compelled to trod in Kennedy's path.

Johnson's National Security Advisor, McGeorge Bundy, advised Johnson to convince key legislators, as well as the public, of continuity. In the summer of 1964, Bundy encouraged him to make sure that Senator Mike Mansfield understood the essential need for heavy U.S. commitment to South Vietnam. Johnson should remind Mansfield, "…the whole history of our support to South Vietnam going back to 1954 makes it inevitable that the U.S. is deeply involved, and this would be true even if we had not made the decision to intervene on a substantial scale in the fall of 1961." [11]

From his first day in office until March 31, 1968, Lyndon Johnson sought to demonstrate continuity with the previous three presidents in terms of Vietnam policy. Johnson demonstrated this need by bringing it to the attention of his advisors, and by attempting to insert a testimony to other presidents' involvement in Vietnam into nearly all of his public addresses on the subject. Most Johnson speeches on foreign affairs referenced Kennedy, Eisenhower, or Truman, if not all three. This repetition emphasizes the importance that continuity played in Johnson's mind.

In preparation for his own speeches, Johnson thoroughly researched past presidential statements so that he might always sound informed (and keep his public reminded) of what his predecessors had to say on the subject. This habit began almost immediately after Johnson entered office; in February 1964, he requested a thorough compilation of Kennedy quotes on Vietnam. Bromley Smith compiled pertinent quotes beginning with the 1961 inaugural address and concluding in September 1963, with the promise of more applicable quotes available by the next morning. It is unclear exactly how aides made these particular selections; perhaps Johnson only requested those snippets that favored intervention in Vietnam. What is clear is that he received a compilation of statements that would have left absolutely no doubt as to what Kennedy intended to do in Vietnam. For example, Johnson read a quote in which Kennedy stated "that the United States is determined that the Republic of Viet Nam shall not be lost to the Communists for lack of any support which the United States Government can render." Kennedy made that statement in early August 1961. Furthermore, the strong declarations Kennedy made in the months prior to his assassination would almost certainly have struck Johnson. In July 1963, Kennedy had informed the American people: "We are not going to withdraw that effort. In my opinion, for us to withdraw from that effort would mean a collapse not only of South Viet Nam, but also of Southeast Asia. So we are going to stay there." In September, Kennedy pointedly told CBS's Walter Cronkite "I don't agree with those who say we should withdraw [from Viet Nam]. That would be a great mistake." [12] Based on this particular compilation of quotes, it is difficult to conceive that Kennedy would not have stayed the course in Vietnam. It is also important to note that public statements such as these were often the only information Johnson, as vice president, received from the Kennedy camp.

USING THE MEDIA TO ESTABLISH CONTINUITY

Johnson's pursuit of a policy based on continuity is understandable, if not necessarily admirable. He did not always convey the proper tone when attempting to portray his feelings to the public. In an address before the members of the New Hampshire Weekly Newspaper Editors Association in the fall of 1964, Johnson attempted to describe a typical dialogue he might have about Vietnam. He related that someone would generally ask, why "are we in Viet-Nam, and how did you get us into Viet-Nam?" Johnson's reply, "Well, I didn't get you into Viet-Nam. You have been in Viet-Nam 10 years," was technically correct. At the same time, these editors might have viewed his response as terse and unnecessary. In typical fashion, Johnson then elaborated on the specific actions taken by Eisenhower and Kennedy (Truman was spared in this particular speech). The crux of his speech was essentially that President Eisenhower committed the U.S. to Diem and Kennedy followed through on that promise. [13] Who was Lyndon Baines Johnson to change course?

The theme of continuity was not one Johnson reserved for small speeches before particular groups of people. He also tended to reiterate it in his major addresses. His 1966 State of the Union Address was no exception; Vietnam was the first topic attended to and continuity was a large part of the explanation for the current policies. Johnson firmly told Americans that the nation would remain in Vietnam, and defended this plan, stating, "We will stay because a just nation cannot leave to the cruelties of its enemies a people who have staked their lives and independence on America's solemn pledge—a pledge which has grown through the commitments of three American Presidents." [14] This time Truman was included, and LBJ emphasized this theme throughout his address.

By late 1967, Vietnam had become not just a major theme in LBJ speeches, but it was often the *only* theme. He began one speech, simply titled "Vietnam," by reiterating why America was still sinking in the quagmire. Again, he linked the situation to the three presidents before him, and he then focused on Eisenhower and Kennedy by reading very specific quotes from them. He followed a lengthy 1959 quote from Eisenhower with several Kennedy quotes, ending with his well-known 1963 statement: "we are going to stay there." [15] Even at this late point in his administration, Johnson was still relying heavily on his predecessors' actions and trying to convince the public that he alone was not to blame for their problems in Vietnam.

Aside from senior members of his administration and the general public, Johnson also sought other sources of support for his efforts to affirm a policy of continuity. Like any modern president, he had a wide circle of unofficial advisors whose thoughts he sometimes solicited. His "outer circle" also tended to reiterate how closely his compared to Kennedy's Vietnam policy. One such advisor, Endicott Peabody, not only offered his own opinions but relayed those of another important figure at the time, John McCloy. Peabody composed a memo to Johnson relating a conversation that took place between himself and McCloy. He reported that Kennedy had solicited McCloy's advice when he was considering committing combat troops to Vietnam. Reportedly, Kennedy felt there were very few other options. Peabody told Johnson "In McCloy's mind, the die was cast at that point." He further reported that McCloy "blamed" Kennedy for making the initial decision to commit troops, and therefore, for all subsequent decisions made. [16] This statement would probably have been encouraging to Johnson, and was perhaps one contributing factor to his reluctance for fully developing his own foreign policy stance.

By late 1967, Johnson's Vietnam policies were under heavy attack. A large part of the criticism stemmed from the "credibility gap" that had emerged between his administration and the media, but another aspect was simply the increasingly crushing cost of waging the war and the shifting mood of the country. Johnson began to attempt some more aggressive public relations strategies; some of those strategies hinged on increasingly making the public aware of the continuity issue.

John Roche was a prominent attorney whom LBJ hired as a consultant to deal with the increasingly difficult credibility problem. Roche spent a significant amount of time studying the past actions of both Kennedy and Johnson and eventually arrived at a straightforward conclusion: Kennedy was wholly to blame. Interestingly, Roche opined that the problems stemmed not from Kennedy's aggressiveness, but from his inability to take proper action. He told Johnson, "Essentially I came to the conclusion that a great deal of our trouble on this has arisen from President Kennedy's virtually total concern with Europe and Cuba, a concentration which led him to ignore the danger signals in Southeast Asia…". However,

Roche argued, Johnson, in his role as VP, had urged Kennedy to more carefully consider the situation. Therefore, any "blame" should be placed on Kennedy. [17] Johnson was merely following his example.

More significant than Roche's observations about JFK was the plan he suggested to Johnson to remedy the situation. Roche wanted to make the point that Kennedy was responsible but he acknowledged that this would be a "matter of incredible delicacy". If not done properly, any action that appeared to "blame" Kennedy could have two negative ramifications. First, Roche noted, "The Kennedy cultists would be up in arms." That, however, was "trivial" compared to what he viewed as the second complication: the involvement of both Rusk and McNamara in the actions of the Kennedy administration. Therefore, Roche offered the following suggestion: "I could prepare an article to be planted (under at least three levels of cover—and I am good at that) which would make the point with minimal reference to Secretaries Rusk and McNamara and with due deference to President Kennedy." He was willing to go to work on this if Johnson did not deem the plot too risky. Roche again reminded Johnson that Vietnam was not at all his fault. The way he saw it, "in large part we have a credibility problem because we are covering for him—we were eight months pregnant in Vietnam before we knew we had been laid." [18]

This memo, and increasing tensions with Robert Kennedy, may have been what led Johnson to request yet another report on consistency between himself and Kennedy. In November 1967, RFK charged that there had been a "switch" between his brother's policies and Johnson's recent actions in Vietnam. Johnson requested a report that would emphatically deny this accusation. He received a document that began with the basic SEATO commitment in 1955 and continued on to quotes from Kennedy that demonstrated how unwavering he was on Vietnam. The report concluded with a compilation of Johnson quotes that demonstrated his acknowledgement of "the deeper meaning of our involvement in Asia." In an accompanying memo, Walt Rostow offered Johnson staunch encouragement. He stated: "I doubt that any reasonable person could read this collection and still believe there had been any 'switch' whatsoever in our policy or our understanding of our commitment." Rostow further scoffed, "And it is hard to understand how a man could have been as close to all this as Bobby was and reach his stated conclusion." [19]

Johnson's pursuit of continuity is not just something evident in the historical record; it was noticed at the time, and was not always viewed as positive. Senator Mike Mansfield took care to warn the president early in his tenure that perhaps continuity was not desirable. Mansfield cautioned, "We are close to the point of no return in Vietnam…there ought to be less official talk of our responsibility in Viet Nam and more emphasis on the responsibilities of the Vietnamese themselves." In Mansfield's opinion, times had changed and peace through diplomacy was the proper course of action. [20]

Mansfield's views were more of the exception, rather than the rule. Johnson was continuously reminded of what Kennedy might have done, and this greatly influenced his decision making on Vietnam. Shortly after Mansfield's warning, Henry Cabot Lodge presented Johnson with a different viewpoint. Lodge recalled the moment in Kennedy's inaugural address when he declared the challenge of the decade was, "not as a call to bear arms, though arms we need—not as a call to battle, though embattled we are—but the call to bear the burden of a long, twilight struggle year in and year out." Lodge wrote that the situation in Vietnam was precisely the type of struggle Kennedy referred to and noted that his words applied directly to the current situation. Lodge encouraged Johnson to stay the course—Kennedy's course. [21]

"Johnson Relying on Ike in Viet Debate"

The reasons for Johnson's desire to continue Kennedy's policies are clear. As not only a member of his party but his vice president, Johnson would have certainly felt pressured to try to accomplish Kennedy's goals. The tragic circumstances surrounding Kennedy's death only made this more necessary; it is doubtful that the American public would have reacted positively to any deviation from Kennedy's course after his assassination. It might have been seen as dishonorable to his memory. The continuity between the two is therefore understandable. It is perhaps more noteworthy that Johnson demonstrated the same obsessive need for continuity with Dwight Eisenhower. Whether or not Johnson truly desired Eisenhower's approval, or whether it was an attempt to benefit from Eisenhower's continued popularity is not entirely clear. In all probability, it was a combination of the two. What is clear is that Johnson spent a significant amount of time attempting to cultivate a positive political relationship with Eisenhower, and that he greatly wanted his support on Vietnam.

From the outset, Johnson's staff encouraged him to link his Vietnam policies to Ike's. In the spring of 1964, McGeorge Bundy advised him to answer questions on the importance of Vietnam by stating: "Ten years ago President Eisenhower rightly decided to support the new government of South Vietnam and we have continued that support ever since in good times and in bad." Bundy included a letter from Eisenhower to Diem, and pointed out that the language Ike used "reminds me very much of the language we still use." He urged Johnson to notice that Eisenhower spoke of the importance of reform and commitment and the need to respond to the Vietnamese people's aspirations. Bundy encouraged Johnson, saying, "In recent months the danger and difficulty in Vietnam have increased, but this is no time to quit, and it is no time for discouragement." [22]

Johnson's attempts to garner Ike's support began in earnest almost immediately after his 1965 inauguration. Presumably, he was working too hard in 1964 adjusting to his new role, and trying to determine his legacy from Kennedy to worry too much about Eisenhower. On the other hand, perhaps he still felt plenty of positive support from the public and did not feel a real need for further bolstering. Whatever the reason, 1965 ushered in a concerted Johnson effort to earn Eisenhower's public support. Johnson ordered his staff to compile Eisenhower quotes on Vietnam, exactly has they had been doing with Kennedy statements. He would have been pleased with the initial results; the first reports yielded quotes such as "Former President Dwight D. Eisenhower said today that President Johnson 'unquestionably has made the correct decision' in ordering a resumption of bombing in North Viet-Nam." [23]

In April, Eisenhower himself noted that the press often raised the continuity question. He wrote to Johnson personally, assuring him that he would not disparage him or his foreign policies publicly. When asked his views on Vietnam, Eisenhower told Johnson his reply had been (and would remain) to say simply that "under the circumstances as I now understand them I believe that you are employing a policy well calculated to serve the best interests of the United States." The closing line of the letter read, "With warm personal regard and great respect." [24] Eisenhower also acknowledged that there had been "continuity of purpose and policy", despite an evolution of the situation and enemy actions. [25] Presumably, this would have at least been somewhat reassuring to Johnson. He used his correspondence with the former president to both thank and flatter Eisenhower. After addressing him as "My dear General," Johnson effused, "I cannot tell you adequately of my deep felt gratitude for the unhesitating support you give to the needs of your country." Johnson then went on to elaborate on how much he and the public needed Eisenhower's wisdom, and assured him that his legacy was now cemented. Johnson told Eisenhower, "But history will surely record that President Dwight D. Eisenhower, both in and out of office, never swerved from what he believed to be the truth nor from giving his courage and his energy to the people he serves as patriot, soldier, President, and now as wise counselor to the nation." [26] It would be interesting to see what Johnson's response would have been if Eisenhower had not been willing publicly to support his policies at that time.

Although Eisenhower's political support was critical for Johnson's popularity, his advice was also considered important from a military perspective. Because of his own military and political experience, Johnson knew Eisenhower could offer a unique perspective on the Vietnam War. Johnson made certain to keep Eisenhower informed, and to gather his advice; of course, Johnson was not always available to brief Ike himself, but he did make certain that other members of his administration tended to the ex-president. For instance, he requested the Ambassador to South Vietnam, Henry Cabot Lodge, to have a personal meeting with Eisenhower. Lodge reported to Johnson that Eisenhower did indeed have specific views not only on how to wage the war, but also on what to tell the public about it. For instance, he suggested that Johnson should expend more effort on developing stronger points along the coast of Vietnam; conversely, he felt there should be "no formal announcements of total U.S. troop strength." [27] Despite his retirement, Eisenhower still followed all aspects of U.S. involvement very carefully.

As Johnson was eager to keep close track of all of his interactions with Eisenhower, he ordered a thorough record of all meetings and conversations. Each notation included a record of how long the conversation lasted. [28] Conversations with Eisenhower totaled 21 during the early years of Johnson's tenure. [29] Johnson had dedicated a significant amount of time to cultivating a relationship with Eisenhower, but as president his schedule simply did not allow as much time as he would have perhaps wished to speak with the former president. The solution was to find a reliable person to be the go between himself and Eisenhower.

The role of intermediary fell to General Andrew Jackson Goodpaster, a soldier and scholar who had a long-time relationship with Eisenhower, most recently as a close adviser during his presidency. Johnson persuaded Goodpaster to meet regularly with Eisenhower with the goal of both briefing him on Vietnam and obtaining his opinions on the situation. As was typical of Johnson (further confirming his penchant for total control), Johnson requested regular updates as to how often Goodpaster was in contact with Eisenhower. Between February, 1965 and June, 1966, there had been 16 formal briefings, three phone conversations, and 30 informal discussions. Goodpaster noted that Vietnam had been discussed at every one of these encounters. [30]

Despite Eisenhower's earlier statements about how successful Johnson's policies in Vietnam were the ex-president eventually began to display some doubts about the direction of the war. Initially, Goodpaster was able to offer him reassurances that positive things were still happening. In a 1967 report to Johnson, Goodpaster began by repeating several of Eisenhower's concerns, which seemed to stem mainly from rumors he was hearing. For instance, Eisenhower told Goodpaster that "many of the people who see him—neither 'Hawks' nor 'doves'—are talking in terms of discouragement about the course of the war in Vietnam. They say that nothing seems to going well and that, perhaps, it would be better to get out of it than to continue." Goodpaster assured Johnson that he had tried to dissuade Eisenhower from this opinion; he had promised Eisenhower that he would soon go over many details of the war with him, and, he had told the former president, "it differs considerably from their premise that nothing seems to be going well." [31]

This report might have been important to Johnson for other reasons. In it, Goodpaster noted that CBS wanted Eisenhower to do an hour-long television presentation on the state of the war in Vietnam. According to Goodpaster, Eisenhower was inclined to give the talk, but wanted to make sure that it remained factual and not opinionated. He would cover topics such as "how our interests are involved, why the area should not be let go to the Communists, why we put in advisers, and increased them, why we introduced our combat forces, why we are bombing the north, etc." [32] For Johnson, this could have been an enormous opportunity to have someone else emphasize the theme of continuity on which he had been focusing so intensively.

Johnson's dependence on Eisenhower did not go unnoticed by the press. In the fall of 1967, *The Washington Post* ran a story headlined: "Johnson Relying on Ike in Viet Debate." According to the article, the purpose of utilizing the Republican war hero was to "help counter the growing opposition to the President's Vietnam policy." By enlisting Eisenhower's support, the administration was in effect attempting to launch a "counterattack against its Vietnam critics." [33] This counterattack was not completely effective and neither did it last long. By early 1968, Eisenhower was becoming very vocal in expressing reservations about Johnson's Vietnam policy. During his meetings with Goodpaster, he consistently questioned him as to why Johnson was doing this or taking that step. He was no longer convinced that the war was being waged the way that it should be. [34]

By that point, Johnson, too, no longer believed that the war was being waged properly, and the majority of Americans were extremely skeptical about Vietnam. The Tet Offensive was a major blow to LBJ's, and the American people's, confidence and is considered by many to be the turning point in the war. Despite the devastating psychological effects of Tet, shifts in Johnson's thinking, and important changes within the administration, continuity was still an important factor in Johnson's decisions. Shortly after taking on the post of Secretary of Defense, Clark Clifford requested a compilation of Kennedy quotes on Vietnam for LBJ's use. Clifford might have especially appreciated Kennedy's stance that, "while we would all like to lighten the burden, I don't see any real prospect of the burden being lightened". [35] Kennedy's dogged determination was yet another way that Johnson could claim continuity.

On March 31, 1968, Lyndon Johnson dramatically announced in a nationally televised address: "I shall not seek, and I will not accept, the nomination of my party for another term as your President." Even knowing that his days in the Oval Office were numbered, the President could not restrain himself from referring once again to continuity as the guiding principle of the policy goals he had tried to achieve. In this address, Johnson chose the words of John F. Kennedy to remind Americans why he had continued to wage war in Vietnam. Johnson recalled that blustery Inauguration Day in 1961 when Kennedy proclaimed that America should "pay any price, bear any burden, meet any hardship, support any friend, oppose any foe to assure the survival and the success of liberty." [36] According to a despondent Johnson, that had been his own primary goal throughout the painful journey of the years since.

CONCLUSION: THE CONTINUED CONSTRAINTS OF CONFORMITY

Perhaps continuity in American foreign relations is unavoidable and, arguably, in most circumstances desirable. The presumption is that a decision previously taken and widely accepted should be specially privileged. Perhaps even more important, presidents will strive to remind the public of their dedication to honoring and maintaining policies enunciated by their predecessors.

At times, this continuity is not sought, nor even desired by the incoming president. Jimmy Carter provides us with an excellent example of a candidate who based his platform largely on reforming foreign policy and getting rid of policies he felt were "highly secretive and partisan, immoral, and overly focused on relations with the Soviet Union." Despite several important successes (notably the Camp David Accords), some historians feel that Carter actually did little other than to expand on policies already in place. For example, his ideas on limiting nuclear weapons had roots reaching back to Truman; his desire to build a constructive relationship with the PRC is easily traced to the Nixon administration. Eventually, Carter did not succeed in altering the structure of foreign policy, or in giving American foreign relations a focus other than the Soviet Union, and cold war tensions had actually escalated by the end of his term. [37]

While in office, Carter was not able to escape the compulsion for continuity despite his good intentions. What makes his an interesting case is the path he chose as an elder statesman after leaving the White House. Carter made international relations his post-presidency priority and has been involved in important mediations in countries such as North Korea, Bosnia, and Somalia. Carter has also not hesitated to criticize his successors' policies when he disagrees with them, something he did not feel comfortable doing while in office. [38] Carter demonstrates that once released from the constraints of conformity, ex-presidents are able to focus on their own foreign policy ideology and goals.

Some contemporary presidents have gone in the opposite direction of Carter and attempted to cite continuity, even where there is none. In recent years, President George W. Bush has come under considerable fire for America's military intervention in Iraq. In attempts to defend his actions, Bush has more than once sought to draw a connection between himself and Harry S Truman. The February 12, 2007, issue of *Newsweek* featured a story about Bush's analysis of the circumstances that brought about the Iraq conflict. As the story reported, the President "compared his situation to the crisis Harry Truman faced in the early days of the cold war. Then, as now, Bush said, the United States confronted a dangerous ideological foe. Truman had answered with the Truman Doctrine, a vow to protect free peoples wherever they were threatened with communist domination." Bush then noted that, as with the situation he now faced, Truman's policies were unpopular at the time, but "history showed he was right."

Just as some questioned Johnson's claims of continuity trumping rationality, many do not see Bush's historical analysis as quite hitting the mark. *Newsweek*'s story offered as a counterweight the reaction of Senator Dick Durbin of Illinois, who pointed out to Bush,

"Harry Truman had allies." [39] There are of course, similarities being drawn between Iraq, the Cold War, and Vietnam that Bush would sooner not be addressed. For instance, some scholars compare the dishonesty of the Johnson administration regarding the Gulf of Tonkin Affair to the post-9/11 atmosphere surrounding the Bush administration. Both instances resulted in "the same manufactured atmosphere of crisis". [40] Others have noted the correlation of "the decent interval", or the idea there should be a clear window between U.S. withdrawal and the collapse of South Vietnam—or Iraq, as the case may now be. Parallels drawn between a "disguised exit" in Vietnam and one in Iraq show the same motive—policy failure. [41]

Tempting as it is (and useful as it may be) it is perhaps too soon to draw definitive parallels between Vietnam and Iraq. As it has done (and continues to do) for Vietnam, the historical record will continue to grow and shed light on the questions that need to be answered about Iraq. One of those questions will certainly be whether or not presidents still feel the compulsion for continuity, as Johnson demonstrated. And whether or not that is always a bad thing. Another question that must be considered is how much impact the cold war consensus played in the compulsion for continuity of recent presidents. Surely it was a large factor, but until historians gain complete access to the papers of the post-cold war presidents, we will not fully understand their foreign policy motivations, including their desire to seek (or avoid) continuity.

REFERENCES

[1] Transcript of Interview with the President Conducted by William H. Lawrence, 15 March 1964. File: "McGeorge Bundy March-4/14/65", Box 3, National Security File Memos to the President McGeorge Bundy, Papers of the President, Lyndon Baines Johnson Library, Austin, Texas. (Hereafter cited as LBJL).

[2] "Statement by the President", 25 March 1965. File: "Deployment of Major U.S. Forces to Vietnam, July 1965", Box 202, National Security File, Papers of the President, LBJL.

[3] See Robert Dallek, *Flawed Giant: Lyndon Johnson and His Times, 1961-1973* (Oxford: New York, 1998), Fredrik Logevall, *Choosing War: The Lost Chance for Peace and the Escalation of War in Vietnam* (Berkeley: University of California Press, 1999), H.W. Brands,*The Wages of Globalism: Lyndon Johnson and the Limits of American Power* (New York: Oxford University Press, 1995), Michael Hunt *Lyndon Johnson's War: America's Cold War Crusade in Vietnam, 1945-1968* (New York: Hill and Wang, 1996).

[4] See Paul R. Henggeler, *In His Steps: Lyndon Johnson and the Kennedy Mystique* (Chicago: I.R. Dee, 1991).

[5] John F. Kennedy to Lyndon Johnson, 28 January 1961. File: "National Security Council—Letter from Pres Kennedy re VP Johnson's Participation", Box 4, Vice Presidential Security File, LBJL

[6] Draft. National Security Action Memo. Undated. File: "National Security Council (II)", Box 4, Vice Presidential Security File, POP, LBJL.

[7] Paul M. Kattenburg, "Orientation Visit to Viet-Nam", 6 January 1964. File: "1963, Paul M. Kattenburg Trip, 11/22/63-12/19/63", Box 24, James C. Thompson Papers, John F. Kennedy Presidential Library, Boston, MA. (Hereafter cited as JFKL)
[8] Paul M. Kattenburg, "Orientation Visit to Viet-Nam", 6 January 1964. File: "1963, Paul M.Kattenburg Trip, 11/22/63-12/19/63", Box 24, James C. Thompson Papers, JFKL.
[9] Speech by Dean Rusk, 24 May 1966. File: "Quotations on Viet-Nam-Dean Rusk", Box 336, Ernest K. Lindley Papers, Spencer Research Library, University of Kansas, Lawrence, Kansas (hereafter cited as "Lindley Papers").
[10] Memo. Walt Rostow to Lyndon Johnson, 15 September 1967. File: "Past Presidential Statements", Box 97, Vietnam Country File, National Security File, POP, LBJL.
[11] Memo. McGeorge Bundy to Lyndon Johnson, 1 July 1964. File: "National Security File: Memos to the President", Box 1,,National Security File Memos to the President, POP, LBJL.
[12] Memo, with attachments. Bromley Smith to Lyndon Johnson, 22 February 1963. [Although this is dated 1963, the salutation "Mr. President" and the opening sentence "The quotations of President Kennedy which you requested are attached" make it clear that this memo was sent after Johnson took office, which means the date should almost certainly be 22 February 1964]. File: "Vietnam, Past Presidential Statements on USG Commitment in SE Asia [1 of 2]", Box 97, Vietnam Country File, National Security File, POP, LBJL.
[13] Lyndon Johnson, "Remarks in Manchester to the Members of the New Hampshire Weekly Newspaper Editors Association", 28 September 1964. File: "Quotations on Viet-Nam Kennedy-Johnson", Box 336, Lindley Papers.
[14] "President's State of the Union Message", 2 January 1966. File: "Vietnam Speeches [2]", Box 17, Files of McGeorge Bundy, National Security File, POP, LBJL.
[15] Lyndon Johnson, "The President's Remarks in San Antonio Before the National Legislative Conference", 6 December 1967. File: "Past Presidential Statements", Box 98, Vietnam Country File, National Security File, POP, LBJL.
[16] Memo. Endicott Peabody to Lyndon Johnson, 6 November 1967. File: "Past Presidential Statements", Box 97, Vietnam Country File, National Security File, POP, LBJL. Endicott Peabody was a prominent political figure from Massachusetts from the early 1960s well into the 1990s. His personal papers are located at the Kennedy Library. John McCloy was a prominent banker who regularly advised Johnson during his tenure in office. McCloy was one of the "wise men" who would eventually recommend de-escalation to Johnson in mid-1968.
[17] Memo. John Roche to Lyndon Johnson, 15 November 1967. File: "Memos to the President", Box 8, Papers of John P. Roche, LBJL. .
[18] Memo. John Roche to Lyndon Johnson, 15 November 1967. File: "Memos to the President", Box 8, Papers of John P. Roche, LBJL. Johnson's response, if there indeed was a written response, has not yet been located at the Johnson Library. Despite his need to place blame elsewhere, there is no clear evidence that Johnson did actually approve a plan like this.
[19] Memo. Walt Rostow to Lyndon Johnson, 28 November 1967. File: "Past Presidential Statements", Box 97, Vietnam Country File, National Security File, POP, LBJL.

[20] Mike Mansfield to Lyndon Johnson, 6 January 1964. File: "National Security File: Memos to the President", Box 1, National Security File Memos to the President, POP, LBJL.
[21] Henry Cabot Lodge, 'Persistance in Viet-Nam" 2 March 1964, File: "McGeorge Bundy, Vol. 2, 3/1-31/64 [1 of 2], Box 1, National Security File Memos to the President, POP, LBJL.
[22] McGeorge Bundy to Lyndon Johnson, 14 March 1964. File: "McGeorge Bundy 3/1-31/64, Vol. 2 [1 of 2]", Box 1, National Security File, POP, LBJL.
[23] Dwight D. Eisenhower quoted in the *New York Times*, 1 February 1965. No page number given. Clipping located in file "Presidential Decisions-Gulf of Tonkin Attacks of Aug., 1964", Box 39,National Security Council Histories, National Security File, POP, LBJL.
[24] Dwight Eisenhower to Lyndon Johnson, 30 April 1965. File: "President Eisenhower [2 of 2]", Box 3, Name File, National Security File, POP, LBJL.
[25] Memo. McGeorge Bundy to Lyndon Johnson, 25 August 1965. File: "McGeorge Bundy, August 1965", Box 4, National Security File Memos to the President McGeorge Bundy, LBJL.
[26] Lyndon Johnson to Dwight Eisenhower, 19 August 1965. File: "Eisenhower, Dwight D., General [1954-1968] [2 of 2]", Box 2, Name File, National Security File, POP, LBJL.
[27] Memo. Henry Cabot Lodge to Lyndon Johnson, 11 August 1965. File: "Eisenhower, Dwight D., General [1954-1968] [2 of 2]", Box 2, Name File, National Security File, POP, LBJL.
[28] Report, "President Johnson's Contacts with President Eisenhower", File: "President Eisenhower [1965-1968] [1 of 2]", Box 3 Name File, National Security File, POP, LBJL.
[29] Memo. Unknown to Lyndon Johnson, 10 June 1966. File: "President Eisenhower [1965-1968] [1 of 2]", Box 3, Name File, National Security File, POP, LBJL.
[30] Memo. Bromley Smith to Lyndon Johnson, 11 June 1966. File: "President Eisenhower [1965-1968][1 of 2]", Box 3, Name File, National Security File, POP, LBJL.
[31] Andrew Goodpaster, Memorandum for the Record, 18 October 1967. File: "Eisenhower, Dwight D. General [1954-1968] [1 of 2]", Box 2, Name File, National Security File, POP, LBJL.
[32] Andrew Goodpaster, Memorandum for the Record, 18 October 1967. File: "Eisenhower, Dwight D.General [1954-1968] [1 of 2]", Box 2, Name File, National Security File, POP, LBJL.
[33] *The Washington Post*, "Johnson Relying on Ike in Viet Debate", 19 October 1967, p. A10.
[34] Andrew Goodpaster, Memorandum for the Record, 14 February 1968. File: "Eisenhower, Dwight D. General [1954-1968] [1 of 2]", Box 2, Name File, National Security File, POP, LBJL.
[35] Robert E. Pursley to Clark Clifford. 11 April 1968. File: "Kennedy on Southeast Asia, 1961-1963", Box 3, Papers of Clark Clifford, LBJL.
[36] Lyndon Johnson. "Address to the Nation Announcing Steps to Limit the War in Vietnam and Reporting His Decision Not to Seek Reelection". 31 March 1968. LBJL,

On-line documents.http://www.lbjlib.utexas.edu/johnson/archives.hom/speeches.hom/680331.asp. Accessed 1 April 2007.
[37] William Stueck, "Placing Jimmy Carter's Foreign Policy" in Gary M. Fink and Hugh Davis Graham, ed., *The Carter Presidency: Policy Choices in the Post-New Deal Era* (The University Press of Kansas: Lawrence, 1998), 244-245.
[38] Douglas Brinkley, *The Unfinished Presidency: Jimmy Carter's Journey Beyond the White House* (Viking: New York, 1998), xvii.
[39] Holly Bailey, Richard Wolffe, and Evan Thomas. "Bush's Truman Show", *Newsweek*, 12 February 2007, p. 24.
[40] Eric Alterman, *When Presidents Lie: A History of Official Deception and Its Consequences*, (Viking: New York, 2004), 302.
[41] David Elliott in Lloyd C. Garner and Marilyn B. Young, ed., *Iraq and the Lessons of Vietnam: Or, How Not to Learn From the Past* (The New Press: New York, 2007), 32-37.

In: White House Studies Compendium. Volume 9
Editors: Anthony J. Eksterowicz and Glenn P. Hastedt
ISBN: 978-1-62618-681-1
© 2013 Nova Science Publishers, Inc.

Chapter 13

LONESOME DOVE: THE POPE, THE PRESIDENT, THE CHURCH, AND VIETNAM, 1963-1969

Lawrence J. McAndrews

ABSTRACT

Thomas Jefferson's "wall of separation" between church and state has never been without major cracks. During wartime, those holes often grow wider, as presidents frequently invoke God and assiduously court clerics. The Vietnam War and Lyndon Johnson were no exceptions. Yet sometimes when the statesman beckons the prelate balks. Pope Paul VI became the first pontiff to journey to the United States, and the first to meet with a president on American soil. But dialogue could not bridge difference, and the Holy Father's often outspoken opposition to the Chief Executive's war alternately annoyed, offended, and even outraged the president. In the end, though, the Pope's prodding converted many skeptical Catholics and non-Catholics alike. Seven years before the United States surrendered to the Communists in Vietnam, Lyndon Johnson surrendered to the Pope over Vietnam. Drawing upon a variety of secondary and primary sources, including documents from the Lyndon Johnson Presidential Library and the United States Catholic Conference Archives, this study examines how and why the world's most powerful Roman Catholic ultimately influenced the Protestant in the White House.

With his imposing stature and outsize arrogance, Lyndon Johnson seemed eager to take on the world as he ascended to the presidency in November 1963. And soon he would have to. Questions of war and peace, especially in Vietnam, would obsess and ultimately overwhelm the president and the nation, as American unilateralism earned international enmity and presaged national humiliation.

Nobody tried harder than Lyndon Johnson to achieve a durable peace in Vietnam and a meaningful respite from the Cold War. Nobody did, except perhaps Pope Paul VI. Just as Johnson often invoked John F. Kennedy in his determination to contain communism yet deepen détente, so too did Pope Paul build on the considerable foundations laid by Pope John XXIII. Pope Paul VI's tireless pursuit of peace prodded the American president, encouraged many American Catholics, and often embarrassed the American Catholic hierarchy, to whom the world remained, even in the wake of the historic Second Vatican Council, less modern than Manichean.

As a result, an American Catholic Church which so enthusiastically welcomed change in other areas seemed terribly frightened by it in this one. It is perhaps unsurprising, then, that when a president uncomfortable with nuance sought refuge from a world grown too complex, he would often find sanctuary in a Catholic church, where the uncertainties of his own faith would give way to the sturdy predictability of another. Yet ultimately neither Johnson nor the American Catholic bishops could escape the challenges to his foreign policy which undid his presidency and unsettled their Church [1]

THE POPE AND THE PRESIDENT

On the night of August 2, 1964, an American destroyer, the *U.S.S. Maddox*, conducting reconnaissance in the Gulf of Tonkin off the coast of North Vietnam, withstood an attack by North Vietnamese torpedo boats. Two nights later, the captains of the *Maddox* and another American ship, the *C. Turner Joy*, reported a second attack. Though the validity of the latter occurrence remained under question, President Johnson asked for, and overwhelmingly received, a Congressional resolution authorizing retaliation for the alleged two incidents. With a November election to win as a "peace" candidate, however, Johnson kept his "blank check" in his pocket while awaiting further provocation.

That moment arrived two months after his landslide victory over Arizona Republican Senator Barry Goldwater, when a Viet Cong assault on an American air force base in Pleiku, South Vietnam killed eight and wounded over one hundred. Over the lone dissent of Catholic Senate Majority Leader Mike Mansfield, Democrat of Montana, Johnson followed the advice of his National Security Council and Congressional leaders by ordering selective American bombing of North Vietnam [2]

Pope Paul VI responded to the American escalation of the Vietnam War first by endorsing a suggestion by French President Charles DeGaulle that the United Nations mediate the conflict. "May international institutions capable of preventing the attacks of force be reinforced," the pontiff pleaded in the week following the Pleiku incident. "May these be adapted, surrounded with general respect, to assure the honest execution, the honest observance of treaties." Two days later the Pope sent a letter to South Vietnam's Catholic bishops urging their efforts to prevent "the horrors of a prolonged and extensive commitment of arms."[3]

The Pope's pleas fell on deaf ears. Johnson showed no inclination to cease the bombing. "Much as I deplore the spread of communism in Asia," Trappist monk Rev. Thomas Merton wrote the president in February, "I hope that peace can be negotiated by an international group," leading to an end to the U.S. military presence. "As you have ignored appeals from Pope Paul, [U.N. Secretary General] U Thant, President DeGaulle, and so many others," Rev. Philip Berrigan, Martin Corbin, and James Forest of the Catholic Peace Fellowship telegraphed the White House in March, "we have little hope our protest will challenge your will to continue and even widen the war in Vietnam." Less than a week later, Johnson dispatched the first American combat troops to join the thousands of advisors already training South Vietnamese forces in the fight against the communists. "I thought you would like to see some of the support we are getting from some of the more level-headed clergy on Vietnam," White House press secretary Bill Moyers wrote Johnson in April, after receiving a copy of a pro-war column by the director of the American bishops' National Catholic Welfare Conference Social Action Department, Monsignor George Higgins, which was to appear in twenty-five diocesan newspapers throughout the country [4]

The Catholic bishops of South Vietnam similarly were more concerned about defeating the communists than accommodating them. White House aide Jack Valenti briefed Johnson on the president's February meeting with the Pope's Apostolic Delegate to the United States, Rev. Egidio Vagnozzi, by noting that "communists have infiltrated the Buddhist movement in South Vietnam," and that Rev. Patrick O'Connor of the National Catholic News Service "has been in Vietnam for over fifteen years [and]…could be useful" to the Administration. Following a meeting with President Phan Huy Quat, the South Vietnamese bishops accused their government of failing to forestall a Buddhist-led purge of Catholic military commanders. Rev. Hoang Quynh, spokesman for the 900,000 Catholic refugees who had fled the communist North, was heading an effort in 116 parishes in the vicinity of Saigon, the Southern capital, to arm young Catholic men with knives and sticks to defend their communities. Not only were South Vietnam's Catholic leaders ignoring the Pope's entreaties for peace, but some of them had even intimated that the Johnson Administration was behind the purge as a step toward a negotiated settlement of the war [5]

Even a papal encyclical could not deter the South Vietnamese Church. In *Mense Maio* (In the Month of May), Paul VI implored the world's governments to "continue at all times to foster and encourage conversations and negotiations at all levels" and to "condemn acts of guerilla war and of terrorism, the practices of holding hostages and of taking repeated reprisals against unarmed civilians." The South Vietnamese hierarchy's reply was to tacitly approve the formation of the Greater Unity Force, a Catholic political organization devoted to "invading and holding" North Vietnam "to deliver our compatriots from the yoke of Communist dictatorship." A month later, the Quat regime fell to a military coup, with Catholic Major General Nguyen Van Thieu in charge of the new government [6]

The Pope did influence the president, however, as Johnson asserted his willingness to negotiate with the enemy in Vietnam. Then he prepared to sit down with Paul himself. "It is of great importance to impress the Pope with our passion for peace in Vietnam," Secretary of State Dean Rusk counselled Johnson, while conceding "faint indications that not all Vatican circles are persuaded on this point" [7]

After publicly urging the United Nations in October to commit itself to "never again war," Paul VI privately pressed Johnson toward that lofty goal. "The entire world is indebted to His Holiness, as I said to him in our private conversation," Johnson told the press, "for the sacrifices he has made in coming on this long trip across the water to provide leadership in the world's quest for peace. His Holiness and I discussed ways and means of advancing that cause" [8]

Yet Pope Paul and President Johnson did not engage in specifics about Vietnam, where the U.S. military presence continued to grow and American peace efforts continued to founder. Majority Leader Mansfield returned in December with four other Senators from a fact-finding mission in Vietnam with a report so pessimistic that Johnson ordered a bombing pause in hopes of igniting peace talks [9]

Without naming either side or even the conflict itself, the Pope's Christmas message deplored the "limits of self-interest or one's own ambitions" as "obstacles to peace," and called instead for "just and sincere negotiation to restore order and friendship." No sooner had the pontiff sent a message to the governments of North Vietnam, South Vietnam, and the United States praising a thirty-hour holiday truce, however, than the fighting resumed [10]

Pope Paul VI ushered in the new year with still another peace proposal, sent this time not only to the combatants in Vietnam but to two of their sponsors, China and the Soviet Union. Johnson began 1966 with an expression of regret – that he had not yet discovered a solution to the Vietnamese imbroglio. "The President believes that if he were to leave office tomorrow," the *New York Times*' John Pomfret wrote, "the judgment of history on him would probably be harsh because of his failure to deal successfully with the conflict."[11]

Having failed to reconcile the competing factions in Vietnam, the Pope turned to neutral parties, advocating an international peace conference convened by the United Nations and conducted by governments with no direct stake in the outcome. Johnson's U.N. Ambassador, Arthur Goldberg, also envisioned a role for the world body in defusing the Vietnam issue – by changing the subject. Goldberg recommended that Johnson travel to Geneva to jumpstart stagnant nuclear nonproliferation talks with the Soviet Union. "If we would get a nonproliferation treaty, the agitation on Vietnam would greatly soften," White House aide Jack Valenti conveyed Goldberg's argument to the president, "and Vietnam would be put in proper perspective." Johnson would reject Goldberg's advice, he would sign a nonproliferation treaty within two years, and the agitation on Vietnam would only harden [12]

After his latest endeavor produced only six months of inaction, Pope Paul VI not only acknowledged that "our sincere and disinterested efforts failed to come to fruition," but he warned of the "possible extension of the conflict" in Southeast Asia. Johnson conceded as much in a letter to Mansfield. "We can get out of Viet Nam. We can get out next week or next month," Johnson wrote the Catholic Senator. "But what happens then?...We know what would then happen to the Catholics, Buddhists, and every other non-Communist group, because we saw it happen in 1954-56." To Mansfield's contention that U.S. policy consisted largely of running in place, Johnson maintained that the enemy was deteriorating, and the end was near. "Once they become convinced that we are not weak; that we are not impatient; that we are not going to falter, that they cannot win; that the cost to them of their continued aggression is rising, that their bargaining position at a conference is getting weaker every day," the president concluded, "then peace will come, whether at the negotiating table or not." [13]

It would not come in 1966. In July Johnson's top commander in Vietnam, Gen. William Westmoreland, accepted the Honor et Veritas Award, the Catholic War Veterans U.S.A.'s highest honor, in appreciation of U.S. bombing of North Vietnamese military targets in Hanoi and Haiphong. In a letter to Johnson, the organization's leader, Martin Riley, expressed the wish for a "speedy and just victory in Viet Nam."[14]

In his strongest language yet, Pope Paul VI's September encyclical *Christi Matri* (To the Mother of Christ) urged "with piercing cry and with tears" an end to the "bloody and difficult war...in areas of East Asia." White House aide Tom Johnson informed the president that the Pope's pleas for peace were winning "considerable sympathy" among the American people. Ambassador to the United Nations Goldberg followed the encyclical with an offer that the world body mediate a settlement predicated upon a U.S. bombing halt, North Vietnamese and U.S. withdrawal from the South, and peace talks which would include the Viet Cong. Though Goldberg's "major policy speech to the [General] Assembly did not mention the Encyclical," the United States Catholic bishops' Office of United Nations Affairs observed, "the Encyclical assured discussion of the question [of Vietnam] within the context of international responsibility."[15]

Pope Paul VI sent a special envoy, Most Rev. Sergio Pignedoli, the Titular Archbishop of Iconio and Apostolic Delegate to Canada, on an October peace mission to Saigon. Then he commemorated the first anniversary of his U.N. speech by exhorting 150,000 Catholics in St. Peter's Square in Rome with words grown tragically ironic over the preceding twelve months: "Never again war." President Johnson also remembered the occasion by attending a special Washington Peace Mass at St. Matthew's Cathedral, where he heard Archbishop Patrick O'Boyle blame the enemy for failing to respond to the president's repeated peace overtures. As Christmas approached, Paul VI reiterated his previous year's hope that a holiday truce would unlock a lasting peace. From Austin President Johnson promised "sympathetic consideration" of the pontiff's latest plea, but from Saigon Secretary of State Rusk conveyed serious doubts [16].

Almost a year after greeting Foreign Minister Andrei Gromyko, the first Soviet official to enter Vatican City, Pope Paul VI hosted Soviet Premier Nikolai Podgorny in January 1967. A week later he appealed to Presidents Johnson, Ho Chi Minh of North Vietnam, and Nguyen Van Thieu of South Vietnam to extend their ninety-six-hour truce in observance of Tet, the lunar new year. Podgorny told Paul VI that his country would never abandon its North Vietnamese ally, and he rebuffed the pontiff's call for direct Soviet-U.S. negotiations on the war. Johnson reiterated his desire to negotiate "at any time and place, in any forum," while adding that surely the Pope "would not expect us to reduce military action unless the other side is willing to do likewise." Condemning the "U.S. imperialists [who] have sent to South Vietnam half a million U.S. and satellite troops and used more than 600,000 puppet troops to wage a war against our people," Ho Chi Minh encouraged Paul VI to "use his high influence to urge that the U.S. government respect the national rights of the Vietnamese people." Thieu joined the Catholic hierarchy in South Vietnam in implicitly supporting a Saigon street protest organized by a Catholic group, the Committee for a Just and Legitimate Peace, in opposition to any peace efforts which would "sell out" South Vietnam to the communists [17]

The Pope pressed on nonetheless. An April meeting with U Thant in Rome preceded the opening of the Pacem in Terris Institute in New York, where the Secretary General admiringly described the pontiff as "obsessed with peace." A month later, Paul VI observed the fiftieth anniversary of the appearance of the Virgin Mary to three shepherd children in Fatima, Portugal, with a call for a U.S. bombing halt and an end to North Vietnamese infiltration of the South. Yet in August, when celebrating the feast of the assumption of the Virgin Mary, the Pope lamented the absence of "the force and coherence and constancy" necessary to achieve them [18]

The Johnson Administration persisted in welcoming the Holy Father's peace efforts without changing its course in Vietnam. In 1967 alone the war would cost $25 billion and over nine thousand American lives. Noting that the Administration has "been getting rapped in many neighborhoods of the world over this Vietnam stuff," *Miami News* editor William Baggs urged Johnson to send another representative to a second Pacem in Terris meeting to be convened by the Center for Democratic Institutions in Geneva in May. While the

Administration had no objection to such peace organizations and had been part of the previous gathering, Special Consultant to the President John Roche replied that it nonetheless had "no special obligation" to serve the group's interests, and would not be sending anyone this time. In a June meeting between Johnson and Soviet Premier Alexei Kosygin in Glassboro, New Jersey, the president extracted a pledge that another U.S. bombing pause would lead to negotiations. Then, Johnson would recall, "Kosygin slammed the door on us. We believe that he talked to North Vietnam, and they told him no"[19].

The president would also meet again with the Pope. This time, unlike in their meeting two years earlier, the two leaders were quite specific in their discussion of the Vietnam War. "You went to South Vietnam to protect your good intentions and your good hopes," Paul VI reassured Johnson in December in Rome. "But you must understand that I can never agree to war." The Pope then encouraged the president to end the bombing of the North.

"We have stopped bombing five times, but this only increases the murder," Johnson replied. "Archbishop [Patrick] Lucey [of San Antonio] went to South Vietnam as one of my observers during the [September] election. He told me that every time we quietened [sic] down they increase[d] their pressure. In the thirty-seven-day bombing pause [of 1965-66], they built up a seven-months' supply."

Charging that "Hanoi is ignoring and violating the Geneva Convention prisoner rules," Johnson urged the Pope to send a representative to visit the prisoners on both sides. He then proposed that the pontiff press South Vietnam and the National Liberation Front, the political wing of the Viet Cong, to engage in informal peace talks in Saigon, exclusive of their North Vietnamese and American sponsors. "Thieu is a good man – honest – and a Catholic," Johnson assured the Holy Father. "As you know, the Catholics are in a minority in South Vietnam. In the recent election, a new Senate was voted in, and a Catholic was elected as President of the Senate....I hope the Pope will encourage them to talk."

Johnson smiled broadly. "Just as the Pope encouraged me to pass my education bills. We are now spending nine billion dollars more on education. And the Pope can claim some responsibility for this."

Paul VI returned the smile, and, reaching out his hands toward the president, promised to try to investigate the treatment of POW's as well as attempt to bring the South Vietnamese government and the NLF together. "I will do whatever is possible. I will study the prisoner situation and see what contacts can be made. This is a cause which is close to my heart."

In return, the Pope inquired, "Is it possible that the truce at Christmas could be extended a day or two? Could you not show the world that on the day of peace January 1 you will also make this a day of truce?"

"My problem is this," Johnson responded. "My military leaders tell me that the North Vietnamese have trucks lined up bumper to bumper, and as soon as the truce begins they start them moving, and those supplies and those men kill our soldiers."

Having been refused yet again in his desperate quest for an end to the Vietnam War, the pontiff relented. "We shall pray for you," he told the president. "And we shall pray for your efforts for peace" [20]

Subsequent events would vindicate both Pope and president. For the first time, the Catholic hierarchy of South Vietnam criticized its government, not for being "soft" on communism, but for standing in the way of peace. The seventeen bishops, representing South Vietnam's two million Catholics, finally fell in line with the Holy Father in calling for an end to U.S. bombing and North Vietnamese aggression. "How can there be peace when those in responsible places mask their false promises behind rhetoric?" the bishops mocked the Thieu government. "How can there be peace if laziness, hypocrisy, and corruption prevail everywhere in society?" [21]

But for the umpteenth time, the North Vietnamese and Viet Cong violated a holiday truce, with a massive assault on some thirty major cities in South Vietnam, including Saigon, during the Tet cease-fire at the end of January. The ferocity of an enemy thought to be on its last legs horrified the millions of Americans witnessing the offensive on their television screens. "Eighty percent of the U.S. either follows the President or wants to do more," Johnson had told Paul VI only two months earlier. After Tet, however, an equal number of Americans wanted their country to leave Vietnam as wanted to win there. In February's New Hampshire Democratic presidential primary, Johnson barely defeated anti-war Catholic Senator Eugene McCarthy of Minnesota. So following two days of meetings with his foreign policy team, Johnson announced to the nation that he would virtually stop the bombing of the North, commence serious peace talks, and, to the amazement of even his closest aides, not seek reelection. The United States would not surrender to North Vietnam and the Viet Cong for another seven years. But on the last day of March in 1968, the president surrendered to the Pope [22]

THE BISHOPS AND THE PRESIDENT

But many American Catholic bishops kept fighting. Their staunch anti-communism and empathy for the Catholic minority in South Vietnam had long produced a sympathetic stance toward the war by most members of the hierarchy. Two weeks before the events in the Gulf of Tonkin, Harmon Burns of the bishops' National Catholic Welfare Conference Legal Department met with Michael Forrestal, Johnson's Assistant Secretary of State for Vietnamese Affairs, to demand that the South Vietnamese government release Major Dang Sy, a prominent Catholic prisoner. The bishops considered Dang Sy a victim of religious discrimination by a pro-Buddhist regime which blamed him for suppressing the Buddhist riots which helped insure President Ngo Dinh Diem's ouster in November 1963. Forrestal assured Burns that although the United States would not request the Major's release for fear of bloody protests by Buddhists in the northern part of South Vietnam, Johnson's Ambassador to South Vietnam Maxwell Taylor had secured from Prime Minister Nguyen Kahnh pledges of a reduction of his life sentence and eventual permission for him to leave the country [23]

The bishops' attention to the Dang Sy case stood in marked contrast to Pope Paul VI's view of the internal divisions within South Vietnam. At the end of August, *L'Osservatore Romano*, the Vatican newspaper, denied that South Vietnamese street clashes leading to the killing of a Catholic youth by a Buddhist mob were signs of a religious conflict [24]

The bishops' fear of communism also precluded a firm statement against nuclear war. Auxiliary Bishop Philip Hannan of Washington D.C. told the November meeting of the bishops' Catholic Association for International Peace that the proposed Schema 13 of the Second Vatican Council's *Constitution on the Church in the Modern World*, which would declare the use of nuclear weapons unjust in any case because their effects "cannot be imagined," fell outside the Church's "just war" tradition. A "just war," the Church had long taught, responds to an unwarranted violation of a legitimate nation's sovereignty only as a last resort and when greater evil would result in the absence of such hostilities. "Certainly we hold war in horror," said Hannan, "but we must state with precision what is prohibited in waging war to those who justly and laudably defend liberty" [25]

At Hannan's urging, a new draft would distinguish between unjust "wars of extermination" and "defensive wars." When Loyola University of Chicago sociologist Gordon Zahn assailed Hannan's dissent for undoubtedly bringing "cheer tonight in some Pentagon quarters as the votive martinis were raised," NCWC Social Action Department Director Msgr. George Higgins chided Zahn and his fellow pacifists for being "so infuriatingly holier than thou." Once and future CAIP president William O'Brien criticized the bishops for not speaking out against nuclear war, but he ultimately blamed the Pope. "There has been no strong, blanket papal condemnation of nuclear war as immoral," O'Brien contended, calling for the Church to "study" the issue [26]

In May Higgins blasted an anti-war vigil at the Pentagon organized by national clergy which "almost inevitably took on the character of an anti-Administration gathering." Lyndon Johnson's favorite Catholic prelate, Archbishop Patrick Lucey of San Antonio, assured Catholic White House aide Jack Valenti that "the situation in Vietnam has...made a turn for the better." The CAIP's World Order Committee issued a July 1965 statement staunchly defending the new U.S. combat role in Vietnam. "We think the United States should be prepared to continue the use of military power as long as the Viet Cong with its supporters continue hostilities," wrote committee chairman Charles O'Donnell. O'Donnell nonetheless concluded his hawkish pronouncement with a nod toward those self-righteous pacifists. Quoting Pope John XXIII in *Pacem in Terris*, O'Donnell expressed the hope "that by meeting and negotiating, men may come to discover better the bonds that unite them" [27]

U.N. Ambassador Arthur Goldberg echoed this mixed message when he addressed the CAIP's annual convention in December. While recognizing the nation's "hard fight on the battlefields of Viet Nam calling for much courage and reserve," Goldberg nevertheless assured the group that "our peace effort is being waged with no less intensity." Though "the tragedy of our times may be that the Pontiff's cry of 'war never again' may be the one condition of survival in our atomic age," Goldberg cited Paul VI, he also lamented that quite possibly "men and nations are too wrapped up in the habits of the past to recognize it."[28]

So, perhaps, were the bishops themselves. A group of fifty college students picketed outside the chancery of New York's Archbishop Francis Cardinal Spellman in a December 1965 protest of Spellman's "silencing" of anti-war Jesuits Revs. Daniel Berrigan, Daniel Kilfoyle, and Frank Keating. Three weeks later Spellman arrived in Saigon for a Christmas visit with U.S. troops. When asked "What do you think about what America is doing in Vietnam?" the Cardinal replied, "I fully support everything it does." Then, paraphrasing the words of nineteenth-century American naval officer Stephen Decatur, Spellman proclaimed, "My country, may it always be right. Right or wrong, my country" [29]

Writing in the *New York Times* in February 1966, Edward Fiske related that the first major declaration of opposition to the Vietnam War by American clergy had emanated not from the pacifist fringe, but from the religious "establishment," in the form of a December 1965 critique by the General Board of the National Council of Churches, which Fiske called "the country's most conspicuous and easily mobilized Protestant institution." On the other hand, the nation's Catholic bishops remained either silent or supportive toward the war, a stance which "contrasts sharply with the peace efforts of Pope Paul," which even the bishops'

Office for United Nations Affairs called "admittedly influential in the recent U.S. bombing pause and its world diplomatic initiative" [30]

A month later the *National Catholic Reporter* distributed a questionnaire on the war to the nation's 225 Catholic bishops. After five weeks, only six had replied, with half expressing support and the other half evading the issue. Rev. John Bennett, president of Union Theological Seminary and a leader of Protestant-Catholic ecumenical dialogue, marked the October anniversary of Pope Paul VI's United Nations speech by recalling that although "the Pope did all in his power…he had no leverage with the North Vietnamese, and apparently not much either with the Roman Catholic hierarchy of the United States on the question of peace." Bennett concluded, "If Pope Paul had been able to get a genuine response from even twenty members of the hierarchy, so that they really threw their weight on the side of peace, his visit might have been much more effective" [31]

Thus did the bishops strive to reconcile their own backing of the war with the Pope's search for peace. Baltimore Archbishop Lawrence Cardinal Shehan's June pastoral, "Peace and Patriotism," while stopping short of criticizing the Administration, nonetheless reminded Catholics of the wartime imperatives of the Second Vatican Council's *Constitution on the Church in the Modern World* to "exert whatever moral and civic influences seem dictated by…conscience." Without accusing the Administration of doing so, Shehan condemned "any act of war aimed indiscriminately at the destruction of entire cities or of extensive areas along with their populations." The bishops' November pastoral toed the same wobbly line. "It is reasonable to argue that our presence in Vietnam is justified," they wrote. "But we cannot stop here….It is the duty of everyone to keep looking for other alternatives" [32]

As evidence of how short a distance the bishops had travelled, the statement passed 169-5. "Your support for the war is accompanied by qualifications," a group of anti-war Catholics addressed the bishops from the nation's capital, "but you have so underemphasized these qualifications that they are being forgotten." The critics then cast their lot with Pope Paul VI, whose *Christi Matri* (Mother of Christ) had summoned both sides in the war to "stop – even at the expense of some inconvenience or loss," and against Cardinal Spellman, whose Christmas eve address to the American troops in Saigon calling for victory in Vietnam provoked unofficial angst in Vatican City, official repudiation in Moscow and Peking, and unusual vitriol from California Episcopal Bishop Kilmer Myers. "I can find no evidence that the Pope's stirring plea has ruffled the surface of American Catholic life," Rev. John Sheerin, editor of *Catholic World*, lamented. "Who speaks for the Church on Vietnam?" [33]

Even when the hierarchy showed signs of straying from its endorsement of Administration policy, it did so haltingly and apologetically. The Christmas message of Boston's Archbishop Richard Cardinal Cushing, while approving of Pope Paul and Secretary General U Thant's peacemaking, refused to disapprove of President Johnson's warmaking. Eleven bishops conveyed some degree of sympathy for the January-February 1967 anti-war gathering in Washington convoked by the ecumenical Clergy and Laity Concerned About Vietnam, yet none accepted the organizers' invitations to attend. Rev. John Cronin, assistant director of the bishops' United States Catholic Conference Social Action Department, did attend, but only to scold the anti-war group for assuming that the Administration wasn't sincere in its quest for peace in Vietnam. Atlanta Archbishop Paul Hallinan spoke at a follow-up meeting of the group, where he called for a "second Selma" to organize for peace, but he would not commit himself to a particular method of attaining it [34].

Catholic Association for International Peace president William O'Brien criticized U.S. air raids around Hanoi and warned of escalation of the aerial war. Yet he refused to oppose the war itself, noting that many of CAIP's members "would agree substantially" with the bishops' peace pastoral. Though "I share your concern about Vietnam," the bishops' Social Action Department director Msgr. George Higgins, one of the authors of the pastoral, wrote John Twohey of the anti-war Catholic Committee on Vietnam in March 1967, he would not sign an open letter indicating such concern. "I respectfully express the earnest hope that the unwillingness of some of us (at the United States Catholic Conference) to sign your open letter will not be interpreted...as *prima facie* evidence that we are not in sympathy with Pope Paul's numerous statements on the crisis in Vietnam," Higgins added, only to take another step back. "This type of criticism, however well-intentioned, can easily degenerate into a crude form of blackmail" [35]

Later the same month Bishop James Shannon of Minneapolis-St. Paul joined ten presidents of Catholic colleges in denouncing the indiscriminate bombing of civilians in Vietnam but neglecting to address the overriding issue of the war itself. "Though the American people are divided on the Vietnamese War," Daniel Callahan wrote in the April *Atlantic Monthly*, for tactical or strategic reasons, "not one bishop has opposed it" [36]

The following year would expose a few cracks in the bishops' façade, however. In July Rochester Bishop Fulton Sheen became the first Catholic prelate to advocate immediate U.S. withdrawal from Vietnam. Though still refusing to break with the Administration, Atlanta's Archbishop Hallinan, Minneapolis-St. Paul's Bishop Shannon, Oklahoma City-Tulsa's Bishop Victor Reed, and Newark's Auxiliary Bishop John Dougherty lent their support in August to the "Negotiation Now" movement, which called for an end to U.S. bombing, a beginning of peace talks, and an enormous economic aid package under U.N. auspices as steps toward an end to the war. Without parting with the Administration, CAIP president William O'Brien decried the resumption of U.S. bombing near North Vietnamese cities, singling out an August 11 bombardment of Longbien bridge less than two miles from downtown Hanoi. "No one who takes seriously the social teaching of the Catholic Church on the moral limits of defensive warfare," O'Brien maintained, "can countenance counter-city warfare in North Vietnam" [37].

In November the bishops promulgated a new "Resolution on Peace," which continued to back "the repeated efforts of our government to negotiate a termination to conflict" while rejecting "peace at any price." The statement nevertheless recognized "considerable division among our people" over U.S. policy while espousing "more rational debate and greater solicitude for mutual understanding." It urged "even greater determination and action in the cause of negotiation" by the Johnson Administration. The following April, in the wake of the Tet Offensive, the bishops applauded Johnson's moves to restrict the bombing and pursue a diplomatic solution to the war, but confessed a "growing anxiety for peace." They formed a Secretariat for World Justice and Peace to better articulate their position on the war [38].

Yet the Administration did not feel threatened by these gathering clouds. "Not all churchmen are by any means opposed to what we are doing in Vietnam," press secretary Bill Moyers reacted to the World Council of Churches' December 1965 resolution. "Now I don't think the Church should abdicate its responsibility to hold men in public life to a very, very rigid standard," added the former Baptist minister. "I know that the President feels that the Church could do that more appropriately if it were more informed and impartial in its judgments"[39]

White House aide Joseph Califano shared with Johnson the September 1967 assessment of his fellow Catholic, Democratic Speaker of the House of Representatives John McCormack of Massachusetts, that "most Catholic clergy" were still "with you on Viet Nam." The president himself acknowledged Cardinal Spellman's death in December by foreshadowing "the first Christmas in many years when our men in uniform will not share the comfort of his presence." And three days before Johnson shocked the world by announcing that he would not seek re-election, Cardinal Cushing advised him that he should. "He said to look out for the Kennedys," Eugene Roscow relayed to fellow White House aide Marvin Watson. "He said he predicted to President Kennedy before he was killed that he would lose the election in 1964," Rostow recounted his conversation with the former president's favorite Catholic prelate. "Bobby had made many enemies for President Kennedy, and the Cardinal didn't think those enemies had forgotten." Though Johnson would not run in 1968, Catholic New York Senator Robert Kennedy would, as an anti-war candidate whose campaign ended with an assassin's bullet in June [40]

THE CHURCH AND THE PRESIDENT

"We must keep the world from being devoured by the Communists," *Commonweal* editor James O'Gera wrote in July 1965, "but we also must keep it from destroying itself." Such was the dilemma which American Catholics faced between the often conflicting aims of President Lyndon Johnson and Pope Paul VI on matters of war and peace. The result was an unsteady excursion between right and left, opposition and obedience [41].

To assist conscientious objectors and oppose the Vietnam War, Rev. Daniel Berrigan joined James Forest of the Catholic Worker Movement and James Douglass, a theology student in Rome, in forming the Catholic Peace Fellowship in the summer of 1964. When poet Daniel and professor Philip Berrigan joined five hundred others in signing a March 1965 "declaration of conscience" against U.S. policy in Vietnam, they became the first priests publicly to protest the war. The statement urged Americans to avoid the draft, refuse to participate in the manufacture or transportation of weapons, and obstruct the mobilization of U.S. troops [42]

But they were not the only Catholics. William Pfaff, formerly an associate editor of *Commonweal*, presciently surmised in April that "there is no evidence that the American public is prepared to sustain a major ground war in Vietnam." Associate editor Jay Neugeboren admonished as early as October 1965 that "there are few illusions left about the prospects of creating a democratic Vietnam out of the present chaos." In November Catholic Worker Roger LaPorte immolated himself in front of the United Nations building. After Rev. Daniel Berrigan eulogized LaPorte, his Jesuit superior exiled him to Mexico. In December, the Catholic Peace Fellowship placed two-page ads in the *National Catholic Reporter*, *Commonweal*, and *Ave Maria* urging Catholics to refuse service in the "unjust" Vietnam War. Rev. John Sheerin concluded in *Catholic World* in March 1966 "that the morality of our involvement in Vietnam is very doubtful." Sheerin marveled, "Is it not strange that so many of our clergy who have no hesitation about making positive moral judgments week after week in confession have no opinions on the great moral problem of our generation?" [43]

Catholic laypeople rushed to fill this void. Father Daniel Berrigan was among over one hundred clergy from many faiths who inaugurated the National Emergency Committee of Clergy Concerned About Vietnam (later Clergy and Laymen Concerned About Vietnam) in January 1966. By the end of the year, the group was advocating a negotiated peace in Vietnam and had grown to sixty-eight chapters. By mid-1966, James Forest, co-chairman of the Catholic Peace Fellowship, an anti-war organization with headquarters in New York, had published a booklet, "Catholics and Conscientious Objection," and his group was counselling up to fifty Catholics per week about how and whether to seek this option to military service. "It should not be left to a small, but happily growing, minority of Catholic priests and laymen to try to redeem the day for the Church in America," wrote war critic Gordon Zahn, author of *German Catholics and Hitler's Wars*. In the United States, unlike in Nazi Germany, where the Catholic Church had been largely silent toward Adolf Hitler's repression, "no Gestapo is likely to be pounding the doors or dragging their priests off to concentration camps. At least not yet." So there was no excuse for Catholic indifference to the horrors of Vietnam. *Commonweal* ended the year by advocating an immediate, unconditional withdrawal of U.S. forces from the "unjust" war in Southeast Asia [44]

"Why in the year 1966 are Catholics getting so involved in peacemaking?" asked Rev. Charles Palms, who answered that the seemingly unending advances in nuclear weapons, the no-holds-barred ambiguity of guerilla warfare, and the empowerment of Catholic clergy and laity by the Second Vatican Council helped explain such activism. "The Catholic Peace Fellowship and others who join in the quest for peace must know that they will not by themselves stop the war in Vietnam," Palms wrote. "But they are resolved to shock the national conscience into realizing the evils of war" [45]

And the newly energized Catholic Left would persist in doing so. Rev. Philip Berrigan of Baltimore was the only Catholic among twelve clergy who criticized the war in an open letter to President Johnson in December 1966. Rev. James Drane of Little Rock, Arkansas engaged in a shouting match in the Washington office of his state's pro-war Democratic Senator John McClellan, then returned home to lead a three-day fast by clergy and students which prompted Democratic State Senator Dan Sprick to label the young priest a "communist." Writing in *Catholic World* in May 1967, Gerhard Elston suggested that it was not too late for the Americans to learn from the French and extricate themselves from a civil war. "Could the United States be as greatminded as France under DeGaulle finally was in Algeria: admit an error, offer a settlement, and offer to help, not on our terms, but on those of the local boys?" [46]

But the Left remained largely left out of the American Catholic consensus on Vietnam. From the right, William Roberts, director of Catholic University's Institute of International Law and Relations, took on Rev. Philip Berrigan in a December 1965 debate in which Roberts declared Vietnam a "just war" in defense of "human rights." The *National Review*'s Anthony Bouscaren in March 1966 attacked the Berrigan brothers and *Catholic Worker* founder Dorothy Day for being soft on communism. *Catholic World*'s Rev. John Clifford asserted in September that it would not be immoral to stay in Vietnam, but rather to leave South Vietnam's sixteen million people helpless against the inexorable communist onslaught. *National Review* inveighed in January 1967 against *Commonweal*'s anti-war stance. "You will find nowhere in the *Commonweal* editorial," Catholic William F. Buckley's journal noted, "of the strategic implications, disastrous for the U.S. and for the world, of the Communist victory the editors announce themselves willing to concede" [47]

Most American Catholics planted themselves firmly in the middle of the Vietnam debate. Rev. Andrew Greeley took issue in June 1965 with those "peaceniks" who equated the escalating resistance to the Vietnam War with the increasing mobilization against racial segregation. "If the peace movement members want to throw up picket lines, if they want to have 'teach-ins' (where mathematicians pontificate on foreign policy), if they want to sound like those who advised us that Mao and Castro were agrarian reformers," Greeley warned, "they are welcome to do their cause more harm than good." But he did not call upon them to cease and desist, for "we surely need a peace movement in this country if only as a counterbalance to the 'war hawks.'" [48]

Father Greeley thus could not have been happy with the tactics employed by a group of Protestant, Jewish, and Catholic seminarians who conducted a two-week peace vigil outside the White House in January 1966. But he would have approved of their message – encouraging more negotiations in Vietnam without attacking the Administration [49].

In July *America* applauded Cardinal Shehan's pastoral, which nimbly avoided criticizing Johnson while warning of any heightened conflict that would unnecessarily endanger civilians. "Has the President overstepped these bounds in Vietnam? We do not believe so," concluded *America*'s editors, while adding that the greater peril to civilians "comes not from the Administration but from those who would pressure the government into casting off the wraps of restraint under which we have been fighting....This the voice of Christian conscience must prevent." As for those disturbed by the other bishops' indifference to the war, Rev. Joseph Gallagher conceded in November 1966, the critics were right, but for the wrong reasons. The hierarchy should indeed speak out, if only to say that the war "is not clearly immoral," but that "the increasing suggestions that North Vietnam (with its fifteen million women and children) should be blasted off the map, turned into a desert, or bombed back to the Stone Age," clearly are [50]

Rev. James Schall similarly distinguished among three categories of "peace" advocates – pacifists represented by groups like the Catholic Worker movement, anti-nuclear organizations, and critics of the U.S. tactics of bombing civilians and the strategy of containing communism in an area outside the American sphere of influence. Father Schall attacked the second group for underestimating the evil of communism and the third for selective outrage not equally directed at violence in the American civil rights movement or the South African struggle against apartheid. But he was respectful, if unsympathetic, toward the first group's position for being "consistent," "religiously motivated," and "lived" [51]

America "has consistently supported the Administration policy in Southeast Asia on the grounds that we have been fighting a limited war for a limited objective – to guarantee the right of the people of South Vietnam to work out their own destiny free from the threat or use of outside force," the editors reiterated in January 1967. But amidst reports of accelerated U.S. bombing of urban areas, they excoriated the "civilian population be damned" attitude of Vietnam hawks. "It is perhaps not a simple matter to keep means proportionate to ends," the editorial concluded, "but the nation with a moral conscience can never cease trying" [52]

The next month the journal's editors rose to the defense of Father Cronin's impassioned dissent at the Clergy and Laity Concerned About Vietnam's anti-war demonstration in the nation's capital. Yet while lauding Cronin's support for the war, the editors again challenged all sides in the Vietnam conflict at home and abroad to press more vigilantly for peace. Cronin himself told the *National Catholic Reporter* that his remarks had intended not to reach either extreme but to ignite a rational dialogue. "Everybody wants peace. Nobody is in favor of napalming children," said Cronin. "But as long as the experts disagree about the facts, I would not join either the hawks or the doves in concrete recommendations with elements of political analysis or factual assumptions" [53]

In June's *Catholic World*, CAIP president William O'Brien offered his rebuttal to Gerhard Elston's Algerian analogy. Unlike a potentially precipitous American exit from Vietnam, O'Brien claimed, France's abandonment of its North African colony portended no deleterious international ripple effect. Yet O'Brien praised Elston's aversion to any significant escalation of the American war [54].

Conclusion

An "argument without end" is how Lyndon Johnson's Secretary of Defense Robert McNamara would characterize the debate over the Vietnam War three decades after its conclusion. Since the United States was losing in Vietnam, the conventional wisdom has come to hold, the Johnson Administration was losing the argument which had put Americans there. To the communists, "we must say in Southeast Asia – as we did in Europe – in the words of the Bible, 'Hitherto shalt thou come but no further,'" the Commander-in-Chief explained the rationale for U.S. military involvement in Vietnam in April 1965. The American Catholic shepherds and much of their flock, who unabashedly or tacitly accepted this argument even at the risk of offending Pope Paul VI, therefore appeared complicit in this national tragedy [55]

After all, a Gallup Poll in late 1966 found far more Catholics than Protestants and Jews on Johnson's side in the Vietnam conflict. At the same time, a survey conducted by *World Campus*, a Maryknoll Fathers magazine, showed one-third of American Catholic college students in favor of U.S. policy in Vietnam, and over half supporting more bombing of North Vietnam while opposing demonstrations against the war. Two years later, American Catholics gave fifty-nine percent of their votes to Johnson's Vice President, Herbert Humphrey, who essentially vowed to continue the Administration's military and diplomatic initiatives in Vietnam [56]

In reassuring its president the American Catholic majority was largely rebuking its Pope. The pontiff himself seemed to recognize the limits of his effectiveness as the Church's and arguably the world's spiritual leader. In his September 1966 encyclical *Christi Matri*, Paul VI acknowledged that the acceleration of his petitions for peace had begotten only escalation on the battlefield. "What is the use of it?" he asked plaintively, answering that despite his many setbacks, he remained convinced that "to pray is not in vain" [57]

The Pope's seemingly hollow words were alienating many non-Catholics as well. *The New York Times*' Edward Fiske reported in December 1967 that many "high Protestant officials" in the United States considered Paul VI "naïve in believing that he can perform a mediator's function in the Vietnam War, in view of the fact that Catholics constitute one of the major political blocs in the country." One cleric was more blunt, contending that "this is too tough a world for activist gimmicks" like the Pope's Vietnam peace proposals [58]

But American Catholics were not always on the "wrong" side of the argument over Vietnam. *Commonweal*'s verdict that President Johnson's mantra of "we cannot just get out" was "not a suitable substitute for a war policy" arrived as early as August 1965, almost eight years before the remaining U.S. troops just got out. The same month, *Life* published a picture of Catholic Worker Christopher Kearns burning his draft card. By the end of August Congress had passed a law prohibiting such actions, and Catholic Worker David Miller would become the first person to go to prison for breaking it. In May 1968 the Berrigan brothers and six other Catholics raided the office of the Catonsville, Maryland draft board and burned the records with napalm [59]

Though most American Catholics repudiated such radical activities, a July 1967 Harris poll showed that they had become more dovish on the war than their Protestant counterparts, with one-quarter of American Catholics now in opposition. Even their bishops finally showed substantial movement in that direction. At their November 1968 annual meeting, the bishops issued a pastoral, "Human Life in our Day," in which they asserted that "one cannot accuse Catholics of either being partisans of any one point of view or of being unconcerned" about Vietnam. While expressing the hope that the Johnson Administration's bombing halt and peace negotiations would soon bear fruit, the bishops nonetheless wondered, "How much more of our resources in men and money should we commit to this struggle?" And they emerged from their anti-nuclear shell to advocate early Senate ratification of the Administration's August 1968 Nuclear Nonproliferation Treaty with the Soviet Union and sixty other nations, a fulfillment of Father Cronin's wish, virtually forgotten in the firestorm over his other remarks at the Clergy and Laity Concerned vigil, that Vietnam not derail nuclear détente [60]

Lest they be charged with undermining their Pope, the bishops voted 121-64 that their pastoral apply the principles of the Vatican II *Constitution on the Modern World* to the Vietnam War and 142-51 to the question of selective conscientious objection. They also voted 153-44 that the pastoral explicitly define the role of conscience during wartime. The results were the document's taut embrace of "Pope Paul's positive, dynamic concept of peace" and advocacy of a new law permitting conscientious objection to a particular war [61]

For his part Pope Paul VI offered American Catholics periodic reminders that in his feverish quest for peace he had not forsaken the Church's traditional anti-communism. On the seventy-fifth anniversary of Pope Leo XIII's *Rerum Novarum* (Of New Things) in May 1966, Paul VI repeated that encyclical's condemnation of Marxism, calling it an "erroneous and dangerous ideology." In October the pontiff refused to accept the resignation of New York's Francis Cardinal Spellman, even though the hawkish first Military Vicar of the United States Armed Forces was two years beyond the retirement age of seventy-five recommended by the Pope only three months earlier. Two years later the Holy Father denounced the Soviet invasion of Czechoslovakia as an affront to the Czechs' freedom and dignity [62]

More important than whether American Catholics were winning or losing the argument on Vietnam during the Johnson era, however, was the reality that the argument, like the war which it spawned, was not yet over. In this way the bishops' statements and their followers' responses to them reflected the extant mysteries of an arduous work in progress. "A careful reading" of the bishops' November 1966 pastoral, war critic Rev. John Sheerin opined in *Catholic World* in January 1967, "reveals that their assent to the policy is so provisioned as to be lacking in any enthusiasm." The fact that the bishops may not be "quite prepared to condemn Administration policy out of hand," *America* observed in March 1967, did not mean that they didn't "deplore war as much as the next Christian" [63]

And though the Vietnam War was fast becoming the paramount moral issue of the day, the question of how and whether American churches should address it remained as inconclusive as the war itself. Somewhere between President Lyndon Johnson's appeal to Americans' "Christian duty" to "help our neighbors" in Vietnam, and Rev. Martin Luther King, Jr.'s anti-war jeremiad from the pulpit of New York's Riverside Baptist Church, lay a religious "no-man's land" which only true believers on either side dared to enter. Despite historic fits and starts, the United States had never seen a Catholic Left before. Dr. Carl Henry, editor of *Christianity Today*, the world's most widely read interdenominational religious periodical, told the *New York Times* in March 1965 that his fellow clergy possessed "neither a divine mandate...nor special competence" to address the nation's burning political issues. "It's a terrible thing," Episcopal priest Rev. G. R. Wheatcroft of Houston told *Newsweek* in July 1967, but on the Vietnam War, "we don't know what to say." Methodist Bishop J. O. Smith of Georgia concurred that on Vietnam, "the position of our church is that we live in a very imperfect world. The church kind of prays about it and hopes by faith we won't get involved next time." Rabbi Henry Siegman, vice president of the Synagogue Council of America, was even more explicit about organized religion's limited role: "I am prepared to accept the contention that Dean Rusk and Robert McNamara speak with no less moral authority than the heads of America's religious establishment." Even the civil disobedience of the civil rights movement, *Newsweek* concluded, had not adequately prepared the churches to confront the moral dilemmas posed by the military draft and conscientious objection [64]

So civil rights champion Patrick Cardinal O'Boyle's instructions to the priests of the Archdiocese of Washington, D.C. that Vietnam not be a subject of their Sunday homilies or the admission by an official in civil rights opponent James Cardinal McIntyre's Archdiocese of Los Angeles that the war "is not a topic of debate in any of our churches" in many ways fell comfortably within the mainstream of American organized religion. And Auxiliary Bishop James Shannon of Minneapolis-St. Paul, himself growing more dovish by the day, could at once lament that his fellow bishops "obviously aren't getting the Pope's message" while at the same time attacking those non-bishops who said essentially the same thing. After Stanford University theologian Robert McAfee Brown deplored the bishops' absence at the January 1967 Clergy and Laity Concerned About Vietnam event, Shannon questioned Brown's authority to do so. "As a Christian he has a moral obligation to follow his conscience and to voice his reservations about American participation in the war in Vietnam," Shannon wrote of Brown in March 1967. "But he does not have the right to decide how his fellow Christians will voice their concern and current agony about this same problem." Thus did Shannon frame his dispute with Brown as not so much about Vietnam as about the hierarchical nature of his Church. "Dr. Brown's style of protest," Shannon succinctly summarized, "is simply not the style of the Catholic bishops" [65]

"We are having an argument within the family," an anti-war Chicago priest explained in December 1965. Many American Catholics would have preferred that it remain there. But a war which would fail to contain communism had shaken a Church which would fail to contain dissent. In this way the American Catholic bishops had more in common with Lyndon Johnson than even they realized [66]

REFERENCES

[1] Paul Conkin, *Big Daddy from the Pedernales: Lyndon Johnson* (Boston: Twayne, 1986), pp. 195-196.

[2] Bruce Schulman, *Lyndon B. Johnson and American Liberalism* (Boston: Bedford, 1995), p. 135; Robert Dallek, *Flawed Giant: Lyndon Johnson and His Times* (New York: Oxford University Press, 1998), pp. 247-248.

[3] Robert Doty, "Pontiff Appeals for Peace Effort," *New York Times*, 12 February 1965, sec. L, p. 1; "Peace in Vietnam is Sought by Pope," *New York Times*, 21 February 1965, sec. L, p. 24.

[4] Letter from Rev. Thomas Merton to President Lyndon Johnson, 20 February 1965, White House Central Files, Name File, Box 377, Lyndon Baines Johnson Presidential Papers, Lyndon Baines Johnson Presidential Library, Austin, TX; Telegram from Rev. Philip Berrigan, Martin Corbin, and James Forest to President Lyndon Johnson, 2 March 1965, White House Central Files, Name File, Box 230, LBJPP, LBJPL; Memorandum from Bill Moyers to "Mr. President," 16 April 1965, White House Central Files, Name File – N, Box 24, LBJPP, LBJPL.

[5] Memorandum from Jack Valenti to President Lyndon Johnson, 26 February 1965, White House Central Files, Subject File – Religious Matters, Box 6, LBJPP, LBJPL, pp. 1-2; Jack Languuth, "Saigon Catholics Fearful of Buddhist Army Purge," *New York Times*, 13 April 1965, sec. L, pp. 1,4.

[6] "Text of Encyclical by Pope Paul Deploring Armed Conflicts," *New York Times*, 1 May 1965, sec. L, p.9; Jack Languuth, "Saigon Catholics Contend Regime is Easy on Reds," *New York Times*, 10 May 1965, sec. L, p.1; Jack Languuth, "Saigon Generals Striving to Form a Stable Regime," *New York Times*, 12 June 1965, sec. L, p.1.

[7] Robert Doty, "Papal Encyclical A Plea for Peace," *New York Times*, 1 May 1965, sec. L, p. 9; "Memorandum for the President: Talking Points for the Pope," n.d., Appointment File (Diary Back-up), Box 23, LBJPP, LBJPL, p.1.

[8] "Excerpts from Papal Address," *New York Times*, 4 October 1965, sec. L, p. 2; Tom Wicker, "Two Leaders Meet: Paul and President Confer Forty-Six Minutes on World Issues," *New York Times*, 4 October 1965, sec. L, p. 2.

[9] E. W. Kenworthy, "Masfield Report Seen as Urging U.S. to Get Peace Pact Quickly," *New York Times*, 9 January 1966, sec. L, p. 1.

[10] Transcript, Bill Moyers Press Conference, 4 October 1964, Appointment File (Diary Back-up), Box 23, LBJPP, LBJPL, p. 7; Robert Doty, "Pope's Christmas Plea: 'Sincere Negotiation,'" *New York Times*, 24 December 1965, sec. L, p. 1; Robert Doty, "Pope Sends Pleas: Pontiff Exhorts Hanoi, Saigon, Washington to Pursue Peace," *New York Times*, sec. L, p.1; Jack Raymond, "U.S. is Pessimistic as War is Resumed," *New York Times*, 26 December 1965, sec. L, p. 1.

[11] Robert Doty, "Pope Appeals to Peking and Moscow on Vietnam," *New York Times*, 2 January 1966, sec. L, p. 1; John Pomfret, "Vietnam 'Failure' Saddens Johnson," *New York Times*, 2 January 1966, sec. L, p. 1.

[12] Robert Doty, "Pontiff Suggests U.N. Arbitration in Vietnam War," *New York Times*, 30 January 1966, sec. L, p. 1; Memorandum from Jack Valenti to President Lyndon

Johnson, 19 March 1966, White House Central Files, Subject File – Peace, Box 3, LBJPP, LBJPL.

[13] "Pope Regrets His Peace Bids' Failure," *New York Times*, 25 June 1966, sec. L, p. 5; Letter from President Lyndon Johnson to Senator Mike Mansfield, 22 June 1966, White House Central Files, Name File, Box 72, LBJPP, LBJPL, pp. 2-3.

[14] Letter from Martin Riley to President Lyndon Johnson, 1 July 1966, White House Central Files, Name File, Box 141, LBJPP, LBJPL.

[15] "Text of Pope's Encyclical on Peace," *New York Times*, 20 September 1966, sec. L, p. 18; Memorandum from Tom Johnson to President Lyndon Johnson, 3 October 1966, White House Central Files, Subject File – Peace, Box 1, LBJPP, LBJPL; "Report to the Bishops," United States Catholic Conference Office for United Nations Affairs, September 1966, General Administration Series, Subseries 3.3, Box 165, Folder: Report to Bishops, United States Catholic Conference Papers, Catholic University of America Archives, Washington, D.C., p. 1.

[16] "Papal Peace Vow Sent to Vietnam," *New York Times*, 1 October 1966, sec. L, p. 4; Robert Doty, "150,000 Join Pope in Plea for Peace by Negotiations," *New York Times*, 5 October 1966, sec. L, pp. 1,4; Robert Doty, "Pope Paul Urges Truce Extension, Then Peace Talk," *New York Times*, 9 December 1966, sec. L, pp. 1,17; "Rusk Pessimistic on Lengthy Truce," *New York Times*, 9 December 1966, sec. L, p. 17.

[17] "Pope to Receive Soviet President," *New York Times*, 4 January 1967, sec. L, p. 6; Robert Doty, "Podgorny Meets Pope at Vatican," *New York Times*, sec. L, pp. 1,16; "The Pope's Message," *New York Times*, 9 February 1967, sec. L, p. 2; "Meeting of the Pope and the President," 13 December 1967, Special Files – Meeting Notes File, Box 2, LBJPP, LBJPL, pp. 4-5; "The President's Reply," *New York Times*, 9 February 1967, sec. L, p. 2; "Ho Chi Minh Reply to Pope," *New York Times*, 14 February 1967, sec. L, p. 8; "Saigon Catholics Stage a Protest," *New York Times*, 25 February 1967, sec. L, p. 3.

[18] "Thant Hails Pope on Peace Efforts," *New York Times*, 27 April 1967, sec. L, p. 9; "Text of Sermon by Pope Paul and Shrine of Fatima," *New York Times*, 14 May 1967, sec. L, p. 47; "Pope Melancholy on Peace Outlook," *New York Times*, 17 August 1967, sec. L, p. 15.

[19] Schulman, p. 139; Letter from William Baggs to Walt Rostow, 27 March 1967, White House Central Files, Subject File – Peace, Box 3, LBJPP, LBJPL; "Meeting of the Pope and the President," p. 7.

[20] "Meeting of the Pope and the President," pp. 4,6,13,9,10,11,12,13,14.

[21] Bernard Weinraub, "Bishops of South Vietnam, Asking Peace, Score Thieu," *New York Times*, sec. L, p. 3.

[22] "Meeting of the Pope and the President," p. 2; Schulman, p. 148.

[23] "Poetic Justice in Vietnam?" *America*, 20 June 1964, p. 837; "Memorandum," National Catholic Welfare Conference Office for United Nations Affairs, 20 July 1964, General Administration Series, Subseries 3.5, Box 173, National Catholic Welfare Conference Papers, CUAA, p. 1; "Protest in Saigon," *America*, 27 June 1964, p. 862.

[24] "Vatican Appeals for Saigon Calm," *New York Times*, 30 August 1964, sec. L, p. 3.

[25] "Council Debates War and Peace," *CAIP News*, January 1965, General Administration Series, Subseries 3.6, Folder: CAIP – News, 1964-65, NCWCP, CUAA, p. 11; "Laymen Lay Low," *National Review*, 10 January 1967, p. 11.

[26] "Denies Schema Thirteen Now Approves Nuclear War," *CAIP News*, May 1965, General Administration Series, Subseries 3.6, Box 174, Folder: CAIP – News, 1964-65, NCWCP, CUAA, p. 9; Msgr. George Higgins, "Pacifist Attack," *CAIP News*, February 1965, General Administration Series, Series 3.6, Box 174, Folder: CAIP – News, 1964-65, NCWCP, CUAA, p. 9; "Church Criticized for Lack of Stand on Nuclear War," *CAIP News*, May 1965, General Administration Series, Subseries 3.6, Box 174, Folder: CAIP – News, 1964-65, NCWCP, CUAA, p. 10.

[27] Msgr. George Higgins, "National Policy and the Clergy," *CAIP News*, May 1965, General Administration Series, Subseries 3.6, Box 174, Folder: CAIP – News, 1964-65, NCWCP, CUAA, pp. 6-7; Letter from Rev. Patrick Lucey to Jack Valenti, 10 May 1965, White House Central Files, Subject File – Religious Matters, Box 6, LBJPP, LBJPL, p. 1; Charles O'Donnell, "Statement on the War in Vietnam by the CAIP World Order Committee," 17 July 1965, General Administration Series, Subseries 3.6, Box 174, Folder: CAIP – News, 1964-65, NCWCP, CUAA, pp. 6-7.

[28] Arthur Goldberg, "Efforts for Peace," 4 December 1965, in *Social Digest*, July-August 1966, General Administration Series, Subseries 3.6, Box 174, Folder: CAIP – Annual Convention, 1965, NCWCP, CUAA, pp. 219, 217-218.

[29] Douglas Robinson, "Catholics Picket Spellman Office," *New York Times*, 5 December 1965, sec. L, pp. 1, 10; "Spellman Arrives for Five Day Visit with Vietnam G.I.'s," *New York Times*, 24 December 1965, sec. L, p. 6.

[30] Edward Fiske, "War and the Clergy," *New York Times*, 15 February 1966, sec. L, p. 2; "Report to the Bishops," United States Catholic Conference Office for United Nations Affairs, February 1966, General Administration Series, Subseries 3.3, Box 165, Folder: Report to Bishops, 1966-1967, USCCP, CUAA, p. 1.

[31] "The Bishops and Vietnam," *Commonweal*, 15 April 1966, p. 93; John Cogley, "'Never Again War'," *New York Times*, 5 October 1966, sec. L, p. 4.

[32] "Peace and Patriotism," *America*, 16 July 1966, p. 50; "Peace and Vietnam," National Council of Catholic Bishops, United States Catholic Conference, 18 November 1966, in J. Brian Benestad and Francis Butler, ed. *Quest for Justice: A Compendium of Statements of the United States Bishops on the Political and Social Order 1966-1980* (Washington, D.C.: United States Catholic Conference, 1981), p. 53.

[33] "Statement on Peace," 18 November 1966, General Administration Series, Subseries 1.1, Box 70, Folder: NCWC Bishops General Meeting Minutes, 1963-66, NCWCP, CUAA, p. 192; "Open Letter to American Catholic Bishops," n.d., General Administration Series, Subseries 1.1, Box 7, Folder: Administration – Letters to Bishops, April-December 1966, NCWCP, CUAA, p. 2; "Text of Pope's Encyclical on Peace," p. 18; "Spellman's View Decried in Rome," *New York Times*, 28 December 1966, sec. L, p. 3; John Cogley, "The Spellman Dispute," *New York Times*, 29 December 1966, sec. L, p. 3; "Spellman's View on War Called Outrageous by Episcopal Bishop," *New York Times*, 4 February 1967, sec. L, p. 3; John Sheerin, "Who Speaks for the Church on Vietnam?" *Catholic World*, November 1966, p. 72.

[34] Cogley, "The Spellman Dispute," p. 3; Robert McAfee Brown, "An Open Letter to the U.S. Bishops," *Commonweal*, 17 February 1967, p. 547; "Challenge for the Churches," *America*, 18 February 1967, p. 234; "A Second Selma," *Christian Century*, 8 March 1967, p. 301.

[35] William O'Brien, "Appeal for Limitation of Vietnam War," *CAIP News*, 30 December 1966, General Administration Series, Subseries 3.6, Box 174, Folder: CAIP – News, 1966-67, USCCP, CUAA, pp. 3-4; Letter from Msgr. George Higgins to John Twohey, 2 March 1967, General Administration Series, Subseries 3.1, Box 172, Folder: USCC Division on Urban Life, 1964-1971, USCCP, CUAA, pp. 1-2.

[36] "Catholics Seek a Review on War," *New York Times*, 19 March 1967, sec. L, p. 3; Daniel Callahan, "America's Catholic Bishops," *Atlantic Monthly*, April 1967, p. 69.

[37] "In Recent Peace Plea Bishop Asks Withdrawal from Vietnam," *CAIP News*, October 1967, General Administration Series, Subseries 3.6, Box 174, Folder: CAIP – News, 1966-67, USCCP, CUAA, pp. 7-8; "Bishops Endorsing Negotiation Now," *CAIP News*, October 1967, General Administration Series, Subseries 3.6, Box 174, Folder: CAIP – News, 1966-67, USCCP, CUAA, pp. 6-7; William O'Brien, "Statement on Bombing Population Centers in North Vietnam," *CAIP News*, October 1967, General Administration Series, Subseries 3.6, Box 174, Folder: CAIP – News, 1966-67, USCCP, CUAA, p. 5.

[38] "On Peace," National Council of Catholic Bishops, United States Catholic Conference, 16 November 1967, in Benestad and Butler, pp. 56-57; "Resolution on Peace," National Council of Catholic Bishops, United States Catholic Conference, Fourth General Meeting, 23-24 April 1968, United States Catholic Conference Papers, United States Catholic Conference Archives, Washington, D.C., pp. 64-65; "Up Bishops' Sleeves," *Newsweek*, 24 April 1967, p. 88.

[39] "White House Rebuttal to Vietnam Critics," *Catholic World*, October 1966, p. 53.

[40] Memorandum from Joseph Califano to President Lyndon Johnson, 18 September 1967, White House Central Files, Subject File – Religious Matters, Box 6, LBJPP, LBJPL; Lyndon Johnson, "Statement by the President," 2 December 1967, White House Central Files, Subject File – Religious Matters, Box 6, LBJPP, LBJPL; Memorandum from Marvin Watson, 28 March 1968, White House Central Files, Subject File – Religious Matters, Box 6, LBJPP, LBJPL.

[41] James O'Gara, "Banning the Bomb," *Commonweal*, 23 July 1965, p. 522.

[42] Charles Meconis, *With Clumsy Grace: The American Catholic Left, 1961-1975* (New York: Seabury Press, 1979), p. 9; "Men of Peace," *Commonweal*, 19 March 1965, p. 779; Anthony Bouscaren, "The Catholic Peaceniks," *National Review*, 8 March 1966, p. 202.

[43] William Pfaff, "No Victory in Vietnam," *Commonweal*, 23 April 1965, p. 137; Jay Neugeboren, "Keeping the Consensus," *Commonweal*, 8 October 1965, p. 8; Meconis, p. 13; Bouscaren, p. 202; John Sheerin, "The Morality of the Vietnam War," *Catholic World*, March 1966, p. 330.

[44] Melvin Small, *Antiwarriors: The Vietnam War and the Battle for America's Hearts and Minds* (Wilmington, DE: Scholarly Resources, 2002), p. 51; Charles Palms, "Peace and the Catholic Conscience," *Catholic World*, June 1966, pp. 145-146; Gordon Zahn, "The Crime of Silence," *Commonweal*, 17 June 1966, p. 356; "Getting Out," *Commonweal*, 23 December 1966, p. 335.

[45] Palms, pp. 149, 152.

[46] Emanuel Perlmutter, "Twelve Clerics Criticize Johnson on Hanoi Bombing," *New York Times*, 27 December 1966, sec. L, p. 6; "Arkansas Priest Leads Fight on War," *New*

York Times, 26 February 1967, sec. L, p. 9; Gerhard Elston, "Vietnam: Some Basic Considerations," *Catholic World*, May 1967, p. 81.

[47] "Says Vietnam War Defends Christian Values," *CAIP News*, January 1966, General Administration Series, Subseries 3.6, Box 174, Folder: CAIP – News, 1966-67, USCCP, CUAA, p. 11; Bouscaren, p. 202; John Clifford, "Some Fallacies About the Vietnam War," *Catholic World*, September 1966, p. 364; "Laymen Lay Low," p. 12.

[48] Andrew Greeley, "Peaceniks Have a Lot to Learn," *CAIP News*, June 1965, General Administration Series, Subseries 3.6, Box 174, Folder: CAIP – News, 1964-65, NCWCP, CUAA, pp. 7-8.

[49] "Seminarians End Two-Week Vigil in Front of White House Today," *New York Times*, 30 January 1966, sec. L, p. 6.

[50] "Peace and Patriotism," p. 50; Joseph Gallagher, "The American Bishops on Modern War," *America*, 11 November 1966, pp. 548-549.

[51] James Schall, "Religion and War," *Commonweal*, 18 November 1966, p. 194.

[52] "Bombs in the North" and "The Moral Issue," *America*, 14 January 1967, p. 32.

[53] "Challenge to the Churches," p. 234; John Donavan, *Crusader in the Cold War* (New York: Peter Lang, 2005), p. 158.

[54] William O'Brien, "Comments on the Vietnam Debate," June 1967, p. 170.

[55] Robert McNamara, James Blight, Robert Brigham, Thomas Biersteker, Herbert Schandler, et al. *Argument Without End* (Washington, D.C.: Public Affairs, 2000); "President Lyndon Johnson Explains Why Americans Fight in Vietnam, 1965," in Dennis Merrill and Thomas Paterson, ed. *Major Problems in American Foreign Relations* (Boston: Houghton Mifflin), p. 450.

[56] James O'Gara, "Catholics and Peace," *Commonweal*, 11 November 1966, p. 158; "Campus Poll Shows Catholics Back War, Decry Draft Lottery," *New York Times*, 20 November 1966, p. 16; Jeffrey Jones, "The Protestant and Catholic Vote," available at *http://www.gallup.com/poll/11911/Protestant-Catholic-Vote,aspx? INTERNET*.

[57] "At a General Audience," *CAIP News*, October 1966, General Administration Series, Subseries 3.6, Box 174, Folder: CAIP – News, 1966-67, USCCP, CUAA, p. 6.

[58] Edward Fiske, "Papal Quest for Peace," *New York Times*, 25 December 1967, sec. L, p. 3.

[59] "Our War in Vietnam," *Commonweal*, 6 August 1965, p. 547; James Hennesey, *American Catholics* (New York: Oxford University Press, 1981), p. 319; Jay Dolan, *The American Catholic Experience* (Notre Dame, IN: University of Notre Dame Press, 1992), p. 451.

[60] "The Churches: What Should We Say?" *Newsweek*, 10 July 1967, p. 82; Dolan, p. 426; "Human Life in Our Day, Chapter II, 'The Family of Nations'," National Council of Catholic Bishops, 15 November 1968, in Benestad and Butler, ed., pp. 65,60; Donavan, p. 187.

[61] "Human Life in Our Day," pp. 59,67-68.

[62] "Pope Paul Warns of Marxist Peril," *New York Times*, 23 May 1966, sec. L, p. 9; Edward Fiske, "Pope Turns Down Cardinal Spellman's Offer to Resign," *New York Times*, 11 October 1966, sec. L, pp. 1,48; Henry ten Kortenar, "Does the Pope Realize?" *Commonweal*, 11 October 1968, p. 49.

[63] John Sheerin, "The Bishops and the Vietnam War," *Catholic World*, January 1967, p. 197; "The Bishops Taken to Task," *America*, 11 March 1967, p. 334.

[64] "Our War in Vietnam," *Commonweal*, 5 August 1965, p. 548; James Fraser, *Between Church and State* (New York: St. Martin's Press, 1999), p. 155; Small, pp. 6-7; Hennessey, p. 320; Dolan, p. 426; Meconis, p. ix; M. S. Handler, "Clergymen Clash on Role in Major National Issues," *New York Times*, 1 March 1965, sec. L, p. 78; "The Churches: What Should We Say?" pp. 81-82.

[65] "The Churches: What Should We Say?" p. 82; James Shannon, "Catholic Bishops and Vietnam," *Commonweal*, 17 March 1967, p. 671; "The Bishops Taken to Task," *America*, 11 March 1967, p. 337.

[66] John Corry, "The Catholic Student Protest: Priest Calls Support of Liberal Clergy 'Argument Within the Family'," *New York Times*, 26 December 1965, sec. L, p. 55.

Chapter 14

"No Winners, No Losers":
Reagan, the Iran-Iraq War and the Gulf's Perpetual Security Dilemma

Bernd Kaussler

Abstract

The central argument of this article is that Reagan's "No Winners, No Losers" policy during the Iran-Iraq war significantly altered the duration of the conflict by shifting the military balance to Iraq's favor and eventually forcing Iran to accept a ceasefire. Guided largely by Cold War strategic objectives and energy security, the Reagan administration first aided Saddam Hussein's regime diplomatically and economically and then effectively entered the war on Iraq's side. In the long term, Reagan's decision to fight Iranian forces in the Persian Gulf significantly affected Iranian strategic and military planning as well as continues to negatively affect relations between the U.S. and Iran. To this day, naval confrontations between U.S and Iranian forces as well as battle tactics implemented against Iraq during the war, continue to inform Iran's basic defense doctrine. Thus, since the end of the war, guided by a deeply entrenched threat perception, deterrence has been Iran's primary strategy. The basic tenets underwriting this doctrine are also direct remnants of Iran's military encounters with Iraqi and U.S. forces during the eight-year long conflict. They constitute continuous efforts to enhance and improve the capabilities of its armed forces, which include an indigenous military procurement program and the threat to use asymmetrical warfare against any potential aggressor or its regional allies. For Iran, the legacy of the war is mistrust and the conviction that only the reliance on its own military capabilities both conventional and asymmetrical preserves territorial integrity, security and regime stability. By and large, it is argued that in terms of diplomacy and military strategy, the Cold War lives on in the Persian Gulf with balance-of-power politics preventing the establishment of a regional collective security framework.

INTRODUCTION

The Iran-Iraq war, which lasted from 1980 until 1988, was the longest conventional war in the 20th Century and claimed the lives of as many as one million soldiers and civilians on both sides. For Iran, the experiences on the battlefield do not only continue to inform current security and foreign policy, but marked the collective memory of an entire generation, fuelling mistrust and animosity vis-à-vis Europe in general and the United States in particular. The Reagan administration's policy during the Iran-Iraq war was as much defined by Cold War strategy and U.S. interests in the Levant and Persian Gulf as it was determined by Reagan himself, who entered office with a deep mistrust and hostility towards the new Iranian regime. By and large, Reagan's official position of neutrality during the war was a carefully guarded veneer of a war policy, which first supported Iraq in economic, diplomatic and military terms but then shifted to actual involvement by U.S. forces against Iran. The central argument of this paper is that Reagan's war policy during the conflict set the foundations for the Persian Gulf's ongoing balance of power politics, by introducing deterrence as the primary tenet of security in the region. Because of these policies and naval confrontations between Iranian and American forces, the major legacy of the war is that the fundamental Cold War concept of deterrence survives in the Persian Gulf, both in its military and diplomatic manifestation. As such, it is argued that a collective security framework is still elusive in that region, largely due to U.S. and Iranian experiences between 1980- 1988.

SADDAM'S MOTIVATIONS

Saddam Hussein's decision to invade neighboring Iran on 22 September 1980 reflected both historical tensions, his self-given role as pan-Arab leader and the Iraqi regime's disastrous assumption that it could bring about the fall of the new Islamic regime. Both Saddam Hussein's unease about new political realities in Iran and his bold, yet inept tactics vis-à-vis Tehran had already manifested themselves months before the invasion when an Iraqi terrorist group, funded by his regime, seized the Iranian Embassy in London in April, demanding the autonomy of the Arab-majority and oil-rich region of Khuzestan in Iran.[1] Whilst territorial and economic gain certainly were certainly vital for Iraq to advance into Iranian territory, Saddam Hussein's biggest grievance was with the Algiers Accord of 1975 in which he and the Shah settled a border dispute on the Shatt al-Arab waterway. With the new Islamic regime still in the early stages, Hussein saw an opportunity to reclaim the entire waterway. [2] Iran's volatile rhetoric coupled with its intent to export the revolution across the region also caused particular concern for regime stability, given Iraq's *Shi'a* majority. Following months of border skirmishes, Hussein eventually responded to Khomeini's open hostility to the Baathist regime, which in his own words "left him no choice but to fight" [3].

IRAQI ADVANCES AND IRAN'S COUNTER OFFENSIVE

Anticipating an easy victory, without ever really stating specific war aims either to Iran or to his own generals, Hussein felt confident that the purge of Iran's military would favor

Iraq's military campaign. [4] Catching Iran's leadership by surprise, the initial phase of the invasion allowed Iraqi forces to advance with three armored and two mechanized infantry divisions into Khuzestan with the aim of securing the major cities and infrastructure with little or no resistance. Failing to launch an extensive air attack against Iranian installations, the Iraqis failed to cripple the Iranian air force, allowing the Iranians to have enough aircrafts for retaliatory attacks. Lacking any real air or naval supremacy, Hussein prematurely declared a "glorious victory against the oppressor clique in Tehran" and stated his readiness to negotiate a ceasefire and negotiations to settle territorial disputes only a week after the invasion. [5] Misreading Iran's political map, the Iraqis failed to garner any support of Khuzestan's ethnic Arabs, who felt more alienated with the destruction and violence of the occupation than they had grievances vis-à-vis the Islamic Republic from which they had also no intention to secede from.[6]. The anticipated two weeks campaign turned into a siege of strategically important cities of Abadan and Khorramshahr. Further north-west, the Iraqis occupied Mehran, advanced towards the Zagros Mountains and were able to cut off a supply corridor to Tehran by securing some territory forward of Qasr-e-Shirin. Overall, Iraq attacked only four targets along a 600 kilometers stretch of the border. [7] Even though the invasion temporarily halted Khomeini's purges of opponents and was under attack by President Bani-Sadr for having disintegrated a once powerful army, [8] the revolutionary regime soon managed to shift the military balance by recruiting thousands of volunteers (*Basij*) and putting them under the command of the Islamic Revolutionary Guards Corps (IRGC). Inspired by revolutionary ferocity as much as nationalism, Iranian forces managed to bring the Iraqi advance to a stall by March 1981. Since military planning in Tehran was still subject to domestic infighting, it was not until September 1981, that a major Iranian counter-offensive, launched by Iran's 16th and 92nd armored divisions, caused Iraqi units to retreat from desert positions and eventually forcing them to pull back its troops west of the Karun River, thus ending Baghdad's costly siege of Abadan. [9]. The purging of the officer corps (the armed forces may have lost as much as 12,000 officers to the revolution) and the shortage of military hardware and their proper maintenance due to the US arms embargo severely impacted both Iranian maneuvering and firepower. However, Khomeini's use of so-called "human waves" substituted for this military imbalance. *Basij* and IRGC units broke through Iraqi lines with subsequent mobile army detachments exploiting breakthroughs. This new, and for Iraqi frightening form of asymmetrical warfare allowed the Iranian military to launch a series of successful campaigns, eventually allowing them to recapture Khorramanshar in May 1982 and forcing Iraqi forces out of Iranian territory by 20 June, 1982. [10]. Interpreting Iraq's retreat as a sign of God, Khomeini took the fateful decision to move the "Army of Islam" into Iraq. Contrary to the counsel of his generals, Khomeini launched a major offensive against the city of Basra on June 21, 1982. [11]. When Iran decided to take the war into Iraq, it was the beginning of a stalemate that would last another six years.

POLICY DETERMINATS FOR THE WHITE HOUSE

When Reagan entered the White House, he regarded the loss of Iran in a rather "orientalist" fashion as the result of Carter's ineptitude and as such "absolved [Iranians] of their responsibility in the revolution […] It was Carter and the Democrats who were responsible for losing Iran, and now a more robust foreign policy, realistic and which a clear idea of friend and foe, would reverse the mistakes of the preceding administration." [12]. Notwithstanding that Reagan's campaign staff had allegedly reached a deal with the Iranians to delay the release of the US hostages held in Iran until after the 1980 election [13], thus allowing Reagan to begin his term on a foreign policy success, the new administration showed nothing but public contempt for the Islamic Republic.

The main determinants for Reagan's policy towards Iran and Iraq were energy security in the Persian Gulf, fears that the Soviets may be able to exert influence in the region, particular exploit the loss of Iran as major U.S. ally, as well as the potential spread of Iran's revolution across the region. [14] Given its poor relations with either of the combatants, U.S. security concerns led immediately to reinforce air defenses by the deployment of AWACS to Saudi Arabia and to block the use of air bases in the Arabian Peninsula by Iraqi aircrafts to reduce the threat of expansion to the war. From the onset of his presidency, Reagan also turned Carter's Rapid Reaction Force into a Rapid Deployment and Joint Task Force, which became the U.S. Central Command (CENTCOM) in charge of the Persian Gulf region and the rest of the Middle East and Central Asia. Up until the reestablishment of diplomatic relations with Iraq, a 1983 U.S. State Department assessment of its position of strict neutrality served US objectives and interests as it: (1) avoided direct great power involvement (2) prevented spread of the war beyond the territory of the combatants to threaten Gulf oil supplies (3) contributed to the current stalemate (4) preserved the possibility of developing a future relationship with Iran while minimizing openings for expansion of Soviet influence [15].

As far as outside influence was concerned, Washington's two main regional allies Egypt and Israel had been instrumental in shaping President Reagan's shift toward Iraq. Even though the Israeli government supplied Iran with arms in the early war years for the purpose of income and in order to keep a stake in Iran, Israeli Defense Minister, Ariel Sharon warned the U.S. government, that Iran's conditions hardened following the success in its March 1982 offensive and may contribute to the demise of the Baathist regime, eventually putting neighboring Arab states, particularly Saudi Arabia, at risk of Iranian influence. [16] Mubarak's demands that the U.S. ought to help Iraq directly or indirectly were eventually heard as it became obvious to the Reagan administration that Iran was in the process of gaining the upper hand in the conflict.[17]. As a prelude to the reestablishment of US-Iraqi relations in 1984, meetings between U.S. representatives and Saddam Hussein paved the way for a working relationship, causing the U.S. to gradually tilt towards Iraq in the conflict whilst pressuring the regime to adopt an evenhanded stand towards the Middle East peace process. Saddam Hussein, for his part, made it clear in February 1983, that the upgrade to full diplomatic relations was contingent on the resolution of the war and a cessation of US support for European and Israeli arms exports to Iran [18] The final determinant causing the tilt towards Iraq was largely the result of Israel's invasion of Lebanon in 1982 and Iran's subsequent support for the country's *Shi'a* population. With *Hezbollah's* quick rise as a key militia in the Lebanese conflict, a fact which can mainly be attributed to Iran's material, financial and operational support, the Reagan administration began to largely frame its Iran policy within the context of Iran's support for international terrorism. The suicide attacks on the U.S. Embassy and the marine barracks in Lebanon in 1983 constituted not only Reagan's first foreign policy crisis but also influenced choices in the White House to eventually resort to military force against Iran [19].

REAGAN'S WAR POLICY

Before the U.S. committed itself militarily in the war, support for Iraq in the conflict manifested itself in financial, economic and diplomatic terms. A cornerstone for US policy was National Security Decision Directive (NSDD) 114, passed on November 26, 1983. Reflecting Reagan's priorities, it called for heightened regional military cooperation to defend oil facilities, and measures to improve U.S. military capabilities in the Persian Gulf, and directed the secretaries of State and Defense and the chairman of the Joint Chiefs of Staff to take appropriate measures to respond to tensions in the area. Concerning energy security, it stated "because of the real and psychological impact of a curtailment in the flow of oil from the Persian Gulf on the international economic system, we must assure our readiness to deal promptly with actions aimed at disrupting that traffic." [20] Confident about U.S. naval supremacy, Reagan noted in his diary in March 1984 "if Iran should try to close the Strait of Hormuz, no real problem- they'll line up with us to keep it open" [21].

By December 1983, Reagan exerted pressure on its allies in Europe, Middle East and Asia to stop any military traffic to Iran, including arms sales by third countries. [22]. Even though U.S. intelligence confirmed Iraq's "use of chemical weapons" [23] against Iran Presidential envoy, Donald Rumsfeld, was dispatched several times to Iraq in order to strengthen bilateral relations, discuss Iraqi military operations, mutual regional security concerns and the construction of an oil pipeline to Jordan and Saudi Arabia.[24]. Overall, through Reagan's diplomatic initiatives, a total of $2 billion worth of US commodity credits were made to Iraq, bilateral trade was actively encouraged, including the sale of military hardware and sophisticated technology to Iraq [25] and Gulf states were pushed to extend financial support to Iraq. In fact, at one point the State Department expressed concern over President Reagan's public disclosure of the magnitude of Western European arms shipments to Iran and Iraq, as it would severely undermine the stated position of neutrality. [26]. As far as U.S. reactions towards Iraq's use of chemical warfare were concerned, the government initially cautioned restraint, instructing the U.S. delegation at the UN Human Rights Commission not to support an Iranian sponsored resolution condemning Iraq's use of chemical weapons. [27]. However, in the light of U.S. intelligence assessments that Iraq will continue to use all weapons in its arsenal including chemicals to dissuade any Iranian attack, [28] the U.S. government eventually condemned the use of WMDs publicly, [29] but avoided, as requested by the Iraqi government a UN Security Council Resolution against Iraq, in favor of a statement by the UNSC President without identifying any particular country for chemical weapons use. The U.S. government did, however, institute foreign policy controls on chemical exports to Iran Iraq, which could be used for chemical weapons manufacturing. It also exerted pressure on allies, in particular Germany, not to export any dual-use equipment to Iran and Iraq. In an effort not to alienate Iraqis, the U.S. Government quietly reiterated its intentions to remain in close dialogue and expanded commercial and eventual full diplomatic relations with Iraq. [30]. Reagan's presidential directive, NSDD 139 in April 1984, paved the way for more assertive U.S. support for Iraq, including the sharing of intelligence and the actual entry of U.S. forces into the conflict. Emphasizing the U.S. objective of ensuring access to military facilities in the Gulf region, and upgrading U.S. intelligence gathering capabilities, Reagan set out policy guidelines "to avert an Iraqi collapse." Reagan's directive further demanded "unambiguous" condemnation of chemical warfare (without naming Iraq), while including the caveat that the U.S. should "place equal stress on the urgent need to dissuade Iran from continuing the ruthless and inhumane tactics which have characterized recent offensives." Deterrence and stepped up U.S. military presence in the Persian Gulf were the fundamental tenets of U.S. policy henceforth. [31] Even though NSDD 139 laid the policy foundations for the use of force against revolutionary Iran by the U.S and its future stake in Persian Gulf security, Reagan continued to be primarily concerned about Tehran's potential shift to Moscow, demanding in a draft NSDD in 1985 to "limit the scope and opportunity for Soviet actions in Iran" [32].

U.S. active involvement was eventually triggered with the "Tanker War" which had started in 1984 and seriously threatened international energy and maritime security. Between 1984 and 1986 Iranian mines and torpedoes damaged sixty-seven oil tankers, including eight registered in Kuwait, eventually forcing the Kuwaiti government in 1987 to ask the U.S. to reflag their vessels under the Stars and Stripes. During a NSC meeting in May 1987, Reagan made it clear that any attack on Kuwaiti ships sailing under American flag will be retaliated forcefully. Notwithstanding U.S. and Israeli arms sales to Iran in exchanges for hostages in Lebanon, Reagan's attitude towards the Iranians had increasingly been defined by contempt and impatience [33].

Reminding critics of Reagan's decision about perceived Cold War and economic realities, Caspar Weinberger stated that unless that the U.S. came to Kuwait's aid " we would be accepting Iran's right to close the international waters of the Gulf and, even worse, opening the door to the Kremlin, which would be more than happy to become the sole guarantor of the security of the small Gulf states." In the National Security Council, Weinberger also proposed to "drop the pretense of even-handedness [and] no longer talk about ending the war "with no winners or losers". Iran is the aggressor in this case and we should not only be supportive of Iraq, but should be seen supportive" [34]. By May 1987, Reagan had six American warships in the Gulf, in 1988 he had doubled the fleet to thirteen.

As far as Iranian tactics were concerned, IRGC and regular Iranian navy attacked Iraqi and international shipping, using F-4 fighters firing Maverick missile, helicopters firing French-made missiles, naval frigates firing Italian anti-ship missiles to the use of small-boat attacks by IRGC operating from islands or offshore oil platforms in the Strait of Hormuz. The Iranian navy also shifted to employing small boats operating in tandem with naval vessels. [35]. Notwithstanding the errant Iraqi missile, which had struck the *USS Stark* on 7 May 1987, killing thirty-seven sailors, and increased congressional criticism over his war policy, Reagan affirmed his support for Iraq's war effort in a personal letter to Saddam Hussein.[36]. President Reagan had completely shifted to the Iraqi camp. By April 1988, the U.S. State Department concluded that given the Iraqi regime's heavily publicized use of chemical weapons on Iraqi civilians at Halabja, the basic nature of the war remained unchanged: "Iraq can't win but need not lose. Iran can win, but probably won't." [37] In order to break this stalemate, the direct involvement of the U.S. navy and Air Force gradually shifted the military balance toward Iraq, which had been facing a series of large-scale Iranian offensives. "Operation Praying Mantis", which was launched by the Pentagon in April 1988, destroyed two Iranian frigates, six high-speed torpedo boats and an Iranian oil platform. The U.S. offensive, which coincided with Iraq's recapture of the strategic *al-Faw* peninsula, constituted a watershed event as it essentially ended the "Tanker War" and largely forced the Iranians to come to terms with UN initiatives for a ceasefire [38]. The shooting down of an unarmed Iranian airliner by the *USS Vincennes* in August 1988, largely the result of incompetence of the captain, killing all 290 passengers on board, was a tragic incident and the last straw for Khomeini to start talks at the United Nations in Geneva [39].

As far as military planers in the White House were concerned, confrontations with the Iranians not only secured the flow of oil through the Strait but also backed U.S. policy of deterrence, showing both superior military capabilities and political resolve. The fact that Reagan had been implementing an "arms-for-hostages" deal with Iran between 1985 and 1986 merely constituted what Weinberger an "aberration" of U.S. policy towards Iran. [40] Reagan later remarked at the Tower Commission that he "let [his] personal concern for the hostages spill over into the geopolitical strategy of reaching out to Iran" and that, by asking "so many questions about the hostages' welfare," he failed to see the implications of the arms transfer for the Iranian regime. [41]. In fact, Washington's tilt towards Iraq after 1987 was as much a result of the above stated strategic determinants, as it was an effort to regain credibility in the eyes of its Arab allies in the region following the "Iran-Contra Affair". To that end, the confrontation with Iran was meant to reassure the Gulf monarchies of America's security umbrella in the region whilst at the same time intended to counter and deter Iranian naval attacks and eventually pressure Tehran to accept a ceasefire on U.S. terms.

Policies adopted by the Reagan administration significantly shifted the military balance towards Iraq, by providing vital intelligence on Iranian movements and diplomatic, financial and direct military support. This did not only prolong the war substantially but eventually forced the Iranian leadership (together with growing domestic dissension) to accept a ceasefire. In the long term, Iraq's import of sophisticated equipment facilitated by U.S. licenses, also proved fundamental for its WMD program. By and large, Reagan's policy of "neither winners nor loser" effectively was a policy of deterrence against Iran in an effort to secure energy security as well as to weaken the Iranian regime. In the immediate term, Reagan's gunboat diplomacy contributed to increased confrontations with Iran's armed forces. Even during the war, Gary Sick, the former principal White House aid for Persian Gulf affairs (1976-1981), criticized Reagan's policy for having deployed U.S. forces "aggressively and provocatively in the hottest parts of the Persian Gulf " which essentially laid the groundwork for the destruction of the Iranian airliner by the USS *Vincennes*. [42]. In the long term, Reagan's policies during the war instilled a deep-grounded suspicion towards successive U.S. administrations amongst Iranian officials. However, it also brought about a newly found confidence about its military capabilities and strategic assets. As far as Iranian leaders were concerned, the end of the war neither brought about territorial loss nor military defeat. Against all odds, in terms of sophisticated weaponry, economic power and America's vast political clout, Ansari argues "this was the first Iranian state not to lose territory in nearly two hundred years." Much more than this, Iran's military planners had learned to adapt on their own terms, fighting a conventional war with unconventional means and limited resources. Far from limiting Iran's military procurement in the long-term, the embargo and diplomatic isolation of the country had encouraged the development of an indigenous arms industry [43]. By and large, Iran's sacrifices on the battlefield not only nurtured the cult of "martyrdom" but also continue to inform the country's basic defense doctrine: deterrence. Even though the end of the war and the death of Khomeini witnessed major changes in Iran's political arena, Iran's security policy remains a direct artifact of the Iran-Iraq war.

Essentially, U.S. policies and the use of force against Iran during the war created a reference point for future bilateral relations (or rather the lack thereof) and further consolidated an American security framework for the Persian Gulf. However, far from creating a sustainable peace after 1988, the Gulf Wars in 1990-91 and 2003 coupled with the policy of dual containment only reinforced the region's balance of power politics and the confrontational course Washington and Tehran had embarked on after 1979 [44]. As will be shown below, during the George W. Bush administration, this bilateral "Cold War mindset" reached new levels with both the U.S. and Iranian governments engaging in openly hostile rhetoric and confrontational actions. As far as the region's security environment is concerned, Reagan's Cold War lives on.

LEGACIES OF WAR:
THE GULF'S PERPETUAL SECURITY DILEMMA

Since the war, Iran's policy towards the Persian Gulf states and the U.S. has largely been determined by security concerns. Despite mutual strategic considerations, the Gulf States still seem unable to create and implement a multilateral regional security structure. With the Gulf Cooperation Council (GCC) member countries being strongly committed to their economic-strategic alliance with the U.S., Tehran's nuclear program and its recent behavior have been watched with increasing unease by the U.S. and its Gulf allies. Beyond the need to maintain popular acquiescence at home, a series of Iranian military maneuvers, actual operations in the region and involvement in Iraq, were meant to repel any possible threat from the U.S. or its GCC allies. Whilst this behavior is being interpreted by both the U.S. and the GCC members as yet another demonstration of hegemonic aspirations, Iran continued to frame these actions and policies in pure defensive terms. Conscious of U.S. capacities to deploy significant naval power in the region, Tehran has made it obvious that, following any U.S. attack on Iran, retaliation would inevitably also target Arab states.

Countering the impact of sanctions as well as defying demands by the UN, EU and U.S. with the above tactics has led to a quandary in the region, in which the GCC states continue to pledge allegiance to Washington's security umbrella in the Gulf, hosting U.S. military and naval bases and underwriting the U.S. economy for their defense. At the same time, they are also unwilling to become pawns in a U.S.-Iranian military show-down. Within this context, Iran's deterrence doctrine proved successful to the extent that GCC states maintain strong trading and diplomatic relations with both the U.S. and Iran whilst at the same time start to accommodate themselves with Iran's growing power [45].

Directly reflecting the realist mindset and defense strategy acquired on the battlefield during the Iran-Iraq war, since 2003, Iran's stepped up defense posture manifested itself on four levels: (1) Iran continued to consolidate its position as regional military power with the launch of new home grown military technology and procurement (2) Iran used a series of large-scale military maneuvers to demonstrate its armed forces' defense commitment and capabilities (3) The Revolutionary Guards took control over Iran's Persian Gulf defense command and were involved in a series of naval "renegade incidents". (4) Lastly, the establishment of an extensive security network in Iraq is as much an expression of Iran's political clout in Baghdad as it serves as a "2nd front" during a potential military confrontation with the US.

Procurement

Since the U.S. imposed weapons embargo, Iran's deterrence doctrine has largely been based on its ability to consolidate indigenous technological military capabilities, which during the last three years predominantly included its nuclear program, various new domestically procured missile systems, the launch of Iranian-built jet fighters as well as a satellite carrier rocket. Reflecting its stepped up defense posture since the U.S.-led invasion of Iraq in 2003, Iran procured missiles from Russia, China and North Korea as well as developed missile systems and other military hardware on their own, which include: *Raad* Anti-Ship Cruise Missile (ASCM), Anti-Tank Guided Weapons (ATGW), various types of surface-to-surface and surface-to-air rockets, a new Russian-made air defense system ("TOR1"), the jet-fighters "*Azaraksh*" and "*Saeqeh*" as well as long-range artillery rockets designed and built in Iran, surface-to-air missiles and ballistic missiles, "Shahab-3" Medium-Range Ballistic Missile (MRBM). As far as major surface vessels are concerned, Iran's three destroyers are over 50 years old and non-operational, the remaining three frigates (Vosper Mark 5) and remaining two Corvettes (30 years old) lack sophisticated weapons. [46] Nonetheless, the launch of an Iranian-built submarine "Qadir" as well as missile-vessels "Jowshan" and "Peykan" all of which are equipped with 533mm torpedoes and mines, has provided Iran with a significant naval deterrent in the Persian Gulf. [47] Notwithstanding above-mentioned technological shortcomings and limits to Iran's defense, the regional military balance (excluding American forces) puts Iran in a dominant position. Quantity and commitment of Iran's armed forces, particularly the Revolutionary Guards Corps (IRGC), continue to be a bulwark and underwrite Iran's basic defense doctrine of total regional retaliation.

Regional military balance in the Persian Gulf	Service personnel	Fighter aircrafts	Main battle tanks	Combat vessels
Bahrain	11,000	29	140	1
Iran	663,000	332	1,710	201
Iraq	162,358	0	127	11
Kuwait	15,700	50	293	0
Oman	39,700	43	117	8
Qatar	12,400	9	30	7
Saudi Arabia	214,500	242	765	72
UAE	65,400	123	567	6

Source: Jane's Security Sentinel: Armed forces, 2008.

The Gulf states' concerns over this kind of procurement and potential Iranian encroachment, which was exacerbated since the election of the Arab world's first *Shi'a* government in Iraq in 2006, eventually culminated in numerous U.S. sponsored declarations condemning Iran's involvement in Iraq as well as demanding the government in Tehran to live up to its commitment under the IAEA and UN Security Council resolutions. American efforts to isolate Iran and rally its Arab allies against what the Bush administration labeled "murderous activities" in Iraq and "nuclear holocaust" initially seemed to be paying off when the U.S. President's proposal of selling defense systems and military aid packages, worth US$20 billion, to the Gulf was welcomed by governments in Saudi Arabia, UAE, Kuwait, Qatar, Bahrain and Oman in 2007. [48] Far from creating a sustainable regional security regime, the deal, which aims to strengthen the maritime, air and missile defenses of these GCC members, seemed to have merely exacerbated the region's security dilemma. The Iranian Supreme Leader's Office was quick to condemn U.S. efforts to "exaggerate the Iranian threat" to the Gulf countries and considered it to yet another tactic to rally Arab countries against Iran. Reminding that Iran's military exercises were never targeted against its neighbors and recalling past Iranian security cooperation initiatives and memoranda of understanding with some Gulf countries, the Supreme Leader, Ayatollah Khamenei's representative in the National Security Council, Hasan Rowhani, called for an end of the arms race in the region and urged regional security cooperation. [49] President Ahmadinejad then presented the Supreme Leader's initiative at a first-ever appearance at the GCC summit in December 2007. However, the proposal of launching a security framework "without foreign influence" continues to be viewed skeptically by the Gulf monarchies, interpreting it as merely a legitimate way for Iran to replace the U.S. as the Gulf's dominant power [50]

Sabre Rattling

Faced with this ongoing mistrust across the Gulf, and, again, in true realist fashion, Iran's leadership used numerous large-scale military maneuvers in Iran as well as in the Persian Gulf to parade both the commitment and capabilities of its armed forces. Massive mobilizations of Iran's IRGC, army, navy and air force not only showed off its indigenous defense systems but also, as a true expression of Iranian power, were meant to strengthen Iran's position during the nuclear negotiation [51]. Whilst such overconfidence certainly antagonized and alarmed the U.S. and EU more than it served as a bargaining chip, Iran's display of power largely catered to the US and its Arab allies in the region, demonstrating that Iran is too powerful a player to be provoked. Numerous military parades and exercises, most notably the "Great Prophet", maneuvers were meant, according to the military leadership, to display the armed forces' deterrence capabilities as well as to exercise new operational tactics and test new weaponry. This kind of projection of strength is, however, also catering to domestic constituents, showing critics of the government and public alike that should Iran enter negotiations again, it would do so from a position of strength [52]. A fundamental part of these deterrence maneuvers has always been the military's stress on its troops' unconditional commitment to defending the country. Official claims that suicide brigades of more than 10,000 trained military personnel can be easily mobilized continue to rank high amongst GCC members' security agendas and did little to defuse concerns over Iranian expansionism [53]. Lastly, a crucial part of Iran's deterrence strategy vis-à-vis the U.S. and the GCC has also always been a certain level of volatile rhetoric, aimed not at seeking military confrontation but questioning the very legitimacy of these pro-Western monarchies. As Iran's Deputy Foreign Minister, Manouchehr provocatively stated in August 2008 that "the next crisis [in] the Persian Gulf is the crisis of legitimacy of the monarchies and traditional systems, which considering current circumstances cannot go on living" [54].

Iran's highly publicized missile tests and military maneuvers served as much as an exercise in deterrence as they catered to domestic constituents. Determined to enter P5+1 negotiations only from a position of strength, Iran's government and military establishment followed a contradictory foreign policy course, combining détente with deterrence. Informed by the regime's inherent raison d'état to avoid appearing making concessions and fearing the impression of weakness, Iran's missile testing has largely overshadowed any diplomatic and conciliatory moves by Iranian diplomats and negotiators [55]. Thus, far from addressing own security perceptions in the Persian Gulf and constructively expressing such concerns [56] during nuclear negotiations, Iranian behavior only exacerbated the regional security dilemma.

IRGC's "Controlled" Renegade Activities

More than ever before, the IRGC has taken on the dominant role in Iran's defense structures and readiness. Whilst naval encounters between IRGC vessels and British and U.S. forces may well be attributed to renegade behavior, it seems more conceivable that these incidents at sea were in fact carefully orchestrated moves. Following the US designation of the Guards as a "foreign terrorist organization", the Supreme Leader appointed Ali Jafari as new IRGC Commander in chief and brought in Mohammad Hosseinzadeh Hejazi as the chair of the Joint Chief of Staff and Ali Akbar Ahmadian as the head of the IRGC Strategic Studies Center, making the Guards' top leadership more homogenous and more answerable to Khamenei [57]. Like many of the country's top military officials, Jafari earned his stripes and combat experience on the battlefield of the Iran-Iraq war. Jafari, who reportedly developed a myriad of "asymmetrical warfare" defense strategies, [58] has already made a number of changes to the Guards' command structure and operational capabilities [59]. The cornerstone of the Guards' strategy remains in the words of a commander "to strike against the interests of any aggressor in any part of the world" through its own forces or proxies, like *Hezbollah* as well as to restrict "movement of enemies in the Persian Gulf."[60] Well aware that with 14 to 17 billion barrels of oil per day, 25 per cent of the world's oil supplies, passing through the Hormuz Strait, a naval blockade or mining of the strait would have severe economic implications for the entire world, Tehran continues to threaten with such naval retaliatory measures [61]. However, the assertion by the IRGC Navy's Rear Admiral Habibollah Sayyari that the Persian Gulf is entirely under Iranian control, [62] seems to be overconfident if not wrong. Even though the IRGC naval units proved themselves during the Iran-Iraq tanker war, targeting civilian oil-carrying maritime traffic as well as continue to display innovative and aggressive tactics and maneuvers, they are no match for U.S. naval power in the Persian Gulf, which would easily neutralize Iran's surface fleet in a matter of hours. At the same time, however, the IRGC could effectively employ tactics, which could limit the U.S. warships' counter-measures. Given the recent activities of small Iranian vessels and past experiences, Iran may well employ tactics used during the "Tanker War" and engage in a sort of "maritime insurgency" which would entail a campaign of mine warfare, missile and small craft attacks to harass and disrupt U.S. and coalition forces and civilian maritime traffic [63]. The arrest of 15 British Navy personnel in March 2007 as well as the encounter between five IRGC speedboats and five U.S. vessels in the Strait of Hormuz in January 2008 should be seen within this context. Both encounters occurred during heightened tensions between Iran and the US in which Tehran's leadership took the possibility of a military confrontation with the U.S. very seriously and as such seemed compelled to retaliate against perceived American belligerency [64]. Both incidents demonstrated in the eyes of hardliners Iran's defense readiness whilst at the same time purportedly uncovered U.S./UK scare tactics as being nothing more than empty bluff. Even though reformists criticized that such affairs would only raise the stakes in the nuclear negotiations and the opening of "new fronts" would only strengthen the consensus against Iran, hardliners in and around the government as well as the Supreme Leader's Office interpreted the "detention and release of the invading British as a mark of Iran's superiority" and a "decisive answer [to the US and UK] that Iran was militarily and politically alert" [65].Undoubtedly, both incidents were carefully orchestrated and served as much as a deterrent to the West and Israel as they catered to domestic audiences. For Iran's leadership this sort of propaganda coupled with actual military incidents seems to serve as a prelude to how a major international standoff in the Persian Gulf could look like. By and large, Iran's strong military presence as well as its controversial control over the three strategically located islands, Abu Mua and Greater and Lesser Tunbs, has largely been seen by the GCC, as a Saudi official put it, as "an hegemonic hold [to gain] control of international navigation routes and the flow of oil to international markets in case it faces a military attack" [66]. Iran's recent installation of additional offices on Abu Musa has been met with strong condemnation by the UAE and the GCC which described it as "flagrant violation of the 1971 memorandum governing the islands' status" [67]. Ongoing Iranian statements claiming sovereignty over the islands and dismissing any arbitration initiatives by the UAE as policies of "extremists in London and Washington" [68] seem to have convinced most Gulf Arab states that Iran's expansionism, fear-mongering and stepped up defense posture is directly targeted against them.

Iranian Involvement in Iraq

Nowhere is this *Sunni-Shi'a* divide more evident than in Iraq where the Gulf states are too aware of an overbearing Iranian presence. The U.S.-led invasion of Iraq in 2003 not only removed one of Tehran's major foes, but in fact provided Iran in the words of Iran's Foreign Ministry with "an epochal shift in Iran's security position in the region", enabling Iran's "soft-power assets to exert considerable religions-political and cultural influence in Iraq. [69] Supporting both the *Shi'a* political-religious establishment in Iraq (the Supreme Council for the Islamic Revolution in Iraq) as well as emerging political heavyweights, Muqtada al-Sadr and his *Shi'a* insurgents, Iran seemed to be pursuing two goals: ensuring that the US occupation would not be used as a launch-pad against Iran, and helping Iraq's *Shi'a* majority to assume a dominant position in the country's new political landscape [70]. Six years after the invasion, Iran maintains very good relations with Prime Minister Nuri al-Maliki, who essentially represents Iraq's political *Shi'a* elite and which looks back on decades of exile in Iran. Iran's military and security establishment also continues to support *Shi'a* militias and has built an extensive religious-military infrastructure in that country, thus fuelling the insurgency and keeping a stake in radical factions should Iraq's transition to democracy fail [71]. Ironically, however, Iranian officials repeatedly stated during security talks with the U.S. that it too, favors Iraq to remain a single political entity, with central authority and without a sectarian civil war. Bearing in mind that like most foreign policy issues, Iran's agenda for Iraq continues to be subject to debate among Iranian factions, Tehran's recent behavior vis-à-vis Baghdad seems to indicate that even though diplomatic and trade links are probably better than with any other Gulf state, the course of U.S.-Iran relations is likely to shape Iran's tactics in Iraq – leaving all options on the table [72]

Essentially, Iran's stepped up defense posture kept the status quo in the region. By exacerbating the region's security dilemma, Arab states continue to remain committed to U.S. guardianship of the Gulf, whilst at the same time felt forced to accommodate themselves with Iran as the emerging regional hegemon.

Thus, despite America's overbearing naval supremacy in the Persian Gulf, Iranians perceive the balance of regional strategic power to be increasingly shifting in their favor: "Operation Iraqi Freedom" has lost support back home and struggles to maintain political and military momentum in Iraq, Israel's military prowess suffered significantly at the hands of Iran's Lebanese ally *Hezbollah* and it is evident that GCC governments are taking the Iranian threat (both conventional and nuclear) seriously. Overall, Iran's policy of deterrence has been somewhat successful. Since the political status quo of the Gulf monarchies fundamentally centers on their ability to distribute oil rents to their constituents, their rulers are not interested in becoming pawns in a US-Iranian conflict but rather seek to bandwagon in order not to jeopardize current and future business prospects. With GCC and individual member states clearly speaking out against any military option towards Iran, U.S. administration's efforts to contain and isolate Iran with help of its regional allies, largely appear to have fallen short of its goal [73]. At the same time, however, the GCC is far from discarding the U.S. as the central pillar of Persian Gulf security, dismissing Tehran's security initiatives as means to consolidate Iranian hegemony and continuing to treat their Persian neighbor with a certain extent of suspicion and ambiguous policies on their own [74].

Conclusion

Reagan's policies during the Iran-Iraq war set the corner stone of contemporary Persian Gulf security, in which the U.S., Iran, the GCC member states and Israel continue to engage a high-stakes game of coercive diplomacy and deterrence. Over thirty years of containing Iran may have maintained security in the Persian Gulf, but has fallen short of creating any collective security framework in the region. Relics of the Cold War, both in their diplomatic and military manifestations continue to determine not only relations between the U.S. and Iran but also between Tehran and its Gulf neighbors. Experiences from the battlefield between 1980-1988 have inherently shaped Tehran's security conceptions vis-à-vis the United States and its Arab allies. Given this rather realist mindset amongst Iran's nomenclature, the leadership continues to embrace military deterrence as its fundamental security doctrine. Iran's rhetoric and demonstration of its striking capabilities in the Persian Gulf seem to have largely deterred GCC states from supporting an attack on Iran. At the same time, the hostile nature of U.S. – Iranian relations continues to prevent the creation of an indigenous regional security arrangement. Remaining committed to America's guardianship of the Gulf, Arab monarchies as well as Iraq are unlikely to engage in any multilateral agreement with Iran any time soon. Even though policies adopted by successive U.S. president towards Iran ranged from neglect and hostility under George H.W. Bush and Bill Clinton to outward belligerency under George W. Bush, it was Reagan's war policy, which determined the course and tenor of current bilateral relations. Hence, as far as international relations in the Gulf are concerned, Reagan's Cold War strategies and rhetoric live on.

Much hope had been placed on Iran's presidential elections in June 2009. Following President Barrack Obama's *Naw Ruz* address to Iran in March 2009, which opened the possibility of rapprochement, it was widely believed that the country's electorate would deny Mahmoud Ahmadinejad a second term due to economic hardship and international isolation, which were largely blamed by Iranians to be the direct results of their president's firebrand rhetoric and hostile foreign policy. Ahmadinejad's re-election was met with massive protests both in the streets and amongst the elite, calling the elections rigged and the new government illegitimate. Now, the alleged usurpation of the election by Ahmadinejad and his hardliner allies is heralding a new chapter in the Islamic Republic. Given its appalling human rights record, which appears to have culminated with massive state sponsored violence against protesters, the arrests of over four thousand and show trials of hundreds of Iranian citizens, including a former Vice-President under Khatami, Ahmadinejad's government seems close to perfecting the hardliners' vision of Iran: the militarization of politics and securitization of society. As much as the IRGC took over control of Iran's international security, so was deterrence and political violence used to stifle opposition domestically. Under Ahmadinejad the *Basij* and the IRG have gained tremendous momentum, creating new fault-lines in Iranian politics: an increasing rift between clergy and the Revolutionary Guards. During his first tenure, the clout of the IRGC network increased significantly, having been awarded by Ahmadinejad with numerous lucrative gas and oil contacts, and former and current officers having taken on cabinet positions and other high-profile government posts. On several occasions, IRGC commanders have openly challenged the clergy and called on them to leave governance to the military and politicians. Ahmadinejad's own interpretation of *Shi'a* eschatology and his claims to have personal contact with the Mahdi, the prophesized Messiah of Islam, infuriated the clergy in Qom as much as it revealed his disconnection from the majority of society. When, in November 2007, Major General Jafari, stated that "the main mission of the *Basij* and the IRG is to fight internal enemies" the new fault lines of Iranian politics were laid open. They would eventually manifest themselves on a large scale in the aftermath of the June 2009 elections [75].

Now the Islamic Republic finds itself in the greatest crisis of legitimacy since its foundation thirty years ago as the once revolutionaries are now transforming themselves to the very regime they once removed. Far from being able to form a cabinet and conduct government business, Ahmadinejad finds itself under fire from mainstream conservatives doubtful over his competency and wary of his domestic and foreign agendas as well as from reformists who largely fight for their political survival. A series of *fatwas* from senior clerics condemning the violence, mass arrests and show trials and calling the government illegitimate further lends support to the notion that the Islamic Republic finds itself at the crossroads. If Iran's nomenclature follows this current path of repression, republican elements of Iran's Islamic government may soon be replaced with a totalitarian interpretation of the *velayat-e faqih*. However, given the political maturity of Iranian society, existing democratic institutions and commitment of stakeholders for democracy, Iran's hardliners may well have started a fight they cannot win.

As far as Iran's foreign relations are concerned, the U.S. has rightly abstained from getting directly involved and taking sides but rather condemned human rights violations. Despite the time-sensitive nature of Iran's ongoing enrichment activities and conventional military procurement, direct U.S.-Iranian engagement seems still elusive. Contrary to his campaign manifesto on a change in foreign policy, President Obama continues the Iran policy of previous administrations. Even before the elections, Obama asked the Pentagon to rejuvenate contingency plans for possible strikes against Iran and maintains a strong U.S. naval presence in the Gulf. Further emphasizing the "deterrence card", U.S. Secretary of State, Hillary Clinton proposed to extend "a defense umbrella" to its allies in the Middle East in order to guard against a nuclear Iran. In her bid for an increased deterrent capability in the Gulf, Clinton stated "if the US extends a defense umbrella over the region, if we do even more to support the military capacity of those in the Gulf, it's unlikely that Iran will be any stronger or safer, because they won't be able to intimidate and dominate, as they apparently believe they can, once they have a nuclear weapon"[76]. Yet again, these are realist deterrence strategies in what continues to be Reagan's Cold War between the United States and Iran.

REFERENCES

[1] See *Washington Post*, May 8, 1990.
[2] FBI Interview with Saddam Hussein, US Department of Justice, Baghdad Operations Center February 8, 2004, Interview Session No.2 available on *http://www.gwu.edu/~nsarchiv/NSAEBB/NSAEBB279/03.pdf*
[3] ibid; In April, Iraq expelled 20,000 Iranians following border clashes whilst Iran put its armed forces on full alert, claiming it was a response to repeated Iraqi attack on border outposts and oil facilities. The Iranian government also accused Iraqi reconnaissance planes of violating Iranian airspace. By April 1980, expulsions and withdrawals of diplomats ended any diplomatic relations between Baghdad and Tehran. *Washington Post*, Wednesday, April 9, 1980; *Washington Post*, April 11, 1980
[4] In his FBI interview, Saddam Hussein called the Iranian military in 1980 "weak and [lacking] leadership. It is also evident that he seriously underestimated Khomeini's grip of power in Iran. FBI Interview with Saddam Hussein, US Department of Justice, Baghdad Operations Center February 8, 2004, Interview Session No.2 available on *http://www.gwu.edu/~nsarchiv/NSAEBB/NSAEBB279/03.pdf*
[5] Kenneth M. Pollack, *The Persian Puzzle – The Conflict between America and Iran* (New York, Random House 2004), pp.185-186; Claudia Wright, "Religion and Strategy in the Iraq-Iran War", *Third World Quarterly*, Vol.7, No4, (Oct. 1985), p. 845; *Washington Post*, September 29, 1980
[6] Claudia Wright, "Religion and Strategy in the Iraq-Iran War", p. 846
[7] Efraim Karsh, *The Iran–Iraq War, 1980–1988*. Oxford, Osprey Publishing. p. 22; Claudia Wright, "Implications of the Iran-Iraq War", *Foreign Affairs*, Vol59, No2, (Winter, 1980), p. 287; Ghassan Salameh and Diane James, "Checkmate in the Gulf War" *MERIP Reports, No. 125/126*, The Strange War in the Gulf (Jul. - Sep., 1984), p. 20.
[8] See Said Amir Arjomand, *The Turban for the Crown*, (Bridgewater, Replica Books, 2000), p.144.
[9] Ghassan Salameh and Diane James, "Checkmate in the Gulf War", p.20.

[10] Kenneth M. Pollack, *The Persian Puzzle – The Conflict between America and Iran*, p.191; Lawrence G. Potter and Gary Sick, *Iran, Iraq, and the Legacies of War*, (New York, Palgrave McMillan, 2004), p.127.

[11] Kenneth M. Pollack, *The Persian Puzzle – The Conflict between America and Iran*, p. 193.

[12] Ali Ansari, *Confronting Iran – The Failure of American Foreign Policy and the Roots of Mistrust*, (London, Hurst, 2006), p. 100.

[13] According to Gary Sick, a White House aide for Persian Gulf affairs from 1976-1981, Reagan's campaign manager William Casey (later indicted for his role in the Iran-Contra scandal) met Iranian representatives in Europe in July, August and October of 1980. The agreed deal was to hand the hostages to the Republicans upon Reagan entering office in return for an immediate arms transfer via Israel and political benefits once the Reagan administration came to office. David Patrick Houghton, *US Foreign Policy and the Iran Hostage Crisis* (Cambridge, Cambridge University Press, 2001), pp. 141-142; Gary Sick, *October Surprise: America's Hostages in Iran and the Election of Ronald Reagan* (New York, Times Books/Random House, 1991), p.11.

[14] *Cover Memorandum from Peter Constable to Peter Tarnoff Dated November 10, 1980, US Department of State*, available at the Digital National Security Archive at George Washington University, Collection: Iraq-Gate, Item No. IG00034. See also Lawrence G. Potter and Gary Sick, *Iran, Iraq, and the Legacies of War*, pp.197-198

[15] *US Department of State, Secret Memorandum, October 7, 1983*, Iraq-Gate, Item No. IG00139.

[16] *Meeting with Israeli Defense Minister Ariel Sharon; US Department of State, Secret Briefing Memorandum, May 21, 1982*, Iraq Gate, Item No. IG00071.

[17] see *Congressional Delegation; White Meeting with Mubarak, Confidential Cable 08835, April 1982*, Iraq Gate, Item No.IG00069.

[18] See *Summary and Transcript of Meeting Between Representative Stephen Solarz and Saddam Hussein, August 25, 1982*, Iraq Gate, Item No. IG00075; By February 193, Hussein fundamentally shifted his position on the Arab-Israeli conflict by stating his willingness to accept any deal which is acceptable to the PLO. see *Letter to the Secretary of State From Tariz Aziz, February 7, 1983, Secret Briefing Memorandum, February 7, 1983*, Iraq-Gate, Item No. IG00103.

[19] See Brian M. Jenkins, "Defense Against Terrorism" in *Political Science Quarterly*, Vol. 101, No. 5, Reflections on Providing for "The Common Defense" (1986), pp. 773-786.

[20] GWU National Security Archive, *http://www.gwu.edu/~nsarchiv/NSAEBB/NSAEBB82/iraq26.pdf (accessed on 12 May 2009)*

[21] Ronald Reagan, *The Reagan Diaries*, (New York, Harper Collins, 2007), p. 224.

[22] *Staunching Iran's Imports of Western Arms and Urging Restraint on Iraq, Secret Cable, 353843, December 14, 1983*, Iraq Gate, IG00152; for particular pressure on the British government on the export of arms and dual-use technology, see *US Department of State, Discussions Points for Visit of Prime Minister Thatcher, December 12, 1984*, Iraq-Gate, Item No. IG00232.

[23] *US Department of State, Iraq Use of Chemical Weapons, Information Memorandum November 1, 1983*, Iraq-Gate, Item No. IG00145.

[24] *US Department of State, Rumsfeld Mission: December 20, 1983 Meeting with Iraqi President Saddam Hussein, Secret Cable, 27572*, Iraq Gate, Item No. IG00156.

[25] In April 1984, the Baghdad interests section asked to be kept apprised of Bell Helicopter Textron's negotiations to sell helicopters to Iraq, which were not to be "in any way configured for military use" even though the order came from the Iraqi Ministry of Defense see GWU National Security Archive *http://www.gwu.edu/~nsarchiv/NSAEBB/NSAEBB82/iraq55.pdf* (accessed 13 May 2009); Lawrence G. Potter and Gary Sick, *Iran, Iraq, and the Legacies of War*, p.198; for recommendations on increasing Iraq's Export-Import Bank and CCC credits, facilitating export licenses, and the pursuit of bilateral economic cooperation see *U.S. Department of State, Briefing Memorandum, July 23, 1986*, Iraq Gate, Item No. IG00346.

[26] *US Department of State, Arms Sales to Iran and Iraq, Memorandum, November 26 1985*, Iraq Gate, Item No. IG00289.

[27] *US Department of State, Confidential Cable, 074411, March 14, 1984*, Iraq Gate, Item No. IG00181.

[28] *US, Defense Intelligence Agency, Intelligence Report, DEB-85-84, September 25 1984*, Iraq Gate, Item No. IG00221.

[29] GWU National Security Archive *http://www.gwu.edu/~nsarchiv/NSAEBB/NSAEBB82/iraq43.pdf* (accessed 13 May 2009).

[30] *US Department of State, Confidential Cable, 094420, April 6, 1984*, Iraq Gate, Item No. IG00197; *US Department of State, Cable 093714, March 31, 1984*, Iraq Gate, Item No. IG00192.

[31] GWU National Security Archive *http://www.gwu.edu/~nsarchiv/NSAEBB/NSAEBB82/iraq53.pdf*, (accessed 13 May 2009).

[32] The White House went so far as "to encourage Western allies […] to help Iran meet its import requirements so as to reduce the attractiveness of Soviet assistance and trade offers. [..] This includes provision of selected military equipment as determined on a case-by-case basis." *Routing Shhet and Draft NSDD Entitled U.S. Policy Towards Iran, Memorandum, June 11, 1985*, Iraq Gate, Item No. IG00254.

[33] Ronald Reagan, *The Reagan Diaries*, p. 470; p.496; p 472.

[34] Douglas Little, *American Orientalism – The United States and the Middle East Since 1945* (London, IB Tauris, 2003), p. 250; *U.S. National Security Council, Secret, PROFS, January 21, 1987*, Iraq Gate, Item No. IG00399

[35] *U.S. Department of State, Information Memorandum, May 18, 1987*, Iraq Gate, Item No. IG00436.

[36] *U.S. Executive Office of the President, Confidential Letter, June 24, 1987*, Iraq Gate, Item No. IG00447.

[37] *U.S. Department of State, Secret Briefing Paper, April 12, 1988*, Iraq Gate, Item No. IG00547.

[38] *U.S. Department of State, SPOT Intelligence Report, April 18, 1988*, Iraq Gate, Item No. IG00553.

[39] See Will Rogers, Gene Gregston, Storm Center: *The U.S.S. Vincennes and Iran Air Flight 655* (Annapolis, Naval Institute Press, 1992).

[40] Lawrence G. Potter and Gary Sick, *Iran, Iraq, and the Legacies of War*, p.198.

[41] Jeffrey D. Simon, "Misunderstanding Terrorism", *Foreign Policy*, No. 67 (Summer, 1987), p. 109.

[42] Gary Sick, "Failure and Danger in the Gulf", 6 July, 1988, *New York Times*.

[43] Ali Ansari, *Confronting Iran*, pp. 116-117.

[44] See Richard L. Russel, "The Persian Gulf's Collective -Security Mirage", *Middle East Policy*, Vol. XII, Winter 2005, Number 4, pp77-88.
[45] See *Jane's Iran Security Sentinel*, accessed 15 December 2008 on *www.janes.com*.
[46] *ibid*; Heinrich Böll Stiftung, *Iran Report*, (Nr.05/2006), p. 15; see statement by Defence Minister Mostafa Mohammad-Najjar, *Vision of the Islamic Republic of Iran West Azarbayjan Provincial TV*, (29 August 2008), BBC Monitoring; Heinrich Böll Stiftung, *Iran Report*, (Nr.0/2007), p.10
[47] see statement by Iran's Defense Ministry, *Fars News Agency website* (26 November 2008), BCC Monitoring; *Voice of the Islamic Republic of Iran*, (6 September2008)
[48] *Washington Post* (28 July, 2007); for congressional scrutiny over the arms deal see CRS Report for Congress, *The Gulf Security Dialogue and Related Arms Sale Proposals* (8 October, 2008) http://www.fas.org/sgp/crs/weapons/RL34322.pdf (website accessed 12 December 2008)
[49] *Al-Alam TV*, (28 April 2007) BCC Monitoring
[50] See "Iran and the Arabs", *The Economist* (19 December 2007)
[51] See comment by Deputy Defense Minister, Nasrollah Esatti, *ISNA*, (14 July 2008) BCC Monitoring
[52] Military officials claimed to have tested a new version of the Shahab 3, with a 2000 km range. *Hemayat*, (15 July 2008) BCC Monitoring; New anti-aircraft defense systems were used during three day long war games by IRGC and regular army, *ISNA*, (8 September, 2008) BCC Monitoring
[53] *Al-Alam TV* (5 November 2006); Iran's Former Ambassador to the UAE, Adel Al Assadi, claims that Tehran also assembled a widespread sleeper-cell network of IRGC infiltrators and collaborators across the Gulf, ready to destabilize the region when needed. *Gulf News*, (15 September, 2008). Kuwait's Defense Secretary dismissed these allegations as "mere rumors" whilst Iranian officials denied them as "lies from enemy Western media." However, the government Dubai, which hosts over 450,000 Iranian expatriates, warned Iran not to drag its Arab neighbors into any conflict. *Kuwait Times*, (23 September 2008).
[54] The statement was immediately condemned by Gulf Cooperation Council Secretary General Abdurrahman al-Attiyah as another effort by Iran to create instability in the region. *Agence France Presse*, (7 August, 2008).
[55] This ambiguous dual track approach was particularly evident when Iran's Foreign Ministry increasingly sought to constructively respond to the 5+1 proposal whilst at the same time the IRGC tested a series of missiles, including the Shahab-3. IRGC Air fore Commander, Hossein Salami stated that the aim was to "demonstrate Iran's determination to respond to any attack" and that "our hands are always on the trigger." see *Iran Press TV*, (8 July, 2008) BCC Monitoring
[56] Such security initiative had been proposed under President Khatami in 2003 which essentially attempted to resolve most bilateral differences between the United States and Iran. In return for US security assurances and a "policy of mutual respect", the Iranians pledged their willingness and commitment to cease enrichment activities and transparency of their nuclear programm, end their military support for Hezbollah and Hamas and support for a democratic Iraq. The offer forwarded to the US by the Swiss Embassy in Tehran was declined by the Bush administration. For the original Iranian

memo see *http://www.nytimes.com/packages/pdf/opinion/20070429_iran-memo-expurgated.pdf*
[57] MENAS, *Iran Strategic Focus*, (October, 2007), Vol.3, No. 10, p.5.
[58] Bernd Kaussler, "Khamenei's Move to Appoint Ali Jafari as Head of Revolutionary Guard" in *Terrorism Focus* Volume: 4 Issue: 31, 2007.
[59] Most important changes included the decision to put Iran's volunteer-militia, the *Basij*, under a single command system of the IRGC. *Basij* amount over 300,000 active volunteers and if mobilized constitute over 1,000,000 personnel, although *Basij* commanders continued to claim that there are over as much as 8 million *Basij*. Given Iran's basic defense doctrine to retaliate any "outside aggression" with outmost force and available manpower, Iran's leadership certainly seems to put much as faith in the *Basij*'s readiness as in their unconditional zeal. see *Vision of the Islamic Republic of Iran Network 2,* (25 November 2008); *Fars News Agency website*, (2 December 2008); *Vision of the Islamic Republic of Iran Ardabil Provincial TV,* (25 November 2008) BCC Monitoring
[60] *Keyhan website*, (23 April 2008); *Islamic Republic News Agency* (20 September 2008) BBC Monitoring.
[61] Tom Ripley, "Gulf of distrust - Naval stand-offs and the Persian Gulf", *Jane's Intelligence Review*, (March 01, 2008).
[62] *Aftab-e Yazd website,* (29 September 2008), BBC Monitoring.
[63] Tom Ripley, "Gulf of distrust - Naval stand-offs and the Persian Gulf"
[64] The detention of the British sailors coincided with the arrest of Iranian officials (allegedly IRGC Quds forces) in Iraq and with Iran's intelligence reports claiming that the US and Britain are fuelling ethnic tensions among Iranian Kurds, Arabs and Baluchis, see MENAS, *Iran Strategic Focus*, (April, 2007), Vol.3, No. 4, p.11.
[65] Statement by Ali Akbar Velayati who was instrumental during negotiations with British officials to get the sailors released. *Tehran-e Emrooz on* (9 April 2007); Criticizing the detention, spokesman of the Organization of the *Mojahedin*, Mohsen Armin, stated "that the opening of any new front will help to divert attentions away from the nuclear issue, and [..] create new arenas and fronts [..]. However, this diplomacy only leads to the creation of a more complete consensus against Iran, and to the worsening of the Iranian nuclear crisis as a whole. Once this happens, we will naturally face a more restricted arena for manoeuvres, and this by extension will be detrimental to the country's national interests." *E'temad website,* (11 April 2007) BCC Monitoring
[66] Statement by Mohammand Ali Zulfa, member of the Saudi Shua Council. *Gulf News*, (5 September, 2008).
[67] *AFP*, (17 August. 2008)
[68] In a speech Foreign Minister Manouchehr Mottaki criticized the UAE for its recent "anti-Iran claims" and called on the emirates "to disavow policies of 'bankrupt' extremists in Washington and London." *Iran Daily,* (6 December, 2008)
[69] Statement by Hamid Reza Dehghani,Garteh Porter, "Iran's Regional Power Rooted in *Shi'a* Ties" *http://www.ipsnews.net/news.asp?idnews=45131* (website accessed 16 December, 2008)
[70] See Kamran Taremi, "Iranian Foreign Policy Toward Occupied Iraq, 2003-05' in *Middle East Policy*, Vol. XII, No.4, Winter 2005, p.30.

[71] On Iran's provision of weapons, logistics and training to *Shi'a* insurgents see testimonies by General David Petraeus who throughout his tenure continued to accuse Iran of providing advanced weaponry to Iraqi *Shi'a* insurgents and essentially charged Tehran with fighting a "proxy war" against the US. New York Times, (12 April, 2008); Report to Congress on the Situation in Iraq, General David H. Petraeus 11 September 2007 *http://www.senate.gov/~foreign/testimony/2007/PetraeusTestimony070911a.pdf*

[72] Iranian reactions to the Iraqi security of forces agreement (SOFA) reflect ongoing domestic tensions over tactics and agenda in Iraq. Whilst factions close to Iraq's SCIRI welcomed the agreement, the Supreme Leader's Office and parliament condemned it as "means of strengthening comprehensive US hegemony in Iraq". MENAS, Iran Strategic Focus, (December, 2009), Vol.4, No.12, p. 3.

[73] See GCC summit statement calling for a diplomatic solution to the nuclear stalemate. *AFP*, (8 December, 2007); see editorial by Saudi Foreign Minister Prince Saud Al-Faisa, "Peace Now" (15 January, 2008) on *http://www.arabnews.com/?page=7and section=0andarticle=105662andd=15andm=1andy=2008* (website accessed, 20 November, 2008); Statement by Jassem al-Kharafi, Speaker of the Kuwaiti parliament, calling US policy towards Iran "provocative" and "threatening" *Reuters*, (15 July, 2008)

[74] Iranian MPs decried the final communiqué of the GCC December summit in 2007 which reasserted UAE sovereignty over the disputed islands. Days later Bahrain hosted a US-sponsored security conference during which US Secretary of Defense, Robert Gates, urged GCC states to protect themselves form Iranian missile threat. MENAS, *Iran Strategic Focus,* (December, 2007), Vol.3, No. 12, p. 3.

[75] Bernd Kaussler, "Iran's Next Leadership", in Foreign Policy in Focus, *http://www.fpif.org/fpiftxt/6131* (accessed 16 August, 2009); Bernd Kaussler, "The End of the Republic?" *http://english.aljazeera.net/focus/2009/08/20098171953790365.html* (accessed 16 August, 2009).

[76] *http://www.nytimes.com/2009/07/23/world/asia/23diplo.html* (accessed 12 August, 2009).

Chapter 15

SPEECH ON THE IMPLEMENTATION OF THE GI BILL EXTENDING EDUCATIONAL BENEFITS TO VETERANS

Barack Obama

PRESIDENT OBAMA:
Hello. Thank you. Thank you. Thank you.

(APPLAUSE)

Please have a seat. Please have a seat.
Good morning, everybody.

AUDIENCE: Good morning.
OBAMA: It is wonderful to see all of you and wonderful to have one of the best partners that anybody could have in elected office, our vice president, Joe Biden. Thrilled to have him here.

(APPLAUSE)

I want to thank Staff Sergeant Miller (ph) for the gracious introduction. I want to thank President Merten for his hospitality.

There are a couple of people here who deserve all the credit, because they got a very tough bill done. And part of the reason they were able to get it done was just because of their extraordinary personal credibility. These are – one is new to the Senate and one had been there a while, and yet together they formed an incredibly formidable team. They're both class acts.

Please give a big round of applause to Virginia's own John Warner and Jim Webb.

(APPLAUSE)

I know that we've got a number of members of Congress who are here, and I want to thank them all for their outstanding work.

I want to point out that Senator Mark Warner could not be here, but we appreciate him.

We've got the secretary of veterans affairs, a hero in his own right, General Eric Shinseki. And I want everybody to please acknowledge him.

(APPLAUSE)

And of the original bill sponsors who could not be here today, we've got Senator Chuck Hagel, Senator Frank Lautenberg, Representative Harry Mitchell, Representative Bobby Scott, Representative Ginny Brown-Waite and Representative Peter King. All of them worked hard, along with the delegation that is present.

OBAMA: And so, we are very grateful to all of them.

I want to join all of today's speakers in thanking those of you who worked so hard to make this occasion possible. But above all, I want to pay tribute to the veterans who are now advancing their dreams by pursuing an education.

Obviously, I'm honored to be here and to renew our commitment to ensure that the men and women who wear the uniform of the United States of America get the opportunities that they have earned.

I was a proud cosponsor of the post-9/11 G.I. Bill as senator. I'm committed to working with Secretary Shinseki to see that it is successfully implemented as president.

And we do this not just to meet our moral obligation to those who've sacrificed greatly on our behalf and on behalf of the country. We do it because these men and women must now be prepared to lead our nation in the peaceful pursuit of economic leadership in the 21st century.

This generation of servicemen and -women has already earned a place of honor in American history. Each of them signed up to serve, many after they knew that they would be sent into harm's way.

Over the last eight years, they have endured tour after tour of duty in dangerous and distant places. They've experienced grueling combat, from the streets of Fallujah to the harsh terrain of Helmand province.

They've adapted to complex insurgencies, protected local populations and trained foreign security forces.

So by any measure, they are the authors of one of the most extraordinary chapters of military service in the history of our nation. And I don't make that statement lightly, for we know that anyone who puts on the uniform joins an unbroken line of selfless patriots that stretches back to Lexington and Concord.

The freedom and prosperity that we enjoy would not exist without the service of generations of Americans who were willing to bear the heaviest and most dangerous burden.

OBAMA: But we also know this: The contributions that our servicemen and -women can make to this nation do not end when they take off that uniform.

We owe a debt to all who serve. And when we repay that debt to those bravest Americans among us, then we are investing in our future — not just their future, but also the future of our own country.

Now, this was the lesson that America was sometimes too slow to learn. After the Civil War and World War I, we saw far too many veterans who were denied the chance to live their dreams; men who were unable to find in peace the hope that they had fought for in war.

And FDR knew this. In 1943, before the beaches of Normandy were stormed and the treacherous terrain of Iwo Jima was taken, he told the nation that the veterans of World War II would be treated differently.

He said that they must not be demobilized, and I quote, "to a place on a bread line" – "demobilized to a place on a bread line or on a corner selling apples."

"Instead," Roosevelt said, "the American people will insist on fulfilling this American obligation to the men and women in the armed forces who are winning this war for us."

That is precisely what the American people did. The G.I. Bill was approved just weeks after D-Day, and carried with it a simple promise to all who had served: You pick the school, we'll help pick up the bill.

And what followed was not simply an opportunity for our veterans. It was a transformation for our country. By 1947, half of all Americans enrolled in college were veterans.

OBAMA: Ultimately, this would lead to three presidents, three Supreme Court justices, 14 Nobel Prize winners and two dozen Pulitzer Prize winners.

But, more importantly, it produced hundreds of thousands of scientists and engineers, doctors and nurses, the backbone of the largest middle class in history.

All told, nearly 8 million Americans were educated under the original G.I. Bill, including my grandfather.

No number can sum up this sea change in our society.

Reginald Wilson, a fighter pilot from Detroit, said, "I didn't know anyone who went to college. I never would have gone to college had it not been for the G.I. Bill."

H.G. Jones, a Navy man from North Carolina, said, "What happened in my rural Caswell County community happened all over the country. Going to college was no longer a novelty."

Indeed, one of the men who went to college on the G.I. Bill, as I mentioned, was my grandfather. And I would not be standing here today if that opportunity had not led him west in search of opportunity.

So we owe the same obligations to this generation of service men and women as was afforded that previous generation. That is the promise of the post-1911 (sic) G.I. Bill. It's driven by the same simple logic that drove the first G.I. Bill: You pick the school; we'll help pick up the bill.

And looking out at the audience today, I'm proud to see so many veterans who will be able to pursue their education with this new support from the American people.

And this is even more important than it was in 1944. The first G.I. Bill helped build a post-war economy that has been transformed by revolutions in communication and technology. And that's why the post- 1911 – 9/11 G.I. Bill must give today's veterans the skills and training they need to fill the jobs of tomorrow.

Education is the currency that can purchase success in the 21st century. And this is the opportunity that our troops have earned.

I'm also proud that all who have borne the burden of service these last several years will have access to this opportunity.

OBAMA: We are including reservists and National Guard members because they have carried out unprecedented deployments in Afghanistan and Iraq. We are including the military families who have sacrificed so much by allowing the transfer of unused benefits to family members. And we are including those who pay the ultimate price by making this benefit available to the children of those who lost their life in service to their country.

This is not simply a debt that we are repaying to the remarkable men and women who have served. It is an investment in our own country. The first G.I. Bill paid for itself many times over through the increased revenue that came from a generation of men and women who received the skills and education that they needed to create their own wealth.

The veterans who are here today, like the young post-9/11 veterans around the country, can lead the way to a lasting economic recovery and become the glue that holds our communities together. They too can become the backbone of a growing American middle class.

And even as we help our veterans learn the skills they need to succeed, I know that all of us can learn something from the men and women who serve our country.

We've lived through an age when many people and institutions acted irresponsibly, when service often took a backseat to short-term profits, when hard choices were put aside for somebody else, for some other time. It is a time when easy distractions became the norm and the trivial has been taken too seriously.

The men and women who have served since 9/11 tell us a different story. While so many were reaching for the quick buck, they were heading out on patrol. While our discourse often produced more heat than light, especially here in Washington, they have put their very lives on the line for America. They've have borne the responsibility of war.

And now, with this policy, we are making it clear that the United States of America must reward responsibility and not irresponsibility. Now, with this policy, we are letting those who have borne the heaviest burden lead us in to the 21st century.

And so today we honor the service of an extraordinary generation and look to an America that they will help build tomorrow. With the post-9/11 G.I. Bill, we can give our veterans the chance to live their dreams, and we can help unleash their talents and tap their creativity, and be guided by their sense of responsibility to their fellow citizens and to this country that we all love so much.

May God bless our troops and our veterans, and may God bless the United States of America.

Thank you very much, everybody.

(APPLAUSE)

END

Chapter 16

THE PRESIDENCY OF JAMES WILSON

Michael H. Taylor and Kevin Hardwick

ABSTRACT

James Wilson envisioned a vigorous and strong presidency premised on popular sovereignty and accountable to the people. This article examines James Wilson's contributions to the creation of the executive branch as adopted by the Constitutional Convention, and explores Wilson's understanding of a properly constituted executive fit for a republic. An understanding of civic virtue, derivative from the Scottish Enlightenment, shaped Wilson's constitutionalism. The habits of sociability introduced into the American polity by an extended suffrage, he believed, would strengthen the civic virtue of the citizenry. Wilson thus saw no contradiction between an extended republic and an enduring republican constitution. For Wilson, the President stood at the symbolic center of the national government, the one representative of the whole American people. Wilson, like other Federalists, presumed the existence of a unified American people, and thus of an American nation. Popular sovereignty was the cement that held the union together and joined the interests and power of the American people with that of their government. In Wilson's constitutional vision, the President was the man of the people, in whom was embodied both national responsibility for the public good and public accountability.

INTRODUCTION

James Wilson, delegate from Pennsylvania at the 1787 Philadelphia Constitutional Convention and a close ally of James Madison, envisioned an energetic and democratic presidency far stronger than that which the delegates consequently approved. Wilson championed an office that would have contained a 3-year term with no limits on reelection, possessed the ability to place judges on the Supreme Court without obtaining consent from Congress, and empowered with an unrestricted veto of legislation passed by Congress. However, it was Wilson's advocacy of a President of the United States who was directly elected by the American people that was remarkable. For Wilson, the President stood at the symbolic center of the national government, the one representative of the whole people. In Wilson's constitutional vision, the President was the man of the people, in whom was embodied both national responsibility for the public good and public accountability. Wilson's vision for the executive seems strikingly modern and democratic.

The history of the drafting and ratification of the United States Constitution has focused on the contributions of a select number of statesmen. James Wilson, often overlooked, was the second most important delegate of the Constitutional Convention of 1787. He was an energetic member of the Philadelphia Convention and James Madison's staunchest ally. After the Convention adjourned he led the fight for ratification of the Constitution as the floor leader of the pro-ratification forces in Pennsylvania's ratification convention. Pennsylvania was the first large state to ratify and Philadelphia was home to the most prolific publishing industry in the country. His arguments *for* and justification *of* the Constitution were disseminated around the country. Wilson's leadership helped to build momentum for adoption of the Constitution in other states.

While Madison and Wilson were allied throughout the convention, one important area of disagreement concerned the structure of the executive. Both men worked from the premises of popular sovereignty. Madison favored a system of indirect election, filtering the *vox populi* through intermediate bodies in the hope that by doing so, men of exemplary character and public virtue would be selected for office. Wilson, on the other hand, was unabashedly democratic. Even as Wilson lent his considerable intellectual and rhetorical gifts to advancing Madison's constitutional construct, he offered a considerably less aristocratic vision than Madison's republicanism. Wilson's nationalism went hand-in-hand with his commitment to democracy, and both shaped in important ways his understanding of the role and function of the executive. Like fellow immigrant Alexander Hamilton, James Wilson was able to perceive beyond loyalty to his adopted state, confident in the existence and desirability of an over-arching national, American identity. He grounded his constitutional thought in the necessity of realizing to the fullest extent possible the sovereign authority of the people. Doing so, he thought, would create the potential for the progressive refinement of American civic character.

I

James Wilson was born on September 14, 1742 in the village of Carskerdo in the Shire of Fife of the Scottish Lowlands. He was the first-born son of pious parents who pledged him to a career in the clergy. Despite the family's meager resources, Wilson acquired an excellent education. He attended a nearby grammar school until the fall of 1757 when he applied for and received a scholarship to the University of St. Andrews. Wilson spent five years at St. Andrews—four as an undergraduate and the first year of seminary school—before he was forced to leave. His father died suddenly in 1762 and the family could no longer support his studies. He did not return home to manage the family farm; instead he sought and found employment as a tutor in a "gentleman's family." Here he remained until his three older sisters found prospects of marriage and his three younger brothers were old enough to assume some of the burden of supporting themselves and their mother. [1]

Wilson quit his job as a tutor in 1765 and sailed for America, after first securing the consent of his mother and eliciting support from friends and relatives to sponsor his journey. Upon arrival, Wilson secured appointment as a tutor at the College of Philadelphia. 1765 was a pivotal year, not only for Wilson, but also for Philadelphia where he lived. The city was coming to terms with the Stamp Act, enacted by parliament while he was at sea. Wilson dutifully discharged his duties as a tutor of Latin and a lecturer in English Literature through the winter of 1765-66. The College recognized his work by awarding him an honorary master's degree at the spring commencement.

Wilson subsequently sought training and employment in law, a profession more suited to his ambition. With the help of a cousin, he secured the financing necessary to pay for his apprenticeship with John Dickenson, one of Pennsylvania's most accomplished attorneys. The working relationship with Dickinson featured prominently in Wilson's life over the next three decades. Wilson spent less than a year with Dickinson before they both agreed that his course of study was complete. Once admitted to the bar, Wilson left Philadelphia and struck out for Reading to begin his career. The legal profession opened a number of new opportunities for him. He quickly emerged as a leading figure in the legal community in Pennsylvania and became active in the civic and political life of the colony.

Wilson's first published works appeared in 1768, in the *Pennsylvania Chronicle*. Together with his friend William White, Wilson penned a series of short moral essays on the subject of politeness, which reveal both his intellectual debt to the Scottish Enlightenment and themes he would later develop in his constitutional thought. Polite conversation, Wilson and White argued, held the potential for moral and social improvement. When diverse people gathered appropriately for discussion, the outcome was refinement of their moral sensibility and consequently of their civic virtue. In these essays, Wilson and White drew generally upon the "Moral Sense" philosophy of Frances Hutchenson, whose works Wilson studied at St. Andrews. Wilson's appreciation of both social diversity and the uplifting potential of sociability, so evident in contemporary Scottish moral philosophy, deeply informed his later constitutional thought. [2]

In August 1774, James Wilson published a pamphlet, entitled *Considerations on the Nature and Extent of the Legislative Authority of the British Parliament*. [3] The paper had actually been written in 1768, but when he showed it to friends, they advised him to await a more receptive political climate before publication. Wilson began the inquiry, "with a view and expectation of being able to trace some constitutional line between those cases in which we ought and those in which we ought not to acknowledge the power of Parliament over us." Reaching the end of his research, he became convinced that the legislative authority of the English Parliament over the colonies must be denied in every instance. [4]

Wilson served as a member of various assemblies and conventions held around the colony before the convening of the Second Continental Congress in Philadelphia in May of 1775. As a member of the Pennsylvania delegation, Wilson again worked with John Dickinson. He joined Dickinson as a leader of the "reconciliationist" faction in Congress, one that sought to build a united front for the clash with Great Britain. Wilson believed that the citizens of the colonies needed to be convinced of the necessity of independence before Congress voted upon a formal break. In July 1776, after the instructions to block a vote on independence were rescinded, Wilson broke with Dickinson and his vote swung Pennsylvania's delegation to support the vote for American independence. [5]

The years Wilson spent working in the Second Continental Congress and later—after the adoption of the Articles of Confederation—the Confederation Congress profoundly shaped his beliefs regarding the role of government. The Congress created by the Articles of Confederation experienced new stresses as the thirteen former colonies, now independent states, felt their way forward towards a new relationship with one another. Wilson was an active member and quickly became a leader of the Nationalist faction in Congress, along with James Madison and Alexander Hamilton. The inability of Congress to coerce the recalcitrant states to adhere to the measures it adopted left a lasting impression and set the stage for his strong support for a national convention that would correct the deficiencies of the Articles by drafting a new constitution. Absent a properly structured national government, American liberties were insecure.

As he subsequently noted, the united colonies "manfully repelled" British attempts to conquer them during the warfare that followed the declaration of independence. "But on another side," he warned, "danger, not less formidable, but more insidious, stole in upon us; and our unsuspicious tempers were not sufficiently attentive, either to its approach or its operation." America, he said, had "neglected to establish among ourselves a government, that would ensure domestick vigour and stability." In consequence, the states "have well nigh become the victims of internal anarchy." Military and diplomatic success during the revolution secured peace, but "the commencement of peace was the commencement of every disgrace and distress, that could befal[l] a people in a peaceful state." The government provided by the Articles of Confederation simply was "inadequate to the government and to the exigencies of the United States."[6]

Wilson experienced first-hand the dangers of weak government. On October 4, 1779, a contingent of militia set out to round up Wilson and many of his friends, including Robert Morris, for defending Tories who were being prosecuted for treason. Accounts of how the violence began differ, but the result was the deaths of four militiamen and a defender. Wilson's efforts to secure a more energetic government, at both the state and national level, were shaped by this traumatic event and a threat of physical violence that appeared in the October 10, 1780 edition of *The Pennsylvania Packet*. The author—identifying himself as "A Plain Dealing Whig"—took issue with Wilson's support of due process for Tories and his desire to amend the Pennsylvania Constitution of 1776. The intent was clear—change your ways or suffer the consequences. Wilson's support for a strong federal government was reinforced by personal experience.[7]

The sincerity of Wilson's commitment to democracy has been a matter of controversy for historians. If his writings and public statements are examined, a politician, constitution maker, and jurist emerges who was of a very democratic bent. However, if we judge him by the conduct of his life, a different portrait comes into view. Wilson was a man intent on being both publically influential and financially successful. "Wilson's democratic faith was philosophical rather than instinctive," Richard Beeman has recently, and judiciously, concluded. "His beliefs were born of a practical understanding of the need to found a strong national government on the sovereign will of an abstracted 'people' more than of any warmth of feeling for the actual people who were to make up the polity." James Wilson, like many other men of the Founding generation, fell short of the rhetorical aspirations he advanced. The concrete contributions that he made to the creation of the Constitution of the United States are nonetheless important, especially to the creation of the office of President of the United States. In judging those contributions, the content of Wilson's rhetoric matters far more than the quality of his personal commitment. Wilson may or may not have been sincere—indeed, the degree of his sincerity is arguably irrecoverable. What we have to analyze are his arguments, and it is on those that we will focus in the remainder of this essay.[8]

II

James Wilson's constitutional thought was guided, at every stage of his career, by an abiding commitment to popular sovereignty. The democratic bent of James Wilson's political thinking became evident early in the Philadelphia Convention, during debate on Thursday, May 31. Delegates had worked their way to the 4th Resolution of the Virginia Plan, which dealt with the election of members of the National Legislature. Roger Sherman of Connecticut took the floor and explained that he "opposed the election by the people, insisting that it ought to be by the State Legislatures. The people ... should have as little to do as may be about the Government. They want information and are constantly liable to be misled."[9] Elbridge Gerry of Massachusetts reinforced Sherman's argument. "The evils we experience flow from the excess of democracy," he said. "He had been too republican heretofore: he was still however republican, but had been taught by experience the danger of the leveling spirit."[10] Gerry emphasized the insecurity even of the provisions of the Massachusetts constitution. As Madison recorded it in his notes, Gerry "mentioned the popular clamour in Massachusetts for the reduction of salaries and the attack made on that of the Governor though secured by the spirit of the Constitution itself."[11]

Wilson, along with George Mason and James Madison, responded to the arguments of Sherman and Gerry by emphasizing the necessity of popular election. Wilson argued "strenuously for drawing the most numerous branch of the Legislature immediately from the people." If a strong national government was to be erected it must rest upon the consent of the people themselves. He explained that "[h]e was for raising the federal pyramid to a considerable altitude, and for that reason wished to give it as broad a basis as possible. No government could long subsist without the confidence of the people." Wilson, like any good engineer, knew that the construction of a strong, tall structure needed to be anchored on a robust foundation or the structure would inevitably topple. If the convention was to construct a national government that touched every citizen of the nation and endure, then it must be sanctioned by the consent of the people. This foundation—the importance of popular consent and public confidence in the new government—underlay Wilson's thinking about the national executive. Where the thinking of many of the delegates at the Philadelphia reflected what they understood to be the corrosive democratic excess of politics in the 1780s, Wilson perceived the necessity of grounding the new Federal constitution in meaningfully democratic institutions.[12]

Wilson sounded this theme most consistently during the Pennsylvania ratifying convention of 1787. As the only representative at the Pennsylvania convention to have served in the Philadelphia convention that had drafted the federal constitution, Wilson naturally played a central role in arguing for its ratification. He opened his commentary with an extended speech on November 26 that aimed, as he put it, to "[prepare] the way for the deliberations of this assembly, by unfolding the difficulties which the late convention were obliged to encounter; by pointing out the end which they proposed to accomplish; and by tracing the general principles which they have adopted for the accomplishment of that end."[13] Popular sovereignty, Wilson emphasized, was the fundamental basis of American government. "The truth is," he affirmed, "that, in our governments, the supreme, absolute, and uncontrollable power remains in the people. As our constitutions are superior to our legislatures; so the people are superior to our constitutions."[14] The animating principle of the proposed federal constitution, Wilson stated, was democracy. "If we take an extended and accurate view of it, we shall find the streams of power running in different directions, in different dimensions, and at different heights, watering, adorning, and fertilizing the fields and meadows, through which their courses are led," he noted. "But if we trace them, we shall discover, that they all originally flow from one abundant fountain. In this constitution, all authority is derived from the people."[15] Wilson repeated this analysis again and again, in speeches of November 28 and December 1, in two extraordinary speeches on December 4, and during his final detailed summary of the debates in two lengthy speeches on December 11.[16]

Wilson summarized his commitment to popular sovereignty and democracy in a striking metaphor, which he first introduced during the Philadelphia convention. On May 31, 1787, early in the Philadelphia convention debates, Wilson spoke in support of popular election of the national legislature. As James Madison recorded his words, "[Wilson] was for raising the federal pyramid to a considerable altitude, and for that reason wished to give it as broad a base as possible."[17] The simile of government as a pyramid was one Wilson found especially useful. He returned to it several times, both in his defense of the federal constitution in the Pennsylvania ratifying convention and in the extended analysis of constitutional thought which he laid out in his famous law lectures, beginning in the winter of 1790. Thus, on the afternoon of December 11, 1787, when Wilson summarized the argument for adopting the proposed Federal constitution, he suggested that "a free government has often been compared to a pyramid."[18] Similarly, in his lecture "On the Legislative Department," Wilson again compared government to a pyramid, adding that "a republican government may well receive that beautiful and solid form."[19]

In each case, the metaphor served to establish a relationship between an extensive nation and a vigorous and powerful government. Describing the federal constitution in the Pennsylvania ratifying convention, Wilson noted that "it is laid on the broad basis of the people." The powers of the proposed federal constitution "gradually rise, while they are confined, in proportion as they ascend, until they end in the most permanent of all forms." The result was a government accountable to the people. In each of its constituent parts, the government created by the proposed federal constitution would retain "a chain of connection with the people."[20] Wilson subsequently refined the metaphor further, in his law lecture "Of the Legislative Department." The foundation of a national government, Wilson suggested, if it is to be trusted with significant power, "must, of consequence, be broad, and strong, and deep." Where in his earlier speeches of 1787 Wilson had suggested that the base of the pyramid was a broad democratic representation, in the lecture Wilson expanded his thinking. "The authority, the interests, and the affections of the people at large are the only foundation, on which a superstructure, proposed to be at once durable and magnificent, can rationally be erected."[21] It was not sufficient, in other words, that the government derive its power from the people. If it was to endure, it needed to retain their affection, a matter distinct in Wilson's thinking from merely representing their interests.

Wilson thus saw no contradiction between democracy and power. Quite the contrary, he viewed an extensive democracy as a precondition for a powerful government, and he viewed a powerful government as necessary for a people to achieve their highest potential. "A progressive state is necessary to the happiness and perfection of man," Wilson stated in the Pennsylvania ratifying convention.[22] "A good constitution is the greatest blessing, which a society can enjoy."[23] Wilson shared the commitment of Federalists like Alexander Hamilton that a strong federal government would promote a flourishing economy. "In a well constituted commonwealth," he noted, "the industry of every citizen extends beyond himself. A common interest pervades society. Each gains from all, and all gain from each."[24] But for Wilson, this meant more than merely the instrumental satisfaction of individual desires. "It has often been observed," he said, "that the sciences flourish all together: the remark applies equally to the arts." For Wilson, the cultivation of "character" and "happiness" remained matters of public concern.[25]

Wilson developed most fully the connections between an extensive nation, a powerful government, and popular sovereignty in his lectures on law, delivered at the College of Philadelphia starting in December 1790. He emphasized the importance of representation, which he defined as "the chain of communication between people and those, to whom they have committed the exercise of the powers of government." For Wilson, the metaphor of government consisting of "chains of connections" signaled an appreciation that in a properly democratic system of government, the relationship between those who governed and those who were governed was reciprocal. The key to the relationship, in Wilson's thought, was the right of suffrage possessed by the "freemen" who constituted the nation's citizens, which, Wilson thought, was a "right of the greatest import, and of the most improving efficacy." Wilson incorporated his earlier reflections on the benefits of polite sociability into his constitutionalism by the mechanism of voting. "The man, who enjoys the right of suffrage, on the extensive scale which is marked by our constitution, will naturally turn his thoughts to the contemplation of publick men and publick measures," Wilson argued. "The inquiries he will make, the information he will receive, and his own reflections on both, will afford a beneficial and amusing employment of his mind." The result was an uplifting patriotism. "A habit of conversing and reflecting on these subjects, and of governing his actions by the result of his deliberations, would produce, in the mind of the citizen, a uniform, a strong, and a lively sensibility to the interests of his country." Wilson asserted, in other words, that the good habits introduced into the American polity by an extended suffrage, operating through the medium of polite sociability, would strengthen the civic virtue of the citizenry.[26]

Wilson's pyramid metaphor signaled his rejection of the small republic argument so common among the opponents of the proposed federal constitution. Wilson had read his Montesquieu, and his language at times echoed passages from that scholar's *Spirit of the Laws*. For example, in his opening speech at the Pennsylvania ratifying convention, Wilson acknowledged the diversity of climate and geography of the United States. "The United States contain already thirteen governments mutually independent," he declared. "Those governments present to the Atlantick a front of fifteen hundred miles in extent. Their soil, their climates, their productions, their dimensions, their numbers are different. In many instances a difference and even an opposition subsists among their interests."[27] But for Wilson, this broad diversity was a source of national strength, not a fact whose existence mitigated against the creation of an enduring, large-scale republic. Repeating the argument advanced a week earlier by Alexander Hamilton, in Federalist Nine, Wilson argued that the proposed federal constitution created a "confederate republick," precisely as Montesquieu himself, properly understood, had advocated. Such a form of government, Wilson said, quoting Montesquieu, is "a convention, by which several states agree to become members of a larger one, which they intend to establish. It is a kind of assemblage of societies, that constitute a new one, capable of increasing by means of farther association."[28]

III

Unlike James Madison, who arrived at the Philadelphia Convention having given little explicit prior thought to the proper constitution of executive authority, [29] Wilson's views were well developed. Thus, while Wilson was closely allied to Madison during the convention and spoke frequently in support of Madison's over-all agenda, Wilson's role in shaping what ultimately became the second article of the United States Constitution was arguably more profound. As Carol Berkin has noted, debate in the Philadelphia Convention "seemed to circle back upon itself, as arguments were fashioned and refashioned, sometimes into incoherence." [30] This recursive character to the deliberations added a certain layered quality to the discussion, as new proposals or topics provided opportunity for older issues to be reopened. During the Convention debates, discussion of the executive clustered in three bursts of deliberation. Starting on June 1 and continuing for the next several days, the delegates opened discussion of the Virginia Plan's seventh and eighth resolutions, which provided for a national executive. A second extended discussion of the national executive began on July 17, and continued until July 26. Late in the Convention, the delegates returned to the executive a third time, in early September. Throughout, the delegates focused on a number of concrete issues. What was the proper number of persons in whom executive authority should be vested? What was the proper method for selecting the executive? For what term of office should he serve? Should the executive be eligible for more than one term? Should the executive possess the power to veto congressional legislation? What was the proper means for removing an ineffective or malicious executive?[31]

Wilson's thinking, as it emerged out of the lengthy debate over these matters, focused on ensuring an appropriate separation of powers, on securing an appropriately powerful executive authority, and on making the executive appropriately representative *of*, and accountable *to*, the people. More than any other delegate, Wilson appreciated the potential of the office to embody the national will. As one scholar has recently remarked, Wilson was the only member of the Convention who "envisioned an American government, and a president, much like those we have today—vigorous and powerful, and based firmly on the will of the people."[32] Thus, defending the proposed Constitution in the Pennsylvania ratifying convention, Wilson emphasized the national character of the executive. "This President, sir, will not be a stranger to our country, to our laws, or to our wishes," he remarked. "He will, under this Constitution, be placed in office as the President of the whole Union, and will be chosen in such a manner that he may be justly styled *the man of the people*."[33]

Wilson's concerns are well illustrated by the debate in the Philadelphia Convention over a unitary versus a plural executive, initiated by Wilson during the first phase of discussion over the constitution of the national executive. On Friday, June 1, Wilson rose and moved that the executive should reside in a single person. Charles Pinckney of South Carolina quickly seconded the motion. A heavy silence fell upon the room as the delegates grappled with the implications of the proposal. Benjamin Franklin "observed that it was a point of great importance and wished that the gentlemen would deliver their sentiments on it before the question was put."[34] Wilson explained that he "preferred a single magistrate, as giving most energy, dispatch and responsibility to the office." One of the shortcomings of the Articles of Confederation was the lack of an executive to carry out the laws adopted by Congress. Wilson's proposal would create an office with powers that he considered the domain of a proper executive, "those of executing the laws, and appointing officers, not appertaining to and appointed by the Legislature."[35]

Vesting the executive powers of the new government in a single man struck a number of the delegates as tending dangerously towards monarchy. Edmund Randolph, for example, challenged Wilson's motion in a June 1 speech. He, "strenuously opposed a unity in the Executive magistracy. He regarded it as the foetus of monarchy." He continued, "[h]e could not see why the great requisites for the Executive department, vigor, despatch and responsibility could not be found in three men, as well as in one man. The Executive ought to be independent. It ought therefore in order to support its independence to consist of more than one." [36] Randolph developed his criticism of a single executive even more forcefully on June 3. He "opposed it with great earnestness, declaring that he should not do justice to the Country which sent him if he were silently to suffer the establishm[ent] of a Unity in the Executive department." Randolph then explained that he "was in favor of three members of the Executive to be drawn from different portions of the Country." [37] Hugh Williamson of North Carolina emphatically echoed Randolph's reasoning in a speech on July 24, declaring that a unitary executive "will be an elective king, and will feel the spirit of one." Williamson went on to add that such an executive "will spare no pains to keep himself in for life, and will then lay a train for the succession of his children."[38]

Wilson insisted on a single executive in order to ensure the unity of power and thus of responsibility. The public would know whom to hold accountable under a single executive, but with Randolph's plan who would be held responsible? Wilson developed his fullest critique of Randolph's arguments on June 4. He emphasized the precedent of the State constitutions, pointing to the fact that "[a]ll the 13 States tho agreeing in scarce any other instance, agree in placing a single magistrate at the head of the Govern[ment]. The idea of three heads has taken place in none."[39] Wilson reiterated arguments earlier articulated by Pierce Butler, noting the potential for disagreement in the executive to distort politics lower down in the pyramid of government. Just as a properly constituted government could refine the character of the people, so one poorly framed could corrupt it. Thus, Wilson remarked that "he foresaw nothing but uncontrouled, continued, and violent animosities; which would not only interrupt the public administration; but diffuse their poison thro' the other branches of Gov[ernment], thro' the States, and at length thro' the people at large."[40] Anything less than a unified office where the executive power of the United States would reside in one person would endanger the national government and threaten faction and disunity. A single executive, situated within a system of balance of powers, would give energy, but more importantly *accountability* to the new national government.

Wilson argued, for similar reasons, against encumbering the executive with an executive council. Roger Sherman pursued Wilson's reference to the state constitutions, noting on June 4 that "in all the States there was a Council of advice, without which the first magistrate could not act." Moreover, Sherman added, "even in G[reat] B[ritain] the King has a Council; and though he appoints it himself, its advice has its weight with him, and attracts the confidence of the people."[41] Hugh Williamson of North Carolina rose and questioned Wilson regarding whether he intended to have an advisory council for the executive? Wilson responded emphatically that he "means to have no Council, which oftener serves to cover, than prevent malpractices."[42] Again, the issue was accountability. As Wilson explained in the Pennsylvania ratifying convention, "the executive power is better to be trusted when it has no screen. Sir, we have a responsibility in the person of our President; he cannot act improperly, and hide either his negligence or inattention; he cannot roll upon any other person the weight of his criminality; no appointment can take place without his nomination; and he is responsible for every nomination he makes."[43]

When Wilson later, in his law lectures, analyzed in some detail differences between the British and American constitutions, he again emphasized the absence of executive councilors. "The British throne is surrounded by counsellors," Wilson noted, with pernicious consequences. "Between power and responsibility, they interpose an impenetrable barrier." In contrast, in the United States Constitution, "our first executive magistrate is not obnubilated behind the mysterious obscurity of counsellors." The result was refinement of the character of the executive. The American President, Wilson stressed, "was the dignified, but accountable magistrate of a free and great people." His tenure in office was "of the noblest kind: by being a man of the people, he is invested; by continuing to be the man of he people, his investiture will be voluntarily, and cheerfully, and honorably renewed." Just as the act of voting induced a kind of civic sociability that refined the character of the citizen who exercised the suffrage, so too service in office held the potential for civic and moral uplift. Executive accountability was fundamental to a properly constituted pyramid of government, as Wilson envisioned it. [44]

A major issue that vexed delegates of the Philadelphia Convention during each discussion of the executive, and that only was resolved in the last days of the Convention, concerned the method of selecting the executive. Early in the Convention, on June 1, Wilson addressed the delegates "that in theory he was for an election by the people."[45] His opinion was informed by the experience of New York and Massachusetts which both provided for an election of their governor by the people; here was precedent that it could be done. Once again Wilson strove to make as clear and direct as possible the accountability of the government to the people. As he explained later that day, "he wished to derive not only both branches of the Legislature from the people, without the intervention of the State Legislatures but the executive also; in order to make them as independent as possible of each other, as well as of the States."[46] Despite his best efforts, however, his arguments received only lukewarm support from other delegates. George Mason, for example, stated that "he favors the idea, but thinks it impracticable."[47] As a compromise, Wilson presented on the following day a system whereby the States would be divided into districts for the selection of "electors of the Executive magistracy," with qualified voters coming from those eligible to vote for members of the House of Representatives. The "electors" would then gather at a predetermined place to select a person "in whom the Executive authority of the national Government shall be vested." Wilson asserted that the selection of the Executive by this process, divorced from dependence upon either the State or the national Legislature would "produce more confidence among the people in the first magistrate."[48]

This notion, the germ of what later became the Electoral College, received little initial support. Elbridge Gerry of Massachusetts "liked the principle of Mr. Wilson's motion, but fears it would alarm and give a handle to the State partisans, as tending to supersede altogether the State authorities." The tangible presence of the States dominated all discussion of the construction of a new government. How would the governments that most Americans were familiar with—the states—fit into the scheme? Gerry gave voice to this thinking when he said, "[h]e thought the Community not yet ripe for stripping the States of their powers, even such as might not be requisite for local purposes." He further doubted that the people could be trusted to make wise choices in the selection of electors, let alone the executive. The people were "too little informed of personal characters in large districts, and liable to deceptions."[49]

Debates over the method for selecting the executive were contentious, and the Convention struggled with the issue well into September. The Committee of Detail, whose job was to come up with solutions to parts of the unfinished Constitution, revived Wilson's idea in the closing days of the Convention. The creation of the Electoral College helped to bridge the gap between Wilson, who pushed for a direct election of the president, and those who advocated the election of the president by Congress. One of the benefits, for delegates concerned about maintaining the viability of the states, of the Electoral College was that it implicitly recognized the role of the states in the selection of a president.

James Wilson favored a strong, independent executive that exercised significant power—power that would be drawn directly from the people and used on their behalf. Securing an executive independent of both national and state legislatures was thus vitally important for his vision. Threats emerged early in the debates, as it became evident that more than a few delegates from the small states feared the loss of state autonomy, and wished to make the national government accountable in various ways to the state governments. For example, on June 2, Wilson's former law mentor—John Dickinson of Delaware—"moved that the Executive be made removable by the National Legislature on the request of a majority of the Legislatures of individual States."[50] The proposal would place the fate of the executive in the hands of forces in control of the state legislatures, not in the hands of a national Congress. Dickinson made his intent clear when he concluded his remarks by asserting that, "[t]he happiness of this Country in his opinion required considerable powers to be left in the hands of the States."[51] This proposal would weaken the federal government and give the state legislatures significant power over the policies pursued by the national government.

Dickenson's proposal stemmed from other concerns as well. His subsequent arguments revealed the extent of distrust of executive authority, shared by many of the delegates. "Such an executive as some seemed to have in contemplation," Dickenson argued, no doubt with Wilson at least partially in mind, "was not consistent with a republic." Dickenson feared monarchy, and looked to federalism as a check on executive authority. "A firm Executive could only exist in a limited monarchy," he claimed. "In the British Gov[ernmen]t itself the weight of the Executive arises from the attachment which the Crown draws to itself, and not merely from the force of its prerogatives. In place of these attachments we must look out for something else." To Dickenson, the sovereignty of the state governments seemed like a logical check on the enlarged executive authority contemplated by the Convention.[52]

In response, Wilson, together with James Madison, mounted a vigorous defense of an independent executive. They argued that Dickinson's proposal would give an undue influence to a minority of the American people over the tenure of the executive by enabling "a minority of the people to prevent the removal of an officer who had rendered himself justly criminal in the eyes of a majority." Moreover, they cautioned "it would open a door for intrigues ag[ainst] him in States where his administration tho' just might be unpopular, and might tempt him to pay court to particular States whose leading partizans he might fear, or wish to engage as his partizans."[53] They believed that it would be "bad policy" to interject the States into determining the fate of the executive. Wilson firmly believed that a *national* executive should only be removed by organs of a *national* government. Dickenson's proposal would have obscured the democratic accountability that was central to Wilson's thought. As Wilson noted later, elaborating in the Pennsylvania ratifying convention on his pyramid metaphor, it was necessary "to preserve that essential mark of free governments—a chain of connection with the people."[54]

Threats similar to Dickenson's, and stemming from similar motives, continued to surface throughout the convention. Thus, for example William Patterson again raised the issue of the involvement of the States in the tenure of the executive when he presented his New Jersey Plan to the Convention on June 15. Patterson's plan provided for the removal of the executive "by Cong[res]s on application by a majority of the Executives of the several States."[55] This provision was one of many in the New Jersey Plan to which Wilson objected in his lengthy discussion of the relative merits of the Virginia and New Jersey Plans to the Convention on June 16. Later, on July 20 when debate returned to the issue of impeachment Wilson again reaffirmed his support for granting Congress the power of impeachment while the executive was in office.[56]

Wilson's work on the Committee of Detail reinforced the placement of the power of impeachment in organs of the national government. The committee's report, presented on August 6, granted to the House of Representatives the power to bring articles of impeachment against the executive and for a trial and possible conviction to be given to the Supreme Court. The details of the mechanisms of impeachment were not yet finalized, but the inclusion of a role for the States was no longer before the Convention.[57]

Wilson thus consistently and repeatedly advocated the need to protect the ability of the executive to ward off encroachment by Congress upon areas reserved for the executive. Another protracted discussion that illuminates Wilson's thinking occurred over the issue of the executive veto, an issue first raised in convention on June 4, when Elbridge Gerry put forth a motion that contained a qualified executive veto. James Wilson and Alexander Hamilton countered with a motion that granted an absolute veto over congressional legislation to the executive. Gerry saw "no necessity for so great a control over the legislature as the best men in the community would be comprised in the two branches of it."[58] Roger Sherman spoke in support of Gerry, noting that he "was against enabling any one man to stop the will of the whole."[59] Sherman worried about substituting the wisdom of the executive for the collective wisdom of Congress. James Madison sided with Gerry, arguing that "a proper proportion of each branch should be required to overrule the objection of the executive, it would answer the same purpose as an absolute negative."[60]

Wilson disagreed with Madison's logic of a qualified veto. He argued that the mere presence of the veto power would dissuade Congress from enacting laws that would trigger an executive veto. "Its silent operation would therefore preserve harmony and prevent mischief." Further, he argued that a qualified veto would be adequate in "peaceable times; but there might be tempestuous moments in which animosities may run high between the Executive and Legislative branches, and in which the former ought to be able to defend itself." [61]

George Mason strenuously objected to Wilson's argument for the absolute veto. Mason warned that it would be used by the executive to obtain acceptance, by the Senate, of his appointments. Mason anticipated a capacity for the executive to corrupt the legislature, much like the experience of the Crown and Parliament in England. Mason warned that if powers, such as an absolute veto, were allocated to the executive, "We are not indeed constituting a British government, but a more dangerous monarchy—an elective one." [62] Benjamin Franklin closed the debate on the subject by remarking, "The first man put at the helm will be a good one. Nobody knows what sort may come afterwards. The executive will be always increasing here, as elsewhere, till it ends in a monarchy." [63] Wilson kept the independence of the executive foremost in his thinking and the absolute veto was a tool to increase the power of the President relative to that of Congress, but in this instance the reservations of the delegates resulted in the defeat of Wilson and Hamilton's motion unanimously. The convention would eventually adopt Madison's proposal of a supermajority to override a presidential veto.

CONCLUSION

James Wilson's political philosophy was predicated upon the necessity of injecting the *vox populi* into the inner workings of any national government. The national government that Wilson helped build rose to a height unimagined by the delegates present on July 4, 1776 when they voted to permanently server formal ties with Great Britain. Wilson's favorite metaphor of a pyramid was apt, as the foundation of the government created by the Constitution of the United States was the consent of the American people. The government of the United States exercised its power directly upon the American people. While neither Wilson nor Madison secured the full degree of independence from State sovereignty in the national government that they desired, in comparison with the Articles of Confederation, the authority of the national government was not filtered through that of the state governments.

Popular sovereignty was the cement that held the federal construct together and joined the interests and power of the American people with that of their government. James Madison conducted exhaustive research in drawing up the Virginia Plan to guide the delegates who gathered in May 1787 in Philadelphia. Madison had a well thought out plan for a national government that would correct the acknowledged deficiencies existing in the Articles of Confederation. James Wilson came to the Philadelphia Convention with very clear ideas of his own regarding what shape a new national government should take. He agreed with Madison's work in many respects, but as he walked the distance from his home to the Pennsylvania State House each morning of the convention he was determined to remodel the plan into a form that was dramatically more democratic than the original. As a leading advocate of a principled, consistent, and comprehensive application of popular sovereignty in government, Wilson advanced his position at every opportunity. This can be seen through his advocacy of the following: (1) a popularly elected House of Representatives by the broadest possible means of suffrage; (2) a Senate elected by a popular vote from electoral districts which crossed state boundaries and gathered popular opinion from a reservoir which saw the American people as a whole; and most importantly (3) a single-person executive which would be elected by a popular vote of the American people. Collectively, Wilson's proposals gathered public opinion through a variety of avenues to breathe life, vigor, and power into a truly national government.

Wilson's advocacy of a strong component of popular sovereignty in the Constitution might seem counterintuitive, as he was not a popular figure in Pennsylvania politics. His political theory would not bring him popular acclaim through the electoral process, but he was a man who acted upon his beliefs and strove to see them become reality. He believed that the two most significant duties of citizens were to vote and serve on juries. Wilson worked to create a President of the United States who would draw his power from and use it on behalf of the American people. He was unsuccessful in constructing a Constitution that he would have supported in every detail, but like any good politician, he secured what he could. For that he deserves our thanks and remembrance.

Wilson was an early advocate of citizenship education, who gave serious attention to the classical republican concern for civic virtue. For Wilson, the "chain of connection" between people and government, personified in an expansive suffrage, was fundamental to the construction of an enduring American republic. He warned in his introductory law lecture in Philadelphia, before an audience consisting of President George Washington and most of the members of the national government, "that the weight of the government of the United States and of each state composing the union, rests on the shoulders of the people."[64] To prepare the people for such an important task Wilson wanted to "convince them, that their duties rise in strict proportion to their rights; and that few are able to trace or to estimate the great danger, in a free government, when the rights of the people are unexercised, and the still greater danger, when the rights of the people are ill exercised." [65] The relationship between people and government needed to be safeguarded by both, from apathy at the base of Wilson's pyramid of government, and from arrogance or overreaching at the pinnacle.

REFERENCES

[1] Page Smith, *James Wilson: Founding Father, 1742-1798*, (Chapel Hill: University of North Carolina Press, 1956), 6. Smith's work remains the necessary starting point for any analysis of Wilson, and the biographical summary in the following paragraphs derives from it, but see also the superb short biographies in Kermit L. Hall and Mark David Hall, eds., *Collected Works of James Wilson*, Volume I, (Indianapolis: Liberty Fund, 2007), "Introduction," xv-xxiv, (hereafter identified as *CWJW*); and Robert G. McCloskey, ed., *The Works of James Wilson*, Volume I, (Cambridge: Harvard University Press, 1967), "Introduction," 1-48. Smith's treatment can be usefully supplemented, for Wilson's intellectual development, by Geoffrey Seed, *James Wilson: Scottish Intellectual and American Statesman* (Millwood, NY: KTO Press, 1978); and Mark David Hall, *The Political and Legal Philosophy of James Wilson, 1742-1798* (Columbia, MO: University of Missouri Press, 1997).

[2] James Wilson and William White's "Visitant" essays are analyzed in Stephen A. Conrad, "Polite Foundation: Citizenship and Common Sense in James Wilson's Republican Theory," *The Supreme Court Review*, Vol. 1984 (1984), 361-65; but see also Stephen A. Conrad, "Metaphor and Imagination in James Wilson's Theory of Federal Union," *Law and Social Inquiry*, 13:1 (Winter, 1988): 1-70; and Arnaud B. Leavelle, "James Wilson and the Relation of the Scottish Metaphysics to American Political Thought," *Political Science Quarterly*, Vol. 57: 3 (September, 1942), 394-410.

For an excellent brief overview of the philosophy of the Scottish Enlightenment, consult the essays in Alexander Broadie, ed., *The Cambridge Companion to the Scottish Enlightenment*, (New York: Cambridge University Press, 2003).

[3] This pamphlet has been reprinted in *CWJW*, Volume I 2007: 3-31.

[4] McCloskey, ed., *The Works of James Wilson*, Volume II 1967: 721.

[5] For a detailed political narrative of these events, see John Ferling, *A Leap in the Dark: The Struggle to Create the American Republic* (New York: Oxford University Press, 2003): 135-76.

[6] *CWJW*, Volume I 2007: 189.

[7] For a detailed examination of the Fort Wilson incident, see John K. Alexander "The Fort Wilson Incident of 1779: A Case Study of the Revolutionary Crowd", *The William and Mary Quarterly*, (3rd Ser., Vol. 31, No. 4. (Oct., 1974), 589-612) and Smith 1956: 133-36.

[8] Richard Beeman, *Plain, Honest Men: The Making of the American Constitution* (New York: Random House, 2009): 133. A dated, but still useful, discussion of Wilson's democratic thought is Geoffrey Seed, "The Democratic Ideas of James Wilson: A Reappraisal," *Bulletin. British Association for American Studies*, New Series, No. 10 (June, 1965), 3-30. For a pithy statement of the contrary view, see John Kaminski's review of Mark David Hall, *The Political and Legal Philosophy of James Wilson, 1742-1798*, in *Journal of the Early Republic*, Vol. 17, No. 4 (Winter, 1997): 693-95. As Kaminski notes, "Those who focus on Wilson's words alone hail him as a democrat; historians and others who chronicle Wilson's actions see him as a talented, elitist, partisan office seeker, who, ever the spendthrift, sold his legal and political skills to the wealthy and died a disgraced runaway bankrupt." (695).

[9] Adrienne Koch, ed., *Notes of Debates in the Federal Convention of 1787 Reported by James Madison,* (New York: W. W. Norton and Company, 1987), 39. Hereafter cited as Madison.

[10] Madison 1987: 39.

[11] Madison 1987: 47.

[12] Madison 1987: 40.

[13] *CWJW*, I 2007: 178.

[14] *CWJW*, I 2007: 191.

[15] *CWJW*, I 2007: 193.

[16] For Wilson's repetition of these themes in subsequent speeches, see *CWJW*, I 2007: 193, 201, 202, 212, 213, 214, 215, 235, 238, 254, 255, 258, 278, 279. For an extended examination of Wilson's analysis of popular sovereignty, see James H. Read, "James Wilson and the Idea of Popular Sovereignty," in Read, *Power versus Liberty: Madison, Hamilton, Wilson, and Jefferson* (Charlottesville: University Press of Virginia, 2000), 89-118; but see also John V. Jezirski, "Parliament or People: James Wilson and Blackstone on the Nature and Location of Sovereignty," *Journal of the History of Ideas*, 32:1 (January to March, 1971), 95-106.

[17] Madison 1987: 40.

[18] *CWJW*, I 2007: 279.

[19] *CWJW*, II 2007: 833.

[20] *CWJW*, I 2007: 279.

[21] *CWJW*, II 2007: 833-34.

[22] *CWJW*, I 2007: 292.
[23] *CWJW*, I 2007: 291.
[24] *CWJW*, I 2007: 290.
[25] *CWJW*, I 2007: 290.
[26] *CWJW*, II 2007: 834-35. See Conrad, "Polite Foundation," pp. 366-374. For an introduction to Wilson's law lectures, see also Mark David Hall, "Notes and Documents: James Wilson's Law Lectures," *The Pennsylvania Magazine of History and Biography*, 128:1 (January, 2004): 63-76.
[27] *CWJW*, I 2007: 179.
[28] *CWJW*, I 2007: 181. For comparison, see Hamilton's discussion of Montesquieu in Federalist Nine, in Alexander Hamilton, James Madison, and John Jay, *The Federalist Papers*, J.R. Pole, ed., (Hackett Press, 2005), 43-46; and Montesquieu, *The Spirit of the Laws*, Anne M. Cohler, Basia C. Miller, and Harold S. Stone, eds., (New York: Cambridge University Press, 1989), 131.
[29] Madison wrote George Washington on 16 April, 1787, to convey what he described as "*some* outlines of a new system," pertinent to "the subject which is to undergo the discussion of the Convention." As Madison went on to confess, "A national Executive must also be provided," but "I have scarcely ventured as yet to form my own opinion either of the manner in which it ought to be constituted or of the authorities with which it ought to be cloathed." Jack Rakove, ed., *Madison: Writings* (New York: Library of America: 1999), 80, 82-83.
[30] Carol Berkin, *A Brilliant Solution: Inventing the American Constitution* (New York: Harcourt, Inc., 2002), 78.
[31] Wilson's thought regarding the constitution of the executive has been the subject of a number of excellent studies: see especially Beeman 2009: 127-37; Robert E. DiClerico, "James Wilson's Presidency," *Presidential Studies Quarterly*, 17:2 (1987), 301-17; and Daniel J. McCarthy, "James Wilson and the Creation of the Presidency," *Presidential Studies Quarterly*, 17:4 (1987), 689-96.
[32] Beeman 2009: 129.
[33] *CWJW*, I 2007: 205.
[34] Madison 1987: 45.
[35] Madison 1987: 46.
[36] Madison 1987: 46.
[37] Madison 1987: 58.
[38] Madison 1987: 357.
[39] Madison 1987: 59.
[40] Madison 1987: 59-60.
[41] Madison 1987: 60.
[42] Madison 1987: 60.
[43] *CWJW*, I 2007: 236.
[44] *CWJW*, I 2007: 729-30.
[45] Madison 1987: 48.
[46] Madison 1987: 48.
[47] Madison 1987: 49.
[48] Madison 1987: 50.
[49] Madison 1987: 50-51.

[50] Madison 1987: 55.
[51] Madison 1987: 55.
[52] Madison 1987: 56.
[53] Madison 1987: 56.
[54] *CWJW*, I 2007: 279.
[55] Madison 1987: 120.
[56] Madison 1987: 125, 331.
[57] Madison 1987: 392-393.
[58] Madison 1987: 62.
[59] Madison 1987: 62.
[60] Madison 1987: 63.
[61] Madison 1987: 63.
[62] Madison 1987: 64.
[63] Madison 1987: 65-6.
[64] *CWJW*, I 2007: 436.
[65] *CWJW*, I 2007: 436.

Chapter 17

POST-FDR REPUBLICAN PRESIDENTS' ADHERENCE TO CORE CONSERVATIVE VALUES

Steven E. Standridge

ABSTRACT

This research tested whether modern Republican presidents from 1953 through 2004 have consistently supported two of the Party's core values: limiting the size of government (as expressed by a decrease in spending and/or lower taxes that result in reduced spending) and minimizing government intrusiveness (as expressed by restricting the expansion of regulatory agencies at the Federal level). The quantitative approach involved analyzing the federal government's growth and intrusiveness. Government growth was quantified by measuring annual spending, as a percentage of GDP. Then, a year-by-year analysis of the federal debt, as a percentage of GDP, was evaluated to provide an added measurement of how closely Republican presidents have limited the size of government. Three key measures were used to establish the level of governmental intrusion at the federal level: the number of Federal Registry pages printed each year; the number of workers employed by the Federal government annually; and, the yearly administrative costs of managing federal rules and regulations. The primary purpose of this research was to measure the modern-era Republican president's adherence to core conservative values contrasted against their rhetorical support found in previous research conducted by the author.

INTRODUCTION

As the 2008 election slowly fades into memory, an army of pundits, scholars and analysts begin the daunting task of studying the proximate causes of what some scholars are presumptively calling a "seismic" political shift. [1] A few pundits have gone so far as to suggest that this election conjoined with the Democratic victories in 2006 were a rebuke of conservative doctrine signifying a much deeper and more protracted ideological shift in the electorate. [2] However, it was not long ago that liberals were lamenting the country's ostensible migration to the right, which wrought, in their collective estimation, social and ethical devastation. [3] To an objective observer these assertions may have seemed accurate as the analysis of such political intellectuals as Micklethwait and Wooldridge reinforced this notion. [4]

Micklethwait and Wooldridge asserted the country had ideologically drifted to right as evidenced by the Republican Party's political dominance from the 1980's through 2004. However, closer examination of the empirical data over the last 25 years may counter this contention. There is substantial evidence to suggest the nation, even before the 2006 and 2008 elections, was more liberally oriented than previously presumed. [5] A more disconcerting revelation for conservatives, though, may be that it is not entirely evident whether the Republican Party has consistently adhered to two of its primary core values (limiting the size of government and minimizing its intrusiveness) in the post-FDR era. It is this proposition that will be tested in the following research project. Specifically, this paper evaluates whether post-FDR Republican presidents have consistently adhered to the precepts of limiting the size and intrusiveness of government. This is an especially salient question as the implications of the 2008 election are examined.

As Americans weighed the merits of each candidate's case for their bid to win the White House many of the same ideological arguments that had been waged over the last four or more decades were being rehashed during the 2008 election.

John McCain, the GOP candidate, showed a particular eagerness to invoke comparisons with Reagan in an unabashed attempt to earn the appellation as an "authentic" conservative. [6] Yet, this was to be expected as most modern-era Republican candidates have freely employed the precepts of limited government as a way to demonstrate their loyalty to the Party's core values. [7] Yet, as the GOP evaluates the lingering effect of the 2006 and 2008 elections and tries to retrace its fall from grace, the party may want to consider whether its misfortunes are tied to how effectively Republican presidents have adhered to these core ideals as they've governed given their enthusiastic support for limited government. Answering these questions may well portend how the party can recapture the electorate's confidence as "guardians" of these long standing precepts.

RESEARCH HYPOTHESIS

The literature on party identification suggests that enduring philosophical doctrines have been embedded in both parties. Conservatives have traditionally supported two broad-based ideological themes: reducing government spending through tax cuts and advocating prudent budget practices; and, limiting government interference through deregulation, encouragement of individualism, support for states' and private property rights as well as advocating local control [8]

Recognizing the enduring strength of these ideological themes, this paper tested whether the Republican Party [9], since 1952 (the year the first post-FDR era Republican president was elected), has developed policies and governed in a manner consistent with two of these core values - limiting the size of government (as expressed by an increase in spending) or minimized its intrusiveness (as evidenced by an expansion of regulatory agencies at the Federal level).

RESEARCH METHODOLOGY

Growth of Government

The growth in the federal government was first quantified by measuring annual spending, as a percentage of GDP, under Republican presidents, starting with the Eisenhower administration. Then, a year-by-year analysis of the federal debt, as a percentage of GDP, was evaluated to provide an added measurement of how closely Republican presidents have adhered to the fiscally conservative doctrine of limiting the size of government by forcing it to live within its means.

Scope of Government

One of the most divisive issues between liberals and conservatives is their differing views on the appropriate role of government, which conservatives often refer to as governmental intrusiveness. Liberals generally defend a more activist role for government in most spheres, including support for redistribution schemes, greater federal regulation of the economy and more direct bureaucratic intervention to assist disadvantaged groups. [10] Conversely, conservatives favor greater reliance on free markets rather than government regulation, less activist policies and lower taxation that encourages economic growth. [11] These ideological differences manifest into diametrically different approaches to governance and funding sources for governmental programs.

Governments typically fund new programs through two primary mechanisms: raising taxes or borrowing money. Increasingly, however, a third scheme has gained favor by legislators and bureaucrats alike, which uses covert funding streams to subsidize various programs. This is accomplished through the imposition of regulation, which impacts individuals and the private sector and imposes unfunded mandates on state or local governments. The expenditures needed to cover the regulatory fees, as well as the expenditures needed for compliance, shift the fiscal burden away from the federal government and onto the affected parties. [12] Moreover, when such financial encumbrances are angrily received, legislators simply transfer the blame to the specific agency and escape responsibility for the increased expense. [13] Of greater concern, however, is that these "off-budget" items do not endure the same formal vetting process that normal budgetary requests experience. As Crews suggests, "Government regulation can advance desired programs without using tax dollars. Because disclosure of and accountability for the regulatory costs are so rare, policy makers are often careless about regulatory costs relative to ordinary government spending" He goes on to state, "Moreover, because regulatory costs are not budgeted and they lack the formal presentation to the public and media that accompanies federal spending, regulatory initiatives can allow manipulation of private sector resources with little public fuss, thus rendering regulation a form of off-budget taxation." Consequently, these off-budget "taxes" lack effective accountability measures, thus increasing the prospect for fiscal mismanagement. The challenge for this research project was finding measures that reliably captured the concept of "intrusive" government, including such schemes as off-budget "unfunded mandates." [14]

Researchers have long debated the concept of "governmental intervention" as it pertains to limits on individualistic endeavors, infringements upon property rights, increased bureaucracy or diminution of local and state control. Although no consensus exists on how best to quantify these concepts, there are measures that can provide a general assessment of the growth of governmental action that can easily be evaluated from president to president. For the purpose of this project, three key measures were used to establish the level of governmental intrusion at the federal level: the number of Federal Registry pages printed each year; the number of workers employed by the Federal government annually; and, the yearly administrative costs of managing federal rules and regulations. [15]

The primary source used for this section of the research project was Dudley and Warren's 2006 report. [16] The authors used expenditures on federal regulatory agencies, as well as staffing levels, as their primary measures of federal governmental regulatory activity. Tracking the total monetary outlays and staffing levels of federal regulatory agencies helped the authors analyze the trends in regulatory activities from 1960 through 2005. Their analysis also assessed the impact of government growth on the private sector, states and other local agencies. As Dudley and Warren suggest, "this information serves as a barometer of regulatory activity, providing policy makers and others with useful insights into the composition and evolution of regulation." [17] The authors also provide the cumulative data for the Federal Registry pages (in graphed format) but spend little time analyzing its relevance or regulatory impact.

To get a more accurate gauge of the Federal government's regulatory activities, the authors segregated federal regulation into two broad categories: social and economic. Social regulation includes regulatory action relating to health, safety and the environment that issues from the Environmental Protection Agency, Occupational Safety and Health Administration, Food and Drug Administration, and Transportation Security Administration. Dudley and Warren state that in order to accurately gauge the extent to which these agencies exert their regulatory influence, it was necessary to subdivide their activities into six subcategories: consumer safety and health, homeland security, transportation, workplace, environment and energy. They continue by stating that these agencies activities', though "generally limited to a specific issue," have "the power to regulate across industry boundaries." [18]

Economic regulation, the second Administrative Cost and Staffing category, includes industry-specific regulations from the Securities and Exchange Commission, Federal Communications Commission and Federal Energy Regulatory Commission. Typically, these agencies regulate a wide variety of activities within specific industries, using largely economic measures, such as "price controls ceilings or floors, quantity restrictions, and service parameters", to exert their control. [19] As with social regulation, Dudley and Warren subdivide economic regulatory categories however into three specific classifications: finance and banking, industry-specific regulation and general business.

The main shortcoming of Dudley and Warren's report for this project is that their data does not include Eisenhower's administration; therefore, no conclusion can be drawn regarding his devotion to reducing federal regulation. However, the analysis garnered from

Dudley and Warren's report serves as an effective indicator of regulatory activity and provides useful insight into the impact and evolution of Federal regulation. [20]

Federal Registry Pages

While the Registry was a useful tool for providing a general sense of how regulatory burdens have expanded from year to year, its reliance as the sole measurement proved to be insufficient. The verbosity of a specific regulation directly correlates to the number of explanatory pages but may obscure the rule's real impact. To illustrate, a new regulation may comprise only a few pages of text, yet might impose a significant financial burden on the affected industry. Conversely, a more detailed rule may be relatively benign and encumber the burdened party very little. Additionally, the Register contains numerous administrative notices, blank pages, corrections, presidential statements and other extraneous material not related to regulatory administration, thus reliance on page count alone provides an incomplete assessment. Due to these limitations, it was necessary to utilize other measures to give a more comprehensive picture of the Federal government's proliferation of regulatory obligations.

Staffing of Federal Regulatory Agencies

Measuring the number of federal workers employed annually is an additional measure that can be used to give greater depth of understanding to just how intrusive the federal government has become. [21] The data reported in Dudley and Warren's document was obtained by counting the number of full-time equivalent employees (FTEs) that 68 Federal regulatory agencies employ every year.

Administrative Costs of Federal Regulation

In addition to examining the number of Federal regulatory employees added yearly, Dudley and Warren's report also tracked the annual spending of the same 68 departments and agencies. The expenditure data contained in the authors' report gives another means by which intrusiveness can measured and was derived from the outlays reported in the Budget of the U.S. Government.

FINDINGS

Since FDR's New Deal, liberal doctrine has increasingly become entrenched in the American political landscape where those principles have even manifested themselves into the Republican Party and its national platform. [22] Starting in the early 1950's, Republicans began to openly embrace these principles, indicating just how influential FDR's philosophy of expanding the size and scope of government had become. To truly appreciate just how integrated the concept of "big" government has become in American politics, one need only examine the growth of the federal government's size and intrusiveness during post-FDR Republican presidencies.

Size of Government

When FDR began his extraordinary expansion of government, few at the time could fully appreciate how massive it would eventually become. In spite of the fact that Dwight Eisenhower was the first of the post-FDR GOP presidents to openly embrace the welfare state, in his eight years in office, he presided over a federal budget that increased by 30 percent. Yet, compared to many of his GOP successors, he was stingy. When Richard Nixon's administration allowed spending to increase by a staggering 70 percent, many fiscal conservatives were apoplectic and began revolting en masse, which precipitated the rise of Ronald Reagan. [23]

When Reagan entered office in 1981, it was under the presumption that fiscal order might be restored and he would be true to the principles of limited government. This rhetoric was apparently stronger than his convictions. He allowed federal spending to increase by 53 percent over his eight years in office. Reagan's successor, George H. Bush, increased spending by only 12 percent in his four-year reign, the smallest increase of any of the Republican presidents. Perhaps the most egregious conservative offender of government expansion may, in the final analysis, be George W. Bush. In his first four years in office his Administration presided over a spending spree that increased federal outlays by 33%, which grew nearly twice as fast as it did under President Clinton. [24] As Stephen Slivinski of the Cato Institute pointed out of his 2006 budget:

> Even if Congress passes Bush's new budget (2006) exactly as proposed, not a single cabinet level agency will be smaller than when Bush assumed office. He [sic] has presided over the largest overall increase in inflation-adjusted federal spending since Lyndon B. Johnson. Even after excluding spending on defense and homeland security, Bush is still the biggest-spending president in 30 years." [25]

Not only have Republican presidents presided over significant expansions in total government spending, they have also been willing to run sizable annual deficits, further abandoning traditional principles of restrained and fiscally prudent governance. One of the most routinely cited statistics for evaluating an Administration's fiscal policies is to examine the difference between what the government takes in (receipts) and what it pays out (outlays) —more accurately, it reflects the government's deficit or surplus on a yearly basis. [26] Figure 3 demonstrates how deficits have consistently been a part of the fiscal management under Republican stewardship, starting with the Ford Administration. Eisenhower is the only post-FDR president, Republican and Democrat alike, to have had an increase in revenues while simultaneously decreasing outlays. Ford and Nixon both have the unenviable distinction as the only presidents in the study period that had a decrease in revenues and an increase in outlays (Table A – Appendix A). This incline stabilized under Carter's reign then continued its steep increase through most of Reagan's tenure, although there was a sharp drop in deficits beginning in 1987 that stabilized for the remainder of his last term. Reagan's successor, GH Bush, oversaw a dramatic increase in the deficit. As with spending, GW Bush has the undesirable distinction of having presided over the largest deficit increase of all post-FDR presidents. In some fairness to him, however, this spike was partly due to the declining receipts and increasing outlays of the Clinton Administration's last half of his second term, which helped contribute to Bush's early deficits (Figure 1).

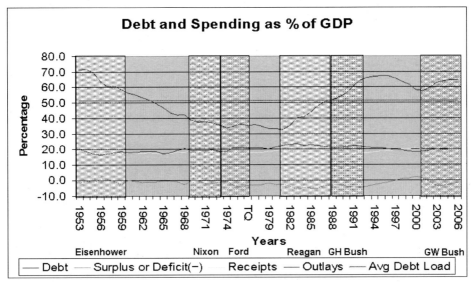

Source: *The Budget of the United States Government and related documents*, various fiscal years. Numbers may not add to totals due to rounding. Data based on annual outlays and receipts found in Appendices A and B.

Figure 1.

Another tool that helps economists evaluate fiscal restraint, which is also closely linked to deficit spending, is the level of debt the federal government amasses annually. The national debt is caused by continuous deficit spending whereby the federal government borrows money, in the form of Treasury bonds, to subsidize ongoing shortfalls in revenues. The bonds are then purchased by U.S. companies, private citizens and foreign entities. By this measure, it is evident that all presidents have experienced some level of debt service to offset their budgetary shortfalls. However, the national debt did not really experience any significant increase until approximately 1982. From that year forward there has been a sharp and consistent increase with a brief decline starting in 2000 (under a Democratic president) through 2001 (Figure 1). Conversely, the sharpest increases have been under Republican presidents, specifically Reagan and G.W. Bush, augmenting the point that the GOP has strayed from its fiscally prudent principles.

A major shortcoming of using deficit spending and its corresponding debt service as a gauge of fiscal temperance is that economists themselves disagree on its accuracy. In fact, Kotlikoff asserts:

> [the] deficit is not a well-defined economic concept. The current measure of the deficit, or any measure, is based on arbitrary choices of how to label government receipts and payments. The government can conduct any real economic policy and simultaneously report any size deficit or surplus it wants just through its choice of words. If the government labels

receipts as taxes and payments as expenditures, it will report one number for the deficit. If it labels receipts as loans and payments as return of principal and interest, it will report a very different number. [27]

Accordingly, it was necessary to utilize another measure to more accurately gauge whether GOP presidents have been successful in limiting government influence on our lives.

Scope of Government

A core philosophical tenet of the Liberal movement is what FDR referred to as the "larger purpose." This shift in belief can arguably be traced back to 1933 when, in his inaugural speech, FDR assured the country that he would use his executive powers to bring about change and stability for the "greater good." [28] His actions enabled governmental bodies to intrude in virtually every aspect of human activity. His sweeping reform brought about new regulations on banking, commerce, food and worker rights. Subsequent Democratic presidents carried forward this heritage and introduced such measures as supplementary labor, environmental, food and workplace safety laws; the Americans With Disabilities Act; the Family and Medical Leave Act; and, product labeling and truth in advertising laws. [29] However, Democrats alone have not been complicit in this expanded intervention into American lives. Republican administrations have happily advocated for and created agencies that have been as "intrusive" as any Democratic originated initiative.

Richard Nixon, for example, embraced affirmative action legislation and imposed price and wage controls; Ronald Reagan created the "Drug Czar's" office in an effort to wage a "war on drugs;" George H. Bush signed the Americans with Disabilities Act; and, finally, G.W. Bush introduced the USA Patriot Act, which the Electronic Frontier Foundation (EFF) characterized as the "most significant threat to civil liberties, privacy and democratic traditions in U.S. history." [30] It is clear that today's Republican representatives and leaders have all made "peace" with the state of large government, thus confirming the notion that big government liberalism has taken root in the Grand Old Party. However, these examples are, at best, anecdotal; therefore, a more definitive measurement must be used in order to determine the true expansion of federal regulations during GOP presidencies. As stated previously, the growth in government regulation can be evaluated on three bases: growth in the number of Federal Register pages, the increase in administrative expenditures related to regulatory activities and the boost in staffing for federal regulatory agencies and departments.

Federal Registry Pages

Figure 2 shows the annual page count of the Federal Register from 1936, when it was first printed, to 2006. While the general upward trends of regulatory expenditures and staffing levels were relatively stable, as will be examined in the next two sections, the Federal Register page count experienced far more volatility. The Nixon and Ford Administrations experienced the sharpest increases in the number of Registry pages, rising from approximately 20,000 pages in late 1970 and reaching 60,000 pages by mid-1975, which represents a 200% increase over this period. Reagan was the only GOP president to have fewer Registry pages upon exit from office than entry and was the only one to experience a sustained decline throughout his entire presidency. [31] To be fair, Reagan's impressive decline began in the Carter Administration and continued through the Reagan presidency. As was stated earlier, use of this data can be misleading as it gives only a partial impression of how significantly the Federal bureaucracies have grown.

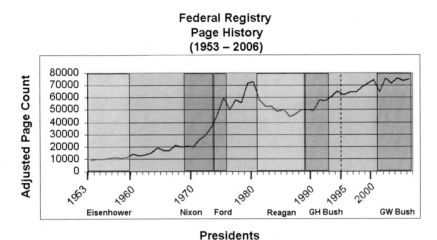

Source: Weidenbaum Center, Washington University and Mercatus Center at George Mason University. Reprinted from *Moderating Regulatory Growth: An Analysis of the U.S. Budget for Fiscal Years 2006- 2007* (Dudley and Warren, 2007).

Figure 2.

Staffing of Federal Regulatory Agencies

One key indicator of regulatory growth is the number of federal employees added annually to administer the labyrinth of federal codes and regulations. Although staffing levels of federal regulatory agencies have fluctuated since 1960 there has been a relatively stable upward trend. As can be seen in Figure 3 and Table C (Appendix C), the 1960 staffing levels were just under 60,000 full-time employees (57,100) dedicated to drafting, managing and enforcing federal regulations.

By 1970, that number had expanded to 90,300 federal regulatory workers, representing a 50.5 % increase. During the decade of 70's, the number of regulatory personnel grew by almost 55,900, or 61.9%. Then beginning with the Carter presidency, and continuing through the first half of the Reagan Administration, staffing levels declined by 12.7% from 1980 through 1985. This striking downward trend reversed itself as the second half of the decade saw an increase of 19.6%. By 1990, staffing at federal regulatory agencies was up by 4.4 % for the entire decade of the 1980's and continued upward into the early 1990's. [32] Between 1990 and 1995, the number of full-time personnel at the various federal regulatory agencies increased by 13.8%. Then in 1996 and 1997, in conjunction with the Republican take-over of the House, there was a precipitous, albeit temporary, decline in staffing levels that once again rose by 14.7% by the end of the decade. [33]

All Republican presidents, excluding Reagan, allowed regulatory staffing levels to grow during their respective terms. Nixon had the largest growth during his time in office (43.96%) whereas Reagan, following through on his pledge to de-regulate, reduced overall regulatory staffing by 11.18%. Although Ford did not reduce aggregate staffing levels, he did, once again, demonstrate a comparatively strong commitment to conservative principles relative to his counterparts by limiting staffing expansion by just 10.11% (Table C).

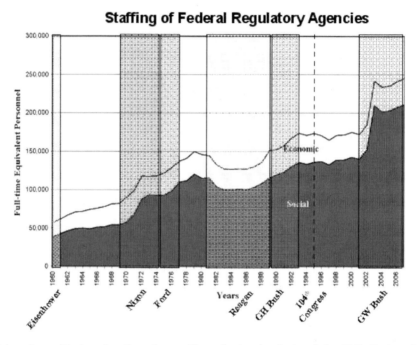

Source. Taken from *Moderating Regulatory Growth: An Analysis of the U.S. Budget for Fiscal Years 2006 and 2007* (Dudley and Warren, 2007) Data based on outlays, which can be found in Appendix C.

Figure 3.

In the first two years of the 21st century it appeared as if historical trends might continue with similar fluctuations in staffing levels with a gradual but overall inclination upwards. However, on September 11, 2001, that radically changed. Due to the creation of the Department of Homeland Security, specifically the formation of the Transportation Security Administration with its corresponding staff of airport screeners, the regulatory workforce jumped by an astounding 31%, the single largest one-year increase in the nation's history. [34]

Administrative Costs of Federal Regulation

Predictably, the rate of growth in regulatory spending has largely been dependent on the philosophical approaches to governance, if not the political whims, of elected officials. [35] What is less evident, though, is the degree to which Republican Presidents have adhered to the precept of reducing government's scope. As has been stated previously, one measure of this is how much regulatory and administrative spending has either grown or contracted from president to president. Figure 4 and Table D (Appendix D) clearly shows a general upward trend in federal outlays for administrative expenses related to regulatory activity. Starting in 1960, the study shows expenditures were roughly $2.5 billion (all figures were adjusted to 2000 dollars; therefore, the actual 1960 expenditures were $533 million). By the end of the decade, total spending at federal regulatory agencies had grown to $5.8 billion ($1,584 million unadjusted). This increase represents a real annual growth rate of 8.6% (adjusted for 2000 dollars). Most of this growth—more than $2 billion—occurred in social regulatory agencies (which experienced a real 136.9% increase in annual budgets over the decade). Economic regulatory programs expanded more slowly, by $0.9 billion or 107.8 percent over the period. [36]

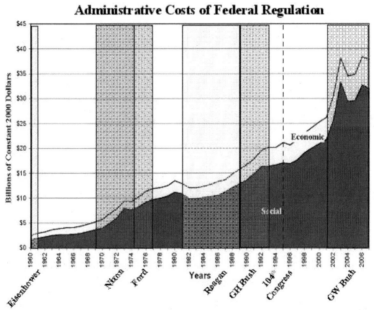

Source. Taken from Moderating Regulatory Growth: An Analysis of the U.S. Budget for Fiscal Years 2006 and (Dudley and Warren, 2007) Data based on outlays, which can be found in Appendix D.

Figure 4.

During the 1970s, the trend in regulatory spending continued upward. Over the ten-year period, real spending on regulatory activities grew by $7.7 billion or 134.5%. Double-digit increases in the first three years preceded much slower growth during the latter part of the decade. This slowed growth rate continued into the early years of the Reagan presidency, where regulatory expenditures declined by 5.26% from 1980 through 1985. As with the staffing patterns seen in the previous section, regulatory spending rebounded and increased by 31.1% between 1985 and 1990. This increase, coupled with the first half decrease, accounted for an overall spending increase of $3.3 billion (in 2000 dollars). Regulatory spending continued to increase in the 1990s, for a total increase of 50.9% over the ten-year span, which amounted to $8.5 billion. Similar to the decline in governmental staffing levels, the

Republican take-over of the House corresponded with a decline in spending from 1994 through 1996, but this regression was transitory. By the end of the decade, total spending had grown by an astounding 53.18%.

The trend continued into the 21st century as regulatory agencies increased their budgets by 37.8% between 2000 and 2005. During this five-year period, the average annual growth in regulatory activities amounted to 6.6% per year. This large spike was primarily due to the fall out from 9-11 and the subsequent formation of the Department of Homeland Security created and expanded in fiscal years 2002 and 2003 (16.5% and 24.6% respectively). The Bush Administration and the Republican Congress were more reserved in their spending in the following two years, as regulatory budgets declined 9.4% in 2004 and grew less than one percent in 2005.

In comparing how loyal the individual Republican presidents have been to the principle of reducing the federal bureaucracy Reagan remained true to his stated contempt for government. He had the lowest increase in regulatory spending of all the presidents since 1960 at 10.3%. Nixon, consistent with the criticism the he willingly embraced the growth of the federal government presided over the greatest expansion in spending of any Republican president (97.06%). [37] G.W. Bush, who has been berated by fellow conservatives for his *Compassionate Conservative* agenda, oversaw the creation of the largest single federal bureaucracy in US history – the Department of Homeland Security. He had the second largest cumulative increase in spending (37.44%) of all the GOP presidents since 1960, which was still a significantly lower aggregate increase than Nixon had and only six percentage points higher than his father's, G.H. Bush, at 31.76%.

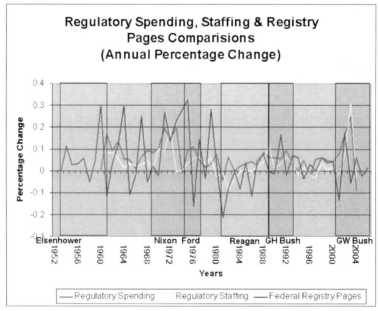

Note. Data taken from data contained in Appendices C and D.

Figure 5.

As an aside, Figure 5 compares the annual changes in regulatory spending, staffing and Registry Page count. What is striking about the comparison is that even though, as mentioned previously, the Registry Page count has far greater volatility than the regulatory staffing and spending levels, there does seem to be some correlation between the three measures. This is particularly clear from the Reagan presidency through G.W. Bush.

Scholars have long debated what measures best indicate a party's ability to limit government's size and scope. [38] Recognizing the enormous difficulty of effectively assessing these two concepts this paper limited its analysis to five measures: the growth in year-to-year spending, the growth in the federal debt, the number of Federal Registry pages added annually, the changes in regulatory staffing levels and the amount of federal money expended on regulatory activities.

In the first area examined (federal spending), it is evident that GOP presidents have generally presided over a systematic expansion in the federal government's budget. This measure, as explained earlier, is too imprecise to definitively ascertain the Party's adherence to minimalist governance; nevertheless, there were some surprising results. For instance, Eisenhower was far more fiscally prudent than his successors and there were a several years his budgets did not have any deficits at all. In fact, he maintained a relatively balanced budget throughout his entire tenure. Two often-maligned GOP presidents, Nixon and Ford, not only increased spending but also had a corresponding decrease in revenues throughout their terms.

Of even greater consternation for devoted fiscal conservatives has to be the revelation that their most beloved conservative figure, Reagan, saw unprecedented spending under his tenure. David Stockman, Reagan's first Director of the Office of Management and Budget and self-proclaimed supply-side advocate, suggests that Reagan sacrificed fiscal discipline to appease powerful interests in Washington and remain politically popular with the electorate. [39] These finding suggest that for all the GOP presidents' sermonizing about the Democrats' irresponsible spending behavior, they have, at least upon a superficial examination, been equally incapable of adhering to their own standards.

DISCUSSION

In the area of federal intrusion it is apparent that, as with spending, GOP presidents have failed to limit the government's intrusion into American's lives. Whether it is evaluating the number of pages added annually to the Federal Register, the number of federal employees hired from year-to-year, or the amount of money spent on managing bureaucracies, Republican presidents have failed to restrain any of these areas.

While it seems evident Republican presidents – despite their rhetoric – have been unwilling or unable to reign in the size and scope of the federal government during their respective tenures, the more interesting question is why? Several plausible theories have surfaced that might help explain the Republicans divergence between words and actions. Perhaps the two most compelling theories are the dominance of Democrats in Congress and the competing priorities of each party.

The Democrat Control Theory. The first justification for explaining the Republican presidents' lack of fiscal discipline and intrusive bureaucratic behavior is directly correlated with the control Democrats enjoyed in both houses of Congress for most of the post-FDR era.

During this period, only three GOP presidents benefited from some level of control by his party in at least one house of Congress: Eisenhower had majorities in both houses for his first two years; Reagan maintained control of the Senate until the last two years of his second term; and, G.W. Bush enjoyed majorities in both houses of Congress in his first six years in office. [40] Nevertheless, all three presidents eventually succumbed to electoral losses, which shifted control back to the Democrats in both the House and Senate after the 2006 elections.

Outside of these three exceptions, all GOP presidents faced Democrat congressional opposition during all or part of their time in office. [41] If then one accepts Gerring's supposition that Democrats generally favor more expansive government, which necessitates a corresponding increase in spending than their GOP counterparts this ostensibly set the stage whereby every GOP president at some juncture in his term faced an ideologically antagonistic House of Representatives that was intent on advancing policies that were at odds with their own stated policy preferences. The significance of this cannot be emphasized enough as the House of Representatives is ultimately responsible for advancing and passing all annual federal budgets. In turn, this frequently leads to situations where a president has to evaluate his willingness to expend his political capital vetoing every unacceptable budget or grudgingly accept approve it so that he might preserve his leverage for more important policy fights. [42] As stated previously, only G.W. Bush enjoyed majorities in both houses for most of his time in office, and yet his budgets expanded government more rapidly and larger than any other president since FDR – largely with the consent of Republican legislators. [43] Some suggest, while not necessarily endorsing his actions, this was largely driven by the need to yield on his stated desire to constrain domestic spending in order to position himself to gain concessions that would benefit the more important "War on Terror," as well as fund the Iraq and Afghanistan conflicts. [44]

As the G.W. Bush years and, to a lesser extent, the GOP take-over of Congress in 1994 demonstrate, Democrat dominance does not alone explain why Republican presidents have been incapable of reigning in government's size and scope. As a compliment to the aforementioned "Democrat Control Theory" another explanation is necessary to more fully explain this incongruence. One creditable hypothesis, this author terms "The Alternate Priorities Theory," asserts Republicans simply have different policy priorities, but that, nonetheless, necessitate the expenditure of equally large sums of taxpayer dollars as the Democratically championed programs; or, their programs/policies require a centrally run bureaucracy to implement and manage.

The Alternate Priorities Theory. It is generally argued that what differentiates conservatives from liberals is their stated distain for government. [45] Yet, the data, as it is presented in this paper, suggests that GOP rhetoric does not comport with their actions – particularly at the presidential level. The Alternate Priorities Theory suggests that Republicans simply trade one policy priority, one that fits their ideological prism, for another. For example, Reagan was singularly focused on national defense, particularly as it related to containing Soviet expansion and influence. Consequently, the policies that flowed from his administration's philosophy reflected this priority, which caused the federal budget to swell as defense spending soared. President G.W. Bush, likewise, increased defense spending to fund the Iraq and Afghanistan wars and enhance homeland security. [46]

With respect to expanding the scope of government, Republican administrations have been equally complicit as their Democrat counterparts. This is particularly evident with right-to-life issues (i.e. - abortions, stem cell research), religious initiatives and cultural matters (i.e. - gay marriage). [47]

Specific examples include Richard Nixon's embrace of affirmative action legislation as well as institution of price and wage controls; Ronald Reagan's creation of the "drug czar's" office designed to wage the "war on drugs;" George H. Bush's signing of the Americans with Disabilities Act; and, finally, G.W. Bush's passage of the USA Patriot Act, which the Electronic Frontier Foundation (EFF) characterized as the "most significant threat to civil liberties, privacy and democratic traditions in U.S. history."[1] It is clear that today's Republican representatives and leaders have made reluctant "peace" with the welfare state.

Unfortunately, the explanations advanced above are largely anecdotal and lack empirical validation. Moreover, the scope of this project did not set out to definitively answer the intriguing question of "why;" rather, its primary purpose was to establish a framework by which future researchers might examine and, hopefully, posit theories that more authoritatively answer this question.

CONCLUSION

When Barry Goldwater penned his groundbreaking book, *The Conscience of a Conservative*, he was in actuality creating a manifesto for the burgeoning conservative movement. His foundational principles of were, and still are, routinely espoused by Republicans including presidential aspirants; however, it seems unmistakable that rhetorically supporting these values and governing by them have yielded disturbing results for ardent conservatives. This may, to some extent, explain why the last two election cycles have so decidedly gone for Democrats: many rank-and-file conservatives feel their elected leaders have betrayed the party's core values. And, as party leaders feverishly try to plot their return to power they must honestly evaluate whether their misfortunes are directly tied to their inability to adhere to these core tenets. Failure to do so may well have implications far beyond the 2008 election - no less than the party's long-term fate may be at stake.

REFERENCES

[1] J.B. Judis, "America the Liberal by Obama's victory marks a radical realignment in American politics. But can the Democrats establish an enduring majority?" *The New Republic* (November 5, 2008). Retrieved November 5, 2008, from *http://www.tnr.com /politics/story.html?id=c261828d-7387-4af8-9ee7-8b2922ea6df0;* and K. Vanden Heuvel, "Transformational Presidency." *The Nation* (November 4, 2008). Retrieved November 5, 2008, from *http://www.thenation.com/blogs/edcut/380292.*

[2] W. Galston, "De-Alignment," *The Democratic Strategist* (November 29, 2006). Retrieved November 16, 2007, from *http://www.thedemocraticstrategist.org/ac/ 2006/11/de-alignment.php;* and R. Teixeira, "Moving Left? Bush's Decline and American Liberalism,". *Dissent Magazine (2007).* Retrieved June 25, 2008, from *http://www.dissentmagazine.org/display.php?id=about.*

[3] K. Phillips, *American Theocracy*. (NY: Penguin Group, 2006).

---

[1] Electronic Frontier Foundation, *The USA Patriot Act.*

[4] J. Micklethwait and A. Wooldridge, *The right nation: Conservative power in America*. (NY: Penguin Press, 2004).

[5] See T.W. Smith, T.W.," Liberal and Conservative Trends in the United States Since World War II," *Public Opinion Quarterly* (1990). Retrieved August 15, 2006, from JSTOR at *http://0-www.jstor.org.skyline.cudenver.edu/*; T.J. Lowi, *The End of the Republican era*. (Norman, OK: University of Oklahoma Press, 1995); and J.B. Judis and R. Teixeira, *The emerging Democratic majority*. (NY: Scribner, 2002).

[6] R.G. Kaiser, 'The Curious Mind of John McCain: Ambition and Emotion Color the Complex Intellect of the Candidate." *The Washington Post* (August 1, 2008) Retrieved August 29, 2008, from *http://www.washingtonpost.com/*.

[7] J. Gerring, J. *Party Ideologies in America, 1828-1996*. rev. ed. (NY: Cambridge University Press, 1998); and S.E. Standridge, "Post-FDR Republican Presidents' Use of Conservative Rhetoric in Platforms, Speeches and Veto Messages," *White House Studies*. 8 (2009).

[8] See L.L. Gould, *Grand Old Party: A History of the Republicans*. (NY: Random House, 2003): J. Gerring, *Party Ideologies in America, 1928-1996*; J.Micklethwait and A. Wooldridge, *The right nation;* and S.E. Standridge, "Post-FDR Republican Presidents' Use of Conservative Rhetoric in Platforms, Speeches and Veto Messages."

[9] It should be clarified that from this point forward any broad reference to the Republican Party, particularly as it relates to ideology, should be interpreted as those libertarian values that are being evaluated in this paper – i.e. limiting the size of government or minimized its intrusiveness.

[10] J. Gerring, *Party Ideologies in America, 1928-1996*.

[11] See note 8.

[12] J.W. Crews, *Ten Thousand Commandments*: *An Annual Snapshot of the Federal Regulatory State*. (Washington, D.C.: Competitive Enterprise Institute, 2007), p. 2. Retrieved July 6, 2007, from *http://www.cei.org/pdf/6018.pdf*.

[13] Ibid.

[14] Ibid., p.3.

[15] Since 1936, the federal government has released a daily Federal Register that publicizes all proposed and newly adopted rules and regulations for any given day. The Federal Register is one of the most frequently cited documents used to evaluate the scope of government intrusion. See S. Dudley and W. Warren, "Moderating Regulatory Growth: An Analysis of the U.S. Budget for Fiscal Years 2006 and 2007,"*Regulators' Budget Report* 28 (2007) published jointly by the Weidenbaum Center and the Mercatus Center. Retrieved July 06, 2007, from *http://www.mercatus.org/*.

[16] The *Moderating Regulatory Growth Report* is a joint document created by the Mercatus Center at George Mason University and the Murray Weidenbaum Center at Washington University in St. Louis. The Weidenbaum Center (formerly the Center for the Study of American Business) began exclusively distributing the report in 1977.

[17] S. Dudley and W. Warren, "Moderating Regulatory Growth: An Analysis of the U.S. Budget for Fiscal Years 2006 and 2007, p. 1.

[18] Ibid, p. 2.

[19] Ibid.

[20] J.W. Crews, *Ten Thousand Commandments*: *An Annual Snapshot of the Federal Regulatory State,* p. 1.

[21] S. Dudley and W. Warren, "Moderating Regulatory Growth: An Analysis of the U.S. Budget for Fiscal Years 2006 and 2007, p. 1.
[22] L. Gould, *Grand Old Party: A History of the Republicans* and J. Gerring, *Party Ideologies in America, 1928-1996.*
[23] Lowi, *The End of the Republican era, pp. 106, 138-139.*
[24] *These statistics were extracted from and validated through secondary sources of data:* B. Ahern, Government Spending = Nearly One-Third U.S. Economy. The Heartland Institute (1999) Retrieved November 25, 2005, from *http://www.heartland.org /archives/ia/ janfeb99/taxes.htm*; J.F. Cogan J. F., Federal budget The Library of Economics and Liberty *(1991). Retrieved November 2, 2005, from http://www.econlib.org/library/Enc/FederalBudget. html;* R. Higgs, "Where figures fail: Measuring the growth of big government," *The Independent Institute* (March 1, 1983).. Retrieved November 30, 2005, from *http://www.independent.org /newsroom/ article.asp?id=1358*; B.M. Riedl, B.M. *(2005, October 7)."Federal spending-By the numbers," H*eritage Foundation (October 7, 2005). *Retrieved November 29, 2005, from http://www.heritage.org/Research/Budget/loader.cfm?url=/commonspot/security/getfile .cfmandPageID=83722;* S. Slivinski, "The Grand Old Spending Party How Republicans Became Big Spenders," *Policy Analysis.* 543 (May 3, 2005) Retrieved, June 7, 2006, from *https://www.cato.org/pubs/pas/ pa543.pdf*; and C.E. Steuerle, and G. Mermin, *The big-spending presidents* (April 10, 1997). Retrieved on November 29, 2005, from *http://www.urban.org/url.cfm? ID=307052.*
[25] S. Slivinski, "The Grand Old Spending Party How Republicans Became Big Spenders," pp. 1-2.
[26] D.N. Weil, "Fiscal Policy,". *The Concise Encyclopedia of Economics.* Library of Economics and Liberty (n.d.). Retrieved October 18, 2007, from *http://www. econlib.org/library/Enc/FiscalPolicy.html.*
[27] L.J.Kotlikoff, "The Federal Deficit," *The Concise Encyclopedia of Economics.* Library of Economics and Liberty (n.d.). Retrieved October 18, 2007 from *http://www.econlib.org/library/ Enc/FederalDeficit.html.*
[28] F.D. Roosevelt, *Inaugural Address, March 4, 1933.* Retrieved November 30, 2005, from *http://www.presidency.ucsb.edu/ws/index.php?pid=14473.*
[29] D. Whitney, *The American Presidents* (Pleasantville, NY: The Reader's Digest Association, Inc., 1996).
[30] Electronic Frontier Foundation, *The USA Patriot Act* (n.d.). Retrieved November 28, 2005, from *http://www.eff.org/patriot/.*
[31] S. Dudley and W. Warren, "Moderating Regulatory Growth: An Analysis of the U.S. Budget for Fiscal Years 2006 and 2007.
[32] Ibid.
[33] Ibid.
[34] Ibid.
[35] J.W. Crews, *Ten Thousand Commandments*: *An Annual Snapshot of the Federal Regulatory State.*
[36] S. Dudley and W. Warren, "Moderating Regulatory Growth: An Analysis of the U.S. Budget for Fiscal Years 2006 and 2007.

[37] S. Hayward, "Nixon Reconsidered," *The Age of Reagan: A Chronicle of the Closing Decades of the American Century* (August, 1999). Retrieved July 1, 2007, from *http://www.ashbrook.org/publicat/dialogue/hayward.html*

[38] K.N. Bickers, K.N., "Programmatic Expansion of the U. S. Government." *The Western Political Quarterly*, 44 (1991), 891-914. Retrieved June 23, 2007, from *http://0-www.jstor.org.skyline.cudenver.edu/*

[39] D. Stockman, *The Triumph of Politics: The story of the Reagan revolution* (NY: Avon Books, 1987).

[40] R.D. Renka, Party Control of the Presidency and Congress, 1933-2006 (UI320 - The Modern Presidency and PS365 - U.S. Congress) *n.d. Retrieved November 30, 2005,* from *http://cstl-cla.semo.edu/renka/ui320-75/presandcongress.asp*

[41] Ibid.

[42] R.S. Conley and A. Kreppel, *Presidential Influence: The Success of Vetoes and Veto Overrides*. Presented at the American Political Science Association, Atlanta, GA (1999). Retrieved October 2, 2005, from http://web.clas.ufl.edu/users/kreppel/types.PDF.

[43] V. de Rugy, *Spending Under President George W. Bush. Tax and Other Fiscal Policy*. Government Accountability Project, Working Papers, Mercatus Center, George Mason University (March 16, 2009).. Retrieved May 1, 2009, from *http://www.mercatus.org/PublicationDetails.aspx?id=26426;* J. Frankel, J. COMMENT and ANALYSIS - Trading places - Republicans' economic policy is now closer to that associated with *Financial Times* (September 13, 2002).. Retrieved March 3, 2009, from *http://www.cid.harvard.edu/cidinthenews/articles/FT_091302.html*; and S. Slivinski, "The Grand Old Spending Party How Republicans Became Big Spenders."

[44] Ibid.

[45] L. Gould, *Grand Old Party: A History of the Republicans* and J. Gerring, *Party Ideologies in America, 1928-1996*.

[46] V. de Rugy, *Spending Under President George W. Bush. Tax and Other Fiscal Policy;* J. Frankel, J. COMMENT and ANALYSIS,and S. Slivinski, "The Grand Old Spending Party How Republicans Became Big Spenders."

[47] J. Micklethwait and A. Wooldridge, *The right nation: Conservative power in America* and K. Phillips, *American Theocracy*.

APPENDIX A

Table A. Summary of Receipts, Outlays and Surpluses or Deficits Current Dollars, Constant [FY 2000] Dollars and As Percentage of GDP: 1953–1976)

President	FY	In Constant (FY 2000 Dollars)					As Percentages of GDP		
		Receipts	Annual % Change	Outlays	Annual % Change	Surplus or Deficit (−)	Receipts	Outlays	Surplus or Deficit (−)
Eisenhower	1953	508.8	-1.6%	556.3	5.2%	-47.5	18.7	20.4	−1.7
	1954	494.7	-2.8%	502.9	-9.6%	-8.2	18.5	18.8	−0.3
	1955	449.8	-9.1%	470.4	-6.5%	-20.6	16.6	17.3	−0.8
	1956	488.8	8.7%	462.9	-1.6%	25.9	17.5	16.5	0.9
	1957	499.6	2.2%	478.3	3.3%	21.3	17.8	17	0.8
	1958	472.1	-5.5%	488.5	2.1%	-16.4	17.3	17.9	−0.6
	1959	453.9	-3.9%	527.5	8.0%	-73.6	16.1	18.7	−2.6
	1960	528.5	16.4%	526.8	-0.1%	1.7	17.9	17.8	0.1
	Total % Δ		3.9%		-5.3%				
	Avg. Yrly % Δ		0.5%		-0.7%				
Johnson	1961	525.8	-0.5%	544.4	3.3%	-18.6	17.8	18.4	−0.6
	1962	552.8	5.1%	592.5	8.8%	-39.6	17.6	18.8	−1.3
	1963	568.9	2.9%	594.3	0.3%	-25.4	17.8	18.6	−0.8
	1964	592.7	4.2%	623.8	5.0%	-31.1	17.6	18.5	−0.9
	1965	605.9	2.2%	613.2	-1.7%	-7.3	17	17.2	−0.2
	1966	662.8	9.4%	681.5	11.1%	-18.7	17.4	17.9	−0.5
	1967	734.6	10.8%	777.2	14.0%	-42.7	18.3	19.4	−1.1
	1968	727.4	-1.0%	847	9.0%	-119.6	17.7	20.6	−2.9
	Total % Δ		38.3%		55.6%				
	Avg. Yrly % Δ		4.1%		5.7%				
Nixon	1969	838	15.2%	823.5	-2.8%	14.5	19.7	19.4	0.3
	1970	815.9	-2.6%	828	0.5%	-12.0	19	19.3	−0.3
	1971	742.9	-8.9%	834.3	0.8%	-91.4	17.3	19.5	−2.1
	1972	770.7	3.7%	857.6	2.8%	-86.9	17.6	19.6	−2.0
	1973	814.7	5.7%	867.3	1.1%	-52.6	17.7	18.8	−1.1
	1974	857.4	5.2%	877.4	1.2%	-20.0	18.3	18.7	−0.4
	Total % Δ (69-74)		2.3%		6.5%				
	Avg. Yrly % Δ		0.4%		1.1%				
Ford	1975	824.7	-3.8%	982.1	11.9%	-157.3	17.9	21.3	−3.4
	1976	818.8	-0.7%	1,021.40	4.0%	-202.6	17.2	21.4	−4.2
	Total % Δ (75-76)		-0.7%		4.0%				
	Avg. Yrly % Δ		-0.4%		2.0%				
	Total % Δ(69-76)		2.3%		-24%				
	Avg. Yrly % Δ		-0.3%		2.7%				

Source: White House Office of Management and Budget (http://www.whitehouse.gov/omb/budget/fy2006/ pdf/hist.pdf). pp. 25-26.

Table A. Summary of Federal Debt as a Percentage of GDP (1976-2006)

President	FY	Receipts (FY 2000 Dollars)	Annual % Change	Outlays	Annual % Change	Surplus or Deficit (−)	Receipts (% GDP)	Outlays (% GDP)	Surplus or Deficit (−)
Carter	1977	903.8	10.4%	1,040.20	1.8%	−136.4	18	20.7	−2.7
	1978	952.5	5.4%	1,093.60	5.1%	−141.1	18	20.7	−2.7
	1979	1,017.80	6.9%	1,107.30	1.3%	−89.5	18.5	20.2	−1.6
	1980	1,028.30	1.0%	1,175.10	6.1%	−146.8	19	21.7	−2.7
	Total % Δ		13.8%		13.0%				
	Avg. Yrly % Δ		3.3%		3.1%				
Reagan	1981	1,077.40	4.8%	1,219.40	3.8%	−142.0	19.6	22.2	−2.6
	1982	1,036.90	-3.8%	1,251.70	2.6%	−214.8	19.1	23.1	−4.0
	1983	961.7	-7.3%	1,294.40	3.4%	−332.7	17.5	23.5	−6.0
	1984	1,016.80	5.7%	1,299.50	0.4%	−282.8	17.4	22.2	−4.8
	1985	1,082.60	6.5%	1,395.70	7.4%	−313.1	17.7	22.9	−5.1
	1986	1,107.30	2.3%	1,425.70	2.1%	−318.4	17.4	22.4	−5.0
	1987	1,196.10	8.0%	1,405.70	-1.4%	−209.6	18.4	21.6	−3.2
	1988	1,235.60	3.3%	1,446.50	2.9%	−210.9	18.2	21.3	−3.1
	Total % Δ		14.7%		18.6%				
	Avg. Yrly % Δ		1.7%		2.2%				
G.H. Bush	1989	1,298.90	5.1%	1,498.90	3.6%	−200.0	18.4	21.2	−2.8
	1990	1,309.30	0.8%	1,589.80	6.1%	−280.6	18	21.8	−3.9
	1991	1,282.60	-2.0%	1,609.90	1.3%	−327.3	17.8	22.3	−4.5
	1992	1,282.70	0.0%	1,623.90	0.9%	−341.2	17.5	22.1	−4.7
	Total % Δ		-1.2%		12.3%				
	Avg. Yrly % Δ		-0.3%		2.0%				
Clinton	1993	1,323.10	3.2%	1,615.50	-0.5%	−292.4	17.6	21.4	−3.9
	1994	1,413.90	6.9%	1,642.20	1.7%	−228.3	18.1	21	−2.9
	1995	1,482.30	4.8%	1,662.10	1.2%	−179.8	18.5	20.7	−2.2
	1996	1,557.70	5.1%	1,673.00	0.6%	−115.2	18.9	20.3	−1.4
	1997	1,661.00	6.6%	1,684.10	0.7%	−23.1	19.3	19.6	−0.3
	1998	1,793.00	7.9%	1,720.90	2.2%	72.1	20	19.2	0.8
	1999	1,874.70	4.6%	1,745.90	1.5%	128.8	20	18.7	1.4
	2000	2,025.20	8.0%	1,789.10	2.5%	236.2	20.9	18.4	2.4
	Total % Δ		53.1%		10.8%				
	Avg. Yrly % Δ		5.5%		1.3%				
G.W. Bush	2001	1,945.90	-3.9%	1,820.60	1.8%	125.2	19.8	18.5	1.3
	2002	1,778.60	-8.6%	1,930.10	6.0%	−151.5	17.8	19.4	−1.5
	2003	1,668.90	-6.3%	2,022.40	4.6%	−353.5	16.4	19.9	−3.5
	2004	1,722.10	2.5%	2,099.70	3.2%	−377.5	16.3	19.8	−3.6
	2005	1,888.2	10.6%	2,167.3	4.1%	-279.1			

President	FY	In Constant (FY 2000 Dollars)					As Percentages of GDP		
		Receipts	Annual % Change	Outlays	Annual % Change	Surplus or Deficit (–)	Receipts	Outlays	Surplus or Deficit (–)
	2006	2,037.1	7.9%	2,247.1	3.7%	-210.0			
	Total % Δ		4.7%		23.4%				
	Avg. Yrly % Δ		0.8%		3.6%				

Source: White House OMB (http://www.whitehouse.gov/omb/budget/fy2008/pdf/hist.pdf). pp. 25-26.

APPENDIX B

Table B. Summary of Federal Debt as a Percentage of GDP: 1953–1976)

End of Fiscal Year	In Millions of Dollars	As Percentages of GDP				
	Gross Federal Debt	Gross Federal Debt	Less: Held by Federal Government Accounts	Equals: Held by the Public		
				Total	Federal Reserve System	Other
1953	265,963	71.3	12.8	58.6	6.6	51.9
1954	270,812	71.8	12.3	59.5	6.6	52.9
1955	274,366	69.5	12.1	57.4	6.0	51.4
1956	272,693	63.8	11.8	52.0	5.6	46.4
1957	272,252	60.5	11.8	48.7	5.1	43.6
1958	279,666	60.7	11.6	49.2	5.5	43.6
1959	287,465	58.5	10.7	47.8	5.3	42.5
1960	290,525	56.1	10.4	45.7	5.1	40.6
1961	292,648	55.1	10.2	44.9	5.1	39.8
1962	302,928	53.4	9.7	43.7	5.2	38.5
1963	310,324	51.8	9.4	42.4	5.3	37.1
1964	316,059	49.4	9.2	40.1	5.4	34.7
1965	322,318	46.9	9.0	38.0	5.7	32.3
1966	328,498	43.6	8.6	35.0	5.6	29.4
1967	340,445	41.9	9.1	32.8	5.8	27.1
1968	368,685	42.5	9.1	33.4	6.0	27.4
1969	365,769	38.6	9.2	29.3	5.7	23.6
1970	380,921	37.6	9.7	28.0	5.7	22.3
1971	408,176	37.8	9.7	28.1	6.1	22.0
1972	435,936	37.0	9.6	27.4	6.1	21.3
1973	466,291	35.7	9.6	26.1	5.7	20.3
1974	483,893	33.6	9.7	23.9	5.6	18.3
1975	541,925	34.7	9.4	25.3	5.4	19.8
1976	628,970	36.2	8.7	27.5	5.5	22.0
1977	706,398	35.8	8.0	27.8	5.3	22.5
1978	776,602	35.0	7.6	27.4	5.2	22.2

Table B. (Continued)

End of Fiscal Year	In Millions of Dollars — Gross Federal Debt	As Percentages of GDP — Gross Federal Debt	Less: Held by Federal Government Accounts	Equals: Held by the Public — Total	Federal Reserve System	Other
1979	829,467	33.2	7.6	25.6	4.6	21.0
1980	909,041	33.3	7.2	26.1	4.4	21.7
1981		32.6	6.7	25.8	4.1	21.8
1982	1,137,315	35.2	6.6	28.6	4.2	24.5
1983	1,371,660	39.9	6.8	33.1	4.5	28.5
1984	1,564,586	40.7	6.7	34.0	4.0	30.0
1985	1,817,423	43.9	7.5	36.4	4.1	32.3
1986	2,120,501	48.1	8.6	39.4	4.3	35.1
1987	2,345,956	50.5	9.8	40.7	4.6	36.1
1988	2,601,104	51.9	11.0	41.0	4.6	36.4
1989	2,867,800	53.1	12.5	40.6	4.1	36.5
1990	3,206,290	55.9	13.9	42.0	4.1	38.0
1991	3,598,178	60.6	15.3	45.3	4.4	40.9
1992	4,001,787	64.1	16.1	48.1	4.8	43.3
1993	4,351,044	66.2	16.8	49.4	5.0	44.4
1994	4,643,307	66.7	17.4	49.3	5.1	44.2
1995	4,920,586	67.2	18.0	49.2	5.1	44.1
1996	5,181,465	67.3	18.8	48.5	5.1	43.5
1997	5,369,206	65.6	19.5	46.1	5.2	40.9
1998	5,478,189	63.5	20.4	43.1	5.3	37.8
1999	5,605,523	61.4	21.6	39.8	5.4	34.4
2000	5,628,700	58.0	22.9	35.1	5.3	29.9
2001	5,769,881	57.4	24.4	33.0	5.3	27.7
2002	6,198,401	59.7	25.6	34.1	5.8	28.3
2003	6,760,014	62.5	26.3	36.2	6.1	30.1
2004	7,354,673	63.9	26.6	37.3	6.1	31.2
2005	7,905,300	64.4	27.0	37.4	6.0	31.4
2006	8,451,351	64.7	27.7	37.0	5.9	31.1

Source: The Budget for Fiscal Year 2008), Historical Tables, pp. 126-127 http://www.whitehouse.gov/omb/budget/fy2008/pdf/hist.pdf).

APPENDIX C

Table C. Total Staffing of Federal Regulatory Activity
(Fiscal Years, Full-time Equivalent Employment)

1981	Reagan	115,528	29,128	144,656	-1.01	
1982		103,781	28,962	132,743	-8.24	
1983		99,997	27,368	127,365	-4.05	
1984		99,974	27,116	127,090	-0.22	
1985		100,818	26,798	127,616	0.41	
1986		99,961	27,396	127,357	-0.20	
1987		103,347	26,942	130,289	2.30	
1988		108,145	27,617	135,762	4.20	-11.18
1989	GH Bush	115,322	35,746	151,068	11.27	
1990		119,459	33,155	152,614	1.02	
1991		123,247	34,284	157,531	3.22	
1992		130,747	36,971	167,718	6.47	23.54
1993		135,804	37,957	173,761	3.60	
1994		133,487	37,499	170,986	-1.60	
1995		136,016	37,594	173,610	1.53	
1996		136,926	33,611	170,537	-1.77	
1997		132,627	32,313	164,940	-3.28	
1998		139,264	31,848	171,112	3.74	
1999		139,271	32,384	171,655	0.32	
2000		142,539	32,548	175,087	2.00	
2001	GW Bush	140,013	32,270	172,282	-1.60	
2002		152,086	32,436	184,522	7.10	
2003		209,801	31,981	241,782	31.03	
2004		201,675	32,341	234,016	-3.21	33.66
1981	Reagan	115,528	29,128	144,656	-1.01	
1982		103,781	28,962	132,743	-8.24	
1983		99,997	27,368	127,365	-4.05	
1984		99,974	27,116	127,090	-0.22	
1985		100,818	26,798	127,616	0.41	
1986		99,961	27,396	127,357	-0.20	
1987		103,347	26,942	130,289	2.30	
1988		108,145	27,617	135,762	4.20	-11.18
1989	GH Bush	115,322	35,746	151,068	11.27	
1990		119,459	33,155	152,614	1.02	
1991		123,247	34,284	157,531	3.22	
1992		130,747	36,971	167,718	6.47	23.54
1993		135,804	37,957	173,761	3.60	
1994		133,487	37,499	170,986	-1.60	
1995		136,016	37,594	173,610	1.53	
1996		136,926	33,611	170,537	-1.77	
1997		132,627	32,313	164,940	-3.28	
1998		139,264	31,848	171,112	3.74	

1999		139,271	32,384	171,655	0.32	
2000		142,539	32,548	175,087	2.00	
2001	GW Bush	140,013	32,270	172,282	-1.60	
2002		152,086	32,436	184,522	7.10	
2003		209,801	31,981	241,782	31.03	
2004		201,675	32,341	234,016	-3.21	33.66

Source: Weidenbaum Center, Washington University and Mercatus Center at George Mason University. Derived from the *Budget of the United States Government* and related documents, various fiscal years. Numbers may not add to totals due to rounding. Data based on outlays.

APPENDIX D

Table D. Total Spending on Federal Regulatory Activity: Constant Dollars Fiscal Years, Millions of 2000 Dollars)

Year	President	Social Regulation	Economic Regulation	Total	Inc/Dec (%)	Total Period Inc/Dec (%)
1960	Eisenhower	$1,682	$851	$2,533	N/A	
1961		1,978	982	2,960		
1962		2,239	997	3,236		
1963		2,532	1,142	3,674		
1964		2,666	1,215	3,881		
1965		2,680	1,402	4,082		
1966		2,786	1,333	4,119		
1967		2,946	1,440	4,385	6.46	
1968		3,297	1,505	4,802	9.51	
1969	Nixon	3,663	1,541	5,204	8.37	
1970		3,985	1,768	5,753	10.55	
1971		4,939	1,940	6,879	19.57	
1972		6,050	1,833	7,883	14.6	
1973		7,937	1,526	9,463	20	97.06
1974	Ford	7,607	1,748	9,355	-1.14	
1975		8,227	2,008	10,235	9.41	
1976		9,207	2,147	11,353	10.92	19.97
1977		9,720	2,219	11,939		
1978		10,010	2,100	12,110		
1979		10,422	2,093	12,515		
1980		11,205	2,284	13,489		
1981	Reagan	10,887	2,045	12,932	-4.13	
1982		9,897	2,196	12,093	6.49	
1983		9,950	2,147	12,097	.03	
1984		10,121	2,242	12,363	2.2	
1985		10,348	2,431	12,779	3.36	
1986		10,550	2,801	13,350	4.47	
1987		11,275	2,418	13,693	2.57	
1988		12,103	2,775	14,878	8.65	10.3

Year	President	Social Regulation	Economic Regulation	Total	Inc/Dec (%)	Total Period Inc/Dec (%)
1989	GH Bush	12,923	2,883	15,806	6.24	
1990		13,644	3,117	16,761	6.04	
1991		14,922	2,999	17,921	5.7	
1992		16,313	3,290	19,603	9.39	31.76
1993		16,411	3,763	20,173		
1994		16,654	3,505	20,159		
1995		17,054	4,075	21,129		
1996		16,883	3,761	20,644		
1997		17,688	4,060	21,748		
1998		19,114	3,972	23,086		
1999		20,040	4,172	24,212		
2000		20,912	4,383	25,295		
2001	GW Bush	21,754	4,486	26,240	8.02	
2002		25,778	4,822	30,600	16.62	
2003		33,433	4,775	38,208	24.86	
2004		29,580	5,185	34,765	-9.01	37.44

Source: Weidenbaum Center, Washington University and Mercatus Center at George Mason University. Derived from the *Budget of the United States Government* and related documents, various fiscal years. Numbers may not add to totals due to rounding. Data based on outlays.

Chapter 18

POLITICIANS UNDER THE MICROSCOPE: EYE BLINK RATES DURING THE FIRST BUSH-KERRY DEBATE

Patrick A. Stewart and Jonathan "Chad" Mosely

ABSTRACT

While Presidential debates during the television era have been more accurately described as "side-by-side press conferences," they offer viewers the opportunity to assess the personality, character and intellect of contending candidates. The 2004 Presidential debates offered just such an opportunity as President George W. Bush and Senator John F. Kerry squared off in a series of three debates in the month before the election. The first debate, focusing on foreign policy, was seen as a "win" for Senator Kerry as President Bush was perceived as anxious by the press and the public in post-debate opinion surveys, while Kerry was seen as more "Presidential." Verbal response has typically been the focus of previous studies, with the candidate providing the most compelling arguments perceived as winning; however, nonverbal behavior has increasingly been seen as key for candidate assessment. Therefore, this study analyzes nonverbal behavior that is reliable in communicating emotional state, that of eye blink rates. Specifically, we measure eye blinks for each candidate in 5-second increments over the course of the debate and analyze it in the context of debate behavior.

There is no doubt that in close elections televised debates can influence electoral outcomes by placing candidates in the spotlight, exposing their strengths and weaknesses in the resulting glare. While presumably focusing on policy positions and intellectual capabilities, modern Presidential debates (and media coverage) arguably focus instead on how "Presidential" candidates look and act. This symbolic theater provided by the debate influences voting outcomes both directly through voter perceptions of the candidates and indirectly through media evaluations of candidate performance. [1]

According to Schrott and Lanoues' analysis of public opinion polling data, presidential debates are not won so much as lost. [2] How they are lost often hinges on verbal mistakes or nonverbal miscues. That debates can hinder presidential aspirations can be traced to the Kennedy-Nixon debates in which a youthful JFK impressed television viewers with his on-screen performance against a haggard Richard Nixon with a "5 o'clock shadow" in a debate that seemed to be determined more by appearances than by the responses themselves. [3] Recent examples include Michael Dukakis' detached response during one of his 1988 Presidential debates with George H.W. Bush to a question asking what he would do if his wife was raped, George H.W. Bush's looking at his watch during Bill Clinton's speaking turn in one of their 1992 debates, and Al Gore sighing during his debate with George W. Bush in 2000. [4] These actions, and more importantly, the media's coverage of them, resulted in changes to the candidates' electoral fortunes.

As a result of the negative effects debates can have on electoral hopes, campaign staffs have attempted to protect their candidate by setting ground rules for the debate. These ground rules presumably lead to candidates being presented in as positive a light as possible while protecting them from potential blunders by structuring how candidates are presented. [5] Due in part to this, recent Presidential debates appear to be less a debate and more side-by-side press conferences with neither candidate directly confronting the other. [6]

The influence of debates on electoral outcomes is a little disputed fact of politics, with Presidential debates being studied by political scientists since at least 1948. While studies considering changes in issue knowledge and attitude toward candidates and their positions find that debates tend to reinforce previous preferences, debates still may sway the opinions of undecided voters. [7] While the quality of arguments put forth by the candidates certainly influences opinions, whether the candidates appear presidential in demeanor and style plays an important role. [8] This is the case, especially in the ever-so important post-debate press analyses that often define who is the winning or losing candidate of the debate. [9]

Key for these public perceptions is the ability of candidates to nonverbally communicate their capacity for leadership. Nonverbal actions reveal an extensive amount of information about a candidate with concomitant effects upon evaluation. According to Jarman in his moment-by-moment analysis of the second George W. Bush-John Kerry debate in 2004: "there is reason to believe that the audience is reacting to the speaker rather than the substance of the comments." [10] Nonverbal information is salient because our political leaders are chosen not just on their policy positions, but also on their appearance and actions. In other words, we likely choose our leaders on the basis of whether they look and act like a leader. [11]

Therefore, while political party plays a powerful role in how individuals determine who wins and loses debates, and policy positions likewise play a role, ultimately it may be how a candidate acts that determines the outcome of a presidential debate. Research considering the impact of nonverbal behaviors during presidential debates on candidate evaluation suggests that it plays an important role, especially when the material is presented in different modalities (text, audio, visual, audiovisual) and that eye blinks are a robust indicator of cognitive effort and emotional stress that are readily apparent to the viewers.[12] Specifically, Exline found that increased eye blink rates negatively affected subject judgments of competency when segments from President Gerald Ford and then-challenger Jimmy Carters' first debate in 1976 were assessed. [13] Likewise, Patterson et al. found that increased eye blink rates by challenger Walter Mondale, in comparison with incumbent President Ronald

Reagan during their second Presidential debate of 1984, was associated with lower evaluations. [14]

The role played by nonverbal behavior, such as eye blinks, in the public's response to Bush and Kerry in their first debate is open for discussion. What is apparent from the first debate is that John Kerry came away the prohibitive winner as post-debate opinion polls showed him winning the debate and reversing the pre-debate public opinion lead held by George W. Bush. [15] While many factors played a role in this reversal, the nonverbal performance of both candidates was implicated by critics and the press with Kerry characterized as acting more "Presidential" than the sitting President, George W. Bush. [16] While this has been attributed to Bush's continual scowling, his eye blink rate, as this study shows, was exceptionally high. Therefore, in this study we consider one robust nonverbal indicator of emotional state and cognitive effort, eye blink rates, and analyze the two candidates and their behavior.

EYE BLINK RATES

Eye blink rates, which may be characterized as a subset of the nonverbal channel of facial expressions, are reliable indicators of psychological and physiological states due to the lesser amount of control that may be exercised over them. Unlike verbal activity, in which subjects are likely to stay "on-message" with relatively minimal effort, the level of cognitive effort necessary for monitoring and controlling of facial expressions and voice tone, pitch and speech rate makes controlling these nonverbal channels, for the most part, prohibitively difficult. This, combined with the automatic fixation of attention on the eyes in attempts to ascertain, attain and/or maintain social attention, makes the eyes a theoretically compelling topic with practical applications. The information eyes provide includes such things as attention, arousal and cognitive activity. [17] As such, we can expect eye blinks to provide insights into a subject's emotional state and cognitive efforts. Although subjects may control eye blinks, they are largely an involuntary response and are readily observable. [18]

Three different types of eye blinks have been identified: reflex blinks which protect the eye from environmental intrusions such as flashes of light, air puffs and foreign articles; voluntary blinks in which there is a modicum of control; and spontaneous/endogenous blinks which are defined as occurring in the absence of identifiable stimuli and being influenced by perceptions or information processing. [19] In the case of endogenous eye blinks, they can provide a reliable indicator of an individual's internal state in terms of level of cognitive activity and/or emotional state due to the relative difficulty of monitoring and controlling the blinks themselves. As stated by Stern et al., "One advantage of the endogenous blink measure is the possibility it offers of baseline assessment. Alterations in the rate, form, or duration of blinks, and the temporal distribution of blinks may be evaluated as changes in either direction from a pre-established level." [20]

Studies suggest that while the baseline blink rate tends to range from 12 to 18 blinks a minute. [21] A variety of factors can influence eye blink rates. The activity an individual is engaged in can lead to increased or decreased eye blink rates. Individuals engaged in a visual task such as operating a moving vehicle, [22] playing videogames, performing a surgical operation, [23] or reading [24] exhibited reduced eye blink rates as they focus on the task at hand.

Blink rate also changes with increased cognitive demands. Speech/conversation and memory tasks lead to increased blink rates. [25] A fascinating study by Mann, Vrij and Bull analyzing videotaped police interviews of subjects compared truthful and deceptive behaviors and found eye blink rates provided a significant indicator of lying/truth-telling. [26] Specifically, over eighty percent of participants blinked less during deceptive behavior than when telling the truth, possibly in hopes of appearing to tell the truth and not indicate emotional stress.

The lack of eye blinks may not just indicate cognitive activity or visual fixation on a task but it may indicate a displayed threat. Threatening stares, in which there are no or few eye blinks and the eyes are focused on the target of displeasure, are a cross-cultural phenomena. Threat stares are present during all stages of life, can be seen in a range of animals as well as humans and are present in the full range of human dominance interactions, including religion. [27] In the case of political competition, threat stares can be expected as the candidates battle to assert dominance. [28]

In terms of emotional state, research dating back to 1928 suggests increasing excitement, anger or anxiety leads to increased blink rate. [29] More recent research suggests blink rate decreases with guilt and increases with emotional arousal and anxiety, with the size of the increase dependent on whether there is visual or auditory stimuli involved. [30] Likewise, research recounted by Stern suggests that the perception of level of threat, such as when witnesses were interrogated in the court of law by unfriendly or friendly lawyers, leads to elevated blink rates when under conditions of high threat. [31]

Perhaps most important is research about Presidential debates suggesting public opinion "winners" and "losers" may, in part, be differentiated by blink rates, with the lower blink rate of "calmer" candidates besting those of "anxious" candidates with higher eye blink rates. [32] Exline's research considering the first debate between President Gerald Ford and challenger Jimmy Carter found differences in the blink rates of the two candidates based upon whether they were responding to moderator questions or rebutting their opponent's response. Ford's blink rate was higher during his rebuttal of Carter's question responses than during his response to moderator questions, whereas with Carter, the inverse was the case. This suggests that for incumbent Ford there was greater cognitive activity and/or "tension leakage" responding to his challenger than defending his record, whereas for Carter, there was greater comfort responding to Ford than to questions from the moderator. [33]

Therefore, while we cannot directly access the innermost thoughts and feelings of political figures, we can infer information about their cognitive activity and emotional state by observing their nonverbal expressions. To this end, this study considers eye blink rates, a robust indicator of cognitive activity and emotional state. By analyzing patterns of George W. Bush's and John F. Kerry's eye blink rates in the first Presidential debate of 2004, we hope to develop inferences concerning the candidates' states as to their overall state of mind and what topics were of greatest concern for them.

METHODS

Data analyzed in this study are taken from C-SPAN's coverage of the first 2004 Presidential debate between President George W. Bush and Senator John F. Kerry. This debate focused on foreign policy issues and was held in Coral Gables, Florida at the University of Miami on the evening of September 30, 2004. It showed both Presidential candidates side-by-side as they answered questions from moderator Jim Lehrer and rebutted each other's responses.

The research design used here is a content analysis of nonverbal behavior by the Presidential candidates. We analyze George W. Bush's and John F. Kerry's nonverbal behavior with the units of analysis consecutive five second sequences starting when the candidates stepped to the podium and ending with their concluding statements. Two coders, each viewing one of the candidates, observed and counted eye blinks. An eye blink is defined here as a "complete blink, in which the upper lid covers more than two-thirds of the cornea." [34]

Due to this being an hour and a half event, there were a total of 1009 five second units per candidate in the side-by-side analysis. While an attempt was made to code every eye blink of each candidate, the behavior of each of the candidates precluded this. Both President George W. Bush and Senator John F. Kerry looked down or away from the camera at various points in the debate. Specifically, President Bush looked away from the camera 2.8 percent of the time while Senator Kerry looked down/away 16.5 percent of the time.

Following protocols of previous nonverbal behavioral studies in which two coders were used to assess convergence of findings by coding 10-25% of all data collected, inter-coder reliability was assessed here by randomly sampling ~10% of the dataset. [35] These 107 cases were then coded by an independent coder. Findings suggest a high degree of reliability in coding both Presidential candidates' eye blinks. President Bush's eye blink inter-coder reliability was quite high, with a Cronbach's Alpha of .917 for the 98 codeable 5-second units ($r=.851$). Likewise, Senator Kerry's inter-coder reliability was high, with a Cronbach's Alpha of .912 for 86 codeable units ($r=.839$). These results are well within expected parameters of previous studies of greater than 80% agreement for nonverbal behavior and comparable with Exline' study. [36]

To analyze behavioral differences between the two candidates, we replicate Exline's study of the first Ford-Carter debate by analyzing differences in candidate blink rates during their responses to moderator questions and rebuttals of their opponent's statements. Furthermore, because we were able to code listening eye blink rate due to the split-screen presentation of the debate, we analyze candidate response to opponent assertions. [37]

FINDINGS

The blink rates for the candidates range from 0 to 13 blinks per five seconds for President George W. Bush and 0 to 9 blinks for the challenger, John F. Kerry. The average eye blink rate for President Bush was 3.62 (SD = 2.23) every 5 seconds, or 43.44 per minute, while that of Senator Kerry was 3.30 (SD = 1.57), or 39.6 blinks every minute. When an independent samples t-test is run, findings suggest there is a highly significant difference in the eye blink rates of the two candidates (df = 1874; t = -3.5398, p>.001), with President Bush exceeding Senator Kerry's blink rate.

Analysis of whether there was a difference in President George W. Bush's blink rates based upon whether he was responding to a moderator question, rebutting a statement by John Kerry, or just listening was carried out using analysis of variance (ANOVA). The overall equation was statistically significant, $F(2, 1006) = 2.5333$, $p = .030$, albeit with a very weak $\eta^2 = .007$.

Comparisons between the response conditions were made using the Tukey HSD test and suggest an interesting, if not anomalous, pattern of behavior by President Bush. Specifically, President Bush's blink rates while listening ($M = 3.57$) were not significantly different during his rebuttals to Senator Kerry's assertions ($M = 3.42$, $p = .662$), and were only marginally significant in response to the moderator's questions ($M = 3.94$, $p = .088$). The only significant difference in the equation was the difference in Bush's blink rates when he was responding to moderator Jim Lehrer's questions when compared to his blink rates during his rebuttals ($p = .030$). Overall, Bush blink was elevated, 42.84 blinks per minute while listening, 47.28 blinks while responding to Lehrer, and 41.04 blinks while rebutting Kerry.

Senator Kerry, for his part, exhibited what could be considered the hypothesized pattern of response. When ANOVA was run, findings suggest highly significant differences for the overall equation, $F(2, 864) = 74.027$, $p < .001$. Furthermore, the effect size was much greater than President Bush's equation, $\eta^2 = .146$.

Comparisons made suggest highly significant differences based upon type of speaking turn. Specifically, Kerry's blink rate when listening ($M = 2.65$) of 31.8 blinks per minute was significantly lower than when he was responding to Lehrer's questions ($M = 3.60$, $p < .001$) or rebutting Bush's assertions ($M = 4.023$, $p < .001$). Furthermore, Kerry's blink rate was significantly higher during his rebuttals, at 48.36 blinks per minute, when compared with his responses to moderator questions ($p < .005$), with a blink rate of 43.2 times every minute.

DISCUSSION

The role of eye blink rates as a largely involuntary indicator of cognitive activity and emotional stress finds a level of support here as the two presidential candidates exhibit differential blink rates depending on the activity they are engaged in. This is especially the case with highly stressful presidential debates, particularly the first one in which candidates face off against each other. While it may be difficult, if not impossible, to know what a politician is thinking or their exact emotional state, analysis of their behavior(s) provides an insight into what internal state they may be experiencing.

When compared with previous studies of eye blink rates, the blink rates of both candidates were substantially higher than the norm of the studies reviewed above. However, when compared with the only published study of eye blink rates during presidential debates, both Bush (44.16) and Kerry (45.72) acquit themselves well during their speaking turns, with comparable blink rates per minute to that of debate winner Jimmy Carter (44.4 blinks per minute), and rates much lower than debate loser Gerald Ford (57.0 blinks per minute). [38] This elevation can be expected, as Presidential debates are highly competitive events that are both cognitively and emotionally demanding.

However, details make the difference. Senator Kerry's eye blink rate during his response to moderator questions suggests he was relatively calmer than during his rebuttals to President Bush's responses. Furthermore, when his blink rates while listening are compared to those when responding, findings fall in line with expectations based upon prior studies. Interestingly, John Kerry's pattern of response resembles that of President Gerald Ford's, that of an incumbent that is likely confident in their positions, but with elevated emotional and cognitive response to challenger assertions during rebuttals.

While President Bush's eye blink rate was lower than Senator Kerry's during their speaking turns, his blink rate was greatly elevated while he was listening, to the point it was anomalous. Whether the increased eye blink rate was due to increased cognitive activity, emotional response of arousal, anxiety or anger in response to the threat posed by his challenger, or other factors, is open for discussion. The only difference was in George W. Bush's eye blink rates when responding to the debate moderator, which were elevated when compared to his rebuttals of John Kerry, suggesting either increased cognitive activity or emotional stress.

The difference in blink rates between the two men may be, in part, due greater visibility of President Bush's face during the debate. Not only does the split-screen view in the debate, with the two candidate's faces presented side-by-side, provide the viewer with a comparative perspective, when missing data is considered on the basis of whether the candidate was listening or talking, Kerry does a better job of masking non-verbal response than does Bush. Specifically, Kerry looks down or away from the camera nearly a third of the time while listening (31.1%) while Bush is looks down/away only 4.9 percent of the time while listening. [39]

The ability of either candidate to successfully mask elevated eye blink rates may have made the difference between winning or losing. News analysis and public opinion surveys of those who watched the first Presidential debate suggests that Senator Kerry appeared to do a better job. [40] While the verbal content of both President Bush's and Senator Kerry's answers, comments and responses should certainly not be discounted, neither should their non-verbal activity, which has been shown to greatly influence public perception. [41] This is especially apparent when comparing Kerry and Bush, as President Bush's eye blink rates and other non-verbal actions made him appear to be anxious and at times angry, whereas Kerry seemed calmer. Even though President Bush's eye blink rate while speaking was slightly lower than Senator Kerry's, Bush's overall eye blink rates were higher than Kerry's, especially when Bush was listening to Kerry. While Kerry indeed might have had higher eye blink rates when he was listening, and hence higher levels of anxiety, his tendency to look down and away from the camera when listening to President Bush's response, which was nearly a third of the time, effectively masked his emotional response in terms of facial affect.

DEBATE ANALYSIS

Analysis of the Presidential candidates' performance during the debate was carried out by considering the mean eye blink rates and their standard deviation during candidates speaking turns. The analytic decision rule of considering speaking turns near or above one standard deviation over or below the mean eye blink rate is based on 5-second units when the candidates are either speaking or listening. Although this is a conservative judgment, it allows us to focus on those speaking turns where there is a sustained increase or decrease in eye blink rates. While the length of their speaking turns vary, analysis by considering those speaking turns near or above/below one-standard deviation from the mean provides cues for analysis of the issues being discussed and how the candidates responded. The expectation is that during the speaking turns in which the candidates exhibited higher eye blink rates, the candidates are experiencing higher levels of excitement, anger, or anxiety and that when lower eye blink rates occur, threat stares may be present.

Senator Kerry's Speech Performance

Analysis of John F. Kerry's trend in eye blink rate during his speaking turns suggests a relatively stable response. Visual analysis of Figure 1 suggests four peaks in his eye blink rate. Two of these peaks are just below one standard deviation above the average eye blink rate of 5.3 blinks in five seconds (63.6 eye blinks per minute), and two of them are just above that rate. The first peak occurred during Kerry's rebuttal to George W. Bush after Kerry's fourth question, which asked whether Kerry thought the United States' involvement in Iraq was a mistake, in light of his stance on the Vietnam War. Here Kerry registered an eye blink rate of 5.00 per five second unit.

Table 1. President Bush & Senator Kerry's Eye Blink Rate per 5 secs

	Question Response	Statement Rebuttal	Listening	Total
Bush Blinks	3.94 (2.51)	3.42 (2.09)	3.57 (2.15)	3.62 (2.23)
Kerry Blinks	3.60 (1.40)	4.05 (1.57)	2.65 (1.41)	3.30 (1.57)

Kerry's specific rebuttal attacked George W. Bush's claims of extensive coalition building and United Nations involvement in Iraq, stating that "It was always American run" and that "Secondly, when we went in, there were three countries: Great Britain, Australia and the United States. That's not a grand coalition".

The second peak eye blink rate of 5.17 (62.04 EBR per minute) occurred during Kerry's rebuttal to Bush after Senator Kerry's sixth question. This rebuttal, which occurred 50 minutes into the debate, dealt with Kerry's plan for ending U.S. military involvement in Iraq. His rebuttal attacked Bush's mode of bringing freedom to Iraq, stating: "the best-case scenario, more of the same of what we see today; worst-case scenario, civil war."

The third and fourth peaks both occurred towards the end of the debate and were both above one standard deviation from the average at an eye blink rate of 5.00. The third peak occurred when Kerry rebutted Bush's response to Kerry's final question which concerned nuclear proliferation and the high priority it held for both candidates. With his rebuttal, Kerry attacked President Bush's pace in dealing with nuclear proliferation in North Korea and Iran and the securing of Russian weapons. The fourth and final peak occurred when Kerry rebutted Bush on the President's final question. While this question dealt with Vladimir Putin's abuse of power in Russia, Kerry redirected his comments to the previous question concerning bilateral talks with North Korea, attacking President Bush's credibility. Specifically, he stated "this is the president who said 'There were weapons of mass destruction,' said 'Mission accomplished,' said we could fight the war on the cheap – none of which were true."

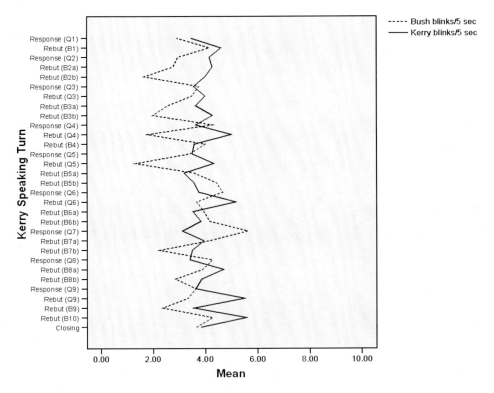

Figure 1. Eye Blink Rates During Kerry's Speaking Turn.

John Kerry's eye blink rate peaked only one time while listening to Jim Lehrer (see Figure 2). This occurred towards the end of the debate when Lehrer asked for a clarification from both candidates concerning their belief that nuclear proliferation would be "the single most serious threat."

Here, Senator Kerry's eye blink rate was 4.00 per five second unit. His eye blink rate underscores the importance of this topic to Kerry, given his elevated blink rates concerning this topic during his final question and his redirection back to this topic in his rebuttal following Bush's response to his final question.

In only one instance during President Bush's speaking turns did Senator Kerry's average blink rate approach one standard deviation above his mean rate (see Figure 3). In George W. Bush's rebuttal to Kerry's response to his second question, Kerry's eye blink rate increased to just below one standard deviation above the mean eye blink rate with an average of 4.00 per five second unit. Here, Bush attacked Kerry for changing his position concerning the use of force, stating "what my opponent wants you to forget is that he voted to authorize the use of force and now says it's the wrong war at the wrong place at the wrong time."

Overall, Senator Kerry's eye blink rate appears to be elevated when he engaged in attacks on President Bush's foreign policy concerning coalition building in Iraq and nuclear proliferation policy, especially in the latter case. Assessing how Kerry responded to attacks on his policy positions was exceedingly difficult due to Kerry looking down and taking notes for a large proportion of the time Bush was speaking. The one time Kerry's eye blink rate elevated to levels of notice occurred when Bush attacked him for changing his policy position, i.e., the "flip-flop" attacks that had been used extensively by the Bush campaign.

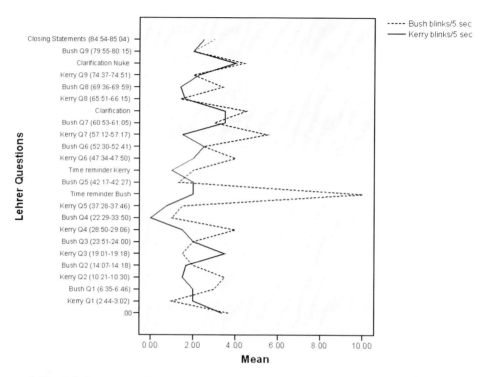

Figure 2. Eye Blink Rates During Lehrer's Speaking Turn.

President Bush's Speech Performance

President Bush exhibited a much higher range of variability in his eye blink rate, both when speaking and while listening. Visual analysis of Figure 3 shows George W. Bush exceeded one standard deviation above the mean blink rate in three of his speaking turns. The first two occurred relatively early in the speech and were rebuttals to Senator Kerry, while the last instance occurred during Bush's closing statement.

The first speaking turn for George W. Bush was also one in which his eye blink rate was elevated, on average, above one standard deviation from his mean blink rate. While the first question, which dealt with whether Senator Kerry could do a better job than President Bush in preventing another "9/11-type terrorist attack in the United States", was not particularly contentious in tone, Bush's eye blink rate averaged 5.64 every five seconds (or 67.68 EBR per minute), as he detailed a successful record by his administration.

The second peak eye blink rate occurred after John Kerry's second question. This question, which followed on comments made by Kerry concerning how Iraq and Afghanistan were being dealt with, asked "what colossal misjudgments in your opinion has President Bush made in these areas?" Kerry's response directly attacked Bush for not going to the United Nations sooner, for not treating war as a "last resort", for "pushing our allies aside" and asserted that Afghanistan, not Iraq, should be the focus of the war on terror. While Bush did not appear to be angered by Kerry during these comments, his response was heated as he defended the commitment of troops to Iraq. George W. Bush's eye blink rate of 7.0 per five second unit (or 84 eye blinks per minute) was underscored by his louder voice tone and aggressive body language, as he emphasized "the world is safer without Saddam Hussein" by gesturing with his right hand.

President Bush's closing comments, while not particularly impassioned in terms of voice tone, body language or verbal content, exhibited his highest average eye-blink rate over a sustained time period. During this two minute time span, Bush's eye-blink rate average 8.7 blinks per five second unit (or 104.4 eye blinks per minute).

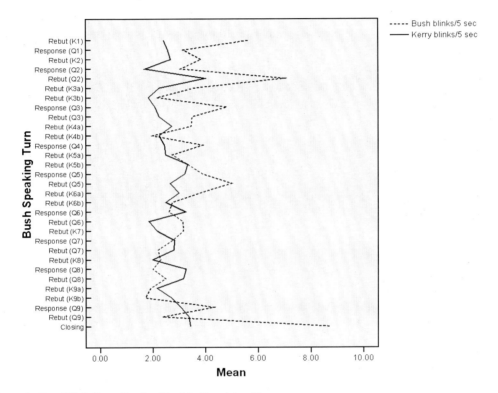

Figure 3. Eye Blink Rate During Bush's Speaking Turn.

Two peak eye blink rates occurred while President Bush listened to moderate Jim Lehrer (see Figure 2). The first occurred when Lehrer gave Bush a time reminder for his rebuttal at the 41:46 mark, with Bush blinking 10 times during a single 5 second unit. This presumably occurred due to John Kerry's accusing Bush of misleading the American public in taking them to war in Iraq, visibly arousing President Bush's ire. Specifically, immediately after Lehrer's time reminder, Bush attacked Kerry's consistency, stating "The only consistent about my opponent's position is he's been inconsistent."

The second peak occurred when Lehrer asked Senator Kerry his seventh question concerning his position on preemptive war. Here Bush averaged 5.62 eye blinks per 5 second unit (or 67.44 EBR per minute). The increased eye blink rate appears to have derived from Kerry's response to the previous question in which he claimed that under Bush the world has gotten more dangerous. During the last few seconds of Kerry's response and during Lehrer's time reminder, Bush jerked his head in an awkward manner twice.

In contrast to the two peaks in Bush's blink rate while listening to Lehrer, there was only one peak in George W. Bush's eye blink rate while he was listening to John Kerry's speaking turns. This peak occurred during Kerry's response to Bush's seventh question and registered 5.62 blinks per 5 second unit. Here, in rebuttal of Bush's response to whether he believed diplomacy and sanctions can resolve the nuclear proliferation problems with North Korea and Iran, Kerry accused President Bush of reversing positions on dialog with North Korea and then not talking to them for two years, during which time they kicked out inspectors and developed nuclear weapons.

Through analysis of both descriptive statistics and consideration of peak eye blink rates, President Bush exhibited a highly aroused disposition during the debate. As sitting President, he came under attack from the challenger, Senator Kerry throughout the debate for his positions and actions. His eye blink rate reflected this, increasing to high levels throughout the debate. Early in the debate this became especially evident as Bush's response to Kerry's questioning his ability to prevent another 9/11-type terrorist attack and his performance in Iraq and Afghanistan led to elevated eye blink rates. Likewise, Bush's increased eye blink rates while listening to Senator Kerry or moderator Jim Lehrer appeared to be in response to Kerry's attacks on Bush's foreign policy decisions. While Bush's eye blink rate peaked during his not particularly impassioned closing statements, this might reflect not the anxiety and/or anger inflamed by Kerry's attacks so much as performance anxiety with a debate that was reported as being won by John Kerry.

CONCLUSION

This study expands on and validates an already extensive research program on eye blink rates that has been building for the better part of a century by applying it to the highly salient topic of presidential debates. [42] In this case we apply the methodology to the first presidential debate between John F. Kerry and George W. Bush, a debate in which President Bush was considered to have given one of the least successful performances since the 1960 presidential debate between Richard Nixon and John F. Kennedy. The findings presented here provide insight into why President Bush may have "lost" this particular debate in terms of public perceptions – his elevated eye blink rate and anomalous eye blink patterns suggest extremely high levels of anxiety and/or cognitive activity. Although presidential debates are understandably highly stressful affairs, in comparison to his opponent, Senator Kerry, President Bush's eye blink rates indicated extremely high levels of stress, especially when listening to his opponent.

While political debates are a much studied phenomena, it is an area that has rarely been studied by focusing on its nonverbal aspects. Due to non-verbal communication being an important, if not the most important, aspect in judging whether a politician has leadership qualities, and thus is competent enough to hold higher office, the lack of research in this area needs to be further redressed. Previous work has done a good job of addressing the role of facial characteristics, facial expressions of emotion, and vocal expressions of emotion in politics; [43] however, little published research has directly considered the eye-blink and its role as indicator of emotional state in the political arena with the exception of Exline and Patterson and colleagues. [44] This study succeeds in establishing a baseline for the Presidential candidates both while they were speaking and while listening to the opposing candidate's responses and attacks and questions from the moderator. This allows for comparison of the candidates with each other and analysis of the debate in greater detail through consideration of those speaking turns in which there were significant deviations from the average eye blink rate. Presumably, based on the findings of previous studies, these deviations indicate issues of higher emotional salience for the candidates.

While this study focuses solely on eye blinks, nonverbal communication is an extensive body of knowledge, including not just characteristics and actions of the facial musculature, but also vocal expression and the rather broad category of body language. As such, this study is an attempt to understand the dynamic aspects of politics and the politicians who compete for power. It is hoped that future studies will consider the eyes to a greater extent, whether the eye-blink itself or gaze direction, threat-stare behavior and pupil dilation, to better understand politicians and their emotional state.

REFERENCES

[1] M. Edelman, *The Symbolic Uses of Politics* (Urbana, IL: University of Illinois Press, 1964) and The Racine Group, "White Paper on Televised Political Campaign Debates," *Argumentation and Advocacy*, 38 (2002), 199-218.

[2] P.R. Schrott and D.J. Lanoue, "Debates are for Losers," *PS: Political Science and Politics*, 41 (2008), 513-518.

[3] R.V. Exline, "Multichannel transmission of nonverbal behavior and the perception of powerful men: the Presidential Debates of 1976," in S.L. Ellyson and J.F. Dovidio (eds.), *Power, dominance, and nonverbal behavior* (New York: Springer-Verlag, 1985).

[4] K.H. Jamieson and P. Waldman, *The Press Effect: Politicians, Journalists, and the Stories That Shape the Political World* (New York: Oxford University Press, 2003); and Schrott and Lanoue, "Debates are for Losers."

[5] The Racine Group, "White Paper on Televised Political Campaign Debates."

[6] The 2004 Presidential debates were no different. Leading up to the debate, the media focused more on the controversy over the rules of the debates and arguably less on the policy positions of the two candidates. The outcome of negotiations between the Bush and Kerry camps led to a 32 page memorandum of understanding concerning such things as height of the podium, presumably to protect the candidates' respective public images. Luckily for the viewers (and the researchers), one set of rules that would have regulated camera angles and shots was disregarded by the broadcasting network, Fox News, with the support of the other networks (see M. Goldberg, "Breaking the Rules," The American Prospect Online. *http://www.opendebates.net/news/relatedarticles/ americanprospect.html* Accessed 2/15/2004). As a result, viewers of the debates were able to see the nonverbal reactions of the candidates as well as hear their policy statements. Probably one of the more interesting controversies to emerge from the first Presidential debate of 2004 was the accusation that the readily apparent square-shaped bulge visible underneath the back of President Bush's suit jacket was a radio receiver

and that he was receiving information cues from his staff through this device. However, his staff denied this, first claiming it was just an odd shaped crease, and later changing this claim to state it was a bulletproof vest. However, no evidence for either has been provided, leaving the mystery of the odd-shaped bulge unsolved.

[7] W.L. Benoit, M.S. McKinney, and M.T. Stephenson, "Effects of watching primary debates in the 2000 U.S. presidential campaign," *Journal of Communication* 52 (2002). 316-331; W.L. Benoit and G.J. Hansen, "Presidential debate watching, issue knowledge, character evaluation, and vote choice," *Human Communication Research,* 30 (2004), 121-144; G.E. Lang and K. Lang, "Immediate and delayed response to a Carter-Ford debate: assessing public opinion," *The Public Opinion Quarterly,* 42(1978), 322-341; and M. Yawn, K. Ellsworth, B. Beatty, and K. Fridkin-Kahn, "How a presidential primary debate changed attitudes of audience members," *Political Behavior,* 20 (1998), 155-181.

[8] Exline, "Multichannel transmission of nonverbal behavior and the perception of powerful men: the Presidential Debates of 1976," and M.L. Patterson, M.E. Churchill, G.K. Burger and J.L. Powell, "Verbal and Nonverbal Modality Effects on Impressions of Political Candidates: Analysis from the 1984 Presidential Debates," *Communication Monographs,* 59 (1992), 231-242.

[9] W.L. Benoit, K.A. Stein, and G.J. Hansen, "Newspaper Coverage of Presidential Debates," *Argumentation and Advocacy,* 41(2004), 17-27; K.H. Jamieson and P. Waldman, *The Press Effect: Politicians, Journalists, and the Stories That Shape the Political World;* J.S. Newton, R.D. Masters, G.J. McHugo, and D.G. Sullivan, "Making up our minds: Effects of Network Coverage on Viewer Impressions of Leaders," *Polity,* 20 (1987), 226-246; and The Racine Group, "White Paper on Televised Political Campaign Debates."

[10] W. Jarman, "Political affiliation and presidential debates: A real-time analysis of the effect of the arguments used in the presidential debates," *The American Behavioral Scientist,* 49 (2005), *239.*

[11] Edelman, *The Symbolic Uses of Politics,* R.D. Masters, *The Nature of Politics* (New Haven, CT: Yale University Press, 1989); and A. Mazur, *Biosociology of Dominance and Deference* (Rowman and Littlefield Publishers, 2005).

[12] R.V. Exline, "Multichannel transmission of nonverbal behavior and the perception of powerful men: the Presidential Debates of 1976," and M.L. Patterson, et. al., "Verbal and Nonverbal Modality Effects on Impressions of Political Candidates: Analysis from the 1984 Presidential Debates."

[13] R.V. Exline, "Multichannel transmission of nonverbal behavior and the perception of powerful men: the Presidential Debates of 1976."

[14] M.L. Patterson, et. al., "Verbal and Nonverbal Modality Effects on Impressions of Political Candidates: Analysis from the 1984 Presidential Debates."

[15] CNN. "Inside Politics- America Votes: Polls – Kerry won Debate," *www.cnn.com/2004/ALLPOLITICS/10/03/election.poll/ Accessed 2/16/2005.*

[16] D. Lothian, D. Bash, J. King, C. Crowley, R. Shumate, and E. Payne, "Debating the first debate: Campaigns assess candidate's performances." CNN.com. *http://www.cnn.com/2004/ALLPOLITICS/10/01/debate.main/index.html* assessed 2/15/2005.

[17] A. Adolphs, F. Gosselin, T.W. Buchanan, D. Tranel, P. Schyns, and A.R. Damasio, "A mechanism for impaired fear recognition after amygdale damage," *Nature,* 433 (2005), 68-72, and H. Kobayashi, and S. Kohshima, "Unique morphology of the human eye and its adaptive meaning: comparative studies on external morphology of the primate eye," *Journal of Human Evolution,* 40 (2001), 419-435.

[18] P. Ekman, W.V. Friesen, M. O'Sullivan, and K. Scherer, "Relative importance of face, body, and speech in judgments of personality and affect," *Journal of Personality and Social Psychology,* 38 (1992), 270-277; and J.A. Stern, L.C. Walrath, and R. Goldstein, "The Endogenous Eyeblink," *Psychophysiology,* 21 (1984), 22-33.

[19] A.R. Bentivoglio, S.B. Bressman, E. Cassetta, D. Carretta, P. Tonali, and A. Albanese, "Analysis of blink rate patterns in normal subjects," *Movement Disorders,* 12 (1997), 1028-1034; L.N. Orchard, and J.A. Stern, "Blinks as an index of cognitive activity during reading," *Integrative Physiological and Behavioral Science,* 26 (1991), 108-116; and J.A. Stern, et. al., "The Endogenous Eyeblink."

[20] J.A. Stern, et. al., "The Endogenous Eyeblink," 22.

[21] F.H. Kanfer, "Verbal rate, eye blink, and content in structured psychiatric interviews," *Journal of Abnormal and Social Psychology,* 61 (1960), 341-347; D.R. Meyer, H.P. Bahrick, and P.M. Fitts, "Incentive, anxiety, and the human blink rate," *Journal of Experimental Psychology,* 45 (1953), 183-187; and K.K.W. Wong, W.Y. Wan, and S.B. Kaye, "Blinking and operating: cognition versus vision," *British Journal of Ophthanmology* 86 (2001), 479.

[22] S. Chollar, "In the blink of an eye," (March 1988) Available: *www.findarticles.com*.

[23] K.K.W. Wong, et. al., "Blinking and operating: cognition versus vision."

[24] A.R. Bentivoglio, et.al., "Analysis of blink rate patterns in normal [eye blink rate {EBR} ~ 4.5]; and L.N. Orchard, and J.A. Stern, "Blinks as an index of cognitive activity during reading."

[25] A.R. Bentivoglio, et.al., "Analysis of blink rate patterns in normal [eye blink rate {EBR} ~ 26]; and R. Goldstein, L.O. Bauer, and J.A. Stern, "Effect of task difficulty and interstimulus interval on blink parameters," *International Journal of Psychophysiology,* 13(1992), 111-117.

[26] S. Mann, A.Vrij, and R. Bull, "Suspects, Lies, and Videotape: An Analysis of Authentic High Stakes Liars," *Law and Human Behavior,* 26(2002), 365-376.

[27] I. Eibl-Eibesfeldt, *Human Ethology* (New York: Aldine de Gruyter, 1989); F.K. Salter, *Emotions in Command: A Naturalistic Study of Institutional Dominance* (New York: Oxford University Press, 1995); and T.B. Ellis, "Natural Gazes, Non-natural Agents: The Biology of Religion's Ocular Behavior," in The Biology of Religious Behavior: The Evolutionary Origins of Faith and Religion, J.R. Feierman (ed.) (New York: Greenwood, 2009).

[28] The authors are indebted to Roger Masters for pointing this out.

[29] J.A. Stern,"The Eye Blink: Affective and Cognitive Influences," in *Anxiety: Recent Developments in Cognitive, Psychophysiological and Health Research,* D.J. Forgays, Sosnowski, and K. Wrzesniewski (eds.), (Washington, DC: Hemisphere Publishing Co., 1992).

[30] F.H. Kanfer, "Verbal rate, eye blink, and content in structured psychiatric interviews," *Journal of Abnormal and Social Psychology,* and E. Weiner, and P. Concepcion,

"Effects of affective stimuli mode or eye blink rate anxiety. *Journal of Clinical Psychology* 31 (1974), 256-259 [EBR ~13; ~24].

[31] J.A. Stern,"The Eye Blink: Affective and Cognitive Influences."

[32] R.V. Exline, "Multichannel transmission of nonverbal behavior and the perception of powerful men: the Presidential Debates of 1976," and M.L. Patterson, et. al., "Verbal and Nonverbal Modality Effects on Impressions of Political Candidates: Analysis from the 1984 Presidential Debates."

[33] R.V. Exline, "Multichannel transmission of nonverbal behavior and the perception of powerful men: the Presidential Debates of 1976."

[34] T.B. Emory, G.W. Ousler III, and M.B. Albelson, MD, "All in the blink of an eye," R*eview of Ophthalmology* (2002). Available: *www.revophth.com*.

[35] J.A. Harrigan, "Proxemics, Kinesics and Gaze," in *The New Handbook of Methods in Nonverbal Behavior Research,* J.A. Harrigan, R. Rosenthal, and K.R. Scherer (eds.), (New York: Oxford University Press, 2005).

[36] Ibid. Exline coded the first ten minutes of a two hour debate (~8% of all data) and achieved intercoder correlation of .956 for Carter and .961 for Ford.

[37] Due to this study being coded into five second units, and there not being a direct correlation between speaking turns and coded eye blink units, the decision was made to code the speaking times for each individual speaker (moderator Jim Lehrer, President George W. Bush, and Senator John F. Kerry). The basis for inclusion as part of the speaking turn is if 2 seconds of speaking occurred during the 5 second unit. While this led to a degree of overlap, and sacrifices some accuracy, for the sake of this study it provides a reasonable coding decision rule.

[38] R.V. Exline, "Multichannel transmission of nonverbal behavior and the perception of powerful men: the Presidential Debates of 1976."

[39] When compared with times talking, Kerry does not look down/away at all, while Bush looks down/away 0.4 percent of the time.

[40] D. Lothian, D. Bash, J. King, C. Crowley, R. Shumate, and E. Payne, "Debating the first debate: Campaigns assess candidate's performances."

[41] R.D. Masters, *The Nature of Politics.*

[42] J.A. Stern, "The Eye Blink: Affective and Cognitive Influences," and J.A. Stern, et. al., "The Endogenous Eyeblink."

[43] R.D. Masters, *The Nature of Politics.*

[44] R.V. Exline, "Multichannel transmission of nonverbal behavior and the perception of powerful men: the Presidential Debates of 1976," and M.L. Patterson, et. al., "Verbal and Nonverbal Modality Effects on Impressions of Political Candidates: Analysis from the 1984 Presidential Debates."

Chapter 19

EXPLORING PARTISAN BIAS IN THE ELECTORAL COLLEGE, 1964-2008

Phillip J. Ardoin

ABSTRACT

The purpose of this work is to examine the sources and impact of partisan bias in the institutional structure of the United States Electoral College. While several analyses of the Electoral College have indicated a lack of partisan bias, conventional wisdom and the results of the 2000 Presidential election suggest the Electoral College is biased in favor of the Republican Party. In order to provide some clarity to this issue, this work provides a *direct* analysis of the multiple sources of bias within the Electoral College and examines their individual impact on each Party's electoral fortunes over the last twelve elections (1964-2008) with particular attention focused on the 2000 Presidential Election. The results of the analyses are in line with previous research which indicates no significant partisan bias within the Electoral College. Ultimately, parties and their presidential candidates are rational political actors which utilize sophisticated campaign strategies that allow them to efficiently employ their resources and limit any institutional disadvantages they may face.

INTRODUCTION

The purpose of this work is to examine the sources of partisan bias within the institutional structure of the United States Electoral College by dissecting the various sources of partisan bias and directly evaluating their individual impact on presidential elections over the last four decades. While several scholars have examined electoral bias in the U.S. House of Representatives [1] only a few have systematically examined bias in the Electoral College. [2]

Conventional wisdom among many pundits, political strategists, and even political scientists suggest the Electoral College is significantly biased in favor of the Republican Party and consequently provides the Republican Party with a near "lock" on the Electoral College. While empirical research by numerous political scientists [3] has challenged the view regarding a Republican Party Electoral College advantage, George Bush's Electoral College victory in 2000 with less than a plurality of the vote revived this debate within the scholarly literature and among political pundits. In order to provide some clarity to this revived debate, my analysis provides a direct exploration of the various sources of partisan bias (malapportionment, turnout differences, and geographic distribution of party vote shares) within the Electoral College and an examination of their individual impact on the Democratic and Republican Party's electoral fortunes over the last twelve presidential elections.

ELECTORAL COLLEGE BIAS

American electoral institutions are of great interest to political scientists and the two most significant and unique elements of our electoral institutions are the winner-take-all system of choosing elected representatives and the Electoral College through which we select presidents. The manner in which the winner-take-all system of elections interacts with the Electoral College creates an interesting electoral dynamic that has led some scholars to speculate about potential biases inherent within the system.

While an unbiased system will yield identical Electoral College votes for equivalent Republican and Democratic vote proportions, a biased system will yield more votes for one party than the other party. For example, if the Democratic Party receives 48% of the Electoral College Votes with 50% of the popular vote and the Republican Party receives 52% of the Electoral College Votes with 50% of the popular vote, the system has a 4% bias in favor of the Republican Party.

While the majority of research regarding partisan bias has focused on bias within the House of Representatives, a small number of scholars have examined the issue with regard to the Electoral College. Borrowing liberally from the work of King and Browning, [4] the initial research on this topic was conducted by Garand and Parent [5] who developed measures of representational form and partisan bias in the relationship between popular vote proportions and electoral vote proportions for each presidential election from 1872 to 1988. The results of their analysis, to the surprise of many observers of the presidential election process, indicated the Electoral College was actually biased in favor of the Democratic Party. Questioning the methods of Garand and Parent, [6] Grofman and Brunell [7] re-examined the influence of partisan bias in the Electoral College. Employing a hypothetical method of analysis, Grofman and Brunell's findings indicate while partisan bias favored the Republican Party from 1900 to 1940, there has been no significant partisan bias in recent elections.

Although the initial work of Garand and Parent [8] and Grofman and Brunell [9] and more recent research by Gelman, Katz, and King [10] provide sophisticated analyses of bias in the Electoral College over the last century, they fail to provide a direct analysis of the sources of bias. The purpose of this work is to feel this void in our understanding of the Electoral College system by examining directly each of the sources of bias and to dissect their individual influences on contemporary presidential elections.

PLAN OF ANALYSES

Before beginning my analysis of partisan bias in the Electoral College, I first define partisan bias and discuss how it differs from the swing ratio. As noted by Grofman et al, [11] confusion between partisan bias and swing ratio has led to much of the confusion regarding Electoral College bias. Second, sources of partisan bias, wasted votes and the votes cast (cost) per Electoral College vote are discussed in detail. Third, whether either party has systematically suffered or benefited more than the other party from these sources of bias in their attempts to win Electoral College votes is examined. Finally, a detailed analysis of the factors which led to George W. Bush's Electoral College victory in 2000, despite his popular vote defeat is provided.

PARTISAN BIAS VS SWING RATIO

Much of the confusion over the issue partisan bias within the Electoral College is due to confusion between partisan bias and swing ratio. In two-party democratic political contests, partisan bias and swing ratio are the two primary measures of the characteristics of the association between a party's vote share and its share of Electoral College votes. The *swing ratio* is a measure of the responsiveness of the electoral system to changes in the proportion of the vote each party receives. In general, the swing ratio is the expected Electoral College vote increase for each percentage point increase in a party's share of the aggregate popular vote. The second measure of the association between a party's vote share and its share of Electoral College votes is *partisan bias*, which represents the degree to which competing political parties receiving the same vote proportions receive dissimilar proportions of Electoral College votes. More specifically, an electoral institution characterized by partisan bias produces differential treatment for the advantaged and disadvantaged party, with the former receiving a higher proportion of Electoral College votes than the latter for any given proportion of popular votes.

SOURCES OF PARTISAN BIAS

What are the sources of partisan bias? There are two basic factors which contribute to partisan bias in the Electoral College. The first factor is a disparity in the vote costs between parties. This is due to differences in the population and/or number of voters per Electoral College vote, which varies as a result of turnout differences and malapportionment. The second factor contributing to partisan bias in the Electoral College is asymmetries in the distribution of wasted votes between the parties which may occur as a result of variation in the distribution of partisan voting strength across states. For instance, if either party consistently wins competitive states and/or the larger states they will waste significantly fewer votes in the United States' winner take all election process.

Ultimately, the number of Electoral College votes a party wins depends on three factors: (1) the number of votes it has available to spend, (2) the number of popular votes casts for each Electoral College vote and (3) the number of votes the party wastes. A party which wins states where the number of votes per Electoral College vote is low and/or wins states by narrow margins will spend their votes most efficiently; and the more efficiently a party spends their votes the more Electoral College votes they will win.

ANALYSES OF BIAS

Vote Costs

The "price" of Electoral College votes varies significantly between states. Because the U.S. Constitution mandates that Electoral College votes are allocated "equal to the whole number of Senators and Representatives to which the State may be entitled in Congress," there is tremendous variation in the cost or rather the number of popular votes cast per Electoral College vote. Since each state, no matter how small its population, is guaranteed by the U.S. Constitution at least one seat in the House of Representatives and two Seats in the U.S. Senate, even the smallest states receive at least three Electoral College votes. Consequently, the Electoral College over represents the least populous states, and the cost of Electoral College votes in smaller states is potentially much lower than the cost of votes in larger states. As noted above, these differences in the cost of votes can provide a significant source of partisan bias when one party consistently wins a significant number of small states.

As one would expect, considering the Constitutional requirement of at least three Electoral College votes to every state, smaller states have substantially fewer citizens per Electoral College vote than larger states. As Table 1 clearly displays, the population per Electoral College vote varies dramatically between the states. For instance, the average population per Electoral College vote in California (534,213) over the last twelve elections is 3.73 times as large as the average population per Electoral College vote in Wyoming (143,108).

These differences in the population per Electoral College vote present the possibility for significant electoral bias. If either party has a significant electoral advantage in smaller states, they are more likely to use their votes efficiently and enjoy an advantage in the competition for Electoral College votes. With this in mind, the average number of victories by each party's presidential candidate in the least expensive and most expensive states is presented in Table 1. When one examines the ten least expensive states (states with the fewest number of votes per Electoral College vote), the results clearly suggest a bias in favor of the Republican Party. Of the twelve elections since 1964, Republicans have been victorious 62% of the time in the 10 least expensive states as compared to only 53% of the time in the most expensive states. However, when one examines the average population per Electoral College vote between the two parties the results indicate only a modest and statistically non-significant Republican Party advantage. Specifically, for the 1964-2008 elections the states which the Republican candidate was victorious had an average population of 372,068 individuals per Electoral College vote compared to Democratic states which had an average population of 376,255 votes per Electoral College vote. This represents a difference of only 4,187 or rather 1.1% of the average population per Electoral College vote.

While state populations are used to determine the number of Electoral College votes allocated to each state, the population per Electoral College vote only provides an indirect measure of the cost of Electoral College votes. As one would expect, turnout varies significantly from state to state and therefore provides the chance for additional variation in the cost of Electoral College votes between states. The more direct and accurate measure of the cost of Electoral College votes can be determined by calculating the average number of *actual votes cast* per Electoral College vote in each state.

Table 1. Top 10 Least Expensive and Most Expensive Electoral College Vote States 1964-2008 by Population

State	EC Pop Rank	Population Per EC Vote	Electoral College Votes 2008	Republican Victories 1964-2008	Democratic Victories 1964-2008
Wyoming	1	143,108	3	11	1
Alaska	2	151,863	3	11	1
Vermont	3	173,009	3	6	6
North Dakota	4	203,457	3	11	1
South Dakota	5	212,165	3	11	1
Delaware	6	212,213	3	5	7
D.C.	7	227,353	3	0	12
Montana	8	228,023	3	10	2
New Hampshire	9	243,504	4	7	5
Rhode Island	10	243,573	4	2	10
Connecticut	Median	401,823	7	5	7
New Jersey	42	472,723	15	6	6
Ohio	43	474,261	20	7	5
Michigan	44	477,041	17	5	7
Georgia	45	477,349	15	10	2
Pennsylvania	46	482,637	21	4	8
Illinois	47	486,677	21	6	6
New York	48	499,598	31	3	9
Florida	49	518,097	27	8	4
Texas	50	529,136	34	9	3
California	51	534,213	55	6	6

Table 2 presents the average number of votes cast per Electoral College vote in the 10 most and least expensive states between 1964 and 2008. Once again these results indicate substantial variation in the votes cast per Electoral College vote between states. While the costs of an Electoral College vote in Alaska averages only 35,845 votes, the average cost per Electoral College vote in Massachusetts is 116,480 votes. The cost of an Electoral College vote from Massachusetts is 3.25 times the cost of an Electoral College vote from Alaska. Clearly, variation in the cost of Electoral College votes provides a potentially significant source of partisan bias.

While Table 2 unmistakably indicates a disparity in the number of votes cast per Electoral College vote between the states, once again this will only produce partisan bias if the system consistently provides one party with a distinct and systematic electoral advantage. In order to examine this issue, we first report the number of times each party has been victorious in the least expensive and most expensive Electoral College vote states. A review of the data parallels the above analysis, once again supporting conventional wisdom and indicating the Republican Party more consistently wins the least expensive states while the Democratic Party relies more heavily on the most expensive states for their support.

Although Table 2 provides a cursory view of the partisan differences in the cost of Electoral College votes, it does not present the complete picture. The more telling and appropriate means of examining this factor is to compare the actual difference in the average number of votes cast per Electoral College vote between the two parties.

Table 2. Top 10 Cheapest and Most Expensive Electoral College Vote States 1964-2004 by Turnout

State	Cost Rank	Popular Votes Per EC Vote	Republican Wins	Democratic Wins
Alaska	1	35,845	11	1
Wyoming	2	37,789	11	1
Vermont	3	44,187	6	6
Hawaii	4	47,519	2	10
Delaware	5	49,647	5	7
South Dakota	6	52,809	11	1
North Dakota	7	52,924	11	1
Nevada	8	53,081	8	4
Montana	9	56,956	10	2
D.C.	10	57,893	0	12
Kansas	Median	88,669	11	1
Ohio	42	104,271	7	5
California	43	105,520	6	6
New York	44	105,721	3	9
Wisconsin	45	105,970	4	8
New Jersey	46	108,310	6	6
Michigan	47	109,407	5	7
Florida	48	110,180	8	4
Illinois	49	110,345	6	6
Minnesota	50	110,369	1	11
Massachusetts	51	116,480	2	10

With this in mind, the average cost each party has paid per Electoral College vote over the period of the analysis (1964-2008) has been calculated. When one examines the overall difference between the parties in costs, there is a small but statistically significant difference in favor of the Republican Party. Specifically, Republican candidates have cast an average of 80,390 votes per Electoral College vote in comparison to Democrats who have cast an average of 87,214. This represents a difference of only 6,824 votes cast per Electoral College or rather 1,842,480 fewer votes for the Republican Party to achieve the 270 Electoral College votes required to win the Presidential election.

Wasted Votes

The second factor contributing to partisan bias in the Electoral College is asymmetries in the distribution of wasted votes between the parties which may occur as a result of variation in the distribution of partisan voting strength across states. Because of the winner take all system employed by the vast majority of states (Maine and Nebraska are the exceptions), all votes above 50% + 1 for a party's candidate can be considered wasted votes. In addition, because of the winner take all system all votes cast in states which the party's presidential candidate is defeated are considered wasted votes.

The number of votes each party wasted in states which they were victorious over the period of this analysis is presented in Table 3. An initial examination of the data suggests the Republican Party has wasted (80,843,674) significantly more votes than the Democratic Party (68,246,195) over the last 12 elections in states which they were victorious. However, upon further analysis the data reveals this difference is actually due to the greater number of Republican Presidential victories over the period of the analysis. More specifically, the party receiving the greatest number of popular votes naturally wins a greater number of states and as a result wastes more votes than the losing party.

A more appropriate means of examining the number of votes wasted by each party is to evaluate separately the average number of votes each party wastes in years which their candidate wins and also loses the general election. In contrast to the analysis of the total number of votes, these more appropriate measures suggest only a slight bias in favor of the Republican Party. In comparing the average number of votes wasted by each party in years which they won the general election, one finds the Democratic Party wasted an average of 401,216 more votes than the Republican Party. Moreover, comparing the average number of votes wasted by each party in years which they lost the general election, the results indicate the Democratic Party wasted more votes with an average of 151,447 more votes.

Table 3. Wasted Votes Over 50% + 1 By Year By Party

Election Year	Sum Democrat	Sum Republican	2 Party Percent Democrat	2 Party Percent Republican
1964 (LBJ)	17,048,665	1,097,287	12.34%	17.81%
1968 (Nixon)	2,212,660	2,838,636	7.54%	6.05%
1972 (Nixon)	312,863	18,312,391	16.34%	14.31%
1976 (Carter)	3,395,138	1,712,168	5.92%	4.22%
1980 (Reagan)	553,166	8,973,436	7.88%	8.51%
1984 (Reagan)	155,160	17,033,050	18.02%	11.33%
1988 (Bush)	1,154,052	8,231,155	6.09%	7.14%
1992 (Clinton)	7,317,348	1,512,092	6.47%	4.86%
1996 (Clinton)	9,791,131	1,587,529	8.70%	4.83%
2000 (GW Bush)	6,477,569	5,937,671	7.36%	8.30%
2004 (GW Bush)	5,373,444	8,675,344	6.48%	9.04%
2008 (Obama)	14,454,999	4,932,915	9.78%	7.87%
Avg Democrat Wins	10,401,456	2,168,398	8.64%	7.92%
Avg Republican Wins	2,319,845	10,000,240	9.96%	9.24%
All Years	68,246,195	80,843,674	9.41%	8.69%

While all votes over 50% +1 can be considered wasted votes, all votes in states which a candidate receives less than 50% are also considered wasted votes. Consequently, if either party consistently loses competitive states they will spend their votes less efficiently which once again may lead to partisan bias.

The number of votes and average percentage of votes wasted by each party in states which their candidate was defeated over the last twelve Presidential elections are reported in Table 4. As one might expect, the results indicate both parties consistently waste more votes in losing states in years which they lose the national popular vote. Moreover, this difference is quite substantial, with the losing party wasting thirty-four times as many votes as the winning party in 1984, twenty-four times as many votes in 1972, and seventeen times as many votes in 1964. Consequently, as a result of losing more Presidential elections, Democratic candidates have wasted a significantly greater number of votes in losing causes than Republican candidates over the 44 year period of the analysis. Specifically, the Democratic Party has wasted 55,095,203 more votes than the Republican Party in states which they have lost. While this suggests a significant bias toward the Republican Party, further analysis shows these results are primarily a consequence of the two landslide victories which the Republican Party enjoyed in 1972 and 1984. In the remaining five elections, which the Republican Party received a smaller margin of victory, the difference in the number of wasted votes between the two parties is significantly smaller and actually favors the Democratic Party. Interestingly, when one compares the average percentage of votes wasted in losing causes between the two parties there is practically no difference. Both parties, on average, receive about 38.5 percent of the vote in states which they lose. Ultimately, neither party is systematically disadvantaged by the number of votes which they waste in losing states.

Table 4. Democratic and Republican Wasted Votes in Losing States

Presidential Year	Sum of Votes Democratic	Sum of Votes Republican	Average Percent Democratic	Average Percent Republican	N Democrat	N Republican
1964 (LBJ)	1,415,718	24,665,183	32.1%	37.5%	45	6
1968 (Nixon)	16,376,224	11,506,776	38.3%	39.1%	17	34
1972 (Nixon)	27,710,216	1,147,304	34.9%	33.4%	2	49
1976 (Carter)	17,013,478	20,422,147	44.5%	43.3%	24	27
1980 (Reagan)	32,080,019	2,850,698	37.9%	38.1%	7	44
1984 (Reagan)	36,360,413	1,061,612	38.3%	31.6%	2	49
1988 (Bush)	31,685,734	8,969,699	42.3%	43.3%	11	40
1992 (Clinton)	11,240,323	26,352,135	35.4%	34.8%	33	18
1996 (Clinton)	10,905,562	26,705,664	40.5%	36.7%	32	19
2000 (GW Bush)	21,836,063	22,682,407	40.1%	40.4%	21	30
2004 (GW Bush)	26,099,985	25,895,833	39.5%	41.9%	20	31
2008 (Obama)	16,093,577	38,908,322	39.6%	41.4%	29	22
Republican Wins	440,965,966	285,282,109	38.8%	38.3%	80	277
Democratic Wins	497,634,624	422,335,560	38.4%	38.7%	163	92
All Years	248,817,312	211,167,780	38.6%	38.5%	243	369

PARTISAN BIAS?

Is the Electoral College biased toward the Republican or Democratic Party? In line with the findings of Grofman and Brunell [12] and Destler, [13] the results of this analyses suggest an absence of any significant partisan bias within the contemporary Electoral College. While it may *appear* that the Republican Party would enjoy an advantage in the Electoral College because of consistently winning more of the cheap Electoral College states, the top 10 least expensive states only represent a total of 32 Electoral College Votes. The Democratic Party can overcome this advantage by simply winning two of the top 10 most expensive states which each represent on average of 26 Electoral College votes. As noted above, while the Republican Party has spent their votes more efficiently over the period of this analysis, the difference between the two parties represents an average of only 6,824 popular votes per Electoral College vote which is not substantially or statistically significant. Regarding the second source of bias, wasted votes, the two parties are relatively even. While the total number of wasted votes for the Democratic Party is significantly greater, the analyses indicate this difference is due to their presidential candidates winning the popular vote less often and losing by landslides in 1972 and 1984.

THE 2000 PRESIDENTIAL ELECTION

While the above discussion and analyses substantiate the findings of previous research which found the Electoral College to be generally unbiased, one must still explain how George W. Bush attained an Electoral College victory in the 2000 Presidential election despite losing the popular vote. Clearly, the Electoral College system did not treat the two parties equally in the 2000 Presidential election. As noted above, there are two basic sources of bias in the Electoral College. The first is based on the price each party pays for Electoral College votes. The second is the number of votes each party wastes in states which they are victorious and states which they are defeated. Tables 5 and 6 display the least expensive and most expensive Electoral College states in the 2000 election and the average number of votes each candidate paid per Electoral College vote. At first glance, the data does not indicate that the Republican Party in 2000 enjoyed the success they normally find among smaller states in presidential elections. In the 2000 presidential election they won only half of the 10 least expensive states. Among the most expensive states, Bush won only 3 states. More importantly, a comparison of the average number of votes cast for each party's 2000 Electoral College votes suggest only a minimal difference favoring George W. Bush. Specifically, the Republican Party in 2000 spent only 4,687 fewer votes per Electoral College vote than the Democratic Party. As with the aggregate analysis, the difference in vote costs is not statistically or substantially significant.

Wasted votes are also an important source of partisan bias and Table 7 displays the sum of votes each party wasted in states which they were victorious and states which they were defeated in the 2000 Presidential election. Not surprisingly, the results are at odds with each other for the 2000 Presidential election. While the Democratic Party wasted more votes in states Al Gore won, the Republican Party actually wasted more votes in the states that George W. Bush was defeated. A comparison, however, of the total number of wasted votes indicates that the Republican Party actually wasted 306,446 more votes than the Democratic Party. Clearly, wasted votes do not explain George W. Bush's 2000 Electoral College victory.

Tables 5. Top 10 Cheapest and Most Expensive Electoral College Vote States 2000/2004

State	Votes Per EC Vote	Cost Rank	Winning Candidate
Wyoming	49,316	1	Bush
Vermont	49,674	2	Gore
Hawaii	51,322	3	Gore
Alaska	55,799	4	Bush
New Mexico	57,357	5	Gore
North Dakota	58,284	6	Bush
Delaware	60,023	7	Gore
Rhode Island	62,377	8	Gore
South Dakota	63,567	9	Bush
West Virginia	67,295	10	Bush
Oregon	102,906	Median	Gore
Maryland	114,401	42	Gore
Florida	116,512	43	Bush
North Carolina	116,512	44	Bush
Minnesota	116,827	45	Gore
Illinois	117,683	46	Gore
Texas	118,739	47	Bush
New Jersey	119,257	48	Gore
Michigan	120,579	49	Gore
New York	124,476	50	Gore
Massachusetts	134,707	51	Gore

Tables 6. Cost of Electoral College Votes in 2000 Presidential Election

	Democratic Electoral College Vote Cost	Republican Electoral College Vote Cost
N	21	30
Minimum	49,674	49,316
Maximum	134,707	118,739
Mean	96,848	92,161

Table 7. Wasted Votes in the 2000 Presidential Election

	Democrats		Republican	
	Wasted Vts Over 50%+1	Wasted Vts in Losing States	Wasted Vts Over 50%+1	Wasted Vts in Losing States
N	21	30	30	21
Mean	308,456	727,869	197,922	1,080,115
Sum	6,477,569	21,836,063	5,937,671	22,682,407
Total Wasted	28,313,632		28,620,078	

Considering the findings of both the cheap votes and wasted votes analyses, the results suggest the Republican Party's advantage in the 2000 Electoral College was primarily due to their spending votes more efficiently by wining more of the least expensive states. While the Republican Party spent only 4,687 fewer votes per Electoral College vote than the Democratic Party, this represents a total of 1,265,454 votes when one multiplies it times the actual number of Electoral College votes required to win the Presidential Election. Clearly this represents a substantial number of votes which had a significant impact in such a close election. The second question which one must answer is whether this was due to a systematic bias in favor of the Republican Party or rather the strategic decisions the Bush Presidential Campaign made during the 2000 election with regards to allocating their resources.

CONCLUSION

In conclusion, this work broadens the understanding of the issue of partisan bias in the Electoral College in providing a fuller analysis of the institutional mechanisms of the Electoral College.

First, the various sources of potential bias in the Electoral College (cheap votes and wasted votes) are clarified.

Second, each of these sources of potential bias are examined and do not present a significant advantage in favor of the Republican or Democratic Party, which supports the previous findings of Grofman and Brunell [14] and Destler. [15]

Third, the analysis suggest the erroneous perception of a Republican Bias in the Electoral College which persists is likely due to the Party's advantage in smaller states (which contributed substantially to Bush's 2000 Electoral College victory) and their historical popular vote success combined with the tendency of our winner take all system to artificially inflate the victorious candidate's Electoral College margin.

While the potential for bias within the institution of the Electoral College is clearly high, neither party over the last half century has been able to consistently take advantage of these potential advantages. This is likely due to the fact that presidential candidates and the parties they represent are rational political actors which understand the opportunities and problems of the institutional structure which they work under. Through the use of sophisticated polling and the strategic allocation of campaign resources each party is able to diminish the inherent inefficiencies which confront their candidate and party.

This has been most vividly displayed in the most recent Presidential elections with the amount of attention and resources each campaign committed to swing states. The Democratic Party knows they are unlikely to achieve an electoral victory in solidly Republican states such as Wyoming and North Dakota and the Republican Party recognizes they are unlikely to achieve electoral success in solidly Democratic states such as California and Massachusetts, so neither party waste limited resources in these states. [16] Ultimately, each party's presidential candidate expends their limited resources (time and money) rationally and as a result the level of partisan bias in the Electoral College is severely restricted.

REFERENCES

[1] See D.W. Brady and B. Grofman, "Sectional Differences in Partisan Bias and Electoral Responsiveness in U.S. House Elections, 1850-1980," *British Journal of Political Science* 27, no. 134-135 (1991); J.Campagna and B. Grofman, "Party Control and Partisan Bias in 1980s Congressional Redistricting.," *Journal of Politics* 52(1990): 1242-57; J.E. Campbell, *Cheap seats : the Democratic Party's advantage in U.S. House elections*, Parliaments and legislatures series. (Columbus: Ohio State University Press, 1996); J.E. Campbell, "Electoral System Bias in the House of Representatives: The Partisan Consequences of District Turnout Variation," (paper presented at the Annual Meeting of the Southern Political Science Association, 1995); B Grofman, B., "Measures of Bias and Proportionality in Seats-Votes Relationships," *Political Methodology* 9(1983): 295-327; G. King and R.X. Browning, "Democratic Representation and Partisan Bias in Congressional Elections," *American Political Science Review* 81(1987): 1251-73; R.G. Niemi, R.G. and P. Fett, "The Swing Ratio: An Explanation and an Assessment," *Legislative Studies Quarterly* 11(1986): 75-90; and E.R. Tufte, "The Relationship between Seats and Votes in Two-Party Systems," *American Political Science Review* 67(1973): 540-54.

[2] See J.E.Berthoud, "The Electoral Lock Thesis: The Weighting Bias Component," *PS: Political Science and Politics* 30, no. 2 (1997): 189-93 (accessed June, 2009); T.L. Brunell and B. Grofman, "The 1992 and 1996 Presidential Elections: Whatever Happened to the Republican Electoral College Lock?," *Presidential Studies Quarterly* 27(1997): 134-35; Destler, I.M., "The Myth of the Electoral Lock," *P.S. Political Science and Politics* 29, no. 3 (1996): 491-94; J.C. Garand and T.W. Parent, "Representation, Swing, and Bias in U.S. Presidential Elections, 1872-1988," *American Journal of Political Science* 35(1991): 1011-31; A. Gelman, J.N. Katz, and G. King, "Empirically Evaluating the Electoral College," in *Rethinking the Vote: The Politics and Prospects of American Electoral Reform*, ed. A.N. Crigler, M.R. Just and E.J. McCaffery (New York: Oxford University Press, 2004); A. Gelman and G. King, "A Unified Method of Evaluating Electoral Systems and Redistricting Plans," *American Journal of Political Science* 38, no. 2 (1994): 514-54; and R. Johnston, D. Rossiter, and C. Pattie, "Disproportionality and bias in US Presidential Elections: How geography helped Bush defeat Gore but couldn't help Kerry beat Bush," *Political Geography* 24(2005): 952-68.

[3] Destler, "The Myth of the Electoral Lock;" J.C. Garand, and T.W. Parent, "Representation, Swing, and Bias in U.S. Presidential Elections, 1872-1988;" A. Gelman, J.N. Katz, and G. King, "Empirically Evaluating the Electoral College," in *Rethinking the Vote: The Politics and Prospects of American Electoral Reform;* and B. Grofman,W. Koetzle, and T. Brunell, "An Integrated Perspective on Three Potential Sources of Partisan Bias: Malapportionment, Tournout Differences, and the Geographic Distribution of Party Vote Shares," *Electoral Studies* 16, no. 4 (1997): 457-70.

[4] G. King and R.X. Browning, "Democratic Representation and Partisan Bias in Congressional Elections."

[5] J.C. Garand and T.W. Parent, "Representation, Swing, and Bias in U.S. Presidential Elections, 1872-1988."

[6] Ibid.
[7] B. Grofman, T. Brunell, and J. Campagna, "Distinguishing Between the Effects of Swing Ratio and Bias on Outcomes in the U.S. Electoral College, 1900-1992," *Electoral Studies* 16, no. 4 (1997): 471-87.
[8] J.C. Garand, J.C. and T.W. Parent, "Representation, Swing, and Bias in U.S. Presidential Elections, 1872-1988."
[9] B. Grofman, B., "Measures of Bias and Proportionality in Seats-Votes Relationships," *Political Methodology* 9(1983): 295-327; B.Grofman, T. Brunell, and J. Campagna, "Distinguishing Between the Effects of Swing Ratio and Bias on Outcomes in the U.S. Electoral College, 1900-1992."
[10] A. Gelman, J.N. Katz, and G. King, "Empirically Evaluating the Electoral College."
[11] B. Grofman, B., "Measures of Bias and Proportionality in Seats-Votes Relationships," *Political Methodology* 9(1983): 295-327; B.Grofman, T. Brunell, and J. Campagna, "Distinguishing Between the Effects of Swing Ratio and Bias on Outcomes in the U.S. Electoral College, 1900-1992."
[12] Ibid.
[13] I.M. Destler, "The Myth of the Electoral Lock."
[14] B. Grofman, B., "Measures of Bias and Proportionality in Seats-Votes Relationships," *Political Methodology* 9(1983): 295-327; B.Grofman, T. Brunell, and J. Campagna, "Distinguishing Between the Effects of Swing Ratio and Bias on Outcomes in the U.S. Electoral College, 1900-1992."
[15] I.M. Destler, "The Myth of the Electoral Lock."
[16] S. Althaus, P.F. Nardulli, and D.R. Shaw, "Candidate Appearances in Presidential Elections," *Political Communication* 19(2002): 49-72; A.Reeves, L. Chen, and T. Nagano, "A Reassessment of 'The Methods behind the Madness: Presidential Electoral College Strategies, 1988-1996," *Journal of Politics* 66, no. 2 (2004): 616-20; and D.R. Shaw, "The Methods behind the Madness: Presidential Electoral College Strategies," *Journal of Politics* 61, no. 4 (1999): 893-913.

Chapter 20

FIRST LADIES AND THE CULTURAL EVERYWOMAN IDEAL: GENDER PERFORMANCE AND REPRESENTATION

Jill Abraham Hummer

ABSTRACT

As symbols of American womanhood, first ladies have become entangled in the public debate about feminism. In particular, when first ladies' roles are tied to the performance of gender, public controversy tends to ensue. What explains this gender-based debate and dissent? What are the consequences? In this article, a construct termed the 'cultural everywoman ideal' is offered as an explanation for this gender-based controversy. The cultural everywoman ideal is an essential component of the first lady's position that obliges her to uphold the dominant cultural belief about American womanhood in all of her acts of political representation. Its process is expouned through the interaction between symbolic and descriptive representation. Drawing on primary source material from presidential libraries and newspaper archives, the existence and function of the cultural everywoman ideal is illustrated through the case studies of Lady Bird Johnson, Betty Ford, and Barbara Bush. The potential and standards for success in meeting the cultural everywoman ideal are evaluated. Consequences of the cultural everywoman ideal include that it tends to set these women up for political failure and circumscribes their ability to act autonomously.

American first ladies have become entangled in the public debate over feminism. The public tends to view the first lady's proper roles dichotomously. The traditionally minded expect the first lady to stay outside of the political fray, to support her husband, and to espouse the virtues of domesticity. Feminists, on the other hand, expect the first lady to speak and act and independently and to engage in politics and public policy. [1] Researchers have also evaluated first ladies, their media coverage, and their public approval according to this dichotomy. [2] When first ladies' public roles are tied to the performance of gender, public controversy tends to ensue. What explains this gender-based debate and dissent? Is it possible for first ladies to be successful in negotiating the crossfire of opposing ideals?

These questions explore the societal and political importance of the first lady. Robert P. Watson has identified the first lady's role as symbol of the American woman as one of her eleven official duties. [3] As such, the first lady reflects the country's notions about womanhood, femininity, and feminism. This role, however, is fraught with complication and contradiction, as the conceptions of American womanhood are different and changing. As Watson states, "Women - and thus first ladies - are no longer just wives and mothers. Women run businesses, serve in elected office, write books, and raise children. The first lady faces the challenge of being simultaneously modern and traditional, a concern with which men, including the president, need not contend." [4] Thus, the first lady's challenges and choices reflect those of women in American society, and cultural beliefs about femininity and feminism are encapsulated in public reaction to the first ladyship.

First ladies and their gender performances have also impacted presidential operations. This was quite evident, for instance, during the Clinton Administration. Throughout her leadership in the failed health care reform effort, Hillary Rodham Clinton faced criticism that was centered on her gender. [5] She blamed her own non-traditional gender performance, including her role in health care reform, for the Democratic losses in the 1994 congressional midterm elections, [6] after which she cut back on her overt policy activity. In addition, her gender performance impacted her husband's own reelection prospects. [7] Thus, the first lady's navigation of gender boundaries can matter for presidential success.

This article seeks to understand the constraint of gender on the first ladyship and its consequences. In so doing, this article introduces a construct termed the cultural everywoman ideal, rooted in the concepts of symbolic and descriptive representation, to explain the controversy that surrounds the first lady's expression of womanhood.

THE CULTURAL EVERYWOMAN IDEAL: LINKING DESCRIPTIVE AND SYMBOLIC REPRESENTATION

The cultural everywoman ideal is an essential component of the first lady's position that obliges her to uphold the dominant cultural belief about American womanhood in all of her acts of political representation. In practice, when the first lady satisfies the dominant cultural ideal of American womanhood, there should exist little to no discussion or debate about how well she fulfills her gender-laden political roles. However, when she fails to live up to this ideal, she becomes a lightning rod for public criticism and her legitimacy as a political representative is called into question. The coexistence of public acceptance and dissent has been the norm because there is no cultural consensus over ideal American womanhood. This section establishes the first lady's role as a political representative, grounds the cultural everywoman expectation in theories of representation, and places this expectation in historical context.

The first lady has historically stood for American women and womanhood as a political representative. This analysis utilizes constructions of representation enumerated by Hanna Fenichel Pitkin. [8] Political representation means "acting in the interests of the represented, in a manner responsive to them." [9] While typically associated with elected representatives, her theories of formal, substantive, descriptive, and symbolic representation can be extended to political officials who are not elected. For example, MaryAnne Borrelli utilizes Pitkin's framework in analyzing the gendered roles of female Cabinet members. [10] Borrelli, through an examination of statutes and case law on first ladies, also confirms their role as formal representatives despite their unelected status. [11] As substantive representatives, whereby first ladies act for women, they have historically served as the primary White House liaison to women's groups, advocated on behalf of women's appointments, and advanced women-centered economic, domestic and foreign policies. [12]

The cultural everywoman ideal and the case studies in this article reveal the first lady as a descriptive and symbolic representative of women. The interrelationship between descriptive and symbolic representation in particular contributes to the exposition of the cultural everywoman ideal. Both forms of representation involve "standing for" the represented. Descriptive representation means "'standing for' something or someone absent by some correspondence of features." [13] Individual representatives or a representative body should be an "'accurate reflection' of the community, or of the general opinion of the nation, or of the variety of interests in society." [14] This standard of 'accurate reflection' implies that there is an *ideal* form of descriptive representation, thereby leaving the possibility that a representative could *deviate* from that ideal. So, an *ideal* form of descriptive representation would occur when a representative forms an exact portrait of the represented in terms of characteristics, opinion, and interests. If a representative is meeting this ideal, there should be no controversy and no reason to discuss how well someone is representing. But if there is a deviation from this ideal, then there should be some kind of debate or dissent over *how well* someone is representing.

Unlike descriptive representation, which focuses on what a representative "*is* or is *like*," [15] symbolic representation refers to the *meaning* implicit in a representative's actions, relationships, and communications, as well as how the represented interpret and react to the meaning that is conveyed. As such, the representative-as-symbol is "the recipient or object of feelings, expressions of feeling, or actions intended for what it represents." Also unlike descriptive representation, symbolic representation does not lend itself to an assessment of how well someone represents. There "is no such concept in our language as 'missymbolizing,' to correspond with 'misrepresenting.' Nor are there accurate and inaccurate symbols." [16] Thus, there is no ideal or bad form of symbolic representation.

Descriptive and symbolic representation interact with one another, and in so doing activate the cultural everywoman ideal. The first lady's deviation from or adherence to an ideal form of descriptive representation, as determined by the gender symbolism she conveys, explains whether public dissent or acceptance flows from the cultural everywoman ideal. To elaborate, the first lady, in nearly all of the representative acts she performs, conveys symbolic gender meaning. The public then receives, interprets, and reacts to that meaning. The nature of that reaction then feeds back into descriptive representation. Recall that descriptive representation relates to the assessment of whether the first lady is an accurate reflection of the thing she represents, in this case American women or womanhood. When her gender symbolism satisfies the dominant cultural gender ideal, a nearly perfect form descriptive representation occurs and she is met with implicit public acceptance. However, when the symbolic gender meaning she conveys deviates from the dominant gender ideal, descriptive representation then has a debate or argument and public dissent ensues. In other words, the first lady, by not satisfying the cultural everywoman ideal, becomes a political lightening rod, and her status as an accurate or legitimate representative of American women is called into question.

The role of cultural everywoman has typically been associated with first ladies since the beginning of presidential history but has been the focus of sustained controversy and conflict with the rise of the second wave women's movement. Before this time, relations between men and women were mainly guided by the mainstream ideology of separate spheres, in which men were the breadwinners and the representatives of their families in the public sphere and women were primarily responsible for taking care of the home and rearing children. [17] Many early first ladies conformed to this gender ideal and therefore fostered little debate about how well they fulfilled their roles. Despite their exclusion from the political realm, some American women rejected the separate spheres ideal, as did some early first ladies, leading to criticism for their gender performances. Dolley Madison, Edith Wilson, and Eleanor Roosevelt are some well-known examples.

These early contradictions were then acknowledged and debated with the second wave of the women's movement. The second wave emerged in the 1960s and witnessed the passage of some of the most important women's rights legislation in history. [18] Correspondingly, this decade rendered the cultural everywoman ideal a source of sustained, unrelenting conflict and controversy for the first lady. Second wave feminism offered up a different, opposite kind of woman, a woman who could perform public roles and duties equal to men. Traditionally feminine women's roles did not disappear as an option. Rather, they were reasserted in the following decades through a conservative backlash against the women's liberation movement. As a result, from the 1960s through the present day, there has been no dominant ideal. Instead, second wave feminism and the conservative backlash forced first ladies ever since to negotiate between the different and opposing kinds of women. The cultural everywoman ideal remains essential to the first lady's character, rendering debate over her representative roles practically inevitable. Therefore, the second wave and its aftermath will be the focus of this analysis.

RHETORIC, PUBLIC OPINION, AND THE CULTURAL EVERYWOMAN

The cultural everywoman ideal encompasses political communication and public opinion. But assessing *how* and *why* a first lady's symbolic words and actions resonate with public opinion poses some challenges. Public opinion polls and survey data would be the obvious place to begin to measure the *how*. Barbara Burrell has used polling data to gauge citizen reaction to the first ladyship of Hillary Rodham Clinton. [19] However, polling data have limits. While survey questions on first ladies have been conducted sporadically since the advent of scientific polling, regular and comprehensive survey questions are not available before Hillary Clinton's tenure. More importantly, while polls can provide insight into *how* the public rates first lady job performance and favorability, they are of limited use because they cannot assess *why*. Polls do not directly ascertain thought processes and reasoning. In other words, if a respondent tells a pollster that she disapproves of a first lady's job performance, we do not know if that disapproval stems from a differing stance on abortion or distaste for how expensive her wardrobe is.

The cultural everywoman ideal cannot be fully explicated without examining language. The first lady's rhetoric is important because it is her primary means of conveying symbolic representation. Within the field of presidential rhetoric, Mary Stuckey has explained how the chief executive is also the nation's interpreter-in-chief and chief storyteller, who tells us who we are as a people and what we stand for as a community. [20] As such, the president's rhetoric is a form of symbol making and conveying. Stuckey claims that as the line between the president's public and private spheres has broken down, presidential families have become more central to the president's role as interpreter-in-chief. [21] Accordingly, as a central actor within the rhetorical presidency and as an interpreter herself, scholars have recently begun to categorize and assess first lady rhetoric. [22] In this analysis, the first lady's rhetoric will be evaluated as her primary means of conveying symbolic representation by interpreting and communicating messages about women's proper roles.

The public's words are important because they convey their lines of reasoning and standards of evaluation for the first lady's role as a descriptive representative. Scholars of the first ladyship have utilized public mail concerning first ladies as a category of analysis. [23] While public mail, whether in the form of letters to officials or to newspaper editors, is problematic in that it is self-selected and derived from a more politically attentive and sophisticated audience, it does provide unique insight into the public's thought processes, which are necessary for understanding the cultural everywoman ideal.

CASE STUDIES

Three examples - Lady Bird Johnson, Betty Ford, and Barbara Bush - are utilized to illustrate the existence, operation, and consequences of the cultural everywoman ideal. These first ladies were chosen for several reasons. The first is to achieve adequate representation in historical timing. Christina Wolbrecht breaks the second wave into smaller historical periods. According to her analysis, the 1960s witnessed a dawning interest in women's rights and escalating controversy, though mainstream parties remained somewhat detached. A full-blown movement with bipartisan support emerged in the early 1970s, followed by a conservative backlash that grew in strength throughout the decade. In the 1980s and beyond, the parties and country were polarized around women's issues, and the family values debate became front and center in American politics. [24] Selecting a first lady from each time period illustrates the sustained conflict over the cultural everywoman ideal since the 1960s, despite uneven partisan attachments and relative prominence of various facets of the movement.

In addition, selecting first ladies who exemplified differing gender ideologies is important to preempt criticism that gender-based controversy is limited to a particular "type" of first lady, as scholars have found that more politically active first ladies tend to be criticized more severely. [25] Barbara Bush exemplified the traditionally conservative first lady and Betty Ford was an outspoken feminist sympathizer, while Lady Bird Johnson veered to neither extreme. Achieving diversity in these areas allows for a more effective evaluation of first ladies' potential for success in negotiating the demands of the cultural everywoman expectation, as discussed in the concluding section.

Comprehensive case studies of each first lady's entire tenure would be too lengthy to include here. Therefore, specific, illustrative examples within their tenures that typified their positions on women's roles have been selected in order to ensure depth of exploration of the cultural everywoman ideal. Lady Bird Johnson's management of her main women's outreach activity, Women Doers Luncheons, illustrates the complications in negotiating the two opposing gender roles that emerged with the second wave. Betty Ford's ERA activism placed her firmly on the side of feminists in the central policy debate of the second wave. Barbara Bush's handling of the Wellesley College commencement address drew focus to her traditionalism by placing it in direct contrast to feminism. All three examples activated the public debate about women's roles, thereby generating sufficient research materials.

Accessibility of source material was also a consideration. In this analysis, primary source material from presidential libraries and newspaper archives are utilized to draw together considerations behind first ladies' symbolic representations, the nature of the public reaction to their descriptive representations, and the consequences of both. I had access to useful, illustrative archival documentation for the Johnson and Ford examples. While similar archival materials are not yet available for Barbara Bush, pertinent data on the Wellesley incident was accessible through newspaper databases. These data resources, while diverse by necessity, do sufficiently capture first lady rhetoric and public responses, the main categories of analysis.

Not every first lady *can* be analyzed here, though every first lady since the 1960s *could* be. After all, this analysis contends that the cultural everywoman ideal has been a source of sustained conflict for her office since the second wave. Lady Bird Johnson, Betty Ford, and Barbara Bush were chosen to ensure representation in timing and gender ideology, as well as because of accessibility of data on illustrative examples. The cases chosen should not to discount the relevance of the cultural everywoman ideal for the other first ladyships of this time period.

LADY BIRD JOHNSON:
WOMEN DOERS, ORDINARY WOMEN, AND NATURAL WOMEN

The Johnson Administration (1963 - 1969) saw the emergence of second wave feminism. This burgeoning revolution challenged the dominant separate spheres ideology by contesting the notion that women are primarily responsible for raising children and caring for men, while offering up the belief that women and men should be social and political equals. With a new feminist ideology vying to displace the dominant ideology, Lady Bird Johnson would have to negotiate between the two to uphold the cultural everywoman ideal. This predicament came to light in the controversy that arose over her Women Doers Luncheons.

The first lady's role as "symbol of American women" includes reaching out to women and their causes, concerns, and issues. [26] The Women Doers Luncheons were perhaps Mrs. Johnson's most comprehensive outreach effort to women. Mrs. Johnson initiated these luncheons in 1964 to focus attention on women's involvement in local and national problems. At a typical Women Doers event, a three-course lunch would be served, then Mrs. Johnson would give brief remarks about the topic at hand, and then a woman activist or expert in a particular field would deliver an address about her work. Liz Carpenter, Mrs. Johnson's staff and press secretary, said that the first lady "didn't want to have luncheons of people to sit around and talk about their ailments and their bridge games." Instead, her goal was to feature "a more vital type of woman." Carpenter further characterized the women honored at the luncheons as "professional career woman types, not always an attractive lot, vital, but not always attractive," and therefore "not always the kind that the average woman can identify with." [27] Carpenter's remarks reference the competing gender ideologies between "professional" or "vital" women versus "average" women. However, Mrs. Johnson, by highlighting the "professional" or "vital" woman, symbolically conveyed to the public that she represented them, while she implicitly failed to represent the "average woman."

According to the cultural everywoman theory, dissent ensues when this type of imperfect descriptive representation occurs. And controversy did soon arise over Mrs. Johnson's representation of activist women at the expense of "average" women. There was an outcry from the public, and many women wrote to the White House complaining that the first lady was not doing enough to acknowledge the contributions of "ordinary" women. The first lady's office tried to ameliorate the outcry, with Carpenter writing a fairly standard reply to such complaints. For instance, she replied to one female citizen,

> Let me assure you that we are not unmindful of the millions of "ordinary women." Both President and Mrs. Johnson are very concerned about the ideas and sentiments of women, in and out of public life....There are so many women in this country that obviously Mrs. Johnson cannot meet with and entertain them all, but there are not so many that she is not vitally interested in what they are doing and thinking. [28]

Carpenter's statement that "there are so many women in this country" points to the competing gender ideologies arising out of the second wave. Her admission that Mrs. Johnson chose to meet with career women signifies her failure to represent "ordinary women." Therefore, since the public interpreted the first lady's symbolic representative actions as failing to meet the cultural everywoman ideal, controversy ensued.

The cultural everywoman theory can also apply to the symbolic and descriptive representation the first lady accords to different types within the larger group of career women. For the Women Doers Luncheons, officials and members of the public constantly wrote the first lady's office recommending that Mrs. Johnson represent various career women she was perceived as ignoring. For example, Carpenter received a purposefully unsigned letter from some female members of the armed forces, who asked, "With parties at the White House for 'women doers,' why are women officers of the armed forces ignored???? We, locally, are involved in all kinds of work." [29] Mrs. Johnson's symbolic representative activities conveyed to the military women that she did not descriptively represent them. Their letter illustrates how dissent can ensue when the first lady was perceived as not representing certain sub-groups of career women even while she attempted to represent career women as a whole.

The public outcry spurred Mrs. Johnson and Carpenter to alter the composition of their luncheons. Afterward, they were careful "to include on these guest lists the average woman, the volunteer," and they tried very hard "to get balanced luncheons." [30] By "balanced luncheons," Carpenter meant that they tried to stage events that bridged the cultural divide by including women who incorporated traditionally feminine activities such as volunteerism along with those who pursued professional careers. For instance, Mrs. Johnson selected Dr. Mary Bunting, a member of the Atomic Energy Commission, to be a featured guest at a

Women Doers Luncheon. In her introductory remarks, Mrs. Johnson was careful to note that Dr. Bunting was both a compassionate mother of four and an inquisitive scientist. [31] By presenting luncheons that "balanced" the activist with the traditional, Mrs. Johnson was evidently trying to avert criticism by living up to the cultural everywoman expectation.

Before she was invited to a Women Doers Luncheon, Dr. Bunting's name was cited by Mrs. Johnson in her Radcliffe College baccalaureate address entitled, "The Total Woman." In this address, Mrs. Johnson cited Dr. Bunting as a good example of such a woman. The Radcliffe speech followed soon after the controversy over the Women Doers Luncheons. The White House intended for it to be a major address in which Mrs. Johnson would substantively define her view of the role of American women, which had become unclear with the emergence of feminism. [32]

Mrs. Johnson began her speech by stating the reality of an emergent gender dualism, acknowledging that the dominant cultural ideal for American women had been shattered. She spoke to her audience about the difficulties the new female graduates will have in navigating "a world of experts on women with every bookstore offering up the joys of emancipation and every newsstand proffering the delights of femininity," stating that women's roles were marked by "confusion" more than anything else. [33]

This lack of a dominant gender ideal posed a problem for the new graduates and the first lady alike. Mrs. Johnson could not advocate either emancipation or femininity and meet the cultural everywoman ideal. Instead, she attempted to fuse both types of women into one total woman:

> But actually, amid all the worries and uncertainties - and the provocative doctrines about the role of the educated woman today, a quite remarkable young woman has been emerging in the United States...She might be called the natural woman, the complete woman. She has taken from the past what is vital and discarded the irrelevant or misleading. She has taken over the right to participate fully - whether in jobs, professions, or the political life of the community. She has rejected a number of overtones of the emancipation movement as clearly unworkable....But she wants to be - while being equally involved - pre-eminently a woman, a wife, a mother, a thinking citizen. [34]

Furthermore, she told her audience of female collegians that they could "happily...marry both man and job." She told them, "If you can achieve the precious balance between women's domestic and civic life, you can do more for zest and sanity in our society than by any other achievement." [35] These statements suggest that Mrs. Johnson believed that women's roles were not necessarily dichotomous, or that women had to pick one of the two competing gender ideologies. In essence, by representing both ideologies but choosing neither, she attempted to meet the cultural everywoman ideal.

As the theory goes, if the first lady lives up to the cultural everywoman ideal, there should be little dissent or controversy expressed through forms such as the news media and public letters. Noted American anthropologist and writer Margaret Mead authored an article for *Redbook Magazine* in high praise of Mrs. Johnson's Radcliffe address. She wrote, "In an age when the question of a 'dual role' has presented problems for so many women, Mrs. Johnson has successfully woven together the several strands of a complicated life. Her assurance that it can be done with pleasure is an earnest that it *can* be done by others." Alluding to the cultural everywoman ideal, she wrote, "While Mrs. Johnson is fully encouraging to the whole range of women's possible roles and gently undogmatic about which of these difficult roles they can or should play, she nevertheless reaches out and touches all of them with hard-working, zestful enthusiasm." [36] This report by Mead, a respected cultural authority writing in a widely publicized women's magazine, provides evidence that Mrs. Johnson had some success meeting the cultural everywoman ideal.

After her Radcliffe address, Mrs. Johnson continued to speak out on the fusion of women's civic and domestic responsibilities. In short, she tried to live up to the cultural everywoman expectation and in so doing engendered very little criticism over her gender roles. In her article, Mead maintained that Mrs. Johnson's new role conception could be a model for future first ladies. However, Mrs. Johnson's successors did not, for the most part, try to reconcile competing gender ideologies. The case of Betty Ford illustrates the dissent and debate that ensues when a first lady provides one-sided representation within the gender culture wars.

BETTY FORD:
THE CULTURAL EVERYWOMAN
COMPROMISED IN THE ERA BATTLE

By the 1970s, the emerging feminism of the Johnson years had grown into a full blown movement. However, the Ford Administration (1974 - 1977) also witnessed a large-scale conservative backlash against this cultural revolution. [37] The women's issues debated around this time "not only gave a focus to the reaction against the changes in child rearing, sexual behavior, divorce, and the use of drugs that had taken place in the 1960s and 1970s, they also mobilized a group, traditional homemakers, that had lost status over the two previous decades...." [38] The ERA, which was the controversial centerpiece of the second wave, "came to be seen as an issue that pitted...women of the Right against women of the Left." [39] Though the Republican Party during the Ford years was moving in line with the conservative backlash against feminism, Betty Ford sided squarely with the Left. Her ERA activism in particular reveals the public debate that ensues when a first lady represents only one side of the gender culture wars.

In her first press conference as first lady, Mrs. Ford announced that she would use her position to push the unratified states to adopt the ERA. During her tenure, she hosted ERA information sessions and strategized with ERA advocacy organizations at the White House. She also made ERA lobbying phone calls from the White House to lawmakers in unratified states including Illinois, Oklahoma, Indiana, Nevada, Arizona, Missouri, North Dakota, and Florida. Her ERA advocacy was a form of symbolic representation that conveyed to the public that she 'stood for' women's liberation.

Furthermore, Betty Ford's symbolic representative activities made it quite clear that she did not 'stand for' socially conservative women. One highly publicized illustration of this was her refusal to meet with Phyllis Schlafly's STOP ERA organization. Schlafly wrote to the First Lady,

> We have heard your statements on television that you are opposed to discrimination against women, and noted that you have met with women's groups representing various

minority points of view. We hope you will not discriminate those of us who hold a contrary view, but will grant us equal rights of visiting with the First Lady. [40]

In this statement, Schlafly insinuated that, as first lady, Betty Ford had an obligation to visit with women representing all different points of view. Her urging Mrs. Ford not to "discriminate" against conservative women points toward the first lady's obligation to meet the cultural everywoman expectation. However, Mrs. Ford repeatedly rebuffed Schlafly's meeting requests. One such reply read, "The First Lady recognizes that every citizen is entitled to discuss what should or should not be the law of the land. Accordingly, she expressed her opinion, just as you did in conveying your thoughts to her." [41] In this reply, Mrs. Ford conceded no obligation to represent socially conservative women. According to the cultural everywoman theory, debate or dissent will ensue when such one-sided descriptive representation takes places.

Schlafly was outraged by the First Lady's refusal to represent their point of view, and so she engaged in a public relations campaign against Betty Ford. Schlafly's protest filtered down to the highly mobilized STOP ERA state organizations. For example, STOP ERA New York published the following in one of its newsletters:

> Mrs. Ford has refused to meet with *ANY* of the LEADERS (other than those who are part of International Women's Year and Women's Lib groups!) These women only represent a small number of voters of this state and nation. I personally have written to Mrs. Ford on three occasions, and to date have not had even the courtesy of an answer! I have constantly requested a meeting with her, and her silence has been my answer, and the answer to the many, many leaders who have attempted to speak with her....Why does she only speak to the Libbers who do not represent the thinking of the majority of the women in this nation?...*WE DEMAND* that the wife of the President of our nation MEET WITH US, THE RESPONSIBLE WOMEN WHO ARE THE MAJORITY IN OUR NATION, FOR IS NOT HER PLACE TO CONSULT.... "*ALL OF THE PEOPLE?*" [42]

Betty Ford's meeting refusals symbolically conveyed to socially conservative women that she did not descriptively represent them. However, by claiming that it was Betty Ford's responsibility as first lady to represent all of the people, this group attempted to bind her to the cultural everywoman expectation by demanding she meet with their side.

Schlafly further protested the use of White House resources for Mrs. Ford's ERA lobbying efforts and demanded an account of how much federal money was spent on her long distance phone calls to legislators. [43] The Republican Convention of Oklahoma passed a resolution requesting that Mrs. Ford abstain from using her office to influence ERA legislation. [44] STOP ERA groups picketed the White House, demanding Betty Ford quit using public resources to lobby for the ERA. However, the White House defended the First Lady, saying it was her "personal prerogative" to make phone calls in her own home, as Betty Ford vowed to stand her ground and keep lobbying. [45] Not only is this evidence of the dissent that accompanies imperfect descriptive representation, here we also begin to see the basis upon which supporters and opponents of Betty Ford grounded their arguments. Betty Ford and her supporters justified her actions as a private, personal prerogative, thereby distancing her ERA lobbying from her official position as first lady. By distancing Betty Ford's "personal" actions from her "political" position, they were attempting to negate the requirements of the cultural everywoman ideal in order to justify her actions and alleviate some of the dissent.

Betty Ford's opponents acknowledged that she was acting in her official capacity, but argued that ERA lobbying was not compatible with her position. For example, a member of the Illinois General Assembly wrote to her,

> I hope you will accept my respectful request that you immediately desist in your long-distance telephone lobbying campaign, and that you refrain from using the prestige of the White House and your position as First Lady of the Land to promote adoption of this extremely controversial, comprehensive and emotionally charged Amendment....In my opinion, this lobbying activity is demeaning to your position as First Lady.... [46]

While this letter could be interpreted as a call to preserve the traditionally feminine notion of the first lady's role, one might also take this as a warning to Mrs. Ford to heed the cultural everywoman ideal by not taking sides in the "emotionally charged" women's movement. Evidence for this is also captured in one citizen's letter that read, "What right do you have as a representative of all women to contact the legislators and put pressure on them to pass the hated ERA? That is certainly below the dignity of the First Lady of the Land and is certainly an all-time low for any First Lady." [47] When any public official is perceived as not living up to the obligations of her office, the dignity of that office is lessened. Here, Betty Ford not living up to the cultural everywoman ideal by picking sides in the gender culture wars caused some segments of the public to think she was disgracing her position. As the above citizen's letter indicates, this public debate and dissent was a consequence of Betty Ford not serving as "a representative of all women."

Betty Ford received thousands of letters from legislators, officials, and members of the public concerning her ERA activism. The bulk of this came in the early months of 1975, when the protest was at its peak. At one point, Mrs. Ford's office reported that letters were running 3 - 1 in opposition to her activism. But the following month, the tide had turned, and the mail was 3 - 1 in favor of the First Lady's ERA activism, with 6,412 letters or wires for and 2,729 against. [48]

Despite the favorable turn in her public mail, by the summer of 1975, Betty Ford's staff began to comprehend the consequences of her not meeting the cultural everywoman ideal, so they began to tailor some of her appearances to reach out to socially conservative women. Her participation as keynote speaker in the Identity in Homemaking conference, which was to give recognition to the importance of homemaking as a profession, was a strategic political move by her staff to counteract the fallout from her ERA activism. They believed that Mrs. Ford's participation "might have a positive effect of focusing her interest in women in the home and diluting some of what has been characterized as her 'radical' stand in support of the Equal Rights Amendment." [49]

The fallout surrounding her ERA activism was compounded by the negative public reaction to her controversial August 1975 *60 Minutes* interview, in which she spoke out in favor of the ERA, abortion rights, and sexual liberation. As a result, going into the 1976 presidential election, she was forced to circumscribe her political activism. [50]

In the fall of 1975, her staff recommended that she decline an invitation to be honored by the National Woman's Party for her ERA activism "due to the recent national discussion following Sixty Minutes [*sic*]." [51] And she told reporters before the New Hampshire primary that, while she would have a speaking role on the campaign trail, she would leave the issues to the president. [52] Here we see the consequences of not meeting the cultural everywoman ideal. After the fallout, Betty Ford was publicly compelled to justify her convictions, alter her representative actions, and circumscribe her political roles.

BARBARA BUSH: WHAT KIND OF ROLE MODEL?

Ronald Reagan's election in 1980 effectively solidified the defeat of the ERA and the end of the second wave, though its legacy would be lasting. By the late 1970s, women who worked outside of the home outnumbered those who did not. [53] Feminists coalesced under the Democratic Party, which advocated reproductive freedom and nontraditional roles for women, while Republicans adopted the family values mantra. During the Bush Administration (1989 - 1993), family values was the cultural standard around which a broad debate over women's roles was waged. [54] Barbara Bush became caught up in this cultural war upon her invitation to deliver the 1990 commencement speech at Wellesley College. The Wellesley incident reveals how difficult it is for first ladies to meet the cultural everywoman ideal in the post-second wave era.

For many Americans, Barbara Bush symbolized the quintessential traditional woman. She dropped out of Smith College in 1944 to marry her husband, mothered five children, and never held a full-time paying job. As first lady, she took on the cause of children's literacy, a traditionally feminine pet project. Therefore, as a symbolic representative, she stood for all that was anti-feminist and pro-family.

Wellesley College also engaged in symbolic representation when it chose Barbara Bush as a commencement speaker. "Graduation marks a transition over which the commencement speaker symbolically presides. The choice of the speaker thus becomes a way an institution signals how it will be sending its graduates into the world and who they should become." [55] When Wellesley announced that Mrs. Bush would be the commencement speaker, 150 students, roughly one-fourth of the graduating class, signed a petition opposing the symbolism the college conveyed with its invitation. The petition stated,

> We, the undersigned, as concerned Senior Class members, are disappointed at the final results of the Commencement Speaker selection process. We are outraged by this choice and feel it is important to make ourselves heard immediately. Wellesley teaches us that we will be rewarded on the basis of our own merit, not on that of a spouse. To honor Barbara Bush as a commencement speaker is to honor a woman who has gained recognition through the achievements of her husband, which contradicts what we have been taught over the last four years at Wellesley. Regardless of her political affiliation, we feel that she does not successfully exemplify the qualities that Wellesley seeks to instill in us. We realize that retracting our offer to Mrs. Bush at this time would be discourteous. Therefore, we propose extending an invitation to an additional guest speaker who would more aptly reflect the self-affirming qualities of a Wellesley graduate. [56]

The first lady's inaccurate descriptive representation is central to the students' petition. The phrases "she does not successfully exemplify...us" and she does not "aptly reflect the self-affirming qualities of a Wellesley graduate" are indicative of this. In essence, the

Wellesley students argued that Mrs. Bush could not stand for them as a commencement speaker because she was not sufficiently like them.

The petition also draws out one crucial aspect of the first lady's fundamental character that automatically disqualifies her as a descriptive representative in the minds of some women, such as the Wellesley graduates. Though many first ladies have been accomplished women in their own right, they occupy their prominent political position by virtue of marrying a powerful man. The Wellesley graduates opposed Mrs. Bush because she had "gained recognition through the achievements of her husband" and not on her own merit. The graduates further protested Mrs. Bush's recognition by means of marriage on graduation day by wearing purple armbands in celebration of the "unknown women who have dedicated their lives to the service of others," according to a letter left on all the folding chairs in the graduation tent. [57] This argument is consistent with the strain of feminism, embraced by some of the students, that wishes to recognize the caring, unpaid contributions made by unknown women around the world. [58] Furthermore, this recognition-through-marriage opposition argument reveals that there are elements of the first lady's essential character that are fundamentally in tension. A first lady cannot possibly meet the cultural everywoman expectation if she is criticized on the grounds of her marital connection to the president, a factor that also essentially defines her position.

The student petition itself is evidence of the dissent that ensues when a first lady fails to descriptively represent a particular demographic. Moreover, the debate about Barbara Bush as an appropriate descriptive representative for Wellesley College women and for American women in general quickly spread from the college campus to the broader public. The petition sparked numerous editorials, opinion pieces, and letters to the editor. Overall, 7,000 print-medium stories on the Wellesley protest were carried around the world. [59] The main theme or question to emerge from this coverage was what kind of gender role model does Barbara Bush offer to Wellesley students?

Some citizens who wrote in reaction to the Wellesley coverage wished to highlight the value of republican motherhood, with its concurrent qualities of sacrifice and selflessness for the betterment of country. Consider the following quotes from editorial writers and letters to the editor of *The Washington Post*:

> Mrs. Bush is being judged on her own merits, not her husband's. **One cannot be unintelligent, undiplomatic and inflexible and become First Lady**....Does Wellesley College teach its students, those young impressionable minds, to abhor being a wife, to avoid any form **of commitment that might sacrifice one's independence**, and that marriage is for those who fail to graduate? [60]

> Are women who have lived their lives in great part in the service of their families and their communities, as opposed to an institution or organization, less entitled to dignity and respect? Come on now. Are we so enthralled with the talisman of salary or the mystique of initials after our names that we see value in no other kind of life? Do we see no worth in mothering? .... One other small point that should be considered by any stable mind is that being the wife of president is very definitely a job, but it is, again, a job without pay....But although the position is one of privilege, it is also one of substantial pressure.... [61]

> In my book, Barbara Bush is beyond price. She can be trusted to handle herself well, to give of her talents and energies to make life better for others. She even knows how to rear

civilized children, a much more noble effort, in my view, than building cars that end up in the junkyard in 10 years or helping corporations merge themselves into overwhelming debt....What we do know about her may, in part, be due to her husband's position. That she is genuinely worth knowing about is due entirely to her own numerous and permanent accomplishments. [62]

These writers who celebrate Barbara Bush as an appropriate gender role model and highlight the value of republican motherhood also downplay or dismiss the fact that the first lady obtained her prominent position by virtue of marrying a powerful man, the key sticking point for feminists.

However, many other writers agreed with the Wellesley graduates that Barbara Bush was an inappropriate role model.

Critics of the students seem to miss the point and are perhaps sidetracked in defending Barbara Bush's many admirable qualities. If Wellesley wants to honor a women [sic] who has chosen family and unpaid work, it should be a woman known for this (or unknown) in her own right in order to properly give value to this type of profession. Being a president's wife is probably not a career field that seniors need to pursue. [63]

Mrs. Bush's lifetime achievements are praiseworthy....Volunteer work, such as Mrs. Bush's efforts in the cause of universal literacy, is laudable. However, these are not the things one goes to college to learn....Women who have studied for their degrees, who have ambitions to make their own way in what is still and will for many years to come (if not eternally) be a man's world do not need to have as their commencement speaker/icon a wife-and-mother, both of which roles are dependent on men. They need a symbol of achievement on less traditional fronts....George Bush would be invited to speak because he's powerful and famous and the president of the United States. His wife has been invited to speak because she too is powerful and famous - but both of these qualities have been derived solely from her husband. [64]

While these writers characterize Mrs. Bush's republican motherhood as admirable, they believe the fact that she derived her position from marrying a powerful man makes her unable to serve as an appropriate gender role model for or a descriptive representative of the college graduates. Thus, the essential position of first lady, in the context of post-second wave feminism, renders the cultural everywoman ideal virtually unattainable.

Barbara Bush's speech was carried live on broadcast and cable networks and was covered by a large entourage of reporters from around the globe. Her speech was reminiscent of Lady Bird Johnson's Radcliffe College commencement address, in that she delicately walked the line between feminist and family values in trying to meet the cultural everywoman expectation. The main theme Barbara Bush carried through her speech was that graduates should resist being pigeonholed into a particular identity or role in society. She used the analogy of Wellesley's Annual Hoop Race to illustrate how gender dualism harmfully routs individualism:

For over fifty years, it was said that the winner of Wellesley's Annual Hoop Race would be the first to get married. Now they say the winner will be the first to become the CEO. Both of these stereotypes show too little tolerance....So I offer you today a new legend: The winner of the hoop race will be the first to realize her dream...not society's dream...her own personal dream. And who knows? Somewhere out in this audience may even be someone who will one day follow in my footsteps, and preside over the White House as the President's spouse. I wish him well! [65]

To Barbara Bush, the cultural everywoman was not necessarily someone who gains acceptance by blending the traditional with the modern but someone who gains acceptance by realizing her own personal dream. However, this view is predicated on societal acceptance of all women's roles. By maintaining that women's variety of choices should be universally accepted, Mrs. Bush was relating an ideal vision of society's view of gender roles. The reality, as Mrs. Bush even recognized in her hoop race analogy, is a gender dualism which binds Wellesley students and the first lady alike and thwarts the first lady's ability to meet the cultural everywoman ideal.

Nevertheless, there is evidence that Mrs. Bush's speech met the cultural everywoman expectation to some extent. Press reports declared it a triumph. "A rock'em-sock'em smash hit," said *The Washington Post*. [66] Another report proclaimed, "They loved it...the crowd cheered, applauded and laughed at her jokes." [67] However, there is also evidence that she met the cultural everywoman ideal only insofar as she represented role choices for elite, married women.

An editorial from *The Washington Post* entitled, "Mrs. Bush Forgot Working Women," discussed how working, poor women could gain nothing from the First Lady's advice to settle the conflict between work and family. For these women, quality time with family is an aspiration, not an option. [68] As another individual editorialized,

> Like countless other women in the country, I missed the live coverage of Mrs. Bush's speech because I was working. I work out of necessity....When Mrs. Bush dropped out of school, she did not put herself at financial risk. If something had happened to her husband, because of death or divorce, she...certainly wouldn't have suffered any economic hardships. She would have continued to be an upper-class woman with plenty of money to educate her children, pursue her volunteer work and live the good life....Mrs. Bush is a woman of grace, style and wit, but she also was born, raised and is still living in the protected world of wealth and privilege. It is from that perspective that she speaks [and] acts.... [69]

All of these writers argue that Mrs. Bush, as a member of the elite class, cannot stand for or descriptively represent poor, working women because she is not sufficiently like them.

Barbara Bush also received criticism for not descriptively representing formerly married women, many of whom are also members of the lower classes. On the day before the Wellesley commencement, the National Displaced Homemakers Network issued a report detailing the increasing ranks of divorced or widowed housewives. As one reporter commented,

> Part of Barbara Bush's considerable charm is that she has a way of saying all the things we wish were true. She is reassuring. For her, the system worked. She left college to marry the man she loved and 45 years later not only are they still married but they seem very much in love. Her investment worked out....The harsh reality, however, is that in too many houses women who believed that these human connections were the most important investments they could make have been fleeced by death or divorce. And they are rapidly plunged into poverty. [70]

As all of this debate indicates, because of her traditional, elite and still married status, Barbara Bush could not stand for all women and thus could not meet the cultural everywoman ideal.

DISCUSSION

There is no societal consensus on what it means to be a woman. Given this, the cultural everywoman ideal, which is premised on a societal consensus about American womanhood, seems to have set first ladies up for political failure. The cultural everywoman ideal creates a double bind for American first ladies: If they act feminist, they are criticized; if they act traditionally feminine, they are likewise criticized. In their political actions and inactions, both activist and traditional first ladies are constrained by their gender. Therefore, this theory seems to present a rather pessimistic framework for first ladies' potential for success. But is this the end of the story? Is it completely impossible for first ladies to free themselves from this double bind?

First it is necessary to answer the question: what might constitute success in overcoming the double bind? While it is probably impossible to totally and completely overcome it, how can first ladies somewhat avoid the pitfalls the double bind presents? The mark of a successful first lady is her ability to negotiate a socially acceptable definition of womanhood and reflect this in her own gender role performance. A socially acceptable definition of womanhood is one that is seen by the public as veering to neither extreme on the feminist – anti-feminist spectrum. In her descriptive and symbolic representations, she should be careful to strike a balance between traditional expectations and a more active role. Clearly preferring neither one, a successful first lady will incorporate elements of both.

Of the cases examined here, Lady Bird Johnson was the most successful in attempting to live up to the cultural everywoman expectation. While she was subject to criticism, she nonetheless explicitly attempted to forge a consensus. Her "total woman" theory, which unified the roles of career women and homemakers, illustrates this. This theory was enunciated in her Radcliffe address but embodied in her overall first lady role even beyond the realm of women's outreach. For example, she was an outspoken activist for the environment yet did not shirk her traditional responsibilities. Yet, when she veered away from "average women" by focusing her attention on "women doers," the delicate gender balance was disrupted and public criticism ensued. Still, she was careful to respond by altering the balance of her luncheons in order to meet the cultural everywoman expectation. Laura Bush is a more recent first lady who has been successful in negotiating the cultural everywoman expectation. As one reporter observed during the 2004 presidential campaign,

> Laura Bush does not stand up at 'W Stands for Women' rallies and hand out her cookie recipes.....She talks about how 'across America, millions of women are raising families, working full time, going to college, starting their own businesses.' If you are in the audience in a business suit, she's speaking to you. If you're pushing the stroller, she's speaking to you." [71]

In Laura Bush's overall role, she was able to forge somewhat of a consensus. She executed the role of traditional wife at home, but pushed for women's liberation abroad, especially in Africa and the Middle East. She was active in the policy realm, but in the traditionally feminine area of education.

Barbara Bush was also somewhat successful in meeting the cultural everywoman ideal, but less so than Lady Bird Johnson. The very thing that ignited the Wellesley controversy was the first lady's anti-feminism expressed both in her life and in her office. She squarely embodied the traditional family values that the Republican Party touted. In her commencement speech, she mainly promoted tolerance for women's chosen and varied life paths. While she did not try to harmonize elements of feminism with anti-feminism to the extent that Lady Bird Johnson did, she did encourage graduates to be non-judgmental about others' choices concerning gender roles. Barbara Bush's speech was generally regarded as a success, showing that in these public remarks at least she was able to meet the cultural everywoman ideal to an extent. However, encouraging tolerance about choices between lifestyles is not quite as effective of a means toward achieving the cultural everywoman ideal. This is evidenced by the criticism in the wake of her speech that many women lack choice. For encouraging tolerance does not necessarily, physically, or practically reconcile the crossfire of opposing ideals, and it simultaneously draws attention to the fact that only a subset of privileged women has had a genuine choice about which gender roles they will pursue. It is also premised on others actually possessing this attitude of tolerance.

Betty Ford was the least successful in meeting the cultural everywoman ideal. In her ERA activism, she encouraged the crossfire of opposing ideals by firmly taking one side in the feminist debate, while refusing to acknowledge the voices on the other side. Her rebuffing of Phyllis Schlafly is illustrative. Hillary Clinton is a more recent example of a first lady who was also not viewed as a cultural everywoman. In the 1992 campaign, she famously told a reporter, "I suppose I could have stayed at home and baked cookies and had teas, but what I decided to do was fulfill my profession, which I entered before my husband was in public life." Hillary Clinton reported that she received hundreds of letters about her "tea and cookies" comment. While some were praiseworthy, she reported that many other were venomous, as her comment had been interpreted as expressing hostility toward stay-at-home mothers. [72] This comment, along with some others made during the campaign, cemented her public image as firmly on the feminist side of the family values debate, impeding her ability to negotiate a socially acceptable definition of womanhood in her future tenure as first lady.

However, while it can be somewhat possible for first ladies to have some success in meeting the cultural everywoman ideal and get around the double bind, the very existence of the ideal still does circumscribe first ladies' freedom to act independently. Betty Ford once said, "I do not believe that being First Lady should prevent me from expressing my ideas. I spoke out on this important issue [ERA] because of my deep personal convictions. Why should my husband's job, or yours, prevent us from being ourselves." [73] Clearly, Betty Ford did not see that the first ladyship does not allow this kind of personal autonomy. The cultural everywoman ideal does in fact prevent first ladies from being themselves and from expressing deeply held personal convictions. The cultural everywoman ideal forced Lady Bird Johnson to alter the nature of her women's outreach activities. It circumscribed Betty Ford's political activism. It forced Barbara Bush to publicly defend and justify her personal choices regarding gender roles.

Individual autonomy is a fundamental liberal ideal on which this country was founded. That the first ladyship lacks capacity to express this ideal raises important questions about the lingering societal constraints of gender on both the first lady and female citizens, especially since the first lady symbolically reflects the country's beliefs about womanhood. Further study will be needed to explore these continued gender-based constraints and whether the first ladyship has the capacity for its occupants to function autonomously, despite the obstacles posed by the cultural everywoman ideal.

REFERENCES

[1] MaryAnne Borrelli, "Competing Conceptions of the First Ladyship: Public Responses to Betty Ford's *60 Minutes* Interview," *Presidential Studies Quarterly* 31, no. 3 (2001), 397-414.

[2] Borrelli, "Competing Conceptions of the First Ladyship"; Erica Scharrer and Kim Bissell, "Overcoming Traditional Boundaries: The Role of Political Activity in Media Coverage of First Ladies," *Women and Politics* 21, no. 1 (2000), 55-83; Betty Houchin Winfield, "From a Sponsored Status to Satellite to Her Own Orbit: The First Lady News at a New Century," *White House Studies* 1, no. 1 (2001), 21-33.

[3] Robert P. Watson, *The Presidents' Wives: Reassessing the Office of the First Lady* (Boulder, CO: Lynne Rienner Publishers, 2000).

[4] Watson, *The Presidents' Wives*, 78.

[5] Mary Ellen Guy, "Hillary, Health Care, and Gender Power," In *Gender Power, Leadership, and Governance*, Georgia Duerst-Lahti and Rita Mae Kelly, eds. (Ann Arbor: University of Michigan Press, 1995), 239-256.

[6] Hillary Rodham Clinton, *Living History* (New York: Simon and Schuster, 2003), 157.

[7] Anthony Mughan and Barry C. Burden, "Hillary Clinton and the President's Reelection," In *Reelection 1996: How Americans Voted*, Herbert F. Weisberg and Janet M. Box-Steffensmeier, eds. (New York: Chatham House Publishers, 1999), 111-124.

[8] Hanna Fenichel Pitkin, *The Concept of Representation* (Berkeley: University of California Press, 1967).

[9] Pitkin, *The Concept of Representation*, 209.

[10] MaryAnne Borrelli, *The President's Cabinet: Gender, Power, and Representation* (Boulder, CO: Lynne Rienner Publishers, 2002).

[11] MaryAnne Borrelli, "The First Lady as Formal Advisor to the President: When East (Wing) Meets West (Wing)," *Women and Politics* 24 (1) (2002), 25-45.

[12] Jill Abraham Hummer, "First Ladies and American Women: Representation in the Modern Presidency," Ph.D. diss. University of Virginia (2007).

[13] Pitkin, *The Concept of Representation*, 80.

[14] Pitkin, *The Concept of Representation*, 61.

[15] Pitkin, *The Concept of Representation*, 61.

[16] Pitkin, *The Concept of Representation*, 99.

[17] Kathleen Dolan, Melissa Deckman and Michele L. Swers, *Women and Politics: Paths to Power and Political Influence* (Upper Saddle River, NJ: Pearson Prentice Hall, 2007), 11.

[18] Christina Wolbrecht, *The Politics of Women's Rights: Parties, Positions, and Change* (Princeton: Princeton University Press, 2000), 31.

[19] Barbara Burrell, *Public Opinion, the First Ladyship, and Hillary Rodham Clinton* (New York: Garland Publishing, Inc., 1997).
[20] Mary Stuckey, *The President as Interpreter-in-Chief* (Chatham, NJ: Chatham House Publishers, Inc., 1991).
[21] Stuckey, *The President as Interpreter-in-Chief*, 139.
[22] Myra Gutin, "Using All Available Means of Persuasion: The Twentieth Century First Lady as Public Communicator," *The Social Science Journal* 37, no. 4 (2000), 563-575; Shawn J. Parry-Giles and Diane M. Blair, "The Rise of the Rhetorical First Lady: Politics, Gender Ideology, and Women's Voice," *Rhetoric and Public Affairs* 5, no. 4 (2002), 565-599; Molly Meijer Wertheimer, *Inventing a Voice: The Rhetoric of American First Ladies of the Twentieth Century* (Lanham, MD: Rowman and Littlefield, 2004).
[23] Borrelli, "Competing Conceptions of the First Ladyship"; Rosanna Hertz and Susan M. Reverby, "Gentility, Gender, and Political Protest: The Barbara Bush Controversy at Wellesley College," *Gender and Society* 9 (October 1995), 594-611.
[24] Wolbrecht, *The Politics of Women's Rights*.
[25] Scharrer and Bissell, "Overcoming Traditional Boundaries."
[26] Watson, *The Presidents' Wives*, 79.
[27] Liz Carpenter, Oral History Interview, April 4, 1969, Lyndon Baines Johnson Library (LBJL).
[28] Carpenter, Oral History Interview.
[29] Unsigned to Liz Carpenter, Undated, Folder: Women Doers Luncheons [2 of 2], Box 71, Liz Carpenter Subject Files (LCSF), White House Social Files (WHSF), LBJL.
[30] Carpenter, Oral History Interview.
[31] Lady Bird Johnson, Press Release, June 29, 1965, Folder: Women Doers Luncheon 6/29/65, Box 16, LCSF, WHSF, LBJL.
[32] Eric F. Goldman to Liz Carpenter, April 21, 1964, Folder: Radcliffe Speech – June 9, 1964, Box 78, LCSF, WHSF, LBJL.
[33] Lady Bird Johnson, June 9, 1964, Press Release, Folder: Radcliffe Speech – June 9, 1964, Box 78, LCSF, WHSF, LBJL.
[34] Johnson, Radcliffe Speech.
[35] Johnson, Radcliffe Speech.
[36] Margaret Mead, "Mrs. Lyndon B. Johnson: A New Kind of First Lady?" *Redbook Magazine* (June 1965), p. 12, Folder: 4/1/65-9/30/65, Box 62. PP5 / Johnson, Lady Bird, White House Central Files (WHCF), LBJL.
[37] Wolbrecht, *The Politics of Women's Rights*, 34-44.
[38] Jane J Mansbridge, *Why We Lost the ERA* (Chicago: University of Chicago Press, 1986), 5-6.
[39] Mansbridge, *Why We Lost the ERA*, 6.
[40] Phyllis Schlafly to Betty Ford, September 16, 1974, Folder: Schlafly, Phyllis, Box 336, Name File (NF), Social Files (SF), WHCF, Gerald R. Ford Library (GRFL).
[41] Nancy Howe to Phyllis Schlafly, February 27, 1975, Folder: Schlafly, Phyllis, Box 336, NF, SF, WHCF, GRFL.
[42] STOP ERA New York Newsletter, March 11, 1976, Folder: 3/20/76 New York City - Women's National Republican Club, Box 23, Sheila R. Weidenfeld Files (SRWF), GRFL.

[43] *Chicago Tribune*, "Alton's Own Challenges Betty on ERA," February 11, 1975, Folder: Ford, Betty - Equal Rights Amendment, Box 21, Patricia Lindh and Jeanne Holm Files (PLJHF), GRFL.

[44] Mrs. Arthur Maddox to Gerald Ford, August 22, 1975, Folder: 6/11/76 - Equal Rights Amendment - State Legislatures, Box 47, SRWF, GRFL.

[45] United Press International, February 14, 1975, Folder: Women—Clippings (1), Box 47, SRWF, GRFL.

[46] Donald E. Deuster to Betty Ford, February 6, 1975, Folder: 6/11/76 - Samples of Public Mail, Box 47, SRWF, GRFL.

[47] "Mrs. Ford's Mail 3-1 Against ERA," *The News* (Mexico City), February 21, 1975, Folder: Ford, Betty - Equal Rights Amendment, Box 21, PLJHF, GRFL.

[48] United Press International, March 3, 1975, Folder: Ford, Betty - Equal Rights Amendment, Box 21, PLJHF, GRFL.

[49] Susan Porter to Sheila Weidenfeld, May 1, 1975, Folder: 9/26/75 Identity in Homemaking Conference (1), Box 7, SRWF, GRFL.

[50] Borrelli, "Competing Conceptions of the First Ladyship."

[51] Susan Porter to Betty Ford, 1975, Folder: Photo Opportunities - National Woman's Party, Box 2, Susan Porter Files, GRFL.

[52] "Betty Ford to Speak out in Campaign," Associated Press, January 12, 1976, Folder: Betty Ford - Campaigning, Box 37, SRWF, GRFL.

[53] Barbara Bergmann, *The Economic Emergence of Women*, 2 ed. (New York: Palgrave McMillan, 2005), 11.

[54] Wolbrecht, *The Politics of Women's Rights*, 62.

[55] Hertz and Reverby, "Gentility, Gender, and Political Protest," 595.

[56] Hertz and Reverby, "Gentility, Gender, and Political Protest," 596.

[57] Donnie Radcliffe, "Barbara Bush, Wowing Wellesley," *The Washington Post*, June 2, 1990.

[58] Abigail McCarthy, "Of Several Minds: The War within—Two Strains of Feminism," *Commonweal* 117, no. 13 (1990), 408.

[59] Hertz and Reverby, "Gentility, Gender, and Political Protest," 596.

[60] Carolyn Frenger, Letter to the editor, *The Washington Post*. May 1, 1990.

[61] Jessica Catto, "...For the Graduates," *The Washington Post*, May 8, 1990.

[62] Carolyn Hinton, Letter to the editor, *The Washington Post*, May 12, 1990.

[63] Doris Rosenbaum Teplitz, Letter to the editor, *The Washington Post*, May 12, 1990.

[64] Grace C. Gilinger, Letter to the editor, *The Washington Post*, May 14, 1990.

[65] Barbara Bush, June 1, 1990, "Remarks of Mrs. Bush at Wellesley College Commencement," http://www.wellesley.edu/PublicAffairs/Commencement/1990/bush.html (May 20, 2008).

[66] Tom Shales, "The First Lady, at the Head of the Class," *The Washington Post*, June 2, 1990.

[67] Donnie Radcliffe, "Barbara Bush, Wowing Wellesley," *The Washington Post*, June 2, 1990.

[68] Richard Cohen, "Mrs. Bush Forgot Working Women," *The Washington Post*, June 5, 1990.

[69] Mary Fay Bourgoin, Letter to the editor, *The Washington Post*, June 15, 1990.

[70] Judy Mann, "The High Risks of Homemaking," *The Washington Post*, June 6, 1990.

[71] Hanna Rosin, "A 'Real Job'? It Works for Laura Bush," *The Washington Post*, October 21, 2004.

[72] Hillary Rodham Clinton, *Living History* (New York: Simon and Schuster, 2003), 109 - 110.

[73] Betty Ford, "Remarks of the First Lady at the Greater Cleveland International Women's Year Congress," October 25, 1975, Folder: 10/25/75 Cleveland (2) Greater Cleveland IWY Congress, Box 19, SRWF, GRFL.

GOVERNMENT DOCUMENTS

Chapter 21

NSC 68: UNITED STATES OBJECTIVES AND PROGRAMS FOR NATIONAL SECURITY (APRIL 14, 1950) (EXCERPTS)

A REPORT TO THE PRESIDENT PURSUANT TO THE PRESIDENT'S DIRECTIVE OF JANUARY 31, 1950

ANALYSIS

I. Background of the Present Crisis

Within the past thirty-five years the world has experienced two global wars of tremendous violence. It has witnessed two revolutions – the Russian and the Chinese – of extreme scope and intensity. It has also seen the collapse of five empires – the Ottoman, the Austro-Hungarian, German, Italian, and Japanese – and the drastic decline of two major imperial systems, the British and the French. During the span of one generation, the international distribution of power has been fundamentally altered. For several centuries it had proved impossible for any one nation to gain such preponderant strength that a coalition of other nations could not in time face it with greater strength. The international scene was marked by recurring periods of violence and war, but a system of sovereign and independent states was maintained, over which no state was able to achieve hegemony.

Two complex sets of factors have now basically altered this historic distribution of power. First, the defeat of Germany and Japan and the decline of the British and French Empires have interacted with the development of the United States and the Soviet Union in such a way that power increasingly gravitated to these two centers. Second, the Soviet Union, unlike previous aspirants to hegemony, is animated by a new fanatic faith, anti-thetical to our own, and seeks to impose its absolute authority over the rest of the world. Conflict has, therefore, become endemic and is waged, on the part of the Soviet Union, by violent or non-violent methods in accordance with the dictates of expediency. With the development of increasingly terrifying weapons of mass destruction, every individual faces the ever-present possibility of annihilation should the conflict enter the phase of total war.

On the one hand, the people of the world yearn for relief from the anxiety arising from the risk of atomic war. On the other hand, any substantial further extension of the area under the domination of the Kremlin would raise the possibility that no coalition adequate to confront the Kremlin with greater strength could be assembled. It is in this context that this Republic and its citizens in the ascendancy of their strength stand in their deepest peril.

The issues that face us are momentous, involving the fulfillment or destruction not only of this Republic but of civilization itself. They are issues which will not await our deliberations. With conscience and resolution this Government and the people it represents must now take new and fateful decisions.

IX. Possible Courses of Action

Introduction. Four possible courses of action by the United States in the present situation can be distinguished. They are:

(a) Continuation of current policies, with current and currently projected programs for carrying out these policies;
(b) Isolation;
(c) War; and
(d) A more rapid building up of the political, economic, and military strength of the free world than provided under a, with the purpose of reaching, if possible, a tolerable state of order among nations without war and of preparing to defend ourselves in the event that the free world is attacked.

The role of negotiation. Negotiation must be considered in relation to these courses of action. A negotiator always attempts to achieve an agreement which is somewhat better than the realities of his fundamental position would justify and which is, in any case, not worse than his fundamental position requires. This is as true in relations among sovereign states as in relations between individuals. The Soviet Union possesses several advantages over the free world in negotiations on any issue:

(a) It can and does enforce secrecy on all significant facts about conditions within the Soviet Union, so that it can be expected to know more about the realities of the free world's position than the free world knows about its position;
(b) It does not have to be responsive in any important sense to public opinion;
(c) It does not have to consult and agree with any other countries on the terms it will offer 'And accept; and
(d) It can influence public opinion in other countries while insulating the peoples under its control.

These are important advantages. Together with the unfavorable trend of our power position, they militate, as is shown in Section A below, against successful negotiation of a general settlement at this time. For although the United States probably now possesses, principally in atomic weapons, a force adequate to deliver a powerful blow upon the Soviet Union and to open the road to victory in a long war, it is not sufficient by itself to advance the position of the United States in the cold war.

The problem is to create such political and economic conditions in the free world, backed by force sufficient to inhibit Soviet attack, that the Kremlin will accommodate itself to these conditions, gradually withdraw, and eventually change its policies drastically. It has been shown in Chapter VIII that truly effective control of atomic energy would require such an opening up of the Soviet Union and such evidence in other ways of its good faith and its intent to co-exist in peace as to reflect or at least initiate a change in the Soviet system.

Clearly under present circumstances we will not be able to negotiate a settlement which calls for a change in the Soviet system. What, then, is the role of negotiation?

In the first place, the public in the United States and in other free countries will require, as a condition to firm policies and adequate programs directed to the frustration of the Kremlin design, that the free world be continuously prepared to negotiate agreements with the Soviet Union on equitable terms. It is still argued by many people here and abroad that equitable agreements with the Soviet Union are possible, and this view will gain force if the Soviet Union begins to show signs of accommodation, even on unimportant issues.

The free countries must always, therefore, be prepared to negotiate and must be ready to take the initiative at times in seeking negotiation. They must develop a negotiating position which defines the issues and the terms on which they would be prepared – and at what stages – to accept agreements with the Soviet Union. The terms must be fair in the view of popular opinion in the free world. This means that they must be consistent with a positive program for peace – in harmony with the United Nations' Charter and providing, at a minimum, for the effective control of all armaments by the United Nations or a successor organization. The terms must not require more of the Soviet Union than such behavior and such participation in a world organization. The fact that such conduct by the Soviet Union is impossible without such a radical change in Soviet policies as to constitute a change in the Soviet system would then emerge as a result of the Kremlin's unwillingness to accept such terms or of its bad faith in observing them.

A sound negotiating position is, therefore, an essential element in the ideological conflict. For some time after a decision to build up strength, any offer of, or attempt at, negotiation of a general settlement along the lines of the Berkeley speech by the Secretary of State could be only a tactic.' Nevertheless, concurrently with a decision and a start on building up the strength of the free world, it may be desirable to pursue this tactic both to gain public support for the program and to minimize the immediate risks of war. It is urgently necessary for the United States to determine its negotiating position and to obtain agreement with its major allies on the purposes and terms of negotiation.

In the second place, assuming that the United States in cooperation with other free countries decides and acts to increase the strength of the free world and assuming that the Kremlin chooses the path of accommodation, it will from time to time be necessary and desirable to negotiate on various specific issues with the Kremlin as the area of possible agreement widens.

The Kremlin will have three major objectives in negotiations with the United States. The first is to eliminate the atomic capabilities of the United States; the second is to prevent the effective mobilization of the superior potential of the free world in human and material resources; and the third is to secure a withdrawal of United States forces from, and commitments to, Europe and Japan. Depending on its evaluation of its own strengths and weaknesses as against the West's (particularly the ability and will of the West to sustain its efforts), it will or will not be prepared to make important concessions to achieve these major objectives. It is unlikely that the Kremlin's evaluation is such that it would now be prepared to make significant concessions.

The objectives of the United States and other free countries in negotiations with the Soviet Union (apart from the ideological objectives discussed above) are to record, in a formal fashion which will facilitate the consolidation and further advance of our position, the process of Soviet accommodation to the new political, psychological, and economic conditions in the world which will result from adoption of the fourth course of action and which will be supported by the increasing military strength developed as an integral part of that course of action. In short, our objectives are to record, where desirable, the gradual withdrawal of the Soviet Union and to facilitate that process by making negotiation, if possible, always more expedient than resort to force.

It must be presumed that for some time the Kremlin will accept agreements only if it is convinced that by acting in bad faith whenever and wherever there is an opportunity to do so with impunity, it can derive greater advantage from the agreements than the free world. For this reason, we must take care that any agreements are enforceable or that they are not susceptible of violation without detection and the possibility of effective countermeasures.

This further suggests that we will have to consider carefully the order in which agreements can be concluded. Agreement on the control of atomic energy would result in a relatively greater disarmament of the United States than of the Soviet Union, even assuming considerable progress in building up the strength of the free world in conventional forces and weapons. It might be accepted by the Soviet Union as part of a deliberate design to move against Western Europe and other areas of strategic importance with conventional forces and weapons. In this event, the United States would find itself at war, having previously disarmed itself in its most important weapon, and would be engaged in a race to redevelop atomic weapons.

This seems to indicate that for the time being the United States and other free countries would have to insist on concurrent agreement on the control of nonatomic forces and weapons and perhaps on the other elements of a general settlement, notably peace treaties with Germany, Austria, and Japan and the withdrawal of Soviet influence from the satellites. If, contrary to our expectations, the Soviet Union should accept agreements promising effective control of atomic energy and conventional armaments, without any other changes in Soviet policies, we would have to consider very carefully whether we could accept such agreements. It is unlikely that this problem will arise.

To the extent that the United States and the rest of the free world succeed in so building up their strength in conventional forces and weapons that a Soviet attack with similar forces could be thwarted or held, we will gain increased flexibility and can seek agreements on the various issues in any order, as they become negotiable.

In the third place, negotiation will play a part in the building up of the strength of the free world, apart from the ideological strength discussed above. This is most evident in the problems of Germany, Austria, and Japan. In the process of building up strength, it may be desirable for the free nations, without the Soviet Union, to conclude separate arrangements with Japan, Western Germany, and Austria which would enlist the energies and resources of these countries in support of the free world. This will be difficult unless it has been demonstrated by attempted negotiation with the Soviet Union that the Soviet Union is not prepared to accept treaties of peace which would leave these countries free, under adequate safeguards, to participate in the United Nations and in regional or broader associations of states consistent with the United Nations' Charter and providing security and adequate opportunities for the peaceful development of their political and economic life.

This demonstrates the importance, from the point of view of negotiation as well as for its relationship to the building up of the strength of the free world (see Section D below), of the problem of closer association – on a regional or a broader basis – among the free countries.

In conclusion, negotiation is not a possible separate course of action but rather a means of gaining support for a program of building strength, of recording, where necessary and desirable, progress in the cold war, and of facilitating further progress while helping to minimize the risks of war. Ultimately, it is our objective to negotiate a settlement with the Soviet Union (or a successor state or states) on which the world can place reliance as an enforceable instrument of peace. But it is important to emphasize that such a settlement can only record the progress which the free world will have made in creating a political and economic system in the world so successful that the frustration of the Kremlin's design for world domination will be complete. The analysis in the following sections indicates that the building of such a system requires expanded and accelerated programs for the carrying out of current policies.

A. THE FIRST COURSE – CONTINUATION OF CURRENT POLICIES, WITH CURRENT AND CURRENTLY PROJECTED PROGRAMS FOR CARRYING OUT THESE POLICIES

1. Military aspects. On the basis of current programs, the United States has a large potential military capability but an actual capability which, though improving, is declining relative to the USSR, particularly in light of its probable fission bomb capability and possible thermonuclear bomb capability. The same holds true for the free world as a whole relative to the Soviet world as a whole. If war breaks out in 1950 or in the next few years, the United States and its allies, apart from a powerful atomic blow, will be compelled to conduct delaying actions, while building up their strength for a general offensive. A frank evaluation of the requirements, to defend the United States and its vital interests and to support a vigorous initiative in the cold war, on the one hand, and of present capabilities, on the other, indicates that there is a sharp and growing disparity between them.

A review of Soviet policy shows that the military capabilities, actual and potential, of the United States and the rest of the free world, together with the apparent determination of the free world to resist further Soviet expansion, have not induced the Kremlin to relax its pressures generally or to give up the initiative in the cold war. On the contrary, the Soviet Union has consistently pursued a bold foreign policy, modified only when its probing revealed a determination and an ability of the free world to resist encroachment upon it. The relative military capabilities of the free world are declining, with the result that its determination to resist may also decline and that the security of the United States and the free world as a whole will be jeopardized.

From the military point of view, the actual and potential capabilities of the United States, given a continuation of current and projected programs, will become less and less effective as a war deterrent. Improvement of the state of readiness will become more and more important not only to inhibit the launching of war by the Soviet Union but also to support a national policy designed to reverse the present ominous trends in international relations. A building up of the military capabilities of the United States and the free world is a pre-condition to the achievement of the objectives outlined in this report and to the protection of the United States against disaster.

Fortunately, the United States military establishment has been developed into a unified and effective force as a result of the policies laid down by the Congress and the vigorous carrying out of these policies by the Administration in the fields of both organization and economy. It is, therefore, a base upon which increased strength can be rapidly built with maximum efficiency and economy.

2. Political aspects. The Soviet Union is pursuing the initiative in the conflict with the free world. Its atomic capabilities, together with its successes in the Far East, have led to an increasing confidence on its part and to an increasing nervousness in Western Europe and the rest of the free world. We cannot be sure, of course, how vigorously the Soviet Union will pursue its initiative, nor can we be sure of the strength or weakness of the other free countries in reacting to it. There are, however, ominous signs of further deterioration in the Far East. There are also some indications that a decline in morale and confidence in Western Europe may be expected. In particular, the situation in Germany is unsettled. Should the belief or suspicion spread that the free nations are not now able to prevent the Soviet Union from taking, if it chooses, the military actions outlined in Chapter V, the determination of the free countries to resist probably would lessen and there would be an increasing temptation for them to seek a position of neutrality.

Politically, recognition of the military implications of a continuation of present trends will mean that the United States and especially other free countries will tend to shift to the defensive, or to follow a dangerous policy of bluff, because the maintenance of a firm initiative in the cold war is closely related to aggregate strength in being and readily available.

This is largely a problem of the incongruity of the current actual capabilities of the free world and the threat to it, for the free world has an economic and military potential far superior to the potential of the Soviet Union and its satellites. The shadow of Soviet force falls darkly on Western Europe and Asia and supports a policy of encroachment. The free world lacks adequate means--in the form of forces in being – to thwart such expansion locally. The United States will therefore be confronted more frequently with the dilemma of reacting totally to a limited extension of Soviet control or of not reacting at all (except with ineffectual protests and half measures). Continuation of present trends is likely to lead, therefore, to a gradual withdrawal under the direct or indirect pressure of the Soviet Union, until we discover one day that we have sacrificed positions of vital interest. In other words, the United States would have chosen, by lack of the necessary decisions and actions, to fall back to isolation in the Western Hemisphere. This course would at best result in only a relatively brief truce and would be ended either by our capitulation or by a defensive war – on unfavorable terms from unfavorable positions – against a Soviet Empire compromising all or most of Eurasia. (See Section B.)

3. Economic and social aspects. As was pointed out in Chapter VI, the present foreign economic policies and programs of the United States will not produce a solution to the problem of international economic equilibrium, notably the problem of the dollar gap, and will not create an economic base conducive to political stability in many important free countries.

The European Recovery Program has been successful in assisting the restoration and expansion of production in Western Europe and has been a major factor in checking the dry rot of Communism in Western Europe. However, little progress has been made toward the resumption by Western Europe of a position of influence in world affairs commensurate with its potential strength. Progress in this direction will require integrated political, economic, and military policies and programs, which are supported by the United States and the Western European countries and which will probably require a deeper participation by the United States than has been contemplated.

The Point IV Program and other assistance programs will not adequately supplement, as now projected, the efforts of other important countries to develop effective institutions, to improve the administration of their affairs, and to achieve a sufficient measure of economic development. The moderate regimes now in power in many countries, like India, Indonesia, Pakistan, and the Philippines, will probably be unable to restore or retain their popular support and authority unless they are assisted in bringing about a more rapid improvement of the economic and social structure than present programs will make possible.

The Executive Branch is now undertaking a study of the problem of the United States balance of payments and of the measures which might be taken by the United States to assist in establishing international economic equilibrium. This is a very important project and work on it should have a high priority. However, unless such an economic program is matched and supplemented by an equally far-sighted and vigorous political and military program, we will not be successful in checking and rolling back the Kremlin's drive.

4. Negotiation. In short, by continuing along its present course the free world will not succeed in making effective use of its vastly superior political, economic, and military potential to build a tolerable state of order among nations. On the contrary, the political, economic, and military situation of the free world is already unsatisfactory and will become less favorable unless we act to reverse present trends.

This situation is one which militates against successful negotiations with the Kremlin – for the terms of agreements on important pending issues would reflect present realities and would therefore be unacceptable, if not disastrous, to the United States and the rest of the free world. Unless a decision had been made and action undertaken to build up the strength, in the broadest sense, of the United States and the free world, an attempt to negotiate a general settlement on terms acceptable to us would be ineffective and probably long drawn out, and might thereby seriously delay the necessary measures to build up our strength.

This is true despite the fact that the United States now has the capability of delivering a powerful blow against the Soviet Union in the event of war, for one of the present realities is that the United States is not prepared to threaten the use of our present atomic superiority to coerce the Soviet Union into acceptable agreements. In light of present trends, the Soviet Union will not withdraw and the only conceivable basis for a general settlement would be spheres of influence and of no influenced "settlement" which the Kremlin could readily exploit to its great advantage. The idea that Germany or Japan or other important areas can exist as islands of neutrality in a divided world is unreal, given the Kremlin design for world domination.

B. THE SECOND COURSE – ISOLATION

Continuation of present trends, it has been shown above, will lead progressively to the withdrawal of the United States from most of its present commitments in Europe and Asia and to our isolation in the Western Hemisphere and its approaches. This would result not from a conscious decision but from a failure to take the actions necessary to bring our capabilities into line with our commitments and thus to a withdrawal under pressure. This pressure might come from our present Allies, who will tend to seek other "solutions" unless they have confidence in our determination to accelerate our efforts to build a successfully functioning political and economic system in the free world.

There are some who advocate a deliberate decision to isolate ourselves. Superficially, this has some attractiveness as a course of action, for it appears to bring our commitments and capabilities into harmony by reducing the former and by concentrating our present, or perhaps even reduced, military expenditures on the defense of the United States.

This argument overlooks the relativity of capabilities. With the United States in an isolated position, we would have to face the probability that the Soviet Union would quickly dominate most of Eurasia, probably without meeting armed resistance. It would thus acquire a potential far superior to our own, and would promptly proceed to develop this potential with the purpose of eliminating our power, which would, even in isolation, remain as a challenge to it and as an obstacle to the imposition of its kind of order in the world. There is no way to make ourselves inoffensive to the Kremlin except by complete submission to its will. Therefore isolation would in the end condemn us to capitulate or to fight alone and on the defensive, with drastically limited offensive and retaliatory capabilities in comparison with the Soviet Union. (These are the only possibilities, unless we are prepared to risk the future on the hazard that the Soviet Empire, because of over-extension or other reasons, will spontaneously destroy itself from within.)

The argument also overlooks the imponderable, but nevertheless drastic, effects on our belief in ourselves and in our way of life of a deliberate decision to isolate ourselves. As the Soviet Union came to dominate free countries, it is clear that many Americans would feel a deep sense of responsibility and guilt for having abandoned their former friends and allies. As the Soviet Union mobilized the resources of Eurasia, increased its relative military capabilities, and heightened its threat to our security, some would be tempted to accept "peace" on its terms, while many would seek to defend the United States by creating a regimented system which would permit the assignment of a tremendous part of our resources to defense. Under such a state of affairs our national morale would be corrupted and the integrity and vitality of our system subverted.

Under this course of action, there would be no negotiation, unless on the Kremlin's terms, for we would have given up everything of importance.

It is possible that at some point in the course of isolation, many Americans would come to favor a surprise attack on the Soviet Union and the area under its control, in a desperate attempt to alter decisively the balance of power by an overwhelming blow with modem weapons of mass destruction. It appears unlikely that the Soviet Union would wait for such an attack before launching one of its own. But even if it did and even if our attack were successful, it is clear that the United States would face appalling tasks in establishing a tolerable state of order among nations after such a war and after Soviet occupation of all or most of Eurasia for some years. These tasks appear so enormous and success so unlikely that reason dictates an attempt to achieve our objectives by other means.

C. THE THIRD COURSE – WAR

Some Americans favor a deliberate decision to go to war against the Soviet Union in the near future. It goes without saying that the idea of "preventive" war – in the sense of a military attack not provoked by a military attack upon us or our allies – is generally unacceptable to Americans. Its supporters argue that since the Soviet Union is in fact at war with the free world now and that since the failure of the Soviet Union to use all-out military force is explainable on grounds of expediency, we are at war and should conduct ourselves accordingly. Some further argue that the free world is probably unable, except under the crisis of war, to mobilize and direct its resources to the checking and rolling back of the Kremlin's drive for world dominion. This is a powerful argument in the light of history, but the considerations against war are so compelling that the free world must demonstrate that this argument is wrong. The case for war is premised on the assumption that the United States could launch and sustain an attack of sufficient impact to gain a decisive advantage for the free world in a long war and perhaps to win an early decision.

The ability of the United States to launch effective offensive operations is now limited to attack with atomic weapons. A powerful blow could be delivered upon the Soviet Union, but it is estimated that these operations alone would not force or induce the Kremlin to capitulate and that the Kremlin would still be able to use the forces under its control to dominate most or all of Eurasia. This would probably mean a long and difficult struggle during which the free institutions of Western Europe and many freedom-loving people would be destroyed and the regenerative capacity of Western Europe dealt a crippling blow.

Apart from this, however, a surprise attack upon the Soviet Union, despite the provocativeness of recent Soviet behavior, would be repugnant to many Americans. Although the American people would probably rally in support of the war effort, the shock of responsibility for a surprise attack would be morally corrosive. Many would doubt that it was a "just war" and that all reasonable possibilities for a peaceful settlement had been explored in good faith. Many more, proportionately, would hold such views in other countries, particularly in Western Europe and particularly after Soviet occupation, if only because the Soviet Union would liquidate articulate opponents. It would, therefore, be difficult after such a war to create a satisfactory international order among nations. Victory in such a war would have brought us little if at all closer to victory in the fundamental ideological conflict.

These considerations are no less weighty because they are imponderable, and they rule out an attack unless it is demonstrably in the nature of a counter-attack to a blow which is on its way or about to be delivered. (The military advantages of landing the first blow become increasingly important with modem weapons, and this is a fact which requires us to be on the alert in order to strike with our full weight as soon as we are attacked, and, if possible, before the Soviet blow is actually delivered.) If the argument of Chapter IV is accepted, it follows that there is no "easy" solution and that the only sure victory lies in the frustration of the Kremlin design by the steady development of the moral and material strength of the free world and its projection into the Soviet world in such a way as to bring about an internal change in the Soviet system.

D. THE REMAINING COURSE OF ACTION — A RAPID BUILD-UP OF POLITICAL, ECONOMIC, AND MILITARY STRENGTH IN THE FREE WORLD

A more rapid build-up of political, economic, and military strength and thereby of confidence in the free world than is now contemplated is the only course which is consistent with progress toward achieving our fundamental purpose. The frustration of the Kremlin design requires the free world to develop a successfully functioning political and economic system and a vigorous political offensive against the Soviet Union. These, in turn, require an adequate military shield under which they can develop. It is necessary to have the military power to deter, if possible, Soviet expansion, and to defeat, if necessary, aggressive Soviet or Soviet-directed actions of a limited or total character. The potential strength of the free world is great; its ability to develop these military capabilities and its will to resist Soviet expansion will be determined by the wisdom and will with which it undertakes to meet its political and economic problems.

1. Military aspects. It has been indicated in Chapter VI that U.S. military capabilities are strategically more defensive in nature than offensive and are more potential than actual. It is evident, from an analysis of the past and of the trend of weapon development, that there is now and will be in the future no absolute defense. The history of war also indicates that a favorable decision can only be achieved through offensive action. Even a defensive strategy, if it is to be successful, calls not only for defensive forces to hold vital positions while mobilizing and preparing for the offensive, but also for offensive forces to attack the enemy and keep him off balance.

The two fundamental requirements which must be met by forces in being or readily available are support of foreign policy and protection against disaster. To meet the second requirement, the forces in being or readily available must be able, at a minimum, to perform certain basic tasks:

(a) To defend the Western Hemisphere and essential allied areas in order that their war-making capabilities can be developed;
(b) To provide and protect a mobilization base while the offensive forces required for victory are being built up;
(c) To conduct offensive operations to destroy vital elements of the Soviet war-making capacity, and to keep the enemy off balance until the full offensive strength of the United States and its allies can be brought to bear;
(d) To defend and maintain the lines of communication and base areas necessary to the execution of the above tasks; and

(e) To provide such aid to allies as is essential to the execution of their role in the above tasks.

In the broadest terms, the ability to perform these tasks requires a build-up of military strength by the United States and its allies to a point at which the combined strength will be superior for at least these tasks, both initially and throughout a war, to the forces that can be brought to bear by the Soviet Union and its satellites. In specific terms, it is not essential to match item for item with the Soviet Union, but to provide an adequate defense against air attack on the United States and Canada and an adequate defense against air and surface attack on the United Kingdom and Western Europe, Alaska, the Western Pacific, Africa, and the Near and Middle East, and on the long lines of communication to these areas. Furthermore, it is mandatory that in building up our strength, we enlarge upon our technical superiority by an accelerated exploitation of the scientific potential of the United States and our allies.

Forces of this size and character are necessary not only for protection against disaster but also to support our foreign policy. In fact, it can be argued that larger forces in being and readily available are necessary to inhibit a would-be aggressor than to provide the nucleus of strength and the mobilization base on which the tremendous forces required for victory can be built. For example, in both World Wars I and II the ultimate victors had the strength, in the end, to win though they had not had the strength in being or readily available to prevent the outbreak of war. In part, at least, this was because they had not had the military strength on which to base a strong foreign policy. At any rate, it is clear that a substantial and rapid building up of strength in the free world is necessary to support a firm policy intended to check and to roll back the Kremlin's drive for world domination.

Moreover, the United States and the other free countries do not now have the forces in being and readily available to defeat local Soviet moves with local action, but must accept reverses or make these local moves the occasion for war – for which we are not prepared. This situation makes for great uneasiness among our allies, particularly in Western Europe, for whom total war means, initially, Soviet occupation. Thus, unless our combined strength is rapidly increased, our allies will tend to become increasingly reluctant to support a firm foreign policy on our part and increasingly anxious to seek other solutions, even though they are aware that appeasement means defeat. An important advantage in adopting the fourth course of action lies in its psychological impact – the revival of confidence and hope in the future. It is recognized, of course, that any announcement of the recommended course of action could be exploited by the Soviet Union in its peace campaign and would have adverse psychological effects in certain parts of the free world until the necessary increase in strength has been achieved. Therefore, in any announcement of policy and in the character of the measures adopted, emphasis should be given to the essentially defensive character and care should be taken to minimize, so far as possible, unfavorable domestic and foreign reactions.

2. Political and economic aspects. The immediate objectives – to the achievement of which such a build-up of strength is a necessary though not a sufficient condition – are a renewed initiative in the cold war and a situation to which the Kremlin would find it expedient to accommodate itself, first by relaxing tensions and pressures and then by gradual withdrawal. The United States cannot alone provide the resources required for such a build-up of strength. The other free countries must carry their part of the burden, but their ability and determination to do it will depend on the action the United States takes to develop its own strength and on the adequacy of its foreign political and economic policies. Improvement in political and economic conditions in the free world, as has been emphasized above, is necessary as a basis for building up the will and the means to resist and for dynamically affirming the integrity and vitality of our free and democratic way of life on which our ultimate victory depends.

At the same time, we should take dynamic steps to reduce the power and influence of the Kremlin inside the Soviet Union and other areas under its control. The objective would be the establishment of friendly regimes not under Kremlin domination. Such action is essential to engage the Kremlin's attention, keep it off balance, and force an increased expenditure of Soviet resources in counteraction. In other words, it would be the current Soviet cold war technique used against the Soviet Union.

A program for rapidly building up strength and improving political and economic conditions will place heavy demands on our courage and intelligence; it will be costly; it will be dangerous. But half-measures will be more costly and more dangerous, for they will be inadequate to prevent and may actually invite war. Budgetary considerations will need to be subordinated to the stark fact that our very independence as a nation may be at stake.

A comprehensive and decisive program to win the peace and frustrate the Kremlin design should be so designed that it can be sustained for as long as necessary to achieve our national objectives. It would probably involve:

The development of an adequate political and economic framework for the achievement of our long-range objectives.

A substantial increase in expenditures for military purposes adequate to meet the requirements for the tasks listed in Section D-1.

A substantial increase in military assistance programs, designed to foster cooperative efforts, which will adequately and efficiently meet the requirements of our allies for the tasks referred to in Section D-1-e.

Some increase in economic assistance programs and recognition of the need to continue these programs until their purposes have been accomplished.

A concerted attack on the problem of the United States balance of payments, along the lines already approved by the President.

Development of programs designed to build and maintain confidence among other peoples in our strength and resolution, and to wage overt psychological warfare calculated to encourage mass defections from Soviet allegiance and to frustrate the Kremlin design in other ways.

Intensification of affirmative and timely measures and operations by covert means in the fields of economic warfare and political and psychological warfare with a view to fomenting and supporting unrest and revolt in selected strategic satellite countries.

Development of internal security and civilian defense programs.

Improvement and intensification of intelligence activities.

Reduction of Federal expenditures for purposes other than defense and foreign assistance, if necessary by the deferment of certain desirable programs.

Increased taxes.

Essential as prerequisites to the success of this program would be (a) consultations with Congressional leaders designed to make the program the object of non-partisan legislative support, and (b) a presentation to the public of a full explanation of the facts and implications of present international trends.

The program will be costly, but it is relevant to recall the disproportion between the potential capabilities of the Soviet and non-Soviet worlds (cf. Chapters V and VI). The Soviet Union is currently devoting about 40 percent of available resources (gross national product plus reparations, equal in 1949 to about $65 billion) to military expenditures (14 percent) and to investment (26 percent), much of which is in war-supporting industries. In an emergency the Soviet Union could increase the allocation of resources to these purposes to about 50 percent, or by one-fourth.

The United States is currently devoting about 22 percent of its gross national product ($255 billion in 1949) to military expenditures (6 percent), foreign assistance (2 percent), and investment (14 percent), little of which is in war-supporting industries. (As was pointed out in Chapter V, the "fighting value" obtained per dollar of expenditure by the Soviet Union considerably exceeds that obtained by the United States, primarily because of the extremely low military and civilian living standards in the Soviet Union.) In an emergency the United States could devote upward of 50 percent of its gross national product to these purposes (as it did during the last war), an increase of several times present expenditures for direct and indirect military purposes and foreign assistance.

From the point of view of the economy as a whole, the program might not result in a real decrease in the standard of living, for the economic effects of the program might be to increase the gross national product by more than the amount being absorbed for additional military and foreign assistance purposes. One of the most significant lessons of our World War 11 experience was that the American economy, when it operates at a level approaching full efficiency, can provide enormous resources for purposes other than civilian consumption while simultaneously providing a high standard of living. After allowing for price changes, personal consumption expenditures rose by about one-fifth between 1939 and 1944, even though the economy had in the meantime increased the amount of resources going into Government use by $60 $65 billion (in 1939 prices).

This comparison between the potentials of the Soviet Union and the United States also holds true for the Soviet world and the free world and is of fundamental importance in considering the courses of action open to the United States.

The comparison gives renewed emphasis to the fact that the problems faced by the free countries in their efforts to build a successfully functioning system lie not so much in the field of economics as in the field of politics. The building of such a system may require more rapid progress toward the closer association of the free countries in harmony with the concept of the United Nations. It is clear that our long-range objectives require a strengthened United Nations, or a successor organization, to which the world can look for the maintenance of peace and order in a system based on freedom and justice. It also seems clear that a unifying ideal of this kind might awaken and arouse the latent spiritual energies of free men everywhere and obtain their enthusiastic support for a positive program for peace going far beyond the frustration of the Kremlin design and opening vistas to the future that would outweigh short-run sacrifices.

The threat to the free world involved in the development of the Soviet Union's atomic and other capabilities will rise steadily and rather rapidly. For the time being, the United States possesses a marked atomic superiority over the Soviet Union which, together with the potential capabilities of the United States and other free countries in other forces and weapons, inhibits aggressive Soviet action. This provides an opportunity for the United States, in cooperation with other free countries, to launch a build-up of strength which will support a firm policy directed to the frustration of the Kremlin design. The immediate goal of our efforts to build a successfully functioning political and economic system in the free world backed by adequate military strength is to postpone and avert the disastrous situation which, in light of the Soviet Union's probable fission bomb capability and possible thermonuclear bomb capability, might arise in 1954 on a continuation of our present programs. By acting promptly and vigorously in such a way that this date is, so to speak, pushed into the future, we would permit time for the process of accommodation, withdrawal and frustration to produce the necessary changes in the Soviet system. Time is short, however, and the risks of war attendant upon a decision to build up strength will steadily increase the longer we defer it.

The foregoing analysis indicates that the probable fission bomb capability and possible thermonuclear bomb capability of the Soviet Union have greatly intensified the Soviet threat to the security of the United States. This threat is of the same character as that described in NSC 20/4 (approved by the President on November 24, 1948) but is more immediate than had previously been estimated. In particular, the United States now faces the contingency that within the next four or five years the Soviet Union will possess the military capability of delivering a surprise atomic attack of such weight that the United States must have substantially increased general air, ground, and sea strength, atomic capabilities, and air and civilian defenses to deter war and to provide reasonable assurance, in the event of war, that it could survive the initial blow and go on to the eventual attainment of its objectives. In return, this contingency requires the intensification of our efforts in the fields of intelligence and research and development.

Allowing for the immediacy of the danger, the following statement of Soviet threats, contained in NSC 20/4, remains valid:

14. The gravest threat to the security of the United States within the foreseeable future stems from the hostile designs and formidable power of the USSR, and from the nature of the Soviet system.

15. The political, economic, and psychological warfare which the USSR is now waging has dangerous potentialities for weakening the relative world position of the United States and disrupting its traditional institutions by means short of war, unless sufficient resistance is encountered in the policies of this and other non-communist countries.

16. The risk of war with the USSR is sufficient to warrant, in common prudence, timely and adequate preparation by the United States.

   a. Even though present estimates indicate that the Soviet leaders probably do not intend deliberate armed action involving the United States at this time, the possibility of such deliberate resort to war cannot be ruled out.
   b. Now and for the foreseeable future there is a continuing danger that war will arise either through Soviet miscalculation of the determination of the United States to use all the means at its command to safeguard its security, through Soviet misinterpretation of our intentions, or through U.S. miscalculation of Soviet reactions to measures which we might take.

17. Soviet domination of the potential power of Eurasia, whether achieved by armed aggression or by political and subversive means, would be strategically and politically unacceptable to the United States.

18. The capability of the United States either in peace or in the event of war to cope with threats to its security or to gain its objectives would be severely weakened by internal development, important among which are:

a. Serious espionage, subversion and sabotage, particularly by concerted and well-directed communist activity.
b. Prolonged or exaggerated economic instability.
c. Internal political and social disunity.
d. Inadequate or excessive armament or foreign aid expenditures.
e. An excessive or wasteful usage of our resources in time of peace.
f. Lessening of U.S. prestige and influence through vacillation of appeasement or lack of skill and imagination in the conduct of its foreign policy or by shirking world responsibilities.
g. Development of a false sense of security through a deceptive change in Soviet tactics.

Although such developments as those indicated in paragraph 18 above would severely weaken the capability of the United States and its allies to cope with the Soviet threat to their security, considerable progress has been made since 1948 in laying the foundation upon which adequate strength can now be rapidly built.

The analysis also confirms that our objectives with respect to the Soviet Union, in time of peace as well as in time of war, as stated in NSC 20/4 (para. 19), are still valid, as are the aims and measures stated therein (paras. 20 and 21). Our current security programs and strategic plans are based upon these objectives, aims, and measures:

19.
a. To reduce the power and influence of the USSR to limits which no longer constitute a threat to the peace, national independence, and stability of the world family of nations.
b. To bring about a basic change in the conduct of international relations by the government in power in Russia, to conform with the purposes and principles set forth in the UN Charter.

In pursuing these objectives, due care must be taken to avoid permanently impairing our economy and the fundamental values and institutions inherent in our way of life.

20. We should endeavor to achieve our general objectives by methods short of war through the pursuit of the following aims:

a. To encourage and promote the gradual retraction of undue Russian power and influence from the present perimeter areas around traditional Russian boundaries and the emergence of the satellite countries as entities independent of the USSR.
b. To encourage the development among the Russian peoples of attitudes which may help to modify current Soviet behavior and permit a revival of the national life of groups evidencing the ability and determination to achieve and maintain national independence.

c. To eradicate the myth by which people remote from Soviet military influence are held in a position of subservience to Moscow and to cause the world at large to see and understand the true nature of the USSR and the Soviet-directed world communist party, and to adopt a logical and realistic attitude toward them.
d. To create situations which will compel the Soviet Government to recognize the practical undesirability of acting on the basis of its present concepts and the necessity of behaving in accordance with precepts of international conduct, as set forth in the purposes and principles of the UN Charter.

21. Attainment of these aims requires that the United States:

a. Develop a level of military readiness which can be maintained as long as necessary as a deterrent to Soviet aggression, as indispensable support to our political attitude toward the USSR, as a source of encouragement to nations resisting Soviet political aggression, and as an adequate basis for immediate military commitments and for rapid mobilization should war prove unavoidable.
b. Assure the internal security of the United States against dangers of sabotage, subversion, and espionage.
c. Maximize our economic potential, including the strengthening of our peacetime economy and the establishment of essential reserves readily available in the event of war.
d. Strengthen the orientation toward the United States of the non-Soviet nations; and help such of those nations as are able and willing to make an important contribution to U.S. security, to increase their economic and political stability and their military capability.
e. Place the maximum strain on the Soviet structure of power and particularly on the relationships between Moscow and the satellite countries.
f. Keep the U.S. public fully informed and cognizant of the threats to our national security so that it will be prepared to support the measures which we must accordingly adopt.

In the light of present and prospective Soviet atomic capabilities, the action which can be taken under present programs and plans, however, becomes dangerously inadequate, in both timing and scope, to accomplish the rapid progress toward the attainment of the United States political, economic, and military objectives which is now imperative.

A continuation of present trends would result in a serious decline in the strength of the free world relative to the Soviet Union and its satellites. This unfavorable trend arises from the inadequacy of current programs and plans rather than from any error in our objectives and aims. These trends lead in the direction of isolation, not by deliberate decision but by lack of the necessary basis for a vigorous initiative in the conflict with the Soviet Union.

Our position as the center of power in the free world places a heavy responsibility upon the United States for leadership. We must organize and enlist the energies and resources of the free world in a positive program for peace which will frustrate the Kremlin design for world domination by creating a situation in the free world to which the Kremlin will be compelled to adjust. Without such a cooperative effort, led by the United States, we will have to make gradual withdrawals under pressure until we discover one day that we have sacrificed positions of vital interest.

It is imperative that this trend be reversed by a much more rapid and concerted build-up of the actual strength of both the United States and the other nations of the free world. The analysis shows that this will be costly and will involve significant domestic financial and economic adjustments.

The execution of such a build-up, however, requires that the United States have an affirmative program beyond the solely defensive one of countering the threat posed by the Soviet Union. This program must light the path to peace and order among nations in a system based on freedom and justice, as contemplated in the Charter of the United Nations. Further, it must envisage the political and economic measures with which and the military shield behind which the free world can work to frustrate the Kremlin design by the strategy of the cold war; for every consideration of devotion to our fundamental values and to our national security demands that we achieve our objectives by the strategy of the cold war, building up our military strength in order that it may not have to be used. The only sure victory lies in the frustration of the Kremlin design by the steady development of the moral and material strength of the free world and its projection into the Soviet world in such a way as to bring about an internal change in the Soviet system. Such a positive program – harmonious with our fundamental national purpose and our objectives – is necessary if we are to regain and retain the initiative and to win and hold the necessary popular support and cooperation in the United States and the rest of the free world.

This program should include a plan for negotiation with the Soviet Union, developed and agreed with our allies and which is consonant with our objectives. The United States and its allies, particularly the United Kingdom and France, should always be ready to negotiate with the Soviet Union on terms consistent with our objectives. The present world situation, however, is one which militates against successful negotiations with the Kremlin – for the terms of agreements on important pending issues would reflect present realities and would therefore be unacceptable, if not disastrous, to the United States and the rest of the free world. After a decision and a start on building up the strength of the free world has been made, it might then be desirable for the United States to take an initiative in seeking negotiations in the hope that it might facilitate the process of accommodation by the Kremlin to the new situation. Failing that, the unwillingness of the Kremlin to accept equitable terms or its bad faith in observing them would assist in consolidating popular opinion in the free world in support of the measures necessary to sustain the build-up.

In summary, we must, by means of a rapid and sustained build-up of the political, economic, and military strength of the free world, and by means of an affirmative program intended to wrest the initiative from the Soviet Union, confront it with convincing evidence of the determination and ability of the free world to frustrate the Kremlin design of a world dominated by its will. Such evidence is the only means short of war which eventually may force the Kremlin to abandon its present course of action and to negotiate acceptable agreements on issues of major importance.

The whole success of the proposed program hangs ultimately on recognition by this Government, the American people, and all free peoples, that the cold war is in fact a real war in which the survival of the free world is at stake. Essential prerequisites to success are consultations with Congressional leaders designed to make the program the object of non-partisan legislative support, and a presentation to the public of a full explanation of the facts and implications of the present international situation. The prosecution of the program will require of us all the ingenuity, sacrifice, and unity demanded by the vital importance of the issue and the tenacity to persevere until our national objectives have been attained.

RECOMMENDATIONS

That the President:

a. Approve the foregoing Conclusions.
b. Direct the National Security Council, under the continuing direction of the President, and with the participation of other Departments and Agencies as appropriate, to coordinate and insure the implementation of the Conclusions herein on an urgent and continuing basis for as long as necessary to achieve our objectives. For this purpose, representatives of the member Departments and Agencies, the Joint Chiefs of Staff or their deputies, and other Departments and Agencies as required should be constituted as a revised and strengthened staff organization under the National Security Council to develop coordinated programs for consideration by the National Security Council.

NOTES

1. Marshal Tito, the Communist leader of Yugoslavia, broke away from the Soviet bloc in 1948.
2. The Secretary of State listed seven areas in which the Soviet Union could modify its behavior in such a way as to permit co-existence in reasonable security. These were:

   - Treaties of peace with Austria, Germany, Japan and relaxation of pressures in the Far East;
   - Withdrawal of Soviet forces and influence from satellite area;
   - Cooperation in the United Nations;
   - Control of atomic energy and of conventional armaments;
   - Abandonment of indirect aggression;
   - Proper treatment of official representatives of the U.S.;

Increased access to the Soviet Union of persons and ideas from other countries. [Footnote in the source text. For the text of the address delivered by Secretary Acheson at the University of California, Berkeley, on March 16, 1950, concerning United States – Soviet relations, see Department of State *Bulletin,* March 27, 1950, pp. 473-478.]

Chapter 22

REPORT TO THE AMERICAN PEOPLE ON KOREA (APRIL 11, 1951)

Harry S. Truman

My fellow Americans:

I want to talk to you plainly tonight about what we are doing in Korea and about our policy in the Far East.

In the simplest terms, what we are doing in Korea is this: We are trying to prevent a third world war.

I think most people in this country recognized that fact last June. And they warmly supported the decision of the Government to help the Republic of Korea against the Communist aggressors. Now, many persons, even some who applauded our decision to defend Korea, have forgotten the basic reason for our action.

It is right for us to be in Korea now. It was right last June. It is right today.

I want to remind you why this is true.

The Communists in the Kremlin are engaged in a monstrous conspiracy to stamp out freedom all over the world. If they were to succeed, the United States would be numbered among their principal victims. It must be clear to everyone that the United States cannot—and will not—sit idly by and await foreign conquest. The only question is: What is the best time to meet the threat and how is the best way to meet it?

The best time to meet the threat is in the beginning. It is easier to put out a fire in the beginning when it is small than after it has become a roaring blaze. And the best way to meet the threat of aggression is for the peace-loving nations to act together. If they don't act together, they are likely to be picked off, one by one.

If they had followed the right policies in the 1930's—if the free countries had acted together to crush the aggression of the dictators, and if they had acted in the beginning when the aggression was small—there probably would have been no World War II.

If history has taught us anything, it is that aggression anywhere in the world is a threat to the peace everywhere in the world. When that aggression is supported by the cruel and selfish rulers of a powerful nation who are bent on conquest, it becomes a dear and present danger to the security and independence of every free nation.

This is a lesson that most people in this country have learned thoroughly. This is the basic reason why we joined in creating the United Nations. And, since the end of World War II, we have been putting that lesson into practice—we have been working with other free nations to check the aggressive designs of the Soviet Union before they can result in a third world war.

That is what we did in Greece, when that nation was threatened by the aggression of international communism.

The attack against Greece could have led to general war. But this country came to the aid of Greece. The United Nations supported Greek resistance. With our help, the determination and efforts of the Greek people defeated the attack on the spot.

Another big Communist threat to peace was the Berlin blockade. That too could have led to war. But again it was settled because free men would not back down in an emergency.

The aggression against Korea is the boldest and most dangerous move the Communists have yet made.

The attack on Korea was part of a greater plan for conquering all of Asia.

I would like to read to you from a secret intelligence report which came to us after the attack on Korea. It is a report of a speech a Communist army officer in North Korea gave to a group of spies and saboteurs last May, 1 month before South Korea was invaded. The report shows in great detail how this invasion was part of a carefully prepared plot. Here, in part, is what the Communist officer, who had been trained in Moscow, told his men: "Our forces," he said, "are scheduled to attack South Korean forces about the middle of June .... The coming attack on South Korea marks the first step toward the liberation of Asia."

Notice that he used the word "liberation." This is Communist double-talk meaning "conquest."

I have another secret intelligence report here. This one tells what another Communist officer in the Far East told his men several months before the invasion of Korea. Here is what he said: "In order to successfully undertake the long-awaited world revolution, we must first unify Asia .... lava, Indochina, Malaya, India, Tibet, Thailand, Philippines, and Japan are our ultimate targets .... The United States is the only obstacle on our road for the liberation of all the countries in southeast Asia. In other words, we must unify the people of Asia and crush the United States." Again, "liberation" in "commie" language means conquest.

That is what the Communist leaders are telling their people, and that is what they have been trying to do.

They want to control all Asia from the Kremlin.

This plan of conquest is in flat contradiction to what we believe. We believe that Korea belong to the Koreans, we believe that India belongs to the Indians, we believe that all the nations of Asia should be free to work out their affairs in their own way. This is the basis of peace in the Far East, and it is the basis of peace everywhere else.

The whole Communist imperialism is back of the attack on peace in the Far East. It was the Soviet Union that trained and equipped the North Koreans for aggression. The Chinese Communists massed 44 well-trained and well-equipped divisions on the Korean frontier. These were the troops they threw into battle when the North Korean Communists were beaten.

The question we have had to face is whether the Communist plan of conquest can be stopped without a general war. Our Government and other countries associated with us in the

United Nations believe that the best chance of stopping it without a general war is to meet the attack in Korea and defeat it there.

That is what we have been doing. It is a difficult and bitter task.

But so far it has been successful.

So far, we have prevented world war III.

So far, by fighting a limited war in Korea, we have prevented aggression from succeeding, and bringing on a general war. And the ability of the whole free world to resist Communist aggression has been greatly improved.

We have taught the enemy a lesson. He has found that aggression is not cheap or easy, Moreover, men all over the world who want to remain free have been given new courage and new hope. They know now that the champions of freedom can stand up and fight, and that they will stand up and fight.

Our resolute stand in Korea is helping the forces of freedom now fighting in Indochina and other countries in that part of the world. It has already slowed down the timetable of conquest.

In Korea itself there are signs that the enemy is building up his ground forces for a new mass offensive. We also know that there have been large increases in the enemy's available air forces.

If a new attack comes, I feel confident it will be turned back. The United Nations fighting forces are tough and able and well equipped. They are fighting for a just cause. They are proving to all the world that the principle of collective security will work. We are proud of all these forces for the magnificent job they have done against heavy odds. We pray that their efforts may succeed, for upon their success may hinge the peace of the world.

The Communist side must now choose its course of action. The Communist rulers may press the attack against us. They may take further action which will spread the conflict. They have that choice, and with it the awful responsibility for what may follow. The Communists also have the choice of a peaceful settlement which could lead to a general relaxation of the tensions in the Far East. The decision is theirs, because the forces of the United Nations will strive to limit the conflict if possible.

We do not want to see the conflict in Korea extended. We are trying to prevent a world war—not to start one. And the best way to do that is to make it plain that we and the other free countries will continue to resist the attack.

But you may ask why can't we take other steps to punish the aggressor. Why don't we bomb Manchuria and China itself? Why don't we assist the Chinese Nationalist troops to land on the mainland of China ?

If we were to do these things we would be running a very grave risk of starting a general war. If that were to happen, we would have brought about the exact situation we are trying to prevent.

If we were to do these things, we would become entangled in a vast conflict on the continent of Asia and our task would become immeasurably more difficult all over the world.

What would suit the ambitions of the Kremlin better than for our military forces to be committed to a full-scale war with Red China?

It may well be that, in spite of our best efforts, the Communists may spread the war. But it would be wrong—tragically wrong—for us to take the initiative in extending the war.

The dangers are great. Make no mistake about it. Behind the North Koreans and Chinese Communists in the front lines stand additional millions of Chinese soldiers. And behind the

Chinese stand the tanks, the planes, the submarines, the soldiers, and the scheming rulers of the Soviet Union.

Our aim is to avoid the spread of the conflict.

The course we have been following is the one best calculated to avoid an all-out war. It is the course consistent with our obligation to do all we can to maintain international peace and security. Our experience in Greece and Berlin shows that it is the most effective course of action we can follow.

First of all, it is clear that our efforts in Korea can blunt the will of the Chinese Communists to continue the struggle. The United Nations forces have put up a tremendous fight in Korea and have inflicted very heavy casualties on the enemy. Our forces are stronger now than they have been before. These are plain facts which may discourage the Chinese Communists from continuing their attack.

Second, the free world as a whole is growing in military strength every day. In the United States, in Western Europe, and throughout the world, free men are alert to the Soviet threat and are building their defenses. This may. discourage the Communist rulers from continuing the war in Korea—and from undertaking new acts of aggression elsewhere.

If the Communist authorities realize that they cannot defeat us in Korea, if they realize it would be foolhardy to widen the hostilities beyond Korea, then they may recognize the folly of continuing their aggression. A peaceful settlement may then be possible. The door is always open.

Then we may achieve a settlement in Korea which will not compromise the principles and purposes of the United Nations.

I have thought long and hard about this question of extending the war in Asia. I have discussed it many times with the ablest military advisers in the country. I believe with all my heart that the course we are following is the best course.

I believe that we must try to limit the war to Korea for these vital reasons: to make sure that the precious lives of our fighting men are not wasted; to see that the security of our country and the free world is not needlessly jeopardized; and to prevent a third world war.

A number of events have made it evident that General MacArthur did not agree with that policy. I have therefore considered it essential to relieve General MacArthur so that there would be no doubt or confusion as to the real purpose and aim of our policy.

It was with the deepest personal regret that I found myself compelled to take this action. General MacArthur is one of our greatest military commanders. But the cause of world peace is much more important than any individual.

The change in commands in the Far East means no change whatever in the policy of the United States. We will carry on the fight in Korea with vigor and determination in an effort to bring the war to a speedy and successful conclusion. The new commander, Lt. Gen. Matthew Ridgway, has already demonstrated that he has the great qualities of military leadership needed for this task.

We are ready, at any time, to negotiate for a restoration of peace in the area. But we will not engage in appeasement. We are only interested in real peace.

Real peace can be achieved through a settlement based on the following factors:

One: The fighting must stop.
Two: Concrete steps must be taken to insure that the fighting will not break out again.
Three: There must be an end to the aggression.

A settlement founded upon these elements would open the way for the unification of Korea and the withdrawal of all foreign forces.

In the meantime, I want to be clear about our military objective. We are fighting to resist an outrageous aggression in Korea. We are trying to keep the Korean conflict from spreading to other areas. But at the same time we must conduct our military activities so as to insure the security of our forces. This is essential if they are to continue the fight until the enemy abandons its ruthless attempt to destroy the Republic of Korea.

That is our military objective—to repel attack and to restore peace.

In the hard fighting in Korea, we are proving that collective action among nations is not only a high principle but a workable means of resisting aggression. Defeat of aggression in Korea may be the turning point in the world's search for a practical way of achieving peace and security.

The struggle of the United Nations in Korea is a struggle for peace.

Free nations have united their strength in an effort to prevent a third world war.

That war can come if the Communist rulers want it to come. But this Nation and its allies will not be responsible for its coming.

We do not want to widen the conflict. We will use every effort to prevent that disaster. And in so doing, we know that we are following the great principles of peace, freedom, and justice.

Chapter 23

REMARKS ON THE CESSATION OF BOMBING OF NORTH VIETNAM (OCTOBER 30, 1968)

Lyndon Baines Johnson

Good evening, my fellow Americans:

I speak to you this evening about very important developments in our search for peace in Vietnam.

We have been engaged in discussions with the North Vietnamese in Paris since last May. The discussions began after I announced on the evening of March 31st in a television speech to the Nation that the United States—in an effort to get talks started on a settlement of the Vietnam war—had stopped the bombing of North Vietnam in the area where 90 percent of the people live.

When our representatives—Ambassador Harriman and Ambassador Vance—were sent to Paris, they were instructed to insist throughout the discussions that the legitimate elected Government of South Vietnam must take its place in any serious negotiations affecting the future of South Vietnam.

Therefore, our Ambassadors Harriman and Vance made it abundantly clear to the representatives of North Vietnam in the beginning that—as I had indicated on the evening of March 31st—we would stop the bombing of North Vietnamese territory entirely when that would lead to prompt and productive talks, meaning by that talks in which the Government of Vietnam was free to participate.

Our ambassadors also stressed that we could not stop the bombing so long as by doing so we would endanger the lives and the safety of our troops.

For a good many weeks, there was no movement in the talks at all. The talks appeared to really be deadlocked.

Then a few weeks ago, they entered a new and a very much more hopeful phase.

As we moved ahead, I conducted a series of very intensive discussions with our allies, and with the senior military and diplomatic officers of the United States Government, on the prospects for peace. The President also briefed our congressional leaders and all of the presidential candidates.

Last Sunday evening, and throughout Monday, we began to get confirmation of the essential understanding that we had been seeking with the North Vietnamese on the critical issues between us for some time. I spent most of all day Tuesday reviewing every single detail of this matter with our field commander, General Abrams, whom I had ordered home, and who arrived here at the White House at 2:30 in the morning and went into immediate conference with the President and the appropriate members of his Cabinet. We received General Abrams' judgment and we heard his recommendations at some length.

Now, as a result of all of these developments, I have now ordered that all air, naval, and artillery bombardment of North Vietnam cease as of 8 a.m., Washington time, Friday morning.

I have reached this decision on the basis of the developments in the Paris talks.

And I have reached it in the belief that this action can lead to progress toward a peaceful settlement of the Vietnamese war.

I have already informed the three presidential candidates, as well as the congressional leaders of both the Republican and the Democratic Parties of the reasons that the Government has made this decision.

This decision very closely conforms to the statements that I have made in the past concerning a bombing cessation.

It was on August 19th that the President said: "This administration does not intend to move further until it has good reason to believe that the other side intends seriously"—seriously—"to join us in deescalating the war and moving seriously toward peace."

And then again on September 10th, I said: "The bombing will not stop until we are confident that it will not lead to an increase in American casualties."

The Joint Chiefs of Staff, all military men, have assured me—and General Abrams very firmly asserted to me on Tuesday in that early, 2:30 a.m. meeting—that in their military judgment this action should be taken now, and this action would not result in any increase in American casualties.

A regular session of the Paris talks is going to take place next Wednesday, November 6th, at which the representatives of the Government of South Vietnam are free to participate. We are informed by the representatives of the Hanoi Government that the representatives of the National Liberation Front will also be present. I emphasize that their attendance in no way involves recognition of the National Liberation Front in any form. Yet, it conforms to the statements that we have made many times over the years that the NLF would have no difficulty making its views known.

But what we now expect—what we have a right to expect—are prompt, productive, serious, and intensive negotiations in an atmosphere that is conducive to progress.

We have reached the stage where productive talks can begin. We have made clear to the other side that such talks cannot continue if they take military advantage of them. We cannot have productive talks in an atmosphere where the cities are being shelled and where the demilitarized zone is being abused.

I think I should caution you, my fellow Americans, that arrangements of this kind are never foolproof. For that matter, even formal treaties are never foolproof, as we have learned from our experience.

But in the light of the progress that has been made in recent weeks, and after carefully considering and weighing the unanimous military and diplomatic advice and judgment rendered to the Commander in Chief, I have finally decided to take this step now and to really determine the good faith of those who have assured us that progress will result when bombing ceases and to try to ascertain if an early peace is possible. The overriding consideration that governs us at this hour is the chance and the opportunity that we might have to save human lives, save human lives on both sides of the conflict. Therefore, I have concluded that we should see if they are acting in good faith.

We could be misled—and we are prepared for such a contingency. We pray God it does not occur.

But it should be clear to all of us that the new phase of negotiations which opens on November 6th does not—repeat, does not—mean that a stable peace has yet come to Southeast Asia. There may well be very hard fighting ahead. Certainly, there is going to be some very hard negotiating, because many difficult and critically important issues are still facing these negotiators. But I hope and I believe that with good will we can solve them. We know that negotiations can move swiftly if the common intent of the negotiators is peace in the world.

The world should know that the American people bitterly remember the long, agonizing Korean negotiations of 1951 through 1953—and that our people will just not accept deliberate delay and prolonged procrastination again.

Well then, how has it come about that now, on November 1st, we have agreed to stop the bombardment of North Vietnam?

I would have given all I possess if the conditions had permitted me to stop it months ago; if there had just been any movement in the Paris talks that would have justified me in saying to you, "Now it can be safely stopped."

But I, the President of the United States, do not control the timing of the events in Hanoi. The decisions in Hanoi really determine when and whether it would be possible for us to stop the bombing.

We could not retract our insistence on the participation of the Government of South Vietnam in serious talks affecting the future of their people—the people of South Vietnam. For though we have allied with South Vietnam for many years in this struggle, we have never assumed and we shall never demand the role of dictating the future of the people of South Vietnam. The very principle for which we are engaged in South Vietnam—the principle of self-determination—requires that the South Vietnamese people themselves be permitted to freely speak for themselves at the Paris talks and that the South Vietnamese delegation play a leading role in accordance with our agreement with President Thieu at Honolulu.

It was made just as clear to North Vietnam that a total bombing halt must not risk the lives of our men.

When I spoke last March 31st, I said that evening: "Whether a complete bombing halt becomes possible in the future will be determined by events."

Well, I cannot tell you tonight specifically in all detail why there has been progress in Paris. But I can tell you that a series of hopeful events has occurred in South Vietnam:

- The Government of South Vietnam has grown steadily stronger.

- South Vietnam's Armed Forces have been substantially increased to the point where a million men are tonight under arms, and the effectiveness of these men has steadily improved.
- The superb performance of our own men, under the brilliant leadership of General Westmoreland and General Abrams, has produced truly remarkable results.

Now, perhaps some or all of these factors played a part in bringing about progress in the talks. And when at last progress did come, I believe that my responsibilities to the brave men—our men—who bear the burden of battle in South Vietnam tonight, and my duty to seek an honorable settlement of the war, required me to recognize and required me to act without delay. I have acted tonight.

There have been many long days of waiting for new steps toward peace—days that began in hope, only to end at night in disappointment. Constancy to our national purpose—which is to seek the basis for a durable peace in Southeast Asia—has sustained me in all of these hours when there seemed to be no progress whatever in these talks.

But now that progress has come, I know that your prayers are joined with mine and with those of all humanity, that the action I announce tonight will be a major step toward a firm and an honorable peace in Southeast Asia. It can be.

So, what is required of us in these new circumstances is exactly that steady determination and patience which has brought us to this more hopeful prospect.

What is required of us is a courage and a steadfastness, and a perseverance here at home, that will match that of our men who fight for us tonight in Vietnam.

So, I ask you not only for your prayers but for the courageous and understanding support that Americans always give their President and their leader in an hour of trial. With that understanding, and with that support, we shall not fail.

Seven months ago I said that I would not permit the Presidency to become involved in the partisan divisions that were then developing in this political year. Accordingly, on the night of March 31st, I announced that I would not seek nor accept the nomination of my party for another term as President.

I have devoted every resource of the Presidency to the search for peace in Southeast Asia. Throughout the entire summer and fall I have kept all of the presidential candidates fully briefed on developments in Paris as well as in Vietnam. I have made it abundantly clear that no one candidate would have the advantage over others—either in information about those developments, or in advance notice of the policy the Government intended to follow. The chief diplomatic and military officers of this Government all were instructed to follow the same course.

Since that night on March 31st, each of the candidates has had differing ideas about the Government's policy. But generally speaking, however, throughout the campaign we have been able to present a united voice supporting our Government and supporting our men in Vietnam. I hope, and I believe, that this can continue until January 20th of next year when a new President takes office. Because in this critical hour, we just simply cannot afford more than one voice speaking for our Nation in the search for peace.

I do not know who will be inaugurated as the 37th President of the United States next January. But I do know that I shall do all that I can in the next few months to try to lighten his burdens as the contributions of the Presidents who preceded me have greatly lightened mine. I shall do everything in my power to move us toward the peace that the new President—as well as this President and, I believe, every other American—so deeply and urgently desires.

Thank you for listening. Good night and God bless all of you.

NSDD 114

NSDD 139

In: White House Studies Compendium. Volume 9
Editors: Anthony J. Eksterowicz and Glenn P. Hastedt

ISBN: 978-1-62618-681-1
© 2013 Nova Science Publishers, Inc.

Chapter 24

U.S. NATIONAL SECURITY DIRECTIVE 114 "U.S. POLICY TOWARDS THE IRAN-IRAQ WAR" (NOVEMBER 26, 1983)

THE WHITE HOUSE
WASHINGTON

SYSTEM II
(91372 Add On)

November 26, 1983

National Security
Decision Directive 114

U.S. POLICY TOWARD THE IRAN-IRAQ WAR

I have reviewed and approved the Terms of Reference to govern our political and military consultations with our key Allies and the Gulf Arab states. Political consultations should begin immediately followed by military consultations with those Allies and regional states which express a willingness to cooperate with us in planning measures necessary to deter or defend against attacks on or interference with non-belligerent shipping or on critical oil productions and transhipment facilities in the Persian Gulf.

In our consultations we should assign the highest priority to access arrangements which would facilitate the rapid deployment of those forces necessary to defend the critical oil facilities and transhipment points against air or sapper attacks. Specific recommendations bearing on U.S. plans and force deployments should be submitted for approval following the consultations.

It is present United States policy to undertake whatever measures may be necessary to keep the Strait of Hormuz open to international shipping. Accordingly, U.S. military forces will attempt to deter and, if that fails, to defeat any hostile efforts to close the Strait to international shipping. Because of the real and psychological impact of a curtailment in the flow of oil from the Persian Gulf on the international economic system, we must assure our readiness to deal promptly with actions aimed at disrupting that traffic. The Secretary of Defense and Chairman, Joint Chiefs of Staff, in coordination with the Secretary of State, are requested to maintain a continuing review of tensions in the area and to take appropriate measures to assure the readiness of U.S. forces to respond expeditiously.

Ronald Reagan

COPY 1 OF 8

In: White House Studies Compendium.Volume 9 ISBN: 978-1-62618-681-1
Editors: Anthony J. Eksterowicz and Glenn P. Hastedt © 2013 Nova Science Publishers, Inc.

Chapter 25

U.S. NATIONAL SECURITY DIRECTIVE 139, "MEASURES TO IMPROVE U.S. POSTURE AND READINESS TO DEVELOPMENTS IN THE IRAN-IRAQ WAR (APRIL, 5 1984)

TOP SECRET   2   SENSITIVE

states, the Secretary of Defense, in consultation with the Secretary of State, is requested to submit specific recommendations on measures to enhance deterrence and reduce the vulnerabilities of U.S. personnel and facilities in the Gulf region and cooperative measures with regional states to improve the defensibility of area facilities. Recommendations should also be submitted on measures which would enhance our near-term readiness to respond to sudden attacks on U.S. interests in the region in a timely, effective, and forceful manner. The forward deployment of additional sea-based forces in the near-term should be weighed against the possibility of deploying land-based forces, specifically tactical air forces, closer to the objective area. With regard to the latter, the possible use of Diego Garcia ▓▓ should be explored as a matter of urgency. (TS)

-- In the recognition of the growing threat of Iranian-sponsored terrorism, the Secretary of Defense will direct the enhancement of the anti-terrorist posture of U.S. military activities and facilities in the Persian Gulf region, ▓▓▓▓▓▓▓▓▓▓ In addition, the Director of Central Intelligence and the Secretary of Defense should examine additional counter-terrorist measures and training we can undertake with regional states. (TS)

-- To obtain complementary actions and support for U.S. efforts to enhance the security of Western interests in the Gulf region, the Secretaries of State and Defense will continue close consultations with appropriate Allied officials, especially the UK and France. (TS)

-- The Secretary of State, in coordination with the Secretary of Defense and the Director of Central Intelligence, will prepare a plan of action designed to avert an Iraqi collapse. The plan of action should include:

- ▓▓▓▓▓▓▓▓▓▓▓▓▓▓▓▓▓▓▓▓▓▓▓▓▓▓▓▓▓▓▓▓▓▓ (TS)

- ▓▓▓▓▓▓▓▓▓▓▓▓▓▓▓▓▓▓▓▓▓▓▓▓▓▓▓▓▓▓▓▓▓▓ (TS)

TOP SECRET   TOP SECRET   SENSITIVE

TOP SECRET   3   **SENSITIVE**

-- The Secretary of State will ensure that the policy of the United States Government condemning the use of chemical warfare (CW) munitions in the Iran-Iraq war is unambiguous and consistent with the 1925 Geneva protocol. Our condemnation of the use of CW munitions by the belligerents should place equal stress on the urgent need to dissuade Iran from continuing the ruthless and inhumane tactics which have characterized recent offensives. (TS)

Ronald Reagan

Congressional Documents

Chapter 26

GULF OF TONKIN RESOLUTION

PUBLIC LAW 88-408
88TH UNITED STATES CONGRESS
GULF OF TONKIN RESOLUTION

JOINT RESOLUTION

To promote the maintenance of international peace and security in southeast Asia

Whereas naval units of the Communist regime in Vietnam, in violation of the principles of the Charter of the United Nations and of international law, have deliberately and repeatedly attacked United States naval vessels lawfully present in international waters, and have thereby created a serious threat to international peace; and

Whereas theses attacks are part of a deliberate and systematic campaign of aggression that the Communist regime in North Vietnam has been waging against its neighbors and the nations joined with them in the collective defense of their freedom; and

Whereas the United States is assisting the peoples of southeast Asia to protect their freedom and has no territorial, military or political ambitions in that area, but desires only that these peoples should be left in peace to work out their own destinies in their own way: Now, therefore, be it.

Resolved by the Senate and House of Representatives of the United States of America in Congress assembled. That the Congress approves and supports the determination of the President, as Commander in Chief, to take all necessary measures to repel any armed attack against the forces of the United States and to prevent further aggression.

Sec. 2.

The United States regards as vital to its national interest and to world peace the maintenance of international peace and security in southeast Asia. Consonant with the Constitution of the United States and the Charter of the United Nations and in accordance with its obligations under the Southeast Asia Collective Defense Treaty, the United States is, therefore, prepared, as the President determines, to take all necessary steps, including the use of armed force, to assist any member or protocol state of the Southeast Asia Collective Defense Treaty requesting assistance in defense of its freedom.

Sec. 3.

This resolution shall expire when the President shall determine that the peace and security of the area is reasonably assured by international conditions created by action of the United Nations or otherwise, except that it may be terminated earlier by concurrent resolution of the Congress.

Approved August 10, 1964

Chapter 27

THE WAR POWERS RESOLUTION

PUBLIC LAW 93-148
93ʳᵈ CONGRESS, H. J. RES. 542
NOVEMBER 7, 1973
JOINT RESOLUTION

Concerning the war powers of Congress and the President.
Resolved by the Senate and the House of Representatives of the United States of America in Congress assembled

Short Title

SECTION 1. This joint resolution may be cited as the "War Powers Resolution".

Purpose and Policy

SEC. 2. (a) It is the purpose of this joint resolution to fulfill the intent of the framers of the Constitution of the United States and insure that the collective judgement of both the Congress and the President will apply to the introduction of United States Armed Forces into hostilities, or into situations where imminent involvement in hostilities is clearly indicate by the circumstances, and to the continued use of such forces in hostilities or in such situations.

(b) Under article I, section 8, of the Constitution, it is specifically provided that the Congress shall have the power to make all laws necessary and proper for carrying into execution, not only its own powers but also all other powers vested by the Constitution in the Government of the United States, or in any department or officer thereof.

(c) The constitutional powers of the President as Commander-in-Chief to introduce United States Armed Forces into hostilities, or into situations where imminent involvement in hostilities is clearly indicated by the circumstances, are exercised only pursuant to (1) a declaration of war, (2) specific statutory authorization, or (3) a national emergency created by attack upon the United States, its territories or possessions, or its armed forces.

Consultation

SEC. 3. The President in every possible instance shall consult with Congress before introducing United States Armed Forces into hostilities or into situation where imminent involvement in hostilities is clearly indicated by the circumstances, and after every such introduction shall consult regularly with the Congress until United States Armed Forces are no longer engaged in hostilities or have been removed from such situations.

Reporting

SEC. 4. (a) In the absence of a declaration of war, in any case in which United States Armed Forces are introduced—
 (1) into hostilities or into situations where imminent involvement in hostilities is clearly indicated by the circumstances;
 (2) into the territory, airspace or waters of a foreign nation, while equipped for combat, except for deployments which relate solely to supply, replacement, repair, or training of such forces; or
 (3) in numbers which substantially enlarge United States Armed Forces equipped for combat already located in a foreign nation; the president shall submit within 48 hours to the Speaker of the House of Representatives and to the President pro tempore of the Senate a report, in writing, setting forth—
 (A) the circumstances necessitating the introduction of United States Armed Forces;
 (B) the constitutional and legislative authority under which such introduction took place; and
 (C) the estimated scope and duration of the hostilities or involvement.
 (b) The President shall provide such other information as the Congress may request in the fulfillment of its constitutional responsibilities with respect to committing the Nation to war and to the use of United States Armed Forces abroad
 (c) Whenever United States Armed Forces are introduced into hostilities or into any situation described in subsection (a) of this section, the President shall, so long as such armed forces continue to be engaged in such hostilities or situation, report to the Congress periodically on the status of such hostilities or situation as well as on the scope and duration of such hostilities or situation, but in no event shall he report to the Congress less often than once every six months.

Congressional Action

SEC. 5. (a) Each report submitted pursuant to section 4(a)(1) shall be transmitted to the Speaker of the House of Representatives and to the President pro tempore of the Senate on the same calendar day. Each report so transmitted shall be referred to the Committee on Foreign Affairs of the House of Representatives and to the Committee on Foreign Relations of the Senate for appropriate action. If, when the report is transmitted, the Congress has adjourned sine die or has adjourned for any period in excess of three calendar days, the Speaker of the House of Representatives and the President pro tempore of the Senate, if they deem it advisable (or if petitioned by at least 30 percent of the membership of their respective Houses) shall jointly request the President to convene Congress in order that it may consider the report and take appropriate action pursuant to this section.

(b) Within sixty calendar days after a report is submitted or is required to be submitted pursuant to section 4(a)(1), whichever is earlier, the President shall terminate any use of United States Armed Forces with respect to which such report was submitted (or required to be submitted), unless the Congress (1) has declared war or has enacted a specific authorization for such use of United States Armed Forces, (2) has extended by law such sixty-day period, or (3) is physically unable to meet as a result of an armed attack upon the United States. Such sixty-day period shall be extended for not more than an additional thirty days if the President determines and certifies to the Congress in writing that unavoidable military necessity respecting the safety of United States Armed Forces requires the continued use of such armed forces in the course of bringing about a prompt removal of such forces.

(c) Notwithstanding subsection (b), at any time that United States Armed Forces are engaged in hostilities outside the territory of the United States, its possessions and territories without a declaration of war or specific statutory authorization, such forces shall be removed by the President if the Congress so directs by concurrent resolution.

Congressional Priority Procedures for Joint Resolution or Bill

SEC. 6. (a) Any joint resolution or bill introduced pursuant to section 5(b) at least thirty calendar days before the expiration of the sixty-day period specified in such section shall be referred to the Committee on Foreign Affairs of the House of Representatives or the Committee on Foreign Relations of the Senate, as the case may be, and such committee shall report one such joint resolution or bill, together with its recommendations, not later than twenty-four calendar days before the expiration of the sixty-day period specified in such section, unless such House shall otherwise determine by the yeas and nays.

(b) Any joint resolution or bill so reported shall become the pending business of the House in question (in the case of the Senate the time for debate shall be equally divided between the proponents and the opponents), and shall be voted on within three calendar days thereafter, unless such House shall otherwise determine by yeas and nays.

(c) Such a joint resolution or bill passed by one House shall be referred to the committee of the other House named in subsection (a) and shall be reported out not later than fourteen calendar days before the expiration of the sixty-day period specified in section 5(b). The joint resolution or bill so reported shall become the pending business of the House in question and shall be voted on within three calendar days after it has been reported, unless such House shall otherwise determine by yeas and nays.

(d) In the case of any disagreement between the two Houses of Congress with respect to a joint resolution or bill passed by both Houses, conferees shall be promptly appointed and the committee of conference shall make and file a report with respect to such resolution or bill not later than four calendar days before the expiration of the sixty-day period specified in section 5(b). In the event the conferees are unable to agree within 48 hours, they shall report back to their respective Houses in disagreement. Notwithstanding any rule in either House concerning the printing of conference reports in the Record or concerning any delay in the consideration of such reports, such report shall be acted on by both Houses not later than the expiration of such sixty-day period.

Congressional Priority Procedures for Concurrent Resolution

SEC. 7. (a) Any concurrent resolution introduced pursuant to section 5(b) at least thirty calendar days before the expiration of the sixty-day period specified in such section shall be referred to the Committee on Foreign Affairs of the House of Representatives or the Committee on Foreign Relations of the Senate, as the case may be, and one such concurrent resolution shall be reported out by such committee together with its recommendations within fifteen calendar days, unless such House shall otherwise determine by the yeas and nays.

(b) Any concurrent resolution so reported shall become the pending business of the House in question (in the case of the Senate the time for debate shall be equally divided between the proponents and the opponents), and shall be voted on within three calendar days thereafter, unless such House shall otherwise determine by yeas and nays.

(c) Such a concurrent resolution passed by one House shall be referred to the committee of the other House named in subsection (a) and shall be reported out by such committee together with its recommendations within fifteen calendar days and shall thereupon become the pending business of such House and shall be voted on within three calendar days after it has been reported, unless such House shall otherwise determine by yeas and nays.

(d) In the case of any disagreement between the two Houses of Congress with respect to a concurrent resolution passed by both Houses, conferees shall be promptly appointed and the committee of conference shall make and file a report with respect to such concurrent resolution within six calendar days after the legislation is referred to the committee of conference.

Notwithstanding any rule in either House concerning the printing of conference reports in the Record or concerning any delay in the consideration of such reports, such report shall be acted on by both Houses not later than six calendar days after the conference report is filed. In the event the conferees are unable to agree within 48 hours, they shall report back to their respective Houses in disagreement.

Interpretation of Joint Resolution

SEC. 8. (a) Authority to introduce United States Armed Forces into hostilities or into situations wherein involvement in hostilities is clearly indicated by the circumstances shall not be inferred—

(1) from any provision of law (whether or not in effect before the date of the enactment of this joint resolution), including any provision contained in any appropriation Act, unless such provision specifically authorizes the introduction of United States Armed Forces into hostilities or into such situations and stating that it is intended to constitute specific statutory authorization within the meaning of this joint resolution; or

(2) from any treaty heretofore or hereafter ratified unless such treaty is implemented by legislation specifically authorizing the introduction of United States Armed Forces into hostilities or into such situations and stating that it is intended to constitute specific statutory authorization within the meaning of this joint resolution.

(b) Nothing in this joint resolution shall be construed to require any further specific statutory authorization to permit members of United States Armed Forces to participate jointly with members of the armed forces of one or more foreign countries in the headquarters operations of high-level military commands which were established prior to the date of enactment of this joint resolution and pursuant to the United Nations Charter or any treaty ratified by the United States prior to such date.

(c) For purposes of this joint resolution, the term "introduction of United States Armed Forces" includes the assignment of member of such armed forces to command, coordinate, participate in the movement of, or accompany the regular or irregular military forces of any foreign country or government when such military forces are engaged, or there exists an imminent threat that such forces will become engaged, in hostilities.

(d) Nothing in this joint resolution—

(1) is intended to alter the constitutional authority of the Congress or of the President, or the provision of existing treaties; or (2) shall be construed as granting any authority to the President with respect to the introduction of United States Armed Forces into hostilities or into situations wherein involvement in hostilities is clearly indicated by the circumstances which authority he would not have had in the absence of this joint resolution.

Separability Clause

SEC. 9. If any provision of this joint resolution or the application thereof to any person or circumstance is held invalid, the remainder of the joint resolution and the application of such provision to any other person or circumstance shall not be affected thereby.

Effective Date

SEC. 10. This joint resolution shall take effect on the date of its enactment.

Carl Albert

Speaker of the House of Representatives.

James O. Eastland

President of the Senate pro tempore.
IN THE HOUSE OF REPRESENTATIVES, U.S.,
November 7, 1973.

The House of Representatives having proceeded to reconsider the resolution (H. J. Res 542) entitled "Joint resolution concerning the war powers of Congress and the President", returned by the President of the United States with his objections, to the House of Representatives, in which it originated, it was Resolved, That the said resolution pass, two-thirds of the House of Representatives agreeing to pass the same.

Attest:
W. PAT JENNINGS
Clerk.

I certify that this Joint Resolution originated in the House of Representatives.
W. PAT JENNINGS
Clerk.

IN THE SENATE OF THE UNITED STATES
November 7, 1973

The Senate having proceeded to reconsider the joint resolution (H. J. Res. 542) entitled "Joint resolution concerning the war powers of Congress and the President", returned by the President of the United States with his objections to the House of Representatives, in which it originate, it was Resolved, That the said joint resolution pass, two-thirds of the Senators present having voted in the affirmative.

Chapter 28

THE IRAQ WAR RESOLUTION

107TH CONGRESS
2D SESSION
H. J. RES. 114

[Report No. 107-721] To authorize the use of United States Armed Forces against Iraq.

In the House of Representatives
October 2, 2002

Mr. HASTERT (for himself and Mr. Gephardt) introduced the following joint resolution; which was referred to the Committee on International Relations

October 7, 2002

Reported with amendments, committed to the Committee of the Whole House on the State of the Union, and ordered to be printed
[Strike out all after the resolving clause and insert the part printed in italic]
[Strike out the preamble and insert the part printed in italic]
[For text and preamble of introduced joint resolution, see copy of joint resolution as introduced on October 2, 2002]

JOINT RESOLUTION

To authorize the use of United States Armed Forces against Iraq.

*Whereas i*n 1990 in response to Iraq's war of aggression against and illegal occupation of Kuwait, the United States forged a coalition of nations to liberate Kuwait and its people in order to defend the national security of the United States and enforce United Nations Security Council resolutions relating to Iraq;

Whereas after the liberation of Kuwait in 1991, Iraq entered into a United Nations sponsored cease-fire agreement pursuant to which Iraq unequivocally agreed, among other things, to eliminate its nuclear, biological, and chemical weapons programs and the means to deliver and develop them, and to end its support for international terrorism;

Whereas the efforts of international weapons inspectors, United States intelligence agencies, and Iraqi defectors led to the discovery that Iraq had large stockpiles of chemical weapons and a large scale biological weapons program, and that Iraq had an advanced nuclear weapons development program that was much closer to producing a nuclear weapon than intelligence reporting had previously indicated;

Whereas Iraq, in direct and flagrant violation of the cease-fire, attempted to thwart the efforts of weapons inspectors to identify and destroy Iraq's weapons of mass destruction stockpiles and development capabilities, which finally resulted in the withdrawal of inspectors from Iraq on October 31, 1998;

Whereas in Public Law 105-235 (August 14, 1998), Congress concluded that Iraq's continuing weapons of mass destruction programs threatened vital United States interests and international peace and security, declared Iraq to be in `material and unacceptable breach of its international obligations' and urged the President `to take appropriate action, in accordance with the Constitution and relevant laws of the United States, to bring Iraq into compliance with its international obligations';

Whereas Iraq both poses a continuing threat to the national security of the United States and international peace and security in the Persian Gulf region and remains in material and unacceptable breach of its international obligations by, among other things, continuing to possess and develop a significant chemical and biological weapons capability, actively seeking a nuclear weapons capability, and supporting and harboring terrorist organizations;

Whereas Iraq persists in violating resolution of the United Nations Security Council by continuing to engage in brutal repression of its civilian population thereby threatening international peace and security in the region, by refusing to release, repatriate, or account for non-Iraqi citizens wrongfully detained by Iraq, including an American serviceman, and by failing to return property wrongfully seized by Iraq from Kuwait;

Whereas the current Iraqi regime has demonstrated its capability and willingness to use weapons of mass destruction against other nations and its own people;

Whereas the current Iraqi regime has demonstrated its continuing hostility toward, and willingness to attack, the United States, including by attempting in 1993 to assassinate former President Bush and by firing on many thousands of occasions on United States and Coalition Armed Forces engaged in enforcing the resolutions of the United Nations Security Council;

Whereas members of al Qaida, an organization bearing responsibility for attacks on the United States, its citizens, and interests, including the attacks that occurred on September 11, 2001, are known to be in Iraq;

Whereas Iraq continues to aid and harbor other international terrorist organizations, including organizations that threaten the lives and safety of United States citizens;

Whereas the attacks on the United States of September 11, 2001, underscored the gravity of the threat posed by the acquisition of weapons of mass destruction by international terrorist organizations;

Whereas Iraq's demonstrated capability and willingness to use weapons of mass destruction, the risk that the current Iraqi regime will either employ those weapons to launch a surprise attack against the United States or its Armed Forces or provide them to international terrorists who would do so, and the extreme magnitude of harm that would result to the United States and its citizens from such an attack, combine to justify action by the United States to defend itself;

Whereas United Nations Security Council Resolution 678 (1990) authorizes the use of all necessary means to enforce United Nations Security Council Resolution 660 (1990) and subsequent relevant resolutions and to compel Iraq to cease certain activities that threaten international peace and security, including the development of weapons of mass destruction and refusal or obstruction of United Nations weapons inspections in violation of United Nations Security Council Resolution 687 (1991), repression of its civilian population in violation of United Nations Security Council Resolution 688 (1991), and threatening its neighbors or United Nations operations in Iraq in violation of United Nations Security Council Resolution 949 (1994);

Whereas in the Authorization for Use of Military Force Against Iraq Resolution (Public Law 102-1), Congress has authorized the President `to use United States Armed Forces pursuant to United Nations Security Council Resolution 678 (1990) in order to achieve implementation of Security Council Resolution 660, 661, 662, 664, 665, 666, 667, 669, 670, 674, and 677';

Whereas in December 1991, Congress expressed its sense that it `supports the use of all necessary means to achieve the goals of United Nations Security Council Resolution 687 as being consistent with the Authorization of Use of Military Force Against Iraq Resolution (Public Law 102-1),' that Iraq's repression of its civilian population violates United Nations Security Council Resolution 688 and `constitutes a continuing threat to the peace, security, and stability of the Persian Gulf region,' and that Congress, `supports the use of all necessary means to achieve the goals of United Nations Security Council Resolution 688';

Whereas the Iraq Liberation Act of 1998 (Public Law 105-338) expressed the sense of Congress that it should be the policy of the United States to support efforts to remove from power the current Iraqi regime and promote the emergence of a democratic government to replace that regime;

Whereas on September 12, 2002, President Bush committed the United States to `work with the United Nations Security Council to meet our common challenge' posed by Iraq and to `work for the necessary resolutions,' while also making clear that `the Security Council resolutions will be enforced, and the just demands of peace and security will be met, or action will be unavoidable';

Whereas the United States is determined to prosecute the war on terrorism and Iraq's ongoing support for international terrorist groups combined with its development of weapons of mass destruction in direct violation of its obligations under the 1991 cease-fire and other United Nations Security Council resolutions make clear that it is in the national security interests of the United States and in furtherance of the war on terrorism that all relevant United Nations Security Council resolutions be enforced, including through the use of force if necessary;

Whereas Congress has taken steps to pursue vigorously the war on terrorism through the provision of authorities and funding requested by the President to take the necessary actions against international terrorists and terrorist organizations, including those nations, organizations, or persons who planned, authorized, committed, or aided the terrorist attacks that occurred on September 11, 2001, or harbored such persons or organizations;

Whereas the President and Congress are determined to continue to take all appropriate actions against international terrorists and terrorist organizations, including those nations, organizations, or persons who planned, authorized, committed, or aided the terrorist attacks that occurred on September 11, 2001, or harbored such persons or organizations;

Whereas the President has authority under the Constitution to take action in order to deter and prevent acts of international terrorism against the United States, as Congress recognized in the joint resolution on Authorization for Use of Military Force (Public Law 107-40); and

Whereas it is in the national security interests of the United States to restore international peace and security to the Persian Gulf region: Now, therefore, be it

Resolved by the Senate and House of Representatives of the United States of America in Congress assembled

Section 1. Short Title

This joint resolution may be cited as the `Authorization for Use of Military Force Against Iraq Resolution of 2002'.

Section 2. Support for United States Diplomatic Efforts

The Congress of the United States supports the efforts by the President to—

(1) strictly enforce through the United Nations Security Council all relevant Security Council resolutions regarding Iraq and encourages him in those efforts; and

(2) obtain prompt and decisive action by the Security Council to ensure that Iraq abandons its strategy of delay, evasion and noncompliance and promptly and strictly complies with all relevant Security Council resolutions regarding Iraq.

Section 3. Authorization for Use of United States Armed Forces

(a) AUTHORIZATION- The President is authorized to use the Armed Forces of the United States as he determines to be necessary and appropriate in order to –

(1) defend the national security of the United States against the continuing threat posed by Iraq; and

(2) enforce all relevant United Nations Security Council resolutions regarding Iraq.

(b) PRESIDENTIAL DETERMINATION- In connection with the exercise of the authority granted in subsection (a) to use force the President shall, prior to such exercise or as soon thereafter as may be feasible, but no later than 48 hours after exercising such authority, make available to the Speaker of the House of Representatives and the President pro tempore of the Senate his determination that –

(1) reliance by the United States on further diplomatic or other peaceful means alone either (A) will not adequately protect the national security of the United States against the continuing threat posed by Iraq or (B) is not likely to lead to enforcement of all relevant United Nations Security Council resolutions regarding Iraq; and

(2) acting pursuant to this joint resolution is consistent with the United States and other countries continuing to take the necessary actions against international terrorist and terrorist organizations, including those nations, organizations, or persons who planned, authorized, committed or aided the terrorist attacks that occurred on September 11, 2001.

(c) War Powers Resolution Requirements-

(1) SPECIFIC STATUTORY AUTHORIZATION- Consistent with section 8(a)(1) of the War Powers Resolution, the Congress declares that this section is intended to constitute specific statutory authorization within the meaning of section 5(b) of the War Powers Resolution.

(2) APPLICABILITY OF OTHER REQUIREMENTS- Nothing in this joint resolution supersedes any requirement of the War Powers Resolution.

Section 4. Reports to Congress

(a) REPORTS- The President shall, at least once every 60 days, submit to the Congress a report on matters relevant to this joint resolution, including actions taken pursuant to the exercise of authority granted in section 3 and the status of planning for efforts that are expected to be required after such actions are completed, including those actions described in section 7 of the Iraq Liberation Act of 1998 (Public Law 105-338).

(b) SINGLE CONSOLIDATED REPORT- To the extent that the submission of any report described in subsection (a) coincides with the submission of any other report on matters relevant to this joint resolution otherwise required to be submitted to Congress pursuant to the reporting requirements of the War Powers Resolution (Public Law 93-148), all such reports may be submitted as a single consolidated report to the Congress.

(c) RULE OF CONSTRUCTION- To the extent that the information required by section 3 of the Authorization for Use of Military Force Against Iraq Resolution (Public Law 102-1) is included in the report required by this section, such report shall be considered as meeting the requirements of section 3 of such resolution. Union Calendar No. 451

INDEX

#

20th century, ix, 128
21st century, 82, 268, 269, 270, 298, 300
9/11, 3, 6, 8, 16, 46, 69, 70, 71, 72, 73, 74, 76, 79, 80, 81, 82, 83, 84, 114, 115, 116, 118, 119, 120, 176, 177, 178, 187, 220, 268, 269, 270, 324, 326

A

abuse, 175, 322
access, 43, 73, 108, 116, 132, 134, 136, 155, 211, 220, 251, 269, 318, 350, 386
accessibility, 350
accommodation, 55, 196, 371, 372, 382, 385
accountability, 79, 166, 271, 272, 279, 280, 282, 291
achievement, 352, 358
activism, 43, 129, 133, 135, 140, 177, 236, 350, 353, 355, 361
acts of aggression, 390
actuality, 303
adjustment, 39
adults, 33
advancement, 140
advertising, 296
advocacy, 80, 154, 155, 164, 239, 271, 283, 284, 353
affirmative action, 296, 303
affirming, 43, 179, 356, 380
Afghanistan, 8, 16, 38, 46, 47, 51, 114, 115, 117, 120, 121, 175, 177, 270, 302, 324, 326
Africa, 195, 361, 379
African-American(s), 1, 4, 5, 6, 11, 12, 17
age, 4, 7, 10, 11, 80, 133, 137, 158, 232, 270, 300, 352
agencies, 56, 75, 76, 156, 211, 292, 293, 296, 297, 299, 416

aggression, 41, 173, 177, 191, 192, 194, 199, 200, 210, 228, 230, 265, 382, 384, 386, 387, 388, 389, 390, 391, 407, 415
aggressiveness, 214
Air Force, 252
airbases, 193
Alaska, 1, 9, 16, 19, 20, 38, 335, 336, 340, 379
Alexander Hamilton, 53, 65, 88, 92, 99, 106, 272, 274, 277, 282, 286
Algeria, 236
ambassadors, 393
American Civil Liberties Union, 78
American culture, 82
American History, 31, 145
American Presidency, 10
American Red Cross, 133, 146
Americans with Disabilities Act, 296, 303
anger, 318, 321, 322, 326
annihilation, 370
ANOVA, 320
anxiety, 8, 234, 318, 321, 322, 326, 329, 330, 370
apathy, 284
appeasement, 379, 383, 390
apples, 269
appointees, 72, 110, 117
appointment process, 110
appointments, 30, 110, 283, 347
appropriations, 74, 75, 76, 176, 201
Arab countries, 256
Arab world, 174, 255
Arabian Peninsula, 250
arbitration, 258
architect(s), xii, 56, 130
armed conflict, 98, 158, 182
armed forces, 179, 182, 186, 201, 247, 249, 253, 254, 255, 256, 261, 269, 351, 410, 411, 413
armed groups, 42
Armenia, 133, 134, 141, 143, 147
Armenians, 133, 134, 137
arms sales, 251, 252

arousal, 317, 318, 321
arrest, 257, 265
arrests, 260
Asia, 193, 194, 195, 197, 200, 202, 215, 221, 226, 251, 374, 376, 388, 389, 390, 407, 408
aspiration, 359
assassination, 116, 138, 213, 216
assault, 111, 226, 231
assessment, 2, 18, 54, 70, 110, 113, 116, 118, 129, 196, 198, 235, 250, 292, 293, 315, 317, 347
assets, 258
Associate Justice, 186
atmosphere, 175, 220, 394
atrocities, 127, 129, 133, 134, 155, 156, 162
attachment, 281
attacks, 323, 326, 327
attitudes, 7, 41, 70, 71, 72, 91, 117, 156, 162, 203, 328, 383
Attorney General, 178, 188, 189
attribution, 165
auditory stimuli, 318
Australia, 322
Austria, 146, 372, 373, 386
authority(ies), 40, 54, 90, 92, 93, 94, 96, 98, 133, 134, 135, 138, 141, 156, 158, 159, 171, 172, 173, 174, 175, 176, 177, 178, 179, 184, 186, 196, 240, 258, 272, 273, 276, 278, 280, 281, 283, 286, 353, 370, 375, 390, 413, 418, 419
authors, 292, 293, 329
autonomy, 136, 138, 139, 142, 143, 172, 195, 248, 281, 361
aversion, 41, 44, 194, 238

B

backlash, 6, 19, 348, 349, 353
baggage, 9
Bahrain, 255, 266
balance of payments, 375, 380
balanced budget, 1, 6, 301
Balkans, 176
ballistic missiles, 255
banking, 292, 296
bankruptcy, 127, 129
banks, 95
bargaining, 166, 211, 228, 256
base, 6, 9, 15, 17, 18, 46, 108, 113, 117, 121, 143, 160, 226, 276, 284, 374, 375, 378, 379
beef, 47
behavior, 301, 315, 317, 318, 319, 320, 327, 328, 330
behaviors, 316, 318
Beijing, 38

beliefs, 274, 284, 362
beneficiaries, 63
benefits, 3, 8, 26, 49, 63, 158, 192, 262, 270, 277, 281
benign, 47, 293
bias, 87, 130, 151, 152, 154, 155, 164, 165, 331, 332, 333, 334, 335, 337, 338, 339, 341, 342
Bible, 238
biological weapons, 416
blame, 3, 22, 23, 32, 93, 96, 105, 133, 153, 162, 192, 209, 214, 215, 221, 229, 291
blockades, 107
blogs, 303
blood, 77, 93
blueprint, 79
bonds, 26, 141, 232, 295
borrowing, 291
Bosnia, 176, 187, 219
bounds, 31, 237
breakdown, 60
breathing, 40, 211
Britain, 49, 106, 107, 108, 109, 112, 123, 134, 169, 170, 198, 265, 273, 283, 322
brothers, 236, 239, 272
brutality, 140
budget deficit, 1, 122, 201
budget surplus, 1, 6
Bulgaria, 196
Bureau of Labor Statistics, 85, 86
bureaucracy, 117, 161, 162, 292, 300, 302
Bush, Barbara, 345, 349, 350, 356, 357, 358, 359, 360, 361, 363, 364
Bush, Laura, 360, 365
Bush, President George W., 306, 315, 319, 320, 330
businesses, 346, 360

C

Cabinet, 97, 136, 166, 347, 362, 394
cabinet members, 104
calculus, 137
Cambodia, 173
Camp David, 84, 219
campaign strategies, 331
campaigns, xi, 1, 5, 6, 9, 24, 26, 58, 97, 249
candidate recruitment, 21, 24
candidates, xiii, 2, 3, 4, 5, 9, 11, 12, 17, 21, 22, 23, 24, 26, 27, 28, 29, 31, 37, 38, 39, 40, 41, 44, 45, 46, 48, 50, 69, 113, 137, 290, 315, 316, 317, 318, 319, 320, 321, 322, 323, 327, 331, 336, 338, 339, 341, 394, 396
capital gains, 31
capitalism, 130

Index

Capitol Hill, 21, 79, 80, 81
carbon, 134
Caribbean, 155, 156, 157, 160, 163
caricatures, 48
case law, 347
case study(ies), 55, 151, 152, 153, 155, 156, 345, 347, 350
cash, 26
cast, 333, 334, 335, 336, 337, 339
casting, 120, 237
category d, 55
Catholic Church, 226, 234, 236
Catholics, 225, 226, 228, 229, 230, 233, 235, 236, 237, 238, 239, 240, 241, 242, 243, 244, 245
caucuses, 2, 5, 17
CBS, 32, 51, 213, 218
ceasefire, 247, 249, 252, 253
cell, 302
censorship, 156
Census, 28, 34
Central Asia, 250
Chad, xiii, 315
challenges, 24, 26, 44, 82, 118, 120, 189, 226, 346, 348
channels, 317
chaos, 138, 235
charm, 359
checks and balances, 90, 183
chemical, 47, 251, 252, 416
chemicals, 251
Chief Justice, 171
Chief of Staff, 117, 186, 188, 202, 257
child rearing, 353
children, 94, 130, 141, 158, 229, 237, 238, 270, 279, 346, 348, 350, 356, 358, 359
Chile, 163
China, 38, 115, 200, 202, 204, 228, 255, 389
Christianity, 140, 240
Christians, 134, 240
CIA, 180
city(ies), 74, 97, 137, 158, 229, 231, 233, 234, 249, 363, 364, 394
citizens, 2, 15, 75, 77, 78, 84, 103, 139, 175, 182, 270, 273, 284, 295, 334, 357, 370, 416, 417
citizenship, 73, 74, 75, 284
civic life, 84, 352
civil liberties, 111, 296, 303
civil rights, 56, 64, 170, 237, 240
civil society, 75, 76
civil war, 115, 136, 137, 236, 258, 322
Civil War (US), 4, 56, 58, 65, 105, 108, 112, 113, 136, 140, 143, 147, 148, 149, 156, 269
civilization, 138, 140, 141, 198, 370

clarity, 43, 143, 331, 332
classes, xii, 359
classification, 55
Clergymen, 246
climate change, 45
climates, 277
Clinton Administration, 79, 295, 346
Clinton, Hillary Rodham, 346, 348, 362, 363, 365
closure, 173
clothing, 95
CNN, 11, 14, 17, 19, 20, 49, 51, 52, 132, 328
coal, 195, 198
coattails, 6, 29, 31, 32, 35, 60, 63
codes, 297
coding, 319, 330
coercion, 108, 200
coffee, 108
cognition, 154, 166, 329
cognitive activity, 317, 318, 320, 321, 326, 329
cognitive effort, 316, 317
coherence, 229
Cold War, xii, 38, 43, 44, 56, 64, 114, 118, 165, 169, 171, 172, 175, 181, 183, 191, 192, 194, 196, 198, 200, 201, 203, 204, 205, 207, 219, 220, 225, 245, 247, 248, 252, 254, 259, 261, 371, 373, 374, 379, 380, 385
college students, 232, 238
colleges, 234
commander-in-chief, 88, 90, 98, 121, 172
commerce, 106, 296
commercial, 157, 159, 169, 170, 251
commodity, 251
communication, xiii, 11, 79, 95, 109, 133, 269, 277, 326, 327, 348, 378, 379
communication systems, 133
communism, 193, 197, 211, 225, 226, 230, 231, 236, 237, 239, 240, 388
communist countries, 382
community(ies), 47, 71, 74, 75, 76, 77, 78, 83, 84, 109, 132, 142, 143, 176, 198, 227, 269, 270, 273, 282, 347, 349, 352, 357
community service, 74, 75, 83
competency, 316
competing candidates, 2
competition, 5, 42, 151, 152, 153, 154, 155, 160, 162, 164, 165, 318, 334
competitors, 6, 17, 42
compilation, 213, 215, 218
complement, 31, 97
complexity, 41, 131, 164
compliance, 173, 291, 416
complications, 350
composition, 10, 62, 63, 66, 98, 292, 351

compounds, 141
compulsion, xii, 209, 210, 219, 220
conception, 142, 353
concise, 305
concrete, 274, 278
conference, 71, 112, 117, 136, 201, 228, 266, 353, 355, 394, 412
confession, 235
confidence, 275, 280, 290
configuration, 31
conflict, 8, 44, 47, 115, 127, 129, 130, 131, 134, 135, 137, 138, 143, 154, 155, 156, 159, 161, 163, 169, 170, 173, 182, 191, 192, 194, 196, 200, 202, 207, 210, 219, 226, 228, 231, 234, 237, 238, 247, 248, 250, 251, 259, 262, 264, 348, 349, 350, 359, 370, 371, 374, 377, 384, 389, 390, 391, 395
conformity, 138, 219
confrontation, 44, 65, 197, 253, 254, 256, 257
confusion, 333, 352
congressional hearings, 187
congressional newspaper, 25
congressional races, 21, 25
consciousness, 70, 133, 134
consensus, 37, 39, 41, 42, 43, 44, 47, 48, 49, 83, 154, 164, 165, 193, 201, 203, 220, 236, 244, 258, 265, 292, 346, 360
consent, 45, 192, 271, 273, 275, 283, 302
conservation, xi
conservative base, 6, 9
conservative principles, 298
consolidation, 90, 372
conspiracy, 91, 116, 387
conspiracy theory, 116
constituents, 26, 93, 97, 136, 140, 210, 256, 259
Constitution, xiii, 59, 88, 90, 98, 99, 100, 122, 169, 170, 171, 172, 173, 174, 177, 178, 179, 182, 183, 184, 185, 186, 189, 231, 233, 239, 272, 274, 275, 278, 280, 281, 283, 284, 285, 286, 334, 408, 409, 416, 418
construction, 119, 172, 174, 251, 275, 281, 284
consumption, 381
contamination, 143
content analysis, 319
Continental, 87, 88, 89, 99, 107, 273, 274
contingency, 261, 382, 395
contradiction, 271, 277, 388
control, 281, 282, 290, 292, 301, 317
controversial, 45, 64, 113, 202, 258, 353, 355
controversies, 49, 327
convention, 5, 88, 232, 272, 274, 275, 276, 277, 278, 280, 282, 283
convergence, 48, 319
conversations, 118, 217, 227

conviction, 43, 169, 170, 247, 282
cooperation, 40, 42, 45, 70, 111, 136, 172, 251, 256, 371, 381, 385
cornea, 319
corporations, 358
correlation, 220, 301, 330
corruption, 231
cost, 51, 76, 85, 97, 105, 109, 112, 164, 199, 201, 212, 214, 228, 229, 333, 334, 335, 336
costs, 289, 291, 292, 333, 335, 336, 339
counsel, 142, 153, 249
counterbalance, 237
counterterrorism, 47, 48
covering, 92, 215
cracks, 225, 234
creativity, 270
credentials, 193
credibility, 322
credit market, 27
criminal activity, 182
criminality, 280
crises, 3, 16, 42, 59, 196
criticism, 78, 96, 120, 214, 234, 252, 279, 300, 346, 348, 349, 352, 353, 359, 360, 361
Cuba, 127, 129, 131, 134, 135, 136, 137, 138, 139, 140, 141, 142, 143, 144, 145, 147, 148, 149, 151, 152, 153, 155, 156, 157, 158, 159, 160, 161, 164, 168, 172, 173, 184, 214
cues, 322, 328
cultivation, 277
cultural beliefs, 346
cultural influence, 258
culture, 73, 74, 78, 82, 201, 353, 355
currency, 137, 269
cycles, 303

D

dailies, 81
danger, 47, 66, 89, 93, 105, 106, 119, 154, 200, 214, 216, 274, 275, 284, 382, 388
Darfur, 47
Darwinism, 131
dating, 318
death, 359
deaths, 274
debt, 273, 289, 291, 295, 301, 358
debt service, 295
debts, 92
decision makers, 118, 154, 163
decisions, 326, 341
defects, 43
defence, 97

defense, 276, 281, 294, 302
deficiencies, 56, 274, 283
deficit, 294, 295
definition, 360, 361
degenerate, 234
delegates, 5, 90, 271, 275, 278, 279, 280, 281, 283
democracy, 10, 39, 42, 43, 105, 109, 111, 114, 115, 116, 119, 120, 195, 196, 258, 260, 272, 274, 275, 276, 277
Democrat, 4, 5, 6, 11, 12, 15, 18, 24, 26, 34, 55, 57, 73, 121, 128, 143, 144, 226, 294, 301, 302, 337, 338
Democratic Party, 9, 17, 31, 58, 64, 66, 120, 121, 332, 336, 337, 338, 339, 341, 342, 356
democratization, 116
demonstrations, 238
denial, 172
Department of Defense, 49, 178, 191
Department of Homeland Security (DHS), 77, 84, 85, 298, 300
Department of Justice, 188, 261
deployments, 270, 410
deposits, 89
depression, 90, 157
depth, 77, 293, 350
deregulation, 290
despair, 198
destiny, 84, 237
destruction, 16, 90, 94, 157, 160, 162, 163, 197, 201, 233, 249, 253, 323, 370
detachment, 129
detainees, 180
detection, 372
detention, 179, 258, 265
deterrence, 114, 120, 200, 201, 247, 248, 253, 254, 255, 256, 259, 260, 261
deviation, 216, 321, 322, 323, 324, 347
dichotomy, 128, 131, 345
differential treatment, 333
dignity, 91, 198, 239, 355, 357
dilation, 327
diplomacy, 38, 39, 41, 44, 45, 49, 76, 92, 152, 155, 156, 157, 160, 215, 247, 253, 259, 265, 326
diplomatic efforts, 104, 115
disappointment, 93, 396
disaster, 77, 95, 97, 374, 378, 379, 391
discipline, 301
disclosure, 33, 251, 291
discrimination, 231, 353
diseases, 142
dislocation, 197
disposition, 202, 326
dissatisfaction, 22, 31

distortions, 191, 192, 194
distress, 91, 107, 142, 198, 274
distribution, 155, 317, 332, 333, 337, 369
district incumbent, 24
divergence, 301
diversity, 29, 273, 277, 349
divorce, 353, 359
doctors, 111, 161, 269
domestic agenda, 117
domestic issues, 121, 136
domestic policy, 3, 81, 156
Domestic Policy Council, 73
dominance, 4, 53, 290, 301, 302, 318, 327
draft, 171, 183, 232, 235, 239, 240, 252
drawing, 275, 283
dream, 358, 359
drought, 132
Drug Czar, 296
drugs, 296, 303, 353
dualism, 352, 358, 359
due process, 274
duration, 317
duties, 273, 284, 346, 348

E

East Asia, 228
Eastern Europe, 194, 195, 204
economic assistance, 203, 380
economic change, 56
economic cooperation, 263
economic development, 375
economic growth, 136, 291
economic incentives, 45
economic policy, 295, 306
economic power, 45, 169, 253
economic problem, 8, 378
economic reform, 56
economics, 381
editors, 133, 134, 143, 213, 236, 237, 349
education, 26, 34, 76, 77, 230, 268, 269, 270, 272, 284, 361
effusion, 93
egoism, 42
Egypt, 3, 250
Eisenhower, Dwight, 294
elaboration, 183
elected leaders, 303
election, 1, 2, 4, 6, 7, 8, 10, 11, 12, 15, 17, 18, 20, 21, 22, 24, 26, 27, 28, 29, 30, 31, 32, 34, 35, 37, 38, 39, 40, 41, 44, 49, 54, 56, 57, 58, 59, 60, 62, 63, 64, 66, 105, 106, 107, 110, 113, 114, 117, 120, 121, 132, 137, 158, 162, 180, 212, 226, 230,

235, 250, 255, 260, 272, 275, 276, 280, 281, 289, 290, 303, 315, 328, 331, 332, 333, 336, 337, 339, 341, 355, 356
electoral coalition, 4
embargo, 107, 108, 169, 249, 253, 255
emergency, 172, 180, 381, 388
emergency preparedness, 77
emergency response, 77, 123
emotion, 71, 326
emotional state, 315, 317, 318, 320, 327
empathy, 231
employees, 78, 293, 297, 301
employment, 10, 81, 90, 272, 273, 277
empowerment, 236
encouragement, 212, 215, 290, 384
endorsements, 140
enemies, 39, 115, 119, 214, 235, 257, 260
energy, 26, 27, 71, 74, 76, 139, 163, 178, 196, 217, 247, 250, 251, 252, 253, 279, 292, 371, 372, 386
energy security, 247, 250, 251, 253
enforcement, 176, 419
England, 89, 106, 107, 169, 283
enrollment, 81
entanglements, 209
enthusiasm, 353
entrepreneurs, 165
environment, 15, 43, 54, 56, 59, 64, 70, 84, 104, 106, 107, 111, 114, 140, 158, 162, 172, 254, 292, 360
Environmental Protection Agency, 292
epidemic, 114
Equal Rights Amendment (ERA), 350, 353, 354, 355, 356, 361, 363, 364
equilibrium, 55, 56, 184, 375
equipment, 110, 111, 251, 253, 263
erosion, 183
espionage, 383, 384
ethics, 26
EU, 254, 256
Eurasia, 194, 375, 376, 377, 382
Europe, 3, 46, 132, 133, 134, 140, 144, 170, 186, 192, 194, 195, 197, 198, 199, 200, 201, 202, 203, 204, 214, 238, 248, 251, 262, 372, 374, 375, 376, 377
evening, 319
evidence, 40, 44, 50, 80, 117, 163, 221, 233, 234, 235, 290, 328, 353, 354, 357, 359, 371, 385
evil, 115, 119, 232, 237
evolution, 135, 192, 217, 292, 293
exclusion, 348
execution, 226, 378, 379, 385, 409
executive branch, 58, 87, 88, 96, 98, 175, 177, 201, 271
Executive Order, 76

executive power, 104, 179, 279, 280, 296
exercise, 2, 87, 97, 170, 171, 173, 179, 181, 198, 200, 256, 277, 419
exertion, 197
exile, 137, 258
exit poll, 8, 17, 26, 27, 28, 29, 33
expenditures, 97, 291, 292, 296, 299, 376, 380, 381, 383
expertise, 1, 3
exploitation, 196, 379
exports, 46, 250, 251
exposure, 142
external relations, 172
extinction, 133
extremists, 46, 258, 265

F

Facebook, 11
facial expression, 317, 326
failed states, 42, 43, 47, 50
failure, 345, 351, 360
fairness, 295
faith, 42, 48, 76, 139, 140, 143, 154, 163, 165, 226, 240, 265, 274, 369, 371, 372, 377, 385, 395
families, 31, 77, 270, 348, 349, 357, 360
family, 272, 349, 356, 358, 359, 361
family members, 270
famine, 128, 129, 133, 135
farmers, 128, 133, 136
FBI, 261
FDR, 4, 16, 18, 57, 59, 60, 193, 269, 289, 290, 293, 294, 296, 301, 302, 304
fear(s), 89, 93, 191, 192, 195, 196, 197, 200, 201, 202, 204, 231, 250, 258, 281, 282, 329
Federal Communications Commission, 292
Federal Convention, 99, 285
Federal Election Commission, 33
Federal Emergency Management Agency, 77
federal funds, 75, 76
federal government, 8, 70, 72, 75, 77, 79, 90, 111, 129, 132, 133, 178, 274, 277, 281, 289, 291, 292, 293, 294, 295, 300, 301, 304, 309, 310
Federal Register, 296, 301, 304
federal regulations, 296, 297
Federal Reserve, 309, 310
federalism, 281
Federalist Papers, 65, 178, 286
feelings, 115, 138, 209, 213, 318, 347
FEMA, 77, 78
femininity, 346, 352
feminism, 345, 346, 348, 350, 352, 353, 357, 358, 361

fever, 152, 156
fights, 302
Filipino, 147
finance, 292
financial, 1, 6, 7, 8, 16, 26, 27, 38, 51, 80, 81, 82, 89, 97, 174, 197, 250, 251, 253, 291, 293, 359, 385
financial crisis, 38, 82
financial institutions, 1, 6, 7, 16
financial resources, 81
financial support, 89, 251
financial vulnerability, 26
financing, 273
first aid, 247
First Amendment, 179
first dimension, 34
first lady, 345, 346, 347, 348, 349, 350, 351, 352, 353, 354, 355, 356, 357, 358, 359, 360, 361
first responders, 77
FISA, 179
fiscal conservative, 294, 301
fiscal policy, 18
fish, 108
fishing, 142
fission, 373, 382
fixation, 317, 318
flexibility, 48, 138, 372
flight, 3, 78
flight attendant, 78
flights, 176
fluctuations, 31, 32, 298
focusing, 315, 326, 355, 360
food, 111, 141, 142, 160, 296
Food and Drug Administration, 292
force, 38, 40, 41, 42, 43, 46, 47, 48, 49, 50, 58, 87, 88, 89, 90, 91, 92, 94, 96, 97, 112, 114, 117, 118, 140, 152, 155, 156, 157, 159, 160, 161, 169, 173, 174, 175, 177, 179, 182, 183, 184, 189, 192, 196, 200, 205, 226, 229, 237, 249, 250, 252, 253, 256, 265, 281, 323, 371, 372, 374, 377, 380, 385, 408, 418, 419
Ford, 55, 99, 174, 186, 294, 296, 298, 301, 307, 312, 316, 318, 319, 320, 321, 328, 330, 345, 349, 350, 353, 354, 355, 356, 361, 362, 363, 364, 365
Ford, Betty, 345, 349, 350, 353, 354, 355, 356, 361, 362, 363, 364, 365
Ford, Gerald, 316, 318, 320, 321, 364
foreign affairs, 9, 39, 50, 159, 169, 171, 177, 178, 179, 180, 185, 210, 213
foreign aid, 383
foreign assistance, 380, 381
foreign language, 76
foreign policy, xi, xii, 1, 2, 3, 8, 9, 37, 38, 39, 40, 41, 42, 43, 44, 45, 48, 49, 50, 56, 64, 82, 104, 114, 116, 118, 119, 127, 128, 129, 130, 132, 133, 134, 135, 136, 140, 143, 151, 152, 153, 154, 155, 158, 160, 161, 162, 164, 172, 176, 178, 179, 186, 195, 202, 209, 210, 211, 214, 219, 220, 226, 231, 237, 248, 250, 251, 256, 258, 260, 261, 315, 319, 323, 326, 373, 378, 379, 383
formation, xiii, 73, 227, 298, 300
foundations, 49, 55, 65, 119, 226, 248, 252
framing, 106
France, 49, 106, 107, 108, 112, 115, 118, 124, 197, 198, 236, 238, 264, 385
franchise, 4
Franklin, Benjamin, 279, 283
free trade, 108, 114, 136
free world, 200, 370, 371, 372, 373, 374, 375, 376, 377, 378, 379, 380, 381, 384, 385, 389, 390
freedom, 43, 71, 85, 114, 119, 130, 165, 180, 198, 211, 239, 268, 322, 356, 361, 377, 381, 385, 387, 389, 391, 407, 408
freedom of choice, 71
friendship, 161, 228
funding, 24, 26, 34, 78, 79, 291, 418
fundraising, 21, 25, 26, 33, 141
funds, 91, 138, 141
fusion, 64, 353

G

Gallup Poll, 67, 238
gambling, 153
gay marriage, 302
GDP, 289, 291, 307, 308, 309, 310
gender, 345, 346, 347, 348, 349, 350, 351, 352, 353, 355, 357, 358, 359, 360, 361, 362
gender balance, 360
gender gap, 4, 11, 12, 17
gender ideology, 350
gender role, 350, 353, 357, 358, 359, 360, 361
general election, 2, 6, 24, 37, 38, 64, 337
generation, 274
Geneva Convention, 131, 132, 133, 180, 230
geography, 42, 163, 277, 342
Georgia, 17, 38, 40, 45, 96, 116, 145, 240, 335, 362
Germany, 49, 115, 157, 192, 194, 195, 196, 198, 199, 204, 251, 369, 372, 373, 374, 376, 386
GI Bill, 267
globalization, 42, 44
glue, 270
God, 138, 140, 143, 157, 225, 249, 270, 395, 397
Gore, Al, 316, 339
governance, xii, 260, 291, 294, 298, 301
government, 88, 89, 131, 197, 227, 228, 254, 255, 259, 271, 272, 274, 275, 276, 277, 278, 279, 280,

281, 282, 283, 284, 289, 290, 291, 292, 293, 294, 295, 296, 299, 300, 301, 302, 304, 305
government policy, 108
government spending, 290, 291, 294
government-financed programs, 76
governor, 1, 5, 9, 16, 64, 91, 117, 129, 137, 158, 280
grants, 75, 171
grass, 121
grassroots, 127, 129
gravity, 176, 417
Great Britain, 110, 112, 115, 123, 124, 171, 192, 194, 196, 197, 204, 273, 283, 322
Greece, 197, 199, 388, 390
Greeks, 137
Grenada, 3
gross national product, 381
grounding, 275
groups, 291, 347, 351, 353, 354
groupthink, 155
growth, 3, 289, 291, 292, 294, 296, 297, 298, 299, 300, 301, 305
growth rate, 3, 299
Guantanamo, 179
guidance, 88, 116
guidelines, 251
guilt, 318, 376

H

Haiti, 3, 114, 175
Hamas, 264
handedness, 252
hands, 281
happiness, 277, 281
hardliners, 257, 260
harm, 282
harmony, 196, 282, 371, 376, 381
Hawaii, 135, 336, 340
hazards, 77
health, 8, 26, 27, 121, 292, 346
health care, 8, 26, 27, 121, 346
hedging, 45
hegemony, 130, 194, 259, 266, 369
height, 194, 283, 327
hemisphere, 193
Hezbollah, 250, 257, 259, 264
high - level party defections, 64
higher education, 75
hip, 346, 361
history, xi, xii, xiii, 3, 39, 50, 66, 72, 75, 82, 95, 96, 104, 111, 114, 127, 128, 129, 130, 135, 141, 163, 178, 181, 185, 212, 217, 219, 228, 268, 269, 272, 296, 298, 300, 303, 348, 377, 378, 387

homeland security, 74, 77, 78, 292, 294, 302
homes, 142
hopes, 316, 318
horses, 91
hospitality, 267
host, 38
hostilities, 91, 93, 173, 174, 175, 178, 179, 192, 193, 232, 390, 409, 410, 411, 413
hostility, 248, 259, 361, 416
hot spots, 47
House of Representatives, ix, xiii, 4, 21, 22, 24, 25, 26, 27, 28, 29, 31, 32, 33, 34, 59, 60, 61, 62, 63, 64, 65, 66, 67, 71, 72, 73, 78, 79, 80, 81, 84, 92, 95, 96, 98, 100, 111, 113, 117, 120, 133, 146, 162, 172, 173, 177, 182, 183, 189, 227, 235, 241, 244, 261, 262, 280, 282, 283, 285, 290, 297, 300, 302, 304, 307, 309, 331, 332, 334, 342, 347, 351, 352, 353, 354, 355, 359, 362, 363, 407, 409, 410, 411, 412, 414, 415, 418, 419
hue, 128
human, xii, 51, 93, 114, 119, 129, 130, 131, 132, 133, 138, 143, 236, 249, 260, 296, 318, 329, 359, 372, 395
human activity, 296
human rights, xii, 114, 119, 129, 236, 260
humanitarian intervention, 127, 129, 132, 133, 134, 140
humanitarianism, 127, 129, 130, 131, 132, 135, 139, 140
hunting, 90
husband, 180, 345, 346, 356, 357, 358, 359, 361
Hussein, Saddam, 16, 115, 116, 117, 174, 175, 247, 248, 250, 252, 261, 262, 325
hypocrisy, 231
hypothesis, 39, 131, 302

I

icon, 358
ID, 86, 305
ideal(s), 49, 131, 134, 143, 199, 290, 345, 346, 347, 348, 349, 350, 351, 352, 355, 356, 358, 359, 360, 361, 381
identification, 22, 31, 290
identity, 58, 272, 358
ideology, xi, 17, 43, 99, 209, 210, 219, 239, 304, 348, 350
illusions, 235
image(s), 3, 37, 39, 47, 72, 75, 115, 118, 132, 133, 159, 327, 361
imagery, 120
imagination, 383
immigration, 117

immunization, 77
impeachment, 95, 282
imperialism, 129, 131, 140, 163, 388
imports, 136
impulses, 43, 44, 54
in transition, 209
inattention, 280
inauguration, 63, 135, 143, 210, 216
incarceration, 179
inclusion, 282, 330
income, 28, 31, 250
income tax, 31
incongruity, 374
increased salience, 2, 27
incumbents, 22, 23, 25, 26, 27, 29, 33, 113
independence, 38, 88, 99, 130, 137, 139, 148, 159, 160, 198, 214, 273, 274, 279, 283, 357, 380, 383, 388
India, 375, 388
Indians, 87, 88, 89, 91, 92, 93, 94, 95, 96, 97, 98, 101, 388
indicators, 317
indirect measure, 335
individualism, 290, 358
individuals, 81, 153, 162, 291, 316, 334, 370
Indonesia, 375
industrial democracies, 10, 17
industrial power, 45
industry(ies), 2, 7, 27, 172, 179, 198, 253, 272, 277, 292, 293, 381
inefficiency(ies), 87, 341
inequity, 92
inertia, 184
inevitability, 110
infancy, 18
inferences, 318
inflation, 294
information processing, 317
infrastructure, 2, 6, 194, 249, 258
initiation, 105
injure, 91
insecurity, 275
insight, 293, 320, 326, 348, 349
inspections, 417
inspectors, 326, 416
institutions, 8, 42, 44, 45, 46, 47, 48, 91, 109, 119, 169, 171, 226, 260, 270, 275, 332, 375, 377, 382, 383
insurgency, 38, 130, 134, 138, 156, 157, 163, 164, 197, 257, 258
integration, 198
integrity, 198, 247, 376, 380
intellect, 315

intelligence, xi, xii, 96, 115, 116, 120, 152, 154, 197, 251, 253, 265, 380, 382, 388, 416
intelligence gathering, 251
interaction, 345
interactions, 318
interdependence, 42, 172
interest groups, 25
interference, 117, 290
internal change, 378, 385
international affairs, 9, 157
international law, 119, 132, 141, 407
international relations, xii, 42, 179, 219, 260, 374, 383
international terrorism, 120, 122, 182, 250, 416, 418
international trade, 41
internationalism, 42, 44, 49, 127, 128, 129, 132, 136
interval, 329
intervention, 77, 116, 127, 128, 129, 132, 133, 134, 135, 137, 138, 140, 141, 142, 143, 144, 159, 172, 174, 176, 193, 200, 210, 213, 219, 280, 291, 292, 296
interview, 355
intrusions, 317
investment, 47, 153, 171, 270, 359, 381
investments, 47, 106, 359
Iowa, 5, 15, 17, 128, 129, 133, 134, 144
Iran, xii, 38, 40, 41, 44, 45, 47, 48, 51, 52, 114, 115, 119, 178, 185, 187, 196, 197, 247, 248, 249, 250, 251, 252, 253, 254, 255, 256, 257, 258, 259, 260, 261, 262, 263, 264, 265, 266, 322, 326, 399, 401
Iraq, 1, 3, 6, 7, 8, 9, 10, 16, 19, 26, 27, 28, 37, 38, 39, 40, 44, 46, 47, 48, 51, 103, 104, 105, 106, 113, 115, 116, 117, 118, 119, 120, 121, 122, 125, 152, 153, 175, 177, 178, 180, 187, 219, 220, 223, 247, 248, 249, 250, 251, 252, 253, 254, 255, 257, 258, 259, 261, 262, 263, 264, 265, 266, 270, 302, 322, 323, 324, 325, 326, 399, 401, 415, 416, 417, 418, 419, 420
Iraq War, 9, 16, 19, 103, 104, 105, 106, 113, 116, 117, 118, 120, 121, 153, 247, 261, 399, 415
iron, 120
irony, 130, 131
Islam, xii, 249, 260
Islamic extremists, 46
Islamic world, 45
islands, 157, 252, 258, 266, 376
isolation, 110, 115, 201, 253, 260, 374, 376, 384
isolationism, 41, 110, 127, 128, 129, 136, 144, 201
Israel, 3, 46, 250, 258, 259, 262
issues, ix, xiii, 2, 7, 8, 10, 21, 22, 26, 27, 30, 34, 38, 39, 40, 42, 43, 45, 48, 50, 56, 71, 76, 83, 88, 89, 92, 95, 118, 136, 190, 196, 240, 258, 278, 291,

292, 302, 319, 322, 327, 349, 350, 353, 356, 370, 371, 372, 375, 385, 394, 395
Italy, 197, 199

J

Jamaica, 156
Japan, 193, 194, 197, 200, 369, 372, 373, 376, 386, 388
Jay, John, 286
Jews, 238
Job Corps, 76
job creation, 74
job performance, 348
jobs, 352
Johnson, Lady Bird, 345, 349, 350, 358, 360, 361, 363
Johnson, Lyndon Baines, 363
Jordan, 251
journalists, 45, 143
judges, 271
judgment, 322
juries, 284
justice, 279
justification, 104, 175, 176, 177, 272, 301

K

Kennedy, John F., 326
kill, 47, 230
Korea, 191, 192, 200, 201, 203, 322, 326, 387, 388, 389, 390, 391
Kosovo, 117, 176
Kurds, 265
Kuwait, 174, 175, 252, 255, 264, 415, 416

L

labeling, 296
labor, 296
land, 354
landscape, 54, 115, 258, 293
language, 277, 325, 327, 347, 349
Latin America, 147
Latinos, 4, 11, 12, 17
law enforcement, 77, 78
laws, 278, 279, 282, 296, 409, 416
lawyers, 318
lead, 2, 26, 31, 38, 42, 48, 82, 107, 109, 110, 137, 153, 200, 202, 230, 236, 268, 269, 270, 316, 317, 318, 338, 374, 376, 384, 389, 393, 394, 419

leadership, 3, 23, 26, 27, 50, 54, 56, 69, 70, 71, 72, 79, 81, 82, 104, 106, 109, 110, 117, 118, 121, 122, 139, 155, 164, 170, 173, 174, 182, 211, 227, 249, 253, 256, 257, 259, 261, 265, 268, 272, 316, 326, 346, 384, 390, 396
leadership abilities, 81, 104
leadership style, 118
leakage, 318
learning, xi, 69, 70
Lebanon, 3, 172, 250, 252
legality, 179
legend, 358
legislation, 27, 30, 159, 184, 271, 278, 282, 296, 303, 348, 354, 412, 413
legislative authority, 273, 410
leisure, 164
liberal states, 45
liberalism, xi, 296
liberation, 199, 348, 353, 355, 360, 388, 416
liberty, 89, 90, 114, 119, 133, 212, 218, 232
lifetime, 358
light, 96, 129, 130, 138, 139, 152, 191, 192, 200, 220, 251, 270, 316, 317, 322, 350, 373, 375, 377, 382, 384, 385, 395
line, 273, 321, 331, 339, 349, 353, 358
liquidate, 377
listening, 319, 320, 321, 322, 323, 324, 326, 327
literacy, 132, 356, 358
literacy rates, 132
livestock, 91, 108
loans, 108, 110, 296
lobbying, 132, 353, 354, 355
local community, 78
local government, 291
logistics, 266
long distance, 354
longevity, 106
Louisiana, 26, 166, 167
love, 79, 140, 270, 359
low risk, 105
loyalty, 55, 272, 290
lying, 318

M

machinery, 136
macroeconomic policy, 18
Madison, Dolley, 348
Madison, James, 271, 272, 274, 275, 276, 278, 281, 282, 283, 285, 286
magazines, 132, 133, 163
magnitude, 199, 251, 417
major issues, 31

majority, 4, 23, 25, 32, 39, 58, 63, 81, 90, 107, 113, 120, 137, 156, 186, 212, 218, 238, 248, 258, 260, 281, 282, 303, 304, 332, 337, 354
man, 82, 107, 109, 135, 138, 143, 170, 215, 230, 238, 240, 269, 271, 272, 274, 277, 278, 279, 280, 282, 283, 284, 352, 356, 357, 358, 359
management, 153, 162, 172, 294, 350
mandates, 291, 334
mania, 131
manic, 210
manipulation, 291
manpower, 194, 195, 265
manufacturing, 107, 251
maritime security, 252
marketplace, 154, 155, 164
markets, 291
marriage, 76, 272, 302, 357
married women, 359
Maryland, 239, 340
masking, 37, 321
mass, 16, 131, 132, 135, 140, 141, 156, 160, 211, 260, 322, 380, 389
mass media, 132, 135
material resources, 372
materials, 46, 96, 180, 350
matter, 79, 96, 98, 106, 120, 165, 184, 212, 215, 237, 257, 274, 276, 334, 346, 394
McCain, Senator John, 290, 304
measurement, 34, 289, 291, 293, 296
measures, 274, 277, 289, 292, 293, 296, 301, 332, 333, 337
media, 8, 9, 10, 21, 132, 135, 142, 152, 153, 155, 159, 162, 214, 264, 291, 315, 316, 327, 345, 352
median, 30
medical, 77, 132, 161
medical care, 132
Mediterranean, 145, 196
membership, 66, 171, 173, 411
memory, 31, 134, 160, 209, 216, 248, 289, 318
men, 272, 274, 277, 279, 282, 321, 327, 328, 330, 346, 348, 350, 358
mentor, 281
messages, 349
metaphor, 276, 277, 282, 283
methodology, 326
Mexico, 24, 235, 340, 364
Miami, 88, 92, 94, 229, 319
middle class, 139, 140, 269, 270
Middle East, xii, 3, 38, 47, 119, 121, 172, 173, 186, 196, 200, 250, 251, 261, 263, 264, 265, 361, 379
migration, 290
militancy, 199
militarization, 260

military aid, 255
military exercises, 256
military spending, 157
military tribunals, 179, 180
militia, 87, 88, 89, 90, 91, 92, 93, 94, 97, 98, 110, 250, 265, 274
militias, 110, 111, 176, 258
minorities, 60, 196
minority, 281, 354
minority groups, 28
missile defenses, 256
mission, 46, 74, 75, 77, 89, 94, 115, 187, 196, 228, 229, 260
missions, 42, 47, 51, 182
Missouri, 284, 353
model, 353, 357, 358
models, 73, 153
moderates, 28
mold, 73
momentum, 5, 58, 259, 260, 272
money, 291, 295, 301, 341, 354, 359
monopoly, 179, 198, 199, 200, 205
Montana, 226, 335, 336
moral judgment, 112, 235
moral reasoning, 163
morale, 374, 376
morality, 127, 129, 235
morning, 283
morphology, 329
Moscow, 196, 199, 233, 241, 252, 384, 388
mothers, 346, 361
motion, 279, 280, 282, 283
motives, 282
movement, 296, 303, 348, 349, 352, 353, 355
multilateralism, 40
multiple factors, 22
murder, 211, 230
muscular philosophy, 39
musicians, 94
mutual respect, 264

N

naming, 228, 251
nation, 271, 275, 276, 277, 290, 298, 304, 306, 347, 349, 354
nation states, 42
national character, 278
national debt, 1, 107, 122, 295
national emergency, 410
national identity, xii
national interests, 39, 41, 47, 105, 265
national parties, 24

national policy, 105, 374
national product, 381
National Public Radio, 83
national security, 37, 38, 39, 40, 41, 43, 46, 48, 49, 82, 114, 115, 116, 117, 118, 119, 121, 159, 169, 170, 171, 185, 194, 201, 211, 384, 385, 415, 416, 418, 419
National Security Council, 195, 211, 220, 222, 226, 252, 256, 263, 386
nationalism, xii, 197, 249, 272
nation-building, 47
NATO, 45, 50, 176, 191, 192, 199, 201, 205, 206
natural disasters, 77, 182
natural resources, 156, 194
naval confrontations, 247, 248
Nazi Germany, 194, 236
negative effects, 316
neglect, 97, 259
negotiating, 45, 89, 112, 228, 232, 346, 349, 350, 360, 371, 395
negotiation, 40, 48, 228, 234, 256, 370, 371, 372, 373, 376, 385
nerve, 132
nervousness, 374
network, 327
neutral, 3, 106, 228
New Deal, 57, 67, 223, 293
New England, 4, 14, 17, 28, 60, 89, 107, 109, 110, 111, 112, 142
New Hampshire primary, 356
NGOs, 141
Nixon, Richard, 294, 296, 303, 316, 326
No Child Left Behind, 122
Nobel Prize, 269
nominee, 5, 7, 11, 12, 64
North Africa, 195, 238
North America, 170
North Korea, 38, 40, 41, 45, 47, 115, 119, 171, 200, 201, 219, 255, 322, 326, 388, 389
Nuclear Nonproliferation Treaty, 44, 239
nuclear program, 254, 255, 264
nuclear weapons, 38, 45, 46, 219, 231, 236, 326, 416
nucleus, 379
nurses, 269
nursing home, 78

O

Obama, 1, 2, 5, 6, 7, 8, 9, 10, 11, 12, 15, 16, 17, 18, 19, 20, 21, 22, 26, 27, 29, 30, 31, 32, 34, 37, 38, 39, 40, 41, 44, 45, 46, 47, 48, 49, 50, 51, 52, 69, 70, 72, 74, 76, 78, 81, 82, 83, 84, 85, 86, 115, 185, 189, 190, 260, 261, 267, 303, 337, 338
Obama Administration, 78
obedience, 235
objective criteria, 203
obligation, 354
obstacles, 228, 362
obstruction, 417
oceans, 41
Office of Management and Budget (OMB), 73, 301, 307, 309
officials, 48, 89, 108, 121, 129, 133, 141, 142, 156, 178, 192, 193, 194, 195, 196, 197, 198, 199, 200, 202, 211, 238, 253, 257, 258, 264, 265, 298, 347, 349, 351, 355
oil, 27, 116, 121, 248, 250, 251, 252, 253, 257, 259, 260, 261
Oklahoma, xiii, 100, 234, 304, 353, 354
openness, 114
Operation Iraqi Freedom, 259
operations, 24, 46, 47, 48, 77, 92, 115, 161, 173, 176, 177, 182, 251, 254, 346, 377, 378, 380, 413, 417
opinion polls, 17, 317, 348
opportunism, 38
opportunities, 2, 21, 41, 44, 56, 65, 70, 71, 75, 76, 77, 78, 79, 81, 86, 111, 159, 165, 182, 268, 273, 341, 373
opportunity costs, 42
oppression, 143
optimism, 39, 79, 164, 212
order, 279, 280, 292, 294, 296, 302, 331, 332, 335, 350, 355, 358, 360
organ, 172, 173, 178
Organization of American States, 173
organize, 111, 141, 198, 233, 384
organs, 282
outreach, 78, 350, 360, 361
overlap, 330
oversight, 188
ownership, 58
ox, 327, 364

P

Pacific, xi, 145, 163, 193, 203, 379
pacifism, 155
pain, 80
paints, 33
Pakistan, 38, 47, 375
Panama, 3
parallel, 29, 171, 200
parameters, 292, 319, 329
paranoia, 154
parents, 272

Parliament, 273, 283, 285
participants, 318
partition, 204
Patriot Act, 117, 296, 303, 305
patriotism, 71, 103, 106, 109, 112, 113, 124, 277
peace, 1, 2, 6, 39, 42, 43, 47, 50, 88, 89, 90, 91, 92, 94, 97, 112, 114, 116, 120, 121, 131, 138, 151, 152, 161, 170, 176, 177, 182, 187, 193, 195, 201, 202, 215, 225, 226, 227, 228, 229, 230, 231, 232, 233, 234, 235, 236, 237, 238, 239, 250, 254, 269, 274, 296, 303, 371, 372, 373, 376, 379, 380, 381, 383, 384, 385, 386, 387, 388, 389, 390, 391, 393, 394, 395, 396, 397, 407, 408, 416, 417, 418
peace process, 250
peacekeeping, 176, 177, 187
Pentagon, 47, 114, 198, 201, 232, 252, 261
percentile, 7
perceptions, 315, 316, 317, 326
permission, 92, 175, 231
permit, 376, 382, 383, 386, 396, 413
perseverance, 396
Persian Gulf, xii, 187, 247, 248, 250, 251, 252, 253, 254, 255, 256, 257, 259, 262, 264, 265, 416, 417, 418
Persian Gulf War, 3, 8, 116, 117
personal autonomy, 361
personal choice, 361
personal contact, 260
personality, 135, 154, 210, 315, 329
Philippines, 130, 144, 152, 153, 156, 162, 163, 164, 168, 375, 388
physiological, 329
pipeline, 251
piracy, 156
pitch, 317
platform, 219, 252, 293
playing, 317
pleasure, 90, 98, 352
poison, 279
Poland, 140, 195
polar, 56
polarization, xiii, 113
police, 114, 196, 318
policy choice, 178
policy initiative, 30
policy issues, 70, 319
policy makers, 291, 292
policy making, 164, 169, 171
policymakers, 105, 106, 133, 199
politeness, 273
political force, 196
political ideologies, xi
political leaders, 316

political opposition, 122
political parties, xi, 1, 18, 22, 333
political party, 81, 316
political power, 197
political system, 21, 31, 169, 170
politics, xi, xii, 4, 7, 10, 18, 19, 22, 30, 31, 37, 41, 42, 43, 48, 54, 55, 56, 70, 72, 99, 110, 112, 118, 119, 120, 122, 134, 137, 139, 143, 152, 158, 161, 163, 169, 170, 189, 190, 201, 247, 248, 254, 260, 275, 279, 284, 293, 303, 316, 326, 327, 345, 349, 381
polling, 7, 316, 341, 348
poor, 359
poor performance, 93
popular support, 23, 183, 375, 385
popular vote, 15, 57, 58, 64, 65, 66, 113, 283, 332, 333, 334, 337, 338, 339, 341
population, 10, 80, 103, 156, 164, 176, 211, 237, 250, 333, 334, 416, 417
populism, 131
Portugal, 115, 229
poverty, 359
power, 271, 273, 276, 277, 278, 279, 280, 281, 282, 283, 284, 292, 303, 304, 306, 322, 327
pragmatism, 171
PRC, 219
precedent, 87, 134, 172, 279, 280
precedents, 98, 134
predictability, 226
preparation, 110, 111, 122, 201, 213, 382
preparedness, 77, 104, 107, 201
preservation, 42, 91
presidency, ix, xi, 2, 3, 4, 5, 6, 10, 15, 16, 17, 21, 23, 53, 55, 56, 58, 60, 64, 65, 66, 69, 70, 104, 111, 113, 117, 135, 169, 171, 178, 183, 185, 196, 210, 217, 219, 225, 226, 250, 271, 297, 299, 301, 305, 349
President Clinton, 294
President Obama, 31, 69, 70, 261
presidential authority, 171
presidential campaign(s), 1, 2, 3, 4, 7, 10, 16, 26, 29, 31, 48, 69, 73, 117, 175, 328, 360
presidential election, xiii, 2, 3, 4, 6, 10, 11, 12, 14, 15, 17, 18, 21, 29, 54, 60, 64, 66, 105, 114, 121, 260, 331, 332, 339, 355
presidential performance, 2
presidential politics, 8
presidential veto, 183, 283
press conferences, 315, 316
pressure, 355, 357
prestige, 109, 355, 383
prevention, 42, 77, 105, 120, 125
price changes, 381

primacy, 41, 49, 119, 169, 171, 178, 180, 184
primate, 329
principles, 38, 39, 40, 42, 55, 75, 79, 88, 89, 107, 109, 132, 140, 171, 196, 198, 201, 239, 276, 293, 294, 295, 298, 303, 383, 384, 390, 391, 407
prisoners, 115, 132, 158, 179, 230
prisons, 115
privacy, 296, 303
private sector, 291, 292
probability, 93, 216, 376
procurement, 247, 253, 254, 255, 261
producers, 33
professional careers, 351
professionals, 28, 77, 87
professions, 352
profit, 93
program, 326
project, 84, 114, 131, 198, 290, 292, 303, 356, 375
proliferation, 132, 293, 322, 323, 326
propaganda, 134, 258
property rights, 290, 292
proposition, 290
prosperity, 39, 41, 49, 114, 268
protection, 88, 89, 91, 94, 97, 105, 106, 108, 121, 138, 176, 192, 374, 378, 379
protectionism, 50, 136
protectorate, 119
Protestants, 140, 238
prototypes, 141
psychology, 153, 163
public administration, 279
public awareness, 77
public concern, 277, 355
public education, 77
public figures, 158
public health, 76, 77, 78
public interest, 96, 142
public life, 234, 351, 361
public opinion, 3, 38, 59, 98, 129, 131, 132, 153, 155, 158, 159, 162, 193, 206, 283, 316, 317, 318, 321, 328, 348, 370
public policy, 18, 56, 345
public resources, 354
public support, 9, 106, 134, 162, 216, 371
publishing, 272
Puerto Rico, 144, 160
punishment, 45, 176
pupil, 327

Q

qualifications, 233
questioning, 98, 256, 326

questionnaire, 233

R

race, 4, 5, 6, 10, 11, 15, 23, 24, 29, 34, 37, 194, 256, 358, 359, 372
radicalism, 119
radio, 80, 327
range, 317, 318, 319, 324, 353
ratification, 90, 170, 239, 272, 275
rationality, 120, 219
raw materials, 180
reactions, 251, 266, 327, 379, 382
reading, 131, 156, 170, 178, 212, 214, 239, 318, 329
Reagan, Ronald, 294, 296, 303, 317, 356
realism, 44
reality, 88, 108, 129, 130, 139, 142, 172, 239, 284, 352, 359
reason, 275, 276, 316, 347
reasoning, 154, 279, 348, 349
recall, 158, 230, 381
recalling, 233, 256
recession, 22
reciprocity, 136, 172
recognition, 2, 75, 76, 158, 159, 329, 355, 356, 357, 374, 380, 385, 394
recommendations, 88, 154, 162, 169, 171, 181, 185, 238, 263, 394, 411, 412
reconcile, 353, 361
reconstruction, 171, 194, 195, 197, 198
recovery, 195, 198, 270
recruiting, 24, 26, 90, 249
redistribution, 291
reelection, 2, 22, 23, 24, 29, 58, 64, 231, 271, 346
reflection, 347
reform, xii, 56, 117, 140, 145, 149, 210, 216, 296, 342, 346
reformers, 237
reforms, 56, 79, 158
refugees, 227
regenerative capacity, 377
Registry, 289, 292, 293, 296, 300, 301
regression, 300
regulation(s), 132, 289, 291, 292, 293, 296, 297, 304
regulatory agencies, 289, 291, 292, 293, 296, 297, 299, 300
rehabilitation, 195, 199
rejection, 42, 277
relationship, 273, 274, 276, 277, 284, 332
relatives, 273
relativity, 376
relaxation, 386, 389
relevance, 169, 171, 292, 350

reliability, 319
relief, 75, 128, 129, 132, 133, 135, 141, 157, 161, 211, 370
religion, 4, 140, 240, 318
religiosity, 139, 140
rendition, 179
renewable energy, 78
repair, 37, 47, 410
repatriate, 416
reporters, 156, 180, 355, 358
repression, 236, 260, 416, 417
Republican Party, 26, 28, 38, 55, 64, 65, 107, 108, 109, 110, 112, 113, 114, 117, 121, 290, 293, 304, 331, 332, 334, 336, 337, 338, 339, 341, 353, 361
reputation, 6, 38, 74, 96, 129, 131, 135
requirements, 174, 263, 355, 373, 378, 380, 420
RES, 415
researchers, 303, 327
resentment, 186
reserves, 384
resistance, 93, 120, 194, 203, 237, 249, 376, 382, 388
resolution, 16, 87, 88, 89, 99, 135, 138, 139, 172, 173, 174, 175, 177, 181, 183, 184, 193, 226, 234, 250, 251, 354, 370, 380, 408, 409, 411, 412, 413, 414, 415, 416, 418, 419, 420
resources, 3, 24, 25, 26, 31, 71, 73, 77, 81, 82, 105, 153, 178, 194, 195, 199, 239, 253, 272, 291, 331, 341, 350, 354, 373, 376, 377, 379, 380, 381, 383, 384
response, 38, 46, 64, 70, 71, 72, 73, 77, 79, 80, 91, 92, 96, 107, 116, 119, 156, 158, 171, 173, 174, 175, 176, 179, 182, 187, 205, 213, 217, 221, 233, 261, 281, 315, 316, 317, 318, 319, 320, 321, 322, 323, 324, 325, 326, 328, 415
responsiveness, 333
restoration, 375, 390
restrictions, 176, 292
retaliation, 107, 173, 199, 226, 254, 255
retirement, 7, 217, 239
retirement age, 239
revenue, 270
Revolutionary Guard, 249, 254, 255, 260, 265
rewards, 155
rhetoric, xi, 40, 46, 69, 70, 75, 79, 81, 89, 117, 176, 191, 192, 231, 248, 254, 256, 259, 260, 274, 294, 301, 302, 349, 350
rights, 106, 107, 108, 111, 112, 131, 138, 159, 169, 179, 180, 198, 229, 240, 284, 290, 292, 296, 348, 349, 354, 355
rings, 44

risk(s), 26, 29, 39, 40, 41, 46, 47, 92, 153, 197, 199, 200, 201, 205, 238, 250, 359, 370, 371, 373, 376, 382, 389, 395, 417
risk-taking, 199, 200, 201
Roosevelt, Eleanor, 348
root(s)s, 121, 136, 139, 212, 219, 296
routes, 42, 142, 258
rubber, 136
rule of law, 183, 198
rules, 120, 154, 162, 180, 230, 289, 292, 304, 316, 327
Russia, 38, 45, 108, 114, 115, 118, 128, 129, 133, 135, 144, 194, 195, 196, 202, 255, 322, 383

S

sabotage, 383, 384
safety, 95, 159, 292, 296, 393, 411, 417
sampling, 319
sanctions, 46, 48, 115, 254, 326
satisfaction, 277
Saudi Arabia, 250, 251, 255
scaling, 42, 47
scholarship, xi, xiii, 272
school, 78, 269, 272, 359
science, xii, 7
scope, 21, 22, 75, 80, 176, 252, 293, 299, 301, 302, 303, 304, 369, 384, 410
Second World, 175
Secretary of Defense, 118, 121, 198, 218, 238, 266
Secretary of the Treasury, 92, 107
security, xii, 38, 39, 40, 41, 42, 43, 45, 47, 49, 77, 89, 90, 91, 114, 116, 119, 159, 177, 212, 247, 248, 250, 251, 252, 253, 254, 255, 256, 257, 258, 259, 260, 264, 266, 268, 292, 294, 302, 305, 373, 374, 376, 380, 382, 383, 384, 386, 388, 389, 390, 391, 407, 408, 416, 417, 418
security forces, 268
security threats, 120
segregation, 237
seizure, 179
selecting, 278, 280, 281, 349
selectivity, 43
self-control, 44
self-doubt, 210
self-interest, 42, 43, 131, 143, 184, 228
Senate, 9, 16, 21, 22, 23, 24, 26, 27, 28, 29, 30, 31, 32, 33, 34, 38, 59, 60, 61, 62, 63, 64, 66, 81, 111, 113, 120, 121, 133, 137, 142, 148, 149, 158, 159, 163, 173, 177, 182, 183, 187, 189, 210, 226, 230, 239, 267, 282, 283, 302, 334, 407, 409, 410, 411, 412, 414, 418, 419

Senate Foreign Relations Committee, 9, 16, 158, 159, 163, 189
sensation, 132
separateness, 172
separation, 278
September 11, 69, 84, 113, 179, 189, 298, 416, 417, 418, 419
Serbia, 176
services, 133, 134
settlements, 91, 109
sex, 24
sexual behavior, 353
shape, 122, 131, 132, 159, 196, 198, 211, 259, 283
shaping, 278
shares, 332
shock, 115, 122, 191, 192, 197, 236, 377
shock therapy, 197
shores, 128, 143
shortage, 107, 111, 249
shoulders, 284
showing, 253, 256, 361
signals, 18, 214, 356
signs, 138, 231, 233, 371, 374, 389
silver, 137, 143
singers, 140
sitting president, 2, 26, 113
skills, 285
slavery, 140, 156
smuggling, 111
snippets, 213
sociability, 271, 273, 277, 280
social institutions, 75
social regulation, 292
social relationships, 154
social security, 121
social structure, 375
society, 2, 71, 72, 97, 114, 196, 231, 260, 269, 277, 346, 347, 352, 358, 359
soil, 277
solution, 72, 88, 93, 152, 153, 155, 159, 161, 162, 183, 217, 228, 234, 266, 375, 378
Somalia, 3, 114, 176, 219
South Africa, 237
South Asia, 163
South Carolina governor, 64
South Dakota, 335, 336, 340
South Korea, 200, 388
Southeast Asia, 153, 164, 186, 212, 213, 214, 222, 228, 236, 237, 238, 395, 396, 408
sovereign state, 176, 370
sovereignty, 90, 138, 141, 171, 232, 258, 266, 271, 272, 275, 276, 277, 281, 283, 284, 285

Soviet Union, 172, 192, 194, 195, 196, 197, 199, 202, 203, 204, 219, 228, 239, 369, 370, 371, 372, 373, 374, 375, 376, 377, 378, 379, 380, 381, 382, 383, 384, 385, 386, 388, 390
Spain, 115, 129, 130, 134, 137, 138, 139, 140, 141, 143, 145, 147, 151, 152, 156, 157, 158, 159, 160, 161, 167, 168
specialists, 127, 128, 129
specialization, xii
specter, 93, 134
spectrum, 360
speculation, 116, 142
speech, 30, 38, 49, 70, 72, 74, 82, 89, 99, 112, 119, 143, 158, 159, 162, 179, 196, 202, 213, 214, 229, 233, 265, 275, 277, 279, 296, 317, 324, 329, 352, 356, 358, 359, 361, 371, 388, 393
spending, 25, 26, 30, 32, 33, 40, 47, 75, 79, 107, 158, 201, 203, 230, 289, 290, 291, 293, 294, 295, 298, 299, 300, 301, 302, 305, 341
spirituality, 140
stability, 41, 42, 48, 114, 115, 198, 247, 248, 274, 296, 375, 383, 384, 417
staff members, 72
staffing, 117, 292, 296, 297, 298, 299, 300, 301
stakeholders, 260
standard deviation, 321, 322, 323, 324
standard of living, 381
standards, 301, 345, 349
Star Wars, 47
starvation, 130, 142, 156
state control, 292
state legislatures, 59, 281
State of the Union address, 72, 74, 76, 78, 82, 92, 118
statistics, 294, 305, 326
statutes, 173, 180, 347
steel, 172, 186
stereotypes, 127, 129, 131, 358
stimulus, 8
stock, 16, 40, 153
strain, 357
Strait of Hormuz, 251, 252, 257
strategic assets, 253
strategic position, 160, 162
strength, 277, 290, 333, 337, 349
stress, 39, 130, 160, 165, 252, 256, 316, 318, 320, 321, 326
stretching, 177
strictures, 141, 170, 174
structure, 54, 74, 80, 88, 130, 151, 152, 154, 155, 164, 166, 219, 254, 257, 272, 275, 331, 341, 384
structuring, 316
students, 356, 357, 358, 359

style, 117, 153, 240, 316, 359
submarines, 390
substitutes, 43
succession, 55, 170, 279
Sudan, 175
suicide, 250, 256
suicide attacks, 250
summer, 355
summer program, xi
Sunnis, 115
supervision, 58, 93
supply, 301
Supreme Council, 258
Supreme Court, 113, 133, 171, 172, 174, 181, 183, 269, 271, 282, 284
surplus, 294, 295
surveillance, 179
survival, 91, 120, 195, 218, 232, 260, 385
survivors, 95
swelling, 78
Switzerland, 10, 146
symbolism, 162, 347, 356
symbols, 345, 347
sympathy, 228, 233, 234
Syria, 45, 47, 114

T

tactics, 58, 115, 120, 193, 237, 247, 248, 252, 254, 256, 257, 259, 266, 383
takeover, 193
Taliban, 16, 38, 114, 115
tanks, 255, 390
target, 9, 12, 115, 254, 318
tariff, 136
task difficulty, 329
Task Force, 77, 250
tax cuts, 57, 74, 122, 290
tax increase, 201
taxation, 31, 291
taxes, 26, 31, 34, 103, 105, 107, 108, 110, 164, 289, 291, 296, 305, 380
teachers, 78
technology, 10, 47, 119, 157, 251, 254, 262, 269
telephone, 78, 355
television, 315, 316, 353
television commercial, 22
tension(s), 54, 108, 130, 175, 210, 215, 219, 248, 251, 257, 265, 266, 318, 357, 379, 389
tenure, 53, 54, 55, 58, 60, 63, 65, 66, 113, 215, 217, 221, 260, 266, 280, 281, 282, 294, 301, 348, 350, 353, 361
territorial, 91, 247, 248, 249, 253, 407

territory, 47, 88, 91, 93, 127, 129, 134, 143, 156, 195, 210, 248, 249, 250, 253, 393, 410, 411
terrorism, 1, 10, 26, 27, 42, 44, 45, 46, 50, 76, 113, 116, 118, 119, 121, 176, 177, 179, 182, 184, 227, 418
terrorist attack, 46, 72, 77, 113, 114, 115, 118, 120, 178, 179, 324, 326, 418, 419
terrorist groups, 42, 114, 418
terrorist organization, 45, 257, 416, 417, 418, 419
terrorists, 43, 45, 47, 48, 114, 118, 119, 182, 417, 418
testing, 257
textbooks, 128
Thailand, 388
thinking, 275, 276, 278, 281, 282, 283, 320, 351, 352, 354
Third World, 261
thoughts, 135, 214, 277, 318, 354
threat(s), 37, 39, 40, 41, 42, 43, 45, 46, 47, 49, 50, 76, 77, 106, 114, 115, 116, 118, 119, 120, 175, 177, 178, 179, 196, 274, 296, 303, 318, 321, 322, 323, 327, 382, 383, 384
Tibet, 388
time commitment, 75
timing, 349, 350
top-down, 162
torture, 156, 179, 180
trade, 1, 6, 41, 64, 106, 107, 108, 109, 129, 132, 136, 205, 251, 258, 263, 302
trade agreement, 136
trade deficit, 1, 6
trade policy, 136
traditionalism, 350
traditions, 48, 296, 303
training, 24, 48, 76, 77, 98, 182, 227, 266, 269, 273, 410
trajectory, 37, 40
transcription, 83
transformation, 71, 131, 269
transition, 356
translation, 71
transmission, 327, 328, 330
transparency, 264
transport, 133
transportation, 235, 292
Transportation Security Administration, 292, 298
Treasury, 27, 195, 295
Treasury Secretary, 27
treaties, 44, 131, 226, 372, 373, 394, 413
treatment, 107, 180, 196, 230, 284, 333, 386
trial, 156, 282, 396
trustworthiness, 97
Tukey HSD, 320

Turkey, 133, 196, 197
turnout, 4, 10, 11, 12, 15, 17, 332, 333, 335
twist, 24, 136

U

U.S. Department of Labor, 85, 86
U.S. economy, 254
U.S. history, 296, 303
U.S. policy, 43, 121, 198, 228, 234, 235, 238, 252, 253
undecided voters, 316
underwriting, 247, 254
unification, 109, 391
uniform, 235, 268, 277
unilateralism, 43, 46, 50, 225
United Kingdom (UK), 203, 204, 257, 379, 385
United Nations (UN), 34, 45, 115, 171, 173, 174, 175, 176, 187, 196, 226, 227, 228, 233, 235, 242, 243, 251, 252, 253, 254, 255, 322, 324, 371, 373, 381, 383, 384, 385, 386, 388, 389, 390, 391, 407, 408, 413, 415, 416, 417, 418, 419
urban, 28, 97, 137, 237, 305
urban areas, 237
USA Patriot Act, 117, 120, 296, 303, 305
USSR, 194, 195, 199, 373, 382, 383, 384

V

vacuum, 136, 162, 165
validation, 303
vandalism, 115
variability, 324
variables, 103, 122
variance, 320
Vatican, 226, 227, 229, 231, 233, 236, 239, 242
vessels, 107, 252, 255, 257, 407
veto, 30, 173, 174, 181, 183, 271, 278, 282
Vice President, 4, 6, 16, 19, 49, 64, 76, 84, 113, 116, 133, 175, 177, 210, 212, 220, 238
victims, 274, 387
Vietnam, 3, 105, 106, 117, 120, 122, 153, 154, 165, 172, 173, 174, 184, 185, 186, 191, 192, 193, 203, 209, 210, 211, 212, 213, 214, 215, 216, 217, 218, 220, 221, 222, 223, 225, 226, 227, 228, 229, 230, 231, 232, 233, 234, 235, 236, 237, 238, 239, 240, 241, 242, 243, 244, 245, 246, 322, 393, 394, 395, 396, 407
Viking, 165, 223
village, 272
violence, xii, 27, 38, 39, 92, 97, 103, 115, 130, 138, 237, 249, 260, 274, 369

vision(s), 37, 41, 39, 48, 135, 152, 161, 164, 169, 170, 171, 183, 260, 271, 272, 281, 329, 359
voice, 281, 317, 325
volatility, 296, 301
volunteer work, 359
volunteerism, 69, 75, 76, 83, 351
volunteers, 77, 83
vote, 3, 4, 5, 8, 10, 12, 15, 17, 25, 27, 29, 57, 58, 64, 80, 96, 97, 99, 111, 113, 133, 137, 176, 181, 183, 273, 280, 283, 284, 328, 332, 333, 334, 335, 336, 338, 339, 341
voters, 1, 2, 3, 4, 7, 8, 9, 10, 11, 12, 15, 16, 17, 18, 21, 23, 26, 27, 28, 29, 31, 32, 38, 56, 64, 113, 117, 133, 136, 280, 316, 333, 354
voting, 4, 6, 7, 10, 11, 17, 27, 29, 113, 277, 280, 315, 333, 337
voting record, 6
vulnerability, 40

W

wages, 136
war hero, 9, 158, 218
War on Terror, 77, 84, 178, 186, 302
war years, 250
Washington, xii, 1, 17, 18, 19, 20, 32, 33, 34, 50, 51, 71, 74, 83, 84, 85, 86, 87, 88, 91, 92, 93, 94, 95, 96, 97, 98, 99, 100, 101, 111, 125, 128, 137, 139, 144, 146, 148, 170, 199, 204, 206, 218, 222, 229, 231, 233, 236, 240, 241, 242, 243, 244, 245, 250, 253, 254, 258, 261, 262, 264, 265, 270, 284, 286, 297, 301, 304, 312, 313, 329, 357, 359, 364, 365, 394
Washington, George, 284, 286
waste, 82, 333, 338, 341
water, 39, 136, 142, 151, 227
watershed, 128, 129, 252
weakness, 26, 130, 159, 184, 194, 200, 202, 257, 374
wealth, 270, 359
weapons, 16, 34, 39, 45, 47, 115, 116, 117, 120, 121, 157, 197, 198, 199, 235, 251, 252, 255, 264, 266, 322, 326, 370, 371, 372, 377, 381, 416, 417, 418
weapons of mass destruction (WMD), 16, 39, 43, 115, 116, 117, 120, 121, 253, 323, 370, 377, 416, 417, 418
wear, 268
web, 50, 306
websites, 25
welfare, 253, 294, 303
welfare state, 294, 303
Wellesley College, 350, 356, 357, 363, 364
West Indies, 108, 123

Western Europe, 131, 132, 197, 198, 199, 251, 372, 374, 375, 377, 379, 390
Whigs, 130, 131, 135, 138, 139
White House, 1, ii, iii, ix, 1, 2, 4, 6, 7, 14, 15, 16, 17, 18, 19, 21, 22, 49, 58, 60, 71, 72, 73, 76, 79, 80, 82, 84, 85, 86, 105, 117, 118, 120, 125, 137, 138, 142, 151, 152, 153, 154, 158, 160, 161, 162, 164, 166, 178, 188, 206, 207, 219, 223, 225, 226, 227, 228, 232, 235, 237, 241, 242, 243, 244, 245, 249, 250, 253, 262, 263, 290, 304, 307, 309, 347, 351, 352, 353, 354, 355, 359, 362, 363, 394
White Paper, 327, 328
WHO, 354
wholesale, 139
wilderness, 91, 93
Wilson, Edith, 348
windows, 70
winning, 315, 316, 317, 321, 338, 339
winter, 273, 276
wires, 355
wiretaps, 120
Wisconsin, xi, 130, 146, 149, 336
withdrawal, 27, 46, 50, 121, 220, 229, 234, 236, 372, 374, 376, 379, 382, 391, 416
witnesses, 318
wives, 346
women, 345, 346, 347, 348, 349, 350, 351, 352, 353, 354, 355, 356, 357, 358, 359, 360, 361

worker rights, 296
workers, 78, 136, 289, 292, 293, 297
workforce, 78, 298
working women, 359
workplace, 292, 296
world order, 56
World Trade Center, 114
World War I, 2, 105, 106, 113, 125, 171, 178, 191, 192, 194, 195, 199, 203, 269, 304, 387, 388
worldview, 47, 139, 140
worldwide, 201
worry, 3, 42, 58, 137, 216
writing, 351, 353

Y

Yale University, 33, 99, 125, 185, 328
yellow journalism, 138
yield, 92, 302, 332
young people, 1, 4, 10
Yugoslavia, 114, 386

Z

zeitgeist, 129